PRINCIPLES

OF

CRIMINAL LAW

Second Edition

By

Wayne R. LaFave
David C. Baum Professor of Law Emeritus
and Center for Advanced Study Professor Emeritus
University of Illinois

CONCISE HORNBOOK SERIES®

WEST®
A Thomson Reuters business

Mat #40904534

© West, a Thomson business, 2003
© 2010 Thomson Reuters
    610 Opperman Drive
    St. Paul, MN 55123
    1–800–313–9378
Printed in the United States of America

ISBN: 978–0–314–91269–5

To
grandson
Jameson

티끌모아 태산

(Tikkul moa tae-san.)

~ Korean proverb

Preface

This text may seem in one respect to be an unlikely product for a law professor, as it has no footnotes—not a single one! The absence of footnotes in this work reflects the fact that it is primarily intended not as a research tool, but rather as a study aid for use by law students during their enrollment in the course on criminal law. By excluding any documentation via footnotes of the various points considered and discussed herein, I have been able to use virtually all of the space in this conveniently-sized paperback volume for textual elaboration of the subjects covered.

While criminal law casebooks currently in use vary considerably in their approach and coverage, I have selected for inclusion in this volume the subject matter that is most commonly included in all basic criminal law courses. What this means, for one thing, is that a relatively small part of this work is devoted to discussion of the definition of particular crimes. Today, most criminal law courses consider in depth some or all of only three offense areas—homicide, rape, and theft—on the theory that they are particularly suited to achieving several of the objectives of a law school course in criminal law. And thus only these three offense categories are extensively discussed herein.

As is true of criminal law courses generally, this volume is devoted primarily to what is usually referred to as the "general part" of the criminal law. And thus the emphasis herein is upon the sources and limitations (including constitutional limitations) of the substantive criminal law, as well as upon general principles concerning mental state, acts and their consequences, defenses to crime, inchoate criminality (solicitation, attempts, conspiracy), and liability for the conduct of others. I have given greater attention to those particular topics that, based upon my own experience in teaching a course in criminal law for a good many years, I have found are most troubling to beginning law students. While this book is about substantive criminal law rather than criminal procedure, some procedural aspects essential to an understanding of the significance of certain criminal law doctrines are considered herein.

Because of the important part that the Model Penal Code has played in the revision and codification of substantive criminal law in recent times, Code sections are often given specific mention in this text; the location of references to a particular section may be found in the table of code sections. When appellate cases are mentioned in the text, they are referred to by name and date only; they are cited fully only in the table of cases. Notwithstanding the lack of footnote references, it must be emphasized that language herein within quotation marks or block indented is that of others who can be readily identified by the interested student (see below).

How does a law professor manage to write a book without footnotes? Easy, first write a much longer work *with* footnotes, and then revise that work down by making many revisions in the text *and* by deleting all the footnotes. Yes, this book is the offspring of another work, published in 2003 and updated annually since, namely, the second edition of a multi-volume treatise for lawyers, judges and researchers called *Substantive Criminal Law* (itself the outgrowth of another work initially published back in 1972). I mention this here so that the student who does want to explore particular topics in the present book in greater depth, especially by finding illustrative cases, applicable statutes, and useful secondary authorities, will have an easy way of doing so. In Westlaw, just go to database SUBCRL and examine the comparable chapter or section, as indicated in the *Table of Cross-References* herein.

WAYNE R. LaFAVE

December 2009

Table of Cross-References

The author of this Book, *Principles of Criminal Law*, is also the author of a three-volume treatise, *Substantive Criminal Law* (2d ed. 2003, with annual updates), available in most law libraries and readily accessible on Westlaw in database SUBCRL. The subjects discussed in this Book are dealt with in greater detail in the Treatise. In addition, while the citation of supporting authority in this Book is extremely limited, citations to appellate cases, legislation and court rules, as well as articles and other secondary authorities, are available in the Treatise. Users of this Book desiring either additional discussion of a particular subject or supporting authority regarding a specific topic will thus find it useful to consult the Treatise. To facilitate such consultation, use this table of cross-references, which indicates for each section of this Book what section in the Treatise deals with the same subject matter. (Even when the section numbers are different, the subsections will usually be identical in both works.)

Principles	Treatise	Principles	Treatise	Principles	Treatise	Principles	Treatise
1.1	1.1	6.1	7.1	11.1	12.1	16.1	19.1
1.2	1.2	6.2	7.2	11.2	12.2	16.2	19.2
1.3	1.3	6.3	7.3	11.3	12.3	16.3	19.3
1.4	1.4	6.4	7.4	11.4	12.4	16.4	19.4
1.5	1.5	6.5	7.5			16.5	19.5
1.6	1.6			12.1	13.1	16.6	19.6
1.7	1.7	7.1	8.1	12.2	13.2	16.7	19.7
1.8	1.8	7.2	8.2	12.3	13.3	16.8	19.8
		7.3	8.3	12.4	13.4		
2.1	2.1	7.4	8.4	12.5	13.5		
2.2	2.2			12.6	13.6		
2.3	2.3	8.1	9.1				
2.4	2.4	8.2	9.2	13.1	14.1		
2.5	2.5	8.3	9.3	13.2	14.2		
2.6	2.6	8.4	9.4	13.3	14.3		
		8.5	9.5	13.4	14.4		
3.1	3.1	8.6	9.6	13.5	14.5		
3.2	3.2	8.7	9.7	13.6	14.6		
3.3	3.3	8.8	9.8	13.7	14.7		
3.4	3.4						
3.5	3.5	9.1	10.1	14.1	15.1		
3.6	3.6	9.2	10.2	14.2	15.2		
		9.3	10.3	14.3	15.3		
4.1	5.1	9.4	10.4	14.4	15.4		
4.2	5.2	9.5	10.5	14.5	15.5		
4.3	5.3	9.6	10.6	14.6	15.6		
4.4	5.4	9.7	10.7				
4.5	5.5			15.1	17.1		
4.6	5.6	10.1	11.1	15.2	17.2		
		10.2	11.2	15.3	17.3		
5.1	6.1	10.3	11.3	15.5	17.4		
5.2	6.2	10.4	11.4				
5.3	6.3	10.5	11.5				
5.4	6.4						
5.5	6.5						

Summary of Contents

Table of Contents

PRINCIPLES
OF
CRIMINAL LAW

Second Edition

Chapter 1

INTRODUCTION AND GENERAL CONSIDERATIONS

Table of Sections

For additional analysis of the above topics and citations to authorities supporting their discussion in this Book, consult the author's 3-volume *Substantive Criminal Law* treatise, also available as Westlaw database SUBCRL. See the Table of Cross-References in this Book.

§ 1.1   The Scope of Criminal Law and Procedure

The substantive criminal law is treated in this book. It is mostly concerned with what act and mental state, together with what attendant circumstances or consequences, are necessary ingredients of the various crimes. Criminal procedure, not covered in this book, is concerned with the legal steps through which a criminal proceeding passes, from the initial investigation of a crime through the termination of punishment. Besides criminal law and procedure, the administration of criminal justice includes such matters as police organization and administration (how most effectively to detect and apprehend criminals), prison administration, and administration of probation and parole.

(a) The Concern of Criminologists. There are, however, groups of people other than lawyers, policemen, probation and parole officers, and prison authorities whose professional work involves the problems of crime and criminals. In particular, criminologists spend their professional lives studying crime and criminals and the administration of criminal justice. Criminologists have varying backgrounds, coming from the fields of sociology, social psychology, medicine (especially psychiatry), anthropology and biology. They are concerned with the study of the phenomenon of crime and of the factors or circumstances—individual and environmental—that may have an influence on, or be associated with, criminal behavior and the state of crime in general. Criminologists are trying to determine why people become criminals, not just to acquire knowledge for its own sake but for the practical ultimate purpose of eradicating the causes of crime and thus reducing if not eliminating crime. The cost of crime in this country is, of course, enormous—doubtless many billion dollars a year if we consider property losses, personal injury losses, the cost of law enforcement (including the cost of maintaining the police, the criminal courts and the prosecutor), the cost of maintaining prisons and parole agencies, and the loss of productive labor of criminals. It is obvious that if crime could be reduced, the savings would be great.

The modern criminologist's method of attacking the problem of crime and criminals is a scientific one, including the collection of statistics on crime and the making of case studies of individual criminals and group studies of criminal classes. What effect does heredity have on crime? What is the effect of environment? What is the effect of poverty, lack of education, unemployment, urban life, poor housing, broken homes, or evil companions? Is there a connection between physique and criminality, between mental defect and crime? Are some racial groups more prone to commit crimes than others? What is the effect of cultural influences—religion, newspapers, comic books, television and radio, moving pictures? In order to take effective steps to combat the crime problem, we must first know with some degree of certainty the answers to such questions. But the field of criminology as a science is relatively new, and the answers are by no means yet certain.

Criminologists are interested not only in the causes of crime and remedies to be taken to eliminate these causes, but also in the treatment to be given the criminal who is caught and convicted. How should we treat him in order to reduce his chances of committing subsequent crimes? It is in this area of criminology (termed penology) that criminologists have had their greatest influence on criminal law and procedure: in the classification of convicts into corrigibles and incorrigibles, and into professionals and casuals, for penal treatment; the establishment of procedures for probation and parole; the indeterminate sentence; the treatment of juvenile delinquency as non-criminal; and to some extent the treatment of alcoholics, drug addicts and sex offenders as sick rather than criminal.

(b) The Concern of Lawyers. Lawyers no less than criminologists are interested in preventing socially undesirable conduct. Their principal weapon in the war on crime is the criminal law. They too are interested in the question of what forms of anti-social conduct should be punished as criminal (i.e., what should be the scope of the substantive law of crimes). And they conceive of punishment for violation of the criminal law as a device for preventing such conduct—by deterring prospective offenders by threat of punishment and by preventing repetition by incapacitating and if possible reforming those who have already committed crimes (see § 1.8). But lawyers also play a part, outside of the criminal law, in the area of crime prevention through laws designed to improve social and economic conditions—those relating to public housing, zoning, public health, industrial working conditions, minimum wages, unemployment compensation and such matters.

In recent years particularly, lawyers have become more conscious of the need for law reform in the administration of criminal justice. This concern has been reflected in several ambitious projects sponsored by the organized bar and other professional groups or otherwise participated in by members of the legal profession.

In the realm of substantive criminal law, by far the most significant development has been the completion of the American Law Institute's Model Penal Code, to which frequent reference is made in this book. The Code is organized into four main parts: (1) the general provisions, which set forth the basic principles that govern the existence and the scope of liability; (2) the definition of specific offenses; (3) provisions governing the processes of treatment and correction; and (4) provisions on the organization of correction. The commentary to the Code, prepared in a desire to place the systematic literature of our penal law upon a parity with that of well-developed legal fields, is in itself a major contribution.

It must be emphasized that the American Law Institute has produced a *model* code, not a *uniform* code. Uniformity is of less importance in penal law than in other fields, such as commercial law. It is appropriate that the several states should have significant variations in their penal laws, based upon differences in local conditions or points of view. The principal contribution of the Model Penal Code is that it represents a systematic re-examination of the substantive criminal law. It identifies the major issues that should be confronted by the legislature in the recodification process and articulates and evaluates alternative methods of dealing with these issues. The intention was to provide a reasoned, integrated body of material that would be useful in such legislative effort.

Perhaps because of the lack of such guidance in earlier years, the criminal codes of most states long suffered from neglect. As one commentator noted in 1956: "Viewing the country as a whole, our penal codes are fragmentary, old, disorganized and often accidental in their coverage, their growth largely fortuitous in origin, their form a combination of enactment and of common law that only history explains." In many codes, some of the most significant crimes (such as murder) were not defined, and it was not uncommon for basic doctrines concerning the scope of liability to have little or no reflection in the statutes. Prior to the time that the work on the Model Penal Code began to be circulated, only two states, Louisiana and Wisconsin, had accomplished over-all reform of their substantive criminal law. But now, largely stimulated by the labors of the American Law Institute, there are a total of thirty eight states which have adopted new substantive criminal law codes. Efforts directed toward similar reform have been undertaken but have faltered in some other states and on the federal level. (The Model Penal Code has also had a substantial impact upon the judiciary; courts have frequently relied upon provisions in the Code when formulating substantive criminal law rules.)

The legal profession has longer shown interest in the realm of criminal procedure. This is reflected in the fact that a number of efforts directed toward reform of criminal procedure antedated the Model Penal Code project. In 1930, the American Law Institute produced a procedure code. The Federal Rules of Criminal Procedure were adopted in 1946, and they have since served as a model for procedure rules in a number of states. In 1952, the National Conference of Commissioners on Uniform State Laws published its Uniform Rules of Criminal Procedure.

This is not to suggest, however, that meaningful reform came earlier in the area of criminal procedure. None of the procedure "models" mentioned above accomplished for the field of criminal procedure what the Model Penal Code has done for the substantive criminal law. The basic defect is that they did not identify and constructively deal with many of the major issues in criminal procedure. In part, this may be attributable to the fact that courts, particularly the United States Supreme Court, have played a leading role in certain procedural areas, such as search and seizure. But, whatever the reason, one characteristic of all the earlier procedure "models" is that they tend to concentrate upon the formal, in-court procedures to the exclusion of other problems of equal or greater importance but of lower visibility. More recently, however, efforts have been made to construct "models" dealing with these problems. One noteworthy effort is the American Law Institute's Model Code of Pre–Arraignment Procedure. Another is the American Bar Association's Standards Relating to the Administration of Criminal Justice. Yet another is the Commissioners' more recent version of Uniform Rules of Criminal Procedure.

As noted earlier, essential to law reform are the identification of major issues and the articulation of alternative ways of dealing with those issues. This, in turn, can be accomplished only through careful scrutiny of existing practices. Such empirical research has been undertaken through the years, but it has been sporadic and sometimes misdirected. A flurry of crime surveys were published in the 1920's and 1930's, and in 1931 a major national survey by the federal government was completed. However, as one writer has aptly pointed out, "the early crime surveys did not produce any clear conception of the kinds of administrative problems which ought to be of greatest concern to legal research." More recently, there has been a renewed interest in the study of the actual processes of criminal justice administration for the purpose of uncovering and analyzing critical problems with which the law ought to be concerned. One of the most ambitious studies is the American Bar Foundation's Survey of the Administration of Criminal Justice in the United States. The President's Commission on Law Enforcement and Administration of Justice also sponsored considerable research into the actual workings of our criminal justice systems.

§ 1.2   Characteristics of the Substantive Criminal Law

The substantive criminal law is that law which, for the purpose of preventing harm to society, declares what conduct is criminal and prescribes the punishment to be imposed for such conduct. It includes the definition of specific offenses and general principles of liability.

"Conduct" in the above statement is used in a broad sense to cover two distinct matters: (1) the act, or the omission to act where there is a duty to act (discussed in ch. 5); and (2) the state of mind that accompanies the act or omission (discussed in ch. 4). Thus the definition of a particular crime will spell out what act (or omission) and what mental state is required for its commission. Furthermore, as we shall see, the definition of a particular crime may require, in addition to an act or omission and a state of mind, something in the way of specified attendant circumstances; and with some crimes the definition also requires a specified result of the act or omission. As the above definition of substantive criminal law implies, conduct cannot be called "criminal" unless a punishment is prescribed therefor.

(a) Specific Crimes and General Principles. The substantive criminal law is to a large extent concerned with the definitions of the various crimes (whether defined by the common law or, far more commonly, by statute)—what conduct, including what state of mind, is necessary for guilt of murder, or rape, or burglary, etc. The definition of specific crimes is dealt with in chapters 13–16 of this book. But the substantive criminal law is concerned with much more than is found in the definitions of the specific crimes, for there are many general principles of the substantive criminal law which apply to more than a single crime—for instance, the principle that an insane person cannot be guilty of any crime, or that one coerced into committing what would otherwise be criminal conduct cannot be guilty of most crimes. Thus criminal battery is sometimes defined as "the intentional or reckless application of force to the person of another, directly or indirectly." The definition does not continue: "... by one who is not legally insane; not legally too young; not too intoxicated to have the necessary state of mind; who was not coerced by threat of immediate death or great bodily harm; and who was not justified because he acted in self-defense, or pursuant to domestic authority, or because the other person consented," and so on.

The general principles of the type represented by insanity, infancy, coercion and self-defense all have to do with *defenses to liability*, which, if applicable, negative the commission of the specific crime. It is customary to distinguish between two different categories of defenses, justification and excuse (see § 8.1 for more on this distinction and on other categories of defenses). Simply stated, the distinction between the two is that "justified action is a morally appropriate action," while excused conduct "is not warranted, but the person involved is not blameworthy." In the case of justification, the harm caused is "a legally recognized harm," but under the circumstances giving rise to the justification "is outweighed by the need to avoid an even greater harm or to further a greater societal interest." In the case of an excuse, on the other hand, the deed is wrong but the actor is excused because suffering from "an abnormal condition * * * at the time of the offense" that creates a condition "render[ing] him blameless for his conduct constituting the offense." In this book, those defenses commonly thought of as being of the justification type are discussed in chapter 9, while those defenses most likely to be characterized as excuse defenses are discussed in chapters 6 and 8. It should be noted, however, that the Model Penal Code does *not* make use of the justification/excuse distinction, reasoning that "the effort to establish precisely in each case whether that conduct is actually justified or only excused does not seem worthwhile, especially since, in regard to the difficult cases, members of society may disagree over the appropriate characterization."

There are other general principles of criminal liability of an *affirmative-liability* sort, which cut across the various specific crimes and which therefore may properly be called "general principles." One type of affirmative-liability general principle concerns the three "inchoate crimes" of attempt, conspiracy and solicitation. Though these crimes are in one sense three specific crimes, yet in another sense they concern all the other specific crimes; thus with attempt the issue may be attempted murder or attempted rape or attempted burglary, etc.; and so with conspiracy to commit murder or to commit embezzlement, and with solicitation to commit any one of the many specific crimes. These inchoate offenses are the subject of chapters 10 and 11 of this book. The second type of general principle of affirmative criminal liability concerns parties to specific crimes, including the liability of accessories as well as of principals—for instance, the liability for murder not only of the one who fired the fatal bullet, but of the other person who urged him to do it, or who supplied him with the gun. Such liability is discussed herein in chapter 12 of this book.

(b) Nature of Criminal Law—Basic Premises. The substantive law of crimes consists primarily of (1) the definitions of the various specific crimes, from murder on down to such minor offenses as speeding, (2) some broader general principles of the substantive criminal law applicable to more than a single crime and so not made a part of the definitions of specific crimes, as just noted above, and also (3) some even broader propositions of law, the basic premises underlying the whole of the Anglo–American substantive criminal law. These basic premises have been of great importance in shaping the criminal law, although we shall see that they have not always been wholly accepted without exception.

The first of these basic premises concerns the requirement of an act; generally, it may be said that conduct, to be criminal, must consist of something more than a mere bad state of mind. This requirement is reflected in court decisions holding that mere status or condition cannot constitutionally be made a crime (see §§ 3.3(d), 3.5(f)). The requirement of an act is discussed further herein (see § 5.1), as is the notion that the failure to carry out a legal duty may also serve as the basis of liability (see § 5.2).

Another basic premise is that conduct, to be criminal, must consist of something more than mere action (or non-action where there is a legal duty to act); some sort of bad state of mind is required as well. This requirement has sometimes been expressed as a constitutional limitation on the power to create crimes (see § 3.3(d)). The various mental states are discussed in more detail herein (see §§ 5.1–5.4). In addition, consideration is given herein to the many statutes that impose liability without fault, i.e., liability without regard to the defendant's mental state at the time he or another engaged in the proscribed acts (see § 5.5).

A third basic premise is that the physical conduct and mental state must concur, and it is also considered later herein (see § 6.3). Generally, it may be said that the defendant's mental state must concur with his act or omission, in the sense that the former actuates the latter. A somewhat different problem of concurrence, also discussed herein, concerns the question of whether the bad results of the defendant's conduct must coincide in type or degree with the results intended or risked. As we shall see, the better view is that one should not be convicted for causing a greater or different harm than is reflected in his mental state, although there are many exceptions to this in current law.

A fourth basic premise concerns harm; only harmful conduct should be made criminal. It is reflected in the substantive due process notion that a criminal statute is unconstitutional if it bears no reasonable relation to injury to the public (see § 3.3). However, substantive due process has not been viewed as necessarily barring criminal statutes grounded merely in "ethical and moral concerns," although a statute proscribing private acts of immorality may be stricken down because it infringes upon a fundamental right. The wisdom of using the criminal law for the promotion and protection of private morality has long been a subject of debate. On the one hand, it is argued that private immorality, like treason, in fact harms society by jeopardizing its existence. On the other, it is contended that any infringement of individual liberty is itself a harm for which there must be justification; that there is no proof that society is harmed by private immorality; that the enforcement of laws against private sin is necessarily impracticable and unevenhanded; and that such laws serve only to present the unscrupulous with an opportunity for blackmail. The subject of harm is not discussed further in the present chapter, although certain aspects of it will be treated later.

Yet another basic premise is that for those crimes requiring not only some forbidden conduct but also some particular result of that conduct, the conduct must be the "legal cause" (often called "proximate cause") of the result. This premise gives rise to problems of considerable difficulty, and they are discussed later herein (see § 6.4).

The sixth basic premise is that a person who has engaged in criminal conduct may only be subjected to the legally prescribed punishment. The role of punishment is considered later (see § 1.5).

The final basic premise of the criminal law is that conduct is not criminal unless forbidden by law providing advance warning that such conduct is criminal. This idea, sometimes termed "the principle of legality," is often expressed by the Latin phrase *nullum crimin sine lege, nulla poena sine lege* (no crime or punishment without law). The various areas of the criminal law in which the principal of legality operates are treated at some length herein. It is reflected in the ex post facto prohibition (see § 2.4), the rule of strict construction of criminal statutes (see § 2.2(d)), the void-for-vagueness doctrine (see § 2.3), and the trend away from open-ended common law crimes (see § 2.1).

(c) Variations in Definitions of Crimes. The various crimes (whether they are statutory crimes or common law crimes) are of course variously defined as to what actions and states of mind are required for guilt. Here we may note that the definitions also often require, in addition, the presence or absence of attendant *circumstances,* and sometimes require that the necessary conduct produce certain *results.* For example, as to circumstances, burglary (at least at common law) requires night-time activity, receiving stolen property requires that the goods received be stolen goods, bigamy requires a previous marriage, statutory rape that the girl be under age, perjury that the witness be sworn, incest that the parties be related. In some cases the necessary circumstances may consist of the absence of something; thus in rape (at least at common law) the victim must be someone who is not the wife of the rapist. Perhaps we might say that in criminal homicide and battery an attendant circumstance necessary for guilt is the absence of any justification or excuse.

In respect to the requirement of a result, some crimes are so worded that a bad result is needed for commission of the crime. For instance, criminal homicide requires the death of a human being, battery the injury of such a person, arson the burning of property, malicious mischief the injury or destruction of property, false pretenses the loss of title to property or money. On the other hand, many crimes are so defined that no bad result is required, it being the policy of the criminal law in these cases to punish activity likely to produce bad results if not nipped in the bud. Thus forgery may be committed although no one other than the forger ever saw the forged document; perjury may be committed although the false testimony was not believed and so did not affect the outcome of the matter in dispute; criminal assault although the bullet intended for the victim missed him; attempt and conspiracy although the crime attempted or agreed upon was never consummated. Similarly, a case holds that one may be guilty of the crime of transporting a woman across state lines for purposes of prostitution although the young lady in question, upon arrival at her destination, refused to perform as expected.

The totality of these various items—conduct, mental fault, plus attendant circumstances and specified result when required by the definition of a crime—may be said to constitute the "elements" of the crime.

(d) Necessity for Prescribed Punishment. We have seen that a crime is made up of two parts, forbidden conduct and a prescribed penalty. The former without the latter is no crime. The modern criminal penalties are: the death penalty, imprisonment with or without hard labor, and the fine. In many cases the section of the statute that describes the forbidden conduct concludes with a statement of the punishment; or perhaps one section sets forth the forbidden conduct and the next section the punishment. Sometimes, however, the statute forbidding the conduct may refer to another statute for the punishment, such as the rather common statute providing that whoever commits embezzlement (defining it) shall be punishable as if he committed larceny, with the larceny statute providing for a certain penalty of fine or imprisonment. Another method sometimes encountered is for the statute, after forbidding certain conduct, to conclude "shall be guilty of a felony" (or "misdemeanor"), without setting forth the penalty; but another catch-all statute provides that one who commits a felony (or a misdemeanor) not otherwise punishable shall be punished in a prescribed way. Similarly, the statute defining certain conduct as criminal may say that this crime is a felony or misdemeanor of a certain classification; another statute then indicates the permissible punishment for each classification. In all of these cases there is little difficulty in concluding that, since the statutes set forth both forbidden conduct and criminal penalty, the legislature has created a crime.

But sometimes the legislature forbids conduct and then omits (in most cases unintentionally) to provide for a penalty; and there is no catch-all statute of the type mentioned above. In such a situation one who engages in the forbidden conduct is not guilty of a crime. However, one case has held that prohibited conduct without a penalty can be punished by a state retaining common law crimes with the same penalty such a state would impose for a common law crime.

(e) Purpose of Criminal Law—Prevention of Harm. The broad aim of the criminal law is, of course, to prevent harm to society—more specifically, to prevent injury to the health, safety, morals and welfare of the public. This it accomplishes by punishing those who have done harm, and by threatening with punishment those who would do harm, to others. Sometimes the harm to be prevented is physical: death or bodily injury to a human being in criminal homicide or battery; burning of a house in arson; loss of property in the theft crimes. Sometimes the harm is to some more intangible interest, as where it consists of the outraged feelings of the victim of indecent exposure. Sometimes the harm to be prevented is simply a mischievous situation, or situation of danger, as in the case of the crime of reckless driving or of the "inchoate" crimes of attempt, conspiracy and solicitation, where, when the defendant's conduct is over, no member of society may have suffered any damage (physical, property or intangible) at all.

Of course, not all harmful conduct is criminal. There is the basic requirement that harmful conduct, to be criminal, must be prohibited by law. And the legislatures have never succeeded in making criminal every sort of harmful conduct.

(f) Criminal Law and Morality. There is no doubt that society's ideas of morality, to the extent that they are held by those members of society who are legislators (in the case of statutory crimes) and judges (with common law crimes), have had much to do with formulating the substantive criminal law. The English judges of long ago shared the feelings of the English public that killing human beings without justification or excuse, and forcible sexual intercourse with a woman other than one's wife, and stealing other people's property were wrongful, and so they created the crimes of murder, rape and larceny to punish such behavior. In more modern times the legislatures of some American states have shared the feelings of the public of those states that it is immoral for gamblers to pay money to athletes to lose games (thus allowing the gamblers to bet on a sure thing), so the legislature has created a new statutory crime, bribery of athletes, to punish that sort of conduct. No doubt at times there are moral issues on which the public is sharply divided, as is true in some places concerning the sale of intoxicating liquor, in which case the side with the more effective lobby may carry the day in creating a crime or defeating its creation. Doubtless too a good deal of criminal law is the result of pressure from narrow groups who are actually concerned with their own best interests much more than they are concerned with thoughts of morality. For instance, automobile dealers in the city, who cannot sell automobiles on Sunday by local city ordinance, have sometimes persuaded the legislature to punish as criminal the Sunday sale of cars anywhere in the state, in order to force the Sunday closing of the out-of-town car dealers, who have been doing a brisk Sunday business to the financial detriment of the city dealers.

But immorality and criminality, though related, are not synonymous. A good deal of conduct that is ethically immoral is not criminal. For example, there are many situations where one has a moral duty to save another's life where it can be done with little danger or inconvenience or expense, but failure to take action to do so is not usually criminal (see § 5.2). In many states one may conjure up some novel and immoral way of injuring others, which the legislature has not yet thought of, and escape criminal liability because there is no criminal statute forbidding it. As we shall see, a few states still hold the threat of "common law crimes" in readiness for just such an emergency.

On the other hand, some conduct that is not immoral may yet be criminal. As we shall see, a modern tendency in the substantive criminal law is to relax the old requirement that there cannot be a crime without a bad state of mind; today we find that many statutory crimes may be committed unintentionally but with negligence or even unintentionally without negligence, as in the case of strict-liability and vicarious-liability crimes (see §§ 4.5, 12.4). As we shall also see, a good motive will not normally prevent what is otherwise criminal from being a crime (see § 4.3). Thus it is nonetheless murder that one intentionally kills a loved one suffering from a painful incurable disease, or larceny that one stole a rich man's money to give his impoverished family a better life. An honest religious belief in polygamy does not serve as a defense to the crime of bigamy.

§ 1.3   Crimes and Civil Wrongs

The criminal law and the civil law have much in common. Criminal statutes have played a part in creating civil liability, while civil statutes have been important in the development of the substantive criminal law. There are, however, a number of differences between criminal law and civil law because of their different functions.

(a) Similarities and Differences. The substantive criminal law and the substantive civil law (such as the law of torts, contracts, and property) have much in common. Civil law, like criminal law, aims to shape people's conduct along lines which are beneficial to society—by preventing them from doing what is bad for society (as by imposing liability for damages upon those who commit torts or break contracts) or by compelling them to do what is good for society (as by decreeing specific performance of contracts for the sale of real property). Society has an interest in preventing killings and rapes; but it also wants to prevent automobile accidents and to discourage breaches of contracts. Civil law, like criminal law, is effective mainly because of the sanctions that the law imposes, through the courts, upon those who commit violations. Even these sometimes do not differ greatly as between the civil and the criminal law. Paying damages (especially "punitive damages") for torts or contract breaches is not much different from paying fines for criminal violations. Confinement of mental defectives in mental hospitals, of juvenile delinquents in reform schools, or of aliens awaiting deportation is not too far removed from imprisonment of criminals in penitentiaries or jails, especially those modern prisons devoted to principles of rehabilitation rather than of revenge and retribution.

Indeed, it has been argued with some force that the only real basis for distinction between crimes and civil wrongs lies in the moral condemnation the community visits upon the criminal but not (at least not so powerfully) upon his civil wrongdoer counterpart. Yet, even aside from differences in moral condemnation, it would seem that criminal punishment, with emphasis on imprisonment, is on the whole more drastic than the sanctions, with emphasis upon paying money, imposed by the civil law, even though in a particular case it may be that the civil sanction imposed is harder on the defendant than the counterpart criminal punishment would be.

(b) Crimes and Torts. Criminal law and the law of torts (more than any other form of civil law) are related branches of the law; yet in a sense they are two quite different matters. The aim of the criminal law, as we have noted, is to protect the public against harm, by punishing harmful results of conduct or at least situations (not yet resulting in actual harm) that are likely to result in harm if allowed to proceed further. The function of tort law is to compensate someone who is injured for the harm he has suffered. With crimes, the state itself brings criminal proceedings to protect the public interest but not to compensate the victim; with torts, the injured party himself institutes proceedings to recover damages (or perhaps to enjoin the defendant from causing further damage). With crimes, as we have seen, there is emphasis on a bad mind, on immorality. With torts the emphasis is more on a fair adjustment of the conflicting interests of the litigating parties to achieve a desirable social result, with morality taking on less importance.

Thus tort law requires pecuniary damage, with but minor emphasis on immorality; while criminal law emphasizes immoral behavior, but often does not require any actual damage. The great difference in function between the two branches of law produces important differences between crimes and torts, even with respect to those crimes and torts that are rather closely related (e.g., tort of deceit, crime of false pretenses)—even, in fact, where they may bear the same name (e.g., assault, battery, libel).

So with assault: to shoot at and miss a sleeping man cannot be a civil assault, as there is no injury, even mental, to the sleeper; but such behavior is socially dangerous enough to constitute a criminal assault. And with libel: a defamatory letter written to the one defamed but seen by no one else cannot be civil libel, because he can suffer no injury where no outsider sees it; but on the criminal side no such publication to a third person is needed, as the evil the crime is designed to prevent is the danger of a breach of the peace caused by the libel victim's anger upon learning of the defamatory matter. Where one person by misrepresentation obtains something of value from another, an action for the tort of deceit will not lie if in fact the victim received all the value that he bargained for and has paid for; in such a case he has suffered no financial loss. But the crime of false pretenses may be committed even if the victim of the misrepresentations suffered no financial loss—in fact, where he got more value than he bargained for (see § 16.7). An innocent converter of another's property (e.g., a bona fide purchaser of stolen property) is liable in tort for conversion. But the crime of embezzlement requires more than simply a conversion; because of the criminal law's emphasis on immorality a "fraudulent" conversion is required (see § 16.6). Ordinary negligence is a common basis of tort liability, but more than ordinary negligence is usually required in the criminal law (see § 4.4).

Turning to matters of defense, we find that in related matters there are differences in defenses to torts and defenses to crimes, because torts are wrongs to private individuals but crimes are wrongs to the public. Thus consent of the adult injured party is a defense to intentionally inflicted torts; but in analogous situations in the field of criminal law consent of the victim may not be a defense. So the consent of the woman to an abortion may be a defense to a tort action for battery, but it is not alone a defense to the criminal action. So too an injured party may condone the tort committed against him; but a victim of crime may not normally obliterate the commission of the crime by forgiving the criminal. Contributory negligence is a well known defense to tort liability based upon negligence; but in the case of crimes based on negligence (e.g., criminal homicide, battery) the contributory negligence of the victim is no defense (although, as we shall see, the conduct of the victim is often important in determining whether the defendant was culpably negligent) (see § 5.5).

There are fundamental differences in matters of responsibility as well. Infants are generally liable for their torts, because tort law is concerned more with compensating the injured party than with the moral guilt of the wrongdoer; but, because of the greater interest of the criminal law in morality, infants below a certain age are deemed incapable of committing crimes (see § 8.6). Much the same thing may be said for the tort and criminal liability of insane persons, who are liable for many of their torts but never for crimes (see ch. 6).

In spite of the differences between tort law and criminal law, however, there are many ideas and concepts common to both branches of the law. Some crimes (e.g., felony-murder and misdemeanor-manslaughter) make use of the idea of "proximate cause," one of the important concepts of tort liability for negligence. We meet the phrase "intervening cause" in crimes as well as torts (see § 5.4). Liability for failure to act where there is a duty to act may be criminal as well as civil, and duty for one purpose is duty for the other. The defense of self-defense is about the same whether the defendant is defending against a suit for the tort of battery or against prosecution for criminal battery.

Frequently the defendant's conduct makes him both civilly and criminally liable: *A* intentionally hits *B* with a baseball bat; or embezzles his property; or publishes defamatory matter about him; or intentionally destroys his watch or burns his house. In any such situation the civil suit need not await the outcome of the criminal proceedings by the modern weight of authority.

On the other hand, sometimes the defendant's conduct renders him criminally but not civilly liable, as is the case with the crime of treason or the crimes of possessing counterfeiting implements or burglar's tools; driving too fast without an accident is a crime but not a tort; and forgery may be committed although no one has lost a cent on account of the forgery. And, conversely, his conduct may render him civilly but not criminally liable, as where he kills or injures another person with but ordinary negligence, or unintentionally commits a trespass, or innocently converts another's property.

Criminal procedure and civil procedure, like the substantive law of torts and crimes, have much in common. A criminal trial, for instance, proceeds along a course greatly resembling that traveled by a civil trial. Most of the rules of evidence (e.g., the hearsay rule) apply equally to both types of cases. But still there are important differences between the two types of procedure, perhaps best illustrated by the requirement that in a civil case the party with the burden of proof must establish his claim "by a preponderance of the evidence," while in a criminal case the state must prove the defendant guilty "beyond a reasonable doubt."

Some substantive criminal law is made in the relatively quiet setting of a civil case. Thus some law of theft has been developed in suits on theft insurance policies, where the insured must show that his property was taken by theft. The law of murder must be considered in the constructive trust branch of the law of restitution declaring that an heir (or legatee, or insurance beneficiary) who obtains property by murdering his ancestor (or testator, or insured) is unjustly enriched if permitted to retain it. Since it is a defense to the tort of malicious prosecution that the plaintiff was actually guilty of the crime charged, these tort cases often go into the question of whether the plaintiff actually committed the crime for which the defendant initiated prosecution. Even federal tax cases have had to decide questions of criminal law because of the formerly-held peculiar notion that one is taxable on the income he derives from larceny or false pretenses or extortion or racketeering but not for what he embezzles.

(c) Interaction of Criminal Law and Civil Law. Criminal statutes have played a part in creating civil liability and defenses to civil liability. Statutes are expressions of public policy, and the common law is, after all, merely the courts' notion of what best promotes public policy. In the absence of any legislative expression of policy, the courts will seek it on their own; but where the legislature has expressed its ideas, the courts will naturally give those ideas great weight. Thus in tort law a criminal statute, designed to protect certain types of people from certain kinds of harms, sets up the standard of conduct of the reasonable man for purposes of negligence liability, so that it is negligence *per se* (or at least evidence of negligence) when a defendant, violating the statute, causes a person of that type to suffer that sort of harm. In contracts law a criminal statute punishing gambling may not spell out that the winner may not sue the loser to recover his winnings, yet the loser has a defense to the civil action. The criminal statute has disclosed a public policy that the courts in civil cases may further effectuate by using that policy in deciding the law in civil cases.

On the other hand, civil statutes have to some extent been important in the development of the substantive criminal law. Thus the common law rule that one cannot be guilty of larceny of his spouse's property (since husband and wife are one individual) has generally been done away with by judicial decision because Married Women's Property Acts (which do not speak of criminal liability at all) have made the wife, in property matters at least, an individual separate from her husband. The common law presumption of coercion, where a wife commits what would otherwise be a crime in her husband's presence, has generally fallen the same way, although the civil statutes freeing the wife from her husband's domination do not themselves directly deal with the matter of coercion as a criminal defense. The criminal law is slower to borrow from civil statutes than civil law is to borrow from criminal statutes, at least in the area of imposing criminal liability where none existed before. This is because of the basic premise of common law, expressed in the maxim *nulla poena sine lege,* that public policy alone (even when disclosed by civil statutes) is not sufficient to make conduct criminal, in the absence of a direct expression of advance warning from the legislature.

§ 1.4   Characteristics of Criminal Procedure

The subject of criminal procedure is not dealt with in this book. It is appropriate, however, to consider at this point some of the basic characteristics of the criminal process in order to understand the significance of the substantive criminal law in terms of day-to-day criminal justice administration. Without such an understanding, the discussion of the substantive criminal law might prompt the inappropriate conclusion that the law of crimes is extremely severe and technical. While it is true that many of the nice technicalities of the substantive criminal law have continued to exist long after the reasons for their existence have disappeared, many of these technicalities (and the severity of them) are overcome through law and practice in the realm of criminal procedure.

Is the assumption underlying the substantive criminal law that all persons whose conduct reasonably appears to be criminal (utilizing the definitions of specific crimes and the general principles of liability) shall be subjected to the full array of criminal proceedings—investigation, arrest, charge, trial, conviction, sentence, and correctional treatment? Even apart from the obvious fact that only a portion of all criminal conduct is detected, the answer is clearly no. For one thing the law has always been concerned with the risk of innocent persons being subjected to criminal proceedings, and thus certain evidentiary tests must be met at several points in the criminal process. The strictest test, that requiring evidence "beyond a reasonable doubt" for conviction, clearly rests upon the notion that it is better to allow some of the guilty to escape conviction than to risk conviction of an innocent person.

Secondly, our systems for criminal justice are pervaded by official discretion; many persons who are guilty of crimes (and who could be proved guilty) are not proceeded against because there appears to be some sound policy reason for such inaction. The authority of the prosecutor to decide on policy grounds whether to prosecute is well known, but there are several other officials who also exercise similar discretion. Finally, some of those who have engaged in criminal conduct are subjected to a part but not all of the criminal process. Sometimes this is done because of serious doubts as to whether the system can effectively deal with certain conduct that the courts or legislatures have declared criminal, while on other occasions the attempt is to reduce the burden upon the limited resources of the criminal justice system.

(a) The Evidentiary Tests. One helpful way of looking at the entire system for the administration of criminal justice is to view it as a series of critical decisions—critical to both the individual concerned and to society as a whole. Taken in their usual chronological order, the key decisions are whether and how to conduct an investigation, whether to arrest, whether to charge, whether to convict, what the sentence should be, and, finally, various decisions in the field of corrections. Although this is somewhat of an oversimplification, many of these decisions, when so ordered, result in what might be called a step profile of the criminal justice system; each succeeding decision point requires a higher degree of evidence of guilt than the immediate preceding decision. As the consequences to the individual being dealt with become more serious, the decision-maker must have a higher quantum of evidence.

In the early stages of the criminal process, the police are limited in what they may do by several evidentiary tests. Some

evidence (sometimes referred to as "reasonable grounds to suspect") must be present before an individual may be stopped and
questioned. Arrests are usually permitted only when the police have
"reasonable grounds to believe" that the person to be arrested has
committed a crime, and searches require "probable cause." Similarly, the prosecutor is limited as to whom he may charge with a
crime. At least in serious cases, an individual may not be required
to stand trial unless a magistrate has found "probable cause" at a
preliminary hearing or a grand jury has returned an indictment
based upon "probable cause." Certain correctional decisions, such
as the revocation of probation or parole, also must be based upon a
required quantum of evidence.

The high point in the evidentiary profile referred to above is
the conviction stage, for it requires admissible evidence that establishes guilt "beyond a reasonable doubt." In a number of instances
this means that the person on trial may not be convicted even
though a layman, on the basis of all available facts, would reach the
conclusion that the individual in question has engaged in criminal
conduct. For good reason, all available facts are not disclosed at
trial. Some evidence, even if it conclusively establishes guilt, may be
excluded from the trial because it was obtained in violation of the
defendant's constitutional rights. Also, much evidence of real and
substantial probative value goes out on considerations irrelevant to
its probative weight but relevant to possible misunderstanding or
misuse by the jury. As to the evidence that *is* received in the case,
the fact-finder (the jury in a jury trial, the judge in a trial without
jury) is to apply a high standard of persuasion, namely, the reasonable doubt test. Although a completely satisfactory definition of this
test has never been developed, it is commonly said that there must
be "an abiding conviction, to a moral certainty, of the truth of the
charge." (By comparison, in civil cases only a "preponderance of
evidence" is required.) There must be proof beyond a reasonable
doubt of all the elements of the crime and of the defendant's
participation or responsibility, but not of each evidentiary fact.

(b) Corpus Delicti. Also deserving mention here is the often
misunderstood concept of *corpus delicti* ("the body of the crime").
Wigmore explains it this way: every crime "reveals three component parts, *first* the *occurrence* of the specific kind of injury or loss
(as, in homicide, a person deceased; in arson, a house burnt; in
larceny, property missing); *secondly,* somebody's criminality (in
contrast, e.g., to accident) as the source of the loss,—these two
together involving the commission of a crime by *somebody;* and
thirdly, the accused's *identity* as the doer of this crime." By the
great weight of authority, the first two without the third constitute
the *corpus delicti.* Although Wigmore has written in terms of those

crimes that require not only bad conduct but also a bad result of conduct (as homicide requires a resulting death, arson a resulting burning and larceny a resulting loss of property in the sense that the property is moved out of the owner's possession), there are many crimes (e.g., attempt, conspiracy, perjury, forgery, reckless or drunken driving) that do not require the doing of any actual harm. Perhaps then it is more accurate to say that the *corpus delicti* embraces the fact that a crime has been committed by someone— i.e., that somebody did the required act or omission with the required mental fault, under the required (if any) attendant circumstances, and producing the required (if any) harmful consequence, without embracing the further fact (needed for conviction) that the defendant was the one who did or omitted that act or was otherwise responsible therefor.

The concept of *corpus delicti* in criminal law is principally used in connection with two rules, both of which are concerned with reducing the possibility of punishing a person for a crime that was never in fact committed: (1) the almost-universal American rule that, in order to convict the defendant of a crime on the basis of his extrajudicial (i.e., out of court) confession or admission, the confession or admission must be corroborated by some evidence (it need not be evidence beyond a reasonable doubt) of the *corpus delicti;* and, (2) the rule of a few states that capital punishment cannot be imposed without direct proof of the *corpus delicti.*

Most *corpus delicti* cases are homicide cases, where the difficulty may be either (a) that, the victim having simply disappeared, no dead body can be produced so as to make it absolutely certain that the victim will not later turn up alive and well, or (b) that, although a dead body is found conveniently lying about, examination of the body and the surrounding circumstances reveals that the death may have been caused as well by accident, suicide or natural causes as by someone's foul play. But the principles concerning *corpus delicti* are equally applicable to other crimes, such as arson, burglary, driving under the influence, possession of drugs, obtaining property by false pretenses, incest, larceny and robbery, and statutory rape.

In its traditional form, the *corpus delicti* rule may have barred the government from introducing the defendant's confession until it had first proved the *corpus delicti*. However, it is now generally accepted that a trial judge has the discretion to vary the order of proof, meaning that the government may introduce the defendant's confession before it has introduced the additional evidence that will establish the *corpus delicti*, so long as the *corpus delicti* is proved before the government rests. Aside from the order of proof, there is also the question of whether the *corpus delicti* rule simply defines the evidentiary foundation needed to support introduction of the defendant's confession, so that the decision is to be made by the trial judge before the case is submitted to the jury, or whether on the other hand it establishes an implicit element of the government's proof, so that the trial judge's evidentiary ruling would be merely preliminary to the jury's later determination of *corpus delicti*. There is a split of authority between the "evidentiary foundation" and "implicit element" approaches, though apparently most courts follow the latter view. It has been cogently argued, however, that the " 'implicit element' approach to corpus delicti is difficult to reconcile with our law's normal view concerning a jury's ability to dispassionately assess a confession."

(c) The Exercise of Discretion. The substantive criminal law has been aptly described as "an island of technicality in a sea of discretion." The substantive law is quite inflexible: if one moves another's property an inch one is guilty of larceny, where the other elements of larceny are present, but not if he fails to move the property; one who breaks and enters a dwelling-house of another at a certain hour may at common law be guilty of burglary, but if he does so a few minutes earlier he is innocent. And so it is with all the various crimes.

On the other hand, the procedural side of the administration of criminal justice is full of situations in which the exercise of discretion plays a large role in determining what happens to the offender. Often the victim of the crime decides not to complain to the authorities. Even if the crime becomes known to the police, they may decide not to seek out the identity of the offender or, if the offender is known, they may decide not to arrest him. Similarly, the prosecutor may exercise his well-recognized discretion and decide that certain offenders should not be prosecuted, or such a decision may be made by the magistrate at the preliminary hearing or by the grand jury. It is well known that juries sometimes refuse to convict persons who have been proved guilty beyond a reasonable doubt, and judges occasionally do likewise when the case is tried without a jury. After the verdict or plea of guilty the trial court usually has some discretion as to probation, the sentencing authority (court or jury) as to the length of sentence if probation is not granted, the parole authority as to release on parole, and the pardoning authority as to pardon or commutation.

It is important to note that in large measure such discretion is exercised because of the scope and state of the substantive criminal law. Because no legislature has succeeded in formulating a substantive criminal code that clearly encompasses all conduct intended to be made criminal and clearly excludes all other conduct, the exercise of discretion in interpreting the legislative mandate is necessary. In part the problem is the result of poor draftmanship and a failure to revise the criminal law to eliminate obsolete provisions, but it also results from the inability of a legislature to envisage all of the day-to-day situations that may arise.

This "administrative interpretation" of the substantive law, however, extends beyond the kind of statutory construction engaged in by courts under recognized principles of legislative interpretation. For example, an unambiguous statute that appears to have been broadly drafted in order to ensure against loopholes through which some offenders could regularly escape may be narrowed, for enforcement purposes, to exclude those persons not the object of real concern by the legislature. Similarly, other penal statutes are not enforced because they are viewed as obsolete or because they are thought to be only "state-declared ideals" rather than definitions of conduct that is to be routinely subjected to penal sanction.

One obvious characteristic of the substantive criminal law is that even the most carefully drafted statute cannot anticipate every situation which might arise under it. Each of the several crimes is defined to encompass a category of activity that may differ from case to case, and even the principles of justification and excuse must be stated in general terms. No more can be expected, as a legal system which seeks to cover everything by a special provision becomes cumbrous and unworkable.

The substantive criminal law, read literally, may thus appear unduly harsh, and for this reason too discretion is exercised because of the special circumstances of the individual case. As one judge has observed, "If every policeman, every prosecutor, every court, and every post-sentence agency performed his or its responsibility in strict accordance with rules of law, precisely and narrowly laid down, the criminal law would be ordered but intolerable."

Finally, the very scope of the substantive criminal law, as compared to the resources that have been allocated for its enforcement, dictate some selectivity in enforcement. Because state and local legislative bodies have not provided nearly enough funds to permit enforcement of all the criminal laws against all offenders, the boundaries of criminal law enforcement are determined more by the size of the appropriations made than by the definitions found in the substantive criminal law. Precisely what crimes deserve priority under these circumstances is a matter on which there is not agreement, although it has been suggested that the maximum sentence authorized for the various offenses might be some guide.

(d) Use of Part of the Criminal Process. Brief mention should also be made of the fact that often certain informal accommodations are resorted to whereby those who have violated the substantive criminal law are subjected to only a part of what is usually viewed as the complete criminal process. These accommodations are resorted to because it is thought that desired objectives may be best accomplished thereby, that subjecting the offender to the total process would be unduly costly in view of the minimal additional benefits to be expected, or that use of the total process is not possible even if desirable because of limited personnel and facilities. Here as well, then, the scope and coverage of the substantive criminal law has had an effect.

As we shall see later, there are constitutional limits on the power of legislatures to declare conduct criminal (see ch. 3). For example, the Supreme Court has held that narcotics addiction may not be made a crime. But even within such limitations, legislatures and courts have made criminal certain conduct that those who administer our systems for criminal justice often believe cannot be effectively dealt with by the usual process of arrest, prosecution, conviction, and sentence. Illustrative is the offense of public drunkenness. Because of a belief that nothing is to be gained by convicting the drunk and imposing a fine or jail sentence on him, it is common practice for drunks to be arrested for their own safety and then released when they are sober. Given this practice, perhaps the continued existence of public drunkenness as a crime in some jurisdictions can best be explained as an instance in which conduct is declared criminal so that the criminal justice process may perform social services not otherwise available.

Another illustration of the use of less than the total criminal process is what is commonly referred to as the negotiated plea of guilty. Very few criminal cases result in a trial; about 90 per cent are disposed of by a plea of guilty, and a good many of these pleas are obtained in exchange for a promise by the prosecutor to seek some concessions for the defendant. The offender may be permitted to plead guilty to an offense less serious than the one he actually committed; he may plead guilty to one of the offenses he has committed in exchange for the prosecutor's promise to drop or not bring other charges; or he may plead guilty in exchange for the prosecutor's promise to recommend a light sentence. Suffice it to note here that one of the explanations for this practice is the state of the substantive criminal law. Thus, when an offense carries a high mandatory minimum sentence, the trial judge may feel that by accepting lesser pleas there may result a finer adjustment to the particular crime and offender than the straight application of the rules of law would permit.

§ 1.5 Purposes of the Criminal Law—Theories of Punishment

The broad purposes of the criminal law are, of course, to make people do what society regards as desirable and to prevent them from doing what society considers to be undesirable. Since criminal law is framed in terms of imposing punishment for bad conduct, rather than of granting rewards for good conduct, the emphasis is more on the prevention of the undesirable than on the encouragement of the desirable.

In determining what undesirable conduct should be punished, the criminal law properly aims more to achieve a minimum standard of conduct than to bring about ideal conduct (say, the conduct of a highly-principled, selfless, heroic person). It is a fine thing for a man, at the risk of his own life, to enter a blazing building in order to rescue a stranger trapped therein; but the law does not (and should not) punish a failure to live up to such a heroic standard of behavior. It is a virtuous thing for an engaged man and woman to refrain from engaging in sexual intercourse until they are married; but it does not follow that the law should punish a failure to adhere to such a highly moral standard of conduct.

The protections afforded by the criminal law to the various interests of society against harm generally form the basis for a classification of crimes in any criminal code: protection from physical harm to the person; protection of property from loss, destruction or damage; protection of reputation from injury; safeguards against sexual immorality; protection of the government from injury or destruction; protection against interference with the administration of justice; protection of the public health; protection of the public peace and order; and the protection of other interests.

The criminal law is not, of course, the only weapon society uses to prevent conduct that harms or threatens to harm these important interests of the public. Education, at home and at school, as to the types of conduct that society thinks good and bad, is an important weapon; religion, with its emphasis on distinguishing between good and evil conduct, is another. The human desire to acquire and keep the affection and respect of family, friends and associates no doubt has a great influence in deterring most people from conduct that is socially unacceptable. The civil side of the law, which forces one to pay damages for the harmful results his undesirable conduct has caused to others, or which in appropriate situations grants injunctions against bad conduct or orders the specific performance of good conduct, also plays a part in influencing behavior along desirable lines.

(a) Theories of Punishment. How does the criminal law, with its threat of punishment to violators, operate to influence human conduct away from the undesirable and toward the desirable? There are a number of theories of punishment, and each theory has or has had its enthusiastic adherents. Some of the theories are concerned primarily with the particular offender, while others focus more on the nature of the offense and the general public. These theories are:

(1) **Prevention.** By this theory, also called *intimidation,* or, when the deterrence theory is referred to as general deterrence, *particular deterrence,* criminal punishment aims to deter the criminal himself (rather than to deter others) from committing further crimes, by giving him an unpleasant experience he will not want to endure again. The validity of this theory has been questioned by many, who point out the high recidivism rates of those who have been punished. On the other hand, it has been observed that our attempts at prevention by punishment may enjoy an unmeasurable degree of success, in that without punishment for purposes of prevention the rate of recidivism might be much higher. This assumption is not capable of precise proof, nor is the assertion that in some instances punishment for prevention will fill the prisoner with feelings of hatred and desire for revenge against society and thus influence future criminal conduct.

(2) **Restraint.** The notion here, also expressed as *incapacitation, isolation,* or *disablement,* is that society may protect itself from persons deemed dangerous because of their past criminal conduct by isolating these persons from society. If the criminal is imprisoned or executed, he cannot commit further crimes against society. Some question this theory because of doubts that those who present a danger of continuing criminality can be accurately identified. It has also been noted that resort to restraint without accompanying rehabilitative efforts is unwise, as the vast majority of prisoners will ultimately be returned to society. The restraint theory is sometimes employed to justify execution or life imprisonment without chance of parole for those offenders believed to be beyond rehabilitation.

(3) **Rehabilitation.** Under this theory, also called *correction* or *reformation,* we "punish" the convicted criminal by giving him appropriate treatment, in order to rehabilitate him and return him to society so reformed that he will not desire or need to commit further crimes. It is perhaps not entirely correct to call this treatment "punishment," as the emphasis is away from making him suffer and in the direction of making his life better and more pleasant. The rehabilitation theory rests upon the belief that human behavior is the product of antecedent causes, that these causes can be identified, and that on this basis therapeutic measures can be employed to effect changes in the behavior of the person treated. Even when there has been more of a commitment to the "rehabilitative ideal" than to other theories of punishment, much of what is done by way of post-conviction disposition of offenders is not truly rehabilitative. Perhaps this is why the theory of reformation has not as yet shown very satisfactory results in practice.

Some have questioned the rehabilitation theory on the ground that "it sees rule-breakers as lacking in dignity, and capable of manipulation." Others have expressed skepticism about reliance upon this theory in practice on "two distinct but related grounds: first, the great uncertainty, indeed ignorance, that presently attends our efforts to reform offenders; second, the injustices, greatly increased by our uncertainty and ignorance, that may be done to offenders who are treated differently because of assumed differences in the needs to which their penal treatment is supposed to respond."

(4) Deterrence. Under this theory, sometimes referred to as *general prevention,* the sufferings of the criminal for the crime he has committed are supposed to deter others from committing future crimes, lest they suffer the same unfortunate fate. The extent to which punishment actually has this effect upon the general public is unclear; conclusive empirical research on the subject is lacking, and it is difficult to measure the effectiveness of fear of punishment because it is but one of several forces that restrain people from violating the law.

It does seem fair to assume, however, that the deterrent efficacy of punishment varies considerably, depending upon a number of factors. Those who commit crimes under emotional stress (such as murder in the heat of anger) or who have become expert criminals through the training and practice of many years (such as the professional safebreaker and pickpocket) are less likely than others to be deterred. Even apart from the nature of the crime, individuals undoubtedly react differently to the threat of punishment, depending upon such factors as their social class, age, intelligence, and moral training. The magnitude of the threatened punishment is clearly a factor, but perhaps not as important a consideration as the probability of discovery and punishment.

(5) Education. Under this theory, criminal punishment serves, by the publicity attending the trial, conviction and punishment of criminals, to educate the public as to the proper distinctions between good conduct and bad—distinctions that, when known, most of society will observe. While the public may need no such education as to serious *malum in se* crimes, the educational function of punishment is important as to crimes that are not generally known, often misunderstood, or inconsistent with current morality.

(6) Retribution. This is the oldest theory of punishment, and the one that still commands considerable respect from the general public. By this theory, also called *revenge* or *retaliation,* punishment (the infliction of suffering) is imposed by society on criminals in order to obtain revenge, or perhaps (under the less emotional concept of retribution) because it is only fitting and just that one who has caused harm to others should himself suffer for it. Typical of the criticism is that this theory "is a form of retaliation, and as such, is morally indefensible."

However, the retribution theory, when explained on somewhat different grounds, continues to draw some support. Some contend that when one commits a crime, it is important that he receive commensurate punishment in order to restore the peace of mind and repress the criminal tendencies of others. In addition, it is claimed that retributive punishment is needed to maintain respect for the law and to suppress acts of private vengeance. For this reason, even some critics of the retribution theory acknowledge that it must occupy a "minor position" in the contemporary scheme.

Although retribution was long the theory of punishment least accepted by theorists, it "is suddenly being seen by thinkers of all political persuasions as perhaps the strongest ground, after all, upon which to base a system of punishment." Today it is commonly put forward under the rubric of "deserts" or "just deserts":

> The offender may justly be subjected to certain deprivations because he deserves it; and he deserves it because he has engaged in wrongful conduct—conduct that does or threatens injury and that is prohibited by law. The penalty is thus not just a means of crime prevention but a merited response to the actor's deed, "rectifying the balance" in the Kantian sense and expressing moral reprobation of the actor for the wrong.

Those who favor the theory claim it "provides an important check against tyranny, for a person is punished only when he deserves it; and the opposite is also true—that he is not punished if he does not deserve it." They are also likely to reject utilitarian approaches to punishment because of the view that punishment may not be inflicted upon a person in order to benefit the collective interests of others.

(7) Restoration. Yet another theory of punishment usually goes under the title of "restorative justice." Restorative justice, it is said, creates an avenue to bring criminals and their victims together rather than keep them apart. It asserts that to right the wrong that criminals have done to victims, criminals must be confronted with the actual human consequences of their actions and acknowledge the harm caused by their wrongdoing. It gives crime victims the opportunity to meet with the criminals who harmed them—to discuss the pain and disruption crime has caused their lives. It also allows sentencing options that require criminals to make some form of restitution to the specific person or persons their crime has victimized. A primary objective is making amends for the offending, particularly the harm caused to the victim, rather than inflicting pain upon the offender. Accountability is demonstrated by recognizing the wrongfulness of one's conduct, expressing remorse for the resulting injury and taking steps to repair the damage.

One central principle underlying the theory of restorative justice is that crime is not just an act against the state but against particular victims and the community in general, with offending viewed primarily as a breach of social relationships and only secondarily as a violation of law. If carried to its ultimate conclusion, restorative justice can be seen as requiring substantial changes in the structures of the criminal process whereby the disposition of a particular case is determined entirely by an agreement reached by the offender, the victim and representatives of the community affected. But even without such dramatic changes, the influence of restorative justice can be seen in the more frequent inclusion of compensation of the victim and service to the community as elements of judicial sentencing.

Restorative justice has been championed as an alternative to traditional punishment theories, particularly retribution, which it is said largely neglect the needs of those directly injured by crime and the resulting damage done to social relationships within an interconnected community. Its advocates claim that restorative practices are more cost effective, more likely to reduce crime rates and recidivism, and more humane than traditional criminal justice, American-style. But, restorative justice also has its critics. It is argued that restorative justice theory would allow disparate treatment of otherwise identical offenders, could encourage arbitrary decisionmaking, and may pay insufficient heed to society's overriding interest in punishing crime. Indeed, it is contended that a restorative justice approach reduces recidivism little, if at all. Others doubt whether restorative justice has any place in the criminal justice system; they note that while there may be powerful reasons for denominating certain behavior a crime, compensating the victim is not necessarily one of them.

(b) Conflict Between the Theories. For many years most of the literature on the subject of punishment was devoted to advocacy of a particular theory to the exclusion of others. Those who espoused the rehabilitation theory condemned the rest, those who favored the deterrence theory denied the validity of all others, and so on. But in recent years the "inclusive theory of punishment" has gained considerable support; there is now general agreement that all (or, at least most) of the theories described above deserve some consideration.

This has given rise to another difficult problem, namely, what the priority and relationship of these several aims should be. This problem must be confronted, as it is readily apparent that the various theories tend to conflict with one another at several points. The retribution, deterrence, and prevention theories call for presenting the criminal with an unpleasant experience; but the chances for rehabilitation are often defeated by harsh treatment. The rehabilitation theory would let the criminal go when (and perhaps *only* when) he had been reformed. This may be a substantially shorter period of time (or a substantially *longer* period of time) than can be justified under the deterrence and retribution theories, which would vary the punishment in accordance with the seriousness of the crime. Because of such conflicts, the legislators who enact the punishment clauses (generally with minimum and maximum provisions) for the various crimes, the judges (or, in some states as to some crimes, the juries) who must sentence the convicted defendant within the limits set forth in legislation, and the administrative officials (parole and pardoning authorities) who are empowered to release convicted criminals from imprisonment, must determine priorities.

It is undoubtedly true that the thinking of legislators, judges and juries, and administrative officers who have a part in fixing punishment, as well as the thinking of the expert criminologist and non-expert layman whose views tend to influence those officials, varies from situation to situation. Sometimes the retribution theory will predominate; most of us share the common feeling of mankind that a particularly shocking crime should be severely punished. Where, for example, a son, after thoughtfully taking out insurance on his mother's life, places a time bomb in her suitcase just before she boards a plane, which device succeeds in killing the mother and all forty-two others aboard the plane, we almost all feel that he deserves a severe punishment, and we reach this result with little reflection about influencing future conduct. Likewise, when a less serious crime is involved and it was committed by a young person who might be effectively reformed, the rehabilitation theory rightly assumes primary importance. And the deterrence theory may be most important when the crime is not inherently wrong or covered by moral prohibition. Illustrative are income tax violations, as to which deterrence is especially important because of our reliance on a system of self-assessment.

Although allowance must be made for such variables, it is fair to say, as a general proposition, that for much of the twentieth century the pendulum was swinging away from retribution and deterrence and in the direction of rehabilitation as the chief goal of punishment; or, to put it differently, away from the philosophy that the punishment should fit the crime toward one that the punishment should fit the criminal. The tendency was to move away from backward-looking and negative theories to the positive goal of influencing future conduct along desirable lines. In part, this may be attributed to the fact that we still know very little about the deterrent effect of punishment on potential offenders, while we have gained increased knowledge of the causes of human conduct as the result of scientific study in such fields as psychology, psychiatry, and criminology.

This emphasis upon rehabilitation is reflected in our criminal justice system in several ways.

Perhaps the most tangible evidences of the dominance of the rehabilitative ideal are found in its legislative expressions. Almost all of the characteristic innovations in criminal justice in this century are reflections of the rehabilitative ideal: the juvenile court, the indeterminate sentence, systems of probation and parole, the youth authority, and the promise (if not the reality) of therapeutic programs in prisons, juvenile institutes, and mental hospitals. * * * [I]t is remarkable how widely the rehabilitative ideal was accepted in this century as a statement of aspirations for the penal system, a statement largely endorsed by the media, politicians, and ordinary citizens.

But skepticism regarding the rehabilitative model began developing in the mid–1960's, and about ten years later there came "an explosion of criticism * * * calling for restructuring of the theoretical underpinnings of the criminal sanction." This rejection of rehabilitation, usually in favor of a "just deserts" theory, was prompted by several considerations. One was the concern with the wide disparity in sentencing that resulted from giving judges broad sentencing discretion to act according to the perceived rehabilitative needs in the particular case. The "just deserts" model was seen as necessary "to counter the capricious and irresponsible uses of state power." The existing system was perceived by many as being arbitrary because rehabilitative efforts were often unsuccessful. When confidence was "lost in the rehabilitative capacities of penal programs and in the ability of parole boards and correctional officers to determine when reformation has been achieved, the rehabilitationist rationale for treatment differentials no longer serves, and the differences are seen as irrational and indefensible." Finally, the retribution or "just deserts" theory, precisely because it "operates from a consensus model of society where the community * * * is acting in the right" and "the criminal is acting in the wrong," had appeal because it seemed to reaffirm our moral values at a time when they were under frequent attack.

This trend is reflected by "a spate of legislative proposals, enacted or advocated throughout the country, that attack the statutory expressions of the rehabilitative ideal. The objects of this attack are sentencing discretion, the indeterminate sentence, the parole function, the uses of probation in cases of serious criminality, and even allowances of 'good time' credit in the prisons." As this trend continues, an increasing number of jurisdictions have adopted sentencing schemes that place the greatest emphasis upon the nature of the crime committed and comparatively little upon the characteristics of the particular offender. Over the course of the present century, there will doubtless be further shifts in emphasis from one theory to another.

§ 1.6   Classification of Crimes

Crimes are classified for various purposes, the principal classification being that which divides crimes into felonies and misdemeanors. Other classifications are: crimes *mala in se* versus crimes *mala prohibita*; infamous crimes versus crimes not infamous; crimes involving moral turpitude versus those not involving moral turpitude; major crimes versus petty crimes; and common law crimes versus statutory crimes. It is important as to each classification to consider: (1) What is the distinction between the one class of crime and the other? (2) What difference does it make whether a crime is classified one way or the other?

(a) Felony and Misdemeanor. The most important classification of crime in general use in the United States is that of felony and misdemeanor. In this country the distinction is usually spelled out by statute or (far less frequently) by the constitution. In the modern codes, it is sometimes provided that a crime punishable by death or imprisonment in the state prison (or penitentiary) is a felony, and that any other crime (i.e., any crime punishable only by fine or by imprisonment in a local jail or both) is a misdemeanor. The practical effect of that dividing line is usually such that these statutes indirectly state what the statutes in almost all other jurisdictions expressly declare: that any crime punishable by death or imprisonment for more than one year (or, occasionally, for one year or more) is a felony and that any other crime is a misdemeanor. The typical provision, in whichever of these two forms it may be found, uses the word "punishable" or the phrase "which may be punished." Under a test so worded it is the possible sentence, not the actual sentence imposed, which controls, by the great weight of authority. There is some authority to the effect that the sentence actually imposed governs, and even a third view that a crime punishable either by imprisonment in the penitentiary or by a fine is a misdemeanor even though the sentence is actually imprisonment in the penitentiary.

Thus in the United States most criminal statutes defining specific crimes do not themselves label as felonies or misdemeanors the crimes that they describe, leaving the matter to be determined by reference to the punishment provided (according to the place or to the length of confinement). Some statutes defining crimes provide that whoever is guilty of certain described conduct shall be guilty of a felony (or shall be guilty of a misdemeanor), sometimes without setting forth any punishment. There is generally to be found, however, some catch-all statute that provides for the punishment to be awarded for crimes which the statutes designate as felonies or misdemeanors but which do not themselves set forth the punishment to be awarded.

What difference does it make whether a particular crime is labeled a felony or misdemeanor? It may be important to make the distinction for purposes either (1) of the substantive criminal law, or (2) of criminal procedure, or (3) of legal matters entirely outside the field of criminal law.

So far as the substantive criminal law is concerned, there are a number of crimes whose elements are defined, or whose punishment is stated, with reference to felonies as distinguished from misdemeanors. Burglary is defined at common law as breaking and entering another's dwelling house at night with intent to commit a felony (a misdemeanor will not do) therein. An accidental death in the commission or attempted commission of a felony may constitute murder under appropriate circumstances, but an accidental death resulting from the commission of or attempt to commit a misdemeanor generally can constitute no more than manslaughter. There exists a common law crime of compounding a felony, which is committed by one who for a consideration agrees not to prosecute for, or agrees to keep quiet about, a felony (but not a misdemeanor) he knows has been committed. At common law parties involved in felonies are divided into principals and accessories, from which fact various consequences followed, whereas with misdemeanors all parties are considered principals. The punishment clauses of criminal statutes are not infrequently worded in terms of felony or misdemeanor; thus a criminal conspiracy (or attempt) statute may provide for one punishment in the case of a conspiracy (or attempt) to commit a felony, and a lighter punishment where there is a conspiracy (or attempt) to commit a misdemeanor. In that part of the substantive criminal law dealing with justifiable homicide, the rule of justification is sometimes worded in terms of felony as distinguished from misdemeanor. Thus it may under appropriate circumstances be justifiable homicide (i.e., no crime at all) intentionally to kill as a last resort in order to prevent the commission of a felony (but not to prevent the commission of a misdemeanor), or in order to effect the lawful arrest of, or prevent the threatened escape of, a felon (but not a misdemeanant).

In the area of criminal procedure, many of the procedural rules depend upon whether the crime in question is a felony or a misdemeanor. A court's jurisdiction over a crime often depends upon whether the crime is classified as a felony or a misdemeanor. The law of arrest distinguishes between arrest for a felony and for a misdemeanor. In some jurisdictions, felonies must be prosecuted upon a grand jury indictment, whereas an information will do for a misdemeanor. An accused felon must generally be present at his trial, though a misdemeanant may agree to be tried in his absence. A witness, including a criminal defendant who testifies in his own behalf, may be impeached on the ground of former conviction of felony, but not of misdemeanor, in some jurisdictions. Habitual criminal statutes normally provide for increased criminal punishment where the defendant has a record of prior convictions of felonies (but not of misdemeanors). The rules relating to probation and parole may differ depending upon whether the defendant has been convicted of a felony or a misdemeanor.

Even outside the area of substantive or procedural criminal law the distinction between felony and misdemeanor is frequently important. One convicted of a felony is in some jurisdictions disqualified from holding public office. He may lose his right to vote or serve on a jury; he may be prohibited from practicing as an attorney. Conviction of felony is often made a ground for divorce. These by-products of conviction of a felony do not generally apply to conviction of a misdemeanor.

The above examples demonstrate that the classification of crime into the two great subdivisions—felony and misdemeanor—is an important one both within and outside the field of criminal law.

(b) Malum In Se and Malum Prohibitum. Crimes are divided for certain purposes into crimes *mala in se* (wrong in themselves; inherently evil) and crimes *mala prohibita* (not inherently evil; wrong only because prohibited by legislation). The distinction, though an ancient one, has survived down to the present time, especially in the area of criminal manslaughter and battery.

Some difficulty has been encountered by the courts in putting particular crimes into one category or the other. Though courts tend to classify common law crimes as *mala in se* and statutory crimes as *mala prohibita,* such a test does not always work, for some statutory crimes have been held to be *mala in se.* It has been said that a crime of which a criminal intent is an element is *malum in se,* but if no criminal intent is required, it is *malum prohibitum;* and that generally a crime involving "moral turpitude" is *malum in se,* but otherwise it is *malum prohibitum.* In a general way, it may be said that crimes which are dangerous to life or limb are likely to be classified as *mala in se*, while other crimes are more likely to be considered *mala prohibita*.

Applying these various generalities to particular crimes, the courts have held these crimes to be *mala in se:* battery, robbery, grand or petit larceny, malicious injury to property, burglary, drunken driving (driving while intoxicated), public drunkenness, possession of drugs, abortion, and attempted suicide. On the other hand, courts have held these crimes to be *mala prohibita:* driving over the speed limit, driving on a suspended or revoked license, failure to yield the right of way, leaving the scene of an accident, failure to wear a seat belt, driving under the influence of intoxicants, sale of intoxicating liquors, public intoxication, hunting without permission, selling unregistered securities, false notarization of a document, carrying a concealed weapon, shooting in a public place, defacing the flag, keeping slot machines, evasion of taxes, and passing through a toll gate without paying the toll.

It may be that the violation of a criminal statute can be considered *malum prohibitum* or *malum in se* depending upon the degree of the violation. Thus speeding a little over the limit may be *malum prohibitum,* but speeding at high speed *malum in se*. Or a violation of a statute prohibiting driving under the influence of liquor might be *malum prohibitum* if the defendant, though under the influence, was not actually intoxicated; but *malum in se* if intoxicated.

What difference does it make whether a crime is classified as *malum prohibitum* or *malum in se?* In the field of substantive criminal law, the principal use of the distinction is with respect to the crimes of manslaughter and battery. One whose criminal conduct *malum in se* causes unintended death (or injury) may be guilty of manslaughter (or battery) without regard to the unlikelihood of that result; but if his conduct is only *malum prohibitum,* he is generally not as readily liable for manslaughter (or battery)—the principal view being that he is liable only if death (or injury) is the foreseeable consequence of his criminal act. Courts faced with the statutory interpretation problem of whether a particular crime may be committed without any sort of bad intent sometimes utilize the distinction by stating that the crime is *malum in se* and so needs a bad intent, or is *malum prohibitum* and so does not. Also, when a statute criminalizes conduct that is *malum in se*, the statute is less susceptible to a challenge of being void for vagueness because the evil being remedied is commonly understood. The distinction also is sometimes used in criminal (or civil) procedure, as under a rule of evidence that a witness may be impeached on account of his prior conviction of a misdemeanor *malum in se,* but not *malum prohibitum*. It is sometimes used in areas of the law outside the field of criminal law and procedure.

When the issue involved in a case is the criminal manslaughter or battery responsibility of the defendant who unintentionally kills or injures another in the commission of some other crime, then, if the concept of crimes *mala in se* is used at all as a basis for liability, the term should be limited to crimes that involve danger of death or injury, and should not include crimes that may be considered morally wrong. Danger and not morality should be the decisive factor here. (Of course, when the issue in a case is disbarment, deportation, impeachment of a witness or the right to recover on an illegal contract, the emphasis ought to be on the morality of the crime in question.) The difficulty of classifying particular crimes as *mala in se* or *mala prohibita* suggests further that the classification should be abandoned, at least in homicide and battery cases. Some cases quite sensibly ignore the distinction and yet reach proper conclusions as to liability on the basis of the danger of death or injury involved in the defendant's criminal conduct.

(c) Crimes Involving Moral Turpitude. For some purposes crimes are divided on the basis of whether or not they involve moral turpitude. Legislation in some jurisdictions has provided for the exclusion or deportation of aliens, or for the disbarment of attorneys or the revocation of the licenses of doctors, or for the impeachment of witnesses, who have been convicted of "crimes involving moral turpitude." These same unfortunate consequences (deportation, disbarment, etc.) do not, by such legislation, follow conviction of crimes not involving moral turpitude. The distinction between crimes that do and do not involve moral turpitude is much the same as the distinction between crimes *mala in se* and crimes *mala prohibita;* so much so that courts often define one phrase in terms of its counterpart. Just as the courts have found it difficult sometimes to distinguish between the crimes that are *mala in se* and those *mala prohibita,* so have the courts been troubled by the vagueness of the phrase "moral turpitude." We have seen that the *malum prohibitum/malum in se* distinction may mean different things in different settings; so too the definition of the phrase "crimes involving moral turpitude" may depend somewhat on the setting in which the phrase occurs.

(d) Infamous Crimes. Crimes are divided for some purposes into infamous crimes and those not infamous. Several American constitutions, including the United States Constitution, require that infamous crimes be prosecuted by indictment. In a number of states, statutes provide for certain consequences (e.g., disbarment of attorneys, disenfranchisement of voters, disqualification of jurors or public officeholders) that follow conviction of an infamous crime. At common law one who had been convicted of an infamous crime was incompetent to testify as a witness; today persons who have been convicted of crime are generally competent witnesses, but modern statutes usually permit impeachment on account of their convictions, sometimes, however, limited to infamous crimes.

Once again, whether a particular crime is to be considered infamous or not may depend, to a large extent, on the purpose for which the distinction is to be made. Where the purpose was in former times to render a witness incompetent (or today to authorize the impeachment of the witness), the term "infamous" properly has reference to those crimes involving fraud or dishonesty or the obstruction of justice (sometimes called *crimen falsi*). Where the term is used in connection with disbarment or disqualification to hold office, vote or serve on a jury, it generally has a similar meaning. Under constitutional provisions relating to indictment, however, the factors of fraud and dishonesty are not especially pertinent. The United States Supreme Court and several states have held that, in this connection, "infamous" refers, not to the nature of the crime, but rather to the kind of punishment that may be awarded. Thus "infamous crime" in the Fifth Amendment concerning indictment includes crime (even a misdemeanor) punishable by imprisonment at hard labor, or in a prison or penitentiary. The states whose constitutional provisions require indictments for infamous crimes generally equate the term "infamous crime" with felony, without emphasis on the hard labor aspects of possible punishment.

(e) Petty Offenses. Crimes are for some purposes divided into major crimes and petty crimes. Generally speaking, petty offenses are a sub-group of misdemeanors; that is, a felony is necessarily a major crime, but a misdemeanor may be either a major crime or a petty offense depending upon the possible punishment. It is commonly a rule of criminal jurisdiction that petty offenses may be tried by a magistrate summarily. Summary procedure means a trial without many of the usual paraphernalia required for criminal trials for the greater crimes—i.e., without a preliminary examination, without an indictment (or probably even on information; the defendant may generally be tried on the complaint) and usually without a jury. Aside from the question of summary jurisdiction of magistrates, the defendant may constitutionally be denied a jury trial for a petty offense even when tried in a regular court of record. In many states the borderline between major crimes and petty offenses is not spelled out by statute, so that the courts themselves have had to draw the line.

A special problem exists as to whether a minor offense that requires for its commission no bad intent and involves only a light punishment should be classified as a "crime" at all, or whether instead it should not be called a "public tort" or a "civil offense" or by some other more pleasant name not involving the stigma inherent in the word "crime." Such strict-liability offenses are in most jurisdictions still considered crimes, however, in spite of the good arguments that have been made to the contrary.

(f) **Common Law Crimes and Statutory Crimes.** Historically, the first step in the creation of crimes was taken by the courts, which invented a few important "common law" crimes, setting forth their definitions and providing for their punishments. Later, as the legislature came to sit more regularly and more often, that body took over more and more the task of creating, defining and punishing new crimes (by statute) and to some extent changing the scope of the old judge-made crimes, until today the law of crimes is mostly statutory law. One question remains to this day: to what extent may a court now create a new crime where the legislature has not done so? Another modern problem concerns the way in which courts interpret statutes defining crimes; the answer sometimes depends upon whether the crime in question involves a statutory definition of one of the old judge-made crimes or whether it concerns a definition of a crime the legislature first created. The classification is sometimes important in other areas of the criminal law.

§ 1.7   Classification of Proceedings

Proceedings to determine the guilt or innocence of those accused of a "crime," as that word is used herein, must be distinguished from other related proceedings, such as those dealing with juvenile delinquency, sexual psychopathy, municipal ordinance violations, statutory penalties, and contempt of court. These other proceedings, though serving objectives not unlike many of the aims of punishment for crime, are usually said to be civil in nature, or perhaps quasi-criminal (or, in the case of criminal contempt, summary). One important reason why such classifications are significant is that those dealt with in other than regular criminal proceedings are not entitled to all of the constitutional and statutory protections provided for criminal defendants.

(a) **Juvenile Delinquency.** As we shall see, at common law and today generally by statute children under a certain age are deemed completely incapable of crime (see § 8.6). Often there is also an age group beyond this age of absolute incapability within which the prosecution must, to convict, prove that the child had the mental capacity to know right from wrong. Aside from these rules concerning capacity to commit crime, every state and the District of Columbia have in modern times created a new type of misbehavior called "juvenile delinquency." Those children under a certain age who commit what would be crimes if committed by adults are instead adjudicated as juvenile delinquents; this is a civil rather than a criminal matter, calling for treatment instead of punishment.

Juvenile courts or family courts have been created by statute (either as separate courts or as branches of existing courts) to handle juvenile delinquency cases. These statutes also set the upper age limit for juvenile court jurisdiction and determine the division of jurisdiction in these cases between the juvenile and criminal courts. Some statutes give the juvenile court discretion, in the case of all offenses that would be criminal if committed by adults, to determine whether to retain jurisdiction or to deliver the juvenile to the criminal courts, while some other states place the decision in the hands of the prosecutor. In some other states the juvenile court has exclusive jurisdiction, although it is common to except certain serious offenses. As to such exceptional crimes, the criminal courts may be allowed to transfer the case to juvenile court, or the juvenile court may be authorized to decide whether the juvenile should be dealt with as a criminal or a delinquent, or the legislature may have conferred no discretion on this matter whatsoever.

The typical juvenile delinquency statute indicates more or less specifically that juvenile delinquency proceedings are designed not for the punishment of the offender but for the salvation of the child. In other words, the proceedings are civil, not criminal. A long-standing consequence of this distinction was that youths proceeded against in juvenile court were not entitled to the many rights recognized for criminal defendants, such as those of confrontation of witnesses, counsel, and the privilege against self-incrimination. However, because of the decision of the United States Supreme Court in *In re Gault* (1967) and subsequent developments, this has changed substantially.

Juvenile courts are often given jurisdiction over offenses committed by adults against juveniles, such as contributing to the delinquency or neglect of children. Such proceedings are criminal in nature, and the ordinary rules of criminal procedure must be followed.

(b) Sexual Psychopathy. About half of the states have enacted statutes establishing special procedures for dealing with the "sexual psychopath" or "sexually dangerous person." These laws provide for the selection of certain persons, those who have committed sex offenses or who are believed likely to do so, for special disposition, which involves their referral to special facilities and their continued custody until they are believed to pose no danger to the community. The sexual psychopath statutes appear to be based upon the assumptions that: (1) they are needed for the protection of society (that is, that the regular processes of the criminal law are inadequate for this purpose); and (2) the designated individuals, more than the ordinary criminal, are susceptible to effective medical treatment. Both of these assumptions have been seriously questioned.

The statutes vary considerably as to the basis for jurisdiction: most require that the person have been convicted of some crime or of a specific sex crime; several others require that the person be charged with some crime or a sex crime; while a few require neither charge nor conviction but only probable cause that the person is a sexual psychopath. Assuming a basis for jurisdiction, the statutes also are not in agreement as to whether the institution of proceedings by prosecutor or judge is discretionary or mandatory. If proceedings are initiated, they usually require a medical examination of the alleged sexual psychopath, which is followed by a judicial hearing. If the individual is found to be a sexual psychopath, then he is committed for an indeterminate term, and release usually comes only upon a finding that the individual no longer represents a danger to society.

The prevailing view is that sexual psychopath proceedings are civil and not criminal in nature. One consequence of this is that it may not be viewed as double jeopardy subsequently to prosecute the individual for the crime that gave rise to the sexual psychopath proceedings (or, where these proceedings are undertaken after conviction, to now require him to serve the sentence for the criminal conviction), although some jurisdictions by statute require termination of the criminal proceedings or give credit on the sentence for the previous confinement. Another consequence of the characterization of the proceedings as civil is that the alleged sexual psychopath may not be granted all of the procedural rights afforded a defendant in a criminal case. There is, however, increasing acceptance of the position that, because one found to be a sexual psychopath is deprived of his liberty as a result of the proceedings, many of the safeguards normal to criminal prosecutions must be followed.

(c) Violations of Municipal Ordinances. By the weight of authority, violations of the ordinances of local governmental organizations (municipalities or counties), although resembling crimes, are not strictly criminal. Pursuant to authorization from the legislature, these local governmental units have the police power to regulate for the protection of the lives, health and property of their inhabitants and the preservation of good order and morals. Thus in most states the typical city or town has passed numerous ordinances on local traffic matters—forbidding speeding, regulating parking, prohibiting careless and reckless driving, requiring stops at stop-signs, within municipal territorial limits; and usually has passed ordinances covering local non-traffic matters as well—curbing dogs, cleaning sidewalks of snow and ice, requiring compliance with health and building regulations and regulating the disposal of trash and garbage. Not infrequently the ordinances forbid some of the same matters that state criminal laws forbid—driving while intoxicated, hit-and-run driving, assault and battery, petit theft. Pursuant to authority from the state, these ordinances frequently provide for fines or imprisonment or both for their violation, although sometimes the power to imprison is limited to imprisonment for failure to pay a fine. A municipal court (variously called municipal court, police court, city court, etc.) is generally created to exercise jurisdiction over cases involving municipal violations committed within the limited territorial jurisdiction of the municipality in question.

Just as a state statute may be invalid because the subject matter has been preempted by the federal government, a municipal ordinance may likewise be held unenforceable because state legislation has occupied the field. And in any event an ordinance is invalid if it is directly contrary to state law—either in purporting to permit that which state law proscribes or in purporting to forbid that which state law expressly permits. Absent preemption, it is not objectionable that a municipal ordinance parallels a state penal statute, and this is so even though there is a difference in the applicable penalties. Given the fact that state and municipal prosecution for the same conduct is impermissible, the existence of such differences can give rise to state-local conflict.

The majority view is that the violation of a municipal ordinance constitutes a civil wrong against the municipality, even though the ordinance authorizes imprisonment as a penalty for violation, and even when the state criminal laws prohibit the same conduct as that prohibited by the ordinance. The consequences of the view that municipal violations are civil wrongs, rather than criminal, arise mainly in determining the procedure to be followed in the proceedings against the violator. Thus it has been held that the prosecution need not be begun by warrant issued upon oath; that the violator is not entitled to a jury trial (even though the offense is such that if it were prosecuted by the state as a crime a jury would be required); that the defendant may be called by the prosecutor as an adverse witness; that proof beyond a reasonable doubt is not necessary for conviction; that (if there is a jury trial) the judge may direct a verdict of conviction; that all the rules of evidence applicable in criminal trials need not be followed; and that the municipality may appeal from an acquittal of the defendant.

On the other hand, some states have taken the view that, at least where imprisonment is an authorized penalty, municipal violations are criminal, not civil, offenses. Another position is that municipal violations are criminal if the conduct forbidden by the ordinance is also forbidden by a counterpart state statute. Other states have stated that municipal violations are quasi-criminal, or partly criminal, and then they apply at least some of the principles of criminal procedure to prosecutions for ordinance violations, especially where the ordinance in question prohibits the same conduct prohibited by the state criminal law (statutory law, or common law if applicable) or where the ordinance provides for imprisonment as a punishment.

The modern trend is away from the notion that municipal violations are civil offenses and in the direction of calling them criminal, especially when violation is punishable by imprisonment as an end in itself, and not simply as a method of collecting a fine. It is perhaps possible to view the collection of a fine as a civil matter, but sixty days in jail is hardly an appropriate remedy for a civil wrong. Even the language of municipal violations is more nearly criminal than civil: the defendant is "prosecuted," he is asked to plead "guilty" or "not guilty," he is "convicted" or "acquitted," he is "sentenced" to fine or imprisonment. It would seem preferable frankly to label such violations as criminal and, as a consequence thereof, afford the defendant the same procedural safeguards to which he would be entitled in criminal cases of equal seriousness.

(d) Statutory Penalties. Statutes, federal and state, not infrequently forbid certain conduct and then provide for pecuniary penalties for violations of the statute. Sometimes the pecuniary penalty is in lieu of the usual criminal penalty of fine or imprisonment, sometimes it is in addition to regular criminal punishment. Under some statutes the penalty may be recovered by the state; in others by an injured party or by an informer. Under some statutes the penalty is a fixed amount; under others it is a percentage of an amount due as a result of the forbidden conduct or a multiple of the damages caused by such conduct. Sometimes the statute provides that the penalty is recoverable in a civil action; sometimes it provides for recovery by indictment or information; often the nature of the proceedings is not mentioned.

The question frequently arises as to whether the proceedings to recover statutory penalties are criminal or civil. Should the action be brought in a court of civil or of criminal jurisdiction? Is the civil or the criminal statute of limitations applicable? Is the defendant entitled to the rights of a criminal defendant at the trial—the right to a jury trial, to be confronted by witnesses, to refrain from taking the stand, to be convicted only on proof beyond a reasonable doubt—or to the rights of a defendant in a civil suit? Is it double jeopardy to sue for the penalty if the defendant had been tried criminally for his violation of the statute? If the verdict is against the suing party, may he move for a new trial or appeal, or is a second trial barred by the prohibition against double jeopardy?

The courts have generally considered that proceedings to recover statutory penalties are civil in nature, and therefore the rules governing civil procedure are applicable. But a number of cases have held the proceedings under particular statutes to be criminal, therefore applying rules of criminal procedure; or to be quasi-criminal, therefore applying at least some of the criminal procedural rules. Insofar as the proceedings are criminal, they are within the scope of this book.

(e) Contempt of Court. Contempt of court is divided into (1) criminal contempt and (2) civil contempt, depending upon whether the purpose of the contempt proceeding is to punish or coerce. It is also divided into (1) direct contempt and (2) indirect (or constructive) contempt, depending upon whether the contempt was in the presence of the court (and perhaps in the judge's view or hearing) or not.

Looking at contempt of court from the point of view of the purpose of the contempt proceeding, contempts may be divided into "two classes,—those prosecuted to preserve the power and vindicate the dignity of the courts, and to punish for disobedience of their orders; and those instituted to preserve and enforce the rights of private parties to suits, and to compel obedience to orders and decrees made to enforce the rights and administer the remedies to which the court has found them to be entitled. The former are criminal and punitive in their nature, and the government, the courts, and the people are interested in their prosecution. The latter are civil, remedial, and coercive in their nature, and the parties chiefly in interest in their conduct and prosecution are the individuals whose private rights and remedies they were instituted to protect or enforce."

Especially when the civil-criminal distinction is being drawn for purposes of determining whether the constitutional protections attendant criminal proceedings must be followed, the classification depends not "on what the underlying purposes are perceived to be," but rather upon "the character of the relief that the proceeding will afford," that is, whether that relief is remedial or punitive. As the Supreme Court stated in *Hicks on Behalf of Feiock v. Feiock* (1988):

> If the relief provided is a sentence of imprisonment, it is remedial if "the defendant stands committed unless and until he performs the affirmative act required by the court's order," and is punitive if "the sentence is limited to imprisonment for

a definite period." If the relief provided is a fine, it is remedial when it is paid to the complainant, and punitive when it is paid to the court, though a fine that would be payable to the court is also remedial when the defendant can avoid paying the fine simply by performing the affirmative act required by the court's order.

Even if the relief imposed is a determinate sentence, the contempt is nonetheless civil if that sentence contains a purge clause allowing the party held in contempt to avoid the balance of such sentence by performing the acts contemplated by the court's order.

Thus it is a civil contempt for one, after having been enjoined by a court from doing a certain act, to do it; or conversely for one, ordered by the court to do some act, not to do it, at least if it is within his power to do it. For his civil contempt he may be imprisoned until he purges himself by compliance with the order (which in the case of a violation of an order prohibitory in nature requires expression of "an intention of future compliance"). On the other hand, one is guilty of criminal contempt if, whether with good aim or bad, he throws a brickbat at the judge sitting on the bench; or, whether an attorney, litigant, juror, witness or spectator, he behaves in a disrespectful or boisterous manner in court; or refuses to obey a lawful order of the court; or commits an assault or battery upon someone (judge, juror, attorney, litigant, witness, bailiff or marshal) in the courtroom.

One who obstructs justice by committing perjury or who procures or tries to procure another to commit perjury, is guilty of criminal contempt. A litigant who tampers with the jury trying his case or with a witness in his case, is likewise guilty of criminal contempt. So too is a juror who is guilty of misconduct in connection with the case he is trying. A witness who, though ordered to do so by the court, refuses to appear in court or to answer a proper question put to him in court or by a grand jury or administrative body, or who refuses to produce before the appropriate body papers in his possession called for by a subpoena duces tecum, is guilty of criminal contempt, unless of course his refusal is based upon a privilege properly invoked by him. Disobedience of the court's order to a defendant on bail to surrender himself to begin serving his sentence is a criminal contempt.

In the case of the criminal contempt, a fine or imprisonment for a definite term may be awarded as punishment. One thus punished by a definite sentence for criminal contempt cannot purge himself of contempt by undoing the wrong he did, as in the case of civil contempt.

A single act or refusal to act in violation of a court order often constitutes both civil contempt and criminal contempt, for which he may be fined or imprisoned for the purpose of coercing him into doing the right thing, and in addition fined or imprisoned for the purpose of punishing him for having done the wrong thing; and principles of double jeopardy do not stand in the way of applying both coercive and punitive sanctions.

For purposes of the appropriate procedure to be used for dealing with civil and criminal contempts, contempts are divided into direct contempts and indirect (sometimes called constructive) contempts. A contempt that is committed in the actual presence of the court (in the courtroom or in chambers) or in its immediate vicinity, whether during a trial or during a recess in the trial, is a direct contempt generally punishable summarily. An indirect contempt, one committed outside the presence or immediate vicinity of the court but which nevertheless improperly interferes with the work of the court, is punishable only after notice (by an indictment or information, or by an order to show cause) and hearing, with an opportunity to be heard in defense to the charge.

It is a direct contempt, for instance, for lawyers or parties to talk disrespectfully to the judge on the bench or to commit assaults or batteries during the course of the trial, or for newspapermen to take surreptitious pictures in court when forbidden to do so. On the other hand, it is an indirect contempt for a litigant or his attorney to tamper with a juror away from the courthouse, to destroy evidence that might be used against the litigant, or to go to the home or office of a prospective witness in a pending case, in order to bribe or intimidate him concerning his testimony. It is generally considered an indirect contempt for a newspaperman falsely to charge in an editorial that a court trying or hearing the appeal of a pending case has been bribed.

It has been said that criminal contempt is a crime, just as much as perjury or any other crime against the administration of justice; or that it is a quasi-crime; or that it is no crime at all. What these conflicting expressions seem to signify is that, on the substantive law side, criminal contempt is very much like an ordinary crime; but procedurally may be treated quite differently. Although it has been held that criminal contempt is a common law crime inherited from England and hence a crime, though no statute makes it so, in those American jurisdictions that recognize common law crimes, yet even in those jurisdictions that do not recognize common law crimes, a power to punish for contempt exists. In some jurisdictions, however, the legislature has enacted an ordinary statutory crime called contempt, sometimes varying the common law elements thereof.

Criminal contempt, like most ordinary crimes, requires something in the way of a bad state of mind: there must be at least an intent to do the act constituting the contempt, or possibly reckless-ly doing the act; it is not necessary, however, that one do the act with any specific intent to be contemptuous or insulting.

Conduct constituting a criminal contempt of court may, of course, also constitute one of the ordinary crimes, as where a disappointed litigant hurls a missile at the judge (a battery if his aim is good, an assault if he misses), or where a witness, intending to obstruct the administration of justice, testifies falsely upon the witness stand (perjury). The fact that the conduct which constitutes criminal contempt is also an ordinary crime does not prevent its punishment as contempt. The rule against double jeopardy forbids punishment both for the criminal contempt and for the ordinary crime.

The procedures that are used to deal with a criminal contempt differ depending upon whether or not the contempt was committed in the actual view or hearing of the judge. If the contempt was committed within the presence of the court, it is then punishable by the judge at once, summarily, on his own knowledge, without a formal written accusation, arraignment, plea, proof, or other trap-pings of an ordinary criminal prosecution. This is because of the "need for immediate penal vindication of the dignity of the court." Other forms of contempt, however, require more elaborate proce-dures, although not all of the safeguards of a criminal trial are necessary. There is no right to a grand jury indictment, but the accused is entitled to fair notice of the charges, and a reasonable opportunity to defend against them with the assistance of counsel, the right to call witnesses, and to confront and cross-examine the witnesses against him. He cannot be compelled to testify against himself, he must be proved guilty beyond a reasonable doubt, and the state or other party may not appeal.

It was long the rule that there was no constitutional right to jury trial in a criminal contempt case. In *Cheff v. Schnackenberg* (1966), however, the Court, in upholding a six-month jail sentence for contempt imposed without jury trial, intimated that the result would have been otherwise had the punishment not been within the "petty offense" exception to the right to jury trial in criminal cases. Finally, in *Bloom v. Ill.* (1968) the Court expressly held that the Constitution requires jury trial for criminal contempt except for those in the "petty offense" category. Moreover, the Court declined to create an exception for direct contempt cases; while the need "to quell a disturbance cannot attend upon the impaneling of a jury," the solution in such a case is summary punishment of not more than six months imprisonment.

§ 1.8   Burden of Proof; Directed Verdict

What are customarily referred to as the elements of crime—a specified act or omission, usually a concurring specified mental state, and often specified attendant circumstances and a specified harmful result caused by the conduct—are described and discussed herein both in general terms (see chs. 4, 5) and with respect to certain crimes against the person and certain crimes relating to property (see chs. 13–16). Considerable attention is also given to the various defenses to crime, both those based upon an alleged lack of responsibility and those based upon a claim of some justification or other excuse (see chs. 6, 8–9). One cannot appreciate the full significance of these elements and defenses without an understanding of the significance of their proof or lack of proof at the criminal trial. It is thus necessary to give some attention to certain matters that are procedural in nature, but which have a large substantive dimension: the burden of proof; and directed verdicts.

(a) Aspects of Burden of Proof. It is a basic policy of Anglo–American criminal law that, in view of the serious consequences following conviction of crime, the prosecution has the burden of proving beyond a reasonable doubt all the facts necessary to establish the defendant's guilt. This burden of proof has two separate aspects: (1) The burden of producing evidence; and (2) the burden of persuading the fact-finder (jury; or judge sitting without a jury). Thus the prosecution must both produce evidence of, and persuade beyond a reasonable doubt of, the existence of certain facts relating to defendant's guilt of the crime charged.

But a question of some difficulty is: what sorts of facts are meant? In a jury trial of A for the battery of B, for instance, the prosecution must certainly introduce evidence, and persuade the jury beyond a reasonable doubt, (1) that A did an act (fired a gun, threw a rock, swung a stick, drove a car), (2) which caused bodily injury to B, (3) which result was either intended by A or was within the risk that A's reckless conduct created—these three items being the elements of the crime of battery. But what about matters of defense that negative guilt, such as self defense, duress and insanity? Must the prosecution, while presenting its side of the case, produce evidence of facts showing that A did not act in self-defense, that A was not coerced, that A was sane, and so on; and must the prosecution convince the jury of the non-existence of facts giving rise to these defenses beyond a reasonable doubt? It would, of course, make the prosecution of A for the simple battery of B a rather cumbersome proceeding if the prosecution had to establish its case by proving, not only the existence of the three elements of the crime, but also the non-existence of every conceivable defense.

The rules that have developed concerning both the burden of production and the burden of persuasion cannot be satisfactorily explained on the basis of any single principle. The exceptional situation in which we place one or both burdens upon the defendant has sometimes been explained in terms of relieving the prosecution of the necessity of proving a negative or in terms of requiring the defendant to prove defenses that are not a part of the definition of the crime. Neither is totally convincing. "What is involved seems rather a more subtle balance which acknowledges that a defendant ought not to be required to defend until some solid substance is presented to support the accusation, but beyond this perceives a point where need for narrowing the issues coupled with the relative accessibility of evidence to the defendant warrants calling upon him to present his defensive claim."

(b) Elements of the Crime. It is everywhere agreed that the prosecution has the burden of proving each of the various elements of the offense in both burden-of-proof senses: it must, to avoid a directed verdict of acquittal, produce evidence of each element; and it must, to secure a conviction, convince the trier of fact of the existence of each element beyond a reasonable doubt. Because this was the law in all jurisdictions, the United States Supreme Court for many years never had occasion to hold explicitly that proof of a criminal charge beyond a reasonable doubt was constitutionally required, although such view was frequently expressed in the Court's decisions. But in the course of holding that due process required this burden of proof to be met in juvenile court cases, the Supreme Court in *In re Winship* (1970) explicitly held "that the Due Process Clause protects the accused against conviction except upon proof beyond a reasonable doubt of every fact necessary to constitute the crime with which he is charged."

In the *Winship* opinion, the Court explained why the reasonable-doubt standard is indispensable in American criminal procedure. The basic point, of course, is that it is "a prime instrument for reducing the risk of convictions resting on factual error." There are several reasons, the Court noted, for reducing the margin of error in criminal cases in this way: (1) because the individual defendant has at stake an interest of immense importance, both in terms of the possibility that he will lose his liberty and that he would be stigmatized by the conviction; (2) because the moral force of the criminal law would be diluted if the public was in doubt whether innocent men were being convicted; and (3) because every individual going about his ordinary affairs should have confidence that the government cannot judge him guilty of a criminal offense without convincing the fact-finder of his guilt with utmost certainty.

The existence of certain facts may call for increased punishment—as under a statute, applicable to a single crime, punishing armed robbery more severely than simple robbery, or under habitual criminal statutes, applicable to many crimes punishing subsequent offenders more heavily than first offenders. The prosecution has the burden of proving the aggravated-punishment facts, which may be considered to be, in a sense, elements of a principal crime. Thus when the prosecution seeks, in connection with defendant's conviction of the crime charged, to impose habitual criminal punishment on account of former crimes committed by the defendant, the prosecution must produce evidence of the facts that these other crimes were committed and that the defendant committed them, and then persuade the fact-finder of these matters beyond a reasonable doubt. (Of course, if the legislature makes a certain issue, e.g., the quantity of drugs possessed, a sentencing issue rather than a guilt issue, then the defendant's "procedural protections are vastly diminished" and the prosecution's burden is only a preponderance of the evidence, which is why there are "constitutional limits on a legislature's ability to designate a particular issue as a sentencing factor rather than as an element of a crime.")

That the *Winship* principle also applies to elements that serve to distinguish a more serious crime from a less serious crime (as compared to elements that serve to distinguish criminal from noncriminal conduct) was settled by the Supreme Court in *Mullaney v. Wilbur* (1975). The defendant there had been convicted of murder in Maine despite his defense of provocation. Under Maine law, as the court explained,

> absent justification or excuse, all intentional or criminally reckless killings are felonious homicides. Felonious homicide is punished as murder—i.e., by life imprisonment—unless the defendant proves by a fair preponderance of the evidence that it was committed in the heat of passion on sudden provocation, in which case it is punished as manslaughter—i.e., by a fine not to exceed $1,000 or by imprisonment not to exceed 20 years.

Consequently, the trial judge instructed the jury that "if the prosecution established that the homicide was both intentional and unlawful, malice aforethought was to be conclusively implied unless the defendant proved by a fair preponderance of the evidence that he acted in the heat of passion on sudden provocation." But the Supreme Court concluded this instruction was constitutionally infirm under *Winship,* and thus held "that the Due Process Clause requires the prosecution to prove beyond a reasonable doubt the absence of the heat of passion on sudden provocation when the issue is properly in a homicide case."

For one thing, the Court noted in *Mullaney,* this conclusion squares with two "important points" that emerged from its "historical review" of heat-of-passion voluntary manslaughter: (i) "the fact at issue here—the presence or absence of the heat of passion on sudden provocation—has been, almost from the inception of the common law of homicide, the single most important factor in determining the degree of culpability attaching to an unlawful homicide"; and (ii) "the clear trend has been toward requiring the prosecution to bear the ultimate burden of proving this fact." For another, this result gives proper recognition to the interests emphasized in *Winship;* considering the substantial differences in the penalty for murder as compared to that for manslaughter, both the individual and the societal interests in a solidly-grounded conviction were no less here than in *Winship.* Finally, the Court stressed it could "discern no unique hardship on the prosecution that would justify requiring the defendant to carry the burden of proving a fact so critical to criminal culpability." (The Court did not question, however, that the state could put the initial burden of production on the defendant, so that the state would not be required as a matter of course to prove absence of heat of passion in each and every murder prosecution.)

Just two years after *Mullaney* came *Patterson v. N.Y.* (1977), where the Court held that the burden of proof could constitutionally be placed on the defendant to establish the affirmative defense of extreme emotional disturbance. *Patterson*'s meaning in the affirmative defense context is discussed below; suffice it to note here that some commentators have found it impossible to reconcile *Patterson* with the *Mullaney* notion that the prosecution must *always* carry the burden of persuasion as to all offense elements. So the argument goes, if the state has it in its power to redefine the crime so as to transform an "element" into an "affirmative defense," then there is no reason—other than excessive formalism—to prohibit the state from instead leaving that particular in the statute as an element and merely assigning the burden of proof as to it to the defendant.

(c) Affirmative Defenses. This book deals with a number of possible defenses that a criminal defendant may use to avoid conviction. Some of these are substantive law defenses that negative guilt by cancelling out the existence of some required element of the crime. For example, certain kinds of mistake of fact, mistake of law, intoxication, or insanity are properly viewed as proof that the defendant did not have the mental state required for the crime charged. Certain other defenses, such as self-defense and necessity, do not negative any of the elements of the crime but instead go to show some matter of justification or excuse that is a bar to the imposition of criminal liability. In addition to these defenses of general applicability, there are also substantive law defenses applicable to individual crimes, in which case the common practice is for the statute defining the crime to contain an exception or proviso setting forth the defense. Thus the typical bigamy statute, punishing one who, though married, marries again, continues with a proviso stating that it is not bigamy if his second marriage occurs after his first spouse has been absent for seven years and is not known by him to be living. An abortion statute, punishing the use of instruments or drugs on a woman to procure a miscarriage, may contain a provision exempting one who does the act on a doctor's orders to save the woman's life.

These various substantive law defenses, whether of the general-principle or of the single-crime type, are often called (somewhat loosely) "affirmative defenses," although they are generally raisable upon a not guilty plea. Who has the burden of proof in connection with these defenses—that is, who has the burden of production, and who has the burden of persuasion and by what measure?

As to the burden of production of evidence, it is uniformly held that the defendant is obliged to start matters off by putting in some evidence in support of his defense—e.g., evidence of his insanity, or of his acting in self-defense, or of one of the other affirmative defenses—unless of course the prosecution, in presenting its own side of the case, puts in some evidence of a defense, in which case the matter of defense is properly an issue though the defendant himself produces nothing further to support it. Experience shows that most people who commit crimes are sane and conscious; they are not compelled to commit them; and they are not so intoxicated that they cannot entertain the states of mind their crimes may require. Thus it makes good sense to say that if any of these unusual features are to be injected into the case, the defendant is the one to do it; it would not be sensible to make the prosecution in all cases prove the defendant's sanity, sobriety and freedom from compulsion. Perhaps experience might show that homicides and battery are, as often as not, committed in self-defense; but even if this is so, it would still be wise (in the interests of simplifying issues and saving time that would be spent in presenting matters on which there is no dispute, and because the defendant normally has greater opportunity to know the facts) to place the burden of production on the defendant. Nothing in *Mullaney* or *Patterson* casts any doubt upon the constitutionality of so allocating the burden of production.

What then of the burden of persuasion? Prior to *Mullaney,* the courts were split into different camps. One point of view was that the defendant has the burden of persuading the fact-finder by a preponderance of the evidence of the existence of facts giving rise to these defenses. The other point of view was that, once the defendant has introduced some evidence of the defense, he need not persuade the fact-finder that the defense exists; instead the prosecution must persuade the factfinder beyond a reasonable doubt that the defense does not exist. But *Mullaney* placed the former view in doubt, as that case could readily be interpreted as meaning that the prosecution now had the burden of persuasion with respect to many (if not all) of the traditional affirmative defenses. Indeed, some lower courts so held.

That *Mullaney* did not go so far was first indicated in *Rivera v. Del.* (1976), where the Court dismissed, as not presenting a substantial federal question, an appeal claiming a state statute burdening the defendant with proving insanity by a preponderance of the evidence was unconstitutional. Any lingering doubts were removed by *Patterson v. N.Y.* (1977), upholding a New York murder conviction obtained in a case in which the jury was told the defendant had the burden of proof as to the affirmative defense of "extreme emotional disturbance," which if proved would reduce the crime to manslaughter. In one sense the *Patterson* circumstances were quite like those in *Mullaney,* for (as the Court conceded) New York's affirmative defense of extreme emotional disturbance was merely "a substantially expanded version of the older heat of passion concept" involved in *Mullaney.* But in another respect *Patterson* was quite different: the crime of murder was defined merely in terms of the defendant having intentionally caused the death of another, and thus the matter of emotional disturbance had nothing to do with any element of the crime but rather involved only an "affirmative defense." This, as it turned out, was a critical difference; the majority in *Patterson* concluded *Mullaney* meant only that "the Due Process Clause requires the prosecution to prove beyond reasonable doubt all of the elements included in the definition of the offense of which the defendant is charged." And thus, as the Court later held in *Dixon v. United States* (2006), the Due Process Clause is not violated by placing on the defendant the burden of proving by a preponderance of the evidence the duress defense where, as would ordinarily be the case, the existence of duress does not controvert the elements of the offense.

Patterson makes some pragmatic sense for precisely the reasons noted by the majority. If the burden must be on the prosecution also to disprove affirmative defenses, then an understandable and likely response from the state legislatures would be to abolish those affirmative defenses that experience showed prosecutors had particular difficulty in disproving. The due process clause, as the Court saw it, does not put any state "to the choice of abandoning those defenses or undertaking to disprove their existence in order to convict for a crime which otherwise is within its constitutional powers to sanction by substantial punishment." *Patterson* thus recognizes that state legislative bodies are in a better position to engage in the "more subtle balancing of society's interests against those of the accused" that is involved in determining whether creation of a particular defense and then imposition of the burden of its disproof on the prosecution "would be too cumbersome, too expensive, and too inaccurate."

The trouble with *Patterson,* objected the dissenters, is that it "allows a legislature to shift, virtually at will, the burden of persuasion with respect to any factor in a criminal case, so long as it is careful not to mention the nonexistence of that factor in the statutory language that defines the crime." This means, they continued, that under *Patterson* a legislature could define murder simply as the causing of another's death and then leave it to the defendant to prove the affirmative defense that he lacked any culpable mens rea. But, unless a crime as serious as murder may constitutionally be made a strict liability offense, which hardly seems likely (see § 4.5), this is not so. *Patterson,* as the majority explained, does not give the legislatures a free hand "to reallocate burdens of proof by labeling" elements as affirmative defenses. The "obvious constitutional limits" to which the majority referred are the various constitutional doctrines that presently exist regarding the way in which crimes may be defined. Thus, if a crime defined by law as consisting of elements *X, Y* and *Z* is reformulated by the legislature so as to consist only of elements *X* and *Y,* with non-*Z* now an affirmative defense to be proved by the defendant, this is permissible under *Patterson* if and only if it is constitutionally permissible to make *X* plus *Y,* standing alone, a criminal offense.

Most lower courts seem to have applied *Patterson* in essentially this way. Thus, based upon an element-versus-defense analysis of particular statutory schemes, it has been held that the burden of persuasion may properly be placed upon the defendant as to insanity, extreme emotional disturbance, intoxication, duress, necessity, self-defense, defense of another, and various other defenses. But, it is essential to note that merely calling something an affirmative defense does not settle the issue; it must appear that the so-called defense does not in actuality negate any element of the crime. Thus, the burden of proof as to the "defense" of alibi may not be placed upon the defendant, for alibi of necessity negates defendant's participation in the conduct defined as criminal. Similarly, there is authority that where the law of criminal homicide is defined in terms of an "unlawful" killing, the burden of proof as to the "defense" of self-defense may not be placed on the defendant, for a killing in self-defense is not unlawful.

Just when a supposed affirmative defense is sufficiently distinct from some element of the crime to come within *Patterson* was the crux of the Court's later decision in *Martin v. Ohio* (1987). The defendant in that case, charged with aggravated murder (defined by statute as "purposely, and with prior calculation and design, caus[ing] the death of another"), had the burden of proving by a preponderance of the evidence the affirmative defense of self-defense. In an effort to distinguish *Patterson,* the defendant claimed that proof of self-defense would, in reality, be proof of the absence of the "prior calculation and design" which was an element of the crime, so that *Mullaney* governed. The Court conceded "that most encounters in which self-defense is claimed arise suddenly and involve no prior plan or specific purpose to take life," so that "evidence offered to support the defense may negate a purposeful killing by prior calculation and design," but ruled against the defendant nonetheless. Because the jury instructions were "adequate to convey to the jury that all of the evidence, including the evidence going to self-defense, must be considered in deciding whether there was a reasonable doubt about the sufficiency of the state's proof of the elements of the crime," there had been no shifting "to the defendant of the burden of disproving any element of the state's case." As for the defendant's alternative argument, that "unlawfulness is an element of the offense that the state must prove by disproving self-defense," it was also rejected by the *Martin* Court. While "unlawfulness is essential for conviction," the state courts had interpreted that term as meaning only that conduct covered by the aforementioned elements set out in the statute, not including the nonexistence of self-defense; as a matter of state law, then, absence of self-defense was not an element of the crime.

One way to assess the *Patterson* rule is in terms of what tasks it does and does not impose upon the courts. In praise of *Patterson,* it might be said that the majority there freed courts from the most difficult task of making individual judgments about various kinds of defenses in the manner apparently contemplated by the dissenters. (The *Patterson* dissenters would have permitted a shifting of the burden of persuasion to the defendant only as to "[n]ew ameliorative affirmative defenses," and thus would have required case-by-case determination of what statutory defenses could be properly so characterized.) But, it appears that *Patterson* raises other, equally challenging questions for courts. For one thing, the majority's approach brings to the fore issues about constitutional limits on defining crime that otherwise would be unlikely to arise. Consider, for example, the defense of self-defense, the major remaining area of uncertainty after *Patterson.* Even if the homicide statute in question does *not* express an "unlawful" killing element, there is certainly room for argument that self-defense nonetheless must be treated for burden-of-proof purposes as an element rather than as an affirmative defense. So the argument goes, to claim otherwise "is to assert that the State may punish a defendant with life imprisonment * * * for [murder] even if the killing was done in the purest self-defense," when in fact "both the Due Process Clause and the Eighth Amendment restrict the State's ability to so punish a defendant whose 'crime,' for example, consisted in an immediate response to a murderous attack upon him." This issue, it should be noted, was not considered in *Martin.*

Secondly, *Patterson* also appears to raise interesting but occasionally difficult questions about the relationship of (even traditional) defenses and the common elements of crimes. For example, if a defendant is charged with an offense that requires a particular mental state but the defendant interposes the defense of voluntary intoxication, statutorily defined as a defense when it "negatives the existence of a state of mind essential to the crime," then must not the burden to disprove that defense be placed on the prosecution beyond a reasonable doubt because it raises the ultimate question of whether the mental state element of the crime existed in the particular case? (Or, if it is thought that the question should be, as some have argued ought be the case, whether the crime *could* constitutionally be defined without including the particular matter at issue, then cases such as this would require courts to resolve the difficult question of the due process limits on strict liability.)

Within the range of what is constitutionally permissible under *Mullaney* and *Patterson,* it remains for each jurisdiction to decide how to allocate the burden of proof in criminal cases as to so-called affirmative defenses. A few of the modern codes put the burden of persuasion on the prosecution as to virtually all issues, while a greater number allocate the burden to the defendant as to any matter that has been designated an "affirmative defense." But many jurisdictions have not adopted any general statutory rules on burden of proof, thus leaving the matter to be worked out by the courts on a defense-by-defense basis. This "seems an inappropriate approach given the lack of consensus on criteria for allocating the burden," for it "invite[s] inconsistency in allocation between similar offenses."

But if the matter were confronted as one of legislative policy, it would seem that imposition of the burden of persuasion upon the defendant is an especially attractive alternative in some circumstances. Just when this should be the choice is difficult to define, though in general it may be said that such allocation is appropriate as a compromise of divergent views on substantive issues. That is, creation of the defense with the burden on the defendant sometimes can be fairly seen to be a sensible middle position between a much broader statute or a strict-liability-type of statute, on the one hand, and, on the other, a statute recognizing the defense and placing an impossible burden on the prosecution to establish the existence of facts within the special knowledge of the defendant. An illustration of such a defense is Model Penal Code § 2.07(5), which provides for exculpation of a corporation on a showing of due diligence by supervising officers to prevent the commission of the offense. It is quite obviously of the "fair compromise" variety, for it is desirable that corporations not be held liable where there was such due diligence, but equally desirable that the prosecution not have to prove an absence of due diligence by every corporate defendant.

(d) Sentencing. If a defendant is charged with armed robbery, one element of which is possession of a firearm at the time of the crime, then under *Mullaney v. Wilbur* (1975) the burden of proof must be on the prosecution to establish such possession beyond a reasonable doubt. On the other hand, if an aggravated robbery statute does *not* make such possession an element but declares that lack of a firearm is an affirmative defense, then presumably under *Patterson v. N.Y.* (1977) it would be constitutionally permissible to place the burden of proof on the defendant to establish this affirmative defense. What then of a third scenario, where the crime itself is simple robbery but the possible sentence is affected by a judge's findings, by less than a beyond a reasonable doubt standard, that the defendant possessed a firearm at the time of the offense? Such was the issue in *McMillan v. Pa.* (1986), where the Court upheld a statute providing that anyone convicted of certain enumerated felonies is subject to a mandatory minimum sentence of five years if the judge finds, by a preponderance of the evidence, that the person "visibly possessed a firearm" during commission of the crime.

McMillan holds that this latter situation is "controlled by *Patterson*" because possession of a firearm could have been, but was not, an element of the underlying crimes. The Court once again declined "to define precisely the constitutional limits noted in *Patterson*," but reasoned that even without such elaboration it could be concluded the Pennsylvania statute did not exceed those limits. For one thing, the challenged statute "does not relieve the prosecution of its burden of proving guilt," as it becomes applicable only after a defendant has been convicted. For another, the statute "neither alters the maximum penalty for the crime committed nor creates a separate offense calling for a separate penalty; it operates solely to limit the sentencing court's discretion in selecting a penalty within the range already available to it without the special finding of visible possession of a firearm." The *McMillan* Court also emphasized that there was no evasion of *Mullaney* in the instant case, as in passing the sentencing statute the state legislature did not reduce the elements of the pre-existing underlying felonies. Moreover, the fact that some states deal with weapons possession as an element of various aggravated offenses "is merely a reflection of our federal system," which allows considerable experimentation by the states. Consequently, proof of the possession by a preponderance of the evidence does not violate due process.

The cautionary observation in *McMillan* that the statute at issue there did not alter the maximum penalty suggested the possibility that the result might be otherwise under a statute like that in *Specht v. Patterson* (1967), where a sexual offense otherwise carrying a 10–year maximum could result in life imprisonment if the judge made certain findings at sentencing. Although *McMillan* was later applied to such a situation in *Almendarez–Torres v. U.S.* (1998), the Court thereafter intimated in *Jones v. U.S.* (1999) that due process requires that "any fact (other than prior conviction) that increases the maximum penalty for a crime must be charged in an indictment, submitted to a jury, and proven beyond a reasonable doubt." *Almendarez–Torres* was explained away in *Jones* because of the "constitutional distinctiveness" of recidivism: "unlike virtually any other consideration used to enlarge the possible penalty for an offense, * * * a prior conviction must itself have been established through procedures satisfying the fair notice, reasonable doubt, and jury trial guarantees."

The very next term, in *Apprendi v. N.J.* (2000), the Court was confronted with a state "hate-crime" statute that, e.g., permitted the maximum sentence for possession of a firearm for an unlawful purpose to double (from 10 years to 20) upon proof by a preponderance of the evidence of defendant's purpose thereby to intimidate a person or group because of, inter alia, race. In a 5–4 decision, the Court held: "Other than the fact of a prior conviction, any fact that increased the penalty for a crime beyond the prescribed statutory maximum must be submitted to a jury, and proved beyond a reasonable doubt." While the *Apprendi* dissenters asserted there were several ways a state legislature could legislate around that holding, this prompted the majority to response that were this to occur the Court "would be required to question whether the revision was constitutional under this Court's prior decisions," such as *Patterson*. Later, in *Ring v. Ariz.* (2002), the Court held that where state law required an additional finding of an aggravating fact before a death sentence could be imposed, that additional fact, after *Apprendi*, must be found by a jury beyond a reasonable doubt. But in *Harris v. U.S.* (2002), concerning *Apprendi*'s application to facts triggering mandatory minimum sentences, the Court reaffirmed *McMillan*. A plurality of four justices reasoned that while "any fact extending the defendant's sentence beyond the maximum authorized by the jury's verdict would have been considered an element of an aggravated crime—and thus the domain of the jury—by those who framed the Bill of Rights [,t]he same cannot be said of a fact increasing the mandatory minimum (but not extending the sentence beyond the statutory maximum), for the jury's verdict has authorized the judge to impose the minimum with or without the finding." And in *Oregon v. Ice* (2009), the Court concluded that the fact the early common law generally entrusted to judges' unfettered discretion the decision whether sentences for discrete offenses should be served consecutively or concurrently, plus the states' historic dominion in this area, counseled against extending *Apprendi* beyond its offense-specific context to the finding of facts necessary to imposition of consecutive sentences.

Blakely v. Washington (2004) involved a presumptive sentencing system where under statutes designated broad sentencing ranges for major classes of felonies and also narrower "standard ranges" for particular offenses. The broad range for Blakely's kidnapping offense was up to 10 years, but the standard range was 49–53 months, from which the judge departed (imposing a sentence of 90 months) upon a finding of "deliberate cruelty," a statutorily enacted ground for departure. The Court held, 5–4, that this violated *Apprendi*, for "the 'statutory maximum' for *Apprendi* purposes * * * is not the maximum sentence a judge may impose after finding additional facts, but the maximum he may impose without any additional findings. Concluding that there was no constitutionally significant difference between the procedures at issue in *Blakely* and the federal sentencing guidelines because in both systems the sentencing rules are mandatory and impose binding requirements on all sentencing judges, the Court in *United States v. Booker* (2005) held *Blakely* applicable as well to the federal guidelines. But a different majority of the Court, addressing the remedial question, severed and excised the statutory provision making the guidelines mandatory, as purely advisory guidelines are constitutional under *Blakely*.

(e) Unconstitutionality of a Criminal Statute. Later in this book there is a discussion of the various constitutional limitations upon the powers of the state and federal government to create crimes (see ch. 3). If this power is exceeded, then the defendant may defend on the ground that the statute defining the crime with which he is charged is invalid, and this may also be thought of as a "defense" to the prosecution. The constitutionality of criminal statutes sometimes hinges upon the existence or nonexistence of underlying facts. It has been held that the burden of proving facts showing unconstitutionality is upon the defendant, partially at least because there is a presumption of validity and a reluctance on the part of courts to strike down legislation as unconstitutional.

(f) Rebuttable Presumptions, Case Law and Statutory. Courts have created some rebuttable presumptions in favor of the prosecution in criminal cases—e.g., the presumption from recent exclusive unexplained possession of stolen property that the possessor stole it, and the presumption from the intentional use of a deadly weapon upon another human being that the user intended to kill his victim with it. In addition, the legislatures have created a great variety of statutory presumptions that aid the prosecution in criminal cases. Often these criminal statutes make proof of a physical fact (or group of facts) "presumptive evidence" or "prima facie evidence" of a mental fact necessary for a conviction—as where, in connection with a crime of receiving stolen property knowing it to be stolen, the statute makes the fact of receiving the stolen property prima facie evidence that the receiver knew it to be stolen. Less frequently, the statutes provide that proof of one physical fact (or group of facts) is prima facie (or presumptive) evidence of another physical fact required for conviction—as where a statute makes it a crime to deface the manufacturer's marks on firearms, and then provides that possession of a firearm on which the marks have been defaced is prima facie evidence that the possessor has defaced it.

The question that now arises is: what is the effect of these case-law and statutory rebuttable presumptions upon the burden of proof, using that term in both its senses—the burden of production and the burden of persuasion? The generally accepted rule is that once the prosecution has proved the underlying fact (or facts) to which the presumption attaches, the case must go to the jury (i.e., there will be no directed verdict for the defendant); but the jury is not compelled, even in the complete absence of rebuttal evidence by the defendant, to find the ultimate fact required for conviction (i.e., the "presumption" is a "permissive" rather than a "mandatory" one). Thus the defendant does not, strictly speaking, have the burden of production to overcome the presumption; yet, as a practical matter, he may well be convicted in some circumstances if he does not do so. As to the burden of persuasion, it is generally held that the defendant is entitled to be acquitted if there is a reasonable doubt in the minds of the jury (or other fact-finders); the burden of persuasion is not shifted by the presumption to the defendant.

(g) Meaning of "Beyond a Reasonable Doubt" and "Presumption of Innocence". The expression "beyond a reasonable doubt" appears most often in the trial court's instructions to the jury, which is generally told: the defendant is presumed to be innocent; the mere fact that he has been charged with a crime is not to be taken as any evidence of his guilt; and the prosecution must prove, beyond a reasonable doubt, all the elements of the crime charged. While some courts have undertaken to define the term "reasonable doubt," other courts have thought that the words themselves are sufficiently clear not to require any embellishment. A jury instruction about reasonable doubt using words that, "as they are commonly understood, suggest a higher degree of doubt than is required for acquittal under the reasonable doubt standard" (e.g., one which equates reasonable doubt with a "grave uncertainty" and an "actual substantial doubt"), violates due process, and thus a conviction obtained pursuant thereto cannot stand.

The so-called "presumption of innocence" is actually not a presumption at all in the legal sense discussed above, that, once an underlying fact has been proved, another (ultimate) fact may (or must) be taken as proved. It is not even a presumption in the popular sense of a thing that is more likely to be true than not, for statistically more people who are charged with crime are convicted as guilty than are acquitted as innocent. It is more properly said that the innocence of the defendant is assumed, which is generally taken to mean no more than that the prosecution has the two burdens of proof discussed in this section: the burden of producing evidence of guilt in order to avoid a directed verdict; and of persuading the fact-finder of guilt beyond a reasonable doubt in order to secure a conviction. However, the customary statement to the jury when the trial court gives instructions is that the defendant is presumed innocent, that the mere fact of accusation is no evidence of his guilt, and that the prosecution must prove guilt beyond a reasonable doubt.

(h) No Directed Verdict of Guilty. After the evidence is in, the trial court may not, on motion of the prosecution, direct a verdict of guilty, no matter how conclusive the evidence of guilt. Nor may the court, without going quite so far as to direct a finding of guilty, direct the jury to find against the defendant on one of the several elements of the crime, even though the prosecution's evidence concerning the evidence is uncontradicted. The notion is that for the court to decide that all elements, or that a single element, of the crime exist would improperly invade the province of the jury, which in fact if not in theory has the power to disregard the applicable law given it by the court by finding, in favor of the defendant, that an element does not exist even when it knows very well that it does exist.

(i) Directed Verdict of Acquittal. If in its opening statement the prosecution omits to state some essential element of its case, the defendant's motion for a directed verdict of acquittal will not be granted without first giving the prosecution an opportunity to embellish its opening statement by adding any missing parts. In a rare case, however, the prosecution's opening statement may affirmatively show that it cannot make out a successful case against the defendant, in which case the court will direct a verdict of acquittal then and there.

In most jurisdictions, the trial court has the power and duty, on the defendant's motion or even on its own motion, after the evidence on either side is closed, to direct a verdict for the defendant if the evidence is insufficient to support a conviction. The prosecution may have proved all of the required elements of the crime except one, but a lack of proof concerning one element requires a directed verdict. Thus a verdict of acquittal is properly directed: in a prosecution for receiving stolen property, where there is no evidence that the defendant knew the property was stolen; or false pretenses, where there is no evidence that the victim relied on the defendant's falsehoods; or for burglary, where there is no evidence of a breaking. Stated more broadly, a verdict should be directed for the defendant if there is no evidence of the *corpus delicti* or, if there is such evidence, there is no evidence connecting the defendant with the crime. In a jurisdiction following the rule that there can be no conviction on the uncorroborated testimony of an accomplice, a verdict must be directed where such corroboration is missing from the prosecution's case.

If the prosecution introduces insufficient evidence to support a conviction, so that the defendant's motion for a directed verdict, made at the close of the prosecution's case, is erroneously denied, but then the defendant, in presenting his own case, himself fills the gap in the prosecution's case, the defendant's renewed motion for a directed verdict, made at the close of his case, is properly denied. This means that a defendant who believes that the prosecution failed to prove a prima facie case is presented with a hard choice. He may present no evidence in his own behalf and thus preserve for appeal the question of whether the trial judge's ruling was erroneous, or else abandon the point by putting in evidence on his side of the case. It has been argued that this rule comes perilously close to compelling the defendant to incriminate himself, and a few courts have declined to follow it.

A defendant is not entitled to a directed verdict at the close of his side of the case just because of plausible and uncontradicted defense testimony of facts that, if true, would constitute a defense, for there is no rule that an unimpeached witness must be believed.

A comparatively modern procedural device in use in civil as well as criminal cases allows a defendant, who has unsuccessfully moved for a directed verdict at the close of all the evidence, to move again, after a jury verdict against him, for a judgment in accordance with his earlier motion for a directed verdict. This motion is popularly known, perhaps a little loosely, as a motion for judgment notwithstanding the verdict ("judgment n.o.v."). A trial judge who has reserved decision on the earlier motion, and who now believes that it would have been proper to have directed a verdict of acquittal at that time, may now enter a judgment of acquittal notwithstanding the jury's verdict of guilty. The question to be determined is exactly the same as that raised by the defendant's motion for a directed verdict of acquittal at the close of all the evidence.

(j) **Test for Passing on Motion.** There is some doubt as to how best to express the question that the court must answer when the defendant moves for a verdict of acquittal. Asking whether the prosecution's "evidence is insufficient to sustain a conviction" is quite vague. Some earlier cases took the view that the motion should be granted unless the evidence was sufficient to "exclude every other hypothesis" except guilt. However, this is unsound, for it would seem to mean that the judge would have to be convinced of guilt beyond doubt before he could submit the issue to the jury, and thus the judge would be pre-empting the functions of the jury. Under another approach, "the standard of evidence necessary to send a case to the jury is the same in both civil and criminal cases," which means that the judge must submit the case to the jury if there is substantial evidence in support of the charge. This view has been rightly criticized and has attracted little support.

The proper test has been stated in the following terms: "If the evidence is such that reasonable jurymen must necessarily have [a reasonable] doubt, the judge must require acquittal, because no other result is permissible within the fixed bounds of jury consideration. But if a reasonable mind might fairly have a reasonable doubt or might fairly not have one, the case is for the jury, and the decision is for the jurors to make." Although there once was some authority to the contrary, the established rule now is that the test previously quoted is also applicable to cases based upon circumstantial evidence.

It must be kept in mind that a defendant may be found guilty of a lesser offense necessarily included in the offense charged. This means that on a motion for a directed verdict the court must consider whether the evidence would be sufficient to sustain a conviction of some lesser offense, for if it would be then the issue of defendant's guilt of the lesser offense should be submitted to the jury.

Chapter 2

SOURCES AND GENERAL
LIMITATIONS

Table of Sections

Sec.
　(b) When Regulations Fix the Penalty
　(c) Delegation of Power to Adjudicate
　(d) Administrative Orders

For additional analysis of the above topics and citations to authorities supporting their discussion in this Book, consult the author's 3-volume *Substantive Criminal Law* treatise, also available as Westlaw database SUBCRL. See the Table of Cross-References in this Book.

---

§ 2.1　Common Law Crimes

Today we find the substantive criminal law in several forms: (1) mostly in statutes; (2) not infrequently in administrative regulations passed pursuant to legislative delegation of authority to an administrative agency; (3) occasionally in constitutions; and (4) sometimes in the common law of crimes. Since historically the substantive criminal law began as common law for the most part, and only later became primarily statutory, it will be well to begin with common law crimes, with a view especially to determining the place of such crimes in modern criminal law.

(a) The Problem. On the civil side of the law we are used to the idea of judges deciding cases where there is no applicable statutory law. If *A*'s dog bites *B*, and *B* sues *A*, the judge who must decide whether a dog-owner is liable to one bitten by the dog may find that no statute covers the situation; but there may well be one or more dog-bite decisions in the reported cases of his state; or if not there may be some cases from other states, as well as from other jurisdictions in the Anglo–American system. He may follow these prior cases, or distinguish them, or choose between them; but he does use precedents to help him decide what the law is.

The situation may be a new one. Perhaps the city has hired a rainmaker to fill its empty reservoirs; the rainmaker seeds the clouds above the mountains where the water for the reservoirs collects; the rain falls; the reservoirs fill up; but a hotel owner in a mountain resort suffers a financial loss when his guests depart because of the dreary weather conditions. When the hotelman sues the city or the rainmaker for damages, what is the law to be applied? The judges who have to decide the law may well find no statute governing rainmaking, no reported case in the state, nor in any other American state, nor any federal case, nor any English, Canadian, Australian, etc., case. Yet the judges do not throw up their hands and say the case cannot be decided; they decide it. Maybe they can utilize some settled law in an analogous situation—

perhaps the law of liability for seeping or collapsing dams may point the way. Even if there is no available analogy or if there are competing analogies, the judges will make (some prefer to say discover) the law to apply to the new situation. The new law will be decided according to the judges' ideas (ideas they acquire as members of society) of what is moral, right, just; of what will further sound public policy, in the light of the customs and traditions of the people of which the judges are members.

A modern theory of jurisprudence suggests, somewhat loftily, that judges select between alternative solutions in order to "satisfy a maximum of human wants with a minimum of sacrifice of other wants [and thus achieve] elimination of friction and waste, economizing of social effort, conservation of social assets, and adjustment of the struggle of individual human beings to satisfy their overlapping individual claims in life in civilized society, so that if each may not get all that he demands, he may at least obtain all that is reasonably practicable in a wise social engineering."

The question in the criminal law field is whether judges can create (or discover) new crimes for which to punish the ingenious fellow who conceives and carries out a new form of anti-social conduct not covered by the criminal code. Today the criminal law of any particular jurisdiction is contained in an imposing mass of statutory material, punishing conduct ranging all the way from murder down to defacing billboards. But it is hard for the legislature in advance to conceive of all possible anti-social behavior that ought to be criminal. If someone intentionally or by chance finds a loophole, may the courts create a new crime to plug that gap?

(b) Common Law Crimes in England. In the beginning, at least, that is exactly what the English judges did. Although there were some early criminal statutes, in the main the criminal law was originally common law. Thus by the 1600's the judges, not the legislature, had created and defined the felonies of murder, suicide, manslaughter, burglary, arson, robbery, larceny, rape, sodomy and mayhem; and such misdemeanors as assault, battery, false imprisonment, libel, perjury, and intimidation of jurors. During the period from 1660 (the Restoration of the monarchy of Charles II after Cromwell) to 1860 the process continued, with the judges creating new crimes when the need arose and punishing those who committed them: blasphemy (1676), conspiracy (1664), sedition (18th century), forgery (1727), attempt (1784), solicitation (1801). From time to time the judges, when creating new misdemeanors, spoke of the court's power to declare criminal any conduct tending to "outrage decency" or "corrupt public morals," or to punish conduct *contra bonos mores;* thus they found running naked in the streets, publishing an obscene book, and grave-snatching to be common law crimes.

Of course, sometimes the courts refused to denote as criminal some forms of anti-social conduct. At times their refusal seemed irrational, causing the legislature to step in and enact a statute; thus false pretenses, embezzlement, incest and other matters became statutory crimes in England. Doubtless the English judges would have declared some other forms of conduct to be criminal but never had the chance because the legislature declared them criminal before the first case arose; such matters might still be considered "common law crimes" even though no court ever declared them so. Some immoral conduct, mostly of a sexual nature (such as private acts of adultery or fornication, and seduction without conspiracy), was punished by the ecclesiastical courts in England. The common law courts never punished these activities as criminal, and thus they never became English common law crimes.

At the same time that judges were developing new crimes, they were also developing new common law defenses to crime, such as self-defense, insanity, infancy, and coercion.

About the middle of the nineteenth century the process of creating new crimes almost came to a standstill in England, and the foremost English criminal law commentator of the time predicted that the era of new common law crimes was over. *Rex. v. Manley* (1932) thus caused quite an uproar in legal circles in England in the 1930's. A woman falsely told the police that she had been robbed—with the result that valuable police time was wasted on a futile search for the non-existent robber, and innocent persons were subjected to suspicion. No statute made such a false report criminal, and no precise common law precedent existed. Yet the judges held that this constituted a common law misdemeanor (the court called the offense "public mischief") and convicted the woman of this new crime.

At the present time it is clear that a new offense will be created by the courts only rarely in England, and any new offense created will be a misdemeanor and not a felony.

(c) Common Law Crimes in the United States. The original colonists in America who emigrated from England brought with them the English common law with its then existing statutory modifications, both civil and criminal, so far as applicable to conditions in America. After the American Revolution the thirteen states retained the English common law where applicable to local conditions. As new states joined the union the common law with statutory modifications generally became the basis of their law, sometimes by an express constitutional or statutory provision to that effect, and sometimes without the aid of such a provision. The rule, whether embodied in a "reception statute" or not, is that the English common law of a general nature, together with the English statutory law in aid of the common law, existing at the time of the founding of the American colonies, if applicable to local conditions, is the law of the state unless repealed expressly or impliedly by statute.

Thus it was that most of the states in the beginning had common law crimes. The states soon began to enact criminal statutes; and in the nineteenth century a number of states undertook to enact comprehensive statutory criminal codes, covering most of the common law crimes as well as new crimes unknown to the common law. Some of these codes expressly provided that there should be no crimes except as found in the code (or, if the code was not meant to be completely comprehensive, except as found in the code or some other statute). Other states without such an express provision held that the comprehensive code by implication abolished common law crimes. In other states common law crimes were retained either by an express "reception statute" or without the aid of any statute. In those states, of course, a particular common law crime might be found to be abrogated by virtue of a statute either conflicting with that common law crime or dealing with the entire subject matter of that common law crime. But in recent years a great many states have enacted comprehensive new criminal codes (see § 1.1(b)), and in the process they have usually but not always abolished common law crimes.

It has long been settled that there are no federal common law crimes; if Congress has not by statute made certain conduct criminal, it is not a federal crime. In spite of this general proposition, Congress has provided for common law crimes in the District of Columbia, and Congress has provided that state criminal law (and this would include state criminal law of the common law variety in the states retaining common law crimes) applies (in the absence of a federal criminal statute) in those "federal enclaves," or islands of federal territory (e.g., army posts, naval bases), located within states. Beyond this, there is a sense in which "federal criminal law is most appropriately viewed as a species of federal common law," for it is "dominated by judge-made law crafted to fill the interstices of open-textured statutory provisions," resulting from the fact that Congress has often "resort[ed] to highly general language that facilitates legislative consensus by deferring resolution of controversial points to the moment of judicial application."

(d) The Common Law in Jurisdictions Abolishing Common Law Crimes. Some of the states that have abolished common law crimes nevertheless have catch-all criminal statutes almost broad enough to bring in the various common law misdemeanors. Moreover, the states rejecting common law crimes often use common law terms in their statutes without defining them, in which case resort must be had to the common law for definition. But such reliance on the common law is inappropriate if the terms at issue had no established meaning at common law.

Jurisdictions that have abolished common law crimes have not necessarily also abolished common law defenses to crime, such as self-defense, prevention of crime, insanity, infancy, coercion and necessity, especially if their statutes do not expressly provide for these defenses. (The reason why common law defenses may exist where common law crimes have been abolished is to be found in the rationale underlying the abolition of such crimes, discussed below.) Even if the statutes *do* provide for these defenses, the nature of the defenses at common law is properly taken into account when the statutes do not appear to depart substantially from the common law approach. So also, the common law of criminal procedure is not abolished in those states that have rejected the substantive common law crimes.

(e) What the Common Law of Crimes Encompasses in States Retaining Common Law Crimes. In the United States the following conduct has been held criminal, although no statute made it so: conspiracy; attempt to commit a crime; solicitation to commit a crime; uttering grossly obscene language in public; engaging in a public affray; burning a body in the cellar furnace; keeping a house of prostitution; maliciously killing a horse; blasphemy; negligently permitting a prisoner to escape; discharging a gun near a sick person; public drunkenness; offenses against the purity of elections; libel; being a common scold; indecent assault; false imprisonment; misprision of felony; creating a public nuisance; eavesdropping; and violations of international law by individuals. This is by no means a complete list of all the cases upholding common law crimes.

We have seen that some activities of a sexual nature were considered offenses against religion not punishable as common law crimes; for instance, private acts of fornication or adultery, and seduction. In general these activities are held not to constitute common law crimes in America.

Several problems have arisen in connection with common law crimes:

1.   There is the problem of the extent of the punishment that may be imposed on one convicted of such a crime. Normally a statute defining a crime states the punishment therefor, but by hypothesis there is no statute creating the common law crime.

Most, if not all, states have general statutes providing for a certain punishment for felonies and misdemeanors where no punishment is otherwise declared. A few have statutes providing punishment for common law crimes. The problem then is to determine whether the common law crime in question is a felony or misdemeanor. As to offenses derived from English precedents, the precedent will generally determine this. As to new offenses not found in English precedents, it would seem that the court should treat the new crime as a misdemeanor. In some of the common law crime states it is theoretically possible to create common law felonies, but it seems that this should be done only if the crime involved was one of the few serious crimes that were common law felonies. Some states by statute provide that all nonstatutory crimes are misdemeanors. (Of course, when a common law crime is enacted into a statute stating the punishment therefor, the punishment prescribed is exclusive.)

2. Another problem in the states retaining common law crimes concerns the effect on the common law of criminal statutes relating more or less directly to the same subject matter: does the statute take over (preempt) the field and thus abrogate the common law crime? Thus a state anti-trust statute makes criminal certain conspiracies in restraint of trade, but it does not mention conspiracy to injure rival businesses by telling lies. Does such a statute abrogate the common law crime of conspiracy to injure the business of another by systematic falsehood? A state statute on conspiracy punishes unlawful agreements to accomplish four or five listed bad things, but at common law the list was greater. Does such a statute abrogate common law conspiracy to produce a result within the common law, but not within the statutory, list? A state statute on conspiracy requires not only an unlawful agreement but also an overt act in furtherance of such an agreement. Does such a statute modify the common law definition of conspiracy? Does a state statute making prostitution (defined as the offering or receiving of the body for sexual intercourse for money) a criminal offense impliedly repeal the common law offense of keeping a house of prostitution? Does a state statute, defining bribery as giving or offering compensation to a witness on his agreement that his testimony shall be influenced thereby, impliedly abrogate common law bribery, which does not require that the witness agree? The problem is similar to that of implied repeal of statutes, where the courts are apt to say that repeals by implication are not favored, but that the earlier statute is repealed by a later statute if the two are so repugnant that they cannot stand together, or if the later statute is such a revision of the entire subject as to manifest a legislative intention to substitute the later for the earlier. So here the courts say that statutes in derogation of the common law are not favored, will be strictly construed, and will not repeal the

common law beyond their terms, unless they are clearly repugnant to the common law or unless they constitute such a revision of the whole subject-matter as to evince an intention by the legislature to substitute statute for common law. And when the legislature simply codifies a common-law crime without articulating its elements, the court must look to the common law for the definition of the crime.

3. The next problem is that of determining what sorts of conduct constitute common law crimes. How does a court determine whether something the defendant has done amounts to a common law crime? Does this mean that the court must find an English case or statutory precedent in point dated before 1607? May the court use post–1607 precedents? What if there is no precedent to be found?

If the court finds an English case directly in point decided before 1607 (or, in some states, 1775), holding that the activity in question constituted a common law crime, clearly this would qualify as a common law crime in a state in this country that recognizes such crimes. A more generally used technique, however, is to look at books by recognized writers on English crimes, especially Blackstone, to determine the existence and definition of a common law crime. To some extent courts look to the case law of other states that retain common law crimes.

The principal difficulty has to do with conduct not covered by any English case law (or statute) dated prior to 1607 (or 1775), the cut-off date in the typical reception statute or reception rule. Perhaps no English case or statute before 1607 can be found punishing false entries in election books because elections were unknown or infrequent in England before that time. Perhaps no English case or statute before 1607 punished the making of false reports to the police because England never got around to dealing with the problem until 1933, being delayed by the fact that it was not until recent times that England had a regular police force. Blackstone could not have mentioned these specific crimes for obvious reasons. Does it therefore follow that these cannot be common law crimes?

Of course, on the civil side of the law we are used to the idea that the common law can grow to meet new situations and to accommodate changing customs and sentiments, but there are difficulties on the criminal side, bound up with the notion, discussed more fully below, that the public is entitled to fair warning of what conduct is criminal.

In one case the defendant was prosecuted for the crime of attempting to obtain property by false pretenses in Colorado, a state that then retained common law crimes by virtue of a reception statute accepting the English common law as it existed in

1607. Colorado had no general statute punishing attempt, so the question was whether attempted false pretenses was a common law crime. The court could find no English case earlier than 1625 so holding, and that case was eighteen years too late to qualify this as a common law crime. An older Kentucky case did much the same thing with the common law crime of conspiracy, the precise question being whether an agreement between competitors to maintain prices constituted such a crime. The court found that as of 1607 common law conspiracy was limited to agreements to promote false indictments and stir up litigation; agreements to do other bad things came later; hence an agreement to maintain prices was not a common law crime.

Most other courts that discuss the problem do not limit themselves to pre–1607 precedents. They may be classified, however, into two groups: (1) those bold spirits willing to create a new crime in the absence of any precedent; and (2) those less bold but willing to follow post–1607 (or post–1775, in some states) English precedents (or perhaps precedents from other American states) but not willing to create a new crime in the absence of all precedent. Illustrative of the first view, it has been held a common law crime to make false entries in election books even though there is no precedent in point from England. "The test is not whether precedents can be found in the books, but whether [defendant's activities] injuriously affect the public policy and economy," and "it is not so much a question whether such offences have been so punished as whether they might have been." As an example of the second point of view, a court held that enticing away a sixteen year old girl for purposes of intercourse did not amount to a common law crime in the absence of any precedent; "it is too late now to assume jurisdiction over a new class of cases, under the idea of their being *contra bonos mores.*" Where the question was whether it is a common law crime to burn a body in the furnace (the criminal statute on dead bodies being limited to disinterring, indecently exposing, and abandoning such a body), the court relied on an 1840 English case and on the general principle that "the common law gives expression to the changing customs and sentiments of the people" whereby such common law crimes have been created as blasphemy, open obscenity and similar indecent offenses against religion and morality that are *contra bonos mores.* The many cases finding that solicitation, attempt and conspiracy (other than conspiracy to indict or stir up litigation) are common law crimes show that pre–1607 English case law is not a prerequisite, since these crimes were developed in England after 1607.

If one takes the view that common law is unwritten law and decided cases serve only to illustrate the law, the existence of common law crimes without early precedent is easy enough. The

Anglo–American notion that case law operates retroactively points to the same result. And it is often difficult to tell what the common law of England before 1607 is without regard to later decisions that have in fact settled the law as, theoretically, it always was. It has been pointed out as a historical fact that in colonial times, when the colonists were applying the common law of England, they did not usually refer to English decisions (doubtless there were few libraries available), but rather to general principles.

It has been said that American courts have no right to invent new crimes but only to declare the common law. Most states accepting common law crimes, however, would agree that the common law can expand to meet a new situation hitherto unknown; and this process is not one of inventing new crimes but of applying common law principles.

4. Another problem concerns the applicability of English criminal statutes in the United States. Such statutes have played a distinctly minor role in American common law crimes. An English criminal statute enacted before 1607, if applicable to our conditions, becomes part of our American common law. Some states have also adopted English statutes enacted after 1607 and before 1775.

5. A final problem concerns whether, if the court finds whatever common law precedent or principle would be necessary in order to recognize a certain common law crime, the court is then obligated to do so. It is possible, of course, that the legislature may have left the courts of the state with no discretion in this regard. But if that is not the case, then the court might well decline to recognize the common law crime if it is deemed not "compatible with our local circumstances and situation and our general codes and jurisprudence." In particular, a court might decline to declare a particular common law crime as the law of the state because of concerns with the due process right to fair warning, or because of a perceived risk that the crime would infringe upon some other constitutional guarantee, such as the privilege against self-incrimination or the equal protection clause.

(f) The Pros and Cons of Common Law Crimes. Finally, there is the question whether it is wiser to retain or wiser to abolish common law crimes. The advantage of retaining such crimes is that there are no gaps. So the argument goes, if something ought to be a crime, but the legislature forgot to declare it a crime, the courts can step in and make it a crime. It is useful to have a reservoir of substantive criminal law to plug loopholes left by the legislative branch. "It is impossible to find precedents for all offences. The malicious ingenuity of mankind is constantly producing new inventions in the art of disturbing their neighbors. To this invention must be opposed general principles, calculated to meet and punish them."

The principal argument against common law crimes is expressed in the maxim *nullum crimen sine lege,* the basis of which is that the criminal law ought to be certain, so that people can know in advance whether the conduct on which they are about to embark is criminal or not. "Although it is not likely that a criminal will carefully consider the text of the law before he murders or steals, it is reasonable that a fair warning should be given to the world in language that the common world will understand, of what the law intends to do if a certain line is passed. To make the warning fair, so far as possible the line should be clear." To require one who intends to tread close to the line of criminality (yet remaining on the side of legality) to study the criminal statutes (and the cases construing those statutes) may be fair enough; but to make him read the English and American cases on common law crimes and speculate on their scope is worse; and it is even more unfair (so the argument runs) to make him guess at his peril as to what a court will hold in a new situation never before encountered by the courts. It is true also that the due process requirement of definiteness in criminal statutes and the policy underlying the ban on *ex post facto* criminal statutes are analogies militating against common law crimes. The fact that Nazi Germany and Soviet Russia once adhered to the policy of punishing as criminal activity that no statute expressly covered tends to make Americans wonder about the democratic basis of common law crimes.

As to the argument that it is necessary to plug loopholes, it has been noted that because of the proliferation of criminal statutes in all American jurisdictions there cannot be very many gaps; "By comparison with lack of discovery of criminal conduct, lack of detection, lack of complaint, and inefficiency in administration, the failure to punish the guilty resulting from gaps in the penal law is an almost trivial defect." Furthermore, whenever a loophole is discovered, the modern legislature can and usually does act quickly to plug it.

To a great extent, a decision on whether it is better to retain or to abolish common law crimes depends upon one's view of the theories of punishment. If punishment is imposed primarily for revenge or retribution, common law crimes punishing anti-social conduct of novel sorts are justified. Likewise, if the primary purpose is to jail and therefore disable for a time persons dangerous to society, or to reform those with anti-social tendencies, it makes greater sense to recognize common law crimes. But if the primary purpose is to deter future offenders through fear of punishment, it has been suggested that new kinds of bad conduct should not be punished, "for if the first wrongdoer had no certain foresight that he would be punished, the threat of punishment could not deter him, and the punishment would be useless." It could be argued, however, that certainty of punishment is not necessary to the deterrent theory (as, indeed, one must recognize from the fact that although many who commit statutory crimes escape punishment for one reason or another, many of us are deterred), and that a substantial chance that punishment will be inflicted for new forms of bad conduct will still deter.

It was only natural that judges should create crimes from general principles in medieval England, because such legislature as there was sat only infrequently and legislation was scanty. Today in the United States, as in modern England, the various legislatures meet regularly. The principal original reason for common law crimes has therefore disappeared. And thus it is not surprising that as more and more states have enacted comprehensive new criminal codes in place of the miscellaneous collection of uncoordinated statutes, they have generally abolished common law crimes.

§ 2.2   Interpretation of Criminal Statutes

Statutes creating crimes are not immune to that malady which so often afflicts legislation of all types—ambiguity. Courts are frequently faced with the problem of the criminal statute that is unclear as applied to the particular fact situation in question. Sometimes the letter of the statute covers the fact situation, but as so applied the statute seems harsh, unjust or even senseless; could the legislature have meant what it seems to have said? In the case of the "administrative crime" it may be that the administrative regulation, the violation of which the legislature has made a crime, is ambiguous.

(a) Use of Canons of Construction. When interpreting an ambiguous statute the court will seek to find the intention of the legislature. At times it is clear that the legislature never thought of the particular fact situation now in question, in which case "intention of the legislature" may mean simply "intention the legislature would have had if it had thought of this problem," to be determined from a consideration of the general purpose the legislature had in mind in enacting the statute. In order to help solve the often difficult problem of the legislature's intention, the courts have a large assortment of rules and maxims at their disposal.

There is something of a dispute among those who like to speculate on the workings of the judicial mind as to whether courts first decide how a defective statute ought to be interpreted and then display whatever canons of statutory construction will make this interpretation look inevitable, or whether the courts actually first use the applicable canons and second reach the result. Doubtless the truth lies somewhere in between—some judges are apt to do it one way, some the other; some cases lend themselves to one technique, some to the other. It is no doubt true that, as applied to a particular fact situation, several rules of interpretation may often be referred to, some looking in one direction and some in the opposite direction. It is also true that most of the rules are stated with an exception indicating the rule does not apply if the meaning of the statute is clear, but a good deal of discretion remains in the courts as to when a statute is clear and when it is ambiguous. At all events, because rules of statutory interpretation sometimes do decide cases and because even in other cases judges must find some applicable rules, one who deals with criminal law (which is, of course, largely statutory) must know something of the techniques of statutory interpretation.

(b) Plain Meaning Rule. Courts often express this thought: "Where the language [of a statute] is plain and admits of no more than one meaning the duty of interpretation does not arise, and the rules which are to aid doubtful meanings need no discussion"; or that if the language is plain and its meaning clear, courts must give effect to it, regardless of what it thinks of its wisdom. This plain meaning rule, it has been noted, "reaffirms the preeminence of the statute over materials extrinsic to it."

The courts, of course, are on even firmer ground in applying the plain meaning rule if they can think of some good reason that the legislature might have had in mind in providing what it literally seems to have provided. On the other hand, courts sometimes conclude that what seems to be clear language is so harsh or foolish or devoid of sense that it is ambiguous after all, and they then proceed to find that the legislature did not mean what it literally said.

(c) Implied Exceptions and Obvious Mistakes. As noted above, courts sometimes do not follow statutes that, though apparently plain, are also harsh or foolish. Courts sometimes speak of an "implied exception" in the statute when they do not wish to apply it literally. Thus a federal statute makes it a crime "knowingly and wilfully to obstruct the passage of the mail." Defendant policeman, with a warrant for the arrest of a mail carrier for murder, arrested the mailman on his appointed rounds. The Supreme Court in *U.S. v. Kirby* (1869) held this was not an obstruction of the mail under the statute; statutes, even plain statutes, should not receive a construction leading to "injustice, oppression, or an absurd consequence. It will always, therefore, be presumed that the legislature intended exceptions to its language, which would avoid results of this character." Similarly, a state criminal statute punishing speeding impliedly excepts a police officer reasonably speeding, in the discharge of his duties, after a fleeing criminal. We shall later see that, generally speaking, a good motive will not excuse criminal conduct, as where a man shoots his beloved but dying wife to end her suffering (see § 4.3). This is perhaps but a way of saying that implied exceptions are not readily to be made for forbidden conduct springing from good motives. There is a general defense, to be dealt with later, called "necessity," whereby one who in an emergency situation commits what would otherwise be a crime may be excused, as where one who is starving takes food belonging to another to save his own life (see § 9.1). Most of the cases on "implied exceptions" could more properly be treated under such a principle.

In the area of entrapment, an implied exception in a criminal statute has been used to explain the defendant's nonliability where the police entrap him into violating the literal terms of a criminal statute—as where a policeman persuades the other to sell him liquor, in violation of a statute forbidding the sale of liquor. One commonly-used explanation of the liquor seller's nonliability is that the liquor statute impliedly excepts the situation where the policeman entraps the other into the act of selling (see § 8.8(c)).

Sometimes a criminal statute is quite obviously worded erroneously—perhaps containing too much, perhaps containing too little. Suppose a health statute makes it a crime for a hotel proprietor to permit someone to sleep in a "hotel, dining room or restaurant." Defendant, a hotel proprietor, lets a guest sleep in his hotel. Literally, the statute makes him a criminal. Quite obviously, however, a comma was erroneously inserted between "hotel" and "dining room"; as the statute is thus corrected by the court, the defendant would not be guilty. Courts are less likely to correct obvious mistakes where the statute's error is in favor of the defendant, though even here courts sometimes interpret statutes to read as they were obviously meant to read.

(d) Strict Construction of Criminal Statutes. Most of the rules of statutory interpretation utilized in construing ambiguous criminal statutes are rules also applicable to civil statutes, but there is one rule that applies only to the former: criminal statutes must be strictly construed in favor of the defendant. The rule grew out of conditions during the period in England before the 19th Century when hundreds of crimes, many relatively minor, were punishable by death. With the decline in the severity of punishment, the rule nonetheless continued in effect in England and in this country. As the Supreme Court has put it in *Rewis v. U.S.* (1971), "ambiguity concerning the ambit of criminal statutes should be resolved in favor of lenity." One modern reason for the rule of strict construction is said to be that criminals should be given fair warning, before they engage in a course of conduct, as to what conduct is punishable and how severe the punishment is. Another is that the power to define crimes lies with the legislatures rather than the courts.

Consistent with these reasons are the now generally accepted limitations upon the rule of strict construction. For one thing, there is no occasion to construe a penal statute strictly or otherwise if the statute is devoid of ambiguity. For another, a statute is "not to be construed so strictly as to defeat the obvious intention of the legislature" or "to override common sense." And in any event, strict construction should not be carried to extremes; it is not necessary that the statute be given its "narrowest meaning" or a "forced, narrow or overstrict construction."

In a number of states legislation has been enacted to abrogate the common law rule of strict construction of criminal statutes. This has very often (but not always) occurred in those states that have adopted a comprehensive new criminal code. Such legislation has doubtless had an effect on courts in some jurisdictions, but in others the rule of strict construction seems to be an attitude of mind that is not readily changed by legislation. No doubt some criminal statutes deserve a stricter construction than others. Other things being equal, felony statutes should be construed more strictly than misdemeanor statutes; those with severe punishments more than those with lighter penalties; those involving morally bad conduct more than those involving conduct not so bad; those involving conduct with drastic public consequences more than those whose consequences to the public are less terrible; those carelessly drafted more than those done carefully.

Numerically, most crimes today are crimes that were unknown to the common law; even the great common law crimes (e.g., murder, manslaughter, rape, mayhem, burglary, robbery, larceny, sodomy, conspiracy, attempt) are reduced to statutory form today in most Anglo–American jurisdictions. But courts construe statutes that spell out common law crimes differently from statutes that create new crimes. As the Supreme Court stated in *Morissette v. U.S.* (1952), when the legislature "borrows terms of art in which are accumulated the legal tradition and meaning of centuries of practice, it presumably knows and adopts the cluster of ideas that were attached to each borrowed word in the body of learning from which it was taken and the meaning its use will convey to the judicial mind unless otherwise instructed." Thus courts interpret common law terminology in statutes according to its common law meaning rather than its everyday meaning, with the result that language which might at first blush seem ambiguous or vague takes on a quite definite meaning. For instance, a statute making it involuntary manslaughter to kill another person by doing a lawful act "without due caution or circumspection" (language that literally sounds almost exactly like the ordinary negligence term "lack of due care") should be interpreted to require a high degree of negligence or recklessness rather than ordinary negligence, in view of the common law requirements of manslaughter. The statute is merely an inartistic legislative attempt to spell out the elements of common law manslaughter, not an attempt to change the negligence element from greater negligence or recklessness to ordinary negligence.

This is not to suggest that common law terms in a statute must inevitably be taken to have their common law meaning, for it may appear that the legislature intended otherwise. Such intent may be discerned by the context within which the term is used or by the fact that the statute has quite clearly expanded upon the common law in other, related respects.

Another rule of statutory interpretation, which may perhaps be considered a special application of the rule of strict construction, is that "where a statute is susceptible of two constructions, by one of which grave and doubtful constitutional questions arise and by the other of which such questions are avoided, [the court's] duty is to adopt the latter." But, as the Supreme Court cautioned in *Almendarez–Torres v. U.S.* (1998),

> those who invoke the doctrine must believe that the alternative is a serious likelihood that the statute will be held unconstitutional. Only then will the doctrine serve its basic democratic function of maintaining a set of statutes that reflect, rather than distort, the policy choices that elected representatives have made. For similar reasons, the statute must be genuinely susceptible to two constructions after, and not before, its complexities are unraveled. Only then is the statutory construction that avoids the constitutional question a "fair" one.

An *ambiguous* criminal statute will often be narrowly construed but, as so construed, upheld by the courts. A *vague* criminal statute is another matter. A criminal statute, federal or state, so vague "that men of common intelligence must necessarily guess at its meaning and differ as to its application" is unconstitutional (see § 2.3). No doubt there is no exact borderline that can be drawn between a statute which is merely ambiguous and one which is unconstitutionally vague.

(e) Legislative History. With a federal statute, whether civil or criminal, there is often a good deal of "legislative history" to aid in finding the intention of the legislature if the statute is ambiguous. The history of a federal statute from the time a bill is introduced until final enactment is generally quite thoroughly recorded in writing. After a bill is introduced by a member of

Congress (say the House of Representatives) it is assigned to a House committee for study and recommendations. The committee holds hearings on the bill, listening to arguments pro and con, which are reduced to writing. The committee makes a written report to the entire House, expressing its thoughts and recommendations. A debate thereafter takes place on the floor of the House, which debate is taken down verbatim in the Congressional Record. Perhaps an amendment is offered and adopted or voted down. The House passes the bill and sends it on to the Senate, where hearings are held by a Senate committee, written reports are made to the Senate as a whole, debate on the bill is recorded for posterity, and the bill is voted upon and passed. Often the Senate votes a bill with somewhat different provisions from the House bill, in which case a "conference committee" of House and Senate members may meet to iron out differences, often writing a report upon the joint product.

The testimony before the committees will often throw light on "the evil to be cured"—the bad situation that required legislative correction—and thus give an indication of the scope of the statute. The committee reports will also usually spell out the existing situation that the legislation is designed to cure; and they may state more or less specifically what the committee thinks the bill means, perhaps giving examples of fact situations coming within or without the statute. Of course, courts are after the intent of Congress, not the intent of a committee of Congress, but it is generally considered that as to details Congress adopts the committee's intent. Courts naturally pay little or no attention to what a single legislator during debate on the floor states he thinks the statute means, unless he happens to be the sponsor of the bill or perhaps a member of the committee that reported on the bill. But resort may be had to the debates to determine a common understanding indicated by many legislators as to what the bill means. If during debate an amendment is offered but voted down, that is generally a clear indication that Congress did not want that provision in the law.

At times a comparison of the wording of an earlier draft with the language of the statute as enacted may throw some light on the meaning of an ambiguous statute. Suppose a state statute makes it bigamy for one already married to remarry; excepting, however, one who marries again after his spouse, whom he does not know to be alive, has been absent for seven years. Defendant's wife leaves on a sea voyage and is reliably reported by shipwreck survivors to have gone down with the ship; so defendant marries a new wife at the end of five years. Thereafter the old wife turns up. It might be argued, though not without some difficulty, that, as a matter of statutory interpretation, it is a defense to bigamy to remarry within seven years honestly and reasonably believing the spouse is dead. But suppose it is found that an earlier draft, otherwise like the statute as enacted, contained a second exception, expressly providing that remarriage after one year in the reasonable belief the spouse is dead is also a defense. The absence of this clause, struck out in the course of enacting the statute, shows pretty clearly a legislative intent that remarriage before seven years is no defense, however reasonable the belief in the spouses' death. (In a similar fashion, it is often useful to compare the wording of a law as originally enacted with that law as it was subsequently amended.)

The use of legislative history as an aid to statutory interpretation has its limits. While a good deal of legislative history can be mined for a federal statute, most state legislatures, although they may go through much the same motions as Congress, do not keep as good a written record of their work. Elaborate committee reports are seldom made, and it is rare for a record to be kept of legislative debates. One incidental benefit to be derived from the complete recodification of a state's criminal code is that the draftsmen (probably not legislators) will often prepare commentary for each section, which will be used by the courts to determine the legislative intent. In the absence of such written evidence, state courts have to ascertain the "evil to be cured" from other sources.

It should be noted also that not all judges are enamored of the use of legislative history in interpreting ambiguous statutes. And in any event, legislative history is less likely to be controlling in construing criminal statutes than civil statutes. If one purpose of a criminal statute is to warn the public of what conduct will get them into criminal trouble—that is, if prospective criminals are entitled to fair warning—then the public should be able to ascertain the line between permitted and prohibited conduct from the statute itself. It is too much to expect the public to delve studiously into drafts of bills, committee hearings and reports and debates on the bill in order to understand the statute. In other words, the rule that criminal statutes should be strictly construed to some extent limits the use of legislative history in the case of criminal statutes.

(f) Title of the Statute. Sometimes a statute's title throws some light on the meaning of an ambiguous statute. Thus, suppose a criminal statute makes it larceny for a chattel-mortgagor to injure, destroy or conceal mortgaged property, with intent to defraud the mortgagee, or to sell or dispose of the same without the mortgagee's written consent. Defendant sells the mortgaged property with the mortgagee's oral consent. Though the result seems harsh, by the literal wording of the statute the defendant is guilty, in spite of his lack of any fraudulent intent, since "intent to defraud" does not go with "sell or dispose." The court, however, thought the statute ambiguous enough in view of the heavy penalty and the fact the crime was labeled "larceny" to warrant a look at the title, which stated: "An act relating to chattel mortgages, providing punishment for selling, destroying or disposing of chattel-mortgaged property, with intent to defraud." Since the title coupled "dispose" and "intent to defraud", the body of the statute was interpreted to require a fraudulent intent to convict a mortgagor who sold or disposed of mortgaged property. So too, the title of the chapter or part within which the statute appears may shed some light, and thus a chapter heading "Offenses Against the Family" lends support to the conclusion that the term "duty of care" in a statute therein on endangering the welfare of a child refers only to persons having a familial or similar supervisory relationship with the victim.

(g) "Striking Change of Expression." When courts interpret wills, contracts, trust instruments and other private documents, they generally look first at the ambiguous word or phrase or clause or sentence that must be construed, and then at the instrument as a whole, to see what light the other parts of the document may throw on the ambiguous portion. So too with statutes, including criminal statutes. If the legislature uses quite different language in two parts of the same statute, that is often an indication of a different legislative intention as to the two parts. Thus in the chattel-mortgage larceny statute, referred to above, comparison of the "injure, destroy or conceal, with intent to defraud" clause with the "sell or dispose without written consent" clause indicates a legislative intent that no fraudulent intent is required for a sale of, as distinguished from an injury to, mortgaged property.

A "striking change in expression" in two different parts of the same statute indicates "a deliberate difference of intent." If the court can in addition think of a good reason why the legislature might want to make the distinction (was there a special danger in the sale situation that did not apply to the injury situation?), this conclusion is almost inevitable.

The change of expression may appear in the comparison of the statute as it used to read with the statute as it reads now after its amendment. For example, a "blue sky" statute, which formerly made it a felony "knowingly" to make a false statement to the Secretary of State in connection with the registration of securities is later amended by striking out "knowingly," thus making it a felony to make a false statement to the Secretary. The defendant thereafter made an untrue statement honestly believing it to be true. The court interpreted the statute to mean that an honest belief in the truth of statement is no defense; by comparing the old and the new it is apparent that the legislature purposely omitted the word "knowingly" so as to catch persons who make honest mistakes.

The "striking change" technique is most applicable when the problem is one of comparing two clauses side by side in the same sentence, as is the case in the above-discussed statute on chattel-mortgages. It is slightly less applicable perhaps when the comparison is between two adjoining sentences of the same section of the statute; still less if the sentences do not adjoin; still less if the sentences are to be found in different sections of the same statute (though passed as two parts of a statute enacted as a whole at the same time); and still less where the two sections were enacted at different times, though dealing with the same subject-matter. So too, the technique is not as apt to be applied by comparing the wording of two statutes dealing with different subjects. But though the rule grows weaker as the two parts to be compared become more remote (as to location, date of enactment and subject matter) from one another, the rule may still be applicable. Thus in the case of the previously mentioned "blue sky" statute that makes it a crime to "make any false statement" in connection with the *registration* of securities, where the question of interpretation was whether the statute required that the maker know the statement to be false, the court discovered that quite another section of the "blue sky" law, dealing with the *sale* of securities, makes it a crime for the seller to "knowingly make any false * * * statements" about the security. The court said that this shows the legislature knew how to use appropriate language for giving the defense of innocent mistake, yet it failed to use the appropriate language in the section on registration of securities; so the statute covers those who innocently make untrue statements.

An invitation to compare the language of two statutes on the same subject, which may point up different expressions indicating different intentions, is given by the following rule of statutory construction: statutes dealing with the same subject-matter are *in pari materia* and must be construed together.

(h) Ejusdem Generis. Sometimes criminal (or civil) statutes (or written documents of private persons) list some specific items followed by a general catch-all phrase, usually introduced by the words "or other." The general phrase may be construed to be limited to things "of the same kind" (*ejusdem generis*) as the specific items. Thus a federal criminal statute makes it a felony for one to transport in interstate commerce an "automobile, automobile truck, automobile wagon, motor cycle, or any other self-propelled vehicle not designed for running on rails" that he knows to be stolen. Defendant flies an airplane he knows to be stolen from one state to another. Is an airplane a "self-propelled vehicle not designed for running on rails'"? Literally, it would seem to be. But the Supreme Court held in *McBoyle v. U.S.* (1931) that an airplane was not covered by the quoted phrase. The theme of the specific objects listed (automobiles, trucks, motorcycles) is vehicles that run on land, so that "other self-propelled vehicles" is limited to land-vehicles, and airplanes are excluded. Similarly, a statute proscribing destruction of property by "use of bombs, dynamite, nitroglycerine or other kind of explosives" was held not to cover igniting a firecracker in a telephone coin return slot, as the named items are all distinguishable from fireworks by being designed to produce an explosion of extreme effect.

The *ejusdem generis* rule is deemed to be especially applicable to penal statutes because of the need for fair warning. But it is to be utilized only when uncertainty exists and not to defeat the obvious purpose of the legislation being construed. For example, if the general language was later added to the statute for the express purpose of broadening its reach beyond the kinds of things specifically enumerated, then clearly the *ejusdem generis* approach is not warranted. And in any event, the canon of *ejusdem generis* cannot be used when a class cannot be ascertained, for that indicates the legislature did not intend for the general term to be limited by the specific terms listed in the statute.

(i) Expressio Unius, Exclusio Alterius. Another maxim of statutory interpretation sometimes used in construing criminal statutes (as well as other types of statutes and documents of private parties) is that the expression of one thing is the exclusion of another (in Latin, *expressio unius, exclusio alterius*). Thus, for instance, a criminal statute that sets forth one exception (or several listed exceptions) to liability impliedly excludes other exceptions. A typical bigamy statute makes it a crime for one who has a living spouse to remarry; provided, however, that one who marries more than seven years after his spouse, whom he does not know to be alive, has disappeared is not guilty. The question that sometimes arises is whether remarriage, after less than seven years' absence but with the affirmative belief that the spouse is dead, is a defense. Many jurisdictions answer no; the statute gives one exception; that impliedly excludes all other exceptions.

The *expressio unius* canon is not limited to questions concerning possible defenses. Illustrative is a case holding that a felony-murder statute permitting conviction where death occurs in the perpetration of an "arson" by the defendant did not extend to a case where the death resulted from the malicious burning of a car. Because the arson statute named only one type of conveyance, "trailer coaches," this indicated it was not intended to cover other vehicles. So too, when the statute at issue actually contains a definition declaring what a certain term means, this generally excludes any meaning that is not stated.

(j) The Special Controls the General, the Later Controls the Earlier. At times courts are faced with the problem of fitting together two statutes (perhaps criminal, perhaps civil) that deal with the same subject matter but which face in opposite directions. One state statute may punish whoever within the state fishes without a license. Another statute permits fishing without a license in Oxbow Lake, which is located within the state. Neither statute refers to the other. Defendant is tried for fishing in Oxbow Lake without a license. A general rule of interpretation of apparently inconsistent statutes is that the special statute controls the general. Putting the two statutes together, then, the result is that fishing without a license anywhere except in Oxbow Lake is a crime. Another such rule is that, with two inconsistent statutes on the same subject, the later statute controls the earlier. If the general fishing statute was passed in 1940, the Oxbow statute in 1950, then *a fortiori* the fisherman in question is not guilty; the Oxbow statute is surely an exception to the general statute, since a later-special statute controls an earlier-general statute. The greater difficulty comes in fitting together an earlier-special statute and a later-general statute. If the Oxbow statute is dated 1940 and the general statute 1950, the question is whether the 1950 statute impliedly repealed the 1940 statute, or whether, though not so worded, it covers all places except the Oxbow Lake, leaving that situation untouched. Here the court might well exhibit another maxim of statutory construction, that "repeals by implication are not favored," and hold that the earlier-special statute controls the later-general statute, in the absence of a legislative intent to cover the subject of fishing entirely in the new statute. This is especially so if the earlier-special statute is in favor of a criminal defendant.

(k) Administrative Interpretation. The written interpretations given to a statute by the administrative officials charged with administering the statute, or even the unwritten administrative practices of those public officials, are sometimes looked to by courts for assistance in the interpretation of ambiguous statutory language. With criminal statutes the interpretation placed thereon by the administrators of the criminal law (attorneys general on a state level; district attorneys on a local level) is similarly entitled to some weight. Thus suppose a statute punishes adultery, without spelling out the detail of whether an unmarried man who has sexual relations with a married woman is an adulterer. A bachelor enjoys such a relationship with a married lady. Though the constant practice in the past has been to prosecute such a man for the lesser crime of fornication, this particular bachelor is tried for adultery.

The court interpreted the ambiguous statute so as not to apply to unmarried men, in view of this constant past practice. It has been questioned whether the same deference is appropriate if the administrative interpretation is an expansive one.

Where a criminal statute has been construed by a court or by the appropriate administrators and thereafter the statute is reenacted without change, it may be argued that the legislature placed its stamp of approval upon (and therefore adopted) the interpretation given by that court or those administrators. This, however, requires an assumption, which may or may not be true, that the legislature knew of the construction placed upon the language by the court or administrators. It has even sometimes been argued that judicial or administrative interpretation, if known to the legislature, followed by long legislative silence (rather than by legislative reenactment) indicates legislative approval of the interpretation.

(*l*) **Borrowed Statutes.** At times one state borrows a statute (criminal or civil) word for word, or nearly so, from another state. It may even borrow a whole criminal code. It has often been held that, when the legislature borrows a statute, it also borrows the prior interpretations placed on the statute by the courts of the state from which the statute is borrowed; though there is always a safety valve: the foreign interpretation is not to be followed if the court thinks it to be quite wrong.

The states that have received, into their criminal law, common law crimes have also adopted those English criminal statutes in aid of the common law enacted before 1607 (or, in some states, 1775). The interpretation put upon these English statutes by the English courts before 1607 (1775) is generally adopted along with the statute.

Courts themselves cannot very well borrow criminal statutes from other jurisdictions, in the absence of any legislative borrowing. Thus if every state but one has a statute making it a crime to bribe an athlete to throw a game, the courts of that one state could not very well make such bribery a crime, unless it has the power to create new common law crimes, in which case it might point to these statutes as indicating such a strong public policy against such conduct that it ought to be criminal. But courts might more readily look to statutes from other jurisdictions giving a criminal a defense, or might look to such statutes when interpreting its own not-borrowed statutes.

A legislature might "borrow" a particular statutory formulation from some other source, in which case a court construing the enactment will understandably place considerable reliance upon authoritative pronouncements concerning the intended meaning of the source formulation. Not at all uncommon these days is a court's reliance upon the Model Penal Code commentary when interpreting a statute following rather closely a section in the Model Penal Code. Similarly, if a state has enacted a criminal statute following the language of a section of the original proposal for recodification of the federal criminal law, then the Working Papers that accompanied that undertaking are an especially relevant source. Likewise, when a state has undertaken to conform some aspect of state penal law to federal law, then federal cases will provide guidance.

(m) Stare Decisis in Interpreting Criminal Statutes. Sometimes a court, having earlier construed a criminal statute strictly in favor of the defendant, later decides that its earlier construction was wrong. Thus, for instance, a state supreme court, in the case of *State v. X*, interprets its false pretenses statute in such a way as to give the defense to the defendant *X*, who obtained property from his victim by false pretenses, that the victim himself was also engaged in some criminality. The great weight of Anglo–American authority, however, is that the criminality of the victim is no defense; and on principle the majority view is sound. Now the case of *State v. Y* is before the state supreme court, and *Y*'s defense is that, under the false pretenses statute as formerly interpreted, the victim was himself a rogue (though of course not so clever a rogue as *Y*). The court now recognizes that its earlier decision was wrong. Can it now overrule its earlier decision and hold that criminality of the victim is no defense? Obviously, other things being equal, courts should interpret statutes correctly, regardless of past mistakes. On the other hand, it may not be fair to *Y*, who may have relied on the decision in the *X* case before he engaged in his scheme to defraud his victim, to change the rule now. The difficulty lies in the Anglo–American theory of precedents that case law operates retroactively, and in particular that case law which overrules earlier precedents operates retroactively. When faced with this very problem—that of overruling or following an earlier erroneous interpretation of the false pretenses statute—the New York court felt obliged in the *Y* case to follow the *X* case precedent, with an invitation to the legislature to change the rule for the future; but the Oregon court made bold to overrule the *X* case even though it meant that *Y*, who may have relied on the *X* case, went to jail. The Oregon court made a distinction between crimes *mala in se* (e.g., false pretenses) and crimes only *mala prohibita;* a person who commits a crime with "a consciousness of wickedness" in doing it has no right to the benefits of *stare decisis.*

The choice, however, is not necessarily between following the precedent (thus letting the defendant off but perpetuating a bad decision) and retroactively overruling it (thus eliminating a bad precedent but putting the defendant behind bars). There are two techniques by which the defendant may go free even if the precedent is overruled. It is not impossible for a court to overrule for the future only, letting the defendant go but stating in the opinion that anyone who from now on conducts himself the way this defendant did will be guilty of the crime. The second method is to overrule the erroneous precedent but to give the defendant the defense of mistake of law induced by an appellate court. Mistake as to the interpretation of a criminal statute is generally no defense. Thus a defendant is ordinarily guilty of burglary if he enters a house by opening wider a partly open window in order to squeeze through to steal the silverware in the house, even though he honestly but mistakenly believes there can be no burglary unless he opens a window entirely shut. But if the state supreme court had previously held that the burglary element of "breaking" is absent in the wider opening of an already partly open window, and the defendant relied on it, he would have the defense of mistake of law. Some courts have even gone so far as to say that the adoption by a court of a new interpretation of an old statute is forbidden by *ex post facto* constitutional provisions if the new interpretation is harder on the defendant than the old.

We have been speaking of the *stare decisis* problem involved when the court decides that its previous interpretation of a criminal statute was too favorable to the defendant. If it decides that its earlier interpretation was too hard on the defendant, it would have no trouble in overruling the earlier case, since the present defendant could not have relied on it to his disadvantage.

§ 2.3   Unconstitutional Uncertainty—The Void-for-Vagueness Doctrine

At common law, it was the practice of courts to refuse to enforce legislative acts deemed too uncertain to be applied. A similar approach was taken by the United States Supreme Court in some early cases where the separation of powers doctrine was invoked to support the proposition that Congress, by the enactment of an ambiguous statute, could not pass the law-making job on to the judiciary. The Court has also reversed convictions under uncertain criminal laws on the basis that the accused was denied his right to be informed "of the nature and cause of the accusation" as guaranteed by the Sixth Amendment. However, today it is the void-for-vagueness doctrine that prevails: the due process clauses of the Fifth Amendment (when a federal statute is involved) and the Fourteenth Amendment (when a state statute is involved) require that a criminal statute be declared void when it is so vague that "men of common intelligence must necessarily guess at its meaning and differ as to its application."

(a) In General. Undue vagueness in the statute will result in it being held unconstitutional, whether the uncertainty goes to the persons within the scope of the statute, the conduct that is forbidden, or the punishment that may be imposed. (While most of the cases have involved statutes, the same principle applies to common law crimes and to administrative regulations that carry penal sanctions.) Ordinarily, a challenge to the statute in this regard is raised in the context of a criminal prosecution, but under limited circumstances an injunction may be obtained barring a prosecution under an unconstitutionally uncertain statute. In any event, the statute is not tested "on its face," but rather with its "judicial gloss," that is, as it has been authoritatively construed by state courts.

The Supreme Court has said, *Lanzetta v. N.J.* (1939), that "[n]o one may be required at peril of life, liberty or property to speculate as to the meaning of penal statutes. All are entitled to be informed as to what the State commands or forbids." And the Court has frequently emphasized that a statute is unduly vague when it gives neither the person subject thereto nor the jury which would try him a basis upon which to safely and certainly judge the result. Nonetheless, it is obviously unrealistic to require that criminal statutes define offenses with extreme particularity. For one thing, there are inherent limitations in the use of language; few words possess the precision of mathematical symbols. Secondly, legislators cannot foresee all of the variations of fact situations that may arise under a statute. While some ambiguous statutes are the result of poor draftsmanship, it is apparent that in many instances the uncertainty is merely attributable to a desire not to nullify the purpose of the legislation by the use of specific terms that would afford loopholes through which many could escape. And thus the Supreme Court has held that statutes are not invalid as vague simply because it is difficult to determine whether certain marginal offenses fall within their language. If the general class of offenses to which a statute is directed is plainly within its terms, the statute will not be struck down because hypothetical cases could be put where doubt might arise.

As the above suggests, there is no simple litmus-paper test for determining whether a criminal statute is void for vagueness. This had led some to question whether there is a thread of consistency running through the Supreme Court's decisions on this subject, although it is probably fair to conclude that a reasonable level of consistency appears once the underlying bases of the void-for-vagueness doctrine are identified. These bases are reflected in three questions often considered by the Supreme Court: (1) Does the statute in question give fair notice to those persons potentially subject to it? (2) Does it adequately guard against arbitrary and discriminatory enforcement? and (3) Does it provide sufficient breathing space for First Amendment rights?

(b) Fair Warning. One rationale underlying the void-for-vagueness doctrine is that of fair warning to persons potentially subject to a statute; the Supreme Court has frequently stressed that everyone is entitled to be informed what the law commands or forbids. Although the Court has said that the law must be clear to the "average man," to "men of common intelligence," and to "ordinary people," such language cannot be accepted at face value. Words of a statute that otherwise might be considered unduly vague may be considered sufficiently definite because they have a well-settled meaning in the common law or in court decisions, or because of their usage in other legislation. These sources of clarification are not likely to occur to the average person. This suggests that the requirement of fair warning is satisfied if a statute suggests the need to seek legal advice and if the statute's meaning might reasonably be determined through such advice.

The language quoted above is somewhat misleading in another respect, as there is no need for legislation to give fair warning except to those potentially subject to it. For this reason, if a penal statute is addressed to those in a particular trade or business, it is sufficient if the terms used have a meaning well enough defined to enable one engaged in that trade or business to apply it correctly. It follows that a statute with uncertain language is more likely to be declared void for vagueness if it is addressed to the general public or to a substantial group of persons who have not voluntarily chosen to subject themselves to a particular regulatory scheme.

One consequence of the fair-warning rationale is that a defendant's chances of mounting a successful vagueness challenge are greater when he can establish an appealing claim to clear notice of the boundaries of the statute in question. This is reflected in the fact that the Supreme Court has given consideration to whether the defendant's conduct is particularly evil and whether the ambiguity being urged appears to be merely a pretext for evading the law. Similarly, while the vagueness objection may be raised in court by one who was totally unaware of the statute prior to his conduct, it should be noted that most of the cases reaching the Supreme Court in which the void-for-vagueness doctrine has been successfully invoked have been those in which it is likely the defendant actually consulted the statute book in advance and was confounded.

Not infrequently the Supreme Court, in passing upon a statute claimed to be unconstitutional for vagueness, has concluded that the statute gives fair warning because scienter is an element of the offense. That is, the statute is upheld because it requires that the prohibited act have been done "intentionally," "knowingly," or "willfully." *Boyce Motor Lines, Inc. v. U.S.* (1952), although it involves an administrative crime, is illustrative. The company was charged with violating an Interstate Commerce Commission regulation that required drivers of vehicles transporting explosives or inflammables to avoid "so far as practicable, and where feasible," congested thoroughfares and tunnels. The Court upheld the indictment because the statute under which it was brought punished only knowing violation of an I.C.C. regulation; the regulation was not vague, the Court concluded, because it would apply only in cases where the defendant was aware of a safer route and deliberately took the more dangerous one or where he willfully neglected to make inquiry about a safer alternate route. But as Justice Jackson correctly pointed out in his dissent, scienter—at least as it has been traditionally defined—cannot cure vagueness in a statute or regulation. One "knowingly" commits an offense when he knows that his acts will bring about certain results (those defined in the statute in question) (see § 4.2), and whether he knows that deliberately causing such results is proscribed by statute is immaterial. Because it is knowledge of the consequences of one's actions and not knowledge of the existence or meaning of the criminal law that is relevant, it seems clear that uncertain language in a statute is not clarified by the addition of a scienter element. Stated in the context of the *Boyce* case, the fact that a conviction may be had only if it is found that the driver willfully failed to take or discover a safer route "so far as practicable, and where feasible," does not require proof of actual knowledge or understanding of the quoted language and thus does not serve to clarify that language. Or, to put it yet another way, it is possible willfully to bring about certain results and yet be without fair warning that such conduct is proscribed.

As noted earlier, it is often difficult to determine whether the uncertain language in a statute renders it ambiguous, so that it may be narrowly construed and thus remain valid, or whether the language makes the statute vague, so that it is void. Consideration of the fair-warning underpinnings of the void-for-vagueness doctrine may be helpful in this regard. If the language of the statute is rather uncertain, but a person potentially subject to the statute could (perhaps with legal advice) reasonably foresee the limited alternative meanings that might be given the statute, then perhaps there is sufficient fair warning to justify subsequent construction and validation of the statute. On the other hand, if the statute is so uncertain that the means by which it might be rehabilitated cannot reasonably be foreseen, then it seems appropriate to invalidate the statute for vagueness.

While the fair-warning principle is one important aspect of the void-for-vagueness doctrine it does not provide a complete rationale of the cases in this area. Particularly because some of the decisions cannot be squared with the notion of fair warning, it may be that the two factors discussed below are more likely to be controlling.

(c) Arbitrary and Discriminatory Enforcement. The decisions of the United States Supreme Court on the void-for-vagueness doctrine also reflect concern with statutes that are so broad that they are susceptible to arbitrary and discriminatory enforcement. Although most of these cases have also reflected a fair-warning concern, the Court on one occasion declared a statute void because of the unlimited discretion given to juries even though no problem of fair warning was present. The objection to a vague statute, then, is akin to a claim of denial of equal protection in law enforcement, although it may more appropriately be said to rest upon the notion that the language of the statute is so uncertain that arbitrariness in its enforcement might not be detected.

This risk of abuse in the administration of the law is present in two forms when the meaning of a criminal statute is unclear. One risk is that the law may be arbitrarily applied by police and prosecution officials, which the Court has characterized as "the more important aspect of vagueness doctrine." The Supreme Court has voided statutes that give the police unlimited discretion, and has evidenced equal concern about laws that furnish convenient tools for discriminatory enforcement by prosecuting officials. The other risk is that the law may be so unclear that a trial court cannot properly instruct the jury. A statute is unconstitutionally vague when it leaves judges and jurors free to decide, without any legally fixed standards, what is prohibited and what is not in each particular case.

This is not to say, however, that a penal statute is void merely because it grants some discretion to those who administer the law. The criminal law is full of instances in which the legislature has passed on to the administrators some responsibility for determining the actual boundaries of the law, as with the frequent occasions when a jury is asked to determine whether the defendant acted "reasonably" in some respect. Account must be taken of what has been called the "principle of necessity": when the concern is with whether the statute provides some opportunity for arbitrary enforcement, it is relevant to ask whether some alternative formulation not carrying this risk reasonably suggests itself. Uncertain statutory language has been upheld when the subject matter would not allow more exactness and when greater specificity in language would interfere with practical administration. On the other hand, statutes that appear to be the result of poor draftsmanship are more likely to be struck down.

(d) Breathing Space for First Amendment Rights. In some of the cases on the subject of unconstitutional indefiniteness, the legislature has not extended its regulation via enactment of criminal statutes into areas protected by the Constitution, but has merely left uncertain exactly what is regulated. That is, even giving the vague statute a most generous reading, it is clear that the legislature could (had it used clear language) proscribe all such conduct. The vice is not legislative overreaching, but merely the lack of fair warning to the public and the lack of standards for those who must enforce and apply the law.

By contrast, in other cases the legislature has undertaken regulation in a "danger zone," in that there are substantive due process limits on how far it may go in regulating conduct without infringing upon, for example, constitutionally protected free speech. If the statute is unclear, there are again likely to be present the two vices of insufficient warning and inadequate enforcement standards. But—of particular importance when the defendant is not in a position to object on either of these two grounds—there is another evil as well: the indefiniteness in the statute, or in the "judicial gloss" placed upon the statute in an attempt to overcome the claim that it prohibits constitutionally protected conduct, may inhibit the exercise of constitutional rights. That is, "there is the danger that the state will get away with more inhibitory regulation than it has a constitutional right to impose, because persons at the fringes of amenability to regulation will rather obey than run the risk of erroneous constitutional judgment."

It is for this reason that the United States Supreme Court has repeatedly applied strict standards of permissible statutory vagueness to legislation in the area of First Amendment rights. "Because First Amendment freedoms need breathing space to survive, government may regulate in the area only with narrow specificity." This bolstering of the void-for-vagueness doctrine by the "breathing space" argument, it should be noted, is somewhat different than a direct attack upon a statute on the ground that it violates constitutional guarantees of the First Amendment. Criminal statutes, of course, may be attacked on the latter basis as well, but the circumstances in which this may be successfully done are in some respects more limited. Thus, when a statute is challenged on this basis it is generally required that the party making the challenge establish that the statute actually infringes upon his own constitutional rights (see § 3.5). This is not so when it is alleged that the statute is vague and that it thus does not afford sufficient "breathing space." Such an attack is permitted even though the person making the attack fails to demonstrate that his own conduct could not be regulated by a statute drawn with the requisite narrow specificity. In appraising a vague statute's inhibitory effect upon First Amendment rights, the Court will take into account possible applications of the statute in other factual contexts.

§ 2.4   Ex Post Facto Laws and Bills of Attainder

The United States Constitution forbids both the federal government and the states to enact any ex post facto law or bill of attainder. Many state constitutions also contain one or both of the same two provisions. While bills of attainder and ex post facto laws overlap to some extent, they do not always mean the same thing and thus are treated here under separate headings.

(a) **Ex Post Facto Laws.** The Supreme Court in *Calder v. Bull* (1798) gave this much-quoted list of ex post facto laws: "1st. Every law that makes an action done before the passing of the law, and which was innocent when done, criminal; and punishes such action. 2d. Every law that aggravates a crime, or makes it greater than it was, when committed. 3d. Every law that changes the punishment, and inflicts a greater punishment, than the law annexed to the crime, when committed. 4th. Every law that alters the legal rules of evidence, and receives less, or different testimony, than the law required at the time of the commission of the offense, in order to convict the offender." The first three are restrictions as to the substantive criminal law, while the fourth—dealing with retroactive changes in the law of evidence—is a limitation on procedural law. And later cases have included procedural changes other than changes in the rules of evidence when the accused is thereby deprived of a substantial right. The subject of ex post facto laws will, however, be treated as a whole in this section rather than divided into its substantive and procedural parts, as the principle underlying the ex post provision applies equally to its substantive and procedural law applications.

The ex post facto prohibition has been recognized by the Supreme Court as furthering two important purposes. For one thing, it serves "to assure that legislative acts give fair warning of their effect and permit individuals to rely on their meaning until explicitly changed." Moreover, the prohibition "also restricts governmental power by restraining arbitrary and potentially vindictive legislation." A third basis has sometimes been stated, namely, that it "assures the legislature can make recourse to stigmatizing penalties of the criminal law only when its core purpose of deterrence could thereby possibly be served."

The ex post facto prohibition is concerned with legislative acts (federal or state), rather than with judicial decisions. It applies only to criminal matters, although retroactive civil statutes have sometimes been held unconstitutional on some other ground, usually as a taking of property rights without due process of law.

The clearest sort of an ex post facto law is one that creates a new crime and applies it retroactively to conduct not criminal at the time committed. This is so obviously true that legislation seldom if ever has attempted to accomplish this result. The same result would follow from a statute that eliminated a former element of the offense (e.g., omitting the word "knowingly" in a statutory crime or the phrase "in the nighttime" in a burglary statute), or that took away a defense formerly available, such as self-defense in battery or lack of pregnancy in abortion.

More difficult problems are frequently encountered under the second aspect of the ex post facto prohibition, which forbids the retroactive application of an increase in the punishment for a crime that carried a lesser penalty when committed. (A lessening of the punishment is not prohibited, and thus a change from the death penalty to life imprisonment may be applied retroactively.) If a statute making grand theft punishable by one to five years imprisonment is amended to increase the punishment to from two to ten years, the amendment would be ex post facto as applied to theft committed before the amendment. And a statute changing the punishment from life imprisonment or death to a mandatory death penalty is ex post facto as applied to a past crime, as is a statute changing the punishment from a fine or imprisonment to a fine *and* imprisonment, one changing a sentencing guidelines presumptive sentence from 3½–4½ years imprisonment to 5½–7 years, one retroactively canceling early release credits, or one increasing defendant's sentence upon revocation of his parole or supervised release. In *Dobbert v. Fla.* (1977), the Supreme Court held that a defendant's sentence of death did not violate the ex post facto prohibition where it was imposed pursuant to valid procedures superceding those which had existed at the time of his crime and which had been thereafter declared unconstitutional. The majority, stressing the fair warning function, deemed it sufficient that the law at the time of defendant's conduct revealed what the legislature wanted to accomplish. The dissenters in *Dobbert,* on the other hand, stressed that at the time of defendant's crime there existed no valid means of imposing a death sentence in Florida.

Although some earlier cases took the view that any change in the kind or manner of punishment is ex post facto as to prior offenses, today it is generally accepted that such a change is permissible if it does not increase the punishment, as with a change in the procedures for arriving at or carrying out a sentence of death. It is not always easy, however, to tell whether the new punishment is greater than or the same as or less than the old. A statute delaying execution for three months has been held not to be ex post facto, but a new law providing for solitary confinement before execution is not valid as to past capital crimes.

An amendment that lowers the maximum punishment but raises the minimum punishment is viewed as increasing the punishment. Likewise, the better view is that the same is true as to a change which reduces the statutory minimum sentence but increases the time that must be served before parole may be granted, although some of the older cases reach the contrary result by viewing release on parole as an act of grace and not a right. A statute reducing the amount of "good time" that can be earned in prison to reduce the sentence imposed is also ex post facto if applied to the sentence on a prior crime; this is so even if "good time" is technically not a part of the sentence, as the change "substantially alters the consequences attached to a crime already completed, and therefore changes 'the quantum of punishment.' " In all such instances, one may object to an ex post facto law that increases the punishment for a past offense even if he actually received a punishment within the old limits.

Some ex post facto questions of the increased-punishment type have arisen in connection with the passage of habitual criminal laws, which impose enhanced penalties for later offenses if the defendant has previously been convicted of one or more crimes. If the defendant commits crime *A* at a time when there is no habitual criminal statute, then such a statute is passed imposing increased punishment for a second offense, and then the defendant commits crime *B,* it is not within the ex post facto prohibition to apply the habitual criminal statute to crime *B.* No additional punishment is prescribed for crime *A,* but only for the new crime *B,* which was committed after the statute was passed. Similarly, it is permissible to define a crime as limited to certain conduct engaged in by persons who have theretofore been convicted of some other offense and to apply the statute to one whose earlier offense and conviction predated the enactment of this statute.

Over the years, some decisions of the Supreme Court have applied the ex post facto prohibition to retroactive changes in evidence or other procedure that operated to the disadvantage of the criminal defendant by making conviction easier. Some cases had to do with the fourth category in *Calder,* concerning alteration of the rules of evidence. Thus, a statute that changed the burden of proof on the prosecution from the usual beyond a reasonable doubt rule to a preponderance of the evidence was deemed ex post facto if retroactive. By comparison, a statute enlarging the class of persons competent to testify was not deemed to be ex post facto as applied to past offenses, for the new rule may be used either for or against criminal defendants as a class. That decision was distinguished in *Carmell v. Tex.* (2000), which involved the retroactive application of a change in the law so that a sex offense victim's testimony alone could support a conviction, without there being the corroborating evidence or timely outcry previously required. The Court in *Carmell* reasoned that this change very definitely fit within *Calder*'s fourth category regarding "less testimony required to convict," and rejected the state's claim that the fourth category is limited to alteration of the burden of proof, noting that laws lowering the burden of proof and laws reducing the quantum of evidence necessary to meet that burden are indistinguishable in all meaningful ways relevant to the concerns underlying the ex post facto prohibition.

As to procedural changes other than changes in the rules of evidence, the Supreme Court once stated the test in this way: a procedural change that does not injuriously affect a substantial right to which the accused was entitled as of the time of his offense is not ex post facto though retroactive; but it is otherwise if it does deprive him of a substantial right. For example, reduction of the number of trial jurors was deemed substantial, but a change in the jurisdiction of courts was not.

Such application of the ex post facto clause in the realm of procedure ended with the decision in *Collins v. Youngblood* (1990). In holding that the retroactive application of a statute which allowed appellate courts to reform an unauthorized verdict without the necessity of remand for retrial did not violate the ex post facto clause, the Court concluded that earlier cases extending that prohibition to the area of procedure were not "consistent with the understanding of the term '*ex post facto* law' at the time the Constitution was adopted" and should be overruled. (Discussion in some of the earlier cases, the Court added, merely supports the still-vital proposition "that by simply labeling a law 'procedural,' a legislature does not thereby immunize it from scrutiny" under the ex post facto clause.) Under this modern view of the ex post facto clause, the *Collins* Court thus concluded, a statute is unobjectionable if it

> does not punish as a crime an act previously committed, which was innocent when done; nor make more burdensome the punishment for a crime, after its commission; nor deprive one charged with crime of any defense available according to law at the time when the act was committed.

However, the Court also made it clear that this last category has to do only with withdrawal of defenses related to the essential elements of a crime, or to matters which a defendant might plead as justification or excuse, and thus it continues to be the rule that extending a statute of limitations period before a given prosecution is barred does not violate the ex post facto clause. But, the Court concluded in *Stogner v. California* (2003), a statute permitting prosecution for sex-related child abuse within one year of the victim's report to police, even as to offenses already time-barred when the law was enacted, *does* violate the ex post facto clause. The Court reasoned that this situation fell within the second category, regarding a law making a crime "greater than it was," understood to include "a statute that 'inflict[s] *punishments*, where the party was not, by *law*, liable to *any punishment*,' " the situation that obtained as to Stogner once the original statute of limitations had expired.

(b) Date of Offense for Ex Post Facto Purposes. With those crimes that consist of both conduct and the result of conduct, as is the case with criminal homicide (a blow with a resulting death is needed), there may arise a question as to the time of the offense for purposes of applying the ex post facto clause. Thus, if the defendant delivers the mortal blow on April 1, a new homicide statute becomes law on April 10, and the victim dies from his wounds on April 20, can the new statute, if disadvantageous to the defendant, constitutionally be applied to his situation? If the theory behind the prohibition on retroactivity is that of giving fair warning, it seems clear that for ex post facto purposes the date of the blow should be the date of the offense.

The problem of determining the date of the offense for ex post facto purposes may also be present when the offense is of a continuing nature, as with an ongoing conspiracy or where the offense is defined in terms of allowing a certain condition to continue or is based upon omissions by the defendant. If the conduct, condition, or failure to act continues after the enactment or amendment of the statute in question, this statute may be applied without violating the ex post facto prohibition. Thus, a statute increasing the penalty with respect to a conspiracy may be applied to a conspiracy that commenced prior to but was carried on and continued beyond the effective date of the new act. Similarly, if a certain condition existed prior to the enactment of a statute making the permitting of such a condition a crime, this does not bar prosecution for the continuance of the condition thereafter. However, if the basis of the prosecution is an omission by the defendant, it must be determined whether the duty to act existed subsequent to the new statutory enactment.

(c) Ex Post Facto Judicial Decisions. It is clear that the ex post facto prohibition in the federal constitution applies only to legislative acts and not to judicial decisions. At the same time, it is

obvious that the rationale behind the ex post facto prohibition—
whether it be stated as a concern for adequate notice to the
defendant or as a concern with the exercise of unfettered power by
public officials—is relevant in the situation where a judicial decision is applied retroactively to the disadvantage of a defendant in a
criminal case. And thus the United States Supreme Court has said
that the due process clause bars an appellate court from doing what
the ex post facto clause prohibits a legislature from doing. Actually,
the proposition cannot be applied that broadly, as all case-law,
including that interpreting criminal statutes, operates retroactively,
and such retroactivity is an essential part of our legal system. It is
fair to conclude that: (1) the prohibition of retroactive judicial
decisions is not as extensive as the prohibition of ex post facto
statutes; and (2) the law regarding the former is not as clearly
developed as that concerning the ex post facto clause.

Perhaps the easiest case is when a judicial decision subsequent
to the defendant's conduct operates to his detriment by overruling
a prior decision that, if applied to the defendant's case, would result
in his acquittal. For example, the later decision may overrule a
prior ruling that the statute under which the defendant was prosecuted is unconstitutional. Or, it may disallow a defense permitted
in an earlier case, or interpret a criminal statute as covering
conduct previously held to be outside this statute. Under such
circumstances, the overruling decision (whether on appeal of the
defendant's case or in another case decided subsequent to his
conduct) is not applied retroactively, at least where the defendant's
conduct is not *malum in se*. This result has been explained on
various grounds—as required by the ex post facto prohibition, by
the prohibition on cruel and unusual punishment, by "principles of
justice," or by the due process clause. If the defendant was actually
aware of the prior decision and relied upon it, then the basis of
decision may be that the defendant has the defense of mistake of
law as a result of being misled as to the existence or interpretation
thereof by the highest court of the jurisdiction.

More difficult are those cases in which the appellate court, in
interpreting a statute that is not unconstitutionally vague or overbroad, decides a question of first impression in that jurisdiction
concerning the meaning and scope of the statute. For example, may
a state supreme court hold for the first time that the felony-murder
statute covers instances in which death is caused by a shot fired by
someone other than the felon, and then apply this interpretation to
conduct that occurred prior to that holding? May an appellate court
do so when deciding, as a matter of first impression, that the word
"arson" in the felony-murder statute must be read to incorporate
not only the arson statute (limited to the burning of dwellings) but
also the malicious burning statute (dealing with the burning of

other buildings)? Is it permissible for a state supreme court to affirm a trespass conviction, based upon a statute that forbids entry upon lands after notice prohibiting same, by resort to a decision subsequent to the defendant's conduct interpreting the statute as also covering failure to leave the property of another after being ordered to do so?

Sometimes the application of appellate decisions on matters of first impression to prior conduct is justified on the ground that nothing in the way of retroactivity is involved because the court has merely decided what the criminal statute has meant from the time of its enactment (and thus prior to the defendant's conduct.) But, even if it may be said that the judicial decision has only explained the statute and not amended it, an element of unfairness may be present if the construction given the statute is one that could not have been reasonably anticipated. Thus, the United States Supreme Court, in *Bouie v. City of Columbia* (1964), reversed the conviction in the trespass case described above because the judicial construction of the statute was "unexpected and indefensible by reference to the law which had been expressed prior to the conduct in issue." Although this standard reflects a concern with fair warning (by the reference to the "unexpected" construction) and also with arbitrary official action (by the reference to the "indefensible" construction), it obviously cannot be applied with ease because it requires a difficult evaluation of "the actual quality of the adjudication" in the case of first impression. For example, if extension-by-analogy is "unexpected" and "indefensible" when a trespass statute, dealing with entry after notice prohibiting same, is held also to cover refusal to leave after notice, why is it not equally so when the word "arson" in a felony-murder statute is held also to cover other malicious burning? Perhaps it is because some defendants have a greater claim to fair warning than others; in *Bouie* the Court noted that the defendants' conduct could not be deemed improper or immoral. In any event, "the promise of *Bouie* has been largely illusory," as "courts have construed the foreseeability requirement generously," and are inclined to "reverse on *Bouie* grounds only when the judicial change seems entirely arbitrary."

There is yet another situation in which a judicial decision may appear to operate retroactively to the detriment of a criminal defendant. The language of a statute defining a crime, as yet without any limiting judicial gloss, may be unduly vague or broad and thus unconstitutional unless clarified or narrowed by judicial interpretation. May a defendant's conviction be affirmed on the basis of such a limiting construction that occurs subsequent to his conduct? That is, is it consistent with the fair-warning principle to charge the defendant with knowledge of the scope of a subsequent, saving interpretation? The United States Supreme Court has assumed that it is, and thus in a number of cases has allowed these statutes the benefit of whatever clarifying gloss state courts may have added in the course of litigation after defendant's conduct. The thrust of these cases seems to be that prospective defendants are not entitled to warning as to the precise way in which the statute will be construed to bring it within the Constitution. In some cases this result is not shocking, as where a defendant is prosecuted for sale of obscene literature and on his appeal the statute is saved by reading in a requirement that the sale be with knowledge of the obscene character of the literature. It has been suggested, however, that this kind of judicial decision should have retroactive effect only when "the limiting construction is a relatively simple and natural one," that is, when there is some warning as to the actual reach of the statute because the way in which it will be construed can be reasonably foreseen. In the *Bouie* case, the Supreme Court intimated it might go at least this far.

(d) Bills of Attainder. The Supreme Court has given this definition: "A bill of attainder is a legislative act which inflicts punishment without a judicial trial." More recently, the Court defined such bills more broadly as "legislative acts, no matter what their form, that apply either to named individuals or to easily ascertainable members of a group in such a way as to inflict punishment on them without a judicial trial." Thus, a statute, federal or state, providing that any public official found guilty of misconduct in office by his superiors should be fined or imprisoned, would be unconstitutional as a bill of attainder.

Actually, most of the cases that have found legislative acts to be bills of attainder have involved punishment in a much broader sense than criminal; thus denial of the right to practice one's profession, or of the right to government or private employment, has been held to be "punishment" within the meaning of the definition of bills of attainder, and this is so whether the legislature's aim was to punish past conduct or to discourage future conduct that it dislikes.

A statute might provide that a named individual (or named individuals, or an identifiable group of individuals), who had in the past done something the legislature thought to be bad but which was not criminal, should be fined or imprisoned. Such a statute would, of course, be a bill of attainder. But it would also be an ex post facto law and thus doubly unconstitutional. The two constitutional prohibitions do tend to overlap somewhat, though they are clearly not identical.

§ 2.5   Repeal or Amendment of Statute

What becomes of the criminal liability of a person, who has violated a criminal statute when that statute was in force, if the statute in question is later repealed? Does the repeal operate retroactively so as to let him go free? Or does the repeal operate only as to future conduct, leaving past conduct to be governed by the law in effect at the time of such conduct? Does it make a difference whether the person in question has been convicted before the repeal, or whether his prosecution is then pending, or whether prosecution has not yet been commenced at the time of repeal? The same questions may be asked, though the answers may be different, in the situation where the criminal statute in question has been amended, rather than repealed, as where the amendment alters the punishment or changes the scope of the statute's coverage.

(a) Common Law Rule. The common law rule is that, in the absence of an effective saving provision, the outright repeal of a criminal statute operates to bar prosecutions for earlier violations of the statute, whether the prosecutions are pending, or not yet begun, at the time of the repeal, on the theory that the legislature by its repeal has indicated an intention that the conduct in question shall no longer be prosecuted as a crime. But such a repeal does not operate to set free a person who has been prosecuted and convicted and as to whom the judgment of conviction has become final before the statute is repealed. This doctrine has been criticized by some as lacking any reasonable basis, and praised by others because it "provides a judicially fashioned rule of statutory construction based upon a reasonable presumption of legislative intent."

The same rules apply where the criminal statute has not been taken off the books, but has been rendered ineffective by other legislation that makes what was criminal a right. Thus, absent an effective saving provision, the passage of a state public accommodations law bars prosecution for trespass of those seeking service in public accommodations and requires release of those convicted for such trespass if their convictions have not become final. And in the controversial case of *Hamm v. City of Rock Hill* (1964), the United States Supreme Court held that, under the supremacy clause of the Constitution, the federal Civil Rights Act of 1964 abated nonfinal state prosecutions for conduct rendered nonpunishable by that Act.

Sometimes the criminal statute is amended to provide a more severe punishment than before. Of course it is clear that the greater punishment cannot be applied to one who violated the statute before the amendment (see § 2.4). But if there is no applicable saving provision, does the amendment impliedly repeal the old statute so as to prevent further prosecutions thereunder, under the common law rule discussed above that repeals operate to bar further prosecutions in the absence of saving provisions? Some cases have so held, but it seems clear that the legislature can hardly have intended by its amendment that the conduct in question should no longer be prosecuted (the rationale of the common law rule of repeal); so other states adopt the better view that the old statute is still available for prosecution of those who violated it before its amendment.

Where, as sometimes happens, the amendment reduces rather than increases the punishment, it is generally held that an offender who violated the statute at the time it carried the heavier penalty may be punished under the amended law; here too the amendment does not serve to free him from all punishment.

There is also a generally recognized simultaneous-repeal-and-reenactment exception to the common law rule. Under this exception, if what was criminal under the repealed statute is also encompassed within the new law, which perhaps carries a different offense label, then prosecution under the repealed statute is permissible. Here as well the result accords with what in all likelihood was the legislature's intent.

(b) Saving Provisions. The common law rule that repeal of a criminal statute bars further prosecution against earlier offenders, being based on the legislature's presumed intent, may of course be changed by an expression of legislative intent that earlier violations may still be prosecuted. So the repealing statute may itself contain a saving clause, or there may be applicable a general saving statute or constitutional provision. Thus most states and the federal government have statutes or constitutional provisions (often applicable to civil statutes as well as criminal) providing in effect that repeal (or either repeal or amendment) of a statute shall not affect prior liability thereunder unless the repealing act expressly so provides. And in the enactment of a new comprehensive criminal code and repeal of prior substantive criminal laws, there is usually included a saving provision to the effect that crimes committed prior to the effective date of the new code are subject to prosecution and punishment under the law as it existed at the time.

Although there is in the jurisdiction a general saving provision, it may be that it is not worded broadly enough to cover the particular repeal situation, in which case the common law applies. Thus when the federal prohibition law was repealed by the Twenty-first Amendment to the Constitution, it was held that the federal saving provision was not applicable to a repeal accomplished by constitutional amendment rather than an act of Congress, with the result that prohibition law violators whose prosecutions were pending at the time of the repeal came under the common law rule and so went free. It was argued before the Supreme Court that the fact that most jurisdictions have expressed dissatisfaction with the common law rule by the enactment of general saving provisions, constitutional or statutory, should persuade the Court to abolish the common law rule even in the absence of an applicable saving provision. The argument was rejected: it took legislation to change the common law rule in other jurisdictions; therefore in the absence of legislation the common law prevails. Similarly, in a more recent case the Supreme Court took the view that the federal saving statute would not apply in the case of a prosecution for prior acts now protected by the Civil Rights Act of 1964; the savings statute was read as being limited to instances of repeal or amendment and not extending to a case in which a new statute substitutes a right for a crime.

There is some variation in these saving provisions. Some declare that a legislative change in a statute will not extinguish penalties or liabilities accrued or incurred under the old law, and others (addressed specifically to criminal cases) state that offenses under the old law shall be punished as if the repeal or amendment had not occurred. Only in a few jurisdictions are the saving statutes expressly limited to the repeal-followed-by-reenactment or changed penalty situations, though it is quite common for the saving statute or some other law to provide that if the penalty is reduced the defendant is entitled to be sentenced (or at least to seek to be sentenced) under the new penalty provisions.

When these saving provisions are applied in instances in which there has been an amendment increasing the penalty or a repeal and substantial reenactment, they produce a sound result. In such circumstances, "the statutes have clearly and consistently been used to prevent unintentional and unwarranted legislative pardons." But the broader provisions have often been applied literally in other situations as well. As a consequence, defendants have been convicted of crimes that no longer existed in any form at the time of their prosecution and have been subjected to penalties more severe than those more recently declared sufficient by the legislature.

When applied to these latter circumstances, it is to be doubted that the saving statutes represent either sound policy or the actual intention of the legislature. "A legislative mitigation of the penalty for a particular crime represents a legislative judgment that the lesser penalty for different treatment is sufficient to meet the legitimate ends of the criminal law. Nothing is to be gained by imposing the more severe penalty after such a pronouncement; the excess in punishment can, by hypothesis, serve no purpose other than to satisfy a desire for vengeance." And if the conduct has been decriminalized entirely because "a new social view decides that certain conduct is no longer to be punished," then again it is anomalous that the saving statute "steps in and imposes the punishment fixed by an earlier generation." Some appellate courts have consequently given seemingly broad saving statutes a narrow reading in order not to deprive the defendant before them of the benefit of a prior legislative judgment that the conduct should not be criminal or should be subjected to lesser punishment.

Although in some jurisdictions violation of a local ordinance may not be a criminal offense, the same principles applicable to the repeal or amendment of a criminal statute apply to the repeal or amendment of an ordinance.

§ 2.6 Administrative Crimes

Sometimes the legislature by statute invites an administrative agency to play a part in formulating substantive criminal law. Thus, Congress may provide that the Interstate Commerce Commission may issue regulations for the safe transportation of certain substances, and further that any violation of the regulations shall be punishable by fine or imprisonment. Or, a state statute may authorize the state food board to issue regulations concerning the importation of food stuff into the state, with the further provisions that a violation of such regulations is a misdemeanor (or, perhaps, that it is a misdemeanor if the regulations so provide). The term "administrative crime" has been applied to define this type of substantive criminal law, and just as administrative law in general is a growing field of law, the administrative crime is becoming more and more important.

As to these administrative crimes, there are three principal questions: (1) May the legislature authorize an administrative agency to issue regulations, the violation of which is punishable as a crime by virtue of penalties set by statute? (2) May the legislature go further and authorize the agency to determine whether criminal penalties should be provided for violation of the rules or to determine what criminal penalties are appropriate? (3) May the legislature go still further and permit the agency to adjudicate individual cases and thus determine guilt?

(a) When Statute Fixes the Penalty. As to question (1), the leading American case is *U.S. v. Grimaud* (1911), holding that Congress may constitutionally delegate to an administrative agency the power to issue regulations the violation of which is punished by statute as a criminal offense. The defendant argued that the statute delegated the power to create new crimes, a power reserved to the legislature, but the Court responded that the violation of the rules had been made a crime by Congress rather than by the agency. Thus, if we consider a crime as being composed of two matters—the elements of the offense (act and mental state) and the penalty—it may be said that Congress may delegate to an administrative agency the task of filling in the elements if Congress itself fixes the penalty. The majority of state courts that considered the problem have followed the lead of the federal courts in this matter.

This is not to suggest, however, that any such delegation will pass muster, for it is commonly asserted that for the delegation to be valid the legislature must provide sufficient standards to guide the agency. But, while the Supreme Court back in 1935 invalidated congressional delegations for lack of sufficient standards, in more recent times the Court has been much less demanding and, indeed, has upheld standards "so vague as to be almost meaningless." The declaration by one federal court that it will now suffice "if Congress clearly delineates the general policy" seems, if anything, an over-statement of current limitations on the federal level.

It is difficult to generalize about the situation on the state level, as there still exists some variation from state to state on the matter of what will be tolerated by way of delegation of the crime-defining function. In some states the wholesale delegation to an administrative agency of power to adopt rules and regulations in a certain area, punishable as the legislature has specified, is deemed an unlawful delegation. But the prevailing view is that such delega-tion is permissible even with minimal guidelines from the legisla-tive branch; the rationale is that such delegation is necessary to assure the flexibility and expertise needed to deal with certain subject matter.

Much less likely to be successfully challenged is a delegation to an administrative agency of responsibility to ascertain certain par-ticulars with respect to a specific criminal statute. Illustrative is the situation in which the legislature declares it a crime to swim in an area not authorized for swimming and then delegates to the Game and Parks Commission the responsibility to designate the no swim-ming areas, and that where the legislature makes the possession of controlled substances a crime and then delegates to the State Board of Pharmacy the responsibility to keep current the list of drugs belonging in that classification. But even here there is not agree-ment as to just what constitutes adequate legislative guidelines. Those court decisions upholding delegation of either type typically emphasize that the problems being dealt with are such as to require more expert or more intense scrutiny than the legislature itself could reasonably be expected to provide.

Although a jurisdiction following the rule that all crimes must be statutory may consistently allow administrative crimes of the sort discussed, in one sense the problem discussed above is similar to that of whether common law crimes should be recognized. One argument against administrative crimes is similar to the argument used against common law crimes: fair warning to the public of what constitutes criminal conduct is a necessary requirement of fair play, and for the most part administrative regulations are not published. Perhaps the best way of dealing with this difficulty would be to give the defendant a mistake-of-law defense when he believed his conduct to be noncriminal and the administrative regulation defining the offense was not reasonably made available (see § 4.6(e)(1)).

While administrative crimes are generally valid where the statute fixes the penalty, the due process requirement that statutes must set forth a reasonably definite standard of conduct applies with equal force to administrative regulations having the effect of law. Likewise, administrative rules in the criminal law field are strictly construed in the same fashion as criminal statutes, and cannot be utilized to create crimes by implication.

The typical delegation statute provides, expressly or by implication, that violations of *valid* regulations are criminal. In such a case, an administrative crime may be invalid (although the statute prescribed sufficient standards, and the regulation definitely set forth the forbidden conduct) because the regulation exceeded the authority set out in the statute. However, a defendant in a criminal prosecution may be foreclosed from raising the invalidity of the regulation as a defense because he failed to take advantage of other established procedures for challenging the regulation.

(b) When Regulations Fix the Penalty. The second problem is the constitutionality of a statute that not only authorizes an administrative agency to issue regulations, but also delegates to the agency the question of whether criminal penalties should be provided for violation of the regulations or the question of what the criminal penalties should be for such a violation. For example, assume that a statute, setting forth proper standards to guide the agency, provides that the agency shall issue regulations and that violation of the regulations shall be a misdemeanor "if the regulation so provides." This type of statute has been held unconstitutional as an invalid delegation of the legislative power to define a crime. If, as in the *Grimaud* case, it is permissible for the agency to determine the elements of a crime, then why is it not permissible for the agency to decide which of its rules are to have criminal penalties attached to them? There is no obvious distinction between the two situations, but it may be that in the latter case the real problem is that the legislature has given no guidance on when a penal sanction should be used.

The kind of statute described above must be distinguished from a statute that makes the violation of every rule adopted under it criminal but delegates to the agency, within fixed statutory limits, the power to set the criminal penalties for each rule. For example, the statute may give the agency authority to issue regulations, all of which are criminal, and then provide that the agency may set penalties for the regulations "not to exceed $500, or six months imprisonment, or both." The courts are not in agreement as to the validity of such a statute, although the chances of such a delegation being upheld appear to be greater when it appears that the range of penalties allowed is reasonable, considering the nature of the regulations. Likewise, such a delegation probably is not valid if the statute fails to set any maximum penalty.

(c) Delegation of Power to Adjudicate. The problems described above must be distinguished from yet another issue regarding delegation, which—although basically a question of procedure and not substantive law—should be briefly noted here. May the legislature delegate to an administrative agency the power of adjudication (that is, the authority to determine guilt or innocence in individual cases) when the proceedings are criminal in nature? The answer clearly is no; as the Supreme Court declared, "[c]ivil procedure is incompatible with the accepted rules and constitutional guaranties governing the trial of criminal prosecutions."

What is not clear, however, is the precise significance of this rule, for the dividing line between criminal penalties and civil or remedial penalties is an uncertain one. Administrative agencies frequently do impose penalties, such as the revocation or suspension of licenses, the withdrawal of privileges (such as second-class mailing privileges), the denial of benefits, or the confiscation of property. Penalties have been held to be civil notwithstanding their severity, and there are a number of cases upholding the power of administrative agencies to levy fines.

(d) Administrative Orders. Although administrative bodies often issue rules and regulations setting forth general rules of conduct within the delegated spheres of action, sometimes they issue specific orders as to particular persons (e.g., an order to deport X, or an order for Y to report for induction into the armed services), the violation of which is criminal. Thus, there is a federal criminal statute providing that an alien who has been ordered deported by the administrative body, and who thereafter wilfully fails to depart or to apply for permission to depart, is guilty of a crime. Another statute provides that one ordered to report for induction by his local selective service board who wilfully fails to do so is guilty of a criminal offense. The administrative agency, by issuing an order to deport or to report for induction, in a sense sets the stage for a violation of the substantive criminal law by establishing one of the elements of the crime.

There is no doubt that such administrative action is valid. A problem may arise, however, as to whether the invalidity of the order is a defense to criminal prosecution. Surely this is a defense if the statute reads "ordered by a valid order of deportation (or induction)." Even without such wording the defense may be allowed as a matter of implied intent of the legislature. But where the legislature makes it clear that a wilful violation of an administrative order, whether valid or invalid, is criminal, the defense of invalidity is probably not available.

Chapter 3

CONSTITUTIONAL LIMITS ON POWER TO CREATE CRIMES

Table of Sections

> For additional analysis of the above topics and citations to authorities supporting their discussion in this Book, consult the author's 3-volume *Substantive Criminal Law* treatise, also available as Westlaw database SUBCRL. See the Table of Cross-References in this Book.

§ 3.1   Generally

While the states have broad authority to create crimes, the federal government has no jurisdiction to create crimes (except in federal territory) unless some provision of the United States Constitution expressly or impliedly gives Congress such power. Thus Congress cannot make it a crime for a manufacturer of or dealer in gambling devices to fail to file a record of sales and deliveries of such devices, if the devices he manufactures or sells do not move in interstate commerce. The federal government has succeeded, however, in accomplishing a good deal of regulation of various activities within the states (with criminal penalties for violations) because of the broad interpretation given to such constitutional provisions as the commerce clause, the taxation clause, and the war power clause.

Both the states and the federal government, therefore, may be said to possess considerable authority (the police power) to declare conduct criminal. But there are constitutional limits, other than those mentioned above, on the exercise of this power. As discussed earlier for purposes of facilitating comparison between those statutes that are vague (see § 2.3) and those that are merely ambiguous and thus subject to clarification by courts using accepted techniques of interpretation (see § 2.2), legislation creating crimes must be fairly definite. Attention has also been previously given (because of its obvious relation to problems concerning the repeal and amendment of legislation, see § 2.5) to the ex post facto clause, which requires that penal legislation operate only prospectively (see § 2.4). In addition, the equal protection clause requires that the police power, even in areas of legitimate governmental concern, not be exercised by resort to arbitrary statutory classifications (see § 3.2). And most important, the police power is also constitutionally limited in the sense that certain activity is beyond regulation by the criminal law. Such a conclusion may be reached via the substantive due process notion that conduct may not be punished unless it bears a substantial relationship to injury to the public (see § 3.3), or by a finding that the legislation in question intrudes upon freedom protected by the Bill of Rights (such as freedom of speech) (see § 3.5). (All of the above limitations flow from provisions of the United States Constitution applicable to both the federal government and the fifty states, although state courts often rely upon similar language in their respective state constitutions.) Finally, in the case of state legislation, the activity may be beyond the reach of the substantive criminal law because the federal government has preempted the area or because prohibition of the activity would impose an undue burden on interstate commerce (see § 3.6).

(a) **Significance of a Successful Constitutional Challenge.** In order to understand better the respective roles of legislatures and appellate courts in determining the actual boundaries of the substantive criminal law, it is necessary to appreciate the significance of a successful constitutional challenge on each of the bases mentioned above. In some instances, for example, it is only the means used by the legislature that gives rise to the constitutional violation; in others the evil lies in the ends sought.

The reversal of a conviction on ex post facto grounds can hardly be viewed as a significant limitation upon the legislature's exercise of its police power, for the objection goes to the retroactive application of the statute rather than its subject matter. Indeed, in most cases such a decision can hardly be viewed as reflecting an instance of legislative overreaching, for it is unlikely that the legislature considered the retroactivity problem. The reversal leaves the statute under which the prosecution was brought intact, available for use prospectively.

By contrast, a successful equal protection challenge to a criminal statute renders the challenged provisions void. Those whose conduct comes within the statute may not be made the object of penal sanctions so long as other conduct, which the legislature may not permissibly distinguish, is exempted. The vice is in the manner in which the legislature has drawn the line between criminal and noncriminal conduct, and depending upon the circumstances the problem may be either that the legislature has gone too far or that it has not gone far enough. A statute proscribing interracial marriages, for example, goes too far; it is void on equal protection grounds, and the legislature can hardly react to the nullification of this statute by a broader enactment prohibiting marriage without regard to race. On the other hand, the voiding of a criminal statute prohibiting interracial cohabitation by members of the opposite sex not married to each other, does not bar the subsequent enactment of a law proscribing all such cohabitation without regard to race. The outer limits of the legislature's power have not been affected, although the manner in which the legislature acted within those limits has been declared arbitrary.

That situation bears some resemblance to those cases in which a statute has been declared void for vagueness. Again, the statute in its present form has been rendered void, but the legislature is still free to enact new laws on the same subject. The court has passed only "upon the legitimacy or illegitimacy of means, invalidating a particular regulation with regard to those as to whom it is indefinite and *because* it is indefinite, and reserving judgment as to whether the end sought to be achieved is achievable through more definite regulation." No decision is reached on the constitutional boundaries of the police power; indeed, the uncertainty as to precisely how far the legislature intended to go removes this question from consideration. A void-for-vagueness finding means only that the extent to which the legislature meant to exercise its power is unclear and that the court, in view of this uncertainty, will not attempt to cure the ambiguity because the matter is one appropriately for the legislature. The message to the legislature is "try again."

In sharp contrast are those cases in which the contention accepted by the appellate court is that the legislature has stepped beyond the outer limits of its power to create crimes, as where it is held that the statute proscribes conduct bearing no substantial relationship to injury to the public. If the only end the statute in question sought to accomplish is one that the legislature may not constitutionally accomplish, then the statute has been completely voided. Often, however, the court will rule in such a way that the statute remains in effect but does not thereafter reach all of the conduct clearly within its terms. Sometimes this is done by merely nullifying a part of the statute, so that some of the conduct proscribed originally is read out of the statute. Or, the court may narrow the reach of the statute by in effect adding something to it, either a new element that must be proved by the prosecution or a new defense that may be raised by the defendant. In any event, the court has dealt with an instance of legislative overreaching, and the clear message to the legislature is "hands off." Certain activity has been insulated from legislative regulation, and the legislature will thereafter be denied access to the protected area absent a stronger showing of need.

It is apparent that it is of some consequence whether the court says "hands off" or "try again." The former is a direct rejection of the legislature's judgment that certain conduct should be within the ambit of the criminal law; the latter only calls for greater care in setting forth what is proscribed. Given the sensitive nature of the relationship between legislatures and courts in developing the substantive criminal law (particularly state legislatures vis-á-vis the United States Supreme Court), courts are often reluctant to erect absolute limits to the police power and thereby foreclose experimentation with some other statutory formulation. This is reflected in the growing hesitancy of courts to circumscribe the police power on substantive due process and equal protection grounds (see §§ 3.2,

3.3), and in their tendency to resort to a void-for-vagueness rationale instead—even when the statute in question is reasonably
specific.

(b) Procedures for Raising Constitutional Objections.
Although primarily a matter of procedure, brief note should be
taken here of the various ways in which the aforementioned constitutional objections might be raised by one who is being threatened
with prosecution, one who is being prosecuted, or one who has been
convicted. Even before one has engaged in the conduct proscribed
by the statute in question, it may be possible to go to court for an
injunction restraining prosecution under an unconstitutional statute or for a declaratory judgment that the statute is unconstitutional. If he has already been charged with violating the statute, he
may seek a writ of prohibition restraining the court from proceeding with the prosecution. Or, when prosecuted for violating the
terms of the statute, he may demur to or move to quash the
indictment or information on the ground of the unconstitutionality
of the statute on which the charge is based. After a verdict of
guilty, he may raise the issue by a motion in arrest of judgment.

A question of some difficulty is whether the defendant, not
having raised the question of unconstitutionality of the statute at
the trial by one of the above devices, may raise the issue for the
first time on appellate review. The courts are not in agreement as
to the answer. A person who has been convicted and is serving his
sentence under an unconstitutional statute may, by the weight of
authority, obtain his release by habeas corpus, but there are some
decisions to the contrary.

It should also be noted here that a person who wishes to
challenge the constitutionality of a state criminal statute may be
able to seek relief in the federal courts. One who is threatened with
state prosecution under a statute alleged to be unconstitutional
might seek federal declaratory and injunctive relief; federal absten-
tion is the general rule here. A person in state custody awaiting
trial under a law claimed to violate the Constitution might also
seek relief via federal habeas corpus. Federal habeas corpus, however, is more likely to be a source of relief following conviction,
although there are procedural hurdles to be surmounted here as
well.

§ 3.2 Equal Protection

The legislatures, both federal and state, in statutes dealing
with civil or criminal liability often make classifications with respect to the persons covered by the statutes or the subject matter
encompassed thereby. In the criminal field legislation has not
infrequently singled out special groups or special types of subject

matter for special treatment. Such statutes are sometimes challenged (rarely successfully) on the ground that they violate the equal protection clause in the United States Constitution or a comparable provision in a state constitution.

(a) Kinds of Classifications. This singling out in penal statutes is accomplished in one of three ways: (1) a statute may define as criminal certain conduct when it is engaged in by certain persons or under certain limited circumstances; (2) a statute may define certain conduct as criminal and then go on to exempt from the statute certain persons or special situations; or (3) a statute (or a number of related statutes) may make distinctions, for purposes of setting the punishment that may be imposed, depending upon the persons engaging in or the circumstances surrounding certain conduct.

Illustrative of the first category are the "joyriding" statutes to be found in a number of states. The ordinary larceny statute requires an intent to deprive the owner permanently of the property, so that taking for temporary use is not larceny, yet the "joyriding" statute covers taking for temporary use when the property taken is an automobile. Similarly, while the typical embezzlement statute requires a fraudulent conversion of another's property, some states have singled out public officials for special treatment: such an official may be punished as severely as the embezzler if he converts (not "fraudulently" converts) public funds under his control. The legislature in each case has concluded that a special evil exists requiring special treatment: a determination that a more serious problem is involved in the unauthorized use of automobiles than in similar use of other types of property; or a determination that a more serious danger exists with respect to treasurers of public funds, who are not as closely watched as, for instance, corporate treasurers.

Illustrative of the second category are the common Sunday closing laws. These statutes require commercial establishments to remain closed on Sunday, but typically go on to exempt certain kinds of businesses, stores of a certain size, or sales of specifically enumerated items. For example, the legislature may exempt the sale of food and medicine on the ground that public health requires that these commodities be available every day of the week. The legislature may exempt businesses employing only one or two employees on the ground that these establishments do not pose the same risk to tranquility as larger retail operations, such as department stores or discount centers. Or, the legislature may permit the sale of recreational items only by stores in designated recreation areas because it is thought that the public need is adequately served thereby.

The third category, which involves distinctions for purposes of punishment rather than distinctions between what is criminal and what is not, may be illustrated by a burglary statute divided into degrees: first-degree burglary is that burglary which occurs during the nighttime; and second-degree burglary, carrying a lesser penalty, is that which occurs in the daytime. Or the distinction may be found in two related statutes dealing with similar conduct but providing different penalties. For example, the taking of property from another with fraudulent intent may be punished as larceny, but the fraudulent appropriation of property held as a bailee may be made criminal under another statute carrying different penalties. Once again, it would appear that the legislature has determined that there is something more reprehensible in burglary by night than by day, and that the technical concept of "trespass" is important for purposes of determining the seriousness of a taking of someone else's property.

Criminal statutes containing such classifications (particularly those in the first category) are sometimes challenged on the ground that they are over-inclusive, that is, that they cover more conduct than the legislature under its police power may reach. The challenge may be that there is a substantive due process violation because the statute prohibits conduct bearing no substantial relationship to injury to the public (see § 3.3), or that the statute is too broad because it infringes upon rights specifically enumerated in the constitution (see § 3.5). Although a claim of over-inclusiveness is sometimes cast in equal protection terms, the typical equal protection case is one in which it is alleged that the defect in the statute is its under-inclusiveness. That is, it is acknowledged that the legislature has the power to reach the conduct covered by the statute, but it is claimed that the legislature has acted in an arbitrary fashion by not including or by specifically excluding other conduct which is not distinguishable. In brief, the argument is that since the classification does not include all who are similarly situated with respect to the purpose of the law, there is a violation of the equal protection requirement of reasonable classification.

(b) Equal Protection and the Supreme Court. The United States Constitution provides that no state may deny to any person within its jurisdiction the equal protection of the laws. Although there is no comparable provision applicable to the federal government, the Supreme Court has taken the view that the federal government is under some equal protection kind of restraint by virtue of the due process clause. These constitutional provisions bar arbitrary enforcement of laws that are fair on their face, and also require that Congress and the state legislatures refrain from arbitrary classifications in legislation. (When a legislative classification or distinction "neither burdens a fundamental right nor targets a suspect class," it is not arbitrary if "it bears a rational relation to some legitimate end.") Only the latter limitation is considered here.

Generally, it may be said that the United States Supreme Court has been quite permissive in allowing state legislatures to draw whatever classifications they choose in enacting criminal laws. This is most clearly reflected in a series of cases involving criminal statutes in the realm of economic and business regulation, where the Court has followed these propositions in testing the statutes challenged: (1) States have a wide scope of discretion in making statutory classifications, and the classifications violated the equal protection clause only when they are without any reasonable basis. (2) A classification with some reasonable basis does not violate the equal protection clause merely because it is not made with mathematical nicety or because in practice it results in some inequality. (3) When a classification is called into question, if any state of facts reasonably can be conceived that would sustain it, the existence of such facts at the time the law was enacted must be assumed. (4) One who questions a statutory classification carries the burden of showing that it does not rest upon any reasonable basis. (5) Classifications of an unusual character deserve closer scrutiny.

It is apparent from these propositions why the Court has said that the claim that state legislation violates the equal protection clause is "the usual last resort of constitutional arguments," for the person challenging the statute must ordinarily prove an elusive negative: that no state of facts can be conceived by which the classification can be said to have some reasonable basis. Such facts are readily assumed by the Court even in the absence of any evidence bearing on the reasons behind the legislature's classification. Thus a regulation prohibiting trucks from carrying advertisements, enacted to prevent distractions to drivers and pedestrians, does not violate the equal protection clause because it excepts advertisements of products sold by the owner of the truck; in response to the argument that the distraction would be the same no matter what the subject of the advertisement, the Court said that local authorities might have concluded that those who advertised their own wares do not present the same traffic problem. Similarly, a statute making it unlawful to solicit the sale of eye glasses but exempting those who sell ready-to-wear glasses selected by the customer was upheld; the Court said it would assume that the ready-to-wear business might present distinct problems of regulation.

It is also important to note that the Supreme Court has taken account of the practical problems of legislating and of enforcing legislation when judging the classifications found in criminal statutes. As a result, even if it may appear that there is inequality resulting from the classification adopted by the legislature, the classification may be upheld because of these practical considerations. For example, a statute challenged as being over-inclusive for exempting some but not all conduct of the same type may be upheld because a broader exemption might create serious enforcement difficulties. Thus a Sunday closing law that permits amusement park vendors to sell selected items but which does not allow department stores to sell the same items is not objectionable, given the fact that it would be most difficult—from an enforcement standpoint—to ensure that the latter establishments so restrict their operations. A statute challenged as being under-inclusive may be sustained on the ground that legislatures must be permitted to take a "piecemeal" approach and to deal with a general problem a step at a time. "The legislature may select one phase of one field and apply a remedy there, neglecting the others." It has been suggested, however, that such selectivity in dealing with only part of a general problem should not be upheld when it appears that the exclusion of other conduct from the statute was motivated by political considerations.

Notwithstanding this considerable deference to the line-drawing by state legislatures between criminal and noncriminal or between various degrees of crime, some classifications have received close scrutiny by the United States Supreme Court. It would appear that when the consequences of the classification are more serious, then something more by way of justification is required. And thus while differing degrees of punishment may be permitted for various forms of theft based upon technical common-law distinctions, the legislature may not go so far as to provide for sterilization of those convicted of three felonious larcenies but not of those convicted of three felonious embezzlements. Classifications by name, rather than by generic category, are permissible, but they receive closer attention because they do not afford flexibility in light of changed circumstances. For this reason, the Supreme Court declared unconstitutional a statute making it an offense to sell money orders without a license but excepting the sale of American Express money orders; although the statute was intended to afford protection to the public, and although American Express might be unique because it is a responsible institution operating on a world-wide basis, the classification did not take account of the possibility that at a later date American Express would not have these characteristics or that some competing company would have them.

Very close scrutiny is given to any classifications based upon race. Given the historical fact that the central purpose of the Fourteenth Amendment was to eliminate racial discrimination emanating from official sources in the states, racial classifications are "constitutionally suspect" and subject to the "most rigid scrutiny," particularly when a criminal statute is involved. As a consequence, the Supreme Court has taken a markedly different approach in cases involving criminal statutes with racial classifications. Instead of the usual position that the statute will be found to violate the equal protection clause only if the person challenging it meets his burden of establishing that no state of facts can be conceived by which the classification can be said to have some reasonable basis, the Court instead places the burden of justifying the classification upon the state. That is, the statute is presumed to be unconstitutional rather than to be constitutional, and the state can overcome this presumption only by clearly establishing some overriding statutory purpose by which the classification is *necessary*—not merely rationally related—to the accomplishment of a permissible state policy.

In *McLaughlin v. Fla.* (1964) the challenged statute provided that: "Any negro man and white woman, or any white man and negro woman, who are not married to each other, who shall habitually live in and occupy in the nighttime the same room shall each be punished by imprisonment not exceeding twelve months, or by fine not exceeding five hundred dollars." Other statutes of general application proscribed adultery and lewd cohabitation, but they required proof of intercourse along with the other elements of the crime. The Supreme Court first rejected the notion in an earlier case that a criminal statute with racial classifications could be justified merely on the ground that it provided for punishment of both the black and white participants in the forbidden conduct. A classification is not necessarily reasonable, the Court emphasized, simply because the law is applied equally to all those within the defined class. The state characterized the challenged statute as intended to prevent breaches of the basic concepts of sexual decency, but this characterization could not save the statute, as the state could not show that illicit intercourse was more likely in cases of interracial cohabitation. Similarly, in *Loving v. Va.* (1967) the Supreme Court struck down a comprehensive statutory scheme aimed at prohibiting and punishing interracial marriages. Because the statutes prohibited interracial marriages only when they involved white persons, it was apparent that they were intended to maintain white supremacy, which is not a permissible state policy.

Strict judicial scrutiny is also given to criminal statutes that draw classifications in terms of the ability to exercise some fundamental constitutional right, such as the freedom of speech. Illustrative is *Carey v. Brown* (1980), striking down a statute prohibiting residential picketing but exempting picketing of a place of employment involved in a labor dispute and declaring: "When government regulation discriminates among speech-related activities in a public forum, the Equal Protection Clause mandates that the legislation be finely tailored to serve substantial stated interests, and the justifications offered for any distinctions it draws must be carefully scrutinized." The Court in *Carey* stressed that it had not been established that there was a valid reason to permit labor picketing but not public protests on other issues.

Gender-based classifications are not "inherently suspect" and thereby subject to "strict scrutiny" in the way that racial classifications are, but at the same time they are not treated with the deference long accorded economic regulation. Such classifications, then, are tested under a third, intermediate approach. Members of the Supreme Court have had difficulty agreeing upon how to state or apply this intermediate test, but it is sometimes said that such a classification will be upheld if it bears a "fair and substantial relationship" to legitimate state ends. Utilizing that approach, the Court in *Michael M. v. Superior Court* (1981) upheld a statutory rape provision that defined the offense as unlawful sexual intercourse with a female under 18. In concluding the test had been met, the Court reasoned (i) that one interest underlying the statute is prevention of illegitimate teenage pregnancies, justifying the legislative conclusion to punish the participant who suffers fewer of the harmful consequences of such a pregnancy, and (ii) that a gender neutral statute would frustrate the state's interest in enforcement because a female would be less likely to report a violation if she was also subject to prosecution.

(c) Equal Protection in the State Courts. State courts, of course, are more frequently called upon to adjudicate claims that some criminal statute contains an arbitrary classification and thus violates the equal protection clause of the Fourteenth Amendment. In addition, it may be claimed that the statute conflicts with an equal protection or similar guarantee in the state constitution, a matter on which the state courts have the last word. And while the cases before the United States Supreme Court have been concerned for the most part with the economic regulations, the state cases also deal with statutes more in the mainstream of the criminal law (e.g., those defining various forms of theft).

Generally, it may be said that state courts have also exercised considerable restraint; they tend to follow the philosophy expressed in the opinions of the United States Supreme Court that the legislature's classification should be sustained if any set of facts can be conceived which would give the classification a reasonable basis. Thus possession of cannabis may be punished in the same fashion as possession of addicting drugs, notwithstanding considerable evidence that it is not addicting, for the legislature may have concluded that it also presents a danger to public safety and welfare. Likewise, the legislature may punish assault with intent to rape as severely as rape, for it may have concluded that one who attempts rape is as much a menace to society as one who succeeds. The legislature may make any theft of livestock a felony, though other theft is graded by the value of the property taken, in order to further "the legitimate purpose of deterring a type of theft easy to commit and difficult to detect." Or, the legislature may properly decide to punish theft by "servants, agents or employees" more severely than theft by others, or assault of family members more severely than other assaults. The legislature may proscribe hazing by colleges and universities but not secondary schools, sexual intercourse with teenagers by older persons but not by teenagers' contemporaries, and driving with a blood alcohol content of .02 when the driver is under 21 but not otherwise.

At least in some states, however, one challenging a statute on equal protection grounds may not have quite as heavy a burden of proving the absence of a rational basis for the classification as he would have before the United States Supreme Court. In part this may be attributable to the fact that the state court is closer to the conditions which prevail in that state, so that it is easier to convince the court that no circumstances justifying the statutory distinction are present. Or, as is also sometimes true when the claim is that the statute violates substantive due process (see § 3.3), it may be because some state courts are less willing to allow the state legislature to regulate business activity. Also, some state courts are more willing to use equal protection analysis to strike down statutes that carry a considerable risk of arbitrary enforcement. A few states have relied upon the equal protection clause in the federal or state constitution in striking down state laws dealing with sodomy or other deviant sexual activity or solicitation thereof where these laws draw distinctions between married and unmarried persons or between different-sex and same-sex activity.

§ 3.3   Substantive Due Process

The United States Constitution forbids both the federal government and the states to deprive any person of life, liberty, or property without due process of law. Most state constitutions also contain a due process clause in identical or similar form. Although the term "due process" might appear to refer only to matters of procedure—requiring that certain procedures be followed and prohibiting others—it is also a substantive limitation on the powers of government. This is as true in the realm of criminal law as elsewhere; the constitutional requirement of due process looms large in criminal procedure, and is also important as a limitation on the manner and extent to which conduct may be defined as criminal in the substantive criminal law. We have already seen, for example, that due process requires that the Congress and the state legislatures be reasonably definite in declaring what conduct is criminal (see § 2.3).

The concern here is with substantive due process as a constitutional limitation on the boundaries of the police power. That is, the question is: when will a criminal statute (one, it may be presumed, which is not vague, retroactive, or arbitrary in its classification of conduct) be declared unconstitutional because of the nature of the conduct it attempts to prohibit? The most obvious answer, perhaps, is that such a constitutional defect will be found to be present when the conduct in question involves the exercise of freedoms and rights protected by the Bill of Rights. For example, freedom of expression may not be abridged by making it an offense to distribute handbills that do not contain the names of the printer and distributor. Situations of this kind are discussed later (see § 3.5).

By contrast, the discussion that follows concerns those instances in which criminal statutes are invalidated without a finding that they constitute a threat to some freedom or right guaranteed by the Bill of Rights. Sometimes this is done, more likely by a state court, on the basis that the statute prohibits conduct that bears no substantial relationship to injury to the public. Or, although this same factor is likely to be present, a court sometimes will strike down a statute on the more specific ground that it does not contain one of the traditional elements of a criminal offense. The objection may be that the statute contains no *mens rea* requirement, that is, that it punishes conduct innocently engaged in without any sort of bad state of mind, or it may be that the statute punishes mere status or condition instead of requiring some specific act or omission to act.

(a) Legislation Bearing No Substantial Relationship to Injury to the Public. At an earlier time, the United States Supreme Court not infrequently held legislation invalid because the Court concluded that the legislation did not have a substantial relationship to some matter of legitimate public concern. The Court's function in this regard, as it was conceived during that period, is expressed in the following quotation from *Mugler v. Kan.* (1887): "There are, of necessity, limits beyond which legislation cannot rightfully go. * * * [T]he courts must * * * upon their own responsibility, determine whether in any particular case, these limits have been passed. * * * If, therefore, a statute purporting to have been enacted to protect the public health, the public morals, or the public safety, has no real or substantial relation to those objects, * * * it is the duty of the courts to so adjudge, and thereby give effect to the Constitution." The Court carried out its duty, as thus conceived, by striking down well over a hundred statutes involving economic regulation during the first third of the twentieth century. Many of these statutes carried criminal sanctions for their violation.

The decline in the Court-asserted control over legislative policy began in 1934 with *Nebbia v. N.Y.* (1934), upholding the conviction of a grocer under a statute prohibiting the sale of milk under established prices. The change in attitude is reflected in the Court's statement in *Nebbia* "that the legislature is primarily the judge of the necessity of such an enactment, that every possible presumption is in favor of its validity, and that though the court may hold views inconsistent with the wisdom of the law, it may not be annulled unless palpably in excess of legislative power." Since 1941, the Court has not once struck down economic legislation as violative of substantive due process; even when there has been no clear evidence of the legislature's purpose, the Court has been willing to reason that the legislature might have reached certain conclusions that would have justified enactment of the challenged criminal statute. This same restraint has usually been reflected in cases involving criminal statutes dealing with other than economic regulation.

This is not to say, of course, that the Supreme Court has withdrawn completely from its role of passing on the constitutionality of criminal statutes. Rather, the point is that the Court is now most reluctant to strike down statutes on a ground which, in effect, necessitates passing judgment on "the wisdom, need and propriety of laws that touch economic problems, business affairs or social conditions." (While the Court upheld a sodomy statute in *Bowers v. Hardwick* (1986) as a legitimate legislative judgment that "a majority of the electorate" deems the prosecuted conduct to be "immoral and unacceptable," the dissent's contention that "the fact that the governing majority in a State has traditionally viewed a particular practice as immoral is not a sufficient reason for upholding a law prohibiting the practice" was later embraced by a majority of the Court in *Lawrence v. Texas* (2003) when overruling the prior decision. But if the statute does not infringe upon a fundamental right, it is still constitutionally permissible for it to be grounded merely in "ethical and moral concerns," *Gonzales v. Carhart* (2007).) Thus, even when a criminal statute is challenged on this basis, the Court is more likely to decide the case on void-for-vagueness or equal protection grounds, which usually affords the legislature some opportunity to proscribe the conduct once again on a somewhat different basis. Or, the Court may prefer to find that the challenged statute infringes upon some guarantee in the Bill of Rights (see § 3.5), even when this requires recognition of "penumbral rights" not specifically enumerated in the first ten amendments. These decisions undoubtedly reflect the attitude that the Court is on more solid ground in finding that a criminal statute conflicts with the Bill of Rights than in finding that it bears no substantial relation to the public welfare. And here as well, the Court's decision is less likely to be as restrictive in terms of the continuing power of the legislature to declare certain conduct criminal. A "pure" substantive due process decision, finding that a particular criminal prohibition is not related to an injury to the public, insulates the prohibited conduct from future legislative restriction unless and until new events occur or new facts are found showing that such a prohibition does serve the public welfare. By contrast, a finding that a statute violates due process on the more specific ground that it intrudes upon the protections of the Bill of Rights, often leaves the legislature with some freedom to again prohibit the conduct, either by reaching new incidents of it or the same incidents plus others.

(b) No Substantial Relation to Injury to the Public: The State Courts. While the United States Supreme Court has all but abandoned the practice of invalidating criminal statutes on the basis that they bear no substantial relation to injury to the public, the same cannot be said for the state courts. This substantive due process basis for invalidating legislation originated in the state courts, and it is perhaps not surprising that it has continued to be used in many states after falling into disuse on the national level. Sometimes the state court decisions purport to be based upon the due process clause of the Fourteenth Amendment, although it is more common for the courts to strike down statutes on the additional or alternate ground that the legislation offends the due process provisions in the state constitution. When the latter rather than the former approach is utilized, the state courts have the last word.

Although the United States Supreme Court has or would find a certain state criminal statute consistent with the Fourteenth Amendment, it does not follow that the highest court of that state will necessarily reach a similar conclusion as to the statute vis-a-vis the state constitution. As one court has said: "What is permissible under the Federal Constitution in matters of State economic regulation is not necessarily permissible under state law. The Constitution of a State may guard more jealously against the exercise of the State's police power." This becomes evident when one compares the state decisions with those of the United States Supreme Court. For example, the Supreme Court has upheld a state criminal statute making debt-adjusting by nonlawyers a crime, but at least one state court has found a comparable statute unconstitutional. Similarly, while the Supreme Court has held that a state may bar the sale of wholesome foods (e.g., imitation skimmed milk) in order to prevent consumer confusion, some state courts have reached the contrary conclusion.

It is difficult to generalize concerning the concept of substantive due process in the state courts, for the various state decisions cannot be harmonized. In some jurisdictions, the courts in recent years have been as reluctant as the Supreme Court to interfere with legislative policies; in others this is not so, as reflected by the fact that the courts there rely upon early Supreme Court decisions which have since been overruled or rejected. To the extent that it may be said that state courts are more likely to find substantive due process defects in challenged criminal statutes, the following factors are important:

(1) In some jurisdictions, a more limited view is taken of the purposes for which the police power may be exercised. Courts in these states are likely to acknowledge that the legislature may act for the protection of public morals, health, and safety, but may balk at the notion that laws may be enacted for the more general purpose of advancing public welfare. Thus, a criminal statute may be invalidated on the ground that it was passed solely for esthetic reasons, although the trend today is away from this view. Or, the state court may adopt the libertarian philosophy of John Stuart Mill that an individual's own welfare, physical or moral, is not sufficient ground in itself to justify the state's interference with the individual's conduct. On this basis, such crimes as becoming intoxicated in private, possession of intoxicants for one's own use, or operating a motorcycle without a safety helmet have sometimes been held to be beyond the state's police power.

(2) State courts, because they are closer to local conditions, are more likely to pass judgment on the legislative conclusion that an evil exists which calls for criminal legislation. Substantive due process cases in the United States Supreme Court for the most part are not based upon a close evaluation of the conditions within the state that might have given rise to the challenged legislation; in the absence of such information the Court is willing to speculate that the legislature might have found facts showing a need for the statute in question. By contrast, the state cases are often based upon a rather extensive consideration of the conditions prevailing in the state, determined by the court through a process of judicial notice or otherwise. One consequence of this, of course, is that state courts often uphold statutes or ordinances by setting forth in some detail the actual conditions that gave rise to and thus justify their enactment. By the same token, a state court will sometimes strike down a statute on the basis of a finding that the evil as perceived by the legislature does not exist. For example, one court invalidated a statute making it an offense to sell imitation cream, apparently enacted because of a concern that consumers would confuse it with

real cream, because it concluded that the average consumer of that state would not be confused.

(3) State courts, because they are closer to local conditions, are more likely to pass judgment on whether the legislature's response is an effective means of dealing with an acknowledged evil. Sometimes a state court will find that a statute violates due process on the ground that those persons at whom the statute is directed will escape detection while others, engaged in innocent pursuits, are likely to be deterred. For example, one court was confronted with a statute that made it a crime to possess cattle hide from which the ears had been removed or the brand obliterated. The court acknowledged that larceny of cattle was a serious problem in the state, and noted that cattle could be identified only by their brands or earmarks. However, the court struck down the statute because, while it would cover persons engaged in the manufacture of leather goods, it would not likely result in the conviction of persons stealing cattle. A cattle thief, the court concluded, would react to the statute by simply disposing of the hide, which is of relatively minor value as compared to the carcass. This approach is in sharp contrast to that of the United States Supreme Court, which refuses to look into "the adequacy or practicability of the law" challenged.

(4) State courts are more willing to pass upon the wisdom of the legislature's response to an acknowledged evil by taking account of other, less restrictive means by which the public interest might be protected. While the United States Supreme Court has repeatedly said that it will not inquire into the wisdom of the legislature's choice of means for dealing with an evil, state courts have not exercised the same restraint. Not infrequently, a state law is invalidated because the court believes that the legislature could have found an equally effective but less severe method of serving the public interest. For example, it has been held that a statute making it an offense to sell certain wholesome products, such as imitation ice cream, violates due process because the purpose of the law—prevention of consumer confusion and fraud—could be just as well accomplished by legislation requiring clear labeling. Similarly, another court has held invalid a law proscribing the use of large signs advertising the price of gasoline at service stations; the statute's purpose of preventing misleading advertising, said the court, could be just as well accomplished by regulating the contents rather than the size of such signs.

(5) State courts, because they are closer to local conditions, are more likely to conclude that the true purpose of a statute is to serve a special interest group rather than the public. The United States Supreme Court has refused to speculate concerning the motives of the legislature when it appears that there is some legitimate purpose upon which the statute in question could be based. By

comparison, state courts sometimes take the view that "if the dominant purpose of the legislation be to serve private interests under the cloak of the general public good, the resulting legislation is a perversion and abuse of power and therefore unlawful." This is not to say, of course, that the mere fact a statute was sponsored and drafted by a private interest group compels the conclusion that it is unconstitutional. But on the other hand, even in the absence of such evidence—indeed, even in the absence of any discussion of legislative motives—it would appear that state courts sometimes strike down criminal statutes because, by their terms, they appear to be intended to aid some special interest group. Some commentators have concluded that, given the pressures which are brought to bear on state legislatures, this kind of judicial interference with legislative policies is most appropriate.

(6) Some state courts still subscribe to the view that the police power may not be utilized to absolutely prohibit a "legitimate" business. At one time this was the philosophy of the United States Supreme Court, which held that the due process clause forbids a state to prohibit a business that is "useful" and not "inherently immoral or dangerous to public welfare." The Supreme Court has long since abandoned that rule, but it is still followed in some of the state due process cases. It has been held, for example, that a statute making it criminal to engage in the business of debt adjusting is unconstitutional; the possibility of fraud by those so engaged, the court held, could not serve as a justification for prohibiting this business.

(c) State Cases: Statutes Covering Harmless Conduct. While much of the preceding discussion has most directly concerned state criminal statutes in the realm of economic regulation, it should not be concluded that the state due process cases are limited to such statutes. Statutes directed at the more traditional problems of the criminal law have also been challenged in many cases. If these decisions are also taken account of, it may be said that the most troublesome recurring problem in the state due process cases is: When may the legislature, in the interest of crime prevention or effective law enforcement, constitutionally enact legislation that proscribes more conduct than that which actually endangers the public? Although this issue is sometimes confused with that of when the legislature may enact strict liability offenses (see § 3.3(d)), we are not here concerned with statutes that punish acts without regard to whether the actor intended or knew he was doing them (e.g., a statute making it an offense to sell liquor to minors without regard to whether the seller knew the buyer was a minor). Rather, the question here is when the legislature may proscribe the knowing or intentional doing of certain acts, even though all who engage in such acts are not bent upon some evil or harmful course.

For example, the legislature might be concerned about street crimes committed by juveniles. Existing laws, of course, adequately cover the commission of these crimes, but they may be thought inadequate; additional legislation may be desired either as a means of preventing these crimes from happening or as a means for prosecuting those who commit but are not apprehended for these crimes. The legislative body may respond by making it an offense for *any* juvenile to be on the street after a certain time of night, or by making it an offense for *any* juvenile to carry a knife or other sharp instrument. Or, the legislature, concerned about the narcotics traffic and the difficulties in apprehending persons while actually in the possession of narcotics, may make it an offense for *any* person to possess certain instruments for taking narcotics (hypodermic needles and syringes) without a doctor's authorization, or to be in a place where it is known narcotics activity is occurring. Similarly, a legislative body, because of a growing fraudulent practice of returning the covers of unsold magazines for credit and then selling the coverless magazines, may make it a crime for *any* person to sell a magazine without a cover. Or, a legislature concerned with credit card fraud might make it criminal to possess a credit card embossing machine. Each of these statutes is admittedly an effective way of reaching those who have engaged or intend to engage in some other conduct that the legislature may unquestionably prohibit, but they obviously also cover persons engaged in innocent pursuits.

It cannot be said that a criminal statute must always be so narrowly drafted that it only covers those persons pursuing the evil objective which is the source of legislative concern. As one court has put it, "it is within the competency of the lawgiver, in the common interest, to declare an act criminal irrespective of the * * * motive of the doer of the act. The Legislature may make the doing of the prohibited act criminal or penal, regardless of a corrupt or criminal purpose * * *. The criminal mind is not essential where the Legislature has so willed." But the legislative power in this regard is not without limits, as evidenced by the fact that each of the statutes referred to above was declared unconstitutional. Generally, it may be said that the vice of these statutes is that they are too sweeping in encompassing activity which is wholly innocent.

Sometimes these statutes, although not drafted in terms of presumptions (as contrasted to a statute which, for example, says that a person in possession of stolen property will be presumed to know that it was stolen), are dealt with in a fashion quite similar to that found when statutory presumptions are challenged (see § 3.4). That is, the question is said to be whether there is a rational connection between the fact proved and fact presumed thereby. Thus the statute on possession of hypodermic syringes and needles was invalidated because it, in effect, created "a conclusive presumption that the possession is for an illegal purpose—an unrebuttable presumption which factually runs counter to human experience." In other cases, essentially the same conclusion has been reached by noting that a fairly high percentage of those engaging in the proscribed conduct would be unlikely to have any evil purpose in mind. The possession cases serve as the best illustration of this point; it is one thing to bar possession of brass knuckles, which are not likely to be found on innocent persons, and quite another to prohibit any kind of knife or sharp instrument. In addition to this matter of probabilities, however, it is sometimes also important to weigh the social utility of the innocent conduct that comes within the statutory prohibition. Thus, even if a statute prohibiting all loitering on the streets is unconstitutional, it does not follow that the same is true of a statute making it an offense to loiter in a school building, for there is no substantial reason for protecting the right of the general public to do so.

(d) Mental State and Act as Constitutional Requirements. Criminal statutes declaring conduct criminal without regard to the evil motives of the actor, discussed above, must be distinguished from strict liability statutes, which make certain acts or omissions criminal without regard to whether the actor intended for the proscribed consequences to occur or knew that they would occur. Illustrative of the latter kind of offense are: (1) a statute that makes it a crime to receive stolen property without regard to whether the receiver knew that the property was stolen; (2) a statute that makes it a crime to convert another person's property to your own use without regard to whether you know that the property in question belonged to another; and (3) a statute that makes it a crime to manufacture tablets or notebooks on which policy-game records are kept without regard to whether the manufacturer intended or knew that the items would be so used. Each of the above statutes was declared unconstitutional as a violation of due process, although none of the three decisions provides much guidance on the question of when, if ever, the imposition of strict liability is constitutionally permissible. It is said, for example, that there exists a basic policy in this country "that a person should not be punished for a crime unless they knew they were committing a crime or intended to commit a crime," but this statement can hardly be accepted in the face of the great many court decisions upholding strict liability statutes (see § 4.5). Sometimes more traditional substantive due process language is used; it may be concluded, for example, that because the statute also covers acts done innocently it does not reasonably relate to the public welfare. This at least suggests that it may be appropriate to consider, as in the evil motive cases, the degree to which persons who are *actually* innocent are likely to come within the reach of the statute. It would also permit the conclusion that there may be instances in which the public welfare is served by imposition of strict liability, as where there is reason to hold those engaged in certain business or other activity to the highest of standards.

The United States Supreme Court has on one occasion held a strict liability law in violation of due process by a somewhat different analysis. In *Lambert v. Cal.* (1957), the challenged provision was a Los Angeles ordinance that made punishable the failure of any convicted felon to register with the police within five days after entering the city. Defendant was convicted of violating this ordinance; there was proof of her failure to register, but her offer to prove that she was unaware of her duty to register was rejected. The Court reversed, emphasizing the unfairness of the ordinance to one in the defendant's position. Because "circumstances which might move one to inquire as to the necessity of registration are completely lacking," the result is an "absence of an opportunity either to avoid the consequences of the law or to defend any prosecution brought under it." Three Justices dissented on the ground that the majority had improperly drawn a constitutional line between acts and omissions, with the result that none of the great many strict-liability-failure-to-act statutes could withstand challenge. Although the intended reach of the *Lambert* decision is far from clear, the dissenters' construction is not necessarily correct. While the reasoning of *Lambert* is most likely to be applicable to omission statutes, there may well be many instances in which it is not unfair to put the burden of inquiry on the defendant. Likewise, an "absence of an opportunity * * * to avoid the consequences of the law" might well be found to exist as to some statutes imposing strict liability for certain acts.

While strict liability offenses are not uncommon, legislatures have not often enacted statutes providing for punishment without proof of a voluntary act or omission by the defendant. When they have done so, these statutes have generally been held to be beyond the police power of the state. Thus, the legislature may not constitutionally make it a crime to have a reputation as a habitual criminal, as one who carries concealed weapons, or as one who associates with such persons. And, although possession of something may qualify as an act, the mere unwitting possession of an item cannot be declared criminal. One common expression is that "an unexecuted intent to violate the law amounts to no more than a thought, and is not punishable as a crime," although this has usually been interpreted as not barring a state from declaring criminal the existence of such unexecuted intent when accompanied by some act. The United States Supreme Court has cast serious doubt upon whether a state may ever criminally punish mere "status" without proof of some irregular behavior in the jurisdiction.

A more detailed consideration of the requirements of a mental state and voluntary act, including the question of what limitations thereon might be appropriate, is to be found in chapters 4 and 5.

(e) Taking Clause Objections Distinguished. Sometimes constitutional objections to criminal statutes have instead been grounded in that part of the Fifth Amendment which declares: "nor shall private property be taken for public use, without just compensation." The claim typically is that by making certain conduct criminal which was theretofore innocent, the government has rendered certain property in the defendant's possession virtually useless, thus amounting to an unconstitutional taking of that property.

The response of the Supreme Court has been that "a prohibition simply upon the use of property for purposes that are declared, by valid legislation, to be injurious to the health, morals, or safety of the community, cannot in any sense, be deemed a taking or an appropriation of property for the public benefit." Thus a law prohibiting the manufacture or sale of intoxicating liquors is not an unconstitutional taking of a manufacturer's buildings and machinery or of a stock of liquor manufactured or acquired before the law went into effect. State courts have responded similarly with respect to challenges grounded in taking clause provisions in the state constitution.

A modern example is provided by *Andrus v. Allard* (1979), concerning the Eagle Protection Act, which makes it unlawful to "take, possess, sell, purchase, barter, offer to sell, purchase or barter, transport, export or import" bald or golden eagles or any part thereof. Possession or transport but not sale of eagles or parts acquired prior to the effective date of the Act were exempted, and the defendants were convicted of selling previously acquired Indian artifacts partly composed of feathers of such birds. In rejecting their claim that this amounted to an unconstitutional taking, the Court reasoned that "where an owner possesses a full 'bundle' of property rights, the destruction of one 'strand' of the bundle is not a taking, because the aggregate must be viewed in its entirety. * * * In this case, it is crucial that appellees retain the rights to possess and transport their property, and to donate or devise the protected birds."

While *Andrus* did not involve a criminal prosecution, its holding has been deemed equally applicable in such a context, even against the claim that the Court's more recent taking clause decisions "demonstrate both a greater solicitude to the burdens placed on property owners by governmental regulations and less willingness to assume a justifying nexus between those burdens and public purpose." But, while "the constitutionality of (uncompensated) contraband laws is taken for granted throughout our legal system," there is some difficulty is squaring those laws with the cautionary language in *Andrus* and with taking clause cases regarding real property.

§ 3.4 Due Process and Statutory Presumptions, Defenses, and Exceptions

As noted in the previous section, criminal statutes are sometimes drafted in broad terms and thus cover persons other than those bent upon some evil purpose, the apparent reason being that the legislature has attempted to relieve the prosecution from the burden of proving some fact which is often difficult to establish. For example, a legislative body, concerned with the fraudulent practice of returning the covers of unsold magazines for credit and then selling the coverless magazines, might make it a crime for any person to sell a magazine without a cover. We have seen that such statutes are often held to violate due process because they encompass much innocent activity. What, then, of a legislative attempt to afford similar assistance to the prosecution by provisions in the substantive criminal law relating to the proof of the crime? For example, given the fact that the statute described above is unconstitutional, would it be permissible for the legislature to redefine the crime as sale of coverless magazines with intent to defraud, and then provide that the mere fact of sale shall be presumptive evidence of intent to defraud? Or, could the legislature make it a crime to sell coverless magazines, and then provide that the defendant might by way of an affirmative defense show the absence of any fraudulent intent? Or, what of a statute that made it an offense to sell a coverless magazine, and then set forth certain exceptions (e.g., where the cover had been destroyed) which the defendant might prove? Although these questions may appear to concern matters of evidence and burden of proof, and thus to be procedural in nature, they also have an important substantive dimension and thus are appropriately dealt with here.

(a) **Forms of Presumptions.** Courts dealing with case law, and legislatures with statute law, have frequently created presumptions in aid of one side of a legal dispute, both in the civil and criminal fields of law. Given the long-accepted notion that the prosecution in a criminal case must prove all elements of the charge and that it must prove its case beyond a reasonable doubt, the constitutional validity of these presumptions is most likely to be challenged on the criminal side of the law. Moreover, these challenges are most likely to be directed to presumptions created by the legislature, apparently because legislatures have been less restrictive than courts in creating rebuttable presumptions.

Statutory presumptions are not uncommon in the criminal law. Thus many "bad check" statutes make it a crime to give a check, with intent to defraud, on a bank wherein the drawer has insufficient funds, and further provide that nonpayment of the check shall be prima facie evidence of the intent to defraud. Some statutes provide that it is a crime to receive stolen property knowing it to have been stolen, and that the possession of stolen goods shall create a presumption of such knowledge. Even in the absence of an expressly stated statutory presumption, courts sometimes hold that the legislature impliedly created a statutory presumption; for example, if the legislature has created a crime without using any expression (e.g., "knowingly," "willfully") requiring a bad intent, the statute may be construed as meaning that the doing of the forbidden conduct is prima facie evidence of a bad intent, which the defendant may rebut by showing he had no such intent.

"Presumption" is a slippery word, but at least it means this: "a presumption is a standardized practice, under which certain facts are held to call for uniform treatment with respect to their effect as proof of other facts." But, precisely what treatment is intended is often not made clear in the statute creating the presumption. For example, what of a statute that makes it an offense for any person who has been convicted of a crime of violence or who is a fugitive from justice to receive a firearm shipped in interstate commerce, and which then provides that possession of a firearm by such a person shall give rise to a presumption that it was shipped in interstate commerce? There are at least four possibilities as to the impact of that statutory presumption:

(1) At a minimum, it must mean that the basic fact (possession) must be allowed to go to the jury as some evidence of the presumed fact (interstate shipment). Such a statutory "presumption," if it can even be called that under such a limited interpretation, does not disadvantage the accused except in the unlikely event that in its absence the basic fact would not have been admissible. Thus, it need not be considered further here.

(2) It is much more likely (particularly if the statute refers to the basic fact as "presumptive evidence" or as establishing a "prima facie case") that the statutory presumption will permit an instruction to the jury that it is authorized to conclude that the presumed fact exists—and thus to convict—if it finds that the basic fact exists. For example, under the statute described above, if the government proved possession and the defendant offered no coun-

ter-proof, the jury would be told that it may but need not convict. This kind of presumption, which the Supreme Court now prefers to call a "permissive inference," tends to operate to the disadvantage of the accused by persuading the jury that it may convict solely upon proof of the basic fact, a conclusion the jury might not otherwise reach.

(3) Another possibility is that the presumption will be said to shift the burden of persuasion, so that defendant will now be required to go forward with evidence negativing the presumed fact. Thus, under the statute described above, once the prosecution proved possession it would be incumbent upon the defendant to offer evidence tending to show the absence of interstate shipment, and if he put in no evidence of this nature the jury would be instructed, in effect, to convict. This is what the Supreme Court has characterized as a "mandatory presumption" of the "rebuttable" kind. Because such foreclosure is a harsh penalty, statutory presumptions in the criminal law have seldom been given this interpretation.

(4) Finally, the presumption might be viewed as removing the presumed element from the case upon proof of the facts giving rise to the presumption. Thus, under the statute described above, once the prosecution proved possession the matter of interstate shipment would no longer be a distinct matter for consideration by the factfinder. As such, it may not even seem like a presumption, but rather more like a redefinition of the crime. Yet, the Supreme Court has chosen to characterize this kind of situation as involving a "conclusive" mandatory presumption.

(b) Permissive Inferences. The law with respect to the constitutionality of presumptions in criminal statutes developed out of a series of cases that, until recently, made no effort to categorize presumptions in the manner set out above. In the first of these cases, *Tot v. U.S.* (1943), involving the statute utilized in the above hypothetical (which the Court has only recently put into the mandatory presumption category), the Court held:

> Under our decisions, a statutory presumption cannot be sustained if there be no rational connection between the fact proved and the ultimate fact presumed, if the inference of the one from proof of the other is arbitrary because of lack of connection between the two in common experience. This is not to say that a valid presumption may not be created upon a view of relation broader than that a jury might take in a specific case. But where the inference is so strained as not to have a reasonable relation to the circumstances of life as we know them, it is not competent for the legislature to create it as a rule governing the procedure of courts.

The Court later stated in *Leary v. U.S.* (1969) that a statutory presumption is irrational "unless it can at least be said with substantial assurance that the presumed fact is more likely than not to flow from the proved fact on which it is made to depend." But when the Court a year later held the requirement that a defendant be found guilty beyond a reasonable doubt was constitutionally compelled as a matter of due process, the sufficiency of the *Leary* test was put into doubt. In *Leary,* as in other statutory presumption cases before and after, the Court dealt ambiguously with the relevance of the beyond a reasonable doubt standard in this context.

Then came *Ulster County Court v. Allen* (1979), in which four persons—three adult males and a 16–year-old girl—were jointly tried for illegal possession of two loaded handguns. When the vehicle in which they were riding was stopped for speeding, police saw the handguns positioned crosswise in an open handbag the girl admitted was hers. Pursuant to a presumption set out in the relevant statute, the jury was instructed that "upon proof of the presence of * * * the hand weapons, you may infer and draw a conclusion that such prohibited weapon was possessed by each of the defendants who occupied the automobile at the time when such instruments were found," but that such presumption "is effective only so long as there is no substantial evidence contradicting the conclusion flowing from the presumption." The Court classified this as a "permissive inference," that is, one which did not remove the burden of persuasion from the prosecution and left the jury free to accept or reject the inference, and concluded that consequently

> it affects the application of the "beyond a reasonable doubt" standard only if, under the facts of the case, there is no rational way the trier could make the connection permitted by the inference. For only in that situation is there any risk that an explanation of the permissible inference to a jury, or its use by a jury, has caused the presumptively rational factfinder to make an erroneous factual determination.

In other words, in testing a permissive inference it is only necessary that, considering *all* the evidence in the *particular* case, there be a rational basis for telling the jury that it may infer one fact from proof of another. Such was the case in *Allen,* the Court next concluded, for the evidence showed that the guns "were too large to be concealed in [the girl's] handbag," and "part of one of the guns was in plain view, within easy access of the driver of the car and even, perhaps, of the other two respondents who were riding in the rear seat."

The trouble with this analysis is that the "Court's heavy emphasis on the evidence adduced at trial appears to * * * transform the analysis of the instructions into a harmless error analysis," as the *Allen* dissenters complained. As one commentator put it: "The Court's look-at-all-the-evidence approach ignores the possibility of the jury's disbelieving all the other evidence and convicting only on the basis of the inference. The jury could have believed that the prosecution had proved the defendants' presence in the car, disbelieved the rest of the evidence, and yet still gone on to convict because of the inference. A harmless error standard that looks heavily to the facts in the record can permit an instruction to be upheld, and a conviction affirmed, primarily on the basis of facts that a jury did not believe beyond a reasonable doubt." It has thus been cogently suggested that a safer form of jury instruction in the so-called permissive inference case, except where the specified proved fact would *alone* support a finding of the presumed fact beyond a reasonable doubt, is one which makes clearer than the instruction in *Allen* the need for the jury to consider the specified proved fact (e.g., presence in the car) with "all surrounding circumstances" in drawing the inference of the presumed fact (e.g., possession of the guns). (Indeed, it may be that the majority in *Allen* was proceeding on the assumption that the instruction in that case was of this character, in which case the above-stated criticism would not apply).

In a civil case context, the Supreme Court on one occasion tested the validity of a presumption on the notion that "the greater includes the lesser." Under this approach, the presumption is translated into a substantive rule, and then that rule is tested by the due process limitations on the police power of the state. Thus a presumption—whether rational or not—would be permitted if the state could constitutionally enact a criminal statute that required no proof of the fact being established by resort to the statutory presumption. This might suggest that a permissive inference, *even if irrational,* should be upheld if the crime could have been defined by the legislature without including the presumed fact as an element (surely not the case in *Allen*). But such reasoning is unsound, for resort to an inference to prove an element presents a problem of rational jury control that total legislative elimination of the element does not. It is one thing to create an offense of carrying a firearm that does not contain any requirement that the gun be loaded. It is quite another to define the crime as the possession of a loaded gun and then provide that upon proof of some irrelevant fact (e.g., that the sun was shining) the jury may infer the gun was loaded.

(c) Mandatory Rebuttable Presumptions. Under the Supreme Court's current terminology, a mandatory rebuttable presumption is one that "does not remove the presumed element from the case but nevertheless requires the jury to find the presumed element unless the defendant persuaded the jury that such a finding is unwarranted." In *Allen,* the Court took pains to point out that the statutory presumption at issue there was not of this sort and that, if it were, then a more demanding test would apply: "since the prosecution bears the burden of establishing guilt, it may not rest its case entirely on a presumption unless the fact proved is sufficient to support the inference of guilt beyond a reasonable doubt."

That statutory rebuttable presumptions are subject to *at least* such a constitutional limitation is apparent from two more recent cases involving presumptions not of the statutory variety. In *Sandstrom v. Mont.* (1979), where the defendant was convicted of deliberate homicide, the jury was instructed that "the law presumes that a person intends the ordinary consequences of his voluntary acts." Because the jury might have interpreted this instruction as shifting the burden of persuasion to the defendant once his voluntary actions were proved, the Court concluded it was unconstitutional; it conflicted with the due process principle that "a State must prove every ingredient of an offense beyond a reasonable doubt, and * * * may not shift the burden of proof to the defendant." Similarly, in *Francis v. Franklin* (1985), where in a murder prosecution the jury was instructed that "a person of sound mind and discretion is presumed to intend the natural and probable consequences of his acts, but the presumption may be rebutted," the Court first concluded that a reasonable juror could have understood this to mean that the burden of proof on the element of intent was shifted to defendant once the predicate acts were proved. Because that was so, the Court concluded, "the challenged language undeniably created an unconstitutional burden-shifting presumption with respect to the element of intent."

Just where this leaves statutory mandatory rebuttable presumptions is not entirely clear. *Sandstrom* and *Francis* (again, neither involving presumptions set out by statute) made no inquiry as to whether the presumptions involved there met the beyond a reasonable doubt test alluded to in *Allen.* Perhaps this is only because they obviously did not meet that standard, so that a mandatory presumption "that shifts the burden of persuasion" to the defendant could pass constitutional muster "if a rational jury could find the presumed fact beyond a reasonable doubt from the basic facts." But another interpretation is that since *Sandstrom* a presumption may never be used to assign a burden of persuasion to the defendant in a criminal case. This would mean, for example, that even if the beyond a reasonable doubt test were satisfied, it would be impermissible to provide by statute that it is a crime to possess heroin with knowledge of its illegal importation and that, upon proof of possession, the knowledge will be presumed unless the defendant proves otherwise.

Some have voiced still broader concern, which is that not even the beyond a reasonable doubt test is appropriate when the legislature could have achieved essentially the same result by recasting the presumed element as an affirmative defense. Under *Patterson v. N.Y.* (1977), when a crime may constitutionally be defined without a particular factual matter being stated as an element, then that matter may be expressed as an affirmative defense and the burden of proof as to it placed on the defendant. *Sandstrom,* which does not disapprove of *Patterson,* thus

> appears to approve of traditionally constructed affirmative defenses, but to regard as constitutionally impermissible the unorthodox method of creating affirmative defenses through presumptions. This distinction, however, is difficult to support because placing a burden of persuasion on a defendant by a presumption is the functional equivalent of creating an affirmative defense in the conventional manner. * * * To be constitutional, the state need only use the correct words in its statute. If the state makes the mistake of effectively creating an affirmative defense through the use of mandatory presumption language rather than in the manner approved in *Patterson,* then the statute is unacceptable even though there is no functional difference between the two methods.

This seeming inconsistency is understandably of less concern to those who believe that imposition of a burden of proof on the defendant as to a matter can be more serious than (and thus should not be equated with) the total elimination of that matter from the legislative scheme defining and classifying crimes.

(d) Conclusive Mandatory Presumptions. A conclusive mandatory presumption, the Supreme Court tells us, "removes the presumed element from the case once the State has proven the predicate facts giving rise to the presumption." In another branch of *Sandstrom,* the Court dealt with the jury instruction there in those terms, for a reasonable juror could well have interpreted that instruction "as an irrebuttable direction by the court to find intent once convinced of the facts triggering the presumption." So viewed, the instruction was declared unconstitutional, for such a conclusive presumption "would 'conflict with the overriding presumption of innocence with which the law endows the accused and which extends to every element of the crime,' and would 'invade [the] factfinding function' which in a criminal case the law assigns solely to the jury."

This analysis has not gone unchallenged:

If the instruction is given in every case of murder, a traditional element of the definition of the crime has been removed. If the instruction accurately describes state law, intent is not included as an element of murder; rather, the state must show only a voluntary act and its ordinary consequences. Alternatively, the instruction may be read to define the crime to require either proof of intent or proof that the defendant's act was voluntary and that the ordinary consequences of that act would be death. In either case, the instruction merely provides an untraditional definition of homicide that foregoes the usual requirement of intent. This involves no burden shifting at all; the issue has simply been removed as an absolute requirement. Consequently, neither alternative should have been objectionable to the Court on the grounds that the reasonable doubt requirement was violated. Montana may very well have defined homicide in an unusual fashion, but under the Court's theory *all* it did was define the crime. Without a constitutional limitation on a state's definition of crime, Montana's statute should have been perfectly acceptable.

In a case like *Sandstrom,* of course, one wonders if the instruction *does* accurately describe state law; surely it does not reflect a legislatively-made judgment as to what it is that constitutes the crime of murder. But this only points up the fact that doubts about *Sandstrom*'s applicability to legislatively-created presumptions are most substantial as to those statutory provisions which encompass a conclusive presumption within a particular crime definition. For example, a statute might provide that it is bigamy for one to remarry knowing his spouse is alive, and also that the fact the spouse is alive shall give rise to a conclusive presumption that he knew the spouse was alive. Such a statute really means that as a matter of substantive law one who actually has a spouse and who remarries is guilty of bigamy whether or not he knows his spouse is alive, and thus the more appropriate constitutional question is whether the legislature may constitutionally so provide (see § 3.3). Yet, even before *Sandstrom* some cases held statutory conclusive presumptions unconstitutional as a violation of due process or an infringement on the rights of the judiciary or a denial of defendant's right to a jury trial, even though the statute, if worded in the form of a rule of substantive law rather than in the fictional language of a conclusive presumption, would probably have been held constitutional. And in one post-*Sandstrom* decision, the Supreme Court has rather summarily applied the rule of that case to a conclusive presumption within a particular criminal statute instead of inquiring whether the proved fact would itself be a constitutional basis for criminal liability.

(e) Affirmative Defenses. As noted above, one point of emphasis in the administration of the criminal law has always been that the prosecution has the burden of coming forward with evidence and the burden of persuading the fact-finder as to the guilt of the accused. Yet, this is not a universal rule, for there are certain excuses or justifications allowed to the defendant that have traditionally been viewed as affirmative defenses. Illustrative are insanity, intoxication, self-defense and similar claims of justification for conduct that would otherwise be criminal, and excuses such as necessity and duress. In some jurisdictions, at least as to some of these defenses, the defendant not only has the burden of first producing evidence but also has the burden of persuasion. Usually the burden is to establish the defense by a preponderance of the evidence, but the Supreme Court has held that it is not a violation of due process for a state to impose upon the defendant the burden of proving his insanity beyond a reasonable doubt.

The question of whether the previously discussed (see § 3.4(b)) *Tot* rational connection rule is applicable to affirmative defenses came before the Supreme Court in *Leland v. Ore.* (1952), involving a conviction under an Oregon statute that imposed upon the defendant the burden of proving the defense of insanity beyond a reasonable doubt. The Court distinguished *Tot* on the basis that there a presumption of guilt rested upon "proof of a fact neither criminal in itself nor an element of the crime charged," while in the instant case the prosecutor was required "to prove beyond a reasonable doubt every element of the offense charged." Because the distinction rests upon "the grammatical point that the defense rests on an exception or proviso divorced from the definition of the crime," it is less than persuasive. If taken seriously, it would mean that legislatures would be free to impose substantial burdens of proof on defendants by merely re-defining crimes, taking out critical elements and fashioning them into defenses instead.

A more convincing distinction might start with the observation that one of the reasons underlying the rational connection test for presumptions—rational jury control—does not arise with affirmative defenses, as no suggestion is made to the jury that it might reach a certain conclusion based upon evidence which is not probative. Once this point is reached, the affirmative defense might then be tested by two inquiries: (1) whether the defense is defined in terms of a fact so central to the nature of the offense that, in effect, the prosecution has been freed of the burden to establish that the defendant engaged in conduct with consequences of some gravity; and (2) whether the need for narrowing the issues, coupled with the relative accessibility of evidence to the defendant, justifies calling upon him to put in evidence concerning his defensive claim. It would appear that most of the traditional affirmative defenses could be upheld on this basis, and this approach would also leave legislatures some room for innovation.

It may also be suggested that the argument that "the greater includes the lesser" carries some force as to affirmative defenses, at least as to relatively minor crimes. For example, consider the public welfare offenses, which impose strict liability as to certain activities, such as the sale of food. If it is permissible to convict a person for sale of impure food without a showing of any intent, knowledge, recklessness, or even negligence on his part, then it is difficult to see what objection could be raised to adding to such statutes an affirmative defense of some kind, such as that the defendant may show lack of knowledge of the impurity or due care in the processing of the food.

However, as discussed in more detail elsewhere herein (see § 1.8(c)), the Supreme Court appears not to have taken such an approach. In *Patterson v. N.Y.* (1977), defendant was charged with murder, defined as intentionally causing the death of another, and was permitted by statute to show by a preponderance of the evidence the affirmative defense that he "acted under the influence of extreme emotional disturbance for which there was a reasonable explanation or excuse," which would downgrade the offense to manslaughter. The Court upheld this allocation of the burden of persuasion, relying largely upon the pragmatic notion that were the rule otherwise legislative bodies might opt to eliminate certain defenses entirely rather than impose upon prosecutors the burden of disproving their existence on a case-by-case basis. As for the Court's prior decision in *Mullaney v. Wilbur* (1975), declaring unconstitutional a state murder statute that imposed upon defendants the burden of proving the heat-of-passion mitigation needed to reduce the crime to manslaughter, it was characterized in *Patterson* as holding only that "shifting the burden of persuasion with respect to a fact which the State deems so important that it must be either proved or presumed is impermissible under the Due Process Clause."

This appeared to mean, the dissenters objected, that (just as in *Leland*) the outcome was determined merely by labels, so that the burden of proof could be put upon the defendant whenever the legislature was ingenious enough to characterize the matter as an "affirmative defense." Not so, the *Patterson* majority objected, for "there are obviously constitutional limits beyond which the States may not go." This suggests that the only limitation here is of the greater-includes-the-lesser type; if the legislature could define a particular crime as consisting only of elements X and Y (rather than X and Y plus Z), then and only then may the legislature instead define the crime as X and Y but allow the defendant to prove non-Z. But some find more promise in *Patterson*. It has been suggested, for example, that the Court's handling of that case reflects "an ambivalence, shared by many scholars, about the insanity defense," in that the Court treated the extreme emotional disturbance defense "as being sufficiently close to insanity to warrant the same burden of persuasion that could have been placed on the defendant to prove insanity." From this, it is reasoned that *Patterson* plus *Mullaney* "require the prosecution to bear the burden of proving those elements necessary to distinguish a greater from a lesser offense among traditionally demarcated degrees of criminal activity."

(f) Statutory Exceptions. Sometimes claims of exemption from a statutory prohibition are based upon some proviso or exception appearing in the statute, in which case courts frequently hold that the burden of coming forward with proof of the exculpatory fact is on the defendant. For example, where a statute made it an offense for a carrier to possess pheasants without being qualified by law to do so, and ten different qualifications were provided by the same laws, it was held that it was for the defendant to establish the qualification he had rather than for the prosecution to prove the absence of all ten.

It is apparent that in many instances these statutory exceptions could not meet the rational connection test; indeed, courts have always explained the placing of the burden on the defendant on a quite different basis, namely that the exculpating facts are peculiarly within the knowledge of the accused. Here again, therefore, the question arises as to whether the constitutional limitations imposed by the *Tot* decision and its progeny are applicable to these statutory exceptions. Although the courts have not given careful attention to this question, it is submitted that the reasons given above for different treatment of affirmative defenses are equally applicable to statutory exceptions. However, in light of the previously discussed tension (see § 3.4(c)) between *Patterson* and *Sandstrom,* in that the legislature cannot do by a device called a "presumption" what it can do by using the words "affirmative defense," there is admittedly somewhat greater chance that a part of a criminal statute characterized as an exception or proviso would not be deemed within *Patterson*'s embrace.

§ 3.5 The Bill of Rights

A criminal statute may be held unconstitutional on its face or as applied to some situations within its terms because it conflicts with some guarantee of the Bill of Rights (which, when a state law is involved, requires an initial determination that the constitutional provision relied upon is applicable to the states through the Fourteenth Amendment). The conflict may be with the freedom of speech, press, assembly, religion, association, or privacy; with the right to be secure against illegal searches; with the privilege against self-incrimination; or with the prohibition on cruel and unusual punishment.

(a) Substantive Due Process and the Bill of Rights. As noted earlier (see § 3.3(a)), the United States Supreme Court has all but abandoned its earlier practice of declaring criminal statutes unconstitutional on the ground that the proscribed conduct bears no real or substantial relation to injury to the public. Thus it would now be most unusual for the Court to hold a law invalid solely upon the basis that no reason *for* prohibiting the delineated conduct has been established. It is not at all unusual, however, for the Supreme Court to strike down a criminal statute (or, at least, to declare it unenforceable as to some fact situations within its terms) because there exists a good reason *for not* proscribing all of the conduct covered by the statute. This happens when it appears that the challenged statute attempts to prohibit conduct which is protected by the Bill of Rights of the United States Constitution. Indeed, it may be said that the latter ground for invalidating statutes has in a sense replaced the former; today the Court is likely to reject a "direct" substantive due process challenge to a criminal statute in favor of a finding that the statute conflicts with the Bill of Rights, even when this result may be reached only by recognition of "penumbral rights" not specifically enumerated in the Constitution.

This is not to say, however, that only the grounds for decision have changed and that the constitutional limits of penal legislation have remained fixed. The Court was once quick to strike down legislative experiments in economic and social reform but slow to assimilate freedoms guaranteed by the Bill of Rights into the due process clause of the Fourteenth Amendment, but now it is criminal statutes imposing restrictions on speech, assembly, religion and the like that are most vulnerable. While some of the reasons that have been given for this "double standard" are less than satisfying, there is general agreement that it is more appropriate for the Supreme Court to determine when legislative policies conflict with the Bill of Rights than to undertake a more general assessment of the wisdom of these policies.

The limitations upon federal and state power flowing from the Bill of Rights are many, and this vast subject today accounts for most of the content of the typical law school course in constitutional law. Accordingly, no attempt will be made here to treat the subject exhaustively. Rather, the purpose of this section is merely to point out some of the most significant limitations on the legislative power to create crimes.

It is well to note, however, that sometimes a substantive due process challenge to a criminal statute will not involve any specific provision in the Bill of Rights but rather only one of the broadly stated interests (e.g., "liberty") in the Fourteenth Amendment itself. A recent example of such a situation, *Wash. v. Glucksberg* (1997), illustrates how especially cautious the Court is in such circumstances. The question in *Glucksberg* was whether the prohibition in Washington's criminal law against causing or aiding suicide offended the Fourteenth Amendment. After cautioning that it "had always been reluctant to expand the concept of substantive due process because guideposts for responsible decisionmaking in this uncharted area are scarce and open-ended," the Court noted that its "established method of substantive-due-process analysis has two primary features." One is that the due process clause specially protects those fundamental rights and liberties which are "deeply rooted in this Nation's history and tradition"; the other is a requirement of a "careful description" of the asserted fundamental liberty interest. The Court in *Glucksberg* thus refused to characterize the right at issue broadly as the "right to die," as had the court of appeals, and instead carefully stated "the question before us" as being "whether the 'liberty' specially protected by the Due Process Clause includes a right to commit suicide which itself includes a right to assistance in doing so." Given the "history of the law's treatment of assisted suicide in this country," the Court concluded "that the asserted 'right' to assistance in committing suicide is not a fundamental liberty interest" and that Washington's assisted suicide ban was "rationally related to legitimate government interests."

(b) Freedom of Expression and Association. The First Amendment provides that "Congress shall make no law * * * abridging the freedom of speech, or of the press; or the right of the people peaceably to assemble," and it has long been clear that this prohibition is also applicable to the states via the due process clause of the Fourteenth Amendment. A literal reading of the language quoted above might well suggest that there is absolutely no constitutional room for a criminal statute which attempts to punish any kind of oral or written communication or any peaceable assembly, but this is not the case. The Supreme Court, by defining what lies within these freedoms and in deciding what constitutes an abridgement of them, has established that certain criminal statutes of this kind are permissible.

Not every form of communication is protected by the First Amendment. "There are certain well-defined and narrowly limited classes of speech, the prevention and punishment of which has never been thought to raise any Constitutional problem. These include the lewd and obscene, the profane, the libelous, and the insulting or 'fighting' words—those which by their very utterance inflict injury or tend to incite an immediate breach of the peace." Because such communications are not an essential part of the exposition of ideas, they are deemed to be of slight social value as compared to the public interest in order and morality. As a consequence, the Supreme Court does not require a showing of need for legislation proscribing such conduct. But even fighting words cannot be proscribed selectively so as to favor one point of view over another.

This is not to suggest, however, that a legislature may proscribe certain speech or writing merely by the use of such labels as "obscenity" and "libel." The question of what communications lie outside the First Amendment is itself an issue of constitutional law, and thus in the last analysis must be answered by the Supreme Court. For example, it is for the Court to decide upon the permissible reach of obscenity statutes and criminal defamation laws. Also, a criminal statute intended to deal with situations outside the First Amendment may not be drafted in such a way that it tends to limit access to constitutionally protected materials; and thus a strict liability statute on possession of obscene literature is unconstitutional because it would tend to influence booksellers to carry only those reading materials they had personally examined as to contents.

Other forms of speech may also be prohibited by the criminal law on the basis of the danger flowing from the content of what is said. "The most stringent protection of free speech would not protect a man in falsely shouting fire in a theatre and causing a panic." The test is often said to be whether there is a "clear and present danger" that the words in question will bring about evils which the legislature has a right to prevent, although more recently the test has been restated in a somewhat more sophisticated form: "In each case [courts] must ask whether the gravity of the 'evil,' discounted by its improbability, justifies such invasion of free speech as is necessary to avoid the danger." Under such a test, it is clear that the First Amendment does not bar the existence of such crimes as solicitation, conspiracy, obtaining property by falsely spoken words, or the grounding of accomplice liability on words giving assistance or encouragement: "There is no question but that the State may thus provide for the punishment of those who indulge in utterances which incite to violence and crime and threaten the overthrow of organized government by unlawful means."

Other criminal statutes and ordinances, while not attempting to proscribe speech on the basis of its content, fix limitations on the time, place, and manner of such expression. In passing upon the constitutionality of these regulations, the Court has frequently employed a balancing-of-interests test; for example, an ordinance banning the practice of summoning occupants of a residence to the door, without their prior consent, for the purpose of soliciting orders for the sale of goods was upheld on the ground that the householder's interest in privacy outweighed the commercial interests of the salesman. However, the law must be narrowly drawn to proscribe only that conduct which interferes with some superior interest; even assuming that the distribution of handbills may be limited to prevent defrauding of the public, this does not warrant a law requiring that handbills of any kind carry the name and address of the persons who printed them and caused them to be distributed. So-called "commercial speech," that which is connected to the selling of a product or service, although also entitled to First Amendment protection, is subject to greater time, place, or manner restrictions.

The expression of ideas through conduct is subject to greater regulation, as the Court has rejected the notion that the Constitution affords "the same kind of freedom to those who would communicate ideas by conduct such as patrolling, marching, and picketing on streets and highways as * * * to those who communicate ideas by pure speech." Therefore, it is permissible for a legislature to proscribe that picketing which unreasonably interferes with ingress or egress to public buildings. Expression by speech or conduct in public parks or streets is subject to regulation in order to protect the primary use of these facilities, but proceeding without a permit may not be punished where the law sets no appropriate standards for the official who is to pass upon the permit application. (As the Court stated in *Va. v. Hicks* (2003): "Rarely, if ever, will an overbreadth challenge succeed against a law or regulation that is not specifically addressed to speech or to conduct necessarily associated with speech (such as picketing or demonstrating).") As to conduct clearly punishable by the criminal law, e.g., battery, a sentence-enhancement provision defined in terms of certain motivating biases or beliefs, e.g., animosity based on race, is constitutional even though the biases or beliefs are themselves protected by the First Amendment.

The right of assembly is protected in much the same way, as is freedom of association and the freedom to travel. While the First Amendment does not expressly mention the latter two rights, it has been construed to include these and other penumbral rights.

(c) Right to Bear Arms. The Second Amendment provides: "A well regulated Militia, being necessary to the security of a free State, the right of the people to keep and bear Arms, shall not be infringed." For a great many years of our history, the precise meaning of this provision was in doubt. Some interpreted it as protecting only the right to possess and carry a firearm in connection with militia service, while others argued that it protects an individual right to possess a firearm unconnected with service in a militia, and to use that arm for traditionally lawful purposes, such as self-defense within the home. The matter was finally resolved in *District of Columbia v. Heller* (2008), where, in a 5–4 decision, the majority adopted the latter interpretation.

The *Heller* majority, reasoning (i) that the term "the people," just as in the First, Fourth and Ninth Amendments, refers "to individual rights," (ii) that "arms" covers "weapons * * * not specifically designed for military use" and "not employed in a military capacity," (iii) that "keep Arms" means only to "have weapons," (iv) that "bear" means to "carry," and (v) that the Amendment's prefatory clause announces a purpose which neither limits nor expands the scope of the operative clause, concluded that the Second Amendment "guarantee[s] the individual right to possess and carry weapons in case of confrontation," not confined by the prefatory clause's stated purpose "to prevent elimination of the militia."

At issue in *Heller* was a D.C. law that totally banned handgun possession in the home and also required that any lawful firearms in the home be disassembled or bound by a trigger lock at all times. Considering that "the inherent right of self-defense has been central to the Second Amendment right," the Court concluded that because "handguns are the most popular weapon chosen by Americans for self-defense in the home, * * * a complete prohibition of their use is invalid." As for the requirement that firearms be inoperable, "[t]his makes it impossible for citizens to use them for the core lawful purpose of self-defense and is hence unconstitutional." However, the *Heller* majority emphasized that "the right secured by the Second Amendment is not unlimited," and gave as examples of "presumptively lawful regulatory measures" "prohibitions on carrying concealed weapons" and "on the possession of firearms by felons and the mentally ill, or laws forbidding the carrying of firearms in sensitive places such as schools and government buildings, or laws imposing conditions and qualifications on the commercial sale of arms," as well as prohibitions on carrying "dangerous and unusual weapons."

The Supreme Court's pre-*Heller* rulings that the Second Amendment is, in any event, not applicable to the states continue to be followed in post-*Heller* decisions of the federal courts, but that issue is currently pending before the Supreme Court.

(d) Freedom of Religion. The First Amendment also provides that "Congress shall make no law * * * prohibiting the free exercise" of religion, and this prohibition has likewise been held applicable to the states. Just as is true of the bar on abridging freedoms of speech, the press, or assembly, the language quoted above has not been interpreted as forbidding any criminal legislation touching upon the protected area.

In *Reynolds v. U.S.* (1878) the Supreme Court applied the secular regulation rule: the First Amendment bestows protection upon religious beliefs, but not upon religious acts that contravene generally applicable legislation. Therefore, because antipolygamy statutes were constitutional as generally applied, the religious practice of polygamy was not protected. Although this decision suggested that any religious belief taking the form of action was outside the First Amendment, the Court later moved to a less restrictive position. While the freedom to believe was absolute and thus subject to no regulation, the freedom to act could be restricted, provided the power to regulate was "so exercised as not, in attaining a permissible end, unduly to infringe the protected freedom." This gave rise to a balancing test; criminal laws that made punishable acts done in the pursuit of religious beliefs would be upheld when so applied if the interest advanced by the statute was of greater importance than the interest in permitting the particular religious practice to continue. For example, a woman may be convicted for allowing her nine-year-old niece to sell religious literature on street corners in violation of the child labor laws, as society's interest in child welfare is more important than this particular form of religious practice. By contrast, a statute permitting prosecution of parents for the failure of their children to salute the flag at school may not be enforced against Jehovah's Witnesses, for there is no genuine interest in obtaining compulsory unification of opinion. In a later case, the Court referred to the need to show a "compelling state interest," but even without relying upon this test later held that application of the compulsory school-attendance law to Amish children who had graduated from the eighth grade would violate their rights under the free exercise clause. The Court stressed that the Amish had supported their claim that such attendance would endanger the free exercise of their religious beliefs, and also that the state's admittedly strong interest would not be adversely affected by an exception for Amish children, in light of the adequacy of the Amish alternative mode of continuing informal education.

In *Employment Division, Dep't of Human Resources v. Smith* (1990), the Court clarified and (four members of the Court objected) altered the approach to be taken when a free exercise challenge is directed at a criminal statute of general applicability. At issue there was the application of a state's controlled substances law, making it a felony to knowingly or intentionally possess the drug, to sacramental peyote use at ceremonies of the Native American Church. The Court concluded: (1) that a state would be prohibiting free exercise if it sought to ban certain acts or abstentions only when engaged in for religious reasons or only because of the religious belief they display (e.g., a ban on the casting of statues to be used for worship purposes); (2) that a state law does *not* prohibit free exercise when the statute, concededly constitutional as applied to others and not specifically directed at religious practice, requires or forbids the performance of an act that a person's religious beliefs forbid or require; and (3) that consequently a claim for a religious exemption to the statute's proscriptions need not be evaluated under a balancing test, even when the conduct prohibited is "central" to the individual's religion.

As the Court later emphasized in *Church of the Lukumi Babalu Aye, Inc. v. City of Hialeah* (1993), what *Smith* means is that a law governing religious practice need not be justified by a compelling governmental interest if it is neutral and of general applicability. But where such a law is not neutral or not of general application, it must undergo the most rigorous scrutiny: it must be justified by a compelling governmental interest and must be narrowly tailored to advance that interest. The ordinances in *Hialeah* did not pass muster under this test. They proscribed animal sacrifice by religious groups but excluded virtually all other animal killings, and thus were not of general application. Moreover, they did not withstand strict scrutiny, as they were both overbroad and underinclusive: the government interests in public health and preventing unnecessary cruelty to animals (i) could be achieved short of total prohibition of religious sacrifice, and (ii) could not be accepted as compelling in light of the failure of the ordinances to proscribe other conduct of the same sort.

Applying one or more of the tests mentioned above, state courts have upheld convictions under statutes of general application notwithstanding the defendant's claim that he was pursuing a religious belief. For example, a father who causes the death of his child by failing to call a doctor, though he honestly believes in prayer rather than doctors as a cure, may be guilty of manslaughter. Criminal laws punishing spiritualism and fortune telling have been held valid, as have statutes punishing the practice of medicine without a license as applied to one who believes he is a divine healer.

Another troublesome kind of case is presented when the criminal statute in question does not attempt to punish acts done in the practice of religion, but instead proscribes other acts and thus makes the practice of religion more burdensome. This happens, for example, when a Sunday closing law is applied to Orthodox Jewish businessmen who because of their religion are also closed on

Saturday. Confronted with such a situation, the Supreme Court upheld this application of the law, emphasizing that the burden was only indirect and that the state was pursuing a secular goal by the only reasonable method available.

(e) Freedom From Unreasonable Search and the Right of Privacy. The United States Constitution also protects "the right of the people to be secure in their persons, houses, papers and effects, against unreasonable searches and seizures," and this protection is likewise granted against both the federal government and the states. The freedom from unreasonable searches and seizures is of primary significance in the realm of criminal procedure, where it is protected by an exclusionary rule which bars from evidence the fruits of an invasion of that right. However, it is also a limitation on the substantive criminal law, in that the failure to permit another to intrude upon your constitutional right against unreasonable searches may not be made criminal. For example, one may not be convicted for refusing entry to a building or fire inspector who is neither acting in an emergency nor armed with a search warrant for the premises.

Other criminal statutes do not attempt to punish directly an assertion of one's constitutional right against unreasonable searches, but do proscribe conduct that ordinarily would not be discovered without inquiry into the individual's most private actions. Illustrative is a law that makes it a criminal offense to use a contraceptive device, which was declared unconstitutional by the Supreme Court in *Griswold v. Conn.* (1965). That decision is based upon the "penumbral" right of privacy, not specifically mentioned in the Constitution, which the opinion of the Court declares flows from the First Amendment right of association, the Third Amendment prohibition on quartering of soldiers, the Fourth Amendment protection against unreasonable searches, the Fifth Amendment protection against self-incrimination, and the provision in the Ninth Amendment that "the enumeration in the Constitution, of certain rights, shall not be construed to deny or disparage others retained by the people." A law forbidding use of contraceptives rather than regulating their manufacture or sale is unduly broad because it invades this right. The *Griswold* Court declared: "Would we allow the police to search the sacred precincts of marital bedrooms for telltale signs of the use of contraceptives? The very idea is repulsive to the notions of privacy surrounding the marriage relationship."

The precise scope of the *Griswold* decision is not entirely clear, and thus it cannot be said with certainty whether many other criminal statutes might also be found unconstitutional as violating the penumbral right of privacy. It is undoubtedly true, as Justice

Stewart noted in dissent, that "even after today a State can constitutionally still punish at least some offenses which are not committed in public." Although it has been noted that *Griswold* furnishes some support for those who argue that the state should not be able to prohibit any private sexual activity between two consenting adults, a majority of the Court in *Griswold* indicated that states may still forbid fornication, adultery, and homosexuality. Because of the emphasis upon marital privacy in *Griswold*, it became apparent that laws attempting to prohibit deviate sexual activity by married couples, when requiring a type of enforcement similar to that condemned in *Griswold*, could be successfully challenged. On the other hand, in the post-*Griswold* case of *Bowers v. Hardwick* (1986), a majority of the Court declared that *Griswold* presented no barrier to criminalizing conduct which has "no connection [with] family, marriage, or procreation." But the holding in *Bowers*, that *Griswold* afforded no protection to consensual homosexual sodomy occurring within one's residence, was later overturned in *Lawrence v. Texas* (2003), which instead embraced the conclusion in the *Bowers* dissent that "intimate choices by unmarried as well as married persons" "concerning the intimacies of their physical relationship, even when not intended to produce offspring, are a form of 'liberty' protected by the Due Process Clause of the Fourteenth Amendment."

Griswold was relied upon by the Supreme Court in *Stanley v. Ga.* (1969), holding that the First Amendment freedom of expression and the penumbral right to privacy together prohibit making private possession of obscene material a crime. However, the Court, while recognizing the defendant's "right to be free from state inquiry into the contents of his library," pointed out that the holding in no way infringed upon the power of the state or federal government to make private possession of "other items, such as narcotics, firearms, or stolen goods, a crime."

Griswold was again relied upon in *Roe v. Wade* (1973), where the Court overturned a statute that proscribed abortion except when necessary to save the life of the mother. The statute was held to violate due process because it unnecessarily infringed upon a woman's right to privacy, declared by the Court to be "broad enough to encompass a woman's decision whether or not to terminate her pregnancy." This right was deemed "fundamental," and thus could be limited only in furtherance of a "compelling state interest." One such interest, that in the existence of the fetus, was held not to arise until the fetus was viable and thus then capable of "meaningful life" independent of the mother. As for the state's interest in the pregnant woman's health, it was held only to permit the establishment of medical procedures for abortions performed after the first trimester, though the Court later held that an "undue burden" test should be used instead of the trimester framework in evaluating abortion restrictions before viability.

(f) Privilege Against Self–Incrimination. The United States Constitution provides that no person "shall be compelled in any criminal case to be a witness against himself," and this prohibition is applicable to both the federal government and the states. This privilege against self-incrimination has had the greatest significance in the area of criminal procedure; its most obvious application is to allow a defendant in a criminal case a free choice as to whether to take the stand in his defense, although more recently it has been held applicable in other procedural contexts, such as police interrogation. Even more recently, however, the privilege has been recognized as a limitation upon the permissible reach of the substantive criminal law.

The thrust of this substantive law aspect of the privilege against self-incrimination is that the failure to do something, such as to register or to pay a tax, may not be punished as a crime when the obligation to so act carries with it a real and appreciable hazard that the individual will thereby incriminate himself by providing information which may be used to support other criminal prosecutions. Thus one may not be convicted for willful failure to pay the wagering occupation tax or to register before engaging in the business of accepting wagers, given the facts that wagering is widely prohibited under federal and state law and that information obtained from the payment of the tax or registering is readily available to assist the efforts of state and federal authorities to enforce these other laws. Similarly, one may not be convicted of knowingly possessing an unregistered firearm or of failure to register a firearm when the information received by compliance with these requirements would readily facilitate prosecution under other sections of the National Firearms Act regarding the making or transfer of such firearms. Such criminal statutes, if defined solely in terms of persons who have violated other laws (e.g., statute *A* requires everyone who has violated statute *B* to register), would undoubtedly be unconstitutional on their face. In other instances, close to the same result is reached by upholding the statute but yet affording those prosecuted thereunder a full defense by merely claiming the privilege.

The United States Supreme Court, relying upon the privilege against self-incrimination, has held that a person under restraint by the police has a constitutional right to remain silent. One procedural consequence of this is that the prosecution may not "use at trial the fact that [the defendant] stood mute or claimed his privilege in the face of accusation." It may well follow that this extension of the privilege has similar significance in terms of what is permissible in the substantive criminal law. It has been suggested that offenses which include as an element the failure to give a reasonable or satisfactory account to a police officer may now be unconstitutional. However, the Supreme Court has not as yet resolved this issue. But the Court has decided that there need not be an "exculpatory no" exception to the false statement statute, for "neither the text nor the spirit of the Fifth Amendment confers a privilege to lie" instead of remaining silent.

(g) Freedom From Cruel and Unusual Punishment. The United States Constitution prohibits the federal government from imposing cruel and unusual punishment for federal crimes; almost all states have similar constitutional provisions forbidding such punishment for state crimes; and the due process clause of the Fourteenth Amendment also prohibits the states from inflicting such punishment for state crimes. While the prohibition on cruel and unusual punishment has sometimes been the basis for challenging action taken in the process of administering the criminal law, it also has considerable significance with respect to the permissible reach of the substantive criminal law. In this regard, the prohibition has three aspects: (1) it limits the methods that may be used to inflict punishment; (2) it limits the amount of punishment that may be prescribed for various offenses; and (3) it bars any and all penal sanctions in certain situations.

As to the first of these, it seems clear that the Eighth Amendment bars those forms of punishment that were considered cruel at the time of its adoption, such as burning at the stake, crucifixion, breaking on the wheel, quartering, the rack and thumbscrew, and extreme instances of solitary confinement. The scope of the amendment is not so limited, however; it "must draw its meaning from the evolving standards of decency that mark the progress of a maturing society." Thus even a punishment that inflicts no physical hardship or pain may be found to be cruel and unusual, as with a deprivation of citizenship which results in the "total destruction of the individual's status in organized society."

Sterilization, found constitutional by some courts, has been declared cruel and unusual by others, which seems more in keeping with the Supreme Court's recent emphasis on the Eighth Amendment as protecting the "dignity of man." Castration constitutes cruel and unusual punishment. Flogging, condemned as cruel in dicta, has been upheld, although the fact that it is unique from all other authorized forms of punishment in that the aim is the infliction of severe pain strongly suggests the Supreme Court would declare it impermissible. But solitary confinement, even when it must be served with no time out-of-doors, does not violate the Eighth Amendment.

Every modern form of carrying out the death penalty—electrocution, hanging, shooting, and lethal drugs or gas—has been upheld. In *Baze v. Rees* (2008), regarding "lethal injection," used by federal government and now adopted "as the exclusive or primary means of implementing the death penalty" in 36 states, the Court concluded "petitioners have not carried their burden of showing that the risk of pain from maladministration of a concededly humane lethal injection protocol, and the failure to adopt untried and untested alternatives, constitute cruel and unusual punishment." As for the question of whether the death penalty is inherently cruel, so as to constitute a per se violation of the Eighth Amendment, the Supreme Court answered in the negative in *Gregg v. Ga.* (1976). In reaching this conclusion, the Court emphasized three factors: (i) that the "imposition of the death penalty for the crime of murder has a long history of acceptance both in the United States and England"; (ii) that it was "now evident that a large proportion of American society continues to regard it as an appropriate and necessary criminal sanction"; and (iii) that the death penalty serves "two principal social purposes: retribution and deterrence of capital crimes by prospective offenders." Regarding the concern expressed a few years earlier by the Court that the penalty of death not be imposed in an arbitrary and capricious manner, the Court in *Gregg* concluded it did not require an absolute prohibition upon capital punishment. Rather, that concern could "be met by a carefully drafted statute that ensures that the sentencing authority is given adequate information and guidance." In upholding the statutory scheme at issue in *Gregg*, the Court stressed that it (1) specified ten aggravating circumstances, any one of which must be found by the jury to exist beyond a reasonable doubt before a death sentence can be imposed; (2) allowed the jury to make a binding recommendation of mercy even without finding any mitigating circumstances; and (3) provided for an automatic appeal at which both the sufficiency of the jury's finding of an aggravated circumstance and whether the sentence was disproportionate compared to those sentences imposed in similar cases would be assessed.

The Supreme Court later concluded that the Eighth Amendment requires that the sentencing authority "not be precluded from considering, as a mitigating factor, any aspect of a defendant's character or record and any of the circumstances of the offense that the defendant proffers as a basis for a sentence less than death." This means it is unconstitutional for a state to mandate the death penalty for a certain degree or category of murder or for those murders accompanied by specified aggravating factors or unaccompanied by a few specified mitigating circumstances, just as it is unconstitutional for a sentencing judge to disregard as a matter of law relevant mitigating circumstances or for such circumstances to be withheld from the sentencing jury. These holdings also reflect the Court's view that under the Eighth Amendment capital punishment must "be imposed fairly, and with reasonable consistency, or not at all," for "a consistency produced by ignoring individual differences is a false consistency." However, a state death penalty statute may give the defendant the burden of proving that the mitigating circumstances outweigh the aggravating circumstances, *Walton v. Ariz.* (1990), from which it follows that a state may direct imposition of the death penalty when the state has proved beyond a reasonable doubt that the mitigators do not outweigh the aggravators, including where the two are in equipoise, *Kansas v. Marsh* (2006).

The prohibition on cruel and unusual punishment also bars punishment authorized by statute which is excessive, that is, out of all proportion to the offense committed. A leading case is *Weems v. U.S.* (1910), involving a public official in the Philippines convicted of falsifying an official record, where the punishment was fifteen years of *cadena temporal* (hard and painful labor and constant enchainment, deprivation of parental authority, loss of the right to dispose of property inter vivos, and continual surveillance for life). Although the Court viewed the punishment as inherently cruel, it also condemned the penalty as excessive in relation to the crime committed, a conclusion that was based upon a comparison of the punishment imposed with the penalties authorized by various American jurisdictions for comparable offenses.

This comparative technique was substantially limited by the Court shortly after the *Weems* decision, which may explain why courts have seldom held that a punishment may be unconstitutionally cruel because of excessiveness. Generally, it may be said that courts have shown considerable deference to the legislative judgment as to how severe a penalty should be authorized for specific classes of offenses. Illustrative of the usual response to a claim of excessive punishment is *Perkins v. N.C.* (1964), where a federal court, although shocked at the sentence of from twenty to thirty years imposed for fellatio, upheld the sentence because it was within "the astounding statutory limit of 'not less than five nor more than sixty years'." While there are cases holding sentences invalid for being clearly out of proportion to the offense—for example, six years for picking flowers in a public park—often these decisions have been based upon state constitutional provisions expressly prohibiting disproportionate sentences.

The Supreme Court has returned to the proportionality issue in recent years, especially with respect to the death penalty. In *Gregg v. Ga.* (1976), where the contention was that capital punishment was per se invalid, the Court proceeded to consider "whether the punishment of death is disproportionate in relation to the crime for which it is imposed." The Supreme Court indicated such an inquiry is particularly appropriate as to the punishment of death, which is "unique in its severity and irrevocability," but then concluded that because "we are concerned here only with the imposition of capital punishment for the crime of murder, and when life has been taken deliberately by the offender, we cannot say that the punishment is invariably disproportionate to the crime. It is an extreme sanction, suitable to the most extreme of crimes."

Gregg created doubt about the constitutionality of the death penalty for offenses other than murder, and soon thereafter the Court confronted that issue in *Coker v. Ga.* (1977). The plurality, concluding "that death is indeed a disproportionate penalty for the crime of raping an adult woman," reasoned:

> Rape is without doubt deserving of serious punishment; but in terms of moral depravity and of the injury to the person and to the public, it does not compare with murder, which does involve the unjustified taking of human life. Although it may be accompanied by another crime, rape by definition does not include the death or even the serious injury to another person. The murderer kills; the rapist, if no more than that, does not. Life is over for the victim of the murderer; for the rape victim, life may not be nearly so happy as it was, but it is not over and normally is not beyond repair. We have the abiding conviction that the death penalty, which "is unique in its severity and irrevocability," is an excessive penalty for the rapist who, as such, does not take human life.

Coker is, to be sure, a most significant decision. "It is the first modern decision in which the Supreme Court has relied on disproportionality to invalidate a punishment under the cruel and unusual punishment clause." Its scope, however, is not entirely clear, which prompted the two *Coker* dissenters to declare that the decision "casts serious doubt upon the constitutional validity of statutes imposing the death penalty for a variety of conduct which though dangerous, may not necessarily result in any immediate death, e.g., treason, airplane hijacking, and kidnapping." One possible view of *Coker* is that it "announced a first principle of morality in law—society may not take the life of a defendant who has not taken the life of his victim." If this is so, then capital punishment would also be barred in all the cases mentioned by the *Coker* dissenters. It seems unlikely, however, that the decision will be so broadly applied. In particular, "since treason, a crime against masses of people, may cause more aggregate harm than a single murder, the greater public injury may justify the imposition of the death penalty."

The *Coker* proportionality inquiry, the Court later noted in *Enmund v. Fla.* (1982), involved the Court looking "to the historical development of the punishment at issue, legislative judgments, international opinion, and the sentencing decisions juries have made before bringing its own judgment to bear on the matter." This same approach was taken by the *Enmund* plurality, which concluded that the Eighth Amendment does not permit imposition of the death penalty on a defendant who aids and abets a felony in the course of which murder is committed by others, but who does not himself kill, attempt to kill, or intend that killing take place or that lethal force be employed. This conclusion that all those guilty of felony-murder (see § 13.5(c)) are not proper candidates for the death penalty was grounded in another part of the *Coker* analysis— that which declared the death penalty is unconstitutional unless it measurably contributes to the goals of retribution and deterrence. As for deterrence, the *Enmund* plurality concluded "there is no basis in experience for the notion that death so frequently occurs in the course of a felony for which killing is not an essential ingredient that the death penalty should be considered as a justifiable deterrent to the felony itself." Moreover, executing Enmund "to avenge two killings that he did not commit and had no intention of committing or causing does not measurably contribute to the retributive end of ensuring that the criminal gets his just deserts." But notwithstanding those comments, the Court later decided "that major participation in the felony committed, combined with reckless indifference to human life, is sufficient to satisfy the *Enmund* culpability requirement."

Another line of cases has to do with the question of whether persons with certain characteristics are inappropriate candidates for the death penalty, no matter what crime they have committed. For example, in *Thompson v. Okla.* (1988), the Court held that the Constitution bars a death penalty sentence for a defendant who was only 15 at the time of the crime. Applying the notion that the Court must be guided by "evolving standards of decency that mark the progress of a maturing society," the Court deemed it relevant that virtually all states with a minimum age for the death penalty required the defendant to be at least 16 at the time of the offense and that since 1948 no jury had imposed the death penalty upon a person under 16. But the Court later held that there was no comparable national consensus sufficient to bar execution of a mentally retarded person with a mental age of seven, although upon revisiting that issue in *Atkins v. Va.* (2002) the Court held that execution of mentally retarded criminals constitutes cruel and unusual punishment prohibited by the Eighth Amendment. The Court in *Atkins* looked to what had happened since the earlier decision, particularly "the consistency of the direction of changes" brought about by state legislatures regarding this issue, and found a "consensus" that "unquestionably reflects widespread judgment about the relative culpability of mentally retarded offenders, and the relationship between mental retardation and the penological purposes served by the death penalty." (*Atkins* left to the states "the task of developing appropriate ways to enforce the constitutional restriction," and thus the Court later held in *Schriro v. Smith* (2005) that a federal habeas court erred in ordering the state in the instant case to hold a jury trial on the issue of mental retardation.) Similarly, in *Roper v. Simmons* (2005), overruling its prior opinion to the contrary, the Court held that the Eighth Amendment prohibits the execution of a juvenile who was under 18 when he committed his crime. The Court again relied upon "the objective indicia of national consensus" (here, the rejection of the juvenile death penalty in a majority of the states, the infrequent use of it elsewhere, and the consistency of the trend toward abolition), and then concluded that, given the diminished culpability of juveniles, neither of the two justifications for the death penalty—retribution and deterrence of capital crimes—provided adequate justification for imposing the death penalty on juveniles.

During the *Coker–Enmund* period, the Court on more than one occasion declined to strike down serious penalties other than death on lack-of-proportionality grounds. But then came *Solem v. Helm* (1983), in which the majority first concluded that the Eighth Amendment "principle that a criminal sentence must be proportionate to the crime for which the defendant has been convicted" was also applicable to felony prison sentences. Proportionality analysis, the Court next cautioned, "should be guided by objective criteria, including (i) the gravity of the offense and the harshness of the penalty; (ii) the sentences imposed on other criminals in the same jurisdiction; and (iii) the sentences imposed for commission of the same crime in other jurisdictions." In the instant case, Helm was convicted of uttering a "no account" check for $100, ordinarily punishable by a five year maximum term, but received a sentence of life imprisonment without parole under the state's recidivist statute because of his prior convictions for six felonies, all of which were minor and nonviolent and none of which was a crime against a person. The Court concluded:

> Applying objective criteria, we find that Helm has received the penultimate sentence for relatively minor criminal conduct. He has been treated more harshly than other criminals in the State who have committed more serious crimes. He has been treated more harshly than he would have been in any other jurisdiction, with the possible exception of a single State. We conclude that his sentence is significantly disproportionate to

his crime, and is therefore prohibited by the Eighth Amendment.

Solem is unlikely to result in the invalidation of many legislatively-determined prison terms; as the Court cautioned, "outside the context of capital punishment, *successful* challenges to the proportionality of particular sentences [will be] exceedingly rare." The first of the *Solem* objective factors, the relation between the gravity of the offense and the harshness of the penalty, is "least capable of objective measurement," but the complexity of the sentencing process is such that reviewing courts are properly cautioned "against injecting their value judgments into the details of legislative sentencing schemes." And in any event, each of the latter two *Solem* objective factors "also limits proportionality review in a manner designed to ensure that only objectively extreme sentences will be invalidated." It is not surprising, therefore, that the Court later rejected a proportionality claim directed at a statute mandating a life term upon conviction for possessing more than 650 grams of cocaine. (However, another part of the Eighth Amendment prohibits "excessive fines"; it "limits the Government's power to extract payments, whether in cash or in kind, as punishment for some offense," and thus necessitates proportionality review.)

If only one punishment is provided by law and that punishment is cruel and unusual, then the whole statute is unconstitutional. On the other hand, if the statute provides in the alternative for both proper punishment and cruel punishment, the statute is no doubt valid as to the proper part.

The third aspect of the constitutional ban on cruel and unusual punishment is that it bars the imposition of penal sanctions of any kind under certain circumstances. As such, the Eighth Amendment not only limits what legislatures may do by way of prescribing penalties for crime, but also what is permissible in terms of defining conduct as criminal. Thus, in *Robinson v. Cal.* (1962) the United States Supreme Court held unconstitutional a statute making it a crime for a person to "be addicted to the use of narcotics." The basis of the Court's decision in *Robinson* is not entirely clear, as emphasis was placed upon three different considerations: (1) the statute created a "status" crime, as it did not require proof of any antisocial conduct within the jurisdiction; (2) the statute made it a crime to suffer the "illness" of narcotics addiction; and (3) the statute made it a crime to suffer from an illness "which may be contracted innocently or involuntarily." Which of these three factors should be considered decisive is, of course, a matter of some importance in determining the implications of the *Robinson* decision.

The Court's emphasis upon the fact that the California statute permits conviction of a defendant "whether or not he has ever used or possessed any narcotics within the State, and whether or not he has been guilty of any antisocial behavior there" suggests that, at least, *Robinson* supports the proposition that crimes of status and personal condition are unconstitutional—a result which has been reached in other cases as a matter of substantive due process (see § 3.3(d)). It may well be, therefore, that many status crimes long recognized in American law, such as the crimes of being a vagrant, common prostitute, common drunkard, and disorderly person, inflict cruel and unusual punishment when interpreted to allow conviction without proof of the commission of some act. On the other hand, if this is all that *Robinson* means, then the scope of that decision is quite limited; it might be held, for example, that narcotics addiction is still punishable when proof of acts is required. In the later case of *Powell v. Tex.* (1968), four members of the Court interpreted *Robinson* as meaning merely that "criminal penalties may be inflicted only if the accused has committed some act * * * which society has an interest in preventing," arguing that were it otherwise the Supreme Court would be "the ultimate arbiter of the standards of criminal responsibility, in diverse areas of the criminal law, throughout the country." On that interpretation of *Robinson,* they concluded that Powell, a chronic alcoholic, was constitutionally convicted of being "found in a state of intoxication in any public place."

The emphasis of the Court in *Robinson* upon the fact that narcotics addiction is an illness has broader implications. From this it would seem to follow, as a few courts have held, that public intoxication cannot be punished when the defendant suffers from the illness of alcohol addiction, notwithstanding the fact that the offense requires an act of sorts—appearing in a public place while in an intoxicated condition. The Supreme Court reached a contrary result in *Powell,* although this was attributable in part to the fact that the record in the case revealed little about the defendant's drinking problem or the nature of alcoholism. As noted above, four members of the Court based the affirmance of Powell's conviction upon a narrow interpretation of *Robinson.* The four dissenting justices in *Powell,* on the other hand, saw *Robinson* as standing for this proposition: "Criminal penalties may not be inflicted upon a person for being in a condition which he is powerless to change." But lower courts have more recently held quite consistently that alcoholism is no defense to a charge of drunkenness.

If the Eighth Amendment prohibits the punishment of antisocial acts which are attributable to an illness, it is apparent that it is of some importance to determine precisely what sort of connection between the illness and the conduct is necessary. For example, does

Robinson prohibit conviction of narcotics addicts for using narcotics or for possessing narcotics for their own use? While lower courts have generally answered this question in the negative, it might be argued that the "illness" rationale of *Robinson* bars conviction for that conduct which is an inevitable consequence of the addiction. This is essentially the position of the dissenters in *Powell*, for they concede that public intoxication is not merely a crime of status, but argue that the defendant, once intoxicated, could not prevent himself from appearing in public places. Concurring Justice White, although concluding there was no showing Powell was unable to prevent himself from appearing in public while intoxicated, observed that "punishing an addict for using drugs convicts for addiction under a different name."

But, if possession and use of narcotics are inevitable for the addict, why cannot it also be said that the commission of other offenses—such as larceny, robbery, burglary, and prostitution—are likewise inevitable because they supply the funds necessary for the continued use of narcotics? It is apparent that courts will be reluctant to extend the cruel and unusual punishment doctrine this far, although it is difficult to articulate a principle upon which to justify not doing so if conviction for possession and use were deemed impermissible. The absence of such a principle is stressed in the opinion of the Court in *Powell*, but the dissenters argued that a constitutional bar on conviction of a chronic alcoholic for being intoxicated in public would not likewise bar conviction for such crimes as theft and robbery because they "are not part of the syndrome of the disease of chronic alcoholism."

The same difficulty is present when one considers the question of whether the *Robinson* decision does not compel the broadening of the definition of insanity to encompass all those who cannot control their behavior because of a mental disease or defect. In *Powell*, four members of the court argued that extension of *Robinson* to that case would have the unfortunate result of raising to constitutional dimension the issue of what test of insanity must be employed in the state courts.

By contrast, the third factor emphasized by the Court in *Robinson*, that addiction is an illness "which may be contracted innocently or involuntarily," probably should not be viewed as critical. It is true that reliance upon this factor would be a convenient way of limiting the reach of the *Robinson* decision. It is also true that such a limitation has some merit, at least in the sense that it identifies a class of cases in which the cruel and unusual punishment argument is most compelling: those in which the defendant was *at no time* at fault for creating his condition. However, the decision in *Robinson* cannot be said to rest upon this factor, as the Court struck down the addiction statute as to all cases rather than recognize that involuntary or innocent addiction could be put forward as a valid defense. None of the various views expressed in *Powell* question that conclusion.

§ 3.6 Other Limitations on the States

State criminal statutes may be found to suffer from constitutional defects other than those discussed in the previous sections. For one thing, state legislation may be challenged on the ground that it violates some provision of the state constitution. Most state constitutions have provisions comparable to those in the federal constitution dealing with due process, equal protection, and the guarantee of specific rights. While state courts often give these provisions essentially the same interpretation as their counterparts in the United States Constitution, they are sometimes construed more broadly, with the result that a state statute which would have withstood challenge before the United States Supreme Court is invalidated by a state court as contrary to the state constitution. In addition, a state criminal statute may be voided because it fails to satisfy certain formal requirements imposed by the state constitution. A number of state constitutions provide that the title of a statute must describe the body of the statute, that no more than one subject may be contained in one statute, and that the legislature must follow certain procedures in enacting bills into law. Such provisions are usually held to be mandatory, with the result that, if they are violated in the case of a criminal statute, the statute will be held unconstitutional. On the other hand, some relatively unimportant formal provisions (such as the rather common state constitutional provision that all statutes should be headed by the clause, "Be it enacted by [the legislature of the state]") have been held to be directory only, so that the failure of the legislature to comply therewith does not make the statute unconstitutional.

In addition, and because of the nature of our federal system, there are certain limitations in the United States Constitution that are applicable only to state legislation. For one thing, state legislatures are expressly forbidden to legislate on certain matters. The Constitution also gives the Congress the authority to legislate on certain subjects (e.g., "To regulate Commerce * * * among the several States"), which must be considered in connection with the provision that the constitution and laws of the United States made in pursuance thereof are the supreme law of the land, notwithstanding anything in the constitution or laws of any state. This gives rise to two difficult problems: (1) Where the Constitution gives Congress a regulatory power, but says nothing about denying such power to the states, may a state regulate on such matters when the Congress has not done so? (2) Where, again, the Constitution gives such power to Congress but does not deny it to the states, but the Congress has regulated on a particular subject, may a state adopt additional regulations on the same subject?

(a) Congress Has Not Acted: The Negative Implications of the Commerce Clause. As to the first of these two questions, the major battleground has been the commerce clause, and the Supreme Court has on innumerable occasions had to pass upon the competing interests of state and national power in the field of commerce—between the police power of the states, on the one hand, and the power of the national government to ensure freedom of interstate commerce, on the other. Many of the Supreme Court cases in this area of the law have involved civil matters, especially the power of the state to tax; but a number of the cases have involved criminal prosecutions for violation of state statutes which, while regulating local matters, also operate as regulations of interstate commerce. The Court has struck down some of these criminal statutes as unconstitutional burdens on interstate commerce.

Over the years, the Supreme Court has set forth a number of different tests for determining the validity of state laws in this context. After an early statement to the effect that the question was whether the particular subject called for uniform regulation or for diversity in regulation, the Court used many other expressions, such as whether the state law was a "burden," or a "substantial" or "undue" burden on commerce; whether the effect on commerce was "direct" or "indirect"; and whether the regulation was or was not imposed "on" interstate commerce itself. However, recently the Court has utilized a three-part inquiry: "(1) whether the challenged statute regulates evenhandedly with only 'incidental' effects on interstate commerce, or discriminates against interstate commerce either on its face or in practical effect; (2) whether the statute serves a legitimate local purpose; and, if so, (3) whether alternate means could promote this local purpose as well without discriminating against interstate commerce. The burden is on the person challenging the statute to show the discrimination against interstate commerce, and the state must then justify the local benefits and unavailability of alternatives.

Illustrative of laws that discriminate against interstate commerce are those which make it an offense to engage in conduct only with respect to goods coming from out of the state or only as to goods leaving the state, those which have "a sweeping extraterritorial effect," and those which bear disproportionately upon out-of-staters. With respect to legitimacy of purpose, it is relevant that the legislation was intended as a protectionist measure or that its contribution to some legitimate objective is speculative at best or minimal in relation to the burden imposed on interstate commerce. As for alternate means, it is of course particularly significant that the local interest could have been just as well protected by restrictions directed more to local activities.

The case of *Edwards v. Cal.* (1941) deserves special mention here, as, unlike almost all the other cases in this area, the concern was not with the regulation of business but rather with the right of individuals to move about. The Court reversed a conviction under a California statute which made it a misdemeanor for any person to bring "into the State any indigent person who is not a resident of the State, knowing him to be an indigent person," holding that an outright ban on immigration into a state by a class of "undesirables" is an undue burden on interstate commerce. On the basis of the *Edwards* decision and others, the Court now speaks of a "constitutional right to travel from one State to another," which appears to be derived from the commerce clause and other constitutional provisions as well, and which might well be used to strike down some current vagrancy statutes and similar criminal laws.

(b) Congress Has Acted: The Preemption Doctrine. A state criminal law, otherwise within the police power of the state, may be invalid because a federal law on the subject has "preempted" (or "occupied") the field to the exclusion of state law. "In the complex system of polity which prevails in this country, the powers of government may be divided into four classes: [1] Those which belong exclusively to the states; [2] Those which belong exclusively to the national government; [3] Those which may be exercised concurrently and independently by both; [4] Those which may be exercised by the states, but only until Congress shall see fit to act upon the subject." The sometimes difficult problem in this area of constitutional law is whether to place a particular state criminal statute within category 3 or category 4, when both a federal and state criminal statute deal with the same subject matter. The problem would be easier to solve if Congress expressly provided that its statute was to be exclusive or not; but it seldom does so.

Not infrequently a state criminal statute exists side by side with a federal statute, both punishing identical or substantially identical conduct. The state statute has often been upheld on the theory that the two statutes do not conflict with one another, and that Congress did not intend to make its law exclusive. The state statute is even more clearly valid if the conduct punished by the state and nation is parallel but not substantially identical. On the other hand, some state criminal legislation has been held unconstitutional under the supremacy clause on the theory that federal legislation has occupied the field. Thus a state perjury statute was held unconstitutional as applied to perjury committed in a federal hearing upon a contested Congressional election. A state statute punishing a banker for accepting a deposit knowing the bank to be insolvent was held invalid as applied to an officer of a national bank, because federal legislation on national banks impliedly indicated an intent to occupy the field to the exclusion of the states. And more recently a state sedition statute punishing advocacy of the violent overthrow of the government of the United States was held invalid in view of the specific federal statute punishing such conduct.

It is not always easy to distinguish the cases decided one way from those decided the other. As the Court has acknowledged, there is no "rigid formula or rule which can be used as a universal pattern to determine the meaning and purpose of every act of Congress. This Court, in considering the validity of state laws in the light of treaties or federal laws touching the same subject, has made use of the following expressions: conflicting; contrary to; occupying the field; repugnance; difference; irreconcilability; inconsistency; violation; curtailment; and interference. But none of these expressions provides an infallible constitutional test or an exclusive constitutional yardstick. In the final analysis, there can be no one crystal clear distinctly marked formula." However, in *Pa. v. Nelson* (1956) the Supreme Court set forth three tests for determining the preemption issue: (1) Is the federal legislative scheme as to the subject matter in question so pervasive as to indicate that Congress must have meant the states were not to supplement the federal legislation? (2) Is the federal interest in the subject matter so dominant that Congress must have meant to preclude the states from dealing with the matter? (3) Would state enforcement in the matter present a serious danger to effective federal enforcement?

Of these three questions, the first two most directly focus upon a determination of what Congress intended. However, in many cases an inquiry into the intent of Congress is not fruitful, as often Congress enacts legislation without anticipating the problem of preemption. It is undoubtedly true, therefore, that the Supreme Court has often invalidated state laws on a preemption theory (often by resort to "intent of Congress" analysis), when in fact Congress did *not* intend to nullify the concurrent jurisdiction of the states. However, although the Court has frequently been criticized on this basis, it can be said that often the result reached has been sound because it in fact rests upon a determination that the continued existence of the state law is not consistent with the general purpose of the federal statute, considering the evil Congress sought to remedy and the methods it chose for this purpose.

Also, it has been pointed out that the preemption decisions of the United States Supreme Court can be better understood if account is taken of the fact that preemption has become a "preferential ground" for decision in cases posing other serious constitutional questions. That is, state statutes are sometimes voided on the ground that they conflict with federal legislation when it might well be argued that, even in the absence of federal legislation, the state laws are unconstitutional. Preemption is often a more attractive ground for decision (in much the same way that void-for-vagueness often is, see § 3.1(a)) because it permits the Court to avoid another very difficult constitutional issue and the necessity of erecting permanent limits on the police power of the states. Thus, whether a state law will be held to be preempted may be influenced to some degree by the presence of other factors, such as:

(1) whether the state law may intrude into an area of exclusive national concern. As noted earlier, even when Congress has not acted, a state law may be invalidated because it intrudes upon an area of Congressional power, such as the power to regulate interstate commerce. When it appears that a substantial argument of this kind might be made, the chances are greater that the fact Congress has legislated will result in a finding of preemption. Thus, such a finding is often made to rest upon facts which have long been utilized to support a finding that the state law burdens interstate commerce, such as the entire halting of the flow of commerce to enforce compliance with state laws or the use of state laws to favor local economic interests. Similarly, in *Hines v. Davidowitz* (1941) a state alien registration law was voided on the ground that it was preempted by the federal alien registration act, but the Court placed considerable emphasis upon the fact that the subject matter appeared to be of exclusive national concern, as reflected in the constitutional provision granting Congress the power to prescribe "a uniform rule of naturalization" and the foreign relations power.

(2) whether the state law may result in the unfair imposition of multiple punishment. Although the double jeopardy clause does not prevent both the federal government and a state from punishing the same act, where that act constitutes a crime against both sovereigns, the thought that such double prosecution and punishment is not altogether fair may influence a finding of preemption. As the Court said in *Nelson*, "We are not unmindful of the risk of compounding punishments which would be created by finding concurrent state power." This factor is apt to receive greater consideration when the penalties provided under the two laws are severe.

(3) whether the state law may violate due process. A finding of preemption sometimes serves as a convenient means of striking down a statute that probably violates due process, as the Court has sometimes hinted. For example, in *Hines,* holding that a state alien registration law was preempted, the Court stressed that "it is also of importance that this legislation deals with the rights, liberties, and personal freedoms of human beings, and is in an entirely different category from state tax laws or state pure food laws regulating the labels on cans."

Chapter 4

MENTAL STATES

Table of Sections

§ 4.1   Generally

It is commonly stated that a crime consists of both a physical part and a mental part; that is, both an act or omission (and sometimes also a prescribed result of action or omission, or prescribed attendant circumstances, or both) and a state of mind. This section discusses generally what is required of crimes in the way of the mental part, variously called *mens rea* ("guilty mind") or *scienter* or criminal intent. The following sections will discuss the various types of *mens rea* in greater detail, including the significance of a defendant's ignorance or mistake of fact or law.

Actually, the terms "mental part" and *"mens rea"* and "state of mind" are somewhat too narrow to be strictly accurate, for they include matters that are not really mental at all. Thus we shall see that, though many crimes do require some sort of mental fault (i.e., a bad mind), other crimes (which are commonly said to require *mens rea*) require only some sort of fault that is not mental. The unadorned word "fault" is thus a more accurate word to describe what crimes generally require in addition to their physical elements.

(a) Common Law and Statutory Crimes. During the early days of the development of common law crimes, the judges often declared conduct to be criminal that did not include any bad state of mind. But in more recent times (i.e., since about 1600), the judges have generally defined common law crimes in terms which require, in addition to prescribed action or omission, some prescribed bad state of mind, although that state of mind has differed from one common law crime to another. The basic premise that for criminal liability some *mens rea* is required is expressed by the Latin maxim *actus not facit reum nisi mens sit rea* (an act does not make one guilty unless his mind is guilty). The words and phrases used by the judges to express the bad mind necessary for common law crimes include "maliciously" (as in murder, arson, malicious mischief), "fraudulently" (forgery), "feloniously" (larceny), "wilfully and corruptly" (perjury), and "with intent to ... " (e.g., "with intent to steal," another phrase used in defining larceny; "with intent to commit a felony therein," in burglary).

Most crimes today, of course, are statutory crimes. In most jurisdictions common law crimes have been abolished; in others common law crimes are sparingly used. In all jurisdictions most of the common law crimes have been stated in the form of statutory law. And of course, in modern times, new statutory crimes, unknown to the common law, far outnumber the relatively few common law crimes originally created by the judges. The "mental" aspects of statutory crimes may be roughly classified as follows as to type:

(1) Many statutes defining conduct that is criminal employ words (usually adverbs) or phrases indicating some type of bad-mind requirement: "intentionally" or "with intent to ... "; "knowingly" or "with knowledge that ... "; "purposely" or "for the purpose of ... "; "fraudulently" or "with intent to defraud"; "wilfully"; "maliciously"; "corruptly"; "designedly"; "recklessly"; "wantonly"; "unlawfully"; "feloniously" and so on. (2) Some of the statutes use words or phrases indicating a requirement of fault, but not necessarily mental fault—e.g., "negligently", "carelessly", or "having reason to know ... " (3) Some statutes define criminal conduct without any words or phrases indicating any express requirement of fault; thus "whoever does so-and-so (or: whoever omits to do so-and-so) is guilty of a crime and subject to the following punishment ..." However, although the statute may contain no adverbs or phrases indicating a requirement of fault, some fault may be inherent in a verb that the statute employs (e.g., whoever "refuses" to do something or "permits" another to do something.)

It may be said of statutory crimes that, so far as the mental element is concerned, (1) some crimes (like most of the common law crimes) require "subjective fault"—actually a bad mind of some sort; (2) others require only "objective fault"—fault which is not a matter of the mind; and (3) others require no fault at all, either subjective (mental) or objective (non-mental), such statutes providing instead for "liability without fault." To illustrate: (1) The statutory crime of receiving stolen property is generally worded in terms of receiving stolen property "knowing the property to be stolen." Such wording requires that the defendant, to be guilty, must know in his own mind (i.e., subjectively) that the property he receives is stolen. If he does not know but ought to know—that is, if a reasonable man in his position would know—that the property is stolen, his objective fault in not knowing what he should know is insufficient for guilt, since a statute so worded clearly requires subjective fault. (2) If, however, the statute reads "having reason to know" the property to be stolen, instead of "knowing" that fact, an objective standard of guilt is set up, and he is guilty, though he does not know, if a reasonable man would have known that the property is stolen. (3) And if the statute reads, "Whoever receives stolen property," without anything further about either "knowing" or "having reason to know," he is, literally at least, guilty when he receives property which is actually stolen, even if he does not know, and reasonably does not know, that the property he receives is stolen property.

(b) Ambiguity as to Requisite Mental State. Much of the difficulty involved in ascertaining what, if any, state of mind is required for a particular crime lies in the ambiguous meaning of the particular word or phrase used. Even "knowingly" is not entirely clear; for instance, does one know a fact (e.g., that property is stolen) when he is 95% sure of it but not completely certain? An even more ambiguous word, but one that legislatures often use in criminal statutes, is "wilfully." "Maliciously" in the definitions of crimes is also a word of many meanings, as is the word "wanton" or the word "corruptly." Least helpful of all are words like "unlawfully" and "feloniously"; statutes using such words say in effect that one is guilty of a crime if he does some defined act or omission guiltily.

Still further difficulty arises from the ambiguity that frequently exists concerning what the words or phrases in question modify. What, for instance, does "knowingly" modify in a sentence from a "blue sky" law criminal statute punishing one who "knowingly sells a security without a permit" from the securities commissioner? To be guilty must the seller of a security without a permit know only that what he is doing constitutes a sale, or must he also know that the thing he sells is a security, or must he also know that he has no permit to sell the security he sells? As a matter of grammar the statute is ambiguous; it is not at all clear how far down the sentence the word "knowingly" is intended to travel—whether it modifies "sells," or "sells a security," or "sells a security without a permit." But, as noted in *Flores-Figueroa v. U.S.* (2009), "courts ordinarily read a phrase in a criminal statute that introduces the elements of a crime with the word 'knowingly' as applying that word to each element."

Yet other difficulty arises when the statute in question contains no mental state words at all. One possibility, considered in more detail later (§ 4.5(a)), is that the statute may fairly be construed as imposing strict liability—that is, liability without any kind of mental state whatsoever. If such a construction is not appropriate, then there remains the question of what mental state should be read into the statute. In such circumstances, courts have often said that a "general intent" is needed, but this is often not helpful because of the ambiguity attending that phrase (see

§ 4.2(e)). Model Penal Code § 2.02(3) solves the latter problem by providing that any of the subjective mental states will suffice.

(c) Basic Types of Mental State. The difficulties inherent in such a variety of expressions as to *mens rea* as is used by the common law and by statutes in defining crimes have led modern thinkers to classify the mental aspects of crime into a few general types; and to urge that, in drafting penal codes, a single expression be used to express a single type of *mens rea* culpability. Model Penal Code § 2.02(2) has thus reduced the matter to four basic types of crimes that require fault: (1) crimes requiring *intention* (or *purpose*) to do the forbidden act (omission) or cause the forbidden result; (2) crimes requiring *knowledge* of the nature of the act (omission) or of the result which will follow therefrom or of the attendant circumstances; (3) those requiring *recklessness* in doing the act (omission) or causing the result (subjective fault in that the actor must in his own mind realize the risk which his conduct involves); and (4) those requiring only *negligence* in so doing or causing (objective fault in creating an unreasonable risk; but, since the actor need not realize the risk in order to be negligent, no subjective fault is required). Most of the modern criminal codes expressly provide for these four basic types of culpability. Of course, there remains the possibility that, for some crimes or for some elements of a crime, a statute may impose strict liability.

Model Penal Code § 2.02(4) deals with the troublesome problem of whether a given culpability requirement applies to all elements of the offense. It provides that when the law defining the offense prescribes the kind of culpability that is sufficient without distinguishing among the material elements thereof, then it is to apply to all the material elements unless a contrary purpose plainly appears in the statute.

(d) Differing Mens Rea Requirements for a Single Crime. Aside from the mental element, we have seen that many crimes are made up not of one but of several physical elements, including not only an act or omission, but also some specific result of that act or omission, or some prescribed attendant circumstances, or perhaps both result and circumstances. Thus the crime of murder requires (aside from its mental ingredients) not only some act or omission (e.g., shooting a gun, wielding an axe, or failing to pull one's infant child out of a bathtub full of water) but also a particular result thereof (the death of the victim). It may properly be said also that lack of justification, such as the justification of self-defense, is a required attendant circumstance in a case where the defendant raises the issue of justification in his defense.

It should be noted that the mental ingredients of a particular crime may differ with regard to the different elements of the crime. Thus in the case of intent-to-kill murder, where the defendant's defense is that he killed in self-defense, the element of conduct causing death requires the intention type of *mens rea* on the part of the defendant; but the element of lack-of-self-defense-justification requires only negligence on his part (i.e., that he unreasonably believed it was necessary to kill to save himself). One might imagine a carefully drafted statutory crime worded: "Whoever sells intoxicating liquor to one whom he knows to be a policeman and whom he should know to be on duty" is guilty of a misdemeanor. Such a statute, aside from its *mens rea* aspects, covers several different physical elements—(1) the sale (2) of intoxicating liquor (3) to a policeman (4) who is on duty. As to elements (1) and (2), the statute evidently provides for liability without fault: if he in fact sells intoxicating liquor it is no defense that he either reasonably or unreasonably thinks he is making a gift rather than a sale, or thinks he is selling Coca–Cola rather than whiskey. As to element (3), however, the statute requires the seller to have actual knowledge that the purchaser is a policeman; so a reasonable or even unreasonable belief that he is a fireman would be a defense. As to element (4), a negligence type of fault is all that is required; a reasonable belief that the policeman is off duty is a defense, but an unreasonable belief is not.

Thus with the various crimes—whether the old common law crimes or the newer statutory crimes not known to the common law—it must be recognized that there may be different *mens rea* requirements as to the different physical elements that go to make up these crimes.

(e) Mental State and the General Principles of Criminal Law. In chapters 6, 8 and 9 consideration is given to the various general principles of criminal law of the defense-to-liability type: insanity, infancy, intoxication, coercion, necessity, consent, self-defense, entrapment and the like. As we shall see, some of these principles operate, when applicable, to eliminate the mental element that a specific crime requires. Thus a defendant's insanity or infancy or extreme intoxication, if any such matter exists, may similarly negative the existence of the necessary mental element that larceny requires. Thus these chapters necessarily deal in some detail with the mental aspects of crime.

The same may be said for the affirmative-liability principles concerning the responsibility of parties to crime and concerning liability for inchoate crimes. Special problems regarding the mental state requirement are often confronted in determining whether a person is a party to a crime committed by another or whether an inchoate offense, such as an attempt, has occurred. Thus chapters 10, 11 and 12 on these subjects will also give attention to the mental aspects of crime.

In chapters 13 through 16 of this book, dealing with the elements of specific crimes rather than with general principles, we shall consider what are the *mens rea* requirements for each of the crimes considered, as well as the physical requirements for those crimes.

§ 4.2   Intent and Knowledge

The meaning of the word "intent" in the criminal law has always been rather obscure, largely as a result of its use in such phrases as "criminal intent," "general intent," "specific intent," "constructive intent," and "presumed intent." Intent has traditionally been defined to include knowledge, and thus it is usually said that one intends certain consequences when he desires that his acts cause those consequences or knows that those consequences are substantially certain to result from his acts. The modern view, however, is that it is better to draw a distinction between intent (or purpose) on the one hand and knowledge on the other.

(a) The Traditional View of Intent. A crime may be defined in such a way that the defendant, to be guilty of it, must intentionally engage in specific conduct (and, perhaps also, intentionally do so under specified attendant circumstances, the intention requirement applying to the circumstances as well), or a crime may be defined in terms of an intention to produce a specified result. Illustrative of the latter are intent-to-kill murder, which requires that a person intend to kill another human being; intent-to-injure battery, which requires that he intend to do bodily injury to another; assault with intent to kill, which requires that he intend to kill the one assaulted; false pretenses, which requires that he intend to deceive his victim; and treason, which requires that he intend to aid the enemy.

The following are examples of the former type of crime: common-law burglary, which requires that the burglar intentionally engage in the conduct of breaking and entering, and perhaps also that he intend that the building thus broken into be a dwelling house; larceny, which requires that the thief intentionally engage in the conduct of taking and carrying away property; and forcible rape, which requires that the rapist intend to engage in sexual intercourse, and perhaps also that he intend to engage in it with a woman not his wife. Although it is true that burglary is not generally expressly defined as "intentionally breaking and entering," etc., larceny as "intentionally taking and carrying away," etc., or rape as "intentionally having sexual intercourse," etc., such an intention is nevertheless a requirement for each of these crimes. Sometimes it is spoken of as a "general intent" to distinguish it from the "specific intent" that a crime may specifically, by its definition, require, over and above any required intention to engage in the forbidden conduct (as burglary requires a specific intent to commit a felony, larceny a specific intent to steal).

With crimes which require that the defendant intentionally cause a specific result, what is meant by an "intention" to cause that result? Although the theorists have not always been in agreement as to the answer to this question, the traditional view is that a person who acts (or omits to act) intends a result of his act (or omission) under two quite different circumstances: (1) when he consciously desires that result, whatever the likelihood of that result happening from his conduct; and (2) when he knows that that result is practically certain to follow from his conduct, whatever his desire may be as to that result.

Thus, to take the first of these circumstances, if A shoots B at such a distance that his chances of hitting and killing him are small, but with the desire of killing him, he intends to kill him; and if by good luck the bullet hits B in a vital spot, A will be held to have intended to kill B, sufficient for guilt of murder of the intent-to-kill variety. Or, if C fails to pull his infant child D off the railroad tracks, desiring to cause D 's death thereby, C intends to kill D though he realizes that the chances are great that someone else will save the child or that the child will crawl away before the next train is due to arrive.

As to the second of the two circumstances listed above, this would cover the case in which E, for the purpose of killing his mother F for her life insurance, places a time bomb on a plane he knows is carrying both F and G. E has an intent to kill G because, though he may regret the necessity of killing G and thus not desire that result, he knows that the death of G is substantially certain to follow from his act. Or if H, who has a legal duty to act affirmatively to aid J in peril, fails to unlock the farmhouse door upon which J is knocking during a blizzard, knowing that J is practically certain to perish in the storm if the door remains locked, H intends to kill J even though he may wish that J by some miracle survive. "Practical" or "substantial" certainty of the result rather than "absolute" certainty is all that is required; H is nonetheless guilty of J's murder (of the intent-to-kill type) though he knows there may be a slight possibility that someone else will happen by in time to rescue J, or that J can make it to another farm without perishing on the way.

Although the matter has received less attention, it would appear that an intention to engage in certain conduct or to do so under certain attendant circumstances may likewise be said to exist on the basis of what one knows. A thief may be said to intentionally take and carry away property when he knowingly does so. And, assuming for the moment that burglary is viewed as requiring that the burglar intend to break and enter some building and also that he intend to do so into a dwelling house, the requirement of intention as to circumstances is satisfied if he knows the building in question to be a dwelling. (Perhaps because it is more apparent that knowledge rather than desire is most significant as to attendant circumstances, it is common for statutes to be drafted in terms of knowledge of these circumstances. Thus, statutes defining the crime of receiving stolen property usually say "knowing the property to be stolen," and statutes on issuing bad checks often say "knowing he has insufficient funds on deposit in the bank" to cover the check.)

(b) The Modern View: Intent and Knowledge Distinguished. As concluded above, the word "intent" in the substantive criminal law has traditionally not been limited to the narrow, dictionary definition of purpose, aim, or design, but instead has often been viewed as encompassing much of what would ordinarily be described as knowledge. This failure to distinguish between intent (strictly defined) and knowledge is probably of little consequence in many areas of the law, as often there is good reason for imposing liability whether the defendant desired or merely knew of the practical certainty of the results. Yet, because there are several areas of the criminal law in which there may be good reason for distinguishing between one's objectives and knowledge, the modern approach is to define separately the mental states of knowledge and intent (sometimes referred to as purpose, most likely to avoid confusion with the word "intent" as traditionally defined). This is the approach taken in Model Penal Code § 2.02(2)(a) & (b).

Thus, as to the results of one's conduct, the Code provides that one acts "purposely" when "it is his conscious object * * * to cause such a result," while one acts "knowingly" if "he is aware that it is practically certain that his conduct will cause such a result." (The former, of course, may exist without the latter.) One is said to act "purposely" as to the nature of his conduct if "it is his conscious object to engage in conduct of that nature," and to act "knowingly" as to the nature of his conduct if "he is aware that his conduct is of that nature." As to the attendant circumstances, one acts "purposely" when "he is aware of the existence of such circumstances or he believes or hopes that they exist," while one acts "knowingly" when "he is aware * * * that such circumstances exist."

Although the foregoing provisions contemplate that one "knows" of present (as opposed to future) events only if he is actually aware of them, an important exception is recognized elsewhere in the Code. This exception has to do with what is commonly termed "wilful blindness," "where it can almost be said that the defendant actually knew," as when a person "has his suspicion aroused but then deliberately omits to make further inquiries, because he wishes to remain in ignorance." Illustrative is *U. S. v. Jewell* (1976), where the evidence was that the defendant was paid $100 to drive a truck with a secret compartment into the United States from Mexico and that he deliberately refrained from looking into the compartment and ascertaining whether there were drugs inside. "Whether such cases should be viewed as instances of acting recklessly or knowingly presents a subtle but important question." The notion that it is properly classified as knowledge in the hierarchy of mental states is grounded in the conclusion "that deliberate ignorance and positive knowledge are equally culpable."

This conclusion is most convincing if the "wilful blindness" category is rather narrowly circumscribed. Such is the case in Model Penal Code § 2.02(7), which states that when "knowledge of the existence of a particular fact is an element of an offense, such knowledge is established if a person is aware of a high probability of its existence, unless he actually believes that it does not exist." Very few of the modern recodifications contain a provision of this type, though it is noteworthy that even in the absence of such an enactment some courts have construed the mental state of knowledge as including such a situation. The Model Penal Code requirement of awareness of a high probability of the existence of the fact serves to ensure that the purpose to avoid learning the truth is culpable. As for the Model Penal Code exception where the defendant actually believes the fact does not exist, it assures that the defendant is not convicted "on an objective theory of knowledge," for example, in *Jewell* "that a reasonable man should have inspected the car and would have discovered what was hidden inside."

It should be noted, however, that the word "knowledge"—used in criminal statutes with some frequency—has not always been interpreted as having the meaning given in the Model Penal Code. Just as we have seen that the word "intent" has not been limited to its dictionary definition, it is also true that the word "knowledge" has likewise sometimes been given a broader definition. Cases have held that one has knowledge of a given fact when he has the means for obtaining such knowledge, when he has notice of facts which would put one on inquiry as to the existence of that fact, when he has information sufficient to generate a reasonable belief as to that fact, or when the circumstances are such that a reasonable man would believe that such a fact existed. Sometimes belief in the existence of an attendant circumstance is deemed sufficient, sometimes it is not. While these decisions, at least in some instances, may have resulted in the setting of desirable limits on the mental state required for various crimes, they have led to considerable confusion because the word "knowledge" has been taken to mean many different things—all the way down to mere negligence in not knowing. But all these variations have to do with the extent of the defendant's understanding of the facts; to "knowingly" engage in certain conduct proscribed by a criminal statute does not require that the conduct be done with knowledge of its illegality.

(c) Disparity Between Intended and Actual Result. With crimes that require that the defendant intentionally cause a forbidden result, it not infrequently happens that there is a difference between the result he intends and the result he achieves, which gives rise to a question as to his criminal liability in such a case. There are four general types of cases:

(1) Unintended Victim. Perhaps the result intended (e.g., harm to the person or harm to property) is exactly as intended except that it happens to someone other than the intended victim. A aims his gun at his enemy B with intent to kill B but, missing, hits and kills A's friend C instead. A throws a rock at B intended to injure B but, missing again, hits and injures D instead. A aims a brick at B's car with intent to damage it, but he misses again, hitting E's car, parked next to B's, and damaging it. Or A sets fire to a wheat field intending to burn B's farm house, but the wind shifts and F's farm house is burned instead. In these cases the problem is whether A is criminally liable for the murder of C, the battery to D, the malicious injury to E's car, or for arson for the burning of F's house.

(2) Unintended Manner. Perhaps the end result that the defendant succeeds in producing is exactly as intended, but it is achieved in an unintended manner. A aims a gun at B's heart with intent to kill, but his aim is bad and he hits B's head, killing him. Or A shoots B with intent to kill, but only wounds him; however, in his weakened condition B catches pneumonia and dies; or a doctor so carelessly treats the wound that an infection sets in, so that B dies; or B catches scarlet fever from a fellow patient at the hospital and dies. Or A shoots at B, with intent to kill, and misses completely; but this unnerving experience causes B to go the long route home, during the course of which he is run over and killed by a truck negligently operated. In each case, A intended to kill B, and the end result was B's death, and B's death would not have occurred but for A's conduct in trying to kill B. But is A criminally liable for murder when the result happens in an unintended manner?

(3) Unintended Type of Harm. Perhaps the result achieved differs from the result intended as to type of harm, as where *A* throws a rock at *B* with intent to injure *B* but misses, unintentionally breaking *B*'s (or *C*'s) window. Is he guilty of the malicious destruction of the window? Or he throws the rock at the window and instead hits the person. Is he guilty of a battery?

(4) Unintended Degree of Harm. Perhaps the result achieved differs from the result intended as to the degree of harm. For example, *A* strikes *B* with a stick, intending only to injure him, but the blow brings about *B*'s death. Is *A* guilty of murder? Or, the situation may be somewhat the reverse; *A* strikes *B* with intent to kill him, but the only result is bodily injury. Of what crime, if any, is *A* guilty under these circumstances?

The first of these situations is often discussed in terms of mental state: it is said that the principle of "transferred intent" applies, so that, for example, *A*'s intent to kill *B* is transferred to *C*, who was actually killed as a result of *A*'s conduct. Actually, it is probably more correct to say that the crime merely requires an intent to kill another, so that there is no problem as to mental state, and no need to resort to the fiction of "transferred intent." Rather, the question is whether the fact a different person was killed somehow makes it unfair to impose criminal liability for murder on *A*, a problem that is more appropriately dealt with as a matter of causation. The same is true of the second situation; the fact the intended result came about in an unexpected manner raises the policy question of whether it is therefore unfair to impose liability on *A*. Because these are matters of causation, they will be dealt with later in § 5.4(d), (f).

The third situation, which concerns an unintended type of harm, might also be discussed in terms of causation, although it seems better to deal with the problem as a matter of the required concurrence between the mental state and harm (see § 5.3(d)). As we shall see, the rule is that ordinarily an intention to cause one type of harm cannot serve as a substitute for the statutory or common-law requirement of intention as to another type of harm. Two notable exceptions are felony-murder and misdemeanor-manslaughter, where the commission of a certain type of felony or misdemeanor will supply the only necessary mental state to support a homicide conviction; here, problems of causation must be confronted (see § 5.4(h)). As to the fourth situation, where the harm caused is of a different degree than intended, the issue might be discussed either in terms of concurrence of mental state and results (particularly when the harm done is greater than intended) or as a question of causation (particularly when the harm done is less than intended). It is dealt with herein as a matter of concurrence (see § 5.3(e)).

(d) Conditional and Multiple Intentions. Where a crime is defined so as to require that the defendant have a particular intention in his mind—as larceny requires that he have an intention to deprive the owner permanently of his property, burglary that he have an intention to commit a felony, and assault with intent to kill that he have an intention to kill—the problem arises whether he has the required intention when his intention is conditional. Thus A takes and carries away B's property intending to restore it to B if A's dying aunt should leave him a fortune. A breaks and enters B's house intending to rape Mrs. B if he finds her at home alone. A points a gun at B telling him he will shoot him unless he removes his overalls, and intending to kill B if he does not comply. Perhaps A's aunt does actually leave him the fortune; and Mrs. B is away from home; and B does remove his overalls. In these cases A is guilty of larceny, burglary, and assault with intent to kill, respectively.

But the condition in some circumstances may be such as to exclude liability. Thus A will not be guilty of larceny if his intention, when taking and carrying away B's property, is to return it if it proves to be B's property, but to keep it if it turns out to be A's own property. Model Penal Code § 2.02(6) sums it up by saying that where a crime requires the defendant to have a specified intention, he has the required intention although it is a conditional intention, "unless the condition negatives the harm or evil sought to be prevented by the law defining the offense." For one to take another's property intending to give it back if he inherits other property involves a condition that does not negative the evil which larceny seeks to prevent; but taking it intending to restore it if it is not his own property does involve a condition which negatives that evil. By like reasoning, the Supreme Court, applying the "core principle * * * that a defendant may not negate a proscribed intent by requiring the victim to comply with a condition the defendant has no right to impose," held in *Holloway v. U.S.* (1999) that the intent requirement in the federal carjacking statute is satisfied by proof that, at the moment the defendant demanded or took control over the driver's automobile, he possessed the conditional intent to seriously harm or kill the driver if necessary to steal the car.

A person often acts with two or more intentions. These intentions may consist of an immediate intention (intent) and an ulterior one (motive, discussed in § 4.3), as where the actor takes another's money intending to steal it and intending then to use it to buy food for his needy family. Sometimes the two intentions are not so distinguishable, but rather are two immediate intentions, as where a man transports a girl across the state line intending that she should on arrival at their destination work as a waitress in the daytime and as a prostitute at night. It may be said that, so long as the defendant has the intention required by the definition of the crime, it is immaterial that he may also have had some other intention. So too, it is possible for a defendant simultaneously to have a primary objective and a secondary, fallback objective even if the two are in a sense inconsistent, as where the defendant assaults a victim intending that the victim die but at the same time intending that if the victim does not die he at least be maimed.

(e) "Criminal," "Constructive," "General," and "Specific" Intent. Much of the existing uncertainty as to the precise meaning of the word "intent" is attributable to the fact that courts have often used such phrases as "criminal intent," "general intent," "specific intent," "constructive intent," and "presumed intent." "Criminal intent," for example, is often taken to be synonymous with *mens rea,* the general notion that except for strict liability offenses some form of mental state is a prerequisite to guilt. As a result, the phrase "criminal intent" is sometimes used to refer to criminal negligence or recklessness. Similarly, the notion of "constructive intent" has been used by some courts; it is first asserted that intent is required for all crimes, and then it is added that such intent may be inferred from recklessness or negligence. It would make for clearer analysis if courts would merely acknowledge that for some crimes intent is not needed and that recklessness or negligence will suffice.

As we shall see, where the definition of a crime requires some forbidden act by the defendant, his bodily movement, to qualify as an act, must be voluntary (see § 5.1(c)). To some extent, then, all crimes of affirmative action require something in the way of a mental element—at least an intention to make the bodily movement that constitutes the act which the crime requires. So too with crimes of omission; the defendant must ordinarily know (sometimes, should know) the facts indicating the necessity of action in order to be criminally liable for his omission (see § 5.2(b)). To this extent, crimes of omission also ordinarily require some sort of mental element (knowledge, or negligence in not knowing). We shall later see that some of the broad defenses to criminal liability (especially insanity, infancy, and involuntary intoxication) operate, when applicable, to relieve the actor from liability because these conditions negative his mental capacity to commit any crime. These notions are sometimes summed up with the expression that all crimes require a "general intent," although the phrase "general intent" is also used on occasion for other purposes as well.

"General intent" is often distinguished from "specific intent," although the distinction being drawn by the use of these two terms often varies. Sometimes "general intent" is used in the same way as "criminal intent" to mean the general notion of *mens rea,* while "specific intent" is taken to mean the mental state required for a particular crime. Or, "general intent" may be used to encompass all forms of the mental state requirement, while "specific intent" is limited to the one mental state of intent. Another possibility is that "general intent" will be used to characterize an intent to do something on an undetermined occasion, and "specific intent" to denote an intent to do that thing at a particular time and place.

However, the most common usage of "specific intent" is to designate a special mental element that is required above and beyond any mental state required with respect to the *actus reus* of the crime. Common law larceny, for example, requires the taking and carrying away of the property of another, and the defendant's mental state as to this act must be established, but in addition it must be shown that there was an "intent to steal" the property (see § 16.5). Similarly, common law burglary requires a breaking and entry into the dwelling of another, but in addition to the mental state connected with these acts it must also be established that the defendant acted "with intent to commit a felony therein." The same situation prevails with many statutory crimes: assault "with intent to kill" as to certain aggravated assaults; confining another "for the purpose of ransom or reward" in kidnapping; making an untrue statement "designedly, with intent to defraud" in the crime of false pretenses; etc. Likewise, criminal attempts require proof of an intent to bring about the consequences set forth in the crime attempted, and this is so even though no such intent is required for the completed crime. Those intents are all of the specific intent variety, while by comparison general intent is only the "intention to make the bodily movement which constitutes the act which the crime requires."

This distinction between "general intent" and "specific intent" is not without importance in the criminal law. For example, the traditional view is that the rules on when mistake of fact or mistake of law will constitute a defense differ depending upon what kind of intent is involved (see § 4.6). Also, some courts have taken the view that the partial responsibility doctrine applies only to specific intent crimes, and some others take the view that intent may be presumed (discussed below) only as to a general intent. It has been suggested, however, that greater clarity could be accomplished by abandoning the "specific intent"-"general intent" terminology, and this has been done in the Model Penal Code.

(f) Proof of Intention ("Presumed Intent"). A maxim much used in criminal law cases states that a person is "presumed to intend the natural and probable consequences of his acts." Thus if *A* fires a gun in the vicinity of *B,* and his bullet kills *B,* it is said that *A* is presumed to have intended the killing of *B* if the circumstances are such that B's death is "natural and probable." If this is taken as a rule of substantive law, it is apparent that it would in effect destroy the concept of intention and replace it entirely with negligence. This is because the defendant would be held to have intended whatever a reasonable man would have foreseen as probable.

In the illustration given above, it certainly will not do to conclude conclusively, from the mere fact that A's bullet killed B, that A intended that result, even though such a result was the foreseeable result of shooting. A may actually have meant to kill B; but he may have intended only to wound B; or he may have intended to miss him completely, wishing only to scare him; or he may have been simply negligent, having no intent to kill, wound or scare. By the same token, it should not be said that the conclusion that A intended to kill *must* be reached in the absence of counter-proof showing that A had no such intent; the so-called presumption of intent does not impose upon the accused any duty to produce evidence. Rather, it merely means that the fact-finder *may* (but need not) conclude under those circumstances that A intended to kill B. Thus the matter is reduced to an inference (or "permissive presumption") rather than a true presumption of the mandatory sort.

The Supreme Court concluded as much in *Sandstrom v. Mont.* (1979). The defendant there was charged with deliberate homicide, which under Montana law consisted of purposely or knowingly causing the death of another. The jury was instructed in accordance with Montana law that the "law presumes that a person intends the ordinary consequences of his voluntary acts." The defendant was convicted, but his conviction was overturned by the Supreme Court on the ground that this instruction violated "the Fourteenth Amendment's requirement that the State prove every element of a criminal offense beyond a reasonable doubt." The state first argued that the instruction "merely described a permissive inference." A cautious instruction of that type would have been permissible, but that clearly was not what had occurred. As the Court correctly noted, the jurors "were not told that they had a choice, or that they might infer that conclusion; they were told only that the law presumed it." The Court likewise rejected the state's claim the instruction merely placed a burden of production on the defendant, properly noting that the jurors were never told that the presumption could be rebutted.

Rather, the Court continued in *Sandstrom,* the jury might "have interpreted the instruction in either of two more stringent ways": one possibility was that the jury took the instruction as "an irrebuttable direction by the court to find intent once convinced of the facts triggering the presumption," and the other was that the jury interpreted the instruction "to find upon proof of the defendant's voluntary actions (and their 'ordinary' consequences), unless *the defendant* proved the contrary." A conclusive presumption here, the Court noted in *Sandstrom,* would be unconstitutional because it "would 'conflict with the overriding presumption of innocence with which the law endows the accused and which extends to every element of the crime,' and would 'invade [the] factfinding function' which in a criminal case the law assigns solely to the jury." Similarly, a presumption that shifted the burden of proof would be unconstitutional as infringing upon the due process requirement that "a State must prove every ingredient of an offense beyond a reasonable doubt."

It is not always easy to prove at a later date the state of a man's mind at that particular earlier moment when he was engaged in conduct causing or threatening harm to the interests of others. He does not often contemporaneously speak or write out his thoughts for others to hear or read. He will not generally admit later to having the intention that the crime requires. So of course his thoughts must be gathered from his words (if any) and actions in the light of all the surrounding circumstances. Naturally, what he does and what foreseeably results from his deeds have a bearing on what he may have had in his mind.

Of course, the defendant, if he elects to take the witness stand, is allowed to testify to what was in his mind at the time he engaged in his harmful conduct. The jury may not believe him, however, if his words and acts in the light of all the circumstances make his explanation seem improbable. Thus, if *A,* charged with murdering *B* on the intent-to-kill theory, testifies that he intended only to scare *B,* but the evidence of bystanders and others show that he was an expert marksman, that he was standing close to *B* when he fired, that he took careful aim before firing, and that his bullets pierced *B* five times in vital areas of his body—under all the circumstances the jury might well disbelieve his testimony and conclude that he meant to kill *B.* This would be especially so if *A* had yelled, just before shooting, "I'll kill you, *B,*" or, without any such words, if it were shown that he had a solid reason for wishing *B* dead.

The legislature sometimes creates statutory presumptions to aid the prosecution in proving the mental side of the crime, including a required intention. Thus it may be provided that it is a crime to give a bad check with intent to defraud, and that nonpayment of the check for lack of funds on deposit gives rise to a presumption that the check-giver intended to defraud. Such a statute provides for more than an inference (or "permissive presumption"); it provides instead for a true presumption of the "mandatory" type, discussed elsewhere herein (see § 3.4).

§ 4.3 Motive

A defendant's motive, if narrowly defined to exclude recognized defenses and the "specific intent" requirements of some crimes, is not relevant on the substantive side of the criminal law. On the procedural side, a motive for committing a crime is relevant in proving guilt when the evidence of guilt is circumstantial, and a good motive may result in leniency by those who administer the criminal process.

(a) Relevance in the Substantive Criminal Law. It is often said that motive is immaterial in the substantive criminal law, and that the most laudable motive is no defense while a bad motive cannot make an otherwise innocent act criminal. On the other hand, it has sometimes been claimed that the substantive law frequently takes account of good and bad motives. These differing viewpoints, it would seem, are attributable to disagreement as to what is meant by the word "motive" and how it differs from "intention," a matter that has caused the theorists considerable difficulty for years. Motive has been variously defined as "the desire coupled with the intention to bring about a certain consequence as an end, by means of other consequences which are also desired and intended but only as means," as "a desire viewed in its relation to a particular action, to the carrying out of which it urges or prompts," and as "ulterior intention—the intention with which an intentional act is done (or, more clearly, the intention with which an intentional consequence is brought about)."

Perhaps because these definitions are less than completely satisfying, it is typical to clarify the definition with an illustration, such as that when A murders B in order to obtain B's money, A's intent was to kill and his motive was to get the money. Such an illustration might well suggest that "intent" is limited to one's purpose to commit the proscribed act (including, as in the illustration, the proscribed consequences), and that all inquiries into why one did the proscribed act are concerned with motive. This view has sometimes been taken. But, if this view is correct, then the notion that motive is immaterial in the substantive criminal law is wrong, for there are a number of instances in which this inquiry into why an act was committed is crucial in determining whether or not the defendant has committed a given crime. For example, if one evening A breaks into B's house, it is most important to know *why* he did so, as it is burglary only if he did so for the purpose of committing a felony. Likewise, if C shoots and kills D, it may well be important to determine *why* he did so, for if he acted in self-defense he is not guilty of murder.

As shown by the burglary example, there are crimes that are defined in terms of certain acts or consequences plus a mental state which is concerned with something beyond the defendant's intent to do those acts or cause those consequences. These are often referred to as "specific intent" crimes which—although itself somewhat misleading—suggests that what is involved is a matter of intention and not motive. While some have taken the contrary view, it is undoubtedly better, for purposes of analysis, to view such crimes as *not* being based upon proof of a bad motive. This can be accomplished by taking the view that intent relates to the means and motive to the ends, but that where the end is the means to yet another end, then the medial end may also be considered in terms of intent. Thus, when *A* breaks into *B*'s house in order to get money to pay his debts, it is appropriate to characterize the purpose of taking money as the intent and the desire to pay his debts as the motive.

The notion that good motives are irrelevant is more complex, although there are numerous examples in the cases where a person has been found guilty of a crime in spite of what might be viewed as a good motive in committing it. A married man who, knowing that he is already married to a living wife, goes through a marriage ceremony with a second woman, is guilty of bigamy (for his conduct and state of mind fulfill the definition of bigamy), though he acts in accordance with an honest religious belief in the rightness of his second marriage. One who intentionally kills another human being is guilty of murder, though he does so at the victim's request and his motive is the worthy one of terminating the victim's sufferings from an incurable and painful disease. One who sends an obscene writing through the mails is guilty of the federal postal crime of depositing obscene matter in the mails, although he is activated by the beneficent motive of improving the reader's sexual habits and thereby bettering the human race. One who intentionally destroys a fence around a graveyard without the owner's consent is guilty of violating the criminal statute on malicious mischief covering such intentional conduct, though he destroys the fence with the praiseworthy motive of building a better fence. And one who, under oath on the witness stand, intentionally tells a lie concerning a material matter is guilty of perjury, although his act is prompted by a desire "to escape the importunities of 'Wall Street.' "

Although it is cases such as these which are frequently cited for the proposition that good motives are no defense, others have relied upon many of the defense-to-liability general principles of criminal law to support the proposition that good motives are sometimes a defense. Thus it is noted that one who commits what is otherwise a crime may have the defense of necessity if his conduct, though it literally violates the law, avoids an immediate harm greater than the harm which the criminal law in question seeks to prevent—as where he steals food because he is starving and will soon die without the food; or where he breaks out of prison, which is on fire, in violation of a statute against prison-breaking, in order to save himself from the fiery death which awaits him if he stays (see § 9.1). He has the mental state that the crime in question requires (an intent to deprive the food owner of his property; an intent to break out of prison); nevertheless, he is not guilty of the crime because his conduct, though literally forbidden by the criminal law, is justified by the policy of the criminal law which, in the limited circumstances covered by the defense of necessity, seeks to promote a value (in the two instances above, the value of human life) greater than the value of the literal obedience to the criminal law.

At this point, it is apparent that it is somewhat difficult to square necessity and the other defenses, such as self-defense, with the proposition that good motives are no defense. Can it be said, on the one hand, that a desire to stop a relative's continued suffering is a matter of motive and thus no defense to a murder charge and, on the other hand, that a desire to obtain food to keep from starving is not a matter of motive and thus a defense to a theft charge? This sounds as if the notion that motives are irrelevant in the substantive law requires that the word "motive" be defined as those purposes, ends, and objectives that are deemed irrelevant, which brings one full circle. One might well take the position that it would be better to abandon the difficult task of trying to distinguish intent from motive and merely acknowledge that the substantive criminal law takes account of some desired ends but not others.

There is, however, at least one good reason to resist characterizing the defenses, such as necessity and self-defense, as instances in which a good motive serves as a defense. Such a characterization leads to analytical difficulties, for it suggests that these defenses are available only if the actor, in each case, had as his primary inducement the objective recognized as lawful by the defense. Although this position has sometimes been taken, the better view is that the law is not concerned with motive once facts supporting the defense have been established. Thus, when a person authorized to carry out a death sentence does so, he is acting lawfully whether he pursues his duties with regret, joy, or indifference. Similarly, when an individual finds himself in a position where the law grants him the right to kill another in his own defense, it makes no difference whether his dominant motive is other than self-preservation. This does not mean, of course, that the defense can be manufactured after the event by resort to facts not known to the actor when he engaged in the conduct. Thus, in the prison-break illustration described earlier, the defendant would not have a defense if he escaped from prison and then later learned, to his pleasant surprise, that when he left it was on fire and that he would have been burned to death had he remained. But, this limitation on the availability of this and other defenses is not based upon the notion that it is the defendant's motive which is critical; rather, it rests upon the policy that motive is not relevant once it is shown that the defendant was aware of facts which would give rise to a defense. Just as the defendant's intent to bring about certain consequences may be established without proof of any motive for it, so too as to a defense to liability.

(b) Relevance in Criminal Procedure. Even though it may be concluded that "motive" (when narrowly defined not to include recognized defenses or certain required "specific intents") is not relevant in the substantive criminal law, an offender's reasons for engaging in proscribed conduct are often relevant on the procedural side of the criminal law. For one thing, the existence of a good motive on the part of the guilty person may be taken into account wherever there is room for the exercise of discretion in the proceedings against that person. The police, taking into account the motives of the offender, may decide not to invoke the criminal process. The prosecutor, for the same reason, may decide not to charge the offender with a crime, or may charge him with a less serious offense than he actually committed. The jury, if the defendant's good motive comes to its attention, might exercise its uncontrolled discretion to acquit. Motives are most relevant when the trial judge sets the defendant's sentence, and it is not uncommon for a defendant to receive a minimum sentence because he was acting with good motives, or a rather high sentence because of his bad motives. Likewise, motive may be taken into account by correctional officials.

Also, especially when the prosecution's case against the criminal defendant is circumstantial, the fact that the defendant had some motive, good or bad, for committing the crime is one of the circumstances which, together with other circumstances, may lead the fact-finder to conclude that he did in fact commit the crime; whereas lack of any discernible motive is a circumstance pointing in the direction of his innocence. And lack of motive, together with other circumstances, may indicate that the defendant was insane and so not criminally responsible for his actions. Nevertheless, it must be emphasized again that a conviction of crime does not require any proof of motive.

§ 4.4 Recklessness and Negligence

We have seen that some crimes require that the defendant intentionally or knowingly do an act or omit to act, or that he intentionally or knowingly cause a specified result of his act or omission. But other crimes may be committed by a reckless act or omission or by recklessly causing a specified result. Still others may be committed by negligence in acting or in omitting to act or in causing some harmful result. Thus, for instance, it is common to make reckless driving and careless driving crimes, without reference to any bad result of such conduct. As to crimes defined in terms of specified harmful results, involuntary manslaughter (and battery) may be committed, among other ways, by reckless conduct that causes death (or bodily injury) to another human being; and malicious mischief by reckless conduct causing injury or destruction to the property of another. Perhaps fewer crimes are defined in terms of negligence, as distinguished from recklessness; but in some states negligent conduct in the operation of an automobile, which causes a death, constitutes a special statutory crime (not manslaughter proper); and there are other special statutory crimes based upon bad results negligently caused.

It came to be the general feeling of the judges when defining common law crimes (not always so strongly shared later by the legislatures when defining statutory crimes) that something more was required for criminal liability than the ordinary negligence that is sufficient for tort liability. The thought was this: When it comes to compensating an injured person for damages suffered, the one who has negligently injured an innocent victim ought to pay for it; but when the problem is one of whether to impose criminal punishment on the one who caused the injury, then something extra—beyond ordinary negligence—should be required. What is that "something extra" that the criminal law generally requires? It might logically be either one or both of two things: (1) Perhaps the defendant's conduct must involve a greater risk of harm to others than tort negligence requires. In other words, perhaps a "high degree of negligence," rather than "ordinary negligence," is necessary. (2) Perhaps, without requiring any riskier conduct than is necessary for ordinary negligence, the criminal law might require that the defendant consciously realize, in his own mind, the risk he is creating—a realization which is not required in the case of ordinary negligence. In other words, perhaps the difference between ordinary negligence and criminal negligence is simply that objective fault will do for the former, while subjective fault is required for the latter. (3) Perhaps the criminal law might require both (a) conduct creating a higher degree of risk than is necessary for ordinary negligence and (b) a subjective awareness that the conduct creates such a risk. The term "recklessness" is sometimes used to designate conduct that involves these two extra factors, (a) and (b), in addition to the requirements of ordinary negligence. The other expression commonly used to indicate something more than ordinary negligence is "gross negligence," but that expression does not give any clue as to whether it is greater riskiness or subjective realization of risk or both which goes into the word "gross."

(a) Negligence. Negligence, which will usually do for tort liability and which will sometimes do for criminal liability, has been defined in various ways, and discussed at great length; but the lowest common denominator of all definitions contains these two items: (1) an expression of the required degree of risk that the defendant's conduct must create, and (2) an expression that that conduct is to be judged by an objective (reasonable man) standard.

(1) Unreasonable Risk. The degree of risk that negligence requires is said to be an "unreasonable" (or "unjustifiable") risk of harm to others (either to their persons or to their property). "Unreasonable risk" is an expression which takes into account the fact that we all create some risk to others in our everyday affairs without subjecting ourselves to liability for negligence. Thus there is always some such risk involved in driving an automobile carefully; but it is not unreasonable to take this small risk in view of the social utility of driving. Driving at a high rate of speed involves even more risk to others, but it may not be unreasonable to take this risk in order to rush a badly injured person to the hospital. The test for reasonableness in creating risk is thus said to be determined by weighing the magnitude of the risk of harm against the utility of the actor's conduct. Under such a test, even a slight risk may be unreasonable. Thus it has been suggested that if there were 1000 pistols on a table, all unloaded but one, and if A, knowing this, should pick one at random and fire it at B, killing him, A's conduct in creating the risk of death, though the risk is very slight (one-tenth of 1%), would be unreasonable, in view of its complete lack of social utility.

Aside from the utility of the actor's conduct, another variable factor involved in the question of whether a particular risk is unreasonable is the extent of the actor's knowledge of the facts bearing upon the risk. A person may or may not create an unreasonable risk of harm to others depending upon what he knows. If A hands a loaded gun to B, who appears normal but whom A knows to be a madman, A creates an unreasonable risk of harm to those within range of the gun; but if A does not know B to be mad, the risk he creates, though identical in amount, is not unreasonable.

Still another variable concerns the nature and extent of the harm that may be caused by the defendant's conduct, and the number of persons who may be harmed. It may not be unreasonable under some circumstances to endanger property though it would be unreasonable, under the same circumstances, to endanger bodily security. It may not be unreasonable to subject persons to the danger of slight injury to their persons, though it would be to subject them to danger of great bodily injury or death. It may not be unreasonable to endanger a single person though it would be to endanger a great many persons. Thus the railroad employee who on

Saturday, erroneously thinking it to be Sunday when no trains run, pulls up the tracks for the purpose of repairing them just in time to cause the wreck of the Saturday Flyer, creates an unreasonable risk (in spite of the social utility involved in repairing the tracks) in view of the fact that the risk is of death and serious injury, not simply of slight injury or property damage, and, more than that, of the fact that it is a risk to many persons, not just to one or a few.

All of this suggests why we cannot measure the risk required for tort or for criminal liability in terms of percentages of chance of harm. The percentages of chance of harming others vary according to the social utility of the defendant's conduct, according to what he knows of the surrounding circumstances, and according to the nature and extent of possible harm resulting from his conduct.

(2) Objective Standard. While negligence thus requires that the defendant's conduct create an unreasonable risk of harm to others, he is nonetheless negligent though he is unaware of the fact that his conduct creates any such risk. All that negligence requires is that he ought to have been aware of it (i.e., that a reasonable man would have been aware of it). Thus negligence is framed in terms of an objective (sometimes called "external") standard, rather than in terms of a subjective standard.

The tort-negligence concept, just discussed, applies in only a relatively few modern statutory crimes. More often, it is a concept applicable to a defense to crime, rather than an element in the crime itself, as in the defense of self-defense. But for the most part, as we have seen, something more than negligence is required for criminal liability. To progress from ordinary negligence to some greater fault (greater than negligence though less than intention or knowledge) that the criminal law ordinarily requires, the components of ordinary negligence which may be varied are the above two—(1) the unreasonable-risk component and (2) the objective-standard component. To repeat: (1) we may require that the defendant's conduct create a risk greater than simply an unreasonable risk, or (2) while requiring only an unreasonable risk, we may require that the defendant have a subjective awareness of the unreasonable risk he creates, or (3) we may require both the higher risk and an awareness of that higher risk.

Before leaving negligence as a basis for criminal liability, it should be noted that there is something of a dispute as to whether criminal liability should, on principle, ever be based upon objective negligence. It has been suggested that the threat of punishment for negligence cannot serve to deter people from negligent conduct; one who is unaware of the risk he is creating cannot be deterred from creating it by thoughts of punishment if he creates it. But others have argued that the threat of punishment for risk-creating does tend to make people think harder about the risks created by their conduct, thus tending to reduce risky conduct and so to promote public safety, the great object of the criminal law.

(b) Criminal Negligence. Though the legislatures and the courts have often made it clear that criminal liability generally requires more fault than the ordinary negligence which will do for tort liability, they have not so often made it plain just what is required in addition to tort negligence—greater risk, subjective awareness of the risk, or both. Statutes are sometimes worded in terms of "gross negligence" or "culpable negligence" or "criminal negligence," without any further definition of these terms. Some manslaughter statutes provide that it is manslaughter to kill another while doing a lawful act "without due caution or circumspection," an expression which literally sounds almost exactly like the term "without due care" so often used to describe tort negligence. "Wilful and wanton disregard of the safety of others" and "recklessness" are other expressions sometimes appearing in statutes—again usually without further definition.

The courts too, when describing the fault that crimes of the negligence type generally require, speak of "gross" or "culpable" or "criminal" negligence, or "wilful and wanton" conduct, or "reckless" conduct, often without pointing out specifically what these adjectives mean. The following is a typical example of a court's plain statement that criminal liability for manslaughter requires more than ordinary (tort) negligence, but making it hazy what that extra something is: "[Criminal liability is always predicated] not upon mere negligence or carelessness but upon that degree of negligence or carelessness which is denominated 'gross' and which constitutes such a departure from what would be the conduct of an ordinarily careful and prudent man under the same circumstances as to furnish evidence of that indifference to consequences which in some offenses takes the place of criminal intent." A requirement of "indifference to consequences" would seem to be another way of requiring an awareness of the risk (i.e., a subjective standard). But the introductory phrase, "as to furnish evidence of," weakens this requirement by seeming to say that the defendant does not actually have to realize the risk and be indifferent to it; he is guilty of criminal negligence if his conduct is so great a departure from that of a reasonable man that the reasonable man would have realized the risk (i.e., an objective standard).

A few cases, however, have spelled out with some clarity what criminal negligence requires in addition to the requirements of ordinary negligence, though they have reached three quite different conclusions: (1) One clearly expressed view is contained in an opinion by Holmes in a manslaughter case. The defendant, not a doctor, in order to cure a sick woman, wrapped her in rags soaked in kerosene, causing burns from which she died. The defendant requested the trial court to instruct the jury that, however much risk of death to the victim his conduct entailed, he could not be guilty if he honestly believed his treatment would cure her. The defendant's defense thus was that he could not be guilty if he was subjectively unaware of the risk he created. Instead, the trial judge charged the jury in effect that the defendant would be guilty if his conduct created a great risk, whether he realized it or not. The appellate court affirmed his conviction, clearly stating that the standard to be applied in a manslaughter case is an objective standard, and urging that such a view of the law is correct on principle since it tends to make people careful. The court thus required that the defendant's conduct be riskier than is required for tort negligence; but, instead of requiring that the defendant be aware of it, it required only that a reasonable man would have been aware of it.

(2) On the other hand, a few cases have quite clearly spelled out that while no greater risk of harm is required for criminal than for tort liability, yet there is a difference between the two: the defendant must realize the risk for criminal law, though he need not for tort law. In applying this subjective test for criminal negligence, it would seem that a person can be said to realize the risk his conduct entails not only (a) when he directly knows it to be risky but also (b) when he knows that he does not know whether it is risky or not, and in fact it is risky.

(3) Lastly, a few cases quite clearly spell out that criminal liability requires both greater risk and subjective realization of that risk. Thus in a case wherein the defendant, having previously suffered blackouts and having been warned by his doctor not to drive alone, was driving alone when he suffered another blackout, so that his car went out of control and killed another motorist, the defendant was held guilty of a statutory crime punishing one who causes death while driving a car "in wilful and wanton disregard for the rights or safety of others." The court stated that one is guilty of "wilful and wanton disregard" where, knowing of the existing conditions "and conscious from such knowledge that injury will likely or probably result from his conduct, and with reckless indifference to the consequences," he goes ahead with his conduct.

Much of the source of the confusion in the law lies in the criminal statutes, which have used expressions like "gross" and "culpable" negligence and "wilful and wanton" disregard of safety without defining these terms. The courts thus have had to do their best with little guidance from the legislature, with varying results. Model Penal Code § 2.02(2)(c) & (d), however, sets forth definitions for the terms "recklessness" and "negligence" (requiring a "substantial and unjustifiable risk" for both, and a subjective "consciously disregards" requirement for recklessness and an objective "should be aware" requirement for negligence), and in most recent recodifications the Model Penal Code approach has been substantially followed.

(c) Violation of Statute or Ordinance. In tort law, one who violates a statute (or ordinance) the purpose of which is to protect a certain class of persons from a certain type of harm, is, by the weight of authority, guilty of negligence *per se* if his victim is a member of that class and receives that type of harm. The notion is that the legislature (or city council) has established the standard of conduct of the reasonable man, so that the violator has necessarily fallen below that standard; or, putting it another way, he has necessarily created an unreasonable risk of harm to others. But violation of a statute (ordinance) does not constitute *per se* that greater negligence (whichever of the three possibilities it is) which criminal law generally requires, though it does constitute some evidence of that negligence. Insofar as criminal negligence is held to require subjective awareness of risk, the defendant's knowledge of the existence and contents of the statute (ordinance), and his knowing disregard of its terms, would of course be relevant. If the objective standard is used, his lack of knowledge of the existence and terms of the law and of its violation is not relevant; but his conduct in committing the violation does not necessarily create that high degree of risk which crimes generally require.

(d) Proof of Subjective Realization of Risk. Just as intention on the defendant's part, when intention is required for criminal liability, must often be inferred from his words and conduct in the light of the surrounding circumstances, so too his subjective realization of risk (when that is a necessary requirement for liability based on criminal negligence) must generally be inferred from his words and conduct in the light of the circumstances. Sometimes the defendant at the time of his risky conduct, or before, or after (in the form of an admission or confession) uses words, overheard by a witness, which show that he actually did realize the risk. But often there are no words to help us. If the defendant's conduct is in fact risky, and if the risk is obvious, so that a reasonable man would realize it, we might well infer that he did in fact realize it; but the inference cannot be conclusive, for we know that people are not always conscious of what reasonable people would be conscious of.

Thus the defendant, if he takes the witness stand, may testify that he did not at the time realize the riskiness of his conduct; and the jury may or may not believe him. Doubtless the jury is more likely to believe him if his conduct, though it involves risk to others, also involves risk to himself or to his loved ones. The seaman aboard the wooden sailing ship, carrying a cargo of rum, who causes the vessel to burn to the waterline when, stealing rum from the hold, his candle sets the rum afire, probably does not realize the risk of burning the ship that his conduct involves, for if the ship should catch fire, he is likely to perish with the rest. The driver of an automobile carrying his children who, to cross the state line and thus prevent his arrest by the sheriff who had jumped on the running board to make the arrest, raced the car across the state-line bridge, having an accident thereon which killed the policeman, probably did not realize that his conduct involved a great risk of an accident; he would not knowingly have subjected his children to such a risk. Of course, sometimes people do consciously take chances with their own lives and those of their families, so that it is not conclusive, because one's conduct endangers himself or his family, that he was not conscious of the danger involved.

Whether or not the defendant was consciously aware of the risk or simply failed to be aware is often a close question. But there are other instances in which the undisputed facts are not at all consistent with a claim of inadvertence. In the latter situation, a defendant charged with a subjective fault crime (e.g., reckless homicide) is not entitled to have the jury consider the alternative of guilt under a lesser objective fault crime (e.g., negligent homicide). Thus, in a manslaughter by recklessness case in which defendant aimed a gun at his wife and pulled the trigger, thinking but not knowing the gun was unloaded, it was proper not to submit a negligent homicide instruction to the jury. But when the defendant who plunged a knife into a person during a religious ceremony testified, as did his followers, that he had performed this ritual in the past without untoward results because of his power to suspend a person's heartbeat, pulse and breathing, an instruction on negligent homicide was required.

(e) Risk of What Harm? With crimes of negligence and recklessness, where a risk of harm to others is required, the type of harm involved is not necessarily the same for all such crimes. Thus the risk of harm that is required for manslaughter is risk of death or serious bodily injury; for battery, it is risk of bodily injury (something less than serious bodily injury); for malicious mischief, it is risk of property damage or destruction. A special statute making it a crime to kill another by driving a car recklessly would require a risk of death or serious bodily injury; another statute making it a crime to injure another by negligent driving while intoxicated would require, so far as risk is concerned, only a risk of bodily injury.

(f) Recklessness vs. Intention and Knowledge. We have seen that crimes defined so as to require that the defendant intentionally cause a forbidden bad result are usually interpreted to cover one who knows that his conduct is *substantially certain* to cause the result, whether or not he desires the result to occur (see § 4.2). "Recklessness" in causing a result exists when one is aware that his conduct *might* cause the result, though it is not substantially certain to happen. One may act recklessly if he drives fast through a thickly settled district though his chances of hitting anyone are far less that 90%, or even 50%. Indeed, if there is no social utility in doing what he is doing, one might be reckless though the chances of harm are something less than 1%. Thus, while "knowledge" and the knowing-type of "intention" require a consciousness of almost-certainty, recklessness requires a consciousness of something far less than certainty or even probability.

A useful illustration is provided by *People v. Hall* (2000), where defendant was charged with recklessly causing the death of another in a jurisdiction using the Model Penal Code definition of recklessness, and the court held that defendant's "conduct—skiing straight down a steep and bumpy slope, back on his skis, arms out to his sides, off-balance, being thrown from mogul to mogul, out of control for a considerable distance and period of time, and at such a high speed that the force of the impact between his ski and the victim's head fractured the thickest part of the victim's skull—created a substantial and unjustifiable risk of death to another person." As for the district court's dismissal of the charges at the preliminary hearing because such actions were not "likely" to cause death, the court responded:

> A risk does not have to be "more likely than not to occur" or "probable" in order to be substantial. A risk may be substantial even if the chance that the harm will occur is well below fifty percent. * * * Some risks may be substantial even if they carry a low degree of probability because the magnitude of the harm is potentially great. For example, if a person holds a revolver with a single bullet in one of the chambers, points the gun at another's head and pulls the trigger, then the risk of death is substantial even though the odds that death will result are no better than one in six.

(g) What Kind of Fault Should Criminal Liability Require? We have noted that some crimes require objective fault while others require subjective fault, and that some require the creation of an unreasonable risk of harm while others require the creation of a higher degree of risk; and we have noted also that statutes are often vague on these requirements and that courts, with so little guidance from the language of the statutes, disagree as to the requirements. Before leaving this topic we should ask: on principle, what should the criminal law require? (1) Should it require a greater risk of harm than tort law generally requires? (2) Should it require a subjective awareness of whatever risk is required, or (as with torts) should it require only that a reasonable man would have realized it?

It is clear that there is no need to choose one answer for all crimes. As to degree of risk, one would naturally expect a higher requirement for murder, with its heavier punishment, than for involuntary manslaughter, which carries a lighter penalty. Thus we shall see that "depraved-heart" murder requires more risk than does manslaughter; if manslaughter requires a "high degree of risk," as many states would say, murder (of the "depraved-heart" type) requires a "very high degree of risk." On the other hand, a state which has had a bad experience of automobile deaths on the highways might logically create a new crime of negligent-death-by-automobile (perhaps carrying a lighter punishment than manslaughter proper), imposing criminal liability on one who creates an "unreasonable risk" of death—something less than a "high degree of risk."

As to the subjective-vs.-objective choice, here too there need not be one answer for all crimes. Subjective fault is greater fault than objective fault; one who consciously does risky things is morally a worse person than one who unconsciously creates risk. But, on the other hand, objective fault is greater fault than no fault at all, and some conduct (as we shall see later in more detail, see § 4.5) is criminal though it involves no fault. It is surely not so startling to punish objective fault as it is to impose criminal liability without fault. The principal policy question is whether the threat of punishment for objective fault will deter people from conducting themselves in such a way as to create risk to others. Though the matter is disputed, it would seem that some people can be made to think, before they act, about the possible consequences of acting, so that the existence of objective-fault crimes does tend to reduce risky conduct. Still, one would hardly wish to impose the death penalty or life imprisonment on one who unconsciously created risk. We might logically require subjective fault for murder while allowing objective fault for manslaughter; or require subjective fault for manslaughter while allowing objective fault for a special situation of danger, such as the driving of an automobile in a risky way. The point is that the legislature might, in the exercise of its police power, require subjective fault for some crimes and objective fault for other crimes. Other things being equal, of course, a lighter punishment should be provided for objective-negligence crimes than for subjective-negligence crimes. Indeed, some state courts have held certain objective-negligence crimes invalid because of the high penalty and lack of any apparent justification in the particular circumstances for such liability.

Another criticism of objective fault is that it is unjust to impose criminal sanctions absent culpability, which is surely lacking when the defendant's doing of harm was not a matter of choice by him. The "moral protest involved when such liability is imposed for negligence is simply that the defendant does not deserve to be subjected to this—which is, to the added burdens of imprisonment or fine and the disgrace and stigma which invariably accompany them—unless he has made a conscious choice to do something he knew to be wrong." In response, it has been argued that there is a form of culpability here—that of failing to bring one's faculties to bear so as to perceive the risks that one is taking. The argument is made that "culpability functions as the touchstone of the question whether by virtue of his illegal conduct, the violator has lost his moral standing to complain of being subjected to sanctions. If his illegal conduct is unexcused, if he had a fair chance of avoiding the violation and did not, we are inclined to regard the state's imposing a sanction as justified."

(h) Disparity Between Foreseeable Result and Actual Result. With crimes requiring that the defendant intentionally cause a forbidden result, we saw that there was a problem of liability when an unintended victim was harmed, when the intended victim was harmed in an unintended manner, or when the resulting harm differed in either type or degree from that intended. The same sort of problem arises in crimes which require that the defendant recklessly or negligently cause the forbidden harm. Here it may arise as to the unforeseeable victim, the foreseeable victim harmed in an unforeseeable manner, an unhazarded type of harm, or an unexpected degree of harm.

(1) Unforeseeable Victim: Perhaps A recklessly or negligently creates a risk of harm to B; as it turns out, B escapes harm; but C is harmed. A recklessly drives a car in such a way as to endanger motorists and pedestrians, but he misses them all; however, a window-washer overlooking the street is so intrigued by watching A's unusual driving that he loses his footing and falls. Is A criminally liable for the window-washer's resulting injury or death?

(2) Unforeseeable Manner: Perhaps A recklessly or negligently creates a risk of a certain type of harm to B, but B is injured in an unusual manner. Thus A recklessly drives his car so as to endanger the lives of pedestrians, but he misses pedestrian B, scaring him to such an extent that he must go to a hospital, where he catches smallpox from another hospital patient and dies. Is A criminally responsible for *B*'s death, which he has in a sense caused?

(3) Unhazarded Type of Harm: *A* acts recklessly toward *B*, foreseeably endangering his property but not his person; but, as it turns out, *B*'s property escapes without injury, yet *B* is killed (or injured). Or the converse situation may occur, as where *A* foreseeably endangers *B*'s person but not his property, but his property and not his person is injured or destroyed. What crime, if any, has *A* committed in these two instances?

(4) Unexpected Degree of Harm: *A* throws a small stone at *B*, giving rise to a foreseeable risk of some minor bodily injury to *B*, but *B* is a hemophiliac and bleeds to death. Is *A* guilty of involuntary manslaughter? Or, *A* recklessly creates a risk of death to *B*, but his conduct unexpectedly only injures *B*. Is *A* guilty of battery?

In the first two of these situations, the results have been essentially the same as the foreseeable harm, and thus the mental state requirement is satisfied. Whether the unexpected victim or unexpected manner should nonetheless present a bar to conviction is a matter of policy best categorized as a question of causation, and it is discussed herein in that context (see § 5.4). Although the latter two situations might also be considered as presenting issues of causation, the more fundamental question is whether the required mental states of recklessness and negligence should somehow be interchangeable from crime to crime, so that one who knows or should know of a particular kind of risk might on that basis be held liable when the harm that actually occurs is of an unhazarded type or unexpected degree. These situations, therefore, are discussed in the section on concurrence (see § 5.3).

§ 4.5 Strict Liability

For several centuries (at least since 1600) the different common law crimes have been so defined as to require, for guilt, that the defendant's acts or omissions be accompanied by one or more of the various types of fault (intention, knowledge, recklessness or—more rarely—negligence); a person is not guilty of a common law crime without one of these kinds of fault. But legislatures, especially in the 20th and 21st centuries, have often undertaken to impose criminal liability for conduct unaccompanied by fault. A statute may simply provide that whoever does (or omits to do) so-and-so, or whoever brings about such-and-such a result, is guilty of a crime, setting forth the punishment. Usually, but not always, the statutory crime-without-fault carries a relatively light penalty—generally of the misdemeanor variety. Often this statutory crime has been created in order to help the prosecution cope with a situation wherein intention, knowledge, recklessness or negligence is hard to prove, making convictions difficult to obtain unless the fault element is omitted. The legislature may think it important to stamp out the harmful conduct in question at all costs, even at the cost of convicting innocent-minded and blameless people. It may expect a lot of prosecutions in a certain area of harmful activity and therefore wish to relieve the prosecuting officials of the time-consuming task of preparing evidence of fault. Doubtless with many such crimes the legislature is actually aiming at bad people and expects that the prosecuting officials, in the exercise of their broad discretion to prosecute or not to prosecute, will use the statute only against those persons of bad reputation who probably actually did have the hard-to-prove bad mind, letting others go who, from their generally good reputation, probably had no such bad mental state.

It should be noted, once again, that crimes are frequently made up of several physical elements, and that a crime may be defined so as to require one type of fault as to one element, another type as to another element, and no fault at all as to a third element. On the other hand, a statute may impose strict liability as to all the elements.

(a) Statutory Interpretation. It is rare if ever that the legislature states affirmatively in a statute that described conduct is a crime though done without fault. What it does is simply omit from the wording of the statute any language ("knowingly," "fraudulently," "wilfully," "with intent to," etc.) indicating that fault is a necessary ingredient. Since crimes usually do require some fault (as expressed by the old maxim *actus non facit reum nisi mens sit rea*), the defendant often argues as to a particular statutory crime of which he is accused that the legislature really meant to require some fault.

Criminal statutes empty of words denoting fault, but not affirmatively providing for liability without fault, have been dealt with in various ways by the courts. Sometimes the court holds that the statute means what it says and so imposes criminal liability without regard to fault. But sometimes the court reads into the statute some requirement of fault, the absence of which fault constitutes a defense; the court may, however, place upon the defendant the burden of coming forward with some evidence of, or perhaps even of persuading the jury of, the absence of this fault (see § 4.5(d)).

A number of factors may be considered of importance in deciding whether the legislature meant to impose liability without fault or, on the other hand, really meant to require fault, though it failed to spell it out clearly. (1) The legislative history of the statute or its title or context may throw some light on the matter. (2) The legislature may have in some other statute provided guidance as to how a court is to determine whether strict liability was intended. (3) The severity of the punishment provided for the crime is of importance. Other things being equal, the greater the possible punishment, the more likely some fault is required; and, conversely, the lighter the possible punishment, the more likely the legislature meant to impose liability without fault. (4) The seriousness of harm to the public that may be expected to follow from the forbidden conduct is another factor. Other things being equal, the more serious the consequences to the public, the more likely the legislature meant to impose liability without regard to fault, and vice versa. (5) The defendant's opportunity to ascertain the true facts is yet another factor that may be important in determining whether the legislature really meant to impose liability on one who was without fault because he lacked knowledge of these facts. The harder to find out the truth, the more likely the legislature meant to require fault in not knowing; the easier to ascertain the truth, the more likely failure to know is no excuse. (6) The difficulty prosecuting officials would have in proving a mental state for this type of crime. The greater the difficulty, the more likely it is that the legislature intended to relieve the prosecution of that burden so that the law could be effectively enforced. (7) The number of prosecutions to be expected is another factor of some importance. The fewer the expected prosecutions, the more likely the legislature meant to require the prosecuting officials to go into the issue of fault; the greater the number of prosecutions, the more likely the legislature meant to impose liability without regard to fault. All the above factors have a bearing on the question of the interpretation of the empty statute, but no single factor can be said to be controlling. Thus some statutes have been held to impose liability without fault although the possible punishment was quite severe, generally because one or more of the other factors pointed toward strict liability.

When, because of the operation of one or more of the factors, the court reads into an empty statute a requirement of fault, that fault may be of the objective (negligence) type, or it may be of the subjective (mental) type. Perhaps the stronger the factors are for requiring fault (heavier punishment, less harmful consequences, etc.), the greater the likelihood that the required fault is subjective fault, though it is often difficult to guess in advance in any case just what requirement of fault if any the court will read into the statute.

The courts that construe empty statutes as requiring some type of fault ordinarily make the prosecution allege and prove that fault in order to secure a conviction, just as if the missing words were written in the statute. But some courts have found another way of dealing with the empty statute that is construed to require fault—a method which falls midway between imposing liability without fault (the prosecution need not allege or prove any fault, and the defendant can raise no defense that he was without fault) and dealing with the statute just as if words of fault were written therein (the prosecution must allege and prove fault, just as it must prove all elements of the crime). These courts say that, though fault is required, it need not be alleged by the prosecution or proved in its presentation at the trial; rather, it is up to the defendant to put in evidence of his lack of fault during his presentation at the trial.

Thus in a bigamy case the statute, devoid of any words requiring fault, provided in effect that one who, having a living spouse, marries someone else is guilty of bigamy unless then divorced. The defendant honestly and reasonably thought he was divorced when he married the second time, but he actually was not divorced. The court held that the bigamy statute requires that the defendant have reason to believe he is not divorced, so that a reasonable belief that he is divorced is a defense. The legislature's omission of any expression of fault in the body of the statute has some effect, however; it was done "to reallocate the burden of proof on that issue [i.e., fault] in a bigamy trial. Thus, the prosecution makes a prima facie case upon proof that the second marriage was entered into while the first spouse was still living * * * and his bona fide and reasonable belief that facts existed that left the defendant free to remarry is a defense to be proved by the defendant." The one point these cases do not ordinarily make clear is whether the rule requires only that the defendant go forward with some evidence of lack of the required fault in order to escape conviction, the prosecution still having the burden of persuading the jury that the defendant was at fault; or whether the defendant actually has the burden of persuading the jury by a preponderance of the evidence that he is free of fault.

(b) Constitutionality. As discussed earlier (see § 3.3(d)), the United States Supreme Court has recognized that as a general matter it is constitutionally permissible to enact strict-liability criminal statutes. "There is wide latitude in the lawmakers to declare an offense and to exclude elements of knowledge and diligence from its definition," the Court stated in *Lambert v. Calif.* (1957), the only occasion when it struck down a strict-liability crime, and only because of rather unusual circumstances. Though it has been argued that the ruling in that case should be extended to proscribe strict-liability offenses more generally, this has not occurred. Rather, *Lambert* has had very little impact.

Constitutional attacks in the state courts have, in the main, been equally unsuccessful. Most of the state decisions reject the notion that there is some general constitutional bar to strict-liability crimes or even that the sanction of imprisonment is consti-tutionally impermissible on a strict-liability basis. But a few states take a somewhat narrower view of what is allowed under their state constitutions. Thus, some authority is to be found to the effect that a strict-liability criminal statute is unconstitutional if (1) the sub-ject matter of the statute does not place it "in a narrow class of public welfare offenses," (2) the statute carries a substantial penal-ty of imprisonment, or (3) the statute imposes an unreasonable duty in terms of a person's responsibility to ascertain the relevant facts.

(c) Pros and Cons of Strict–Liability Crimes. Aside from the question of constitutionality, there is the question of wisdom in providing for strict-liability crimes. The reasons for having statutes imposing criminal liability without fault are those of expediency: in some areas of conduct it is difficult to obtain convictions if the prosecution must prove fault, so enforcement requires strict liabili-ty. If the conduct to be stamped out is harmful enough, or if the number of prosecutions to be expected is great enough, the legisla-ture may thus wish to make the absence of fault no defense, in order to relieve the prosecution of the task of going into the matter.

For the most part, the commentators have been critical of strict-liability crimes. "The consensus can be summarily stated: to punish conduct without reference to the actor's state of mind is both inefficacious and unjust. It is inefficacious because conduct unaccompanied by an awareness of the factors making it criminal does not mark the actor as one who needs to be subjected to punishment in order to deter him or others from behaving similarly in the future, nor does it single him out as a socially dangerous individual who needs to be incapacitated or reformed. It is unjust because the actor is subjected to the stigma of a criminal conviction without being morally blameworthy. Consequently, on either a preventive or retributive theory of criminal punishment, the crimi-nal sanction is inappropriate in the absence of *mens rea*."

As to the argument of necessity in support of strict liability, "the answer, among others, is that (a) maximizing compliance with law, rather than successful prosecution of violators, is the primary aim of any regulatory statute; (b) the convenience of investigators and prosecutors is not, in any event, the prime consideration in determining what conduct is criminal; (c) a prosecutor, as a matter of common knowledge, always assumes a heavier burden in trying to secure a criminal conviction than a civil judgment; (d) in most situations of attempted control of mass conduct, the technique of a first warning, followed by criminal prosecution only of knowing violators, has not only obvious, but proved superiority; and (e) the common-sense advantages of using the criminal sanction only against deliberate violators is confirmed by the policies which prosecutors themselves tend always to follow when they are free to make their own selection of cases to prosecute."

Dissents to some of these propositions have occasionally been registered. For example, it has been suggested that a strict-liability offense may be a more efficacious deterrent than an ordinary criminal statute because "a person engaged in a certain kind of activity would be more careful precisely because he knew that this kind of activity was governed by a strict liability statute" and because "the presence of strict liability offenses might have the added effect of keeping a relatively large class of persons from engaging in certain kinds of activity." Also, it is contended that strict-liability offenses often do require "fault" in a restrictive sense, in that they "can be interpreted as legislative judgments that persons who intentionally engage in certain activities and occupy some peculiar or distinctive position of control are to be held accountable for the occurrence of certain consequences."

Yet, it is generally agreed that conviction for strict-liability offenses should be insulated "from the type of moral condemnation that is and ought to be implicit when a sentence of imprisonment may be imposed." Thus, Model Penal Code § 2.05(1)(a) would permit strict liability only for "offenses which constitute violations"; violations under the Code are not crimes, may be punished only by a fine, forfeiture, or other civil penalty, and may not give rise to any disability or legal disadvantage based on conviction of a criminal offense. Likewise, others have urged that a strict-liability crime should carry a label with less sinister connotations, such as "public tort," "public welfare offense," or "civil offense." Reforms along these lines have seldom been adopted. Consequently, as things now stand some crimes that may be committed without fault are punishable by imprisonment, and those who commit them are labeled as criminal.

(d) Alternatives to Strict Liability. In light of the criticisms that have been made of strict liability, it is appropriate to take note of possible alternative approaches. One would be only fault liability but with substantially higher penalties, on the theory that in terms of deterrent efficacy the reduced likelihood of conviction would thereby be offset by the increased magnitude of the punishment. But if the nature and circumstances of the activity in question is such that proof of fault is extremely difficult and likely to be largely a matter of chance, it might be questioned whether this would be a fairer system. Assume, for example, that the choice is between convicting all 100 defendants who have sold food later shown to be impure and fining each $250, or convicting the five out of the 100 the prosecutor can show had knowledge of the impurities and fining them each $5,000. The increased penalties for the five (contrasted to no penalty at all for others known to have sold impure food but whose fault cannot be proved) might seem more unjust than the imposition of a $250 fine without regard to fault in all 100 cases.

Secondly, it has been argued that between liability based upon subjective fault and strict liability, "there is a 'half-way house': criminal liability predicated upon negligence. * * * [T]he idea of criminal responsibility based upon the actor's failure to act as carefully as he should affords an important and largely unutilized means for avoiding the tyranny of strict liability in the criminal law." Doubtless there are circumstances in which the strict liability approach is now utilized where the negligence alternative would suffice, but this is not inevitably the case. As to certain forms of conduct, even the negligence standard may present insurmountable problems of proof for the prosecution. Moreover, as suggested earlier, sometimes strict liability is grounded in the notion that the activity engaged in by the defendant is so hazardous to the general public that simply performing in a non-negligent fashion should not be deemed sufficient.

Another possible alternative is shifting the burden of proof. As one commentator has put it: "It is fundamentally unsound to convict a defendant for a crime involving a substantial term of imprisonment without giving him the opportunity to prove that his action was due to an honest and reasonable mistake of fact or that he acted without guilty intent. If the public danger is widespread and serious, the practical situation can be met by shifting to the shoulders of the defendant the burden of proving a lack of guilty intent." To the extent that strict liability in a particular area is grounded in the prosecutor's difficulties in proving fault, this is an attractive alternative when constitutionally permissible (see § 1.8). Here again, however, it is a less than satisfactory measure when the basis of the strict liability is the imposition of an absolute standard upon high-risk activity. And some object that this alternative would result in a significant loss of deterrence but yet the conviction of many blameless defendants who were unable to muster proof of their innocence.

Finally, it has been suggested that strict liability could be replaced with a "prior warning method," whereby a warning is issued upon discovery by the authorities of a violation, after which any subsequent violations of the same type by the same person would be subject to prosecution on a strict liability basis. As a matter of administrative practice, this is precisely the approach now used with apparent success by various specialized enforcement agencies. Whether formalizing this "one-bite" limitation into the substantive law would reduce the deterrent effect of the law is unclear. However, some feel that "under such an alternative, those merchants who believe that their fault in selling prohibited food-stuffs is unprovable, and who would be deterred by absolute liability statutes will not be deterred," meaning such a system "spares faultless individuals from punishment at the cost of increased harm to victims of undeterred, but deterrable, crime."

§ 4.6   Ignorance or Mistake

Ignorance or mistake as to a matter of fact or law is a defense if it negatives a mental state required to establish a material element of the crime, except that if the defendant would be guilty of another crime had the situation been as he believed, then he may be convicted of the offense of which he would be guilty had the situation been as he believed it to be. (A quite different kind of mistake of law, whereby the defendant believes that his conduct is not proscribed by the criminal law, is generally not a defense.)

(a) Generally. No area of the substantive criminal law has traditionally been surrounded by more confusion than that of ignorance or mistake of fact or law. It is frequently said, on the one hand, that ignorance of the law is no excuse, and, on the other, that a mistake of fact is an excuse. Neither of these propositions is precisely correct, and both are subject to numerous exceptions and qualifications. Uncertainty as to the precise significance of the defendant's mistake or ignorance of the surrounding facts is attributable in part to assertions, usually unexplained, in some decisions that the error must be a reasonable one or that the defendant is subject to conviction notwithstanding the mistake. Another source of confusion is the indiscriminate use of the phrase "ignorance of the law" to encompass both the situation in which the defendant is unaware of the existence of a statute proscribing his conduct, and that where the defendant has a mistaken impression concerning the legal effect of some collateral matter and that mistake results in his misunderstanding the full significance of his conduct (as where, in a bigamy case, the defendant mistakenly believes that his prior divorce is valid). These two situations call for quite different analysis and, frequently, different results.

In actuality, the basic rule is extremely simple: ignorance or mistake of fact or law is a defense when it negatives the existence of a mental state essential to the crime charged. Indeed, it is so simple because, unlike the defenses discussed in later chapters, it is merely a restatement in somewhat different form of one of the basic premises of the criminal law. Instead of speaking of ignorance or mistake of fact or law as a defense, it would be just as easy to note simply that the defendant cannot be convicted when it is shown that he does not have the mental state required by law (see

§ 4.1) for commission of that particular offense. For example, to take the classic case of the man who takes another's umbrella out of a restaurant because he mistakenly believes that the umbrella is his, it is not really necessary to say that the man, if charged with larceny, has a valid defense of mistake of fact; it would be more direct and to the point to assert that the man is not guilty because he does not have the mental state (intent to steal the property of another, see § 16.5) required for the crime of larceny. Yet, the practice has developed of dealing with such mistakes as a matter of defense, perhaps because the facts showing their existence are usually brought out by the defendant, even though (for the reasons stated above) it is commonly accepted that the prosecution is required to disprove the mental state-negating mistake beyond a reasonable doubt.

Once the basic rule is understood, it is then apparent why the two different kinds of mistake of law mentioned earlier call for different results. If, instead of the mistake of fact in the umbrella hypothetical, the defendant took the chattel through a mistake of law, such as that his prior dealings had vested ownership of it in him, he would again not have the intent-to-steal mental state required for the crime of larceny. By contrast, this intent to steal would be present if the defendant took the umbrella he knew was owned by another but he could honestly say that he was unaware that such a taking was proscribed by the criminal law. It is in this latter sense that it may be correctly said that ignorance of the law is no excuse, although even here, as will be discussed later, there are exceptions when the defendant reasonably believes his conduct is not proscribed by law and that belief is attributable to an official statement of the law or to the failure of the state to give fair notice of the proscription.

(b) Ignorance or Mistake Negating Mental State; Reasonableness. The rather simple rule that an honest mistake of fact or law is a defense when it negates a required mental element of the crime would appear to be fairly easy to apply to a variety of cases. One merely identifies the mental state or states required for the crime, and then inquires whether that mental state can exist in light of the defendant's ignorance or mistake of fact or law. For example, on a charge of receiving property knowing it to be stolen, the critical mental element is knowledge concerning the illegal means by which the property was obtained. If the defendant knew that the goods were stolen, but believed them to be television sets when they were in fact radios, it would be apparent that this mistake of fact would be no defense because it does not negate the mental element of the crime. On the other hand, if the defendant by a mistake of either fact or law did not know the goods were stolen, even though the circumstances would have led a prudent man to believe they were stolen, he does not have the required mental state and thus may not be convicted of the crime. Frequently, however, the cases do not proceed along this easy route, for two reasons: (1) because of uncritical acceptance of the general statement that the mistake must be reasonable; and (2) because imprecise drafting has left it uncertain what mental element is actually required for the offense in question.

Illustrative of the first point is the case of *U.S. v. Short* (1954). The defendant was convicted of assault with intent to commit rape, and he appealed on the ground that the court had erred in refusing a defense-requested instruction that he could not be convicted if he believed the girl had consented. The conviction was affirmed, and it was held that the requested instruction was too broad because it failed to qualify the defendant's belief by stating the belief must be reasonable. In support of this conclusion, the court noted that on a charge of rape the defendant would only be entitled to an instruction that reasonable belief as to consent was a defense.

As the dissenting judge in *Short* pointed out, the notion that a mistake of fact is a defense only when reasonable is far too general and does not apply in many cases. One example cited was where the defendant is charged with knowing possession of marijuana; because such possession denotes conscious knowledge of the thing possessed, even negligent ignorance of the character of the cigarettes would be a defense, for knowledge is a higher and different statutory requirement than negligence (see § 4.2(e)). As for the majority's reliance upon the reasonable belief requirement under the crime of rape, the dissenting judge contended that the crime of rape was distinguishable from assault with intent to rape because the former requires only a general criminal intent while the latter requires a specific intent. As discussed earlier, the phrases "general intent" and "specific intent" only tend to cause confusion, and thus the dissenting judge's point can be best related by avoiding those terms and by instead going directly to the kind of mental element required for these two crimes. First of all, at least under the case relied upon by the majority in *Short,* the crime of rape must be understood as *not* including an element of knowledge of the woman's lack of consent, from which it follows that not every mistake by the defendant by which he believes the woman is consenting will be a defense. But, the crime of assault with intent to rape clearly sets forth a mental element; the defendant's purpose in assaulting the woman must be rape. This purpose of intercourse against the woman's will cannot be present if the defendant believes—even unreasonably—that the woman is consenting. (This fundamental point has gone unrecognized even in some of the modern codes.)

The second factor mentioned earlier, uncertainty in criminal legislation as to precisely what mental state, if any, is required—has also accounted for much of the confusion in this area, as is aptly illustrated by the offense of bigamy. Many of the bigamy statutes in this country are silent on the matter of *mens rea*. As a consequence, a common view of the crime of bigamy is that none of the following constitutes a valid defense: reasonable belief that the first spouse is dead; reasonable belief that the first marriage was illegal; reasonable belief that a decree concerning the first marriage was a divorce decree; or reasonable belief that a foreign divorce would be recognized in the jurisdiction. Such results have been reached through a process of statutory construction of bigamy statutes, often based upon these principles: (a) that when the legislature specified certain defenses (e.g., belief in the death of the other spouse based upon seven years absence) it intended to exclude all others; (b) that if the legislature had intended to require *mens rea* for the crime of bigamy it would have explicitly indicated this in the statute; and (c) that the statutory language justifies the assumption that the legislature favored the policy that those who remarry do so at their peril.

These three principles are highly questionable, however, and they have been rejected in the more carefully reasoned decisions. As to the notion that the enumeration of certain defenses indicates an intention to bar other defenses, it is more logical to conclude that the legislature merely intended to set forth special defenses applicable to this particular crime while at the same time permitting resort to defenses which are applicable to crimes generally. Likewise, the absence of words in the statute requiring a certain mental state does not warrant the assumption that the legislature intended to impose strict liability; to the contrary, at least for an offense as serious as bigamy, it should be presumed that the legislature intended to follow the usual *mens rea* requirement "unless excluded expressly or by necessary implication." The implication that the legislature favored the remarry-at-your-peril doctrine certainly is not "necessary." Indeed, consideration of the matter on policy grounds justifies the conclusion that no good purpose would be served by punishing those who remarry honestly believing their prior spouse to be dead or reasonably believing that their prior marriage was terminated by a valid divorce.

Of course, if an offense is truly of the strict liability variety (see § 4.5), then the most obvious consequence of that fact is that there is no mental state to be negated and no mistake or ignorance of fact or law will suffice to exonerate. Illustrative is the offense of selling liquor to a minor or permitting him to stay upon premises licensed for the sale of liquor, which in most jurisdictions is viewed as imposing absolute liability upon those who operate establishments licensed to sell intoxicating beverages. Under such a strict liability provision, it is no defense that defendant believed the minor was of age, and this is true even if the minor appeared to be of age, represented himself as having reached the requisite age, or produced false credentials showing that he was of age. So too with the crime of statutory rape, which in the majority of states "impose[s] strict liability for sexual acts with underage complainants." Under such a provision, a conviction may be obtained "even when the defendant's judgment as to the age of the complainant is warranted by her appearance, her sexual sophistication, her verbal misrepresentations, and the defendant's careful attempts to ascertain her true age."

The possible harshness of the strict liability approach is made most apparent when the defendant can show that he made a reasonable mistake of fact or law. For this reason, cases in which such a mistake is in evidence have sometimes influenced appellate courts to accept such a mistake as a defense notwithstanding the regulatory nature of the offense and the absence of any *mens rea* requirement in the statutory formulation. For example, even where the statute provided that no person should sell liquor to any minor "actually or apparently, under the age of eighteen years," it was interpreted to mean "actually *and* apparently" on the ground that otherwise a businessman would be penalized for acting in good faith in selling intoxicants to one who appeared to be over the statutory age. Similarly, a conviction for transporting undersized fish was reversed because the defendant truck driver established that he did not know the fish were undersized and the cargo was so packed that he could not have reasonably been expected to examine it. These courts, in effect, have concluded that the statute is *not* an absolute liability statute but rather requires negligence, and thus their holdings do not conflict with the general principle that ignorance or mistake of fact or law is a defense only if it negates a required mental state.

(c) The "Lesser Legal Wrong" and "Moral Wrong" Theories. It sometimes happens that because of ignorance or mistake of fact or law, the defendant is unaware of the magnitude of the wrong he is doing. That is, if the circumstances were as the defendant believed them to be, then he would be guilty of some lesser crime or else a noncriminal but (in the eyes of society) immoral act. For example, assume that the defendant, in a jurisdiction which by statute makes burglary of a dwelling a more serious offense than burglary of a store, reasonably believes that the building he has entered is a store when it is in fact a dwelling. Is he guilty of the crime of burglary of a dwelling, or of the crime of burglary of a store, or neither? Or, assume a defendant is charged with the crime of statutory rape, but he shows that he reasonably believed the girl had reached the age of consent so that, at most, he thought he was merely engaging in an immoral act. Is he, or is he not, guilty of the crime of statutory rape?

Some cases appear to support the general proposition that in such instances the mistake by the defendant may be disregarded because of the fact that he actually intended to do some legal or moral wrong. For that reason, the assumption seems to be, he is not deserving of the usual ignorance or mistake defense. Thus, in the leading English case of *Reg. v. Prince* (1875), where the defendant, charged with unlawfully taking a girl under the age of sixteen out of the possession of the father against his will, acted on the reasonable belief that the girl was eighteen, it was held no defense that he "thought he was committing a different kind of a wrong from that which in fact he was committing." And in *White v. State* (1933), where the defendant was convicted of the statutory offense of abandoning a pregnant wife, it was held that his defense that he did not know his wife was pregnant was properly refused, for in any event his abandonment was "a violation of his civil duty," and thus he acted at his peril. Similar reasoning accounts in part for the nearly unanimous view that a reasonable mistake of age is not a defense to a charge of statutory rape. As one court explicitly stated, even under his own understanding of the circumstances the defendant intended to commit the crime of fornication, and on that basis he may be held accountable for a crime different and more serious than he intended.

Although the matter is sometimes not made entirely clear, the assumption in these cases is not merely that the crimes involved are of the strict liability variety, thus barring ignorance or mistake of fact or law as a defense. Rather, they rest upon the notion that *some* varieties of ignorance or mistake should not be a defense, namely, those which indicate that the defendant still intended to do what constitutes a legal or moral wrong. (In the *Prince* case, for example, it was noted that the defendant would have a valid defense if he were to show that he mistakenly believed the girl's father had consented, for then he "would not know he was doing an act wrong in itself.") The lesser legal wrong and moral wrong theories, then, are grounded upon the proposition that a "guilty mind," in a very general sense, should suffice for the imposition of penal sanctions even when the defendant did not intentionally, knowingly, recklessly or even negligently engage in the acts described in the statute. That is, the defense of ignorance or mistake of fact or law "rests ultimately on the defendant's being able to say that he has observed the community ethic."

That position is unsound, and has no place in a rational system of substantive criminal law. As noted herein (see § 5.3), it is generally true that crimes defined in terms of causing a certain bad result require mental fault of the same kind and intensity, and mental fault sufficient for some other kind of crime will not suffice. (For example, acts done with an intent to injure a person, if they unexpectedly result in injury to property, may not result in conviction of the actor for an intent-to-destroy-property type of crime.) This is because considerations of deterrence, correction, and just condemnation of the actor's conduct all focus attention upon the harm intended rather than the harm actually caused. In the above example, the actor's conduct deserves condemnation, he stands in need of correction, and official response to his actions is warranted as a deterrent—*not* because of the property damage, but because of the actor's intent to harm a person. Clearly, the same analysis is called for when, because of ignorance or mistake of fact or law, the defendant's mental state is not of the same kind or intensity as the bad results his conduct has brought about.

If this is true, then it obviously follows that there is no justification for failing to take account of the defendant's ignorance or mistake when as a result he thought he was doing something which at most may be labeled immoral. "Moral duties should not be identified with criminal duties," and thus when fornication is itself not criminal it should not become criminal merely because the defendant has made a reasonable mistake about the age of the girl with whom he has intercourse. Moreover, the moral wrong theory poses the added difficulty of determining precisely what the "community ethic" actually is, not an easy task in a heterogeneous society in which our public pronouncements about morality often are not synonymous with our private conduct.

This is not to say, however, that the law should always recognize as a defense ignorance or mistake of fact or law by which the actor believes he is only committing a lesser degree of crime or merely an immoral act. There may be sound policy reasons for, in effect, imposing strict liability as to certain elements of particular crimes. Indeed, illustrations of this are to be found in the Model Penal Code, which clearly rejects the lesser legal wrong and moral wrong theories as general principles. For example, the Code § 213.6(1) position on sex offenses is that when criminality depends on a child's being below the age of 10, it is then and only then no defense that the actor believed the child to be older, "for no credible error regarding the age of a child in fact less than 10 years old would render the actor's conduct anything less than a dramatic departure from societal norms." The point is that such judgments should be made as matters of policy on an offense-by-offense basis, as in the Code, in lieu of uncritical acceptance of the more general lesser legal wrong and moral wrong theories.

When one of those exceptional situations is not present, so that ignorance or mistake of fact or law is a defense, yet the defendant would be guilty of some other crime if the facts had been as he believed them to be, there remains the question of what disposition is appropriate. To return to an earlier illustration, what if the defendant is on trial for burglary of a dwelling, but he shows by way of defense that he believed the building to be a store, and burglary of a store constitutes a lesser crime? As already concluded, conviction for burglary of a dwelling would not be possible because the mistake negates a required mental state. Moreover, conviction for burglary of a store might appear to be precluded because the required *actus reus* is not present; and even conviction of attempted burglary of a store might be in doubt under some versions of the impossibility doctrine (see § 10.5). Under Model Penal Code § 2.04(2), the defendant in these circumstances may be convicted "of the offense of which he would be guilty had the situation been as he supposed." Such a provision avoids some procedural difficulties, and permits an appropriate result whereby the defendant is found "guilty of the lesser crime which on his own assumptions he committed."

(d) Belief Conduct Not Proscribed by the Criminal Law.

It bears repeating here that the cause of much of the confusion concerning the significance of the defendant's ignorance or mistake of law is the failure to distinguish two quite different situations: (1) that in which the defendant consequently lacks the mental state required for commission of the crime and thus, as explained above, has a valid defense; and (2) that in which the defendant still had whatever mental state is required for commission of the crime and only claims that he was unaware that such conduct was proscribed by the criminal law, which, as explained below, is ordinarily not a recognized defense.

Except for one particular situation explored later in this section, it is usually an easy task to determine in which of these two categories the defendant's mistake belongs. For example, the crime of larceny is not committed if the defendant, because of a mistaken understanding of the law of property, believed that the property taken belonged to him; it is committed, however, if the defendant believed it was lawful to take certain kinds of property belonging to others because of the custom in the community to do so. The requisite mental state (intent to steal, see § 16.5) is lacking only in the first of these two cases, for it "is not the intent to violate the law but the intentional doing the act which is a violation of law" that is proscribed.

Why is it that neither ignorance of the criminal law (in the sense that the defendant is unaware of the statute proscribing his conduct) nor mistake of the criminal law (in the sense that the defendant has mistakenly concluded that the relevant statute does not reach his conduct) is a defense? Upon the early notion that the law is "definite and knowable," one common explanation is provided by the maxim that everyone is presumed to know the law. But even if there was once a time when the criminal law was so simple and limited in scope that such a presumption was justified, it is now an "obvious fiction" and "so far-fetched in modern conditions as to be quixotic." No person can really "know" all of the statutory and case law defining criminal conduct. Indeed, the maxim has never served to explain the full reach of the ignorance-of-the-law-is-no-excuse doctrine, for the doctrine has long been applied even when the defendant establishes beyond question that he had good reason for not knowing the applicable law.

A somewhat more satisfying explanation for the doctrine is the pragmatic proposition that if all defendants were entitled to raise an ignorance-of-the-criminal-law defense, then the finders of fact in criminal cases would repeatedly be confronted with an issue which in most instances could not be readily resolved. Both commentators and courts have argued that such a defense would become a shield for the guilty because (a) the defendant's claim of ignorance could not ordinarily be refuted, and (b) assuming the defendant was in fact ignorant, it would require a far-reaching inquiry to ascertain whether the defendant was at fault in not knowing the law. Holmes questioned whether "a man's knowledge of the law is any harder to investigate than many questions which are gone into," as have others, and thus it may be doubted if part (a) of the above argument is sound. The same may not be said for part (b) of the argument, however; the questions involved in pursuing an inquiry into whether or not the defendant was at fault in his ignorance would be "even more complicated than those raised by the defenses of insanity and infancy, where the justification for the defendant's failure to know of the law and mores is not in issue, being assumed to be due to mental disease or youth."

Another argument in favor of the present rule is that while it may be harsh upon the individual defendant who was reasonably ignorant or mistaken concerning the penal law, "public policy sacrifices the individual to the general good." The "larger interests on the other side of the scales" include realization of the educational function of the criminal law. So the argument goes, conviction of defendants for violation of new or forgotten criminal laws serves to bring home to the general public the existence of these rules and aids in establishing them as the social mores of the community. If individuals were acquitted because of their own unawareness of the law, such acquittals would—if anything—only increase the public uncertainty and confusion as to what conduct has been made criminal.

A related point, on a somewhat more theoretical plane, is that it would conflict with the principle of legality to treat a defendant in a criminal case as if the law were as the defendant thought it to be. Under the principle of legality, rules of law express objective meanings that are declared by competent officials and are then binding. There "is a basic incompatibility between asserting that the law is what certain officials declare it to be after a prescribed analysis, and asserting, also, that those officials *must* declare it to be * * * what defendants or their lawyers believed it to be. A legal order implies the rejection of such contradiction. It opposes objectivity to subjectivity, judicial process to individual opinion, official to lay, and authoritative to nonauthoritative declarations of what the law is."

Whatever the merit of these several arguments in support of the general rule that ignorance or mistake as to the penal law is no defense, several commentators have expressed concern with the harshness of the rule when applied to the lesser regulatory crimes involving conduct not inherently immoral. The early criminal law was "well integrated with the mores of the time," so that "a defendant's mistake as to the content of the criminal law * * * would not ordinarily affect his moral guilt." But the vast network of regulatory offenses that make up a large part of today's criminal law does not stem from the mores of the community, and so "moral education no longer serves us as a guide as to what is prohibited." Under these circumstances, where one's moral attitudes may not be relied upon to avoid the forbidden conduct, it may seem particularly severe for the law *never* to recognize ignorance or mistake of the criminal law as a defense. Moreover, some would question whether it is desirable to characterize as criminal an individual who has not demonstrated any degree of social dangerousness, that is, a person whose conduct is not anti-social because (i) he reasonably thought the conduct was not criminal, and (ii) the conduct is not by its nature immoral.

The United States Supreme Court was confronted with this issue in *Lambert v. Cal.* (1957), where the defendant had been convicted under an ordinance making it unlawful for any convicted person to remain in Los Angeles for more than five days without registering with the police department. The ordinance was held to violate the notice requirements of due process when applied to a defendant "who has no actual knowledge of his duty to register," for "circumstances which might move one to inquire as to the necessity of registration are completely lacking." This language is significant, for it emphasizes that the defendant was in no way at fault in not being aware of the legal duty in question. Thus, the holding in *Lambert* would be inapplicable to a defendant who could rightly be said to be under an obligation to ascertain the legality of his conduct. For example, it would certainly be proper to hold to the position that an individual has a "duty to keep informed about the legal regulation governing conduct in which [he] is peculiarly engaged," so that one engaged in the manufacture of dairy products could not defend on the ground of his ignorance of an available statute or administrative regulation prohibiting the sale of butter without a certain percentage of fat.

It is important to note, however, that the *Lambert* decision does not require legislative tampering with the doctrine that ignorance of the criminal law is no excuse. Ignorance of the law, after all, *is* an excuse when it negatives a required mental element of the crime, so it would be fairly simple to redraft legislation of the kind condemned in *Lambert* so that guilt depends upon a knowing violation of a legal duty. Illustrative is a statute making it an offense knowingly to attempt to evade the payment of income taxes, properly interpreted in *Cheek v. U.S.* (1991) as not reaching a defendant who was unaware of his duty under the law to pay taxes. As the Supreme Court explained, the "proliferation of statutes and regulations has sometimes made it difficult for the average citizen to know and comprehend the extent of the duties and obligations imposed by the tax laws," and accordingly the Congress made "intent to violate the law an element of certain federal criminal tax offenses." Analytically, this approach is to be preferred over that of creating an exception to the general rule that ignorance of the criminality of the conduct is no excuse, for neither Lambert nor Cheek should escape conviction merely because of ignorance that their conduct was punishable under the criminal law. Rather, the important matter is ignorance of the legal duty—in *Lambert* the duty to register, and in *Cheek* the duty to pay taxes.

(e) Belief Conduct Not Proscribed Because of Governmental Action or Inaction. Under the better view, there are limited situations in which the defendant's belief that his conduct was not proscribed by the criminal law is a defense. These exceptions are somewhat akin to the void-for-vagueness (see § 2.3) and ex post facto (see § 2.4) doctrines, in that the government is rightly barred from obtaining a conviction because the government (through its representatives acting in an official capacity) is responsible for the inability of the defendant to know that his conduct was proscribed.

(1) Enactment Not Reasonably Made Available. A mere claim by the defendant that the statute under which he is being prosecuted had not come to his attention prior to the time he engaged in the conduct charged is, of course, not a valid defense.

But, in some instances the defendant may show more—either that his conduct occurred very soon after the statute was enacted and before it was made generally available, or that his conduct occurred later but still before the usual formalities of official publication had been fully complied with. Although the earlier decisions recognize no defense even under these circumstances, the more rational position is that the defendant's belief that his conduct is not criminal is a defense when "the statute or other enactment defining the offense is not known to [him] and has not been published or otherwise reasonably made available prior to the conduct alleged."

Such a situation is unlikely to arise today with respect to national or state criminal legislation; all such enactments are published, and normally these laws carry an "effective date" that affords time for publication prior to their actually becoming law. The same is not necessarily true as to local legislation. Particularly in smaller communities, local ordinances may never be printed or otherwise made generally available. Nor is it often true of regulations promulgated by administrative agencies, violation of which may carry criminal sanctions (see § 2.6). While "substantive rules of general applicability" of federal administrative agencies must be published in the Federal Register, many states have not attempted a systematic publication and codification of their administrative regulations.

(2) Reasonable Reliance Upon a Statute or Judicial Decision. An individual should be able reasonably to rely upon a statute or other enactment under which his conduct would not be criminal, so that he need not fear conviction if subsequent to his conduct the statute is declared invalid. A contrary rule would be inconsistent with the sound policy that the community is to be encouraged to act in compliance with legislation. Thus, just as it is no defense that the defendant mistakenly believed the statute under which he was prosecuted to be unconstitutional, it is a defense that he reasonably relied upon a statute permitting his conduct though it turned out to be an unconstitutional enactment.

For essentially the same reason, the better view is that it is a defense that the defendant acted in reasonable reliance upon a judicial decision, opinion or judgment later determined to be invalid or erroneous. The clearest case is that in which the defendant's reliance was upon a decision of the highest court of the jurisdiction, later overruled, whether the first decision involved the constitutionality of a statute, the interpretation of a statute, or the meaning of the common law. A contrary rule, whereby the subsequent holding would apply retroactively to the defendant's detriment, would be as unfair as ex post facto legislation (§ 2.4).

There are several decisions supporting the proposition that reasonable reliance upon a decision of a lower court is likewise a defense. Thus, if the lower court has found a repealer statute constitutional, has declared the relevant criminal statute unconstitutional, or has enjoined enforcement of the statute, there may be a basis for reasonable reliance. However, in the case of lower court decisions there is more likely to arise a question of whether the reliance is reasonable. It has been suggested, for example, that reliance should not be a defense when it was known that the decision of the lower court was on appeal. Some modern codes only recognize reliance upon appellate decisions.

(3) Reasonable Reliance Upon an Official Interpretation. Consistent with the above, the better view is that if a defendant reasonably relies upon an erroneous official statement of the law contained in an administrative order or grant or in an official interpretation by the public officer or body responsible for interpretation, administration, or enforcement of the law defining the offense, then his belief that the conduct was not criminal is a defense. This is most obviously so when the defendant is prosecuted for engaging in activity without a license, as required by state law, and he shows that upon application for such a license to the proper authority he was advised that no license was required. In such a situation, the defendant has done everything that may reasonably be expected of him.

But what if the defendant, not in the context of seeking a license or permit, obtains an advisory opinion from some enforcement official, most likely the local prosecuting attorney, that his contemplated conduct would not be in violation of the criminal law? "Local prosecuting attorneys and law officers have a duty to give legal opinions to the local officials within their district, and it is only natural for private citizens as well to come to them for advice on questions of criminal liability." Thus, it would seem that here as well a defense of reasonable reliance should be available. But in *Hopkins v. State* (1949), the defense was rejected on the ground that otherwise the prosecutor's advice "would become paramount to the law." Such an objection is ill-founded, for the law would still be paramount; the advice would establish a defense of good faith only for the individual who received it and only so long as that individual was not authoritatively advised to the contrary.

Indeed, the result in *Hopkins* would appear to be contrary to due process, for to permit conviction of a person for conduct that he has been told by state officials is permissible "would be to sanction an indefensible sort of entrapment by the State." Thus, as the Supreme Court held in *Cox v. La.* (1965), demonstrators may not constitutionally be convicted of parading "near" a courthouse when they did so after the highest police officials of the city told them, in effect, that they could lawfully meet 101 feet from the courthouse steps. Similarly, due process was held to bar conviction of persons for refusing to answer questions of a state investigating commission when they relied upon assurances of the commission that they had a privilege to refuse to answer, although in fact they did not.

It does not follow, of course, that one would be justified in seeking out any public official for such advice and then proceeding in reliance upon the opinion received. Whether viewed in terms of the requirement that the reliance itself be reasonable or, as also provided in Model Penal Code § 2.04(3)(b), that the interpretation be obtained from one "charged by law with responsibility for the interpretation, administration or enforcement of the law defining the offense," such a broad interpretation of the defense is unwarranted. Thus, for example, a tavern keeper could not rely upon advice from the mayor as to the meaning of the state law concerning the closing of bars on election day, nor could a policeman rely upon the court clerk who administered his oath of office for an opinion about the lawfulness of the officer carrying a concealed weapon. On the other hand, a chemical company could reasonably rely upon a Corps of Engineers' interpretation that the River and Harbor Act only prohibits water deposits that affect navigation, as the Corps "is the responsible administrative agency under the * * * Act."

(4) Reliance Upon Advice of Private Counsel. In each of the situations heretofore described, the general objections to recognizing a mistake-of-the-criminal-law defense are inapplicable, for "the possibility of collusion is minimal, and * * * a judicial determination of the reasonableness of the belief in legality should not present substantial difficulty." Is this not equally true if the defendant has reasonably relied upon a private attorney for advice? It has been argued with some persuasion that the answer is yes, at least when the defendant can show that he consulted a reputable attorney, he had a good faith belief in the legality of his conduct, and the conduct is not obviously antisocial in character. Here as well, so the argument goes, the defendant has clearly shown that his actions have been entirely consistent with law-abidingness.

Yet, the cases uniformly hold that no defense is available under these circumstances, and Model Penal Code § 2.04 is in accord. The principal reason for this position apparently is that the risk of collusion is greater and that those desiring to circumvent the law would shop around for bad advice. "Lawyers are under enough temptations toward dishonesty already, without giving them the power to grant indulgences, for a fee, in criminal cases. Nor is the private attorney an 'officer of the state' for whose advice the state is responsible, whatever may be his status as an 'officer of the court' for other purposes." It has been forcefully argued, however, that the rule should be otherwise (as it is in one jurisdiction) because (i) reliance upon one's own counsel, as compared to a government official, is not inherently more blameworthy, and (ii) the potential for abuse, given the necessity for reasonable reliance, is not that great and, in any event, any problems of proof "may be reduced significantly * * * by giving the defendant the burdens of production and persuasion."

Chapter 5

ACTS; CONCURRENCE AND CONSEQUENCES

Table of Sections

For additional analysis of the above topics and citations to authorities supporting their discussion in this Book, consult the author's 3-volume *Substantive Criminal Law* treatise, also available as Westlaw database SUBCRL. See the Table of Cross-References in this Book.

---

§ 5.1   Requirement of an Act

Bad thoughts alone cannot constitute a crime; there must be an act, or an omission to act where there is a legal duty to act. Thus the common law crimes are defined in terms of act or omission to act, and statutory crimes are unconstitutional unless so defined. A bodily movement, to qualify as an act forming the basis of criminal liability, must be voluntary.

(a) Meaning of "Act." The word "act" has been defined in many different ways, often depending upon the purpose for which the word is used. Sometimes, for example, there are said to be both positive and negative acts, the latter referring to leaving undone something that ought to be done. Similarly, the word has sometimes been defined so as to encompass both internal and external acts; internal acts are said to be "acts of the mind" that do not necessarily "realize themselves in acts of the body." The view has also been taken that an act includes three constituent parts: (1) its origin, such as bodily activity; (2) certain surrounding circumstances; and (3) certain consequences. For example, in a situation in which *A* shoots and kills *B,* this "act" might be said to include the muscular contraction by which the trigger was pulled, the circumstances that the weapon was loaded and that *B* was in the line of fire, and the consequence of *B*'s death.

Other theorists have subscribed to a much narrower definition; to them, acts are merely bodily movements. This, of course, excludes what was referred to above as negative acts, internal acts, surrounding circumstances, and consequences. This is the modern view, as reflected in Model Penal Code § 1.13(2), and is adopted here because it is this definition of act that is most meaningful in discussing the requirement of an act. There are analytical difficulties in calling an omission an act, and thus it is better simply to acknowledge that either an act or an omission to act contrary to a legal duty suffices. For the reasons explained later, internal acts (that is, mere thoughts) cannot constitute a crime, which means that it is better to exclude them from the definition of act.

In favor of defining acts to include the circumstances and consequences, it has been argued that this approach is desirable because offenses are often defined in terms of circumstances (e.g., in perjury, that the witness is sworn; in bigamy, that the defendant is already married) and consequences (e.g., in homicide, the killing of a human being), and because a more limited view as to the meaning of the word "act" may result in a holding that no mental state is necessary as to these circumstances or consequences. As to the latter, this problem may be avoided (as in Model Penal Code §§ 1.13(10), 2.02(1)) by merely recognizing certain circumstances and consequences as material elements of an offense and then requiring some mental state as to each material element. A definition of act that encompasses circumstances and consequences, on the other hand, presents a serious problem in determining the termination point of one's acts, and also poses serious analytical difficulties in discussing "voluntary" acts.

(b) Necessity for an Act. One basic premise of Anglo–American criminal law is that no crime can be committed by bad thoughts alone. Something in the way of an act, or of an omission to act where there is a legal duty to act, is required too (see § 5.2). To wish an enemy dead, to contemplate the forcible ravishment of a woman, to think about taking another's wallet—such thoughts constitute none of the existing crimes (not murder or rape or larceny) so long as the thoughts produce no action to bring about the wished-for results. But, while it is no crime merely to entertain an intent to commit a crime, an attempt (or an agreement with another person) to commit it may be criminal; but the reason is that an attempt (or a conspiracy) requires some activity beyond the mere entertainment of the intent.

Mere thoughts must be distinguished from speech; an act sufficient for criminal liability may consist of nothing more than the movement of the tongue so as to form spoken words. Some crimes are usually committed by the act of speech, such as perjury and false pretenses and the inchoate crimes of conspiracy and solicitation. Other crimes, usually committed by other forms of activity, may nevertheless be committed by spoken words; thus one person can murder another by maneuvering him into the electric chair by giving perjured testimony at his trial for a capital crime. And, because one is guilty of a crime if he encourages or commands or hires another to commit it (see § 12.2), it would seem that practically all crimes may be committed by conduct which includes no voluntary bodily movement other than speaking.

The common law crimes all require an act or omission in addition to a bad state of mind. A statute purporting to make it criminal simply to think bad thoughts would, in the United States, be held unconstitutional. And a statute that is worded vaguely on the question of whether an act (or omission), in addition to a state of mind, is required for criminal liability will be construed to require some act (or omission).

Several reasons have been given in justification for the requirement of an act. One is that a person's thoughts are not susceptible of proof except when demonstrated by outward actions. But, while this is doubtless true in most instances, it fails to take account of the possibility that one might confess or otherwise acknowledge to others the fact that he has entertained a certain intent. Another reason given is the difficulty in distinguishing a fixed intent from mere daydream and fantasy. Most persuasive, however, is the notion that the criminal law should not be so broadly defined to reach those who entertain criminal schemes but never let their thoughts govern their conduct.

It should also be noted that even bad thoughts plus action do not equal a particular crime if the action is not that which the definition of the crime requires. No doubt, for instance, the legislature can make it a crime to put poison in a well with intent to cause injury or death; if so, such a crime can be committed though no one comes close to taking a drink before the poison is discovered. But if the statute most nearly in point punishes "assault with intent to kill," such a statute is not violated under the above circumstances, the reason being that the action taken is not the action which the crime, by its definition, requires. Some crimes are so defined that a series of acts is required for their commission. Burglary, for instance, at common law (and by some modern statutes) requires both a "breaking" and an "entering" of a dwelling house; the defendant normally first opens a closed door or window and then walks or climbs through the open door or window. Doing the first act without the second (or the second without the first) would not satisfy such a definition of burglary.

(c) Voluntary Nature of Act. The word "act" might be defined in a broad sense to include such involuntary actions as bodily movements during sleep or unconsciousness, or in a narrow sense to mean only voluntary bodily movement. At all events, it is clear that criminal liability requires that the activity in question be voluntary. The deterrent function of the criminal law would not be served by imposing sanctions for involuntary action, as such action cannot be deterred. Likewise, assuming revenge or retribution to be a legitimate purpose of punishment, there would appear to be no reason to impose punishment on this basis as to those whose actions were not voluntary. Restraint or rehabilitation might be deemed appropriate, however, where individuals are likely to constitute a continuing threat to others because of their involuntary movements, but it is probably best to deal with this problem outside the criminal law.

Just what is meant by the term "voluntary" has caused the theorists considerable difficulty. Sometimes a voluntary act is said to be an external manifestation of the will. Or, it may be said to be behavior that would have been otherwise if the individual had willed or chosen it to be otherwise. There are those who believe that the term is indefinable, and also those who take the view that a voluntary act must be defined in terms of conditions which render an act involuntary. Model Penal Code § 2.01(2) comes closest to the last approach, as it identifies certain movements that are deemed not to be voluntary acts: a reflex or convulsion; those during unconsciousness or sleep; those during hypnosis or resulting from hypnotic suggestion; and others which are not a product of the effort or determination of the actor, either conscious or habitual.

The cases, though few in number, lend support to most of the specific classifications. It has been held, for example, that one is not guilty of murder if he killed the victim while asleep or in the clouded state between sleeping and waking. Even assuming that "the conduct of a sleep-walker may be purposive (though not recollected on waking), and may be regarded as expressing unconscious desire," it is nonetheless undoubtedly sound not to impose liability for an unconscious desire manifested in this way. Similarly, it has been held that there is no voluntary act as to movements following unconsciousness, and the defense of hypnotism has been allowed. As to the latter, it should be noted that there is a difference of opinion as to whether acts during or resulting from hypnosis are actually involuntary, stemming largely from differing views on whether a hypnotized person will engage in acts that are repugnant to him. The residual category in the Model Penal Code formulation also covers the classic case in which one person physically forces another person into bodily movement, as where A by force causes B's body to strike C; under these circumstances, there is no voluntary act by B. But it does not include so-called "brain-washing," whereby attitudinal changes are produced through a process of coercive persuasion. Nor does it include instances in which the defendant ingested drugs or alcohol, or the situation that in some jurisdictions falls within the insanity defense and is called "irresistible impulse" (see § 6.3(a)).

There is general agreement that a mere reflex is not a voluntary act. It should be noted, however, that the term "reflex" does not cover all instances of bodily movement in quick response to some outside force or circumstances. A reflex is a muscular reaction "in which the mind and will have no share," such as a knee jerk or the blinking of the eyelids. It does not include, for example, the case in which A, finding himself about to fall, reaches out to seize some object in order to avoid falling, for in that instance A's mind has quickly grasped the situation and dictated some action.

Although a voluntary act is an absolute requirement for criminal liability, it does not follow that every act up to the moment that the harm is caused must be voluntary. Thus, one may be guilty of criminal homicide (or battery) even though he is unconscious or asleep at the time of the fatal (or injurious) impact, as where A, being subject to frequent fainting spells, has such a spell while driving his car (or, after becoming aware that he is sleepy, continues to drive and falls asleep at the wheel), with the result that the car, out of control, runs into and kills (or injures) B while A is unconscious or asleep. Here A's voluntary act consists of driving the car, and if the necessary mental state can be established as of that time (e.g., finding recklessness on the basis of A's knowledge that he was very sleepy or subject to epileptic seizures), it is enough to make him guilty of a crime.

(d) Crimes of Personal Condition. A few crimes—notably the crime of vagrancy—are often defined in such a way as to punish status (e.g., being a vagrant) rather than to punish specific action or omission to act. Statutes creating crimes of this sort, though occasionally held invalid as creating an unreasonable restraint on personal liberty or on account of vagueness in definition, have often been upheld notwithstanding their definition of crime in terms of "being" rather than "acting." There is a growing body of authority, however, that such statutes are unconstitutional, either as a violation of substantive due process (see § 3.3(d)) or on cruel and unusual punishment grounds (see § 3.5(f)).

(e) Crimes of Possession. Some crimes are defined in terms of possession. Thus, possession of intoxicating liquor or of narcotics or of counterfeiting dies, or possession of burglar's tools with intent to commit a burglary therewith, may be made criminal. Though possession is not, strictly speaking, an act (bodily movement) or an omission to act, crimes based upon possession are generally upheld. For legal purposes other than criminal law—e.g., the law of finders—one may possess something without knowing of its existence, but possession in a criminal statute is usually construed to mean conscious possession. So construed, knowingly receiving an item or retention after awareness of control over it could be considered a sufficient act or omission to serve as the proper basis for a crime. This knowledge or awareness, however, concerns only the physical object and not its specific quality or properties; one may be said to be in possession of narcotics even when he believes that the substance is not a narcotic, although this belief might well bar conviction because the required mental state is lacking.

The word "possession" is often used in the criminal law without definition, which perhaps reflects only the fact that it is "a common term used in everyday conversation that has not acquired any artful meaning." Certainly the term encompasses actual physical control, although even as to this "something more than momentary control" is said to be necessary (though the persons's involvement with the article need not constitute "use," another common term in criminal statutes). However, possession need not be exclusive in a single person; joint possession is possible in the criminal law. Both statutes and court decisions sometimes define possession more expansively as covering any exercise of dominion and control over the property in question. This approach, it has been noted, "is simply not informative in any functional manner" because the "terms 'dominion' and 'control' are nothing more than labels used by courts to characterize given sets of facts."

Certainly a part of the problem, as the Supreme Court noted some years ago, is that the word possession "is interchangeably used to describe actual possession and constructive possession which often so shade into one another that it is difficult to say where one ends and the other begins." Constructive possession, which is simply a doctrine used to broaden the application of possession-type crimes to situations in which actual physical control cannot be directly proved, is often described in terms of dominion and control, or more loosely as the power to exert dominion and control. It is not uncommon, however, for constructive possession to be even more broadly defined to include as well circumstances in which the defendant had the ability to reduce an object to his control. Various factors are utilized by courts to support a finding of constructive possession.

(f) Vicarious Liability. It is a general principle of criminal law that one is not criminally liable for how someone else acts, unless of course he directs or encourages or aids the other so to act. Thus, unlike the case with torts, an employer is not generally liable for the criminal acts of his employee even though the latter does them in furtherance of his employer's business. In other words, with crimes defined in terms of harmful acts and bad thoughts, the defendant himself must personally engage in the acts and personally think the bad thoughts, unless, in the case of a statutory crime, the legislature has otherwise provided (see § 12.4).

§ 5.2   Omission to Act

Most crimes are committed by affirmative action rather than by non-action. But there are a number of statutory crimes that are specifically defined in terms of failure to act; and other crimes that, though not specifically so defined, may be committed either by affirmative action or by failure to act under circumstances giving rise to a legal duty to act.

Illustrative of the former are statutes making it a crime for a taxpayer to fail to file a tax return, for a parent to neglect to furnish medical care for his sick children, for a motorist to fail to stop after involvement in an automobile accident, or for a draftee to fail to report at the appointed time and place for induction into the armed forces. Such crimes of omission give rise to little difficulty so far as criminal liability for omission is concerned. The criminal statute itself imposes the duty to act, and breach of the duty is made a crime.

More difficult, however, are crimes that are not specifically defined in terms of omission to act but only in terms of cause and result. Murder and manslaughter are defined so as to require the "killing" of another person; arson so as to require a "burning" of appropriate property. Nothing in the definition of murder or manslaughter or arson affirmatively suggests that the crime may or may not be committed by omission to act. But these crimes may, in appropriate circumstances, be thus committed. So a parent who fails to call a doctor to attend his sick child may be guilty of criminal homicide if the child should die for want of medical care, though the parent does nothing of an affirmative nature to cause the child's death. Even accomplice liability may be grounded in an omission to act.

(a) Duty to Act. For criminal liability to be based upon a failure to act it must first be found that there is a duty to act—a legal duty and not simply a moral duty. As we have seen, some criminal statutes themselves impose the legal duty to act, as with the tax statute and the hit-and-run statute. With other crimes the duty must be found outside the definition of the crime itself— perhaps in another statute, or in the common law, or in a contract.

Generally one has no legal duty to aid another person in peril, even when that aid can be rendered without danger or inconvenience to himself. He need not shout a warning to a blind man headed for a precipice or to an absent-minded one walking into a gunpowder room with a lighted candle in hand. He need not pull a neighbor's baby out of a pool of water or rescue an unconscious person stretched across the railroad tracks, though the baby is drowning or the whistle of an approaching train is heard in the distance. A doctor is not legally bound to answer a desperate call from the frantic parents of a sick child, at least if it is not one of his regular patients. A moral duty to take affirmative action is not enough to impose a legal duty to do so. But there are situations that do give rise to a duty to act:

(1) Duty Based Upon Relationship. The common law imposes affirmative duties upon persons standing in certain personal relationships to other persons—upon parents to aid their small children, upon husbands to aid their wives, upon ship captains to aid their crews, upon masters to aid their servants. Thus a parent— or, indeed, another person standing in loco parentis—may be guilty of criminal homicide for failure to call a doctor for his sick child, a mother for failure to prevent the fatal beating of her baby by her lover, a husband for failure to aid his imperiled wife, a ship captain for failure to pick up a seaman or passenger fallen overboard, and an employer for failure to aid his endangered employee. Action may be required to thwart the threatened perils of nature (e.g., to combat sickness, to ward off starvation or the elements); or it may be required to protect against threatened acts by third persons.

Aside from the relationships mentioned above, perhaps other relationships may give rise to a duty to act. If two mountain climbers, climbing together, are off by themselves on a mountainside, and one falls into a crevasse, it would seem that the nature of their joint enterprise, involving a relationship of mutual reliance, ought to impose a duty upon the one mountaineer to extricate his imperiled colleague. So also if two people, though not closely related, live together under one roof, one may have a duty to act to aid the other who becomes helpless.

(2) Duty Based Upon Statute. A statute (other than the criminal statute whose violation is in question) sometimes imposes a duty to act to help another in distress. Thus it is commonly provided that a driver involved in an automobile accident must stop and render whatever assistance is necessary to others who may be injured in the accident. Failure to stop after an accident would of course be a violation of the hit-and-run statute itself; but furthermore, if an injured party should die for lack of this assistance, the driver might well be criminally liable for the homicide as well. Here the duty to act to preserve life is to be found in the hit-and-run statute. The same result would follow from statutes making it a criminal offense not to provide safety measures, if, as a result of such omission, someone should die. Statutes sometimes impose upon a person the duty to furnish necessaries to other persons; and failure to do so may lead to criminal liability for a resulting death. No doubt a duty to act may be imposed by a non-criminal statute, by an ordinance, or by an administrative regulation or order.

(3) Duty Based Upon Contract. The duty to act to aid others may arise, not out of personal relationship or out of statute, but out of contract. A lifeguard employed to watch over swimmers at the beach, and a railroad gateman hired to safeguard motorists from approaching trains, have a duty, to the public they are employed to protect, to take affirmative action in appropriate circumstances. The lifeguard cannot sit idly by while a swimmer at his beach drowns off shore; the gateman must lower the gate when a train and automobile approach his crossing on collision courses. Omission to do so may make the lifeguard or gateman liable for criminal homicide. So too a nurse may be contractually obligated to act to aid her patient, and an asylum superintendent to aid those in his charge. For a duty to act, by virtue of a contract, to exist, the victim need not be one of the contracting parties.

A more difficult problem concerns the duty, not of the one who is employed to safeguard the public in a particular way, but rather of his fellow employee, whose employment contract does not specifically require him to act in that way. What if, for instance, a locomotive engineer standing near a crossing sees a train and car approaching the crossing; does he owe a duty to the motorist to wake up the sleeping gateman, in view of his employment by the railroad to operate trains? It would seem that a duty to act might be imposed on him, though there is authority to the contrary.

(4) Duty Based Upon Voluntary Assumption of Care. Although one might not, as an original matter, have a duty to act to rescue a stranger in peril, yet once he undertakes to help him he may have a duty to see the job through. Thus, although he may have no duty to pick an unconscious person off the railroad tracks as a train is approaching around the bend, yet if he once lifts him off the track, he cannot thereafter lay him down again in his original position; if he should do so, and the train should kill him, he would be criminally liable for the homicide. A more difficult problem is involved if he starts to aid the other but does not go so far as to improve the other's position, as where a good swimmer starts to swim out to a drowning bather but turns back on recognizing the bather as his enemy. Perhaps here he would be liable only if his conduct in starting to go to the other's rescue induced other prospective rescuers to forego action. So too if one voluntarily and gratuitously assumes responsibility for a helpless person—such as for a child or an insane or infirm person—he has a duty thereafter to act to protect the other from harm.

(5) Duty Based Upon Creation of the Peril. If one person himself places another in a position of danger—either intentionally or negligently or without fault—does he have an affirmative duty to safeguard the other from that danger? The clearest case of such a duty is that in which the defendant is himself at fault in creating the danger. But there may perhaps be a duty to act even if the defendant innocently creates the situation of danger, as where one accidentally starts a fire in a building and then fails to take steps to rescue another person trapped therein. It has been argued, however, that one who innocently creates danger is on principle in the same position as that of a bystander who happens by when a situation of danger has developed.

By way of contrast, where a duty to act to save an imperiled person otherwise exists, it is no defense to a crime based upon failure to act that the victim was at fault in negligently getting himself into his predicament, as where a seaman negligently falls overboard.

(6) Duty to Control Conduct of Others. One may stand in such a personal relationship to another that he has an affirmative duty to control the latter's conduct in the interest of the public safety, so that omission to do so may give rise to criminal liability. A parent not only has a duty to act affirmatively to safeguard his children, but he also has a duty to safeguard third persons from his children; an employer has a similar duty to curb his employee while the latter is performing his employer's business. Thus a car-owner may be criminally liable to third persons injured or killed as a result of his failure to control his speeding chauffeur.

(7) Duty of Landowner. A landowner may have a duty to act affirmatively to provide for the safety of those whom he invites onto his land. A night-club owner may be criminally liable, for instance, for the deaths of his patrons killed as a result of the owner's failure to provide proper fire escapes.

Over the years of the development of tort and criminal law, the trend has been in the direction of creating new situations wherein an affirmative duty to act is imposed. No doubt the trend will continue in the future.

(b) Knowledge of Legal Duty and Facts Giving Rise to Duty. Although part of the larger problem of when the imposition of strict liability should be permitted and when a mistake of fact or law should be recognized as a defense (see §§ 4.5, 4.6), some attention should be given here to the question of whether liability may be imposed for an omission when the defendant was either unaware of the facts giving rise to the duty to act or unaware of the existence or scope of the legal duty.

Though one might otherwise be under a duty to act, so that omission to do so would ordinarily render him criminally liable, the prevailing view is that he may not be held liable if he does not know the facts indicating a duty to act. Thus, while a father normally has a duty to rescue his young child from drowning, if he does not know the child is in the water then his ignorance may relieve him from criminal responsibility for the child's death. And while a parent has a duty to obtain medical attention for a seriously

ill child, the parent's ignorance of the child's condition may likewise relieve him or her of responsibility for the child's death.
Similarly, most courts have taken the view that one may not be
convicted under a hit-and-run statute if he was unaware of the fact
that an accident has occurred. Of course, sometimes there may be a
duty to take care to know the facts, as well as a duty to go into
action when the facts are known. Thus a grandmother, who undertook the care of her infant grandchild, who did not know that the
child was smothering to death because, after taking charge of the
child, she had put herself into a drunken stupor, was held criminally liable for the child's death.

Some courts have taken the position that the imposition of
strict liability in omission cases is inappropriate. Basically, the
argument is that, notwithstanding whatever reasons might be given
for saying that those who engage in certain activity should be held
to act at their peril (e.g., those engaged in the sale of liquor should
be held strictly liable for sales to minors), it is unfair to hold
individuals liable for failing to act when they were unaware of the
circumstances that ought to prompt such action. As one court has
put it, one cannot be said to have a duty to report something of
which he has no knowledge. On the other hand, the imposition of
strict liability in omission cases has sometimes been justified on
essentially the same basis as in other cases. This approach is
reflected in one case which held that one might be convicted under
a hit-and-run statute without proof that he was aware that an
accident had occurred; the court viewed driving on the highways as
a high-risk activity that merited the imposition of liability without
regard to knowledge of the specific facts, and also expressed concern over the problems of proof that would be presented if the
prosecution had to establish scienter beyond a reasonable doubt in
every hit-and-run case.

What, then, of the case in which the defendant, though aware
of the facts, was unaware of the existence or scope of the duty to
act? For example, could a parent who, finding his small child
drowning in the bathtub, fails to pull the child out, successfully
defend on the ground that he did not know that a parent has a duty
to act to protect his small children from the perils of drowning? Or,
could a driver successfully defend a prosecution for failure to report
an accident on the ground that he mistakenly believed that the
statutory reference to "accident" was intended to cover only cases
of collision and not the present instance of a passenger falling while
alighting from the vehicle? By application of the general principle
that ignorance of the law is usually no excuse (see § 4.6(d)), the
answer would seem to be no. An exception, of course, may be where
the statute only covers "wilful" or "knowing" failure to carry out a
duty, for there ignorance of the existence or scope of the duty

negates the required mental state, as has been held as to certain omissions covered by the Internal Revenue Code.

The critical question, then, is when a legislature may impose liability for failure to perform some duty even in the absence of knowledge as to the existence or scope of that duty, which the Supreme Court confronted in *Lambert v. Cal.* (1957). The defendant was convicted because she, a convicted felon, failed to register with the Los Angeles authorities as required by ordinance, and she was not permitted to raise ignorance of the registration requirement as a defense. The Supreme Court reversed on the ground that due process requires that ignorance of a duty must be allowed as a defense when "circumstances which might move one to inquire as to the necessity of [taking certain affirmative action] are completely lacking." The dissenters, erroneously it seems, criticized the majority for drawing a distinction between acts and omissions; the distinction is actually between omissions involving duties of a highly unusual and unforeseeable nature and all other cases. The *Lambert* defense would most likely not be available when the legal duty is consistent with a strong moral duty, as in the drowning hypothetical described above. Likewise, it probably would be unavailable in the case described above involving the mistaken interpretation of the accident-reporting requirements.

(c) Possibility of Performing the Act. Just as one cannot be criminally liable on account of a bodily movement that is involuntary (see § 5.1(c)), so one cannot be criminally liable for failing to do an act that he is physically incapable of performing. A father who cannot swim need not dive into deep water to rescue his drowning child. But impossibility means impossibility. Thus, though a poverty-stricken parent would not be criminally liable for his child's death resulting from failure to provide food and shelter if it is impossible for him to obtain these necessaries, he would be liable if he failed to go to an available welfare agency for help.

A related question concerns the amount of inconvenience and expense and risk that the rescuer must undergo in order to fulfill his duty to act. A parent must doubtless leave his companions in the middle of an interesting bridge hand to rescue his smothering baby. Must he risk his life by diving into a dangerous whirlpool to save his drowning child? Probably the amount of risk that a person must take depends to some extent upon the fact situation giving rise to the duty to act. Thus a parent, to carry out his duty to aid his child, might be required to take a greater chance with his own life than would be required of a motorist who has innocently injured a stranger in an automobile accident.

A somewhat different problem concerns the chance one should take with a third person's life: should a parent endanger the third person's life to save his own child; should a ship captain endanger the lives of all on board in order to pick up a seaman or passenger fallen overboard? In such a choice-of-evils situation, the omission to act may be excused because of the risk to third persons involved in acting.

(d) Causation. Most of the criminal cases on omission to act deal with criminal homicide—murder or manslaughter. Homicide crimes require not only conduct (act or omission, with accompanying state of mind) but a certain result of conduct (the death of the victim). It must therefore be shown, in the homicide-by-omission cases, not only that the defendant had a duty to act, but also that his failure to act caused the death.

The problem of causation in omission cases has been a matter of real difficulty for many theorists. For example, it has been claimed that when a speeding train runs over a child that the father failed to rescue, the cause of death is the train and not the forbearance of the father. However, problems of this nature disappear once it is acknowledged that the question of causation is not solely a question of mechanical connection, but rather a question of policy on imputing or denying liability.

Legal or "proximate" cause, at the very least, requires a showing of "but for" causation: but for the omission the victim would not have died (see § 5.4(b)). Failure on the part of a parent to call a doctor for a sick child may often make the parent criminally liable for the child's death; but only if the doctor could have saved it, not if it would have died in spite of medical attention. It is apparent that this is a matter which often is not susceptible of easy proof, and convictions have sometimes been reversed because of what the appellate court viewed as less than adequate proof of causation. It has been argued that the courts have been somewhat too demanding in this regard, and that it should suffice if the prosecution establishes a serious sickness and a failure to summon aid. This approach, it is claimed, would bring the omission-causation cases in line with the act-causation cases, where an act may be said to cause another's death notwithstanding the fact that the victim's life would have soon been taken by some other cause.

(e) Crimes That May be Committed by Omission to Act. Other than the crimes that are specifically defined in terms of omission to act (e.g., failure to file a tax return; failure to stop and aid after accident), what possible crimes may be committed by failure to act? Most of the actual cases are, as already noted, homicide cases, wherein someone died by reason of a failure to act. The homicidal crime thus committed may be murder or manslaughter depending upon state-of-mind factors applicable generally to these crimes. Thus one's failure to act to save someone toward whom he owes a duty to act is murder if he knows that failure to act will be certain or substantially certain to result in death or serious bodily injury. If he does not know that death or serious injury is substantially certain to result, but the circumstances are such as to involve a high degree of risk of such death or injury if he does not act (in some jurisdictions he must, in addition, be conscious of this risk), his failure to act will afford a basis for liability for involuntary manslaughter. A failure to act that, under the circumstances, amounts to no more than ordinary negligence would not, by the general rules of criminal homicide, make him liable for either murder or manslaughter. Thus it cannot accurately be said that an omission to act (assuming a duty to act) plus death equals murder, or equals manslaughter, without considering the *mens rea* requirements of those crimes.

It would seem that criminal battery may be committed by an omission to act (if there exists a duty to act), as well as by an affirmative act. If a parent, knowing that injury is substantially certain to result to his infant child unless he acts to prevent it, fails to act, and the infant is injured but not killed as a result, the parent would doubtless be guilty of battery. The same result should follow if his omission amounted to recklessness, though he did not intend any injury to the child.

In a case already noted an omission to put out a fire accidentally started, with intent to cause the building to burn down, was held to amount to arson. A father was held guilty of "abandoning and exposing" his infant child to the elements when, after his estranged wife had deposited the child, poorly clad in cold weather, on his doorstep, he carefully stepped over the child and proceeded on his way out the door. A driver was said to be guilty of the crime of "ill-treating" a dog by failing to stop his car and render aid after hitting the animal.

(f) A Broader Duty to Rescue? The traditional Anglo–American position on criminal omissions, which confines the duty to act in saving others from harm to certain narrowly-defined categories, has long been the subject of serious debate. Note has frequently been taken of the fact that many European codes adopt a much broader view, imposing a duty to rescue on anyone who could do so without danger to himself, and this has led to the recommendation that duty and liability should be based upon "the defendant's clear recognition of the victim's peril plus his failure to take steps which might reasonably be taken without risk to himself to warn or protect the victim." Those who subscribe to this view ask, for example, why criminal sanctions should not be imposed upon an expert swimmer who fails to come to the rescue of a drowning child.

One long-standing explanation for not expanding legal duty to conform to moral duty is that the latter notion is extremely vague. Precisely how does one define a doctor's moral duty, in terms of the effort and expense that must be undertaken, to aid one known to be in need of medical attention? Does everyone who knows of the existence of a starving person have a moral duty to give that person food? But in response to the argument that no broader rule can be formulated, it is contended that an appeal to common decency is no less specific than the standard of liability for negligent acts. Another argument made against a more general duty to rescue is that it would unduly broaden the "circumstances under which the ordinary citizen will be exposed to the hazards of legal prosecution" because "omissions are so inherently ambiguous that speculation about the omitter's guilt and dangerousness is more of a threat to society than is the preventable harm by omission." Others question whether this would be so, and also label as speculation the related claim that a broader duty to rescue would influence people to interfere officiously in the affairs of others.

Finally, the point is made that, despite frequent avowals to the contrary, we really do not view death-causing omissions in the same way as death-causing acts, so that what is in fact a distinction on moral grounds is appropriately also a distinction in the criminal law. However, this does not necessarily mean that omissions outside existing legal duty categories should be ignored by the criminal law; it may only mean that such omissions should be subject to lesser sanctions than those provided for acts that bring about the same results. For example, causing the death of a stranger by failing to rescue him would not be considered homicide, and thus would not be punished as severely as affirmative acts with the same mental state and the same consequences. Some of the European "Good Samaritan laws" operate in this way, and similar legislation has been adopted in a few states.

§ 5.3 Concurrence of Acts and Results With Mental Fault

This section deals with two different problems concerning concurrence of the mental fault (intent, knowledge, recklessness, or negligence) with other elements of the various crimes. One problem is that of the necessary concurrence of the mental fault with the act or omission which is the basis for liability—that is, the act or omission which constitutes the "legal cause" of the bad result, when the crime in question is defined in terms of a certain bad result. This is sometimes referred to as concurrence in time, although we shall see that actually concurrence in time is neither required nor sufficient; the true meaning of the requirement that the mental fault concur with the act or omission is that the former actuate the latter.

The second problem concerns concurrence of the mental fault with the bad results, which arises as to those crimes defined in terms of bad results. This is often spoken of as the requirement of concurrence in kind and intensity, which reflects the notion that ordinarily the mental fault (intent, recklessness, etc.) must be of the same order as the harm caused. Or, to put it another way, mental states are not interchangeable between crimes; if one sets out with intent to cause the harm covered in crime A and then inadvertently causes the harm covered by crime B, neither crime A nor crime B has been committed. There are a number of important exceptions to this, however, in that some crimes are defined in terms of causing one result while having a mental state concerning another, quite different result.

(a) Concurrence of Act or Omission and Mental Fault. With those crimes that require some mental fault (whether intention, knowledge, recklessness, or negligence) in addition to an act or omission, it is a basic premise of Anglo–American criminal law that the physical conduct and the state of mind must concur. Although it is sometimes assumed that there cannot be such concurrence unless the mental and physical aspects exist at precisely the same moment of time, the better view is that there is concurrence when the defendant's mental state actuates the physical conduct. That is, mere coincidence in point of time is not necessarily sufficient, while the lack of such unity is not necessarily a bar to conviction.

The easiest cases are those in which the bad state of mind follows the physical conduct, for here it is obvious that the subsequent mental state is in no sense legally related to the prior acts or omissions of the defendant. Thus it is not a criminal battery for A accidentally to strike and injure his enemy B, though A, on realizing what has happened, rejoices at B's discomfiture. It is not burglary for A to open the door and enter B's house at night with an innocent intention, though A later decides to steal B's property therein. The crime of receiving stolen property knowing it to be stolen is not committed when A receives from B property that he does not know to be stolen, though when A later learns it is stolen he decides to keep it. It is not larceny for A to take possession of and carry off B's property with an innocent mind, although later A, overcome by temptation, converts the property with an intent to steal it. Similarly, it is not robbery if the act of force or intimidation by which the taking is accomplished precedes the formation of the larcenous purpose. And one who expresses approval to his employee for the latter's prior crime is not held accountable for the crime, as he could have been had he directed his employee to commit the crime.

With crimes committed by conduct in the form of omission to act, as well as with those committed by conduct of the affirmative-action sort, the state of mind must concur with the conduct. Thus, under a statute making it a crime (arson) to burn one's own building with intent to defraud an insurance company, one who accidentally starts a fire in his own building is not thereby guilty, for his affirmative conduct in starting the fire is unaccompanied by any intent to defraud. But his further omission-to-act conduct in departing the premises without taking steps to extinguish the fire or to sound the alarm, intending that the building should burn so as to enable him to collect the insurance money, constitutes arson, for here his criminal omission to act coincides with his intent to defraud.

Of course, in some of the illustrations given above it may appear that the activity in question ought to be criminal. Often it can be and has been made criminal, without violence to the basic premise of concurrence, by redefining the crime or creating new crimes to cover other physical conduct that does concur with the defendant's mental state. This development is most evident in the area of larceny, where the offense was broadened by the courts by such doctrines as "breaking bulk" and "continuing trespass," and where such crimes as larceny by bailee and embezzlement were brought into being.

What, then, of the case in which the bad state of mind exists prior to the defendant's act or omission? Certainly one who at one time has such a state of mind cannot be convicted for having it merely because at some later date the acts or results that he once intended accidentally occur. Thus if A forms an intent to kill B, then abandons that intent, but at some later date inadvertently runs over B and kills him, A can hardly be considered to be guilty of murder merely because the results of his conduct coincide with his former intent. The imposition of criminal liability on this basis would be essentially the same as imposing liability for bad thoughts alone, which, for reasons we have noted earlier (see § 5.1), is not done.

One way to explain the above situation is simply to say that there is no concurrence because the mental state, being abandoned, did not actuate the physical conduct. But this may also be true when the mental state has not been abandoned. Assuming again that A forms an intent to kill B, but now that he has not abandoned that intent, and that he accidentally runs over B and kills him, the result still should be that there is no concurrence of the mental and physical elements. This is because "his moving and steering of his car were not done in order to give effect to desire to kill." Even this language must be narrowly read, it would seem, to mean that the acts must be done for the actual carrying out of the intent and not merely to prepare for its execution. In the above illustration, for example, it would not appear to make any difference that, at the time of the accident, *A* was driving to a store to purchase a gun with which to kill *B*.

Consider next the case in which *A* decides to kill *B*, and then voluntarily becomes intoxicated for the purpose of nerving himself for the accomplishment of his plan, and then, while intoxicated, kills *B*. Assuming that *A* had the required mental state prior to intoxication, but then became so intoxicated as to be unable to have such a mental state, is he guilty of murder? Most courts have said yes, disposing of the problem with the maxim that voluntary intoxication is not a defense under these circumstances, but in one case the defendant was acquitted on the ground that there was no concurrence of mental fault and act. But, if—as suggested above— the requirement of concurrence is not one of coexistence at a particular point of time, but rather of the state of mind actuating the physical conduct, then it would appear that *A* may be convicted of murder if there is this latter connection between the death-causing acts and his prior mental state. Just as in the previous illustration, if the killing were inadvertent and thus not attributable to the prior mental fault there would be no murder; but if the defendant's death-causing acts were more directly a consequence of the prior mental fault, then the basic premise of concurrence is satisfied.

(b) Attendant Circumstances and Results. With crimes that require physical conduct, mental fault, and attendant circumstances, the circumstances must concur with the conduct and fault. For example, it is not burglary, which requires that the dwelling broken into and entered be that of another, if one enters a house with intent to steal when, unknown to him, the former owner has just died and left the house to him. And, because the crime of rape under its traditional definition requires that the victim not be the defendant's wife, it is not rape for one to have sexual intercourse with his wife against her will an hour before their divorce.

With crimes defined in terms of conduct that produces a bad result (such as murder, manslaughter, and battery), there may be a time lag between the conduct and the result. In such a case it is the concurrence of the state of mind with the conduct, not with the result, which is necessary. Thus *A* may shoot *B* with intent to kill him; but if *B* lives on for a month before dying from the wound, by which time *A*, having repented of his earlier conduct, has employed some leading doctors in a vain attempt to save B's life, A is guilty of intent-to-kill murder, for his intent to kill B concurred with his act of shooting B, and his later reformation is irrelevant on the issue of guilt. Similarly, when A drives his car toward B's car with the intent of injuring B, but at the last moment he changes his mind and puts on the brakes but yet skids into B's car, the change of heart is no bar to conviction. There was an intent to injure that concurred with the injury-causing acts, and the fact that the results occurred only after a change in intent and ineffectual acts to avoid the results is immaterial. Likewise, one may be found guilty of reckless homicide notwithstanding a last-moment attempt to avoid the accident.

(c) What Act Must Concur With the Mental Fault? With crimes defined in terms of a mental state, act or omission, and a certain bad result, a particular kind of act or omission is seldom required. The emphasis is upon results caused by the defendant, and any act or omission (with the prescribed state of mind) which causes that result will do. Thus, intent-to-kill murder may be committed by an infinite variety of acts, though the act must both concur with the mental fault (here intent) and be the "legal cause" of the results (here the death of another). If attention is not focused upon the proper act, it may appear that the requirement of concurrence has not been met.

For example, consider the case in which the defendant, aware that he is extremely sleepy and in danger of falling asleep at the wheel of his car, drives on, then falls asleep, and then drives into the rear of another car, resulting in the death of one of the passengers. It might be contended that the awareness which makes up the mental fault existed prior to the time he went to sleep, and that the death-causing acts occurred subsequent to the time he fell asleep, so that there is not that concurrence of act and mental state needed for commission of a crime. But, we know that the acts subsequent to his falling asleep are not acts upon which criminal liability is based, as they do not even qualify as voluntary acts. Rather, the act—which is the cause of death—is continuing to drive while knowing that he is very sleepy, which obviously concurs with the required mental state.

The same kind of analysis can be utilized in dealing with the mistake-as-to-death cases, which have been a considerable source of difficulty to courts and commentators. The basic facts common to all of these cases are that the defendant has engaged in two separate acts: first, an act done with intent to kill that, unknown to the defendant, does not bring about death; and second, an act done to conceal the crime or dispose of what is thought to be a dead body, which does bring about death. For example, A poisons B and then, thinking B dead, decapitates her; the poison was insufficient to cause death, and B dies from the decapitation. C strikes D on the head, and then rolls what is thought to be D's dead body over a cliff in order to give the appearance of an accident; C did not give D a killing blow, and D dies from exposure at the bottom of the cliff. Numerous cases from foreign jurisdictions provide many other grisly illustrations.

In all of these cases in which there was an intent to kill and an attack on the victim in furtherance of that intent, there is no question but that the defendant could be convicted of attempted murder. But, what about a charge of murder? Is it not true that a murder conviction is foreclosed because of a lack of concurrence, in that the act done with intent to kill did not kill and the act which did kill was not done with intent to kill? Some courts have so held, although the weight of authority is to the contrary.

The rationale of some of the cases is obscure, but convictions in such cases have been upheld on the ground that disposal of the body was part of the original plan, or on the notion that the two acts were part of a single transaction with a common intention. Although it has been said that "ordinary ideas of justice and common sense require that such a case shall be treated as murder," other commentators have been firmly of the view that there is no concurrence in these cases. It is argued, for example, that no one would be guilty of murder when A strikes B with intent to kill and then departs erroneously believing B to be dead, and then C causes B's death by mutilating what he believes to be a dead body; and that the same should be true when there is but one actor.

It does seem clear that one cannot merely couple the prior intent to kill with the acts done with intent to dispose of a dead body, as the former intent did not actuate these acts, and to the extent that the cases rest upon this or similar notions they conflict with the principle of concurrence. However, there is no need to make such a connection, for there is an earlier act (A giving poison to B, and C striking D, in the illustrations given above) that clearly does concur, and if that act can be said to be the "legal" or "proximate" cause of death, then all the requirements for a crime are met. In short, the best approach to the mistake-as-to-death cases is to try to establish that the act which does concur with the intent was the legal cause of death, rather than to try to establish concurrence between the intent and the subsequent act which, admittedly, could more readily be found to be the legal cause of death.

(d) Concurrence of Results and Mental Fault—Difference as to Type of Harm. An intention to cause one type of harm cannot serve as a substitute for the statutory or common-law requirement of intention as to another type of harm. Thus where *A* intentionally steals a gas meter out of a house, and as a result a woman is made ill by the escaping gas, it cannot be said that the intent to steal suffices also to establish the intent to injure another. And where *A* throws a rock with intent to hit *B* and misses, unintentionally breaking *B*'s (or *C*'s) window, *A* is not guilty of malicious destruction of property of the intent-to-destroy type. Similarly, where *A* intends to steal rum from the hold of a ship and lights a match in order to see better, causing a fire that destroys the ship, *A* is not guilty of arson of the intent-to-burn type. (By like token, one type of knowledge will not suffice where the statute requires knowledge as to a different type of harm.) In all of these instances, however, the fact that *A* intended another type of harm does not foreclose the possibility that he might be found to have acted recklessly or negligently (if that is the required mental state) as to the harm caused, so that he might be convicted on this basis.

As these cases illustrate, what has sometimes been referred to as "transferred intent" is applicable only within the limits of the same crime; *A*'s intent to kill *B* may suffice as to his causing the death of *C*, but *A*'s intent to steal from *C* will not suffice as to his causing the burning of *C*'s property. That is, while a defendant can be convicted when he both has the *mens rea* and commits the *actus reus* required for a given offense, he cannot be convicted if the *mens rea* relates to one crime and the *actus reus* to another. Although the courts have not carefully articulated the reasons why this is so, the basic point is that a contrary rule would disregard the requirement of an appropriate mental state. The distinctions now drawn between various kinds of crimes in terms of their seriousness, as reflected by the punishments provided for them, would lose much of their significance if an intent to cause any one specific type of harm would suffice for conviction as to any other type of harm that is criminal when intentionally caused. There is no rational basis, for example, to support the conclusion that one who inadvertently burns a house while attempting to steal property therein should have his conduct classified in the same way as that of one who intentionally burns the house of another.

The same result should be reached when the mental state is recklessness or negligence. For example, it may happen that *A* acts recklessly toward *B*, foreseeably endangering his property but not his person; but, as it turns out, *B*'s property escapes without injury, yet *B* is killed (or injured). Or the converse situation may occur, as where *A* foreseeably endangers *B*'s person but not his property, but his property and not his person is injured or destroyed. It would seem that in either case *A* would not be criminally liable on account of the actual result, for manslaughter or battery in the first situation or for malicious mischief in the second.

There are a few notable exceptions to this general rule that a mental state as to one type of harm will not suffice for a crime involving another type of harm, and they come into play when the unintended harm is the death of another. Under the felony-murder rule, one may be guilty of murder if he causes the death of another in the course of committing a felony (or, at least, one of certain dangerous felonies); and, under the misdemeanor-manslaughter rule, one may be guilty of involuntary manslaughter if he causes the death of another while committing a *malum in se* type of misdemeanor. These rules, however, are not based upon notions of "transferred intent," but rather stem from certain peculiarities in the law of homicide, which will be discussed later (see §§ 13.5, 14.5).

It should also be noted that there are some crimes which contain, as part of their mental element, the intent to commit some other crime. Thus common-law burglary requires the intent to commit a felony within the dwelling. These crimes should not be viewed as exceptions to the rule that intent cannot be transferred between crimes, as the intent to commit another crime is an additional requirement and not a substitute for the required mental state as to the *actus reus* of the crime. In burglary, for example, intent to commit a felony is an additional element of the offense rather than an alternative to the necessary mental state for the acts of breaking and entering another's dwelling.

(e) Concurrence of Results and Mental Fault—Difference as to Degree of Harm. With many crimes that are defined so as to require some forbidden harmful result, the degree of harm, within fairly broad limits, may not be relevant to the question of criminal liability. For A intentionally to strike B without justification is a battery, and it makes no difference as to A's guilt of simple battery whether B is lightly scratched or seriously injured. So if A intends a light injury but actually inflicts a serious injury, or intends a serious injury but inflicts only a light injury, we need not worry about the difference between his intent and his achievement so far as simple battery is concerned. And if one intends to kill his enemy painlessly but succeeds in inflicting pain before death, he is guilty of nothing more than murder. With the crime of malicious mischief, it makes no difference whether A intends to injure B's property but actually destroys it, or intends to destroy but actually only injures it.

On the other hand, some crimes differ from others according to the degree of the resulting harm, as battery (requiring only bodily injury) differs from criminal homicide (requiring death), or a battery (requiring only slight injury) differs from mayhem (requiring loss of a bodily member or—today generally—disfigurement), or as a simple battery differs from statutory aggravated battery with intent to kill or maim. It is as to such crimes that the problem arises of what significance should be attributed to a difference in degree between the harm intended and the harm done. For example, *A* may intend to injure *B* but by mistake succeed in killing him, and the question is whether *A* is guilty of murder or manslaughter. Conversely, *A* may intend to kill but succeed only in wounding *B;* is *A* guilty of simple battery or aggravated battery-with-intent-to-kill? *A* may strike at *B*'s jaw with his fist with intent merely to knock him down, but instead he shatters *B*'s glasses and causes *B* to lose his eyesight; is *A* guilty of mayhem? Conversely, *A* aims at his glasses with intent to put out the eyes but merely succeeds in connecting with *B*'s jaw, knocking him down but causing no permanent injury; is he then guilty of simple battery?

The easier problem is the one involved where the harm inflicted is less in degree than the harm intended. Here *A* is clearly guilty of the lesser crime—of simple battery (or of battery-with-intent-to-kill under a common type of statute) where he intends to kill but only injures; of simple battery (or of statutory battery-with-intent-to-maim) where he intends to put out the eye but only bruises the victim's jaw. On principle, there seems to be no reason for refusing to recognize an intention to do a greater degree of harm as an equivalent of an intention to do the amount of harm that actually resulted. Indeed, it can often be said that the latter is necessarily encompassed in the former; if one intends to do *serious* bodily harm to another, then he intends to do bodily harm to him.

Where the harm inflicted is greater in degree than that intended, and the criminal law divides the matter into two separate though related crimes according to the degree of harm, there is greater difficulty in holding *A* criminally liable according to the harm actually done. But it is quite well settled (though perhaps not inherently just) that if *A,* intending merely to inflict mild bodily harm upon *B,* actually but unexpectedly succeeds in killing *B,* he is guilty of criminal homicide—not murder, to be sure, but involuntary manslaughter. *A* intentionally strikes *B* a light blow on the mouth; unknown to *A, B* is a hemophiliac ("bleeder"); the doctors are unable to stop the bleeding so that *B* dies; *A* is guilty of involuntary manslaughter though he never intended to kill *B* and though *B*'s death from so light a blow is entirely unforeseeable (see § 14.5(d)). And it is equally well settled that if *A,* intended to do *B* serious bodily injury but not to kill him, actually inflicts a fatal wound, *A* is guilty of murder, in spite of the difference between the degree of harm intended and that achieved (see § 13.3). Similarly, if *A* throws a stone at *B* intending to strike his body, but by bad luck the stone strikes *B*'s eye and puts it out, *A* is guilty of the greater crime of mayhem, as an intent merely to injure plus actual maiming or disfiguring will do. (Some statutes, however, define mayhem as maiming or disfiguring with intent to maim or disfigure; under such a statute, of course, there must be an intent to maim or disfigure.)

It has been rightly pointed out that the doctrine that when one intends a lesser crime he may be convicted of a graver offense committed inadvertently would lead to anomalous results if generally applied. Actually, it appears there is no such doctrine, and that the results described above are attributable to unique concepts which have developed as to the offenses mentioned. Even as to these crimes, it would doubtless be better to abandon the notion that an intent to cause some lesser harm will suffice for conviction of the greater crime, as done in Model Penal Code §§ 210.2, 210.3. "Whether the matter is viewed in relation to the just condemnation of the actor's conduct or in relation to deterrence or correction," there is no basis for imposing on a defendant either the label or the sanctions applicable to one who intentionally caused the results that the defendant fortuitously caused while intending some lesser degree of harm. In short, the better result when the actual harm exceeds the intended harm is to deal with the actor's conduct in terms of harm intended.

The same issue may arise as to crimes involving recklessness and negligence, as where A recklessly endangers B's limbs but not his life and yet succeeds in killing B. Thus A, by throwing a relatively small stone in the vicinity of B without any intent to hit him, creates a risk of injuring him but not of killing him; unfortunately he hits B and so is guilty of recklessness-battery; but B is quite unforeseeably a hemophiliac and bleeds to death. Is A guilty of involuntary manslaughter? Given the fact that the battery is an unlawful act, the result might well be yes, although here as well it is clear that the better policy is not to hold the defendant liable for the fortuitous fatality.

§ 5.4 Causation

With crimes so defined as to require not merely conduct but also a specified result of conduct, the defendant's conduct must be the "legal" or "proximate" cause of the result. For one thing, it must be determined that the defendant's conduct was the cause in fact of the result, which usually (but not always) means that but for the conduct the result would not have occurred. In addition, even when cause in fact is established, it must be determined that any variation between the result intended (with intent crimes) or hazarded (with reckless or negligent crimes) and the result actually achieved is not so extraordinary that it would be unfair to hold the defendant responsible for the actual result.

(a) The Problem. We have already noted that some crimes are so defined that conduct accompanied by an intention to cause a harmful result may constitute the crime without regard to whether that result actually occurs. Thus it is perjury to tell a material lie on the witness stand with intent to mislead judge and jury, though the lie is so transparent that no one who hears it believes it and thus the outcome of the case is not affected. It is forgery to make a false writing with intent to defraud, though no one except the writer sees it, so that no one is actually defrauded. So too reckless or negligent conduct may constitute a crime though no one is harmed, as is true of the crimes of reckless driving and careless (negligent) driving. With all such crimes there is no need to worry about causation.

On the other hand, some crimes are defined in such a way that the occurrence of a certain specific result of conduct is required for its commission. The crime (or one way to commit the crime) may require an intention to produce that result. Thus the intent-to-kill type of murder requires that the defendant intend to produce a death; the intent-to-injure type of battery that the defendant intend to cause a bodily injury; the intent-to-injure type of malicious mischief that the defendant intend to cause an injury to property; arson that the defendant intend to cause a burning of property; and false pretenses that the defendant intend to cause the victim to pass title to his property. Some crimes may be committed by recklessness in producing the necessary result. Manslaughter and battery, for instance, may be committed by reckless conduct that produces death or injury respectively; and there is a type of murder ("depraved-heart" murder) as to which a very high degree of recklessness causing death constitutes murder. Reckless conduct that brings about property damage may constitute malicious mischief. Probably false pretenses may be committed by one who recklessly makes a false statement knowing he does not know whether the statement is true or false, on the basis of which the victim hands over his property to him. Still other crimes may be committed by negligence in causing the required result, as is the case with some modern statutes punishing persons who negligently cause death or injury by driving an automobile (or by driving an automobile while intoxicated).

With those crimes which require that the defendant intentionally or recklessly or negligently cause a certain result, there exists the problem of causation. With these crimes it is not enough for criminal liability that the defendant conduct himself with an intention to produce the specified result, or that he conduct himself in such a manner that he recklessly or negligently creates a risk of that result. A is not liable, of course, for murder though he shoots at B intending to kill, so long as his bullet hits no one; nor for manslaughter or battery though he drives his car recklessly, if his conduct fails to harm an endangered pedestrian or motorist. For these crimes of cause-and-result we must have at the very least the required fatal or injurious consequence. Suppose, therefore, in addition to the element of A's intentional or reckless conduct, we add the element of a death or injury to B. It is still not enough for criminal liability that A so conducted himself and that B simultaneously died or was injured. Thus if A shoots at B intending to kill but misses, but at that moment B drops dead of some cause wholly unconnected with the shooting, A is not liable for the murder of B, in spite of the simultaneous existence of the two required ingredients, A's intentional conduct and the fatal result. What is missing is the necessary causal connection between the conduct and the result of conduct; and causal connection requires something more than mere coincidence as to time and place. It is required, for criminal liability, that the conduct of the defendant be both (1) the actual cause, and (2) the "legal" cause (often called "proximate" cause) of the result.

In brief, this ordinarily means (1) that the defendant's conduct must be the "but-for" cause (sometimes called the "cause in fact") of the forbidden result (the word "cause" in the phrase "legal cause" or "proximate cause"), and in addition (2) that the forbidden result which actually occurs must be enough similar to, and occur in a manner enough similar to, the result or manner which the defendant intended (in the case of crimes of intention), or the result or manner which his reckless or negligent conduct created a risk of happening (in the case of crimes of recklessness and negligence) that the defendant may fairly be held responsible for the actual result even though it does differ or happens in a different way from the intended or hazarded result (the word "legal" or "proximate" in the phrase "legal cause" or "proximate cause").

When causing a particular result is an element of the crime charged, it must be proved by the prosecution beyond a reasonable doubt. In the usual case there is no difficulty in showing the necessary causal connection between conduct and result. A with intent to kill B aims his gun at the heart of B, a person in good health, and pulls the trigger. No one else is trying to kill B at that moment. A's aim is good and B, pierced through the heart, dies in a few moments. Here A's conduct in fact caused B's death (i.e., but for A's conduct B would have lived), and the actual result, the death of B from a wound in the heart, is exactly the result intended. (Since A not only legally caused B's death, but intended to do so, he is guilty of murder in the absence of circumstances of mitigation or justification). Or A, driving his car at a reckless speed, and aware that his conduct is creating a substantial and unreasonable risk of death and injury to other motorists on the road he travels, crashes his car into another car, killing its driver *B*. Here *A*'s conduct in fact caused *B*'s death and the result that occurred (*B*'s death in a car crash) is exactly the kind of result, both as to the type of victim and the type of harm to him, which falls within the risk that *A* created by his conduct. (Since *A*'s conduct legally caused *B*'s death, and was accompanied by recklessness, he is guilty of manslaughter.)

It is the unusual case—numerically in the minority, yet arising often enough to warrant considerable attention by the courts—that gives difficulty in the area of causation. Perhaps at the moment when *A* fired at *B* and hit him in the heart, *X*, acting independently, also shot at *B* and hit him in the head, either wound being sufficient by itself to kill *B*. Or (leaving out the existence of a third person) perhaps the wound that *A* inflicted upon *B* would not have been fatal except for the fact that *B* was already weakened by sickness or prior injury. Or the wound that *A* inflicted upon *B* would not have been fatal if properly treated, but the doctor or nurse called to attend *B* so negligently treats the wound that *B* dies. Or the fatal (or non-fatal) wound is so painful to *B* that he commits suicide to escape the pain. Or *B* successfully dodges *A*'s bullet by diving into the river where, unable to swim to shore, he drowns. In another class of cases, *A* misses *B* and instead hits and kills or wounds *C*. These out-of-the ordinary cases raise the causation problem—is there in the eyes of the law a sufficient causal connection between the defendant's conduct and the result of his conduct?—and the answers are generally spelled out in the terms of "concurrent cause," "intervening cause," "superseding cause," "preexisting weakness," "transferred intent" and the like.

(b) Cause in Fact. In order that conduct be the actual cause of a particular result, it is almost always sufficient that the result would not have happened in the absence of the conduct; or, putting it another way, that "but for" the antecedent conduct the result would not have occurred. So where *A* shoots at *B*, who is hit and dies, we can say that *A* caused *B*'s death, since but for *A*'s conduct *B* would not have died. However, although but-for causation explains almost all of the cases wherein it is held that the conduct in question causes the result in question, it does not explain them all.

In torts law there is the situation where *A* wrongfully (intentionally or negligently) starts a fire that by itself is sufficient to burn *B*'s property, while at about the same time *X* (wrongfully or innocently) or lightning starts another fire also sufficient to burn *B*'s property. The two fires meet and combine and burn *B*'s property. Here one cannot say that but for *A*'s conduct *B*'s property would not have been burned. Yet *A* is held to have caused the injury to *B*'s property.

In the criminal law too the situation sometimes arises where two causes, each alone sufficient to bring about the harmful result, operate together to cause it. Thus A stabs B, inflicting a fatal wound; while at the same moment X, acting independently, shoots B in the head with a gun, also inflicting such a wound; and B dies from the combined effects of the two wounds. It is held that A has caused B's death (so he is guilty of murder if his conduct included an intent to kill B, manslaughter if his conduct constituted recklessness). (X, of course, being in exactly the same position as A, has equally caused B's death.) So the test for causation-in-fact is more accurately worded, not in terms of but-for cause, but rather: Was the defendant's conduct a substantial factor in bringing about the forbidden result? Of course, if the result would not have occurred but for his conduct, his conduct is a substantial factor in bringing about the result; but his conduct will sometimes be a substantial factor even though not a but-for cause.

What if A shoots and instantaneously kills B who, from disease or from a prior mortal wound independently inflicted by a third person X, was at death's door, with but an hour more to live, at the moment A killed him. Here we can properly say that but for A's conduct B would have lived (though only for an hour); thus A has caused B's death. So one who hastens the victim's death is a cause of his death.

A difficulty is presented in the situation where A inflicts a mortal wound on B, who, though dying, has an hour to live; then X, acting independently, kills B instantaneously. Can it be said that A has in fact caused B's death? (X, by substantially hastening B's death is surely a cause of B's death.) Or is A saved from criminal liability because X's conduct somehow cut off A's conduct as a cause of death? Some cases have held as to such a situation that A's conduct is not a cause of B's death, but there is some authority to the contrary. Although the commentators have generally approved the former view, it has been questioned whether a different result is not called for on somewhat different facts, as in this situation: A is entering a desert; B secretly puts a fatal dose of poison in A's water keg; A takes the water keg into the desert where C steals it; both A and C think it contains water; A dies of thirst. It is argued that " 'causing death' normally involves the notion of shortening life and not merely determining the manner of dying," so that B and not C is the cause of death.

Of course, in all these cases involving two assailants, if A and X are not acting independently, but are working together to cause B's death, one is as guilty as the other on general principles concerning accomplices in crime, no matter which one actually applies the coup de grace.

Finally, special mention must be made of a frequently recurring situation that might appear to be of the type previously described. It is that in which A's conduct has very seriously injured B, ultimately resulting in B's condition deteriorating to the point where his heart and breathing action can be continued only with a life support system, use of which is finally terminated by Dr. X because B's condition is irreversible. In such circumstances, A will of course contend that Dr. X was the cause of death. Often this contention is rebuffed by use of the concept of "brain death" to conclude that B's death occurred before Dr. X terminated the system. But courts have indicated that in any event A is still the cause of B's death, for Dr. X's actions are not to be viewed as an independent intentional killing but rather as a foreseeable consequence of B's medical treatment.

(c) Legal (Proximate) Cause Generally. We have already noted that, even though A's conduct may actually cause B's death (or injury), his conduct is not necessarily the "legal" (or "proximate") cause of B's death (injury). The problems of legal causation arise when the actual result of the defendant's conduct varies from the result which the defendant intended (in the case of crimes of intention) or from the result which his conduct created a risk of happening (in the case of crimes of recklessness and negligence). The variance may be (1) as to the person or property harmed, or (2) as to the manner in which the harm occurs, or (3) as to the type or degree of the harm. Although most of the actual cases concern homicide, where the result in question was someone's death, the same principles apply to other cause-and-result crimes involving some injury or loss other than death—such as bodily injury to the person (as in criminal battery) or injury to or loss of property (as in malicious mischief, arson, false pretenses).

The problems of legal causation arise in both tort and criminal settings, and the one situation is closely analogous to the other. Although the courts have generally treated legal causation in criminal law as in tort law, on principle they do not have to, for the issue is not precisely the same in the two situations. In tort law, it would seem, one might logically require one who actually injured another (especially if he intended to cause an injury to another, but also even if he only negligently caused such an injury), to pay for the damage actually caused without regard to the likelihood or unlikelihood of the particular result achieved, on the theory that of the two of them he, rather than the innocent victim, should bear the cost. (The trend in tort law has, in fact, been in the direction of expanding liability, though courts still talk in terms of legal or proximate cause).

But with crimes, where the consequences of a determination of guilt are more drastic (death or imprisonment, generally accompanied by moral condemnation, as contrasted with a mere money payment) it is arguable that a closer relationship between the result achieved and that intended or hazarded should be required. The most obvious difference in this regard between the two areas of law, of course, is that in tort law the defendant may be held responsible for harms different than those actually risked by his conduct, while this is generally not the cause in the criminal law (see § 5.3). It is significant that it is in the limited areas of the criminal law where this is possible—felony-murder and misdemeanor-manslaughter— that there has been the greatest move away from the notion that legal cause in tort cases is controlling (see § 5.4(h)).

There is yet another reason for taking a somewhat different view of causation in criminal law than in tort law. The requirement of causation in criminal law, more often than not, serves not to free defendants from all liability but rather to limit their punishment consistent with accepted theories of punishment (see § 1.5). It is generally accepted, for example, that these theories support the conclusion that when A shoots at B with intent to kill and misses, he should not be punished as severely as would have been appropriate had he killed B. This being so, the same should be true when B's death results from a series of events too extraordinary or too dependent on the acts of another to be attributed to A. A should not suffer the penalty for murder, nor should he be entirely free of criminal sanctions.

The problem of legal causation arises in respect to both crimes of intention and crimes of recklessness and negligence. A shoots at B with intent to kill him; perhaps he misses B but kills an unintended victim C; or perhaps he does hit B, who dies in quite an unintended manner (e.g., B, only injured, goes to the hospital, where his doctor negligently dresses the wound, which leads to gangrene and death). Or A recklessly endangers B's life; perhaps, however, it is an unexpected victim C, not B, who dies; or perhaps B dies but in an unexpected manner. Though the two situations are analogous, they do not necessarily call for precisely the same treatment. One might logically, it would seem, be harder on those who intend bad results, more readily holding them criminally liable for results that differ from what they intended, than on those (morally less at fault) whose conduct amounts only to reckless or negligent creation of risk of bad results. For this reason, cause-and-result crimes of intention must be treated separately from those of recklessness and negligence.

(d) Intentional Crimes—Unintended Victim ("Transferred Intent"). In the unintended-victim (or bad-aim) situation—where A aims at B but misses, hitting C—it is the view of the criminal law that A is just as guilty as if his aim had been accurate. Thus where A aims at B with a murderous intent to kill, but because of a bad aim he hits and kills C, A is uniformly held guilty of the murder of C. And if A aims at B with a first-degree-murder state of mind, he commits first degree murder as to C, by the majority view. So too, where A aims at B with intent to injure B but, missing B, hits and injures C, A is guilty of battery of C. On similar principles, where A throws a rock at B's property intending to injure or destroy it but instead hits and injures or destroys C's property, A should be guilty of malicious mischief to C's property. And if A sets a fire with intent to burn B's property, but because of a shift in the wind the fire burns C's property, A should be guilty of the arson of C's property.

These proper conclusions of law as to criminal liability in the bad-aim situation are sometimes said to rest upon the ground of "transferred intent": To be guilty of a crime involving a harmful result to C, A must intend to do harm to C; but A's intent to harm B will be transferred to C; thus A actually did intend to harm C; so he is guilty of the crime against C. This sort of reasoning is, of course, pure fiction. A never really intended to harm C; but it is not necessary, in order to impose criminal liability upon A, to pretend that he did. What is really meant, by this round-about method of explanation, is that when one person (A) acts (or omits to act) with intent to harm another person (B), but because of a bad aim he instead harms a third person (C) whom he did not intend to harm, the law considers him (as it ought) just as guilty as if he had actually harmed the intended victim. In other words, criminal homicide, battery, arson and malicious mischief do not require that the defendant cause harm to the intended victim; an unintended victim will do just as well. But, it may be that the transferred-intent theory will be applied even when the result is a greater degree of criminal liability than if the intended victim had been hit, as where (in the above example) the law makes harm to C a more serious offense than harm to B, or where the intent is transferred to more than one unintended victim.

It may be extraordinary when A takes aim on B with a gun or rock, that anyone except B should be within gunshot or rock throwing range; or, when A sets his fire, that the wind should shift so as to blow toward C's property. Thus A and B are not, as they suppose, alone on the desert; C, a tramp, is asleep nearby behind some sagebrush, and he is struck and killed by the bullet A intended for B. Is A guilty of murder? In tort law this fact makes no difference to A's liability; there is no requirement, in order to hold A liable for the harm he causes to C as a result of a bad aim at B, that the harm he causes be likely or even foreseeable. It has sometimes been argued, however, that "the plain man's view of justice" requires that the notion of transferred intent in the criminal law be limited to those cases where the defendant was negligent as to the actual victim.

Whether such a limitation is a sensible one depends upon the rationale behind what is often referred to as transferred intent. If it is simply that one who intends to kill and who does cause death is rightly viewed as a murderer, then the limitation should not be imposed. But it is questionable whether this is the rationale; at least this view has not been followed when the person the defendant intended to kill actually dies but the result is an abnormal and unforeseeable one. In the bad-aim cases, the actor may be convicted of attempting to murder his intended victim, so the rationale behind transferred intent must somehow explain why a higher penalty should be permitted merely because he killed a third person. One suggestion is that while, in a moral view, one who attempts a crime is as bad as one who succeeds, the penalties are not as great for attempts because the public would not tolerate the severe punishment imposed when the harm is done (e.g., the penalty for murder) for one who did not actually bring about the harm. When a third person is killed this barrier is not present, although, to complete the argument, it must be assumed that it is present when the defendant was not even negligent as to the person killed.

There are, of course, some situations where, though A intentionally kills or injures B, A is not guilty of murder or battery. Though he kills B, he may be guilty only of voluntary manslaughter (e.g., when B has provoked A into a reasonable rage to kill) (see § 14.2); or he may be guilty of no crime at all (e.g., when he is privileged to kill or injure B in self-defense, or to prevent B's commission of a felony) (see §§ 9.4, 9.7). Now suppose A shoots at B under these circumstances but, missing B, hits and kills or injures C, an innocent bystander. If A aims at his attacker B in proper self-defense, but hits C instead, he is not generally guilty of murder or battery of C. Once again, he is only as guilty as to C as he would have been had his aim been accurate enough to have hit B. So too if A aims at B with intent to kill under circumstances that would make him guilty of voluntary manslaughter of B, but he hits and kills C instead, A is guilty of voluntary manslaughter of C.

The situation, discussed above, concerning the unintended victim of an intentional crime—which we have referred to for short as the bad-aim situation—is to be distinguished from an entirely different unintended-victim case—the mistaken-identity situation—which is governed by a quite separate set of legal rules. Thus in the semi-darkness A shoots, with intent to kill, at a vague form he supposes to be his enemy B but who is actually another person C;

his well-aimed bullet kills *C*. Here too *A* is guilty of murdering *C*, to the same extent he would have been guilty of murdering *B* had he made no mistake. *A* intended to kill the person at whom he aimed, so there is even less difficulty in holding him guilty than in the bad-aim situation. And of course *A*'s conceivable argument that his mistake of fact (as to the victim's identity) somehow negatives his guilt of murder would be unavailing: his mistake does not negative his intent to kill; and on the facts as he supposes them to be *A* is just as guilty of murder as he is on the facts that actually exist (see § 4.6). The transferred intent case must likewise be distinguished from the case in which there is no primary target at all, in that the defendant acted with the intent to kill any member of a group of persons.

(e) Reckless and Negligent Crimes—Unhazarded Victim ("Transferred Negligence"). An analogous problem exists as to crimes of recklessness or negligence. Thus suppose *A* recklessly creates a risk of death or bodily injury to another person *B* (or to a whole class of persons, including *B*), so that he would be liable for involuntary manslaughter (or battery) if he killed (or injured) *B*. But he misses *B;* instead, *C*, who was not the person foreseeably endangered or a member of a foreseeably endangered class, is killed or injured. Is *A* guilty of involuntary manslaughter if *C* is killed, or of battery if *C* is injured? Or (if one likes to speak in fictions) is the recklessness that *A* directed toward *B* to be "transferred" to *C*, with the result that *A* was reckless with respect to *C* so as to afford the basis for manslaughter or battery liability? To give two illustrations: (1) *A* puts household poison in a whiskey bottle and places the bottle in a locked drawer to which, as *A* knows, only *A* and *B* have keys, thereby recklessly endangering *B;* but *C*, a burglar breaks into the drawer by force, takes a drink and dies. (2) *A* drives a car through town so fast that he creates a high degree of risk of death to other motorists (a class of persons), but not to people within buildings along his route. He crashes into what appears to be an ordinary pleasure vehicle but which actually is full of explosives. The resulting explosion causes a window to shatter over *C*, sitting near the window; the glass cuts *C*'s artery, causing death.

In these situations, the better view may be that *A* is not criminally liable for *C*'s death. If one accepts the argument, discussed above, that negligence to the person killed should be required in the transferred intent cases, then it seems to follow that the same result should be reached here, particularly in view of the fact that a narrower view of legal causation is often taken when the defendant is a reckless or negligent wrongdoer rather than an intentional wrongdoer. To hold *A* criminally liable for *C*'s death would extend the criminal law beyond tort law, where one is not liable to the "unforeseeable plaintiff."

If the above view is correct, then there would be no "transferred negligence" in criminal law. The mental state for a negligence crime would encompass all those persons the defendant *should* foresee as endangered by his conduct, and he would not be held to be the legal cause of the harm resulting to other persons from his conduct. There could, however be "transferred recklessness," by which the defendant's conscious awareness of the danger to one person would suffice when another person is harmed *and* the defendant was negligent as to that person. For example, *A* recklessly fires a gun in the general direction of *B*, of whose presence *A* is actually aware, but the shot hits *C*, who *A* did not see but should have seen. This would be an appropriate case for what some would call "transferred recklessness"; more appropriately, it might be said that here *A* is the legal cause of *C*'s injury.

(f) Intentional Crimes—Unintended Manner. It sometimes happens that the defendant successfully brings about the end result he intends (e.g., death or injury to a certain person), but he does so in a manner which he never contemplated. The variation between intended manner and actual manner may be relatively slight, as where *A* with intent to kill shoots at *B*'s heart but hits him in the head, killing him. It may on the other hand be very great, as where *A*, shooting at *B* with intent to kill, misses him completely, but causing him to turn north rather than continuing south; then, while traveling north, *B* is struck by lightning and killed—a result that would not have happened but for *A*'s shot at *B*. Or it may be somewhere in between these extremes, as where *A*, shooting at *B* with intent to kill, merely wounds *B;* but the doctor who tends his wounds negligently treats him, with death resulting from the infection that a careful doctor would have prevented.

We have already noted that courts are somewhat more willing to find the defendant's acts to be the legal cause of the results when the defendant actually intended those results, albeit they came about in a manner other than he intended. It does not follow, however, that the law should hold the defendant criminally liable for those results in every case in which what he intended actually came about, no matter how abnormal or unforeseeable the chain of events might be. In the second illustration given above (where *B* was struck by lightning), "most people would not only refuse to say that the man had caused [the] death but would recoil at the prospect of punishing him with the same severity as that reserved for murder." When intended results come about in a highly unlikely manner, the defendant should not be punished for those results (as opposed to punishment for attempting to bring them about), for to do otherwise would bring the criminal law into sharp conflict with our sense of justice. Thus, Model Penal Code § 2.03(2)(b) appropriately deals with this situation by putting the issue squarely to the jury's sense of justice; the inquiry is whether the actual result is "too remote or accidental in its occurrence to have a [just] bearing on the actor's liability or on the gravity of his offense." The decided cases, discussed below, generally conform to this view, although many of them rest upon difficult distinctions between intervening, concurrent, natural, human, and other classifications of causes.

(1) Direct Cause. Where the only difference between the intended manner and the actual manner lies in the precise nature of the injury inflicted, there is no difficulty in holding the defendant liable. *A* is thus guilty of murdering *B* where he intentionally inflicts a fatal wound, or of battery if he non-fatally wounds *B* (whether with intent to kill or merely to injure *B*), though he hits another part of *B*'s body than the precise spot at which he aims. So too if *A* should aim a rock at *B*'s right eye with intent to put it out; it would be mayhem though his aim was off and the rock struck the left eye, putting it out.

(2) Pre-existing Weakness. Sometimes *A* attacks *B* with intent to kill, but succeeds only in inflicting what would be a non-fatal wound in a person of ordinary health. But *B* is in a weakened condition from disease or prior wounds or exposure or intoxication, and so he dies. (Sometimes, in addition, he would have died sooner or later anyway from this disease or other condition, but *A*'s murderous attack carries *B* off sooner than otherwise.) It is held that *A* is guilty of murdering *B,* his act being a direct cause of *B*'s death.

(3) Intervening Cause: Generally. The intended result achieved in an unintended manner often happens as a consequence of some intervening act (a) of the victim himself, (b) of a third person, (c) of the defendant, or (d) of a non-human source. We are not concerned here with the case, discussed earlier, in which the defendant's act and some other act concur to bring about the victim's death (e.g., *A* stabs *C, B* shoots *C, C* expires by bleeding to death from both wounds). Rather, the question here is the significance of subsequent acts from any of these four sources when they are more than a concurring cause of death, as where the defendant did not inflict a fatal wound and the victim died only from the effects of the subsequent act.

The significance of acts from each of these four sources is discussed in some detail below. As a preliminary matter, however, it is important to note in a general way how courts have dealt with these kinds of cases. As might be expected, courts have tended to distinguish cases in which the intervening act was a *coincidence* from those in which it was a *response* to the defendant's prior actions. An intervening act is a *coincidence* when the defendant's act merely put the victim at a certain place at a certain time, and because the victim was so located it was possible for him to be acted upon by the intervening cause. The case put earlier in which *B*, after being fired upon by *A*, changed his route and then was struck by lightning is an illustration of a coincidence. However, it is important to note that there may be a coincidence even when the subsequent act is that of a human agency, as where *A* shoots *B* and leaves him lying in the roadway, resulting in *B* being struck by *C*'s car; or where *A* shoots at *B* and causes him to take refuge in a park, where *B* is then attacked and killed by a gang of hoodlums.

By contrast, an intervening act may be said to be a *response* to the prior actions of the defendant when it involves reaction to the conditions created by the defendant. The most obvious illustrations are actions of the victim to avoid harm, actions of a bystander to rescue him, and actions of medical personnel in treating the victim. But, while a response usually involves a human agency, this is not necessarily the case; infection of a wound inflicted by the defendant may be said to be an instance of germs responding to the victim's condition.

As common sense would suggest, the perimeters of legal cause are more closely drawn when the intervening cause was a matter of coincidence rather than response. There is less reason to hold the defendant liable for the bad results when he has merely caused the victim to be at a particular place at a particular time, than when he has brought other agencies into play in response to a danger or injury. Thus—though the distinction is not carefully developed in many of the decided cases—it may be said that a coincidence will break the chain of legal cause unless it was foreseeable, while a response will do so only if it is abnormal (and, if abnormal, also unforeseeable). If *A* shoots *B* and leaves him disabled and then *C* runs over *B* with his car (coincidence), the question is whether *A* could not have reasonably foreseen this possibility; if *A* shoots *B* and then Dr. *C* gives *B* improper medical treatment (response), the basic question is whether the treatment was abnormal (generally, negligent medical treatment is not so viewed). If *A* shoots *B* and *B* is taken to the hospital, where he comes into contact with some communicable disease that causes his death (coincidence), *A* is not guilty of murder unless this was foreseeable (unlikely, unless it was generally known that there had been an outbreak of this disease); if instead *B*'s wounds became infected and he died (response), *A* is guilty of murder (infection not abnormal).

(4) Intervening Cause: Acts of the Victim. Suppose that *A* approaches *B* with a deadly weapon and a murderous intent to kill, so that B, in order to escape, "voluntarily" jumps out a window, or precipitates himself into a ravine, or plunges into a river, with fatal consequences to B. Here A is held guilty of murdering B. Similarly, if A comes at B with an intent to injure but not to kill, causing B to jump to escape the threatened injury, A is liable for manslaughter if B is killed, and battery if B is only injured. Such impulsive acts to avoid harm are quite normal, and thus A may be said to be the legal cause of the consequences. Similarly, where A, intending to kill, merely inflicts a non-fatal wound, but A in a delirium rips off the bandages and dies from the loss of blood, the involuntary intervening act of B would not cut off A's liability for murder. The same is true of various instinctive, impulsive or reflexive acts of B that bring about the death of C.

More difficult are cases where the victim's act is voluntary rather than instinctive, as where he refuses to go to a doctor who could save his life, or refuses to submit to a lifesaving operation; and so he dies when he might have been saved. It has been held that, even here, A's act constitutes the legal cause of B's death. Even where the victim's refusal is unreasonable it may nonetheless not be abnormal, as where the victim refuses to consent to amputation of a leg; there may well be instances, however, in which the refusal is so extremely foolish as to be abnormal.

What, then, of suicide by the victim? If A wounds B with intent to kill, but thereafter C shoots B with intent to kill and does kill him instantly, we know that A is not the cause of B's death. If, instead, B takes his own life, we again have a deliberate act directed toward killing B that has intervened, so one might expect the same result. Such a result is certainly appropriate when B commits suicide from some motive unconnected with the fact that he is wounded, but suicide is not abnormal when B acts out of the extreme pain of wounds inflicted by A or when the wound has rendered him irresponsible. Although voluntary harm-doing usually suffices to break the chain of legal cause, this should not be so when A causes B to commit suicide by creating a situation so cruel and revolting that death is preferred.

(5) Intervening Cause: Acts of a Third Person. The most common case involves the negligent treatment of wounds by a doctor or nurse. A, intending to kill B, merely wounds him; but the doctor so negligently treats the wound that B dies. It is generally held that A is guilty of murdering B, i.e., that A's act legally caused B's death, unless the doctor's treatment is so bad as to constitute gross negligence or intentional malpractice. In short, mere negligence in medical treatment is not so abnormal that the defendant should be freed of liability. (Indeed, it has been held that the "act of disconnecting life support systems of a person who is brain dead with little chance of recovery is medically reasonable and is not the death producing cause or a sufficient intervening cause of death to negate the act of the defendant as the cause of death.'') It might seem to follow that the same result would be reached when, for example, *B* dies in a traffic accident attributable to the negligence of the ambulance driver who is taking *B* to the hospital. But, it is very likely that *A* would not be held to be the legal cause of *B*'s death in such a case, as the death is from new injuries; the medical negligence cases have usually emphasized that the negligence aggravated the wound inflicted by the defendant.

This kind of accident must be distinguished from a somewhat different situation, as where *A*, with intent to kill *B*, only wounds *B*, leaving him lying unconscious in the unlighted road on a dark night, and then *C*, driving along the road, runs over and kills *B*. Here *C*'s act is a matter of coincidence rather than a response to what *A* has done, and thus the question is whether the subsequent events were foreseeable, as they undoubtedly were in the above illustration.

(6) Intervening Cause: Acts of the Defendant. Assume that *A*, with intent to kill *B*, strikes *B* and renders him unconscious, and then, mistakenly believing *B* to be dead, hangs *B* to give the appearance of suicide; *B* actually dies of strangulation. As noted earlier, this kind of case has usually been thought to present a problem of concurrence in that the act done with intent to kill did not kill and the act that did kill was done without intent to kill (see § 5.3(c)). Courts have usually responded to this issue by declaring that there was concurrence because *A*'s actions were all part of a single transaction. It may be suggested, however, that instead of resorting to this artificial device to establish concurrence, it might be better to ask whether the act which clearly concurs with the intent (*A*'s striking of *B*) is not properly viewed as the legal cause of death.

Although this act by *A* was not in itself sufficient to cause death, we know from the medical treatment cases that this in itself is no bar to finding legal cause. What then of the defendant's mistaken belief, whether reasonable or unreasonable, that his victim is dead? While this belief bars a finding of intent to kill at the time of the acts done to avoid detection, it should not bar a finding of legal cause. Although the defendant's awareness of certain facts may extend legal cause farther than would otherwise be the case, it has never been assumed that legal cause requires that death occur in a way that the defendant actually anticipated. In the negligent medical treatment cases, for example, it would appear to make no difference that the treatment was not anticipated by the defendant because he left his victim thinking him dead; legal cause would be found to exist in such a case because the medical treatment, though unanticipated, is not an abnormal response. By the same token, acts by the defendant himself to dispose of the body are not abnormal and thus do not break the causal chain, and this is so even though it might be acknowledged that mutilating what is thought to be a corpse, if done by another person, is such an unusual occurrence as to break the chain of causation.

(7) **Intervening Cause: Non-human Acts.** Assume that *A* intends to kill *B* but only wounds him, leaving him unconscious in a pasture, where he is kicked in the head by a grazing horse or struck by lightning or snowed under by a blizzard, in any event with fatal results. This is properly labeled a coincidence, and thus if the intervening factor is foreseeable—as if the pasture is crowded with lively horses or if a blizzard is obviously blowing up—*A* would be liable for murder, though the horse or the blizzard, not *A*'s bullet, applied the coup de grace to *B*. On the other hand, if the event that actually kills *B* is quite unexpected—as if lightning strikes *B,* or the storm or the horse-kick is highly unlikely—*A* will not be considered the legal cause of *B*'s death.

In one well-known case *A* attacked *B* with intent to kill, but he only wounded *B,* sending him to the hospital for treatment; at the hospital he caught scarlet fever from his doctor and died. It was held that *A* was not criminally liable for *B*'s death. This is the proper result, as again, we are dealing with a matter of coincidence, and it cannot be said that what happened was foreseeable.

(g) **Reckless and Negligent Crimes—Unforeseeable Manner.** The courts have tended to apply the same rules to recklessness and negligence crimes as they have to intent crimes, although the number of cases in the former category are not great. Again, it is usual for courts to distinguish direct cause from intervening cause cases, and, in the latter group, to separate out coincidence cases from response cases. Nonetheless, there is some reason to believe that where the harm (which, it may be assumed, came about in a somewhat out-of-the-ordinary way) was merely risked or knowingly risked, rather than intended, courts are likely to take a more limited view of what constitutes legal cause.

For crimes requiring proof of recklessness or negligence by the defendant, it must be established that the reckless or negligent conduct (not just any conduct of the defendant) caused the prohibited result. Thus where driver *A* struck pedestrian *B* and then drove on, but only *A*'s conduct after impact was culpably negligent, *B*'s manslaughter conviction was reversed for lack of proof as to whether *B* died from the initial impact or from being dragged by *A*'s car thereafter. Moreover, where there is no intervening cause the defendant's recklessness or negligence can be the proximate cause of the result notwithstanding *prior* recklessness or negligence that produced a preexisting condition.

(1) Direct cause: As noted earlier, where *A* intends to shoot *B* in the heart but instead hits *B* in the head, or where *A* intends to put out *B*'s left eye but instead puts out his right eye, the courts have had no difficulty in finding *A* to be the legal cause of the harm. The same would likely be true where the crime was one of recklessness or negligence, although the problem is unlikely to arise because the knowing or inadvertent creation of risks is not likely to be as specific as the intents mentioned above.

We have also seen that where *A* intends to kill *B,* he takes his victim as he finds him, so that if *B* would not have died but for some highly unusual condition (as where *B* is a hemophiliac) *A* is still the legal cause of *B*'s death. The same result has been reached in the "constructive homicide" cases, as where *A* only intended to do a minor injury to *B* but this battery serves as a basis for a homicide conviction under the misdemeanor-manslaughter rule. Such a result in the latter case is unfortunate, for it does violence to the principle of *mens rea*. What then of the case in which *A* does not intend to kill *B* but only proceeds with conscious awareness of an unreasonable risk that he might do so, as where *A* drops a large object from a window down in the general direction of *B*? If the object strikes *B* and crushes him *A* is clearly guilty of recklessness-manslaughter; but what if the object causes *B* a very minor injury but *B* bleeds to death because he is a hemophiliac?

The same issue may arise when it is not the victim's unusual condition that brings about his death. Suppose that *A,* a stevedore loading a vessel, very carelessly handles a plank suspended over the ship's hold, thereby recklessly creating a risk that *B,* at work below in the hold, will be killed by virtue of being struck by the falling plank. As it turns out, because of *A*'s conduct the plank does fall into the hold, but it misses *B*; however, it causes a spark that ignites gasoline fumes (the existence of which *A* was reasonably unaware of) in the hold, burning *B* to death. Is *A* to be held for recklessness-manslaughter of *B*?

Notwithstanding the fact that if in either of these cases *A* had intended to kill *B* he would be held to be the legal cause of *B*'s death, a different result might be reached where *A* was only reckless or negligent and the victim was harmed in a way that was not foreseeable. Although a completely convincing basis for such a distinction probably cannot be articulated, it rests upon the notion that the issue of legal cause is largely one of "the plain man's sense of justice" and that the issue should be put "to the jury's sense of justice." So viewed, it would seem that legal cause is more likely to be found lacking when the defendant was only reckless or negligent and the manner of the harm was not foreseeable.

(2) **Intervening Cause:** Most of the cases involving crimes of recklessness or negligence where the manner of achieving the actual result differs from the manner that was foreseeable are those where some factor intervenes between the defendant's conduct and the result. Thus A recklessly fires a gun in the vicinity of a rowboat on a dangerous river; B and C are in the boat; B in fright jumps overboard, capsizing the boat; and C drowns. A was held guilty of recklessness-manslaughter, for B's instinctive response to the situation was a normal consequence of A's conduct. So too, if A recklessly point's C's shotgun toward B and holds his finger on the trigger during an argument with B, prompting C to intervene by grabbing the gun, which then fires and kills B, A is guilty of reckless manslaughter. Or A recklessly endangers B's life, but his reckless conduct only causes a non-fatal injury; however, a doctor (or nurse) negligently treats the wound, so that B dies. A is liable for B's death (i.e., he is guilty of manslaughter of the recklessness type) if the doctor's treatment is merely negligent, but not if his treatment is grossly negligent or intentionally wrong. Similarly, a police officer's conduct in pursuing a fleeing perpetrator, even if it was negligently performed and resulted in the death of the officer or a third party, is not deemed conduct "so unusual, abnormal or extraordinary" as to constitute an superceding cause.

Although "one who intentionally inflicts a wound calculated to destroy life, and from which death ensues, cannot throw responsibility for the act either upon the carelessness or ignorance of his victim or upon unskillful or improper treatment which aggravated the wound and contributed to his death," is the same true when the defendant merely recklessly or negligently inflicts a wound? That is, are intervening causes dealt with in precisely the same way, without regard to the nature of the defendant's mental state? Most of the cases reflect no obvious differences, and courts tend to apply the same principles whether the defendant was acting with intent to injure or kill or was merely reckless or negligent. Of course, if there was prior negligence by both the defendant and the victim, then the jury will have to decide whether or not the latter was the sole cause of the injury. But it also appears that there is a greater likelihood of the victim's subsequent acts to avoid harm being found abnormal when the defendant is only charged with acting recklessly or negligently. It is less apparent that any such distinctions are drawn when the intervening act is medical treatment, although it may be suggested that what has sometimes been viewed as less than gross negligence in treatment when the defendant acted with intent might not be so viewed if the defendant had only been reckless or negligent. The one instance in which the cases do reflect a clear difference is where the intervening act is that of the defendant himself; subsequent acts to conceal a crime, causing the death of one the defendant believes to be dead, are considered normal only when the defendant originally acted with intent to kill.

If the intervening cause is merely a coincidence rather than (as with medical treatment) a response, then the question is whether it was foreseeable. Illustrative is the case where A, driving recklessly, caused passenger B to be thrown from the car at night onto an icy, snow-packed country road, where B was struck by C's car. In such circumstances, A is quite properly viewed as the proximate cause of B's death. But if B, after being thrown from the car, left the roadway to a position of apparent safety and then later, on his own, walked out into the roadway and then was struck by C's car, the result might well be otherwise.

(h) Unintended Type of Harm—Felony–Murder and Misdemeanor–Manslaughter. Where A intends one type of harmful result, but his conduct causes quite another type of harm to the intended victim (or to an unintended victim), A has generally been held not criminally liable for the harm actually caused. This is not because legal cause is lacking; indeed, often the connection between the defendant's actions and the harm is very close, as where A throws a rock at B's window and instead the rock hits C. Rather, it is the principle of *mens rea* that bars conviction. A's intent cannot be "transferred" from his actual purpose to the result—that is, from one kind of crime to another—because this would destroy the meaningful distinctions between crimes of varying seriousness carrying quite different penalties (see § 5.3).

There are the felony-murder and misdemeanor-manslaughter situations in criminal homicide, however, where liability for a caused death may result, not from the fact that the defendant intended to kill the victim, but because he had some quite different bad intention in his mind and was acting to carry out that bad intention. Thus, if A, while committing or attempting a felony such as robbery, unintentionally kills B, he may be guilty of murder; if he unintentionally kills B in the commission of a misdemeanor (such as speeding) he may be guilty of manslaughter (see §§ 13.5, 14.5). This is so not because of any transfer of intent to (say) rob B, bad though that intent is, to the death of B, thus leading us wrongly to conclude that A intended to kill B so as to be guilty of murder of the intent-to-kill variety. It is so because there are several types of murder in addition to intent-to-kill murder, and one type is the felony-murder.

It is not sufficient that A, who has committed a felony or misdemeanor, has somehow caused B's death; the causation link must be to that conduct by A constituting the requisite felony or misdemeanor. Thus, if A engages in a heated argument with B and then commits a battery upon B, after which B dies from a cerebral hemorrhage, but the medical evidence cannot establish whether the hemorrhage was prompted by the battery or the excitement of the prior argument, A may not be convicted of misdemeanor-manslaughter. Sometimes the point, though expressed in terms of causation, is that the nature of the offense (especially in misdemeanor-manslaughter cases) is such that the violation of it really cannot be said to have caused the resulting harm. This is particularly true as to violation of licensing requirements where the absence of the license appears not—in a "but for" sense—to have caused the bad results.

It has sometimes been claimed, perhaps because the felony-murder and misdemeanor-manslaughter rules border on strict liability, that the only casual relationship that must be established in such cases is cause-in-fact, which ordinarily only requires proof that but for the defendant's acts (here the felony or misdemeanor) the harm would not have occurred. Thus it is said that if a kidnapper is carefully driving a car in which the kidnaped person is a passenger, and an accident occurs in which that person is killed, then the kidnapper is guilty of murder because kidnaping is a felony. This is not so. Generally, it may be said that rules of causation are the same in felony-murder and misdemeanor-manslaughter cases as in the areas previously discussed, and thus, for example, legal cause will not be present where there intervenes (1) a coincidence that is not reasonably foreseeable (which disposes of the above case) or (2) an abnormal response.

For instance, if A sets fire to his home to collect the insurance and as a consequence someone in the building or a fireman fighting the blaze is killed, then A is clearly guilty of murder; A is the direct cause of the death of those trapped in the building, and in the case of the fireman the intervening act of fire-fighting could hardly be viewed as abnormal. Assume no such person is killed, but instead, although the firemen have roped off the area, a foolhardy bystander B ducks under the rope and dashes into the house, disregarding the fire chief's warning cries, in order to rescue some articles for the owner, and B is killed when the fiery building collapses on top of him. It would seem that this is such an abnormal response that A would not be held to be the legal cause of B's death, although a contrary result would be reached in the case where a member of A's family, after reaching a position of safety outside the house, rushes back in to retrieve some items of property and then cannot escape from the burning building. Similarly, if A sets out to rob B's store it is normal for B to try to protect his property, and if as a result there is an exchange of gunfire in which a shot from B's gun hits and kills a bystander, A is the legal cause of this death. The same is true where the shot comes from the gun of a policeman; appearance of the police in response to a robbery is just as normal as appearance of firemen to fight a fire. In these two cases, however, even though causation is established, a limited interpretation of the felony-murder rule might result in A not being convicted of murder.

Two Pennsylvania homicide cases—one involving the felony-murder doctrine, the other the misdemeanor-manslaughter doctrine, and both imposing limitations thereon—have given rise to a good deal of discussion. In the former case, *Commonwealth v. Redline* (1958), A and B, after robbing X, were fleeing the scene when policeman P appeared and, in the ensuing gunfire, justifiably shot B to death. At his trial for the felony-murder of B, A was convicted on the theory that the death of B in the manner of its occurrence was a natural and foreseeable result of the commission by A and B of the robbery of X. On appeal A's conviction was reversed, however; the court, without specifically saying that tort notions of proximate cause are inapplicable in criminal cases, stated that A could not be guilty of felony-murder of one whose death constituted a justifiable homicide by P. In the misdemeanor-manslaughter case, *Commonwealth v. Root* (1961), A and B raced their cars in a drag race as a result of a challenge by A accepted by B. During the 70–90 m.p.h. race B, trying to pass A's car, hit an oncoming truck driven by C and was killed. A was convicted of manslaughter of B on the theory that the death of B in the manner it occurred was a foreseeable consequence of the unlawful and reckless conduct of A and B in racing as they did. On appeal A's conviction was reversed, however, the court stating that the tort concept of proximate cause is inapplicable in criminal cases, "a more direct causal connection being required." No explanation of the required "more direct causal connection" was given.

It is submitted that the true reason for the holding in these two cases is the court's feeling, not clearly expressed in the two cases, that A should not, in all justice, be held for the death of B who was an equally willing and foolhardy participant in the bad conduct that caused his death. Thus, in the first case, the court suggests that perhaps A would have been held guilty of felony-murder had the policemen shot a bystander to death instead of A's co-felon B, although on principles of legal causation there is no basis for this kind of distinction. And, in the second case, if C, the driver of the truck that B hit, had been killed rather than B, the court might well have thought that A ought to be guilty of manslaughter of C, although here again the distinction cannot be justified in terms of legal cause. The two Pennsylvania cases no doubt illustrate a growing dissatisfaction with the felony-murder and misdemeanor-manslaughter doctrines, concerning which there is a slowly-emerging trend toward legislative abolition (see §§ 13.5(h), 14.5(e)). However, to the extent that these cases rely wholly or in part upon the requirement of legal cause as a means of limiting these doctrines, they tend to distort the meaning of legal cause.

As a general matter, proximate cause questions in felony-murder and misdemeanor-manslaughter cases have been worked out in much the same way as previously described. Where, for example, the injury defendant inflicted upon the victim or the surgery or treatment necessitated thereby brings on not abnormal complications resulting in the victim's death, the defendant is the proximate cause of death. The same is true where the defendant's conduct brings about the victim's death because of a pre-existing weakness of the victim. Impulsive acts of the victim in an effort to escape being harmed by the defendant's conduct, simple negligence by the victim in not avoiding the risk defendant created, or self-inflicted harms attributable to the victim's weakened condition, are quite normal and thus do not break the causal chain. Nor do responses of third parties that are not abnormal, such as those previously mentioned, efforts at rescue, or negligent medical treatment. And if the defendant's felony or misdemeanor causes the victim to be at a certain place at a time when some nonresponsive harm befalls him, proximate cause still exists if the events were foreseeable, as where a speeding driver strikes and kills an intoxicated man robbers left helpless in the middle of the road at night in a snowstorm.

This is not to suggest, however, that the basic premise of legal causation might never be employed to keep the felony-murder and misdemeanor-manslaughter cases within reasonable bounds. As noted earlier, if the basic inquiry is whether the result was so unusual in its occurrence "to have a [just] bearing on the actor's liability or on the gravity of his offense," it is not inappropriate to give some consideration to whether the defendant intended that result or was merely reckless or negligent as to that result. In felony-murder and misdemeanor-manslaughter cases, the defendant need not even have been reckless or negligent as to the result of death, although, to the extent that these two doctrines have any real justification, it may be that the commission of the felony or misdemeanor tends to show recklessness or negligence in this regard. Thus if, as has been suggested, a more limited view of legal cause might be taken as to reckless and negligent crimes, this may also be true as to felony-murder and misdemeanor-manslaughter cases.

For example, assume that A shoots at B with intent to kill, misses him, but B dies of fright. Since it is true that in cases where A inflicts a very minor wound and B is so weak that he dies from it, A is said to take his victim as he finds him, it is not inconceivable that A would be found to be the legal cause of B's death in the above example. However, if B were to die from fright or excitement as a consequence of A's commission of a misdemeanor in B's presence, then legal cause might well be found to be lacking.

(i) Year-and-a-Day Rule in Homicide. Several centuries ago, when doctors knew very little about medicine, the judges created an absolute rule of law: one cannot be guilty of murder if the victim lives for a year and a day after the blow. (Sometimes the rule was deemed applicable in manslaughter cases as well.) The difficulty in proving that the blow cause the death was obviously the basis of the rule. Now that doctors know infinitely more, it seems strange that the year-and-a-day rule should survive to the present, but it has done so in some jurisdictions. The great majority of states, however, have abrogated the rule, judicially or legislatively.

(j) Absolute Liability Crimes. Assume that a strict liability statute makes it an offense to pollute rivers or streams with certain substances, which of course means that it is not necessary to conviction that the defendant be shown to have intended to do so or that he was reckless or negligent in this regard. A (a company that produces this substance) fills one of its own tank-cars with this substance and then arranges for shipment of this tank-car to its destination via B railroad. The train on which this car is carried travels for some distance along the side of a stream, during which time some of the substance leaks out of the car and into the stream. Is A guilty of the strict-liability pollution offense?

A, of course, might show that he used due care to prevent his tank-car from leaking, but we know that such evidence does not disprove any required mental state, as none is required. What of causation? If only the but-for tests were used, it would appear that A is guilty, as but for A's conduct in having the material shipped the pollution would not have occurred. In a tentative draft, the Model Penal Code only required that the but-for test be met in absolute liability cases, but in response to criticism the following was added to Code § 2.03(4): "When causing a particular result is a material element of an offense for which absolute liability is imposed by law, the element is not established unless the actual result is a probable consequence of the actor's conduct." This is an appropriate way in which to handle legal cause in strict liability cases, and is certainly preferable to the approach in a few such cases of dispensing with the causation requirement.

(k) Causation and the Jury. In *Kibbe v. Henderson* (1976), the habeas corpus petitioner had been convicted of extreme recklessness murder on evidence he left his robbery victim intoxicated and helpless at night during a snowstorm in the middle of a road, where the victim was struck and killed by a speeding car. The court held that since the Constitution requires proof beyond a reasonable doubt on every element of the crime, the failure to instruct the jury on causation created an impermissible risk that the jury had not made a finding on that element. In *Henderson v. Kibbe* (1977), the Supreme Court reversed, noting that the jury had been read the statutory requirement that defendant "thereby cause the death" and had been told of the meaning of recklessness (including that the defendant must have been aware of and disregarded "a substantial and unjustifiable risk"), that both counsel had vigorously argued the causation issue, and that a more elaborate instruction on causation would likely have favored the prosecution on the facts of this case. The Court did not say that what was done below was sound procedure, but only that Kibbe, who had not requested a causation instruction at the close of the trial, thus had failed to meet his heavy burden on this collateral attack to show prejudice.

There is state authority to the effect that, at least when a somewhat complex causation question is present in the case, it is not sufficient merely to tell the jury that they must find the defendant was the cause or the proximate cause of the results. "The definition of 'proximate cause' is clearly a term which is not within the common and ordinary knowledge of a layman. Its meaning has been the subject of much lengthy litigation. It is asking too much to expect a jury, without proper definition, to understand and apply such a technical term." Of course, a highly sophisticated set of instructions elaborating upon such concepts as intervening cause and superceding cause may, as a practical matter, be of little help. Noteworthy in this regard is the approach in Model Penal Code § 2.03(2)(b), (3)(b) of having the jury determine whether the result "is not too remote or accidental in its occurrence to have a [just] bearing on the actor's liability or on the gravity of his offense." The advantage of thereby "putting the issue squarely to the jury's sense of justice is that it does not attempt to force a result which the jury may resist." The disadvantage is that there may be inequality in application of this flexible standard by juries.

§ 5.5 Consequences: Significance of Consent, Conduct, or Condonation by Victim

Consent of the victim is a defense only when it negatives an element of the offense or precludes infliction of the harm to be prevented by the law defining the offense. Neither the victim's guilt of a crime nor his contributory negligence is per se a defense. Likewise, the victim's subsequent condonation or ratification of the crime or acceptance of restitution is not a defense, although statutes in some jurisdictions permit the "compromise" of certain minor crimes by restitution.

(a) Consent. Generally, it may be said that consent by the victim is not a defense in a criminal prosecution. The explanation most commonly given for this rule is that a criminal offense is a wrong affecting the general public, at least indirectly, and consequently cannot be licensed by the individual directly harmed. Thus, it is no defense to a charge of murder that the victim, upon learning of the defendant's homicidal intentions, furnished the defendant with the gun and ammunition. Nor is it a defense to the statutory offense of fraternity "hazing" that the pledges consented to the activity.

Certain crimes, however, are defined in terms of the victim's lack of consent, and as to these the consent of the victim is obviously a bar to conviction. Rape, for example, is typically defined as the "unlawful carnal knowledge of a woman without her consent," and thus consent by the woman to sexual intercourse negatives an element of the offense. Similarly, the crime of trespass is sometimes defined in terms of entry without consent.

More troublesome are other crimes that, while not defined in terms of lack of consent by the victim, are concerned with the infliction of certain types of harm which may sometimes not occur if the victim has given some degree of consent. Larceny, for example, requires a trespassory taking, which is not present when the victim's consent is obtained in certain ways. Likewise, the requirement of "unlawful" application of force for the crime of battery is sometimes not present because of the consent of the victim. But consent to a battery is a defense only if "the bodily harm consented to or threatened by the conduct consented to is not serious."

Assuming a situation in which consent is a defense, what constitutes consent? This question has been most frequently confronted, as might be expected, in cases where the charge was rape. Submission to physical force or to a threat of great and immediate bodily harm is not consent. Assent by one "who is legally incompetent" or "who by reason of youth, mental disease or defect or intoxication is manifestly unable or known by the actor to be unable to make a reasonable judgment as to the nature or harmfulness of the conduct charged to constitute the offense" is not effective consent.

As to assent by deception, the distinction that has traditionally been drawn (but which currently is much disputed, see § 15.3(c)) is between fraud in the factum and fraud in the inducement. Fraud in the factum involves a form of deception that results in a misunderstanding by the victim as to the very fact of the defendant's conduct, while fraud in the inducement merely involves deception as to some collateral matter; the former cannot result in effective consent, but the latter can. For example, if a doctor engages in sexual intercourse with a female patient under circumstances in which she does not know what is occurring and believes that she is only submitting to an examination or operation, this is fraud in the factum and the woman cannot be said to have consented. On the other hand, if the doctor convinces the woman that she should submit to intercourse because this would be effective treatment for her illness, the woman has given effective consent because this is only fraud in the inducement. Just what is a "collateral matter" under this approach is sometimes a matter of dispute, as is reflected by the split of authority on the question of whether it is rape for a man to have intercourse with a woman by misrepresenting himself as her husband. Perhaps it is more helpful to ask, as does Model Penal Code § 2.11(3)(d), whether the deception was "of a kind sought to be prevented by the law defining the offense."

This same distinction between fraud in the factum and fraud in the inducement is also relevant as to other crimes defined in terms of lack of consent. However, as to other offenses where consent is only sometimes a defense, such as battery, both forms of deception may be considered unlawful and thus a bar to effective consent.

Because persons engaging in certain types of activities subject themselves, to some degree, to the risk of harm, the question naturally arises as to whether and to what extent the election to participate in certain activity amounts to consent to bodily harm. The issue is sometimes addressed by a statute declaring, for example, that one has consented to the "reasonably foreseeable hazards" of joint participation in a lawful athletic contest or competitive sport, of medical or scientific experimentation conducted by recognized methods, of a certain occupation or profession, or of other lawful activity. Under this test, it would appear that a participant in an athletic contest consents to that harm which is inflicted within the rules of the game and also that which occurs as a result of minor and common deviation from the rules, but not that attributable to deviations amounting to unprovoked exceedingly violent attacks. As for medical or scientific experimentation, much depends upon the extent to which the subject has been made aware of the risks involved.

(b) Guilt of the Victim. The fact that the victim of a crime was himself engaged in criminal activity is not, in and of itself, a defense. As explained in the leading case of *State v. Mellenberger* (1939), the doctrine of *particeps criminis* (whereby one party to a crime may not recover in a civil suit against another party thereto) has no place in the criminal law, for the purpose of the criminal law is the suppression of crime and the punishment of criminals. Criminal prosecutions are not brought for the protection and benefit of the victim, and thus the victim's status as a criminal is not relevant.

Thus, the crime of false pretenses may be committed by cheating the operators of an illegal lottery, larceny by trick by inducing the victim to part with embezzled funds, and robbery by taking the fruits of a burglary. So too, larceny may be committed by taking items of contraband, such as bootleg liquor or slot machines, from the person who is committing a crime by possessing them.

For a time, an exception to the general rule was recognized in some jurisdictions. The exception was limited to cases in which one party induced another person to join in an illegal scheme and then defrauded him of his money or property, and was based upon the assumption that the protection of the law should not extend so far as to protect those who surrender their goods in the hope of obtaining a benefit by illegal means. Such reasoning is incorrect, for it would permit swindlers to operate with immunity by drawing their victims into illegal schemes. Fortunately, statutory enactments have put an end to this minority position.

Notwithstanding the rule that guilt of the victim is no defense, it must be remembered that the victim's criminal activity may give rise to circumstances whereby another may act with justification for the purpose of thwarting or terminating the criminal actions. These circumstances are described herein under the headings of self-defense (see § 9.4), defense of another (see § 9.5), defense of property (see § 9.6) , and law enforcement (see § 9.7). In light of these defenses, some have argued in favor of a nonspecific victim liability defense, or that victims' actions should be considered a liability mitigator in all appropriate cases and not merely in the context of a few distinct defenses.

(c) Contributory Negligence by the Victim. In the law of torts, contributory negligence by the plaintiff is a defense to an action based upon the defendant's negligence. This defense "does not rest upon the idea that the defendant is relieved of any duty toward the plaintiff. Rather, although the defendant has violated his duty, has been negligent, and would otherwise be liable, the plaintiff is denied recovery because his own conduct disentitles him to maintain the action. In the eyes of the law both parties are at fault; and the defense is one of the plaintiff's disability, rather than the defendant's innocence."

Given this rationale for the contributory negligence defense, it is apparent that it has no place in the criminal law. Negligence by the victim, just as with criminal conduct by the victim, "does not bar an action against another for the wrong which he has committed against the peace and dignity of the state." Thus it has been frequently held, for example, that it is no defense to a charge of manslaughter or reckless homicide arising out of defendant's operation of an automobile that the deceased driver or pedestrian was also negligent.

This is not to say, however, that negligence by the victim is inadmissible in a criminal prosecution. As discussed earlier (see § 5.4(f)(6)), such negligence may have a bearing upon the issue of whether the defendant's conduct was the proximate cause of the injury, and it is also significant in determining whether the defendant was criminally negligent. For these reasons, it would be incorrect for the trial judge to instruct that the victim's negligence is totally immaterial on all aspects of the case, or, at the other extreme, to instruct in a manner that treats the negligence as a defense for which the burden of proof is on the defendant.

(d) Condonation, Ratification, and Settlement. Condonation, the forgiveness of a criminal offense by the victim, is no defense. Sometimes this is explained on the ground that condonation is after-the-fact consent by the victim and thus cannot be any more effective than before-the-fact consent. This, however, might suggest that condonation is a defense in those circumstances where before-the-fact consent would bar conviction, but this is not the case. While before-the-fact consent may negative an element of the offense or preclude infliction of the harm to be prevented by the law in question, this is not true of subsequent condonation. Such forgiveness "has no proper place in the criminal law. The interest of the state is paramount and controls prosecutions * * * [f]or it is the public, not a complainant, that is injured by the commission of a crime." Acts by the victim alleged to constitute ratification (formal sanction, not necessarily involving forgiveness) are for the same reason no defense.

So too, it is no defense that the victim has been made whole by recovering a judgment in a civil action against the defendant. Nor is it a defense that the defendant has voluntarily made restitution; "satisfaction of a private wrong is not a bar to a criminal prosecution." Once again, the dominant theme is that when a crime has been committed the principal injury, in the contemplation of the law, is that which has been suffered by the public.

In some jurisdictions, condonation or settlement has by legislation been made a defense to certain crimes. Some of these enactments deal with specific offenses where the legislature has presumably made the judgment that conviction is unwise if the victim has otherwise obtained satisfaction, perhaps because the crime is in reality more private than public in nature. Thus, in some states a subsequent marriage of the parties following seduction is proof of condonation and a bar to prosecution. Likewise, statutes in certain jurisdictions permit a prosecution for adultery only upon the complaint of an offended spouse, so that if the aggrieved spouse condones the offense the husband or wife may not be convicted.

Twelve states have much broader compromise statutes, covering most or all misdemeanors, which provide that if the injured party appears in court and acknowledges that he has received satisfaction for the injury, then the prosecution may be terminated. Only a few of these statutes expressly provide that no such termination may be permitted but upon agreement by the prosecutor. If the court orders that the prosecution be so terminated, that is a bar to another prosecution for the same offense. These statutes have been strictly construed so that, for example, it must appear that the injured party in fact appeared in court and made the necessary acknowledgment of satisfaction; mere evidence of compromise is not sufficient. More important, these provisions are applicable only to those crimes that overlap a civil remedy. Thus, compromise with a person injured in an automobile accident is no defense to a charge of leaving the scene of an accident, nor is compromise with the owner of a damaged aircraft a bar to prosecution for operating an aircraft under the influence of liquor.

It is undoubtedly true that there are certain crimes which are more private than public, as to which settlement is to be encouraged in lieu of prosecution. "In one class of cases, the public wrong is merged in that of the individual, and compensation to him is accepted as the adequate measure of redress. In the other, the individual grievance is swallowed up in the greater wrong done to society; and nothing but public punishment will suffice, to vindicate the violated law." Yet, it may be questioned whether indiscriminate compromise statutes, covering a wide range of offenses and involving restitution by the defendant, represent sound policy.

For one thing, reliance upon the misdemeanor-felony distinction as a basis for deciding when compromise should be permitted is highly questionable. There is nothing inherent in the label "misdemeanor" or in the characteristics of misdemeanors generally (see § 1.6(a)) which suggest that settlement is to be preferred. This point is aptly illustrated by *State v. Garoutte* (1964), where the court, after noting that it "was never thought that the taking of a human life could be paid for and forgotten," reluctantly concluded that the defendant's compliance with the misdemeanor compromise statute barred prosecution for manslaughter by motor vehicle because the crime had been changed from a felony to a misdemeanor (apparently without any legislative consideration of the significance of this change in relation to the 85–year-old compromise statute).

There has been some degree of legislative recognition of this problem, for the compromise statutes usually set out various exceptional circumstances in which disposition of criminal charges by compromise is proscribed. The most common exceptions are where: (1) the offense was committed by or upon a police officer or judge; (2) the offense was committed "riotously"; (3) the offense was committed with intent to commit a felony; or (4) the offense was a crime of domestic violence.

Even assuming there is something to the misdemeanor-felony dichotomy, it is apparent that a statutory policy of permitting compromise of most or all misdemeanors involving an "injured party" is indiscriminate. As noted in *Garouette:*

> The present state of the law has this incongruous result. If a drunk or reckless driver does not hit anyone, he may go to jail * * *. If guilty, he cannot escape punishment. There is no "injured person" or "injured party" or possible "remedy by civil action," and the compromise statute may not be invoked. But if he damages property, hits someone, or even kills them, under the compromise statute he may completely escape punishment by paying civil damages.

Finally, these statutes might be questioned on the ground that they discriminate against the indigent, who are unable to make a private settlement and in that way avoid conviction. "The law should treat rich and poor alike, and the fact that a man might be able to pay for damages due to his negligence should not save him from criminal prosecution." Indeed, these compromise statutes may violate the equal protection clause of the United States Constitution.

(e) Administration of the Criminal Law. Subject to the exceptions which have been noted, it may be concluded that the substantive criminal law does not recognize as a defense the victim's consent, guilt of a crime, contributory negligence, condonation or ratification of the defendant's conduct, or acceptance of a settlement. However, these factors not infrequently have a significant impact upon the administration of the criminal law. Because of their presence, it sometimes occurs that the police decide not to arrest, the prosecutor decides not to charge, or the judge or jury decides not to convict.

There are undoubtedly a variety of reasons why this happens. Most likely, however, the presence of such circumstances leads the decision-maker to conclude that (a) the harm to be prevented by the statute has thus not occurred; (b) prosecution, conviction, and punishment would serve no purpose or would be harmful to the present relationship between the offender and victim; or (c) the limited resources of the criminal justice system are better devoted to other, more serious matters.

Chapter 6

INSANITY DEFENSE

Table of Sections

For additional analysis of the above topics and citations to authorities supporting their discussion in this Book, consult the author's 3-volume *Substantive Criminal Law* treatise, also available as Westlaw database SUBCRL. See the Table of Cross-References in this Book.

---

§ 6.1 Theory and Purpose

The insanity defense is quite different from other defenses in that the result, if it is successfully interposed, is not acquittal and outright release of the accused but rather a special form of verdict or finding ("not guilty by reason of insanity") usually followed by commitment of the defendant to a mental institution. Thus, its purpose is usually said to be that of separating from the criminal justice system those who should only be subjected to a medical-custodial disposition.

(a) Insanity as a Defense. "Insanity" is a word frequently encountered in legal situations quite outside the criminal law. One test for insanity for the purpose of civil commitment, for example, is whether the person sought to be committed can properly take care of himself and his affairs. A person who is insane cannot make a valid will, but here the test is whether the testator understands the nature of his property and its disposition. One who is insane cannot make a contract, or testify in court, or serve on a jury, but in each instance the test for insanity differs somewhat because of the circumstances involved. Insanity is also a ground for divorce in some jurisdictions, and here again a different test is likely to be used.

The word "insanity" is also used in different criminal law settings, and once again the meaning of the word differs depending upon the circumstances. There is, for instance, insanity as a defense to a criminal prosecution, which is the kind of insanity we are principally concerned with in this book. Although such insanity may be defined in one of several ways, depending upon the law of the jurisdiction, none of those definitions will suffice for other uses of the word "insanity" in the criminal process, such as (1) to determine who is incompetent to stand trial (see § 7.1(a)); (2) to determine who is incompetent to submit to execution (see § 7.1(c)); (3) to determine who is to be committed following a successful insanity defense (see § 7.4(a)); or (4) to determine who is ineligible for release following such commitment (see § 7.4(c)).

As for insanity as a defense, under the prevailing *M'Naghten* rule (sometimes referred to as the right-wrong test) the defendant cannot be convicted if, at the time he committed the act, he was laboring under such a defect of reason, from a disease of the mind, as not to know the nature and quality of the act he was doing; or, if he did know it, as not to know he was doing what was wrong. A few jurisdictions have supplemented *M'Naghten* with the unfortunately-named "irresistible impulse" test, which—generally stated—recognizes insanity as a defense when the defendant had a mental disease that kept him from controlling his conduct. For several years (but no longer) the District of Columbia followed the so-called *Durham* rule (or product test), whereby the accused is not criminally responsible if his unlawful act was the product of mental disease or mental defect. And in recent years a substantial minority of states have adopted the Model Penal Code approach, which is that the defendant is not responsible if at the time of his conduct as a result of mental disease or defect he lacked substantial capacity either to appreciate the criminality of his conduct or to conform his conduct to the requirements of law. These might be said to represent four different definitions of insanity for purposes of the substantive criminal law, but, as will be noted when these tests are discussed in greater detail (see § 6.2–6.5), some believe that the practical differences between them are not great.

(b) Purpose of the Defense. There exist in the criminal law a number of substantive defenses to a charge of criminal conduct (see chs. 8 & 9). These defenses are usually defined in terms of unusual circumstances that, when raised by the defendant, evidence a situation in which the purposes of the criminal law would not be served by conviction of the defendant. For example, take the defense of self-defense (see § 9.4). For *A* intentionally to kill *B* is murder, and the various purposes of the criminal law (see § 1.5) are served by convicting and punishing *A* for his crime of taking a human life. But if *A* killed *B* to prevent *B* from killing him, then the defense of self-defense comes into play because the purposes of the criminal law are better served by *A*'s acquittal; "authorizing the potential victim to kill his assailant constitutes a sanction which may be assumed to fulfill punitive, restraining, and deterrent functions in the service of the community's objective to safeguard human life."

In some respects, at least, the insanity defense is like self-defense and the other defenses. Again we are dealing with an unusual situation that is ordinarily raised by the defendant and that, if it in fact existed, means the purposes of the criminal law would not be served by conviction. (The insanity defense, as it relates to these purposes, is discussed herein.) Yet, the actual consequence of a successful insanity defense is quite different than with respect to any other defense; in every other case, a successful defense results in acquittal and outright release of the defendant, but with the insanity defense the probable result is commitment of the defendant to a mental institution until he has recovered his sanity (see § 7.4). Acceptance of the defendant's insanity defense is specially noted by a jury verdict (or, in a trial without jury, a judge's finding) of "not guilty by reason of insanity," after which he will (in some jurisdictions) be automatically committed or (in others) be subjected to proceedings that are most likely to result in commitment.

It is apparent, then, that the insanity defense serves a unique purpose. Few efforts to articulate that purpose have been made, although the general assumption seems to be that the defense makes it possible to separate out for special treatment certain persons who would otherwise be subjected to the usual penal sanctions that may follow convictions:

> The problem is the drawing of a line between the use of public agencies and force (1) to condemn the offender by conviction, with resultant sanctions in which the ingredient of reprobation is present no matter how constructive one may

seek to make the sentence and the process of correction, and (2) modes of disposition in which the condemnatory element is absent, even though restraint may be involved. * * * Stating the matter differently, the problem is to etch a decent working line between the areas assigned to the authorities responsible for public health and those responsible for the correction of offenders.

Another view, however, is that the "real function" of the insanity defense "is to authorize the state to hold those 'who must be found not to possess the guilty mind *mens rea,*' even though the criminal law demands that no person be held criminally responsible if doubt is cast on any material element of the offense charged." That is, the defense is seen as a device whereby certain persons are singled out for commitment, not as an alternative to conviction and imprisonment, but rather as an alternative to outright acquittal. Under this theory, the insanity defense is unlike the other defenses in that it does not apply only to persons against whom each of the elements of the offense charged could be established.

There is actually some truth to both views, and this is because the circumstances which give rise to a defense of insanity *sometimes* also warrant the conclusion that the defendant did not commit the acts with the mental state required for conviction of the crime charged. But this is not always the case, for "the insanity defense is broader than the mens rea concept," as evidenced by the fact that the defense would in theory even be available in a prosecution for a strict-liability crime that required no proof of the defendant's mental state.

Thus, at one extreme, if the effect of the defendant's mental disease was that he did not even know what he was doing—if, to take an oft-cited example, he strangled his wife but believed that he was squeezing lemons—he would certainly have a valid insanity defense under any of the insanity tests now in use. But, in a homicide prosecution which included as an element of the charge that the defendant killed his wife intentionally, knowingly, or recklessly (defined in subjective terms, in that the defendant was actually aware of the risk attending his actions), it would also be correct to say that this defendant is simply not guilty for lack of *mens rea.* At least to the extent that courts have declined to admit evidence of mental disease except in the context of an insanity defense, it could be said that in this situation the defense serves as a device for committing those who would otherwise be acquitted.

At the other extreme, if the effect of the defendant's mental disease was that he was significantly lacking in the ability to control his actions, he would again have an insanity defense under at least some of the insanity tests. But it is unlikely that it could be said that this defendant, merely because of limitations upon his powers of self-control, did not act with intent (that is, with a purpose of bringing about the harmful result), knowledge (awareness that the harmful result would follow), or recklessness (awareness of a substantial risk that the harmful risk will follow), whatever the relevant mental state is for the offense charged. In such a situation, the insanity defense serves as a means to bring about commitment of the defendant in lieu of conviction and imprisonment.

(c) Theories of Punishment and the Defense. Another helpful way of looking at the defense of insanity is in relation to the various theories of punishment (see § 1.5), for the philosophical reasons for allowing the defense are tied up with these theories.

(1) Prevention. One theory underlying punishment of those who commit crimes is that by subjecting them to an unpleasant experience they will be less likely to commit other crimes in the future. But, this "can be effective only with men who can understand the signals directed at them by the [criminal] code, who can respond to warnings, and who can feel the significance of the sanctions imposed upon violators." Punishment, therefore, is not at all likely to deter the insane individual from future antisocial conduct. The insanity defense diverts these persons to what is hopefully a process of treatment directed at the causes of their actions and intended to overcome the mental disability that might bring about future harmful conduct.

(2) Restraint. Another purpose of punishment is protection of society from dangerous persons; those convicted of serious crimes are usually incarcerated for a substantial period of time, during which they cannot endanger society by more criminality. The insanity defense is quite consistent with this notion, for if the defense is successfully interposed, the defendant is not merely incarcerated for a fixed period of time but is instead committed until such time as he no longer is dangerous.

(3) Rehabilitation. Under this theory, sanctions are imposed upon the convicted defendant for the purpose of altering his behavior pattern and making him a more useful citizen in the community. It is generally assumed that the rehabilitation of the insane person should be accomplished through means which differ from those that are useful for the rehabilitation of others. The insanity defense diverts the insane person to a mental hospital instead of a prison so that he may receive rehabilitation through treatment.

(4) Deterrence. Punishment of those who violate the criminal laws also serves as a means of general prevention, in that the law-abiding tendencies of the general public are reinforced by the example of punishment of those who have not been law abiding. This purpose would not be served by conviction and punishment of the insane, for "the examples are likely to deter only if the person who is *not* involved in the criminal process regards the lessons as applicable to him," which he is likely to do "only if he identifies with the offender and with the offending situation." It is unlikely that the sane person (or even the insane person who believes himself to be sane) will identify with the insane defendant, and thus the insane cannot be effectively used as a deterrent example to others. Or, if one accepts the argument that such identification will nonetheless occur because the public will not scrutinize that closely the characteristics of those punished, it may still be argued that the objective of deterrence should not be enhanced by punishment of the insane. "It would be widely regarded as incalculably cruel and unjust to incarcerate men who are not personally responsible in order to serve social functions."

(5) Education. Yet another theory of punishment is that the process of prosecution, conviction, and imposition of sanctions serves to educate the general public by making known what conduct is prohibited by the criminal law. This function, however, is most important as to relatively minor offenses that do not involve inherently bad conduct; there is no need to educate the public about those crimes, such as murder, for which the insanity defense is most frequently interposed. Moreover, the punishment of individuals who, because of their insanity, would be viewed by the general public as not blameworthy would only blur the distinction between good and bad conduct and thus work against the education theory.

(6) Retribution. The oldest theory of punishment, that the criminal owes the community a measure of suffering because of that which he inflicted, still persists at least to some degree. Assuming there is some current validity to this theory, it may nonetheless be said that the purpose of retribution would not be served by conviction and punishment of the insane. Indeed, the insanity defense developed as a means of saving from retributive punishment those individuals who were so different from others that they could not be blamed for what they had done.

(d) Abolish the Insanity Defense? Yet another way of viewing the insanity defense is through consideration of the arguments that have been made over the years—pro and con—concerning whether the defense should be abolished. Of course, if the insanity defense were abolished there would have to be substituted some other mechanism to deal with the insane person who has engaged in harmful conduct, perhaps by merely taking mental condition into account after conviction in deciding what is to be done with the offender (and, perhaps also by establishing and utilizing commitment procedures for those whose insanity negates the mental state needed for conviction and who thus have nonetheless been found not guilty).

The following arguments have been made in favor of abolishing the insanity defense:

(1) Insanity is in practice only a "rich man's defense" in that only the wealthy can afford the array of experts needed to mount a convincing defense—experts who are in short supply and whose time would be better spent in treatment of those who have been committed or imprisoned.

(2) The key terms in the various insanity tests are so vague that they "invite semantic jousting, metaphysical speculation, intuitive moral judgments in the guise of factual determinations."

(3) The function of the insanity defense remains uncertain, but even accepting the common assertion that the purpose is to remove from the criminal process those who are not blameworthy, "there is just no basis in psychiatry to make a differentiation between * * * the man who is personally blameworthy for his makeup from the man who is not."

(4) The crucial decision to be made concerns the proper disposition of mentally abnormal persons who commit criminal acts, and this is a matter that is better dealt with in a direct way following conviction than indirectly during trial.

(5) Persons channelled out of the criminal process following a finding of not guilty by reason of insanity are not protected against administrative abuse of their rights to the same degree that they would be if they remained within the criminal justice system.

(6) "A number of informed observers believe that it is therapeutically desirable to treat behavioral deviants as responsible for their conduct rather than as involuntary victims playing a sick role."

(7) As a practical matter, the insanity defense is most often utilized to avoid the harshness of the death penalty. A more direct response would be to abolish the death penalty.

(8) "The insanity defense discriminates against persons who commit crimes because of influences on their personalities other than mental disease or defect."

(9) The insanity defense sometimes serves as a means of facilitating detention of those who did not have the *mens rea* required and whose present dangerousness has not been determined.

In favor of retaining the insanity defense, these points have been made:

(1) Efforts to keep the insanity question out of the criminal trial have been largely unsuccessful. Under the bifurcated trial system, whereby the issue of guilt is first tried and the issue of insanity is then tried separately, evidence essentially equivalent to that which would be entered for purposes of the insanity defense frequently is brought out in the first part of the trial on the issue of *mens rea*. This could be avoided by eliminating *both* the *mens rea* requirement and the insanity defense, but the few efforts to do so have been held to deny due process.

(2) Defendants who now go free because they lacked *mens rea* would, if the insanity defense were abolished, be more likely to be convicted on the assumption that they would be weeded out at the disposition stage, resulting in their premature labeling as an offender.

(3) "[E]liminating the insanity defense would remove from the criminal law and the public conscience the vitally important distinction between illness and evil, or would tuck it away in an administrative process." So the argument goes, it is extremely important that we retain the concept of responsibility in the criminal law and "that 'blame' be retained as a spur to individual responsibility." Moreover, we would rebel at the notion of labeling as criminal those who are generally conceded not to be blameworthy.

(4) If the choice between sanctions, the official condemnation of conviction and punishment on the one hand and the indeterminate detention for treatment and its accompanying stigma on the other, is to be made in a way that will be acceptable to the public, then the decision must "be made by a democratically selected jury rather than by experts—because the public can identify with the former but not with the latter." Moreover, the receipt of psychiatric input in a trial, subject to traditional adversary procedures, is the best approach "for exposing differences in professional judgments."

A few states have by statute abolished the defense of insanity by legislation providing that evidence of mental disease or defect is admissible only to negate the mental state required for the offense charged. Some case authority is to be found holding such abolition constitutional. In *State v. Korell* (1984), the court rejected the defendant's contention that the insanity defense was so firmly established in the common law at the time our Constitution was adopted that it was a fundamental right protected by the Fourteenth Amendment due process clause. The court noted that the Supreme Court, in *Powell v. Tex.* (1968), characterized the defense as one of those doctrines which "have historically provided the tools for a constantly shifting adjustment of the tension between the evolving aims of the criminal law and changing religious, moral, philosophical, and medical views of the nature of man," a process always "thought to be the province of the States." Early court decisions holding abolition of the insanity defense unconstitutional were distinguished because the statutes there challenged, unlike their modern counterparts, did not even permit trial testimony on mental condition to cast doubt on whether a defendant had the requisite mental state.

As for the contention that abolition of the insanity defense constitutes cruel and unusual punishment under the Eighth Amendment, the *Korell* court concluded this was not so because the Supreme Court's teachings in *Robinson v. Cal.* (1962) and *Powell* were merely that neither status nor illness could themselves be made criminal (see § 5.1(d)). Some commentators support that line of reasoning, but others do not. They read *Powell* as merely rejecting the notion that a particular "test of insanity is constitutionally required," while indicating a willingness "to require at least some defense based on the impairment of free will."

While the Supreme Court has not passed directly upon the question of whether the insanity defense may constitutionally be abolished, it has on one occasion considered whether a particular narrowing of the defense violated due process. In *Clark v. Arizona* (2006), the defendant's first claim was that the state, which at one time had the usual two-pronged *M'Naghten* rule, had created an unconstitutional variety of the insanity defense when the legislature redefined the defense so that it was stated solely in terms of "a mental disease or defect of such severity that the person did not know the criminal act was wrong." As for defendant's contention that the full *M'Naghten* rule was a constitutional minimum, the Court took note of the considerable "diversity of American standards" regarding the insanity defense and thus concluded: "History shows no deference to *M'Naghten* that could elevate its formula to the level of fundamental principle, so as to limit the traditional recognition of a State's capacity to define crimes and defenses." And in any event, the Court added, the Arizona version of the test was actually not significantly different from the full *M'Naghten* standard, for one way a defendant could show that he did not know that his act wrong was by showing (as would otherwise suffice under the omitted part of the test) that he did not appreciate the nature and quality of his act.

§ 6.2 The M'Naghten "Right–Wrong" Test

In a majority of the jurisdictions in this country, what is most often referred to as the *M'Naghten* rule has long been accepted as the test to be applied for the defense of insanity. Under *M'Naghten,* an accused is not criminally responsible if, at the time of committing the act, he was laboring under such a defect of reason, from disease of the mind, as not to know the nature and quality of the act he was doing, or if he did know it that he did not know he was doing what was wrong.

(a) The *M'Naghten* Case. In 1843 Daniel M'Naghten shot and killed Edward Drummond, private secretary to Sir Robert Peel. M'Naghten, believing that Peel was heading a conspiracy to kill him, had intended to take Peel's life, but he instead shot Drummond because he mistakenly believed him to be Peel. At the trial of his case, M'Naghten claimed that he was insane and could not be held responsible because it had been his delusions which caused him to act. The jury agreed, and M'Naghten was found not guilty by reason of insanity.

Due to the importance of both the victim and the intended victim, the decision was not a popular one. The House of Lords debated the decision and posed to the justices of the Queen's Bench five questions concerning the standards for acquitting a defendant due to his insanity. The answers to these questions were appended to the report of the original case, *M'Naghten's Case* (1843), and have come to be considered as if they were a part of that decision.

It should be noted that four of the five questions of the House of Lords referred only to the proper test and procedures for acquitting one who was "affected with insane delusions respecting one or more particular subjects or persons." Only question three, regarding what should be left for the jury to decide, did not have such a reference in it. But regardless of whether the House of Lords meant to inquire only about a specific facet of insanity, a portion of the judges' answers has come to be the most widely accepted test for the type or degree of mental disorder that will absolve a person from criminal responsibility.

The majority of the justices stated: "[T]o establish a defense on the ground of insanity, it must be clearly proved that, at the time of the committing of the act, the party accused was laboring under such a defect of reason, from disease of the mind, as not to know the nature and quality of the act he was doing, or if he did know it that he did not know he was doing what was wrong." This advisory opinion soon became known as the *M'Naghten* test of insanity. It is clear, however, that the judges were merely attempting to state the law as it then existed; the right-wrong test had previously been utilized in both England and the United States.

Taken literally, the *M'Naghten* rule appears to refer to a certain mental disability that must produce one of two conditions, both of which are defined in terms of lack of cognition. Thus the elements of *M'Naghten* might be distinguished in this way:

> (1) (disability) that the accused have suffered a defect of reason, from a disease of the mind; *and*

(2) (result) that consequently at the time of the act he did not know

   (a) the nature and quality of the act, *or*

   (b) that the act was wrong.

The *M'Naghten* test (sometimes with slight variations) has become the predominant rule in the United States. It is the rule in the federal courts and also remains the rule in more than thirty of the states, occasionally supplemented with a test for loss of volitional control. But a substantial minority of states has rejected the *M'Naghten* test, usually in favor of the Model Penal Code approach (see § 6.5).

(b) The Meaning of *M'Naghten*. Although the *M'Naghten* rule has been one of the most widely debated topics in the criminal law, there is very little explanation or clarification of the rule to be found in the case law. This is probably due to the small percentage of defendants who raise an insanity defense and the extreme rarity of appeals by these defendants.

(1) "Disease of the Mind." There has never been a clear and comprehensive determination of what type of mental disease or defect is required to satisfy the *M'Naghten* test. Some believe that only a few types of psychoses will suffice. However, it would seem that any mental abnormality, be it psychosis, neurosis, organic brain disorder, or congenital intellectual deficiency (low IQ or feeblemindedness), will suffice *if* it has caused the consequences described in the second part of the test. Thus, although many psychiatrists apparently believe that only a few psychoses will give rise to a successful insanity defense under the *M'Naghten* rule, this is not because certain illnesses or defects are per se excluded but rather because they do not produce the lack of cognition required under *M'Naghten*.

While there "has been almost no judicial definition of mental disease in cases concerned with the *M'Naghten* rule," courts have not hesitated to "reject efforts to assert insanity by persons whose mental conditions are clearly marginal." Thus the requisite mental disease is not present in the case of "bodily demand for drugs during withdrawal" or of so-called "temporary insanity" resulting from intoxication (as compared to "an alcoholic psychosis such as delirium tremens, resulting from long continued habits of excessive drinking"). So too, courts have warned that "the utmost care should be taken not to confuse such mental disease with moral obliquity, mental depravity, or passion arising from anger, hatred, revenge and kindred evil conditions," meaning that "a mere moral, or emotional insanity, so-called," as in the case of a defendant who acted because he was "insanely jealous," will not suffice.

Despite the fact that the "cases are relatively silent * * * on which diseases would qualify," some judgment is possible regarding certain conditions that have often received attention in more recent years. For example, in the case of post-traumatic stress disorder (PTSD), as experienced by some combat veterans, courts and commentators are in agreement that this constitutes a mental disease, at least when the impairment is severe, and thus it is not surprising that PTSD evidence has produced not guilty by reason of insanity verdicts in *M'Naghten* jurisdictions. There is also a body of opinion to the effect that "[u]nder *M'Naghten*, postpartum psychosis satisfies the criteria of a mental disease or defect by preventing the defendant from understanding the nature and quality of her act or knowing that her act was wrong." Insanity pleas based upon the presence of this psychosis have been entered in several cases, although the results when mothers have relied upon it in defense when charged with killing their recently-born children have been mixed. So too, the multiple personality disorder (MPD), also known as the dissociative identity disorder, has been deemed a mental disease under a *M'Naghten*-style statute. The complicating factor here is that courts have applied three different approaches in dealing with MPD—the prevailing alter approach, which considers the culpability of the personality that allegedly committed the crime; the seldom-used unified approach, which focuses upon the person as a whole without regard to which personality was in control at the relevant time; and the host approach, where a finding of not guilty by reason of insanity can be grounded in the fact that the host personality did not plan or participate in the offense. It is unlikely that a defendant in a *M'Naghten* jurisdiction could prevail except under the latter theory.

As for "homosexual panic," "the idea that a latent homosexual—and manifest 'homophobe'—can be so upset by a homosexual's advances to him that he becomes temporarily insane," the issue has not been squarely addressed in appellate decisions. Sometimes insanity defenses so grounded have been permitted to go to the jury, and sometimes they have succeeded. But the correctness of these cases has been questioned by many commentators. As one put it: "Homophobia differs from recognized mental illnesses because it is a product of culturally imposed values rather than abnormal psychological traits. Homosexual panic should therefore not be accepted as a mental defect negating or reducing individual culpability."

As for "the new-syndrome-suffering defendants," it is doubtless true that a great many of them "are clearly not legally insane by any of the traditional tests," for "what is generally striking about virtually all the new syndromes is that they are extremely rarely associated with or characterized by a massive, psychotic break with reality," and instead "involve mood or conduct problems, impaired judgment and reasoning, and other lesser forms of psychopathology." It is not surprising, therefore, that courts and commentators have in the main declared that the battered woman syndrome, whatever its relevance as to a self-defense claim, is not a mental disease for purposes of the insanity defense. As for the premenstrual syndrome (PMS), it will not suffice under *M'Naghten* for two reasons: it is not a mental disease, and it does not "affect individual's ability to appreciate the 'nature and quality' of criminal conduct, or to understand whether it is right to wrong." As for the Munchausen syndrome by proxy, "a form of child abuse wherein the perpetrating parent (almost always a mother) fictitiously induces illnesses or symptoms in a child by fabricating evidence," usually resulting "in numerous and extensive diagnostic procedures that in themselves can often harm the child," it is regarded by the criminal justice system "as a form of behavior, not as a true mental disease," and, indeed, is relied upon not by way of defense but rather by the prosecutor to show the mother's guilt.

Another disorder, the psychopathic personality, would clearly appear to be excluded by the requirement that the accused have suffered from a disease of the mind. Although it is virtually impossible to define adequately a psychopathic personality, it is commonly asserted that a psychopath is one who exhibits an abnormality only in the repetitious performance of antisocial or criminal acts. Such a person differs from others only in the quantity or types of his actions and not by the quality of his mental facilities, and thus he would not have an insanity defense under *M'Naghten*. But even in this situation the "disease of the mind" element of *M'Naghten* is not itself a unique limiting factor, as the psychopath likewise could not qualify under the lack-of-cognition requirement.

One commentator has made the argument that a defendant's criminal conduct may have been significantly influenced "by his exposure to social environmental factors * * * affecting his mental functioning," and that when this is the case the use of such theories as urban psychosis, television intoxication, and black rage "to support an insanity defense requires little substantive expansion with respect to established criminal law doctrine." It is open to serious question, however, whether they meet either the mental disease or other requirements of *M'Naghten*, and the same may be said with perhaps even greater confidence as to some other proposed defenses, such as the so-called "cultural" defense and "rotten social background" defense. (Of course, it is doubtless true that many of these proposed defenses are based not on the assumption that they involve mental disease, but rather on the claim that they establish a legitimate showing of nonresponsibility on some other basis, but even so viewed they have often been subjected to severe and telling criticism.)

Before leaving this discussion of what mental disease will suffice under *M'Naghten*, note must be taken of the language used in the federal *M'Naghten*-type statute and also adopted in a few states, namely, that there must be a "severe mental disease or defect." As the legislative history of the federal act reveals, the "concept of severity was added to emphasize that non-psychotic behavior disorders or neuroses such as an 'inadequate personality,' 'immature personality,' or a pattern of 'antisocial tendencies' do not constitute the defense," and also that "the voluntary use of alcohol or drugs, even if they render the defendant unable to appreciate the nature and quality of his acts, does not constitute insanity." If that was the only concern, then this addition is of no significance, for the "mental diseases cited to justify the addition of the term 'severe' constitute legal insanity only under tests which employ the volitional element," which the *M'Naghten*-style federal statute does not. And thus the severity requirement has not prevented a showing of the requisite mental disease where the defendant was afflicted, for example, with a multiple personality disorder or post-traumatic stress disorder, or, indeed, any mental disease or defect characterized by a mental state that involves hallucinations or delusions. A court's severity analysis is not determined by whether the word "severe" does or does not appear in the diagnosis, for the statute "contemplates a more thoroughgoing approach, in which a court reviews the diagnosis for overall indications of the severity of defendant's mental disease or defect." It is not necessary that the defendant's mental illness be of a recent vintage, was diagnosed shortly before or shortly after the crime, or must require medication or prevent a defendant from holding down a job.

(2) "Know." It is the word "know" in the test that has been the source of most of the criticism of *M'Naghten*. The test has been described as unrealistic on the assumption that "know" refers only to intellectual awareness. It has been contended that few if any individuals have existed who do not have any intellectual awareness of what they are doing, and that a test phrased merely in terms of such cognition is unduly restrictive. It is impossible, so the argument goes, to separate a man's intellect from his will in testing his mental capabilities.

Others have contended that the word "know" encompasses more than just the minimal awareness of facts or the ability to mechanically repeat what has happened. To them, "know" refers to "affective" or "emotional" knowledge, "so fused with affect that it becomes a human reality," knowledge that "can exist only when the accused is able to evaluate his conduct in terms of its actual impact upon himself and others and when he is able to appreciate the total setting in which he is acting." That is, the person must be able to grasp the underlying significance of what he did and not just be able to register and repeat physical surroundings and the actions he took. Some have even gone so far as to assert that a person must have the capacity to choose between acts in order to know what he is doing, although this would seem to stretch the term beyond all limits.

As one study has shown, there is no basis for the claim that the *M'Naghten* test has been strictly applied so as to extend only to intellectual awareness. Very few appellate decisions are to be found taking that limited view, and as to some of these the limitation may be of little significance because of the availability of the "irresistible impulse" control test in addition to *M'Naghten*. In most of the *M'Naghten* jurisdictions the word "know" is not defined at all, leaving the jury free to determine the meaning on the basis of the expert testimony received at trial. Of the lesser number of jurisdictions that have addressed the question of what "know" means, the great majority have favored a broad construction of the word.

(3) "Nature and Quality of the Act." Many courts feel that knowledge of "the nature and quality of the act" is the mere equivalent of the ability to know that the act was wrong. Indeed, in many jurisdictions the *M'Naghten* rule is stated merely in terms of the defendant's ability to distinguish right from wrong, and there is no mention of or instruction on knowledge of the nature and quality of the act. When mentioned, it is usually by mere repetition of the wording in *M'Naghten,* although the phrase has also turned up in other forms, such as "nature or quality" and "nature and consequences."

When considered at all, the entire phrase has been typically held to mean that the defendant must have understood the physical nature and consequences of the act. Thus, an accused must have known that holding a flame to a building would cause it to burn, or that holding a person's head under water would cause him to die. Only a few courts have indicated that the phrase refers to something more than knowledge of physical consequences. In *State v. Esser* (1962), for example, the Wisconsin court held that the phrase implied a true insight into the nature of the conduct and that it was forbidden. This, of course, is another way of reaching the result which is also possible by giving the word "know" a broad construction. "To know the quality of an act, with all its social and emotional implications, requires more than an abstract, purely intellectual knowledge. Likewise, to talk of appreciating the full significance of an act means that 'nature and quality' must be understood as including more than the physical nature of the act."

It is error to instruct the jury that to be insane the defendant must not have known the nature and quality of the act *and* that it was wrong. This is because a person might well be able to appreciate the physical consequences of the act and yet be incapable of understanding that it was forbidden.

(4) "Wrong." If the defendant does not know the nature and quality of his act, then quite obviously he does not know that his act is "wrong," and this is true without regard to the interpretation given to the word "wrong." For example, a madman who believes that he is squeezing lemons when he chokes his wife to death does not know the nature and quality of his act and likewise does not know that it is legally and morally wrong. On the other hand, as noted above, a defendant might know the nature and quality of his act (especially if that is taken to refer only to the physical consequences), but yet not know that it is "wrong." The extent to which such situations might arise, however, depends upon whether the *M'Naghten* test refers to legal wrong or moral wrong: "A kills B knowing that he is killing B, and knowing that it is illegal to kill B, but under an insane delusion that the salvation of the human race will be obtained by his execution for the murder of B, and that God has commanded him (A) to produce that result by those means. A's act is a crime if the word 'wrong' means illegal. It is not a crime if the word wrong means morally wrong."

The *M'Naghten* judges did not make clear what construction they were giving to the word "wrong." At one point they said that a person is punishable if "he knew at the time of committing such crime that he was acting contrary to law; by which expression we * * * mean the law of the land." But at another point they observed: "If the question were to be put as to the knowledge of the accused solely and exclusively with reference to the law of the land, it might tend to confound the jury by inducing them to believe that an actual knowledge of the law of the land was essential in order to lead to a conviction; whereas the law is administered on the principle that everyone must be taken conclusively to know it, without proof that he does know it. If the accused was conscious that the act was one which he ought not to do, and if that act was at the same time contrary to the law of the land, he is punishable."

In England, *M'Naghten* is now read as requiring that the defendant know that the act was legally wrong. In this country, however, the question of whether wrong means legally or morally wrong has not been clearly resolved. The issue has very seldom been raised; this part of the *M'Naghten* test is simply given to the jury without explanation. In the few cases in which the matter has been put into issue, some have held that the defendant must not have known that the act was legally wrong, while others have interpreted "wrong" to mean morally wrong. Some courts have held that the defendant must not have realized that the act was wrong *and* punishable, but have not made it clear whether this refers to both moral and legal wrong or only one of the two.

In the unlikely event that the defendant knew that his act was morally wrong but did not know that it was illegal, then it would seem that the *M'Naghten* test for insanity has not been met. In this instance, as is true generally, "knowledge of the law is presumed." The concern is instead with the case in which the defendant knew that his acts were contrary to law but yet believed that they were morally correct. Some have asserted that this is also an unlikely circumstance, given the fact that "the vast majority of cases in which insanity is pleaded as a defense * * * involve acts which are universally regarded as morally wicked as well as illegal." But whether this is so will depend upon how another ambiguity is resolved—that is, "whether 'moral wrong' is to be judged by the personal standards of the accused or by his awareness that society views the act as wrong." Society's moral judgment will usually be identical with the legal standard, and thus interpretation of "wrong" in the *M'Naghten* test as moral wrong will not significantly broaden the test if moral wrong is to be determined by an objective standard. But interpretation of "wrong" as moral wrong has nonetheless been opposed because it "invites * * * jury nullification" and conflicts with the principle that criminal sanctions are proper for "all who might be deterred."

One final observation about the meaning of the word "wrong" is required. The question under *M'Naghten* is only whether (because of a disease of the mind) the defendant did not know that the act he performed was wrong. An inability to differentiate generally between right and wrong is not necessary.

(5) Insane Delusions. In responding to the questions put to them by the House of Lords, the *M'Naghten* judges discussed the situation of persons who labor under "partial delusions only, and are not in other respects insane." As to such a person, he was said to be "nevertheless punishable according to the nature of the crime committed, if he knew at the time of committing such crime that he was acting contrary to law." Later, the judges explained that "he must be considered in the same situation as to responsibility as if the facts with respect to which the delusion exists were real. For example, if under the influence of his delusion he supposes another man to be in the act of attempting to take away his life, and he kills that man, as he supposes in self-defense, he would be exempt from punishment. If his delusion was that the deceased had inflicted a serious injury on his character and fortune, and he killed him in revenge for such supposed injury, he would be liable to punishment."

This has given rise to the question of whether, under the *M'Naghten* test, there is a separate and distinct rule that is to be applied in the case of a defendant suffering from insane delusions. Although some American cases might be read as if they were following somewhat different standards in such a case, it is undoubtedly fair to conclude that this particular part of *M'Naghten* does not set up a unique formula differing from the right-wrong test. The significant considerations are these:

(i) The *M'Naghten* judges were merely attempting to state the law of England as it then existed. The right-wrong test had been utilized in the earlier cases, but in no prior case can there be found a separate rule for defendants suffering from delusions. Thus it would seem that the judges did not intend to state a test which was inconsistent with the right-wrong test they had set forth.

(ii) The person described by the *M'Naghten* judges simply does not exist. "There is not, and never has been, a person who labors under partial delusion only and is not in other respects insane." This is because a delusion is not an isolated disorder, but rather a symptom of a widespread disorder.

(iii) If the affirmative part of the *M'Naghten* judges' statement about insane delusions is considered alone, it is clearly compatible with the right-wrong test. If a person suffering from delusions imagines facts which, if true, would justify his acts, then it would seem that this person is not in a position to discriminate between right and wrong with respect to his acts.

(iv) If the negative part of the statements in *M'Naghten* is taken as an exclusive test in delusion cases, thus barring an insanity defense if the facts regarding which the delusion exists would not constitute a defense if true, this would constitute an inroad upon the right-wrong test. But it is unlikely that any courts would so hold today. Rather, the better view is that a mental disease may qualify under the right-wrong test even though its primary symptom is a delusion concerning imagined facts which, if true, would not themselves constitute a defense.

(c) The Criticism of *M'Naghten*. The *M'Naghten* test has long been the subject of controversy. Although the critics of *M'Naghten* have been far more vocal than the defenders, at least until recently, the extensive literature on the subject provides more than an adequate exploration of the issues involved. Only the major criticisms will be briefly considered here.

(1) Based Upon Outmoded Concepts. The criticism of *M'Naghten* most frequently heard is that it is "based on an entirely obsolete and misleading conception of the nature of insanity, since insanity does not only, or primarily, affect the cognitive or intellectual faculties, but affects the whole personality of the patient, including both the will and the emotions." Typical is this statement from *Durham v. U.S.* (1954): "The science of psychiatry now recognizes that a man is an integrated personality and that reason, which is only one element in that personality, is not the sole determinant of his conduct. The right-wrong test, which considers knowledge or reason alone, is therefore an inadequate guide to mental responsibility for criminal behavior." Or, as the point was expressed by another court, it is an "absurdity" to determine the insanity issue by only asking the right-wrong question "when one surveys the array of symptomatology which the skilled psychiatrist employs in determining the mental condition of an individual."

In response, it has been argued that this criticism is misdirected in that it erroneously assumes that *M'Naghten* is intended to provide a medical definition rather than a legal definition. "[I]t is always necessary to start any discussion of *M'Naghten* by stressing that the case does not state a test of psychosis or mental illness. Rather, it lists conditions under which those who are mentally diseased will be relieved from criminal responsibility. Thus, criticism of *M'Naghten* based on the proposition that the case is premised on an outdated view of mental disease is inappropriate. The case can only be criticized justly if it is based on an outdated view of the mental conditions that ought to preclude application of criminal sanctions."

(2) Inconsistent With Purposes of Criminal Law. As the immediately preceding comments suggest, a more appropriate criticism of *M'Naghten* might be that it is inadequate to the task of selecting those mentally disabled persons who ought not be subjected to punishment under our system of criminal law. This criticism has also been voiced with considerable frequency. As most often stated, the concern is that the right-wrong test is not sufficient to exclude all insane nondeterrables because it only takes account of impairment of cognition and ignores impairment of volitional capacity. "Volitional ability to choose the right and avoid the wrong is as fundamental" in this regard, so the argument goes, "as is the intellectual power to discern right from wrong and understand the nature and quality of [one's] acts."

Supporters of *M'Naghten,* on the other hand, argue that the objectives of the criminal law are better served by an insanity test that is concerned with cognition rather than self-control. For example, one argument is that the goal of general deterrence is best served by a rule that declares irresponsible only those persons who quite clearly could not have been deterred because they could not have employed reason to restrain the act. Fundamental to this view is the proposition that "it is essential to maintain the threat" of punishment "so long as there is any chance that the preventive influence [of the criminal law] may operate." By starting from that point, it appears "safe" to exempt from punishment those who did not know what they were doing, for such individuals are quite clearly not deterrable and may be exculpated without diminishing the pressure on ordinary men to conform with the law. This is not true, so the argument goes, if exculpation is possible because of lack of self-control; especially because a complete inability to resist seldom exists, the threat of punishment must be maintained against those who because of mental disease are strongly tempted to break the law—just as it is against those who are for other reasons under a strong compulsion to engage in criminal conduct.

Others have taken a somewhat different approach in contending that *M'Naghten* is consistent with the purposes of the criminal law. They begin with the proposition that deterrability is *not* the touchstone of responsibility; it is noted that in one sense all offenders are nondeterrable (i.e., they were not deterred). Rather, responsibility rests upon "moral blameworthiness." But, how is moral blame to be determined? Not by asking whether it was reasonable, on the facts of the individual case, to expect compliance with the law, for the criminal law frequently imposes moral condemnation in the absence of such an expectation. Instead, moral blameworthiness "is less a quality of the offender, resting on his actual ability or inability to conform, than of the normative judgment of others that he ought to have been able to conform." The *M'Naghten* test is then found an appropriate device for identifying those without moral blame, for it isolates "that group that is popularly viewed as insane" and whose "acquittal will not offend the community sense of justice."

(3) Asks Questions Psychiatrist Cannot Answer. A common objection among psychiatrists to the right-wrong test is that it is directed to ethical and moralistic rather than scientific concerns. It is claimed that the question of the defendant's knowledge of right and wrong is more of a problem for a theologian and that it requires the psychiatrist to forsake his objective role and make value judgments. This criticism, however, is based upon a misunderstanding of what is being asked of the experts. "We are not being asked whether a defendant acted according to our accepted standards of morality or whether his own theoretical standards were the generally accepted ones. What we are asked is whether the defendant had sufficient intellect or sufficiently clear mind at the time of the crime to know what these generally accepted standards were." The psychiatrist is not being called upon to respond to the ethical question of what *is* right or wrong, but only to indicate whether the defendant was able to make moral and ethical discriminations.

(4) Restricts Expert Testimony. Yet another criticism of the *M'Naghten* test is that it unjustifiably restricts expert testimony and thus keeps from the factfinder much relevant information concerning the defendant's mental condition. The "true vice" of *M'Naghten* is said to be that "the ultimate deciders—the judge or the jury—will be deprived of information vital to their final judgment."

This contention has been totally debunked by one study, which concluded after a thorough analysis of the relevant appellate opinions that there is "virtually no support in law for the view that *M'Naghten* is responsible for inhibiting the flow of testimony on the insanity issue." Rather, the policy of the courts has been to admit any evidence that is probative of the defendant's mental condition, and this has been so even when the evidence appears to relate solely to defendant's lack of self-control. A similar conclusion was reached by the Model Penal Code draftsmen: "No American case has been found where a trial court excluded evidence or refused to charge on the defense of insanity merely because the evidence in support of the defense related to neurosis or psychopathic personality or other mental disturbance rather than a psychosis."

The study mentioned above also documents the conclusion that psychiatrists have not been forced to testify in terms of a definition of "know" which is limited to intellectual awareness. Based upon an analysis of numerous transcripts, that study found that expert witnesses were regularly permitted to explain their interpretation of this word in *M'Naghten* and to assert that the defendant did not have the requisite knowledge because of his lack of normal emotional awareness.

§ 6.3 The "Irresistible Impulse" Test

A few of the jurisdictions that follow *M'Naghten* have supplemented it with another test which is unfortunately labeled the "irresistible impulse" rule. Those two words suggest limitations upon the rule which are not strictly adhered to in practice, so that the "irresistible impulse" rule may more accurately be described as a test whereby the accused is not criminally responsible if he had a mental disease which kept him from controlling his conduct.

(a) Meaning of "Irresistible Impulse." Of the jurisdictions in this country that still follow the *M'Naghten* rule, a few have also adopted what is commonly (but unfortunately) termed the "irresistible impulse" test. Broadly stated, this rule requires a verdict of not guilty by reason of insanity if it is found that the defendant had a mental disease which kept him from controlling his conduct. Such a verdict is called for even if the defendant knew what he was doing and that it was wrong; the defendant's mental condition need not satisfy both the *M'Naghten and* "irresistible impulse" tests.

The notion that an "irresistible impulse" should qualify as an insanity defense even predates the *M'Naghten* case. Prior to the time that the *M'Naghten* judges responded to the inquiries from the House of Lords, writings in the field of medical jurisprudence emphasized that an individual might know what he was doing and that it was wrong but nonetheless be unable to control his conduct. And in 1840, just a few years before *M'Naghten,* an English judge instructed the jury as follows concerning one Oxford, charged with treason for firing a pistol at Queen Victoria: "If some controlling disease was, in truth, the acting power within him which he could not resist, then he will not be responsible." When the judges were later consulted about the law of insanity in *M'Naghten,* no mention was made of the test used in *Oxford,* but this is probably attributable to the fact that their answers were confined to the questions put to them in a particular case which concerned a defendant who had acted because of a delusion. After *M'Naghten,* English trial judges instructed juries only in terms of the right-wrong test, and "irresistible impulse" was expressly rejected as "a most dangerous doctrine" in 1863.

In the United States, a lack-of-control type of test may be traced back as far as 1834. The phrase "irresistible impulse" was apparently first used in 1844, but the context in which it was used left it uncertain whether such a test separate and distinct from *M'Naghten* was actually being adopted. A few jurisdictions accepted the test in the 1860's and 1870's, but the leading judicial exposition of the "irresistible impulse" test came in *Parsons v. State* (1887). The court held that in every criminal trial where the defense of insanity is interposed the jury should receive the following inquiries:

> 1. Was the defendant at the time of the commission of the alleged crime, as a matter of fact, afflicted with a *disease of the mind,* so as to be either idiotic, or otherwise insane?

> 2. If such be the case, did he know right from wrong as applied to the particular act in question? If he did not have such knowledge, he is not legally responsible.

> 3. If he did have such knowledge, he may nevertheless not be legally responsible if the two following conditions concur:

> (1) If, by reason of the duress of such mental disease, he had so far lost the *power to choose* between the right and wrong, and to avoid doing the act in question, as that his free agency was at the time destroyed.

(2) and if, at the same time, the alleged crime was so connected with such mental disease, in the relation of cause and effect, as to have been the product of it *solely.*

In one very important respect the *Parsons* case is representative of the test as it is used in the United States. The courts have generally stated the rule in terms of the defendant's inability to resist doing wrong or to control his acts, and the phrase "irresistible impulse" is very seldom used. This means that in practice the test is broader than the misleading "irresistible impulse" language suggests, for the jury is not ordinarily told that the defendant must have acted upon a sudden impulse or that his acts must have been totally irresistible. Rather, the jury is given the rule in terms of the capacity for self-control or free choice.

(b) Criticism of the "Irresistible Impulse" Test. As the "irresistible impulse" test grew in popularity, it received praise from both lawyers and psychiatrists who believed that *M'Naghten* standing alone was too restrictive because of its failure expressly to encompass the defendant who was unable to control his conduct. However, it did not escape criticism. On the one hand, as is evidenced by the fact that most *M'Naghten* jurisdictions did not also adopt a control test, the "irresistible impulse" rule was sometimes viewed as an unnecessary or unwise broadening of the criteria for determining irresponsibility. At the other extreme, there were those who came to believe that the "irresistible impulse" test was inadequate because it did not go far enough beyond *M'Naghten.* Some of the major criticisms are discussed below.

(1) "Impulse" Requirement Too Restrictive. One of the complaints about the "irresistible impulse" test is that it is too restrictive because it covers only impulsive acts. The test is described as applicable only to those crimes that "have been suddenly and impulsively committed after a sharp internal conflict," and is said to give "no recognition to mental illness characterized by brooding and reflection."

It has been clearly established that this criticism is unfounded. As noted above, the word "impulse" is only rarely used. Even if used in a jury instruction, it has not been established that jurors will take the word as requiring suddenness. The jury is *not* told that the "irresistible impulse" defense requires proof of sudden, unplanned action, and any evidence tending to show loss of control because of a mental disease is freely admitted.

(2) "Irresistible" Requirement Too Restrictive. Another objection which has been voiced focuses more upon the word "irresistible." It is claimed that the test is too restrictive because it requires a total impairment of volitional capacity. If this is a fair statement of the limits of the test, then it is indeed restrictive, for conditions where an absolute inability to resist exists are rare, and individuals in such circumstances "would in all probability be sufficiently out of touch with reality to meet" the *M'Naghten* test of irresponsibility.

This criticism may also be questioned on the ground that it is based more upon the "irresistible impulse" label than upon the test as it is determined. Given the facts that juries are usually instructed in terms of loss of self-control or free choice, evidence is freely admitted, and experts are not prevented from explaining what they mean by loss of control, it seems unlikely that juries are led to believe that an absolute inability to resist is required. The requirement set forth in the *Parsons* case that the impulse must be the sole cause of the act has seldom been followed, nor is there any evidence of a tendency to follow the practice of the military courts in inquiring whether the acts would not have been inhibited even by a "policeman at the elbow" of the defendant.

(3) Inconsistent With Purposes of Criminal Law. Others feel that the supplementing of *M'Naghten* with the "irresistible impulse" test broadens the insanity defense too much. Their position, in brief, is that deterrence is an important objective of the criminal law and that this purpose is not served by declaring irresponsible those who—even because of a mental disease—fail to control their impulses toward wrongdoing. As one commentator observed: "The possibly resistible but abnormally compelling urge may justify a marked difference in treatment of an offender after conviction. The point here insisted upon, is that assuming deterrence to be the objective and the basis of liability, such a resistible urge can not logically exonerate from liability itself. On the contrary it is the very type of case where the will to resist most needs strengthening and development through example." Similar reasoning has often been used by courts that have refused to adopt the "irresistible impulse" test.

In response, it has been questioned whether conviction of a person actuated by an insane impulse would deter others from the commission of crime. Experience, it is said, has shown that acceptance of the "irresistible impulse" test does not diminish the deterrent effect of the criminal law. Indeed, the most compelling reason for recognizing the test is that it comports better with the objectives of the criminal law; it describes "persons who could not respond to the threat of sanction and who would readily be perceived by others as incapable of responding."

(4) Presents Issue Incapable of Proof. Yet another objection to the "irresistible impulse" test, found mainly in the earlier cases rejecting the test, is that it is too vague and uncertain and thus too difficult to prove or disprove. It has been said, for example, that "the difficulty would be great, if not insuperable, of establishing by satisfactory proof whether an impulse was or was not 'uncontrollable.'"

This does not appear to be an adequate reason for rejecting the "irresistible impulse" test, for a similar objection may be made about any insanity test. The objection was fully considered and rejected in the *Parsons* decision, the leading case on the subject: "It is no satisfactory objection to say that the rule above announced by us is of difficult application. The rule in *M'Naghten's Case* is equally obnoxious to a like criticism. The difficulty does not lie in the rule, but is inherent in the subject of insanity itself."

§ 6.4 The Durham "Product" Test

Under what was usually referred to as the *Durham* rule, utilized by the District of Columbia Court of Appeals for nearly twenty years, an accused was not criminally responsible if his unlawful act was the product of mental disease or mental defect. As originally formulated this rule was criticized because of the ambiguity in the words "product" and "mental disease or defect." Subsequent cases defined those terms in such a way that the *Durham* rule began to resemble the American Law Institute Model Penal Code insanity test, which ultimately supplanted *Durham*.

(a) The *Durham* "Product" Test. In 1871, New Hampshire became the first state to reject completely the *M'Naghten* test. Influenced by the writings of Dr. Isaac Ray, who contended that insanity "is never established by a single diagnostic symptom, but by the whole body of symptoms, no particular one of which is present in every case," *State v. Jones* (1871) held that a defendant was to be found not guilty by reason of insanity if his crime "was the offspring or product of mental disease." The New Hampshire solution was praised by some, but was criticized by others on the ground that its inherent ambiguity left juries with insufficient guidance on the critical issue of responsibility. Subsequent experience in New Hampshire did not afford a basis for evaluating that criticism, nor did it provide any further elucidation of the "product" test. For the next eighty-three years, no other American jurisdiction adopted the New Hampshire rule or even gave it serious consideration.

Then the United States Court of Appeals for the District of Columbia decided the case of *Durham v. U.S.* (1954). In an opinion by Judge Bazelon, the court held "that an accused is not criminally responsible if his unlawful act was the product of mental disease or defect." This broader test of criminal responsibility, the court concluded, was preferable to the tests then in use in the District—

M'Naghten and irresistible impulse. Also relying upon the writings of Dr. Ray, the court found the *M'Naghten* rule wanting "in that (a) it does not take sufficient account of psychic realities and scientific knowledge, and (b) it is based upon one symptom and so cannot validly be applied in all circumstances." As for the so-called irresistible impulse test, it was found inadequate "in that it gives no recognition to mental illness characterized by brooding and reflection." The "product" rule, on the other hand, would give psychiatrists greater leeway to put before the factfinder all relevant information concerning the character of the defendant's mental disease or defect, while leaving the jury free to perform its traditional function of applying "our inherited ideas of moral responsibility" to the circumstances of the individual case.

No effort was made in *Durham* to explain the meaning of the word "product" in this context, nor were mental disease and mental defect defined. "Disease" was merely distinguished from "defect"; the former, but not the latter, was a condition capable of either improving or deteriorating. Some indication of how the new rule should be applied in practice was given by this suggested jury instruction: "If you the jury believe beyond a reasonable doubt that the accused was not suffering from a diseased or defective mental condition at the time he committed the criminal act charged, you may find him guilty. If you believe he was suffering from a diseased or defective mental condition when he committed the act, but believe beyond a reasonable doubt that the act was not the product of such mental abnormality, you may find him guilty. Unless you believe beyond a reasonable doubt either that he was not suffering from a diseased or defective mental condition, or that the act was not the product of such abnormality, you must find the accused not guilty by reason of insanity. Thus your task would not be completed upon finding, if you did find, that the accused suffered from a mental disease or defect. He would still be responsible for his unlawful act if there was no causal connection between such mental abnormality and the act. These questions must be determined by you from the facts which you find to be fairly deducible from the testimony and the evidence in this case."

(b) The Response to *Durham*. The *Durham* decision brought forth a flood of commentary from both lawyers and psychiatrists. The psychiatrists, generally, applauded the decision, although some were sharply critical. As for the legal profession, *Durham* was usually viewed with considerable skepticism; some lawyers, however, were most sympathetic to the decision.

In praise of *Durham* it was said that the new rule would "expand the area of inquiry and communication of the medical expert as a witness." Now a psychiatrist could present his testimony in regard to the mental condition of the accused in concepts familiar to him and which actually exist in mental life. As a result, a proper allocation of the duty of determining insanity had been achieved among the judge, jury and expert psychiatric witness.

The critics of *Durham* saw it as a "non-rule" in that it provided the jury with no standard by which to judge the evidence and left the jury entirely dependent upon the testimony of the experts. For one thing, the word "product" was not defined in *Durham,* an omission that some deemed indefensible. Given the *Durham* court's rejection of the irresistible impulse test, it seemed fair to conclude that the product requirement could be satisfied by something less than total destruction of the defendant's capacity for self-control. If "product" was intended as a but-for test of causation, so that the question would be whether the accused would have committed the criminal acts if he had not suffered from a mental disease or defect, then *Durham* called for an answer that could rarely be given. Moreover, a but-for test would leave the prosecution with the impossible burden of proving beyond a reasonable doubt that the defendant's acts were *not* the product of his mental disease or defect. The uncertainty about the meaning of "product" made the "mental disease or defect" part of *Durham* more critical than under *M'Naghten* or the irresistible impulse test. Thus, *Durham* was also criticized because of its failure to define this phrase.

The *Durham* court disapproved of *M'Naghten* and irresistible impulse as insanity tests on the ground that they made absence of responsibility depend upon particular symptoms of mental disease or defect (lack of cognition, lack of capacity for self-control). This, said the critics, was the "fundamental error" in *Durham,* for it rested upon the assumption that the concern is simply with mental disorder rather than with the question of when the disorder should be accorded the specific legal consequence of a defense to criminal conviction. The symptoms cannot be disregarded, for it is only by reference to them that responsibility criteria can be properly limited so as to exclude only the nondeterrables from criminal sanctions. Such a limitation has been defended in these words:

> So long as there is any chance that the preventive influence may operate, it is essential to maintain the threat. If it is not maintained, the influence of the entire system is diminished upon those who have the requisite capacity, albeit that they sometimes may offend. * * * The category must be so extreme that to the ordinary man, burdened by passion and beset by large temptations, the exculpation of the irresponsibles bespeaks no weakness in the law. He does not identify himself and them; they are a world apart.

The *Durham* rule did not gain acceptance in other jurisdictions. Defense counsel frequently sought approval of the "product" test in lieu of *M'Naghten* and irresistible impulse, but appellate courts uniformly declined to follow *Durham*. Finally, in 1972, the *Durham* rule was abandoned even in the District of Columbia. But the 18 years of experience with *Durham* remain instructive on the fundamental question of how the insanity defense should be defined.

(c) The *Durham* Test Defined. The *Durham* decision was far from the last word on the application of the "product" test in the District of Columbia. In the decade following *Durham,* over one hundred appellate opinions involving the sanity issue were decided by the United States Court of Appeals for the District of Columbia. It became apparent that many of the criticisms of *Durham* were not without substance, and thus the court set about the task of responding to them by giving greater content to the *Durham* test. In this interval, *Durham* "traveled a remarkably circuitous path toward the conclusion that the jury needed some guidance, that words like 'mental disease' and 'product' were inadequate, and that the standard would have to incorporate somehow a description of the sorts of effects of disease that were relevant to compliance with the criminal law."

(1) The Definition of "Product." In *Carter v. U.S.* (1957), the court had occasion to explain the meaning of "product" in the *Durham* test. The trial judge's instruction in terms of "the consequence, a growth, natural result or substantive end of a mental abnormality" was held to be neither adequate nor accurate:

> When we say the defense of insanity requires that the act be a "product of" a disease, we mean that the facts on the record are such that the trier of the facts is enabled to draw a reasonable inference that the accused would not have committed the act he did commit if he had not been diseased as he was. There must be a relationship between the disease and the act, and that relationship, whatever it may be in degree, must be, as we have already said, critical in its effect in respect to the act. By "critical" we mean decisive, determinative, causal; we mean to convey the idea inherent in the phrases "because of," "except for," "without which," "but for," "effect of," "result of," "causative factor"; the disease made the effective or decisive difference between doing and not doing the act. The short phrases "product of" and "causal connection" are not intended to be precise, as though they were chemical formulae. They mean that the facts concerning the disease and the facts concerning the act are such as to justify reasonably the conclu-

sion that "But for this disease the act would not have been committed."

This definition of "product" as a but-for test of causation, of course, did not still the critics, who had already said that use of a but-for test would require an answer which could seldom be given. Nor did it satisfy those who believed that a test of criminal responsibility should be narrowly drawn so as to exclude from penal sanctions only non-deterrables. This latter objection was also voiced from within the court:

> Apart from all other objections the product aspect of *Durham* is a fallacy in this: assuming arguendo that a criminal act can be the "product" of a "mental disease" that fact should not per se excuse the defendant; it should exculpate only if the condition described as a "mental disease" affected him so substantially that he could not appreciate the nature of the illegal act or could not control his conduct.

Although the court did not abandon the but-for definition of product, the criticisms of it were overcome indirectly by the court's later action in defining the term "mental disease and defect."

Another objection made concerning the but-for definition was that it placed the prosecution in an impossible position because if a psychiatrist could come to a firm opinion on the product issue it would almost invariably be in the defendant's favor: "while occasionally one can say that an act *was* a product of mental disease, one can rarely if ever say that an act was *not* a product. To analogize, one can sometimes find a needle in the haystack, but one cannot find that there is *not* a needle in the haystack." That this criticism had merit was clearly reflected in the cases decided under *Durham*. However, that problem was largely overcome by the court's later holding in *Washington v. U.S.* (1967) that psychiatrists could no longer testify whether the alleged offense was the product of mental illness:

> The term "product" has no clinical significance for psychiatrists. Thus there is no justification for permitting psychiatrists to testify on the ultimate issue. Psychiatrists should explain how defendant's disease or defect relates to his alleged offense, that is, how the development, adaptation and functioning of defendant's behavioral processes may have influenced his conduct. But psychiatrists should not speak directly in terms of "product," or even "result" or "cause."

(2) The Definition of "Mental Disease or Defect." *Durham* was intended to enable psychiatrists to testify freely and completely without what were believed to be the evidentiary limitations of the right-wrong and irresistible impulse tests. But when test cases under *Durham* arose, raising such questions as whether psychopathy or neurosis were mental diseases, "disputes about nomenclature arose which were strikingly reminiscent of those which had previously characterized trials under *M'Naghten.*" Prosecution psychiatrists would classify the defendant's behavior as not psychotic; defense psychiatrists, on the other hand, would claim that it was psychotic or else the product of a lesser mental disorder claimed to qualify as a "mental disease or defect."

Illustrative of the problems that resulted is the case of *Blocker v. U.S.* (1959). Blocker, on trial for murder, interposed an insanity defense. Three psychiatrists on the staff of St. Elizabeth's Hospital testified on the issue; one found nothing wrong with the defendant, the other two testified that he suffered from a sociopathic personality disturbance, and all three agreed that a sociopathic personality disturbance was not considered a mental disease or defect. Less than a month after Blocker's conviction, the Assistant Superintendent of St. Elizabeth's testified in another case that he believed a sociopathic personality disturbance was a mental disease, and Blocker then sought a new trial because of this new medical evidence. The court of appeals held that he was entitled to a new trial so that he might have "the most mature expert opinion available on an issue vital to his defense." As one of the participants in that decision later acknowledged, "we tacitly conceded the power of St. Elizabeth's Hospital Staff to alter drastically the scope of a rule of law by a 'week-end' change in nomenclature which was without any scientific basis, so far as we have any record or information."

Blocker intensified the criticism that the undefined "mental disease or defect" part of *Durham* left the jury without standards to guide it and unduly dependent upon the experts' classifications of mental abnormalities. Two subsequent developments, however, substantially overcame these difficulties: (1) the court announced a judicial definition of what is included in the term "mental disease or defect"; and (2) the court developed guidelines to govern expert testimony on the issue.

In *McDonald v. U.S.* (1962), the court agreed with the proposition, often stated theretofore by critics of *Durham,* that "what psychiatrists may consider a 'mental disease or defect' for clinical purposes, where their concern is treatment, may or may not be the same as mental disease or defect for the jury's purpose in determining criminal responsibility." Consequently, the court concluded "the jury should be told that a mental disease or defect includes any abnormal condition of the mind which substantially affects mental or emotional processes and substantially impairs behavior controls." Because under *McDonald* a mental condition had to have behavioral consequences in order to qualify as a "mental disease or defect," *Durham* was in effect limited in such a way that it was not significantly different from the American Law Institute "substantial capacity" test. Moreover, *McDonald* also overcame the difficulties with the "product" portion of *Durham,* for the requirement that the defendant's abnormality have behavioral consequences made relatively unimportant the second issue of whether (on a but-for analysis) the mental disease caused the defendant's acts.

In *Washington v. U.S.* (1967), the court again noted that "the classifications [the medical profession] has developed for purposes of treatment, commitment, etc., may be inappropriate for assessing responsibility in criminal cases." This being the case, it was imperative that the roles of the psychiatrist and the jury be kept separate and distinct. Each, said the court, has "different judgments to make": the psychiatrist is concerned with "the medical-clinical concept of illness"; while the jury must decide "the legal and moral question of culpability." And thus the court provided an explanatory instruction to guide the expert, counsel, and the jury on the kind of expert testimony which was expected.

§ 6.5 The A.L.I. "Substantial Capacity" Test

About a year following the *Durham* decision, the American Law Institute's Model Penal Code project produced yet another test for the insanity defense. Although its psychiatric advisory committee recommended adoption of *Durham,* the Institute instead approved a formulation consisting of a modernized version of the *M'Naghten* and irresistible impulse tests.

(a) The A.L.I. Test. This A.L.I. test in Model Penal Code § 4.01 reads as follows:

(1) A person is not responsible for criminal conduct if at the time of such conduct as a result of mental disease or defect he lacks substantial capacity either to appreciate the criminality [wrongfulness] of his conduct or to conform his conduct to the requirements of law.

(2) As used in this Article, the terms "mental disease or defect" do not include an abnormality manifested only by repeated criminal or otherwise anti-social conduct.

As indicated in the accompanying commentary, the Code draftsmen rejected the *Durham* rule because of the ambiguity of the word "product." *M'Naghten* and irresistible impulse, however, were not totally rejected; these two tests combined were seen as properly focusing upon impairment of cognition and impairment of volitional capacity—conditions that must be taken into account in an effort to exclude nondeterrables from penal sanctions. The result, therefore, was a broader statement of the concepts basic to the *M'Naghten* and irresistible impulse tests.

Most significant is the fact that the A.L.I. test only requires a lack of "substantial capacity." This is clearly a departure from the usual interpretation of *M'Naghten* and irresistible impulse, whereby a complete impairment of cognitive capacity and capacity for self-control is necessary. Substantial capacity, the draftsmen noted, is all "that candid witnesses, called on to infer the nature of the situation at a time that they did not observe, can ever confidently say, even when they know that a disorder was extreme." Moreover, even if witnesses could be more specific, it is undoubtedly true that there are many cases of advanced mental disorder in which rudimentary capacities of cognition and volition exist but which clearly present inappropriate occasions for the application of criminal sanctions. The draftsmen acknowledged that the word "substantial" imputes no specific measure of degree, but concluded that identifying the degree of impairment with precision was "impossible both verbally and logically."

The A.L.I. test uses the word "appreciate" instead of "know," a term that has been responsible for much of the criticism and misunderstanding of *M'Naghten*. It thus seems apparent that expert testimony concerning the emotional or affective aspects of the defendant's personality is clearly relevant on this aspect of the A.L.I. formulation. As to the "conform" part of the test, it avoids the implication (often drawn from the irresistible impulse test) that the loss of volitional capacity can be reflected only in sudden or spontaneous acts as distinguished from those accompanied by brooding or reflection.

As to paragraph (2) of the A.L.I. test, the draftsmen explained that it "is designed to exclude from the concept of 'mental disease or defect' the case of so-called 'psychopathic personality.' " They noted that the psychopath differs from a normal person only quantitatively and not qualitatively, and that there is considerable difference of opinion on whether psychopathy should be called a disease. Thus the draftsmen favored "excluding a condition that is manifested only by the behavior phenomena that must, by hypothesis, be the result of disease for irresponsibility to be established," and avoiding "litigation of what is essentially a matter of terminology."

(b) The Response to the A.L.I. Test. The Model Penal Code test (sometimes with minor variations) was adopted by virtually all of the United States Courts of Appeals, only to be repudiated by Congress in 1984 in favor of a *M'Naghten*-style statutory formulation. A significant minority of the states have accepted the A.L.I. test, usually by statute but sometimes by court decision.

(1) Paragraph (1) of the Test. The "substantial capacity" test has also been criticized by some commentators. Certain critics of *M'Naghten* and irresistible impulse have asserted that the defects in those two tests are also present in the A.L.I. formulation. It is claimed, for example, that the A.L.I. test is only a "refurbishing" of the two traditional rules, and that it has failed to "bridge the gap that now exists between legal and psychiatric thinking."

Others have been critical of the A.L.I test on the ground that it is ambiguous. Thus, it has been asserted that the word "result" introduces the most objectionable aspects of the *Durham* "product" test. Use of the words "substantial capacity" and "appreciate" has been questioned on the ground that they do not have a common, absolute meaning. These words, it is said, are bound to encourage differences among expert witnesses and also among jurors over whether the defendant's degree of impairment or depth of awareness was sufficient.

In the main, however, the A.L.I. test has drawn praise from the commentators. As to the objections summarized above, it has been noted that "the *Durham* experience has taken much of the bite from such criticisms. It is now apparent that a precise definition of insanity is impossible, that the effort to eliminate functional definitions deprives the jury of an essential concreteness of statement and that it is entirely sensible to leave 'mental disease' undefined, at least so long as it is modified by a statement of minimal conditions for being held to account under a system of criminal law." The Model Penal Code formulation has rightly been praised as achieving the two important objectives of a test of responsibility: (1) giving expression to an intelligible principle; and (2) fully disclosing that principle to the jury.

(2) Paragraph (2) of the Test. Much of the criticism of the A.L.I. proposal has been directed at paragraph (2), which excludes from the definition of "mental disease or defect" an abnormality manifested only by repeated criminal or otherwise anti-social conduct. As noted earlier, the draftsmen's purpose was to exclude the psychopath.

Such a fixed, rigid exclusion from the definition of mental disease or defect has been opposed on several grounds. One objection is that such an exclusion is unwarranted in the face of existing doubts as to whether the psychopathic personality constitutes a valid psychiatric classification. Another is that psychopaths are generally not deterrable and thus are not deserving of penal sanctions. Also, it has been noted that some headway is now being made in the treatment of psychopaths by psychiatric therapy and that therefore they are fit subjects for medical-custodial disposition. Others have expressed approval of paragraph (2) of the A.L.I. test, arguing that such a limitation is essential to keep the defense from swallowing up virtually all of criminal liability.

Whether paragraph (2) does in fact exclude the psychopathic personality from the insanity defense is questionable. A psychiatrist is unlikely to base his diagnosis of the criminal psychopath solely upon his criminal or antisocial conduct. Thus, the actual impact of paragraph (2) may be to exclude only those psychopaths who received a routine examination, but not those affluent and fortunate enough to receive a more careful diagnosis.

Because of doubts about the soundness or effectiveness of paragraph (2), some courts adopted a modified form of the A.L.I. test in which there are no express exclusions from "mental disease or defect." But most of the legislative enactments of the A.L.I. test include paragraph (2).

Chapter 7

INSANITY—PROCEDURAL CONSIDERATIONS

Table of Sections

For additional analysis of the above topics and citations to authorities supporting their discussion in this Book, consult the author's 3-volume *Substantive Criminal Law* treatise, also available as Westlaw database SUBCRL. See the Table of Cross-References in this Book.

---

§ 7.1 Incompetency at Time of Criminal Proceedings

If a defendant is suffering from a mental disease or defect that renders him unable to understand the proceedings against him or to assist in his defense, he may not be tried, convicted, or sentenced so long as that condition persists. Rather, he is ordinarily committed to a mental institution until such time as he recovers. In practice, these commitments have to a significant respect displaced the process of trial, acquittal on grounds of insanity, and commitment following acquittal.

If a defendant sentenced to death is suffering from a mental disease or defect that renders him unable to understand the nature and purpose of the punishment about to be imposed, he may not be executed until such time as he has recovered from that condition.

(a) Incompetency to Stand Trial. For a variety of reasons, the insanity defense is raised in only a very small percentage of criminal cases. In part, this is because many individuals who might raise the defense never go to trial. Some are screened out very early as a part of the discretion exercised by the police and prosecution. Persons arrested for minor crimes by the police may be diverted to the civil commitment route when it appears that their conduct resulted from mental illness. Even in more serious cases, the prosecutor may decide to initiate civil commitment proceedings (or, influence the bringing of such proceedings by others) or to place the apparently mentally ill person on a form of administrative probation on the condition that he seek psychiatric assistance. Also significant is the fact that of those charged, the overwhelming majority (in some jurisdictions over 90%) will plead guilty, often as a result of a process of "plea negotiations" whereby the defendant enters a guilty plea in exchange for the prosecutor's promise to seek or obtain sentencing concessions. There are certain to be included in this large number of cases many in which an insanity defense might be raised with at least a reasonable chance of success. And, just as some defendants plead guilty instead of defending on grounds of insanity, some go to trial without raising the defense because of a tactical decision that the risk of conviction and sentence is more appealing than the risk of indeterminate commitment to a mental institution.

Of particular interest here, however, is yet another reason: because the person who was insane at the time of his conduct is likely to be incompetent at the time of trial, he may be declared incompetent to stand trial and then committed. If he does not recover, he will never be tried; if he does ultimately recover but a substantial interval of time has elapsed, the prosecutor may dismiss the prosecution either (a) because essential witnesses to or evidence of the crime are no longer available, or (b) because of a judgment that no purpose would now be served by prosecution. It is precisely those individuals who are most likely to be able to make a clear showing of insanity at the time of their conduct—the persistently and obviously psychotic—who are withdrawn from the criminal process in this way. Commitment for incompetency to stand trial thus appears to have displaced the insanity defense to a significant degree.

This is not to suggest that the legal test of incompetency to stand trial is the precise equivalent of any of definitions of the insanity defense. Apart from the obvious fact that the concern is with the defendant's mental condition at a different point in time, the question of competency to stand trial is not concerned with the defendant's responsibility but rather with his ability to participate in the proceedings in a meaningful way. "[I]t is not enough for the * * * judge to find that 'the defendant [is] oriented to time and place and [has] some recollection of events' "; rather, "the 'test must be whether he has sufficient present ability to consult with his lawyer with a reasonable degree of rational understanding—and whether he has a rational as well as factual understanding of the proceedings against him.' " This, essentially, is the common law test of competency to stand trial, which has been codified in many jurisdictions and in others continues as a result of judicial interpretation of competency statutes that merely refer to the defendant's "insanity" or "unsound mind."

Under this test, there are two distinct matters to be determined: (1) whether the defendant is sufficiently coherent to provide his counsel with information necessary or relevant to constructing a defense; and (2) whether he is able to comprehend the significance of the trial and his relation to it. The defendant must have an "ability to confer intelligently, to testify coherently and to follow the evidence presented." It is necessary that the defendant have a rational as well as a factual understanding of the proceedings. This necessitates a level of comprehension going beyond surface knowledge, but does not require functioning at normal levels.

Sufficient competency can exist even though achieved only by compelled medication, but such medication has sometimes been viewed as impermissibly infringing on the defendant's ability to establish an insanity defense. In *Riggins v. Nev.* (1992), the Supreme Court held that a defendant's interest in avoiding compelled medication is a liberty interest protected by the due process clause, such that such medication "is impermissible absent a finding of overriding justification and a determination of medical appropriateness." The Court went on to assert that due process would be satisfied if the court below "had found that treatment with antipsychotic medication was medically appropriate and, considering less intrusive alternatives, essential for the sake of [the defendant's] own safety or the safety of others." The *Riggins* Court took note of but had no occasion to decide the more critical issue noted above: "whether a competent criminal defendant may refuse antipsychotic medication if cessation of medication would render him incompetent at trial."

Building on *Riggins*, the Court in *Sell v. United States* (2003) set out a standard that "will permit involuntary administration of drugs solely for trial competence purposes in certain instances," which "may be rare," as under the standard: (1) "a court must find that *important* government interests are at stake," which includes the government's interest "in bringing to trial an individual accused of a serious crime"; (2) "the court must conclude that involuntary medication will *significantly further* those concomitant state interests," i.e., "that administration of the drugs is substantially likely to render the defendant competent to stand trial" and "substantially unlikely to have side effects that will interfere significantly with the defendant's ability to assist counsel in conducting a trial defense"; (3) "the court must conclude that involuntary medication is necessary to further those needs," i.e., "that any alternative, less intrusive treatments are unlikely to achieve substantially the same results"; and (4) "the court must conclude that administration of the drug is *medically appropriate*, i.e., in the patient's best medical interest in light of his medical condition." The Court added that it is unnecessary to follow this standard in the interest of rendering the defendant competent to stand trial if forced medication is needed for another purpose, e.g., because of defendant's dangerousness, an inquiry that "is usually more 'objective and manageable.'"

It has sometimes been suggested that the ability to consult meaningfully with counsel requires a capacity on the part of the defendant "to remember the facts surrounding the occurrence of the alleged offense." Were this literally true, then in any case in which the defendant could not recall relevant events because of amnesia it would be necessary to delay the trial because of the defendant's incompetency. But this is not the case; rather, the courts have held that the loss of memory due to amnesia is not alone an adequate ground upon which to base a finding of incompetency to stand trial. As one court quite frankly put it: "When it is considered that the result of an order finding defendant unfit for trial in these circumstances would be outright release, assuming the amnesia is permanent and there is no other mental defect sufficient to warrant commitment, it can be more easily understood why all the courts which have passed on this question have refused to allow amnesia to be classified as the sort of mental defect causing incapacity to stand trial." But trial of an amnesiac defendant can be fundamentally unfair in some circumstances, and consequently trial judges must determine, on a case-by-case basis, whether the defendant could likely receive (and, at the conclusion of the trial, whether he in fact did receive) a fair trial.

The notion that a defendant who is incompetent may not be tried, which is a requirement of due process, has several reasons underlying it. For one, it ensures the accuracy of the proceedings, as an incompetent defendant is not in a position to exercise several rights (e.g., to testify in his own behalf, to confront opposing witnesses) that are intended to accomplish that end. Second, it ensures the fairness of the proceedings, as it avoids the situation of a trial in which the defendant is unable to make certain basic decisions concerning the course of his defense. Third, it aids in maintaining the dignity of the proceedings, for an incompetent defendant is likely to conduct himself in the courtroom in a manner that would disrupt the trial. Finally, under our theory of the criminal law it is important that the defendant know why he is being punished, a comprehension which is greatly dependent upon his understanding what occurs at trial.

The issue of the defendant's competency to stand trial is usually raised at the time of arraignment, when the defendant is called upon to plead, although it may be raised at any time during the course of the trial. The issue may be raised by the defendant, of course, but his failure to do so does not constitute a waiver of the due process right not to be tried when incompetent, for "it is contradictory to argue that a defendant may be incompetent, and yet knowingly or intelligently 'waive' his right to have the court determine his capacity to stand trial." It may also be raised by the prosecutor (which is frequently the case because in this way the prosecutor can also obtain psychiatric evidence about the defendant to rebut an insanity defense) or by the court, and this is so even if the defense would prefer to go to trial without an inquiry into competency (an understandable desire in some instances, in that the defendant would prefer conviction and sentence to a definite term instead of indefinite commitment).

The issue must be raised in such a way to create a reasonable doubt in the judge's mind concerning the defendant's present capacity to stand trial; a mere unsupported suggestion that defendant is insane will not suffice. If a reasonable doubt does exist, then the judge must take the appropriate steps for determination of the issue. In most jurisdictions there exists statutory authority for the judge to have the defendant committed while he is examined by court-appointed experts or the staff of a public hospital. At common law, the judge had discretion to determine the method to be used to try the issue; he could either decide the question himself or impanel a jury. Today, the great majority of jurisdictions require that this issue be decided by the judge, though in a few states the matter may or must be determined by a jury. Although the burden of proof is sometimes upon the defendant to show his incompetency, this is probably not the case in practice, particularly when the issue has not been raised by the defendant. The Supreme Court held in *Medina v. Cal.* (1992) that a statute placing the burden of proof on the party asserting incompetency of the defendant to stand trial does not violate the procedural due process right of the defendant. The Court, first emphasizing that neither history nor contemporary practice reflected a settled view on where the burden should lie, concluded that once a state has met its due process obligation of providing a defendant access to procedures for making a competency evaluation, there is no basis for requiring it to assume the burden of vindicating the defendant's constitutional right not to be tried while legally incompetent. The preponderance-of-the-evidence standard is usually utilized, but some states require clear and convincing evidence. The Supreme Court held in *Cooper v. Okla.* (1996) that this latter standard, if imposed on the defendant, allows a defendant to be put on trial even though it is more likely than not that he is incompetent, and that consequently it violates due process.

If the defendant is found incompetent, the criminal proceedings are suspended and he is invariably committed to a mental institution until he recovers. Most states place the responsibility for determining whether a defendant has recovered with the court, although a few jurisdictions at least sometimes have the decision made by a jury or by medical personnel.

Upon a post-conviction determination that an error occurred earlier in not holding a competency inquiry or in conducting it improperly, the question then becomes whether the issue of defendant's competency at trial can now be ascertained retrospectively. While retrospective competency hearings are generally disfavored, they are permissible whenever a court can conduct a meaningful hearing to evaluate retrospectively the competency of the defendant. In deciding whether a retrospective competency hearing is feasible, four factors deserve consideration: (1) the passage of time, (2) the availability of contemporaneous medical evidence, including medical records and prior competency determinations, (3) any statements by the defendant in the trial record, and (4) the availability of individuals and trial witnesses, both experts and non-experts, who were in a position to interact with defendant before and during trial, including the trial judge, counsel for both the government and defendant, and jail officials.

(b) Commitment for Incompetency: The Risk of Unfairness. Although the traditional procedures described above are intended to protect the defendant's due process right not to be tried while incompetent, they do not always operate to the benefit of the individual committed. For one thing, the commitment is based upon a charge of a crime that he may not have in fact committed or for which he could not be convicted if he was afforded the opportunity to prove his innocence or to establish some defect in the prosecution's case. Secondly, he is being held for the purpose of getting him into a state of mind whereby he can be prosecuted, but the commitment might continue for years without a serious attempt at treatment or even when it is reasonably certain that his condition is untreatable. Moreover, in most jurisdictions the practice has been to institutionalize because of incompetence to stand trial without regard to whether there is really any need for custody, that is, without reference to the legal criteria for civil committability (generally, whether the person is dangerous to society or is in need of treatment and unable to care for himself). Finally, the critical decisions of incompetency and, perhaps more important, recovery or nonrecovery have often been made without sufficient procedural safeguards to ensure their accuracy. For all of these reasons, it has been said that the process "poses a very real risk of abuse and of being bent to punitive purposes."

The Supreme Court addressed many of these problems in the most important decision of *Jackson v. Ind.* (1972). The case involved a mentally defective deaf mute with a mental level of a preschool child who, after being charged with two robberies, was found incompetent to stand trial because he lacked "comprehension sufficient to understand the proceedings and make his defense." On that basis alone he was committed to a state mental hospital, and it appeared the commitment would be for life, as there was little likelihood that his condition would ever improve. Jackson challenged his commitment on both equal protection and due process grounds, and the Court held in his favor on both theories.

On the equal protection question, the Court first noted it had previously held in *Baxstrom v. Herold* (1966) that a person civilly committed upon completion of his prison sentence was denied equal protection when not afforded the same procedural guarantees as others subjected to the civil commitment process. This meant the equal protection claim was, if anything, just as strong here. "If criminal conviction and imposition of sentence are insufficient to justify less procedural and substantive protection against indefinite commitment than that generally available to others, the mere filing of criminal charges surely cannot suffice." The state countered that commitment of a defendant incompetent to stand trial is only temporary, pending his recovery, and thus need not be subject to the same limitations as indeterminate civil commitments. But the Court rejected this contention, noting that the statutory scheme did not make the likelihood of improvement a relevant factor and also that the record did not suggest any possibility that Jackson would recover.

The Court in *Jackson* thus applied to this context the teaching of *Baxstrom* that "the State cannot withhold from a few the procedural protections or the substantive requirements for commitment that are available to all others." This means, for one thing, that the *procedures* for commitment of a defendant not competent to be tried must (at least if the commitment is other than "temporary") be "substantially similar" to those made available to those persons subjected to the civil commitment process. (This was not a problem in *Jackson,* the Court concluded, as the procedures in the two contexts—notice, examination by two doctors, judicial hearing, representation by counsel, right to introduce evidence and to cross-examine, decision by court alone, and appellate review were essentially the same.) For another, this means that the *standards* for commitment and release must likewise be substantially the same as for other persons. Jackson had thus been denied equal protection, as he was subject "to a more lenient commitment standard and to a more stringent standard of release than those generally applicable to all others not charged with offenses."

Similar considerations underlie the *Jackson* Court's second holding that "indefinite commitment of a criminal defendant solely on account of his incompetency to stand trial does not square with the Fourteenth Amendment's guarantee of due process." Because "Jackson's commitment rests on proceedings that did not purport to bring into play * * * *any* of the articulated bases for exercise of Indiana's power of indefinite commitment," it violated the due process requirement "that the nature and duration of commitment bear some reasonable relation to the purpose for which the individual is committed." Specifically, the Court held

> that a person charged by a State with a criminal offense who is committed solely on account of his incapacity to proceed to trial cannot be held more than the reasonable period of time necessary to determine whether there is a substantial probability that he will attain that capacity in the foreseeable future. If it is determined that this is not the case, then the State must either institute the customary civil commitment proceeding that would be required to commit indefinitely any other citizen, or release the defendant. Furthermore, even if it is determined that the defendant probably soon will be able to stand trial, his continued commitment must be justified by progress toward that goal.

The Supreme Court declined "to prescribe arbitrary time limits," but merely noted that Jackson's three and one-half years of confinement "establishes the lack of a substantial probability that he will ever be able to participate fully in a trial." It thus remains unclear exactly to what extent automatic commitment for incompetency to stand trial may still be utilized. Some states permit such commitment for up to a year or 18 months. At least one court has held that the "reasonable period" language in *Jackson* does not permit confinement for competency determination alone for a time exceeding the maximum possible sentence for the offense charged, while another court has ruled to the contrary.

Yet another noteworthy aspect of the *Jackson* case is the Court's pronouncement that its prior decisions on the due process requirement of a competency inquiry do not "preclude the States from allowing at a minimum, an incompetent defendant to raise certain defenses such as insufficiency of the indictment, or make certain pretrial motions, through counsel." It had theretofore been generally assumed that if the defendant is found incompetent to stand trial, then no aspect of the criminal proceedings may be pursued until he has regained his competency. The harshness of this view is clearly reflected by the decision in *U.S. v. Barnes* (1959). Four defendants were indicted for a murder allegedly committed over ten years earlier, and three of them successfully moved to dismiss the indictment on the ground that they had been denied a speedy trial. The fourth defendant's motion, based upon exactly the same ground, was denied because he was found to be "presently insane and so mentally incompetent as to be unable to understand the proceedings against him." The court acknowledged that there would be no need for the defendant to assist his counsel in making the speedy trial defense, but concluded that this made no difference because the test of incompetency was stated in the alternative. The curious result: because this defendant was unable to understand the proceedings at which the charge against him would be dismissed, he should be committed until such time as he would be able to participate in a trial that would not occur.

Preferable to *Barnes* is the Model Penal Code § 4.06(3) approach, which would allow the unfit defendant to pursue "any legal objection to the prosecution which is susceptible of fair determination prior to trial and without the personal participation of the defendant." Under this view, counsel for an incompetent defendant would often be permitted to present those motions ordinarily determined at the pretrial stage, such as to quash the indictment or to suppress critical evidence.

It might even be desirable to go beyond this and sometimes permit the incompetent defendant to present defenses that ordinarily are only raised at trial. For example, if the examination of the accused to determine incompetency also discloses that he has a valid insanity defense, there is much to be said for permitting the court to enter a judgment of acquittal on that ground. This avoids the possibility of having to try that issue long after the event, and has the added advantage that a defendant committed following such acquittal is much more likely to respond to treatment than a defendant whose status is uncertain because of an outstanding criminal charge. Similarly, it makes sense to hear such defenses as alibi at this early stage, for the witnesses might well be unavailable at a trial held following a substantial period of commitment for incompetency.

One commentator has made yet another proposal, one that would afford the defendant a no-lose full trial in these circumstances. If the defendant were found not guilty, that would be the end of the matter; if he were found guilty, the verdict would be set aside and he would be committed "until he is sufficiently recovered to be retried or until other appropriate disposition can be made of the case." A few jurisdictions allow procedures along these lines. An even more extreme proposal contemplates

> abandonment of the traditional rule against trying incompetent defendants. Incompetency should instead be grounds for obtaining a trial continuance during which the state must provide resources to assist the defendant toward greater trial competence. If trial competence is not achieved within six months, the state should be required to dismiss the charges or proceed to a trial governed, where necessary, by procedures designed to compensate for the incompetent defendant's trial disabilities.

Finally, note must be taken of the recognition in *Jackson* that the petitioner had a "substantial" claim that the charges against him should be dismissed. The Court did not reach this claim, but did take note of the bases upon which it could be grounded: "the Sixth–Fourteenth Amendment right to a speedy trial, or the denial of due process inherent in holding pending criminal charges indefinitely over the head of one who will never have a chance to prove his innocence." Of course, it is also possible that dismissal of charges following a substantial period of incompetency will be permissible under state law even if not constitutionally compelled. In such circumstances, there remains the troublesome question of whether the charges should be dismissed with or without prejudice (that is, with or without a bar to subsequent reinstatement). But because of the concern "that the dismissal of serious criminal charges against an incompetent defendant who may regain competency to stand trial in two or three years would constitute a grave public disservice," there is a disinclination to dismiss with prejudice unless it presently appears likely a fair trial would not later be possible.

(c) Incompetency at Time Set for Execution. It is the rule in all jurisdictions that a sentence of execution cannot be carried out if the prisoner is insane at the time set for execution. The common law was quite vague on the meaning of insane in this context, but it is usually taken to mean that the defendant cannot be executed if he is unaware of the fact that he has been convicted and that he is to be executed. Stated another way, he must be so unsound mentally "as to be incapable of understanding the nature and purpose of the punishment about to be executed upon him." Whether this is a correct or complete statement of the rule remains somewhat unclear because of continuing uncertainty about the reasons underlying it.

One traditional explanation for the rule is that if the defendant were sane he might be in a position to urge some reason why the sentence should not be carried out. The logic of this has been questioned on the ground that it is unlikely a defendant who by hypothesis was sane during trial and at the time of sentencing would thereafter think of a reason not previously considered. Even less convincing is the explanation that the prisoner's insanity is itself sufficient punishment, for when he regains his sanity he is subject to execution. Yet another reason is that it is a rule of humanity—a refusal to take the life of an unfortunate prisoner— but this has been characterized as "inverted humanitarianism." Then there is the theological rationale that a person should not be put to death while insane because he is unable to make his peace with God while in that condition, which is at best difficult to assess in our theologically pluralistic society.

Perhaps the most acceptable explanation is "simply that it is unnecessary to put the insane prisoner to death." For one thing, the insane prisoner may be spared the death penalty without weakening the deterrent effect of that penalty. Taking the life of an insane person does not serve as an example to others, for a potential offender would not consider the possibility of escaping the death penalty by becoming insane following conviction. Likewise, the retributive function of punishment is not served by execution of the insane prisoner. Viewing retribution in the sense of exacting a punishment equivalent to the harm done, it may be said that killing an insane person does not have the same moral quality as killing a sane one. Or, if retribution is taken to mean that punishment serves to give law-abiding citizens a form of release, then the answer is that this will occur only if the public is able to identify with the prisoner, which they cannot do if he is insane.

In *Ford v. Wainwright* (1986), the Supreme Court held that the Eighth Amendment ban on cruel and unusual punishment prohibits a state from inflicting the death penalty upon a prisoner who is insane. After taking note of the common-law restriction and the reasons for it recited above and the unanimous restriction upon such executions in the states, the Court declared: "Whether its aim be to protect the condemned from fear and pain without comfort of understanding, or to protect the dignity of society itself from the barbarity of exacting mindless vengeance, the restriction finds enforcement in the Eighth Amendment." Later, in *Penry v. Lynaugh* (1989), *Ford* was said to cover one who is "unaware of the punishment they are about to suffer and why they are to suffer it," not the case as to the prisoner in the instant case, a mentally retarded person with the reasoning capacity of a 7–year-old child, and the Court concluded "there is insufficient evidence of a national consensus against executing mentally retarded people convicted of capital offenses for us to conclude that it is categorically prohibited by the Eighth Amendment." But upon revisiting that issue in *Atkins v. Va.* (2002), the Court concluded otherwise. Looking at what had happened since *Penry*, particularly "the consistency of the direction of changes" brought about by state legislatures regarding this issue, the Court found a "consensus" that "unquestionably reflects widespread judgment about the relative culpability of mentally retarded offenders, and the relationship between mental retardation and the penological purposes served by the death penalty."

Ford was revisited again in *Panetti v. Quarterman* (2007), where the Court, though declining to set down a rule governing all competency determinations, concluded that the lower court's competency standard had been too restrictive. Defendant's experts concluded that, although he claimed to understand the state wanted to execute him for murder, his mental problems had resulted in the delusion that the stated reason was a sham and that the state actually wanted to execute him to stop him from preaching, but the lower court deemed such delusions to be irrelevant. Not so, the Supreme Court decided, considering that capital punishment is imposed because it has the potential to make the offender recognize at last the gravity of his crime and to allow the community to affirm its own judgment that the prisoner's culpability is so serious that the ultimate penalty must be sought and imposed. Both those objectives, the Court observed, are called into question if the prisoner's only awareness of the link between the crime and punishment is so distorted that it has little or no relation to the understanding shared by the community as a whole.

There was no established procedure at common law for trying a claim that the defendant was insane and thus not subject to execution. If facts were brought to the attention of the court that sentenced the defendant raising a reasonable doubt in the mind of the judge, then he could "take such action as, in his discretion, he deemed best"; he could try the issue himself or empanel a jury to do so. Most jurisdictions have now enacted statutes on the subject. Many of these statutes permit only the warden to initiate proceedings to determine insanity for the purpose of staying execution, and this has been held not to violate due process. Some statutes follow the common law procedure of petition to the court, and some others allow the claim to be made to the governor. Several statutes require trial of the issue after a plausible claim of insanity is raised, but others merely require examination of the prisoner by a psychiatrist, delegating the ultimate decision to the governor, warden or state hospital director. Some of the statutes expressly provide for jury trial of the issue, although there is no constitutional right to jury trial. In the post-*Atkins* era, most states have placed the burden of proof on the defendant, usually by a preponderance of the evidence but occasionally by clear and convincing evidence. Notwithstanding earlier Supreme Court decisions to the contrary, it has been argued that a hearing on a claim of insanity should be constitutionally required. But, while *Ford v. Wainwright* (1986) makes it clear that the due process right to be heard applies to the decision on incompetency at the time set for execution, it remains uncertain exactly what is necessary for a constitutionally-sufficient procedure. But *Ford* does require a fair hearing, including an opportunity to submit "expert psychiatric evidence that may differ from the State's own psychiatric examination," and thus the *Ford* rule was violated when the state court reached its competency determination without holding a hearing or providing the prisoner with an adequate opportunity to provide his own expert evidence. *Panetti v. Quarterman* (2007).

In some states, the question of recovery is judicially determined. Elsewhere, the practice is merely for the superintendent of the hospital where the prisoner is held to certify that he has recovered, after which the governor sets a new date for execution. It is very likely, however, that the prisoner has a constitutional right to a hearing on the question of his recovery. Whether the government may forcibly medicate an incompetent prisoner on death row in order to make him legally sane and thus executable has not been authoritatively resolved.

§ 7.2   Procedures for Raising the Insanity Defense

It is the defendant who usually raises the insanity defense, although it is not uncommon for the defendant deliberately not to do so for the reason that the consequences of conviction are preferred over commitment following a verdict of not guilty by reason of insanity. There is some questionable authority that in such an instance the court or prosecutor may force the insanity issue into the case. In some states the defendant must give advance warning by plea or notice of his intention to rely upon the insanity defense.

It is to the advantage of both the prosecution and defense to have the defendant examined by a psychiatrist whose orientation and examination procedures are such as will probably support their side of the case. In most states the prosecutor can obtain a court-ordered examination, which is usually conducted by a psychiatrist in the employ of the state. The indigent defendant is constitutionally entitled to the services of a psychiatrist.

There is a general presumption of sanity, and thus the initial burden (called the burden of going forward) is on the defendant to introduce evidence creating a reasonable doubt of his sanity. As to the burden of convincing the jury (called the burden of persuasion), some states require the defendant to prove insanity by a preponderance of the evidence, while others require the prosecution to prove sanity beyond a reasonable doubt. At the close of all the evidence, the jury is instructed on the insanity test and is given several verdict alternatives: guilty; not guilty; not guilty by reason of insanity; and (in a minority of jurisdictions only) guilty but mentally ill.

(a) Who and Why. Unlike other defenses that, if successful, will result in acquittal and outright release (see § 6.1(b)), the insanity defense may not appear to be an appealing alternative to the defendant. Except for the defendant who is charged with a crime punishable by death, the disadvantages of a finding of not guilty by reason of insanity may seem just as great or even greater than those which would flow from a verdict of guilty. In the former instance the defendant is not formally condemned and may gain some satisfaction from the fact that he was not responsible for what he did and that he is now being sent to an institution which is supposed to provide treatment for his illness. "But he must weigh those advantages against the fact that his detention is for an entirely indeterminate period; that he may be kept in a hospital as long as or longer than he would have remained in prison; and that being regarded as mentally ill may bring him as much stigma, economic deprivation, family dislocation, and often as little treatment or physical comfort as being a criminal."

This being the case, it is apparent that the decision of defense counsel in deciding whether or not to raise the insanity defense is likely to be influenced substantially by his assessment of the consequences of a finding of criminality as opposed to a finding of insanity. The stigma will probably appear to be just as great in one instance as the other, so that counsel will focus his attention on the matter of length of incarceration. If conviction would be followed by a very long sentence, then commitment for an indefinite term may seem preferable. But, except in such a situation, the imposition of a fixed sentence within legislatively-set limits and the possibility of probation or parole is certain to seem a better course than the risk of a commitment that could last the rest of the defendant's life. Counsel is also likely to lean in the direction of a criminal disposition because he is more familiar with that process; he may be able to predict with reasonable accuracy how much time the defendant would actually have to serve if convicted of the instant crime under the known circumstances, but he may know little or nothing about whether his client's impairment could readily be corrected by treatment or whether effective treatment is available. It is common, therefore, for defense counsel *not* to put the insanity question into issue notwithstanding the availability of some evidence indicating that the defense would be successful.

The facts suggesting that the defendant may have a valid insanity defense may nonetheless come to the attention of the prosecutor or the court. Indeed, if the prosecutor is uncertain whether the defense will be raised at trial he will seek out such facts in order to determine whether he should be prepared to prove the defendant's sanity. He may obtain information about the circumstances surrounding the crime or of defendant's psychiatric history by police investigation, his own investigation, the subpoena of witnesses before the grand jury, or commitment of the defendant for a determination of his competence to stand trial (see § 7.1(a)). At trial, testimony of a witness may bring to the attention of the prosecutor and judge the possibility of an insanity defense that the defendant has already decided to forego.

In these circumstances, may the prosecutor or court interject the insanity defense into the case over the wishes of defendant and defense counsel? Some decisions indicate that the answer is yes, although their current status is in doubt as a result of *Lynch v. Overholser* (1962). The defendant, with a history of passing bad checks, understandably preferred to plead guilty to a bad check charge and receive a sentence that could not exceed one year, but the court refused the plea because the defendant appeared to have an insanity defense. At trial, the prosecution introduced evidence of the defendant's insanity, resulting in a verdict of not guilty by reason of insanity and, as provided for under District of Columbia law, the defendant's mandatory commitment. The court of appeals approved on the ground that "society has a stake in seeing to it that a defendant who needs hospital care does not go to prison," but the Supreme Court reversed. Noting that the result was automatic commitment on the basis of merely a reasonable doubt of defendant's sanity, a doubt not raised by the defendant himself, the Court interpreted the commitment statute as not reaching such a situation.

It must be emphasized that the Court in *Lynch* did not pass directly upon the question of whether the defendant is entitled to keep the insanity defense out of the case entirely. But several recent decisions have held that the defendant is so entitled, and thus it appears that *Lynch* has emerged "as authority for the proposition that neither prosecutor nor judge can assert the insanity defense when a competent defendant, who is adequately represented, has chosen not to do so." This proposition draws support from other, more recent Supreme Court decisions recognizing the importance of allowing the defendant to make strategic decisions on his own behalf.

Whether such a proposition is a sensible one is a matter on which opinions differ. On the one hand, it is argued that this defense should be subject to abandonment for tactical reasons in the same way as alibi or entrapment. On the other, it is contended that judge and prosecutor must be allowed to raise the defense as part of their general obligation to see that justice is done—in this instance, to see that those not responsible do not go to jail and that they are not returned to society uncured. The latter argument may lose some of its force if the fairness and effectiveness of the procedures for commitment, treatment, and release are in doubt (see § 7.4).

(b) When and How. The earliest point in the criminal process at which the insanity defense might be raised in a formal way is at the preliminary hearing. At that hearing, the magistrate is to determine whether there is probable cause to believe that the defendant committed a crime, and thus it might be thought that defense counsel could challenge the existence of probable cause by attempting to show that the defendant was insane at the time of the crime. Having the issue resolved in the defendant's favor at this early stage might be supported on the notion that "persons who are blameless should not have to suffer the sanctions of the criminal process for a moment longer than necessary." But in practice, the defense is seldom raised at this stage of the process. The preliminary hearing is very frequently waived, and even when it is not defense counsel usually prefer not to expose the nature and dimensions of their defense at this early stage. Considerable uncertainty currently exists as to the place of the insanity defense at the preliminary hearing, as well as to the larger question of the extent to which the defendant may raise any affirmative defenses at this time. Several persuasive arguments have been presented in opposition to permitting the defense to be litigated at the preliminary hearing: (1) The magistrate is unlikely to be qualified to try such an issue. (2) He ordinarily would have no authority to institute commitment procedures against a defendant who negated probable cause with an insanity defense. (3) The trial of defenses, and particularly a defense as complicated as the insanity defense, would require more refined and lengthy procedures, which in turn would frustrate the objectives of the hearing and add to trial delay.

Close to a quarter of the states have enacted statutes providing that if the grand jury fails to return an indictment on the ground of insanity, then that fact is to be certified to the court and the court may (in some states, must) initiate commitment proceedings. But these statutes are of little practical significance, for in most jurisdictions the defendant is not entitled to appear before the grand jury or to present evidence to that body. Because the prosecutor exercises considerable control over the business of the grand jury and its decision-making, a case is not likely to be terminated at this point on the ground of defendant's insanity unless the prosecutor desires such a disposition. Moreover, an insanity determination by the grand jury that serves as the basis for a subsequent commitment is vulnerable to attack on constitutional grounds.

Thus, arraignment (the time at when the defendant is called upon to enter his plea) is the earliest point at which the defendant is likely to be able to interpose the defense of insanity. In most jurisdictions, however, he is under no obligation to do so at that time; under the prevailing rule the defendant may respond to the charge against him simply with a plea of not guilty, and he need not disclose in advance the nature of the defense upon which he is going to rely. This means that the prosecutor must resort to the various means described earlier in order to determine the likelihood of the insanity defense being raised at trial and to obtain psychiatric data about the defendant for use in rebutting that defense.

A majority of jurisdictions, in recognition of the fact that it is extremely important for the prosecution to know in advance of trial whether an insanity defense will be raised, have adopted legislation requiring the defendant to give advance notice. In some states this legislation requires a special plea of not guilty by reason of insanity as a prerequisite to raising the defense at trial. But much more common is a requirement that the defendant file a written notice at a certain time prior to trial manifesting his intention to defend on the ground of insanity. Some of these statutes go on to provide that the defendant must set forth in his notice the names of his witnesses and the substance of his defenses. Unless the matter is put into issue by the prosecution's evidence or the defendant establishes good cause for his failure to so plead or give notice, the defendant may not thereafter defend on grounds of insanity. These statutes usually also provide that the trial court may commit the defendant for examination after his indication of an intention to raise the insanity defense.

The requirement that the defendant by plea or notice disclose in advance of trial his intention to rely upon the insanity defense has been challenged on the ground that it infringes upon the defendant's constitutional privilege against self-incrimination. The argument, in brief, is that this right frees the defendant from any obligation to provide the prosecutor with information which might be useful to the prosecution's case and, particularly, to identify the nature of the defense before the prosecution has put in its case. The claim has been consistently rejected in the state courts, and this result would seem to be bolstered by the Supreme Court holding that the defendant may constitutionally be required to give advance notice of his intention to rely upon an alibi. It has been argued, however, that a notice-of-insanity requirement is more vulnerable than a notice-of-alibi statute, in that the former, unlike the latter, involves an admission by the defendant that he did the acts charged.

(c) Court–Ordered Psychiatric Examination. Lay testimony is unlikely to be sufficient either in effectively presenting an insanity defense or in rebutting such a defense. Thus, in a case in which the issue of insanity is to be litigated both the defense and the prosecution will be interested in having the accused examined well in advance of trial.

One common complaint about the procedure for trying the insanity defense issue is that "it lacks the impartiality which should be characteristic of scientific inquiry." In an attempt to eliminate the so-called "battle of the experts," most jurisdictions have enacted statutes providing for examination of the defendant by a court-appointed psychiatrist. Appointment under these provisions may come because the defense, prosecutor, or court has asserted that the defendant is not competent to stand trial (in which case the examination will nonetheless probably result in the psychiatrist gaining information relating to the accused's condition at the time of the alleged crime), or it may be triggered by the defendant's action of pleading or giving notice of an insanity defense. Under the most common type of procedure, the court designates a specific psychiatrist who will thereafter examine the defendant in his office or in a court clinic or the jail. Elsewhere, the defendant is temporarily committed to a mental hospital for examination by a member of the hospital staff. Under both procedures, "the examination is ordinarily made by a psychiatrist employed by the government, either because the statutes require it or because a government psychiatrist is the only one available." Upon completion of the examination, a report is prepared and copies are furnished to the court, the prosecutor, and defense counsel.

The report is likely to have a very significant impact upon the outcome of the case. It has been established that if there is a conflict between the conclusions reached by the so-called impartial expert and by an expert retained by one of the parties, the jury will in almost every instance accept those of the former. As a result, both the prosecutor and defense counsel are influenced by his findings. This would be a desirable result if the appointed expert could be counted upon to bring the "truth" into court, but this is not the case. "An impartial expert, and the added credibility he brings with him, could be justified only if there was a high degree of consensus among psychiatrists on the answers to questions likely to arise in the courtroom, on the qualifications of persons competent to present such answers and on the techniques to be used at the various stages of examination. No such consensus can be said to exist." In part, the problem arises out of the fact that the statutes concerning examination by an impartial expert often do not set forth the minimum qualifications required of the examiner, do not stipulate the kind of examination which is to be conducted, and "give the examining expert little or no guidance as to what his report must contain." But the more fundamental point is that the single expert only represents the point of view of his particular school of psychiatry.

One other problem relating to court-ordered mental examinations is this: to what extent, if at all, is the defendant who is ordered to submit to such an examination protected by the constitutional privilege against self-incrimination? This issue, which took on much greater significance once the privilege was held applicable to the states and interpreted as extending to pretrial questioning of a detained suspect, can arise in various ways. One question is whether a defendant's incriminating admissions to the examiner tending to show that he engaged in the conduct charged (e.g., "yes, I shot him") are admissible at trial against him. (It is not unlikely that such an admission will be made, as one accepted technique of examination is to ask the defendant "about his view of the facts and the feelings which he experienced at the time of the crime.") There is general agreement that the privilege extends to such admissions, although courts have differed upon the means by which the privilege is to be enforced. Statutory provisions to the effect that such admissions by the defendant are not admissible at trial on the issue of guilt are usually thought to be adequate, and in the absence of such provisions some courts have held that the defendant may refuse to submit to the examination without penalty.

But are such admissions properly admitted as a part of the basis for the expert's opinion on the defendant's sanity? The courts have quite consistently answered in the affirmative, at least where the defendant has asserted an insanity defense and introduced supporting psychiatric testimony. The Supreme Court has not had occasion to rule on this precise point, but has referred to these lower court decisions with apparent approval. The view typically taken is that consequently it suffices if, after such a statement is admitted into evidence, the jury is instructed that it is not to consider the admission on the question of guilt. This view has been justly criticized on the ground that the jury is unlikely to be able to obey such an instruction. Another approach is to permit such evidence to be admitted on the issue of insanity only if that issue is tried in a separate hearing following determination of the issue of guilt. This bifurcated trial procedure (see § 7.3(b)) has the unique advantage that defendant's statements cannot operate to his prejudice on the issue of guilt, but yet they are brought to the attention of the factfinder as a very relevant part of the examination process.

But the broader issue is just why it is that the entire examination process is not contrary to the defendant's privilege against self-incrimination. That is, why is it not a violation of the privilege to require the defendant to submit to an examination that may very well provide the prosecution with information which can be admitted for the purpose of defeating the defendant's insanity defense? Some courts have simply accepted without question the notion that the privilege is inapplicable in this context, while other courts have offered a variety of explanations. Sometimes that conclusion has been grounded upon the proposition that the defendant's mental condition is real evidence and thus for that reason not within the privilege. (In defining the scope of the privilege, the Supreme Court has held that it only protects the accused from providing "evidence of a testimonial or communicative nature," and thus has upheld such practices as the taking of a blood sample, placing the suspect in a lineup, requiring him to speak for voice identification, and requiring him to provide a handwriting exemplar.) But in *Estelle v. Smith* (1981) the Supreme Court rejected this argument out of hand, noting that the privilege against self-incrimination is "directly involved" when the state uses as evidence against the defendant "the substance of his disclosures during the pretrial psychiatric examination." In short, mental examinations are unlike these other practices in that "examinations impinge on values protected by the privilege."

Another reason sometimes given for not extending the privilege to the court-ordered examination concerns the concept of "waiver." That is, the problem is sometimes resolved on the ground that the defendant has waived the protection of the privilege by raising the insanity defense or by submitting to examination without protest. *Estelle* can easily be read as approving this theory, for the court went out of its way to distinguish the instant case, in which the defendant had not interposed an insanity defense or offered psychiatric evidence for any purpose, from one in which "a defendant asserts the insanity defense and introduces supporting psychiatric testimony." But the waiver theory has been severely criticized. As *U.S. v. Byers* (1984) put it:

> It seems to us at best a fiction to say that when the defendant introduces his expert's testimony he "waives" his Fifth Amendment rights. What occurs is surely no waiver in the ordinary sense of a known and voluntary relinquishment, but rather merely the product of the court's decree that the act entails the consequences—a decree that remains to be justified. Even if the average defendant pleading insanity were aware of this judicially prescribed consequence (an awareness that the

doctrine of waiver would normally require), his acceptance of it could hardly be called unconstrained.

Yet a third theory, which may be what the Supreme Court in *Estelle* was actually referring to in noting that if a state could not examine an insanity-defense defendant then it would be deprived "of the only effective means it has of controverting his proof on an issue that he interjected into the case," has to do with not giving the defendant an unfair advantage. Thus, courts that have rejected the Fifth Amendment claim in this context have not infrequently referred to the need for a "fair state-individual balance" or for "fundamental fairness" or "judicial common sense" in resolving the issue. These courts have thus "denied the Fifth Amendment claim primarily because of the unreasonable and debilitating effect it would have upon society's conduct of a fair inquiry into the defendant's culpability." As the matter was explained in *Pope v. U.S.* (1967):

> It would be a strange situation, indeed, if, first, the government is to be compelled to afford the defense ample psychiatric service and evidence at government expense and second, if the government is to have the burden of proof, * * * and yet it is to be denied the opportunity to have its own corresponding and verifying examination, a step which perhaps is the most trustworthy means of attempting to meet that burden.

Such practical considerations of what constitutes a fair but effective criminal process are rightly taken into account in determining the reach of the Fifth Amendment privilege against self incrimination.

If, on the basis of one or more of the above theories, a defendant has no constitutional right not to submit to a court-ordered psychiatric examination, then of course it follows that the defendant is not exercising a constitutional right if he refuses to talk with the court-appointed psychiatrist. Sanctions are thus permissible in the event of such noncooperation. Some courts permit the prosecutor to comment on the defendant's silence in this respect at trial. But this alone is insufficient, for "it permits the defendant to present expert testimony that cannot be effectively challenged." Thus the better approach is to bar the noncooperating defendant from presenting any psychiatric testimony on his own behalf.

Yet another question is whether a defendant has a constitutional right to the assistance of counsel in connection with a court-ordered psychiatric examination. Some courts have held that a defendant is entitled to notice of and an opportunity to consult with counsel regarding an examination by a government psychiatrist, a conclusion which finds support in the Supreme Court's decision in

Estelle v. Smith (1981). As explained in *U.S. v. Garcia* (1984), counsel can render meaningful assistance prior to the interview:

> A defendant facing such an exam must make decisions with significant legal consequences and is in obvious need of counsel. * * * He may wish to refuse to submit to the government examination and risk exclusion of his own expert testimony at trial, and rely instead on lay testimony to establish insanity. * * * A defendant may need advice regarding what sort of questions he should expect, the need to cooperate, and the possible ramifications of his answers. He may have legitimate fifth amendment concerns regarding use of statements made in an examination * * * and may well be unaware that his statements may not be admitted for the purpose of establishing any issue except mental condition.

A few courts have ruled that a defendant also has a right to have his attorney present during the psychiatric examination. However, the overwhelming majority of the cases hold to the contrary. These cases very often stress that the presence of counsel would limit the effectiveness of the examination, which is a practical consideration of the kind the Supreme Court has acknowledged must be taken into account in determining the scope of the Sixth Amendment right to counsel. Denial of counsel at the examination is also consistent with the Court's other reasoning concerning the need for assistance of counsel. In *U.S. v. Ash* (1973), holding there is no right to have defense counsel present at a photograph identification, the Court declared that for the Sixth Amendment to apply the defendant must find himself "confronted, just as at trial, by the procedural system, or by his expert adversary, or by both." But a defendant who was allowed to consult with counsel before the examination is not in such a situation during the examination; at that time "he had no decisions in the nature of legal strategy or tactics to make," and the "examining psychiatrist is not an adversary, much less a professional one," in the sense in which that phrase is used in the right to counsel cases.

(d) Examination of Defendant by Own Psychiatrist. If the defendant can afford to do so, he will be examined by a psychiatrist of his own choosing. However, the effectiveness of the examination in terms of constructing a convincing defense of insanity will be determined in large measure by the defense counsel. He must select a psychiatrist whose orientation is such as to favor the defendant's position, and he must develop a close working relationship with him and adequately inform him as to the kinds of information that are needed concerning the defendant's past condition.

In this respect the indigent defendant will sometimes be at a significant disadvantage. Statutes in some states authorize payment of reasonable expenses related to the defense of indigent defendants, which are at least sometimes construed to cover a psychiatric examination by a defense psychiatrist. But, especially absent a statute clearly authorizing the granting of such assistance at state expense, courts have generally not looked with favor upon assertions that an indigent defendant is denied a fair trial of his insanity defense if he is not provided with a psychiatrist of his own choosing. Such assistance is said to be merely "collateral" and thus not something that must be provided at public expense. Moreover, it is assumed to be adequate that the defendant was examined by a state psychiatrist; the state is said to have no "constitutional obligation to promote * * * a battle of experts by supplying defense counsel with funds wherewith to hunt for other experts who may be willing, as witnesses for the defense, to offer the opinion that the accused is criminally insane." It has been suggested that the equal protection approach developed in *Griffin v. Ill.* (1956) undercuts these cases, but courts have been most reluctant to extend the *Griffin* holding to situations in which the indigent defendant requested appointment of his own psychiatrist. In so doing, some argue, they have failed to recognize that substantial equality cannot be accomplished unless the indigent defendant has a psychiatrist whose orientation and preparation is such as to support the defense theory of the case.

In *Ake v. Okla.* (1985), the Supreme Court held "that when a defendant demonstrates to the trial judge that his sanity at the time of the offense is to be a significant factor at trial, the State must, at a minimum, assure the defendant access to a competent psychiatrist who will conduct an appropriate examination and assist in evaluation, preparation, and presentation of the defense." The Court added that it was leaving "to the States the decision on how to implement this right," but failed to indicate clearly whether implementation requires that a defendant who makes the requisite showing is inevitably entitled to a psychiatrist *of his own*. Indeed, *Ake* appears to have been written so as to be deliberately ambiguous on this point, thus leaving the issue open for future consideration, as comments supporting a move in either direction appear throughout the majority opinion in the case.

On the one hand, the reference in the above holding to a psychiatrist assisting "in evaluation, preparation, and presentation of the defense" certainly suggests that a psychiatrist serving exclusively in the defense camp is necessary. This position is also bolstered by the Court's recognition that "psychiatrists disagree widely and frequently" on the various questions related to the insanity defense and that consequently juries "must resolve differences in opinion" after hearing from "the psychiatrists for each party." Also significant is the fact that the Court makes reference to existing statutes concerning provision of assistance to the defense, rather than those which merely provide for examination of the defendant by a court-appointed "neutral" psychiatrist. Finally, it is relatively clear that in the other branch of *Ake,* concerning the right to psychiatric assistance at a capital sentencing proceeding, the Court has given express recognition to the need for a separate psychiatrist on the defense side.

On the other hand, it must be noted that the *Ake* case involved a fact situation in which there was *absolutely no* psychiatric testimony available on the insanity defense. The defendant had been denied a psychiatrist of his own, and the court-ordered examination had been limited to defendant's competency to stand trial, so that even the psychiatrists at the state hospital were unable to testify about defendant's mental condition at the time of the offense. Moreover, the Court in *Ake* did caution that an indigent defendant has no "constitutional right to choose a psychiatrist of his personal liking or to receive funds to hire his own," and also restated the now-familiar doctrine that a state need not "purchase for the indigent defendant all the assistance that his wealthier counterpart might buy." Finally, the Supreme Court distinguished the cases relied upon by the court below by characterizing them as instances in which the defendant had been examined by "neutral psychiatrists" who "were not beholden to the prosecution," though the psychiatrists in those cases were the court's witnesses—not appointed for defendant's exclusive use and, at least in one instance, permanent employees of the state's psychiatric facility who were unlikely to view the insanity defense from a defendant's perspective.

§ 7.3   Procedures at Trial Re Insanity Defense

(a) **Burden of Proof.** The phrase "burden of proof" is somewhat ambiguous and is often used for different purposes. To avoid confusion, it is helpful to distinguish between (1) the initial burden of going forward with the evidence (sometimes called the production burden), and (2) the burden of persuasion. Failure of the party who has the burden of going forward to meet that burden will result in the factual matter being foreclosed adversely to him, either by a directed verdict or by an instruction to the jury. The burden of persuasion, on the other hand, involves the situation in which the factual matter is before the jury for decision; the burden is that of convincing the jury to accept the version of those facts alleged by the party bearing the burden.

On the issue of lack of responsibility because of insanity, the initial burden of going forward is everywhere placed upon the defendant. This proposition is often stated in terms of a presumption of sanity; most men are sane, and thus the defendant in this particular case is presumed to be sane until some amount of evidence to the contrary is produced. Were it otherwise, the prosecution would be confronted with the intolerable burden of establishing the defendant's sanity in every criminal case. The burden of going forward is usually met by testimony of lay or expert witnesses for the defense tending to show that the defendant was insane at the time of the conduct charged, although this is not of necessity so. It sometimes happens that the insanity defense will become an issue in the case because of testimony elicited by the prosecutor from his own witnesses or by the defense on cross-examination of prosecution witnesses.

The states are not in agreement on the quantum of evidence required to discharge the burden of going forward. The prevailing rule is that the evidence must raise a reasonable doubt of the defendant's mental responsibility for the criminal act. A few jurisdictions, however, appear to require a lesser standard sometimes stated as merely "some evidence," "slight evidence," or a "scintilla" of evidence. This latter view leads to some difficult questions. For example, if the defendant meets this lesser burden but the prosecution does not thereafter produce any evidence of the defendant's insanity, should the court direct a verdict of not guilty by reason of insanity? Yes, answered one court, for once the defendant met his production burden the defendant's sanity became an essential element to be proved by the government beyond a reasonable doubt. No, answered another, for a directed verdict requires not merely some evidence but rather proof sufficient to compel a reasonable juror to entertain a reasonable doubt.

Once the defendant has met his burden of going forward with the evidence, it then must be determined which party has the burden of persuasion. In about ten states, this burden rests with the prosecution; in these jurisdictions the prosecution must then proceed to prove responsibility beyond a reasonable doubt. In the other states, the burden of persuasion is on the defendant to convince the jury of his insanity, usually by the civil standard of a preponderance of the evidence. But in the federal system, recent legislation has placed upon the defendant the burden of proving his insanity defense by "clear and convincing evidence," and this is now true in a minority of states as well. When "a defendant fails to present sufficient evidence to sustain his assigned burden of proof * * *, he clearly has no right to have the insanity question submitted to the jury in the hope that they will acquit him based on sympathy, caprice, or compromise."

In those states in which the burden of persuasion rests upon the defendant, the most common explanation is that insanity is an affirmative defense rather than an element of the crime and that the presumption of insanity justifies the requirement that the defendant prove his sanity. A supporting consideration is the fear that if the rule were otherwise it would be too easy for a defendant who was sane to create a reasonable doubt concerning his sanity. Some, however, have questioned the propriety of placing the burden on the defendant. It is argued that the fundamental proposition that the state must prove the defendant's guilt beyond a reasonable doubt should logically extend to the issue of criminal responsibility, in that the essential element of *mens rea* is not proven unless it is shown that the defendant was capable of entertaining the requisite mens rea. Another contention is that it is more equitable to place the burden on the state, which has resources available to obtain the necessary psychiatric evidence, than on the defendant, who is likely to be indigent.

In *Leland v. Ore.* (1952), the Supreme Court upheld a since-repealed Oregon statute which required the accused to establish his insanity beyond a reasonable doubt. The Court could see "no practical difference of such magnitude as to be significant in determining the constitutional question" between the Oregon statute and the provisions found in about half the states requiring the defendant to prove his sanity by a preponderance of the evidence. The fact the latter rule was followed in a large number of states was deemed quite relevant under the test then utilized for due process violations—whether the practice "offends some principle of justice so rooted in the traditions and conscience of our people as to be ranked as fundamental." The Supreme Court later held in *In re Winship* (1970), relying in part upon the dissent in *Leland,* that "the Due Process Clause protects the accused against conviction except upon proof beyond a reasonable doubt of every fact necessary to constitute the crime with which he is charged." Yet the Court thereafter dismissed, as not presenting a substantial federal question, an appeal claiming a state statute burdening the defendant with proving insanity by a preponderance of the evidence was unconstitutional. As the Court later explained in *Patterson v. N.Y.* (1977), "once the facts constituting a crime are established beyond a reasonable doubt, based on all the evidence including the evidence of the defendant's mental state, the State may refuse to sustain the affirmative defense of insanity unless demonstrated by a preponderance of the evidence." The same result has been reached where the defendant's burden is to establish insanity by clear and convincing evidence. As the *Patterson* language suggests, special steps may be required by trial courts to ensure that shifting the burden of proving insanity to the defendant does not, as a practical matter, lessen the constitutionally-imposed burden on the prosecution to prove beyond a reasonable doubt all elements of the crime, including the requisite mental state.

(b) Witnesses and Their Testimony. In almost every jurisdiction, a lay witness who is sufficiently acquainted with the defendant to form an intelligent opinion as to his sanity may testify to that opinion, although it is common to require that the witness precede or accompany his opinion with a statement of the facts and circumstances upon which it is founded. Just how much exposure the lay witness must have had to the defendant is a matter that has caused considerable disagreement. Sometimes such testimony is permitted on the basis of a single meeting of only a few minutes duration, while on other occasions such a brief observation has been held inadequate. A lay witness may testify as to the defendant's sanity based upon observation of usual or normal human behavior by him, but may testify as to his insanity only if he has seen the defendant engage in irrational or abnormal behavior. Although "a persuasive case is unlikely to be made on lay testimony alone," courts have not infrequently upheld verdicts based upon a jury's acceptance of lay testimony of sanity over expert testimony of insanity, and have likewise indicated that an insanity defense may be supported by lay witnesses alone.

As for expert testimony, the testimony of a psychiatrist is ordinarily the most useful, although even physicians in general practice are often allowed to testify as experts on the insanity question. In most jurisdictions qualified clinical psychologists are also permitted to give expert testimony relating to an insanity defense. The expert's opinion may be based upon (1) his personal examination of the defendant, (2) his evaluation of all the testimony in the case, or (3) a hypothetical question propounded by counsel. The latter technique has been the subject of considerable criticism, and it is not frequently used.

It is generally agreed that the witness may not be asked the ultimate question of whether the defendant was responsible, for this, like an inquiry into whether a person was negligent, seeks a legal conclusion and thus invades the province of the jury. For a time, courts were for the same reason also inclined to hold that the witness could not be asked the "test questions," that is, that he could not be permitted to state his opinion in terms of the applicable legal test of insanity (e.g., "I believe that defendant had a disease of the mind which deprived him of knowledge of right and wrong"). The prevailing rule is now to the contrary.

The rule permitting the asking of the test questions rests upon the assumption that the resulting testimony, particularly from a psychiatrist, will better advance the jury's inquiry. It has been questioned, however, whether this is the case. "The essential vice of allowing the test questions is that they tend to supplant the factual detail upon which the decision on responsibility should ideally be based. * * * The jury is left with the impression that it must choose between the experts, because it is not told enough about the defendant's mental life to enable it to make an intelligent judgment about *him,* rather than about the psychiatric witnesses."

In addition to opinion evidence, a defendant's mental condition may be proved by circumstantial evidence. This can ordinarily be done: (1) by evidence of the defendant's actions and declarations prior to, at, and subsequent to the time of the conduct charged; (2) by evidence of facts that sometimes cause or predispose one to insanity (e.g., circumstances which might cause psychic stress, hereditary insanity, the presence of substances in the body likely to affect the mind); or (3) by evidence of prior or subsequent insanity, such as civil adjudication of insanity at a time not too remote from the time of the alleged crime.

(c) The Bifurcated Trial. In a few jurisdictions, the defense of insanity is tried separately from the other issues in the case. Under California law, for example, a defendant may plead (1) not guilty, (2) not guilty and also not guilty by reason of insanity, or (3) merely not guilty by reason of insanity. If the second form of plea is entered, the guilt-stage of the trial is first concluded without any reference to the insanity defense, after which (if defendant was found guilty) a separate proceedings takes place before the same or a different jury for purposes of trying the insanity defense. If the third form of plea is entered, this has the effect of a plea of guilty with reservation of the insanity defense, so that only the insanity issue is tried. Such procedures have been upheld whether the insanity issue is determined before or after the main trial, and even though the insanity issue is tried before a different jury.

The purpose of the mandated bifurcated trial procedure is to eliminate from the basic trial on the issue of whether the defendant engaged in the conduct a great mass of evidence having no bearing on that question and which may confuse the jury or be made the basis of appeals to the sympathy or prejudice of the jury. In California, at least, this objective was not realized. As a result of the ruling in *People v. Wells* (1949) that evidence of mental disease or defect was admissible on the issue of whether the defendant had the requisite mental state (see § 8.2), this mass of evidence was often heard at both the guilt-stage and insanity-stage of the trial. A very few states have invalidated their bifurcated trial statutes, precisely because the legislation was deemed to bar such evidence at the guilt-stage of the trial.

A different question is whether a defendant who plans to interpose an insanity defense should be entitled to a bifurcated trial if he prefers to proceed in that fashion. On occasion it has been held that bifurcation is called for to protect the defendant's privilege against self-incrimination, as where the defendant made an inculpatory statement during a compulsory pretrial psychiatric examination. Several states take the position that whether to grant the defendant's bifurcation request is a matter within the sound discretion of the judge, with bifurcation called for only when "a defendant shows that he has a substantial insanity defense and a substantial defense on the merits to any element of the charge, either of which would be prejudiced by simultaneous presentation with the other." In one other state, a defendant may opt for a bifurcated trial as a matter of right. But it has frequently been held that failure to allow a defendant asserting an insanity defense to have a bifurcated trial does not violate his constitutional rights.

(d) Instructions and Verdict. At the conclusion of all the evidence, the trial judge instructs the jury on the law. Now, for the first time and *after* hearing what may be a vast amount of evidence on the insanity issue, the jury is finally authoritatively told what the legal test for the insanity defense is and who has the burden of proving what. Particularly in those jurisdictions where there does not exist a standard "pattern" jury instruction on the insanity defense, the judge's oral instructions may be rambling, imprecise, or even downright misleading.

In most jurisdictions, if the insanity issue reaches the jury then it will be given three alternative verdict forms: guilty; not guilty; or not guilty by reason of insanity. If properly instructed, the jury will be told that their first order of business is to determine whether the defendant committed the acts charged and that they should reach the insanity question only if they make that initial determination in the affirmative. Occasionally, however, the jury is told to reach the insanity issue first and to proceed to the issue of guilt or innocence only if the defendant is not found not guilty by reason of insanity, which makes possible the curious result of commitment without a finding that the defendant had even done the acts charged.

One might think, simply as a matter of logic, that if the insanity issue is in the case the jury would be told of its significance, that is, of the fact that commitment must or may follow a finding of not guilty by reason of insanity. However, the view taken in many jurisdictions on this matter is that the jury should *not* be told of the consequences of an acquittal by reason of insanity. The questionable explanation for this position is that such an instruction would distract the jury from the insanity issue and would invite compromise verdicts. The better view is to the contrary, for, as explained in *Lyles v. U.S.* (1957), it does not make sense that a jury should be presented with three verdict choices (guilty, not guilty, and not guilty by reason of insanity) but know the consequences of only the first two. Fortunately, the *Lyles* position has gained support from other courts and some legislatures. But in *Shannon v. U.S.* (1994), the Supreme Court rejected *Lyles* and held that absent some misstatement to the jury on the subject, a federal trial judge is not to instruct the jury on the consequences of a not guilty by reason of insanity verdict. The Court in *Shannon* reasoned (i) that such information is "irrelevant to the jury's task" when, as there, the jury "has no sentencing function"; and (ii) that defendant's claim otherwise some jurors would harbor a mistaken belief such a verdict would result in defendant's immediate release is beside the point, as it is assumed jurors follow the instructions they receive "to apply the law as [instructed] regardless of the consequences."

In recent years, a substantial minority of states have enacted legislation requiring that in trials involving an insanity defense a fourth alternative verdict form be provided: "Guilty but mentally ill." The jury is given both an insanity defense instruction and an instruction as to what lesser or different type of mental illness permits a GBMI verdict. If a GBMI verdict is returned, the defendant is then sentenced just as if an unqualified guilty verdict had been returned. The only significance of the GBMI verdict is that the defendant is examined by psychiatrists before beginning his prison term and, if he is found to be in need of treatment, is transferred to a mental health facility. If the defendant's mental illness persists, absent civil commitment he may be held only until his sentence expires; if the defendant regains his sanity he nonetheless serves the balance of his sentence.

Several commentators have questioned the constitutionality of these provisions. However, GBMI statutes have been upheld against claims that they deny equal protection, violate due process and impose cruel and unusual punishment, and also against the contention that the statutes are impermissibly vague in setting out two ambiguous and overlapping definitions of insanity. These provisions have been praised in some quarters. It is said, for example, that "the GBMI verdict provides a workable middle ground for factfinders who must face the vagaries of conflicting psychiatric opinion." But most of the commentary has been critical, and deservedly so.

For one thing, the GBMI procedure is not a sensible way to go about achieving its purported purpose of determining which prisoners need psychiatric treatment:

It surely makes no sense for commitment procedures to be triggered by a jury verdict based on evidence concerning the defendant's past rather than present mental condition and need for treatment. Decisions concerning the proper placement of incarcerated offenders should be made by correctional and mental health authorities, not by juries or trial judges.

For another, the incidental effect of the GBMI procedure (doubtless intended by most of its proponents) is likely to be that of weakening the insanity defense by working "to deceive juries into rejecting valid insanity pleas." "Jurors faced with the GBMI alternative may be tempted to adopt it as a compromise verdict based on the assumption that dangerous offenders would be neutralized by incarceration, while still receiving psychiatric treatment." Such an indirect attack upon the insanity defense has been condemned even by those who are not sympathetic to the defense.

§ 7.4 Procedures After Finding of Not Guilty by Reason of Insanity

After a finding that the defendant is not guilty by reason of insanity, he is usually committed to a mental institution for treatment. In some jurisdictions commitment is mandatory following such an acquittal, but the majority view is that commitment is to be ordered only if it is found (usually, by the trial judge) that the defendant's insanity continues or that he is dangerous. Because of limited resources and the emphasis upon security, the individual committed may receive little or no treatment. Some courts have recognized a "right to treatment" for those who have been committed.

In most jurisdictions the release decision is vested in the committing court or some other court, although often the court will not have occasion to consider the matter unless the patient or the authorities having custody of him seek release. Four different standards for release have been used: (1) sanity; (2) lack of dangerousness; (3) sanity and lack of dangerousness; (4) sanity or lack of dangerousness. Considerable uncertainty exists as to the meaning of each standard. The burden of proof is usually placed upon the patient.

(a) Commitment. In a minority of states and also in the federal courts, statutes require automatic, mandatory commitment of a defendant who has been found not guilty by reason of insanity. The judge is left with absolutely no discretion; he has no authority to conduct an inquiry into the defendant's present mental condition, nor can he fail to commit on the ground that the defendant was recently declared sane in civil proceedings. In all other jurisdictions, commitment is possible but not mandatory. This is because of statutory provisions allowing commitment only upon a showing of grounds for such action.

There is considerable variation in the procedures and standards that have been prescribed. As to who makes the decision, virtually all states have given this responsibility to the trial judge, though a few have provided for a jury determination of this issue. The statutes vary somewhat as to the criterion for decision, but most of them are construed to mean "that the defendant must be insane and be dangerous to himself or others." In some states the defendant has the burden of proving he should not be committed, but more often the burden is on the state. The state usually has to make its showing by clear and convincing evidence, but in some states the preponderance-of-the-evidence standard is followed, while in one jurisdiction the grounds for commitment must be shown beyond a reasonable doubt.

Whether mandatory commitment or discretionary commitment is the most sound procedure is a matter of debate. In favor of mandatory commitment it is argued that it "not only provides the public with the maximum immediate protection, but may also work to the advantage of mentally diseased or defective defendants by making the defense of irresponsibility more acceptable to the public and to the jury." It is also said that mandatory commitment will deter spurious claims of insanity. Discretionary commitment is thus criticized on the grounds that it may provide insufficient protection for society and that jurors will be reluctant to acquit on grounds of insanity.

The objection to mandatory commitment is more fundamental. Under this practice, the operative assumption is that the trial of the insanity defense has established something about the defendant which justifies his being kept in custody. That is, he is treated as if the crime had been proved against him, as if he had been proved insane at the time of the crime, and as if the insanity continued to the time of disposition.

> In the mandatory commitment jurisdictions, these assumptions present difficult problems for legal theory. For one thing, there is ordinarily no explicit finding by the jury that the defendant would have been guilty of the crime but for the insanity. For another, in half the states, an acquittal by reason of insanity does not mean that the defendant was proved insane. It means only that there was a reasonable doubt on the question. Even in jurisdictions where the defendant must prove his insanity to win acquittal, the presumption of continuity is applied across the board without regard to whether the insanity was of the sort which is likely to have continued. The inflexibility of the assumption is made dramatically evident by the fact that the

defendant who has just won his acquittal is presumably competent to stand trial and, therefore, at least superficially "sane."

Because the mandatory commitment procedure is theoretically unsound, so the argument goes, it will appear to be punitive and for
that reason have an adverse effect upon efforts to treat the individual committed.

Commitment procedures following a finding of not guilty by
reason of insanity have frequently been challenged on constitutional grounds where, as is not uncommon, those procedures either
involve mandatory commitment or otherwise differ from the procedures required in the civil commitment process. These challenges
have only rarely succeeded, and such a result is even more unlikely
today in light of *Jones v. U.S.* (1983). The defendant in that case
was automatically committed following the not guilty by reason of
insanity finding in his trial for attempted petit larceny, and under
District of Columbia law could only obtain his release by showing
by a preponderance of the evidence that he was no longer mentally
ill or dangerous. Relying principally on *Addington v. Tex.* (1979),
where the Supreme Court held that the government in a civil
commitment proceeding is constitutionally required to demonstrate
by clear and convincing evidence that the individual is mentally ill
and dangerous, the defendant in *Jones* claimed the D.C. procedures
were constitutionally defective as a matter of due process and equal
protection. The Supreme Court did not agree.

The Court in *Jones* turned first to the question of whether a
D.C. verdict of not guilty by reason of insanity, necessitating both
(i) a finding beyond a reasonable doubt that defendant committed
an act that constitutes a criminal offense and (ii) a finding by a
preponderance of the evidence that defendant committed the act
because of mental illness, "is sufficiently probative of mental illness
and dangerousness to justify commitment." The Court declared
that the first of the above two findings "certainly indicates dangerousness" and is generally "at least as persuasive as any predictions
about dangerousness that might be made in a civil-commitment
proceeding." As for defendant's claim that this was not so in the
present case because of the nature of the crime charged, the Court
responded that dangerousness was not limited to acts of violence.
The Court next concluded "that the insanity acquittal supports an
inference of continuing mental illness" so as to justify automatic
commitment. "It comports with common sense," said the *Jones*
majority, "to conclude that someone whose mental illness was
sufficient to lead him to commit a criminal act is likely to remain ill
and in need of treatment."

As for the defendant's claim his commitment was unconstitutional because based on a preponderance of the evidence standard,

while *Addington* had required proof by clear and convincing evidence, the Court responded that in "equating these situations, petitioner ignores important differences between the class of potential civil-commitment candidates and the class of insanity acquittees that justify differing standards of proof." For one thing, the insanity acquittee has himself advanced the insanity defense and proved his mental illness, meaning "there is good reason for diminished concern as to the risk of error." For another, the proof he committed a criminal act eliminates the risk, as it was put in *Addington,* that he is being committed for mere "idiosyncratic behavior."

The final issue considered in *Jones* was whether the defendant "nonetheless is entitled to his release because he has been hospitalized for a period longer than he could have been incarcerated if convicted." As to this, the Court reasoned:

> A particular sentence of incarceration is chosen to reflect society's view of the proper response to commission of a particular criminal offense, based on a variety of considerations such as retribution, deterrence, and rehabilitation. * * * The State may punish a person convicted of a crime even if satisfied that he is unlikely to commit further crimes.
>
> Different considerations underlie commitment of an insanity acquittee. As he was not convicted, he may not be punished. His confinement rests on his continuing illness and dangerousness. * * * There simply is no necessary correlation between severity of the offense and length of time necessary for recovery. The length of the acquittee's hypothetical criminal sentence therefore is irrelevant to the purposes of his commitment.

Central to the *Jones* decision is the notion, as theretofore stated by some lower courts, that defendants acquitted on the basis of an insanity defense constitute an "exceptional class" entitled to no hearing because their prior insanity is presumed to continue. But such analysis is unsatisfactory for many reasons: (1) Where the burden of proof is on the prosecution to prove sanity (see § 7.3(a)), the jury's verdict only means that there was a reasonable doubt as to sanity, and thus the only presumption is one of a continuing reasonable doubt. (2) The presumption is only prima facie evidence and thus is rebuttable, but without a hearing there is no opportunity for rebuttal. (3) The presumption continues only for a reasonable time, and thus should not be applicable when considerable time has passed since the occurrence giving rise to the criminal charge. (4) The defendant was more recently found or presumed to be sane, for otherwise he could not have been placed on trial.

(b) Treatment and the "Right to Treatment." An individual who is committed following his acquittal on grounds of insanity may, nonetheless, be improperly characterized as in the "criminal insane" category and be dealt with in essentially the same way as the convicted defendant who becomes insane while serving his sentence and the charged defendant who is found incompetent to stand trial. One survey showed that he would be confined in a separate ward or unit of the state mental hospital in twenty-seven states, unsegregated in the hospital in five states, held in a ward or unit of the penal institution in two states, confined in either the penal institution or state hospital in three states, and committed to a separate institution for the criminally insane in nine states.

Wherever confined, he may receive little or no treatment. Most of these institutions are severely overcrowded and lack sufficient competent personnel to undertake an effective treatment program. Moreover, the administrators of these institutions find themselves confronted with the irreconcilable functions of therapy and security.

> The therapeutic ideal calls for allowing patients more and more responsibility for their own actions and judgments, with correlative diminishing restrictions and controls, which inevitably means accepting greater or less security risk. Any type of institutionalization, even in the best of hospitals, militates against therapy. A warmer, closer, family environment would be better. Maximum security in practice means close confinement in a cell or cell-like room, and there is little in the nature of a treatment program that can be carried on under such conditions.

The conflict is usually resolved by favoring security over therapy. One reason for this is that effective therapy may appear impossible due to the rapid turnover and limited training of the professional staff. More important, perhaps, is the fear of public criticism should an insane killer or rapist escape.

In recent years, increased attention has been given to the notion that an individual held in custody on grounds of insanity, particularly one committed following a finding of not guilty by reason of insanity, has a "right to treatment." A leading case is *Rouse v. Cameron* (1966), in which the habeas corpus petitioner (committed upon a finding that he was not guilty by reason of insanity of carrying a dangerous weapon) objected to the district court's refusal to consider his allegation that he had received no psychiatric treatment. The court of appeals indicated that absence of treatment might render mandatory commitment unconstitutional under various theories: (1) commitment without an express finding of present insanity might violate due process if treatment were not promptly undertaken; (2) confinement longer than would have been permissible upon conviction might violate due process if no treatment was provided; (3) failure to provide treatment might constitute a denial of equal protection; and (4) indefinite confinement without treatment may be so inhumane as to be cruel and unusual punishment. However, the right to treatment recognized by the court was based upon language in the 1964 Hospitalization of the Mentally Ill Act: "A person hospitalized in a public hospital for a mental illness shall, during his hospitalization, be entitled to medical and psychiatric care and treatment."

The dimensions of the right were stated by the *Rouse* court in these terms:

> The hospital need not show that the treatment will cure or improve him but only that there is a bona fide effort to do so. This requires the hospital to show that initial and periodic inquiries are made into the needs and conditions of the patient with a view to providing suitable treatment for him, and that the program provided is suited to his particular needs.

The case was remanded for a hearing on whether petitioner was receiving adequate treatment, with instructions that if he was not the hospital should be afforded a "reasonable opportunity" to initiate treatment, but the court declined "to detail the possible range of circumstances in which release would be the appropriate remedy." Elaboration is also lacking in *Youngberg v. Romeo* (1982), concerning the claim of a person involuntarily committed to a state institution for the mentally retarded that he had a due process right to "habilitation." The Court did hold, however, that "the minimally adequate training required by the Constitution is such training as may be reasonable in light of respondent's liberty interests in safety and freedom from unreasonable restraints."

Several commentators have expressed doubts as to whether the right to treatment concept can actually have a significant impact. It has been questioned whether many courts will be willing to recognize such a right in the face of the unavailability of sufficient medical personnel and medical health appropriations, and whether legislative bodies would in any event respond with the necessary resources in light of other priorities. However, litigation in the federal courts has prompted several states to overhaul their institutional mental health facilities.

It has also been questioned whether the courts are in a position to define and enforce the right to treatment. Psychiatrists have objected that "the definition of treatment and the appraisal of its adequacy are matters for medical determination," while legal commentators have asserted "it would assign too great a role to litigation and to the judiciary to superintend treatment processes."

To this, the author of the *Rouse* decision, Judge Bazelon, responded that courts can define and superintend treatment in the same manner that they now review other administrative action based upon special expertise. "[T]he judge must decide only whether the patient is receiving carefully chosen therapy which respectable professional opinion regards as within the range of appropriate treatment alternatives, not whether the patient is receiving the best of all possible treatment in the best of all possible mental hospitals." But, as the Supreme Court cautioned in *Youngberg,* courts should not "second-guess the expert administrators on matters on which they are better informed."

(c) Release. In most jurisdictions, the decision whether to release a person who was committed following acquittal on grounds of insanity is vested in the committing court or some other court. In some jurisdictions the matter comes up for decision as a matter of course after some period of time has passed since the commitment, while elsewhere it must be initiated by some official, usually the superintendent of the facility where the person is confined, or by the patient himself. The patient may seek his release by way of a writ of habeas corpus except where some similar procedure is specifically required by statute. To avoid the necessity of repeated hearings upon the same patient's claims, some jurisdictions permit challenge of the continuation of the commitment only after a specified time following the date of commitment or the time of the last hearing on the matter. Such restrictions have been upheld as constitutional. In a minority of jurisdictions, some other agency or person, usually the superintendent of the facility in which the patient is confined, may make the release decision.

There is disagreement on whether it is best to put the release decision (when the issue is not raised by the patient directly) in the hands of the court or in those of the administrator of the facility where the patients are confined. Some argue that the psychiatrist should be the exclusive judge of a patient's fitness for release, which may be correct if it is properly assumed that only a medical question is involved. However, the quality of decision-making at that level has been criticized on various grounds, and at least to the extent that those criticisms are valid and in response to a practice of too liberal release practices, there is something to the notion that the judiciary must be involved to ensure that the release decision will "be made by a politically responsible group whose concern will be for community as well as individual welfare."

But since it is difficult to assess who should make the decision unless it is known what the decision involves, it is important to also consider the statutory criteria for release. The standards governing both the administrative and the judicial decisions whether to release the patient fall into four groups: (1) Is the patient sane? (2) Is the patient not dangerous? (3) Is the patient sane *and* not dangerous? (4) Is the patient sane *or* not dangerous? The first of these rests upon an assumption that the basis for commitment was a therapeutic one, and the second on an assumption that commitment is a form of preventive detention. The third standard serves both objectives, for an individual who has regained his sanity but is still dangerous cannot obtain release, nor can one who represents no danger if his mental illness persists. The last standard is difficult to explain, for it would seem to serve neither objective adequately; the dangerous individual may be released if he has recovered his sanity, and the individual who still requires treatment to restore him to sanity may be released if he is not dangerous. Perhaps it rests upon the assumption that a sane person will not be dangerous while an insane person is assumed to be if he cannot prove to the contrary, and that only a person who is both dangerous and insane can justifiably be subjected to continued confinement.

The meaning of the critical words "sane" and "dangerous" in this context is somewhat obscure. As to the former, the applicable statutes differ considerably. They may put the issue in terms of whether the patient is no longer mentally ill, whether he is cured, whether he is restored to sanity, whether he is entirely and permanently recovered, whether he has recovered sufficiently to be released, whether a recurrence of insanity is improbable, or simply whether he is sane. The critical terms are undefined, and thus "they are usually broad enough to allow administrators free rein in the first instance and to give reviewing courts little guidance."

The dangerousness test is most often stated in terms of whether continued detention is necessary for the safety of the patient or the public, but this is also ambiguous.

> Dangerous behavior might be construed to include: (1) only the crime for which the insanity defense was successfully raised; (2) all crimes; (3) only felonious crimes (as opposed to misdemeanors); (4) only crimes for which a given maximum sentence or more is authorized; (5) only crimes categorized as violent; (6) only crimes categorized as harmful, physical or psychological, reparable or irreparable, to the victim; (7) any conduct, even if not labelled criminal, categorized as violent, harmful or threatening; (8) any conduct which may provoke violent retaliatory acts; (9) any physical violence toward oneself; (10) any combination of these.

It is clear that the choice which is made among these alternatives can have a very substantial impact upon release policies, particularly in those jurisdictions where automatic commitment follows acquittal on the basis of a broadly-stated definition of insanity. Under such circumstances, it may happen that the only "danger" is that the patient will again engage in conduct of a nonviolent nature. Although it has been questioned whether confinement can be justified under those circumstances, release was denied upon such facts in *Overholser v. Russell* (1960), where apparently the only risk was that the patient might again write bad checks (the crime for which he was found not guilty by reason of insanity):

> The danger to the public need not be possible physical violence or a crime of violence. It is enough if there is competent evidence that he may commit any criminal act, for any such act will injure others and will expose the person to arrest, trial and conviction. There is always the additional possible danger—not to be discounted even if remote—that a nonviolent criminal act may expose the perpetrator to violent retaliatory acts by the victim of the crime.

As noted earlier (see § 7.4(a)), the Supreme Court has since adopted this position in *Jones v. U.S.* (1983).

The most debated issue concerning the tests for release is whether the sane but dangerous patient should be entitled to release. No, says Model Penal Code § 4.08(2), and this position is explained in this way:

> It seemed preferable to the Institute to make dangerousness the criterion for continued custody, rather than to provide that the committed person may be discharged or released when restored to sanity as defined by the mental hygiene laws. Although his mental disease may have greatly improved, such a person may still be dangerous because of factors in his personality and background other than mental disease. Also, such a standard provides a means for the control of the occasional defendant who may be quite dangerous but who successfully feigned mental disease to gain an acquittal.

In response, it is argued that

> to hold a patient solely for potential dangerousness would snap the thin line between detention for therapy and detention for retribution. * * * Not to release such persons would in effect be to equate an undefined "dangerousness" with an undefined mental illness. Since there can be no such equation, a decision not to release solely on the basis of *potential* dangerousness would be like a decision not to discharge a tubercular patient— though no longer infectious—because he is a potential killer or check forger.

Essentially the latter position prevailed in *Foucha v. La.* (1992), where the Supreme Court found "constitutional significance" in its *Jones v. U.S.* (1983) declaration that "the committed acquittee is entitled to release when he has recovered his sanity or is no longer dangerous." In *Foucha,* information from medical authorities indicated the acquittee's mental illness was in remission but that because of an antisocial personality (an untreatable condition, not a mental disease) he had been engaged in several altercations, but the lower court denied release merely because he was dangerous to himself and others. The Court concluded this violated the due process requirement "that the nature of the commitment bear some reasonable relation to the purpose for which the individual is committed." Because he was not suffering from mental illness, Foucha could not be held as a mentally ill person. Nor could he be imprisoned for purposes of deterrence and retribution, for Foucha had not been convicted of a crime and thus "the State has no such punitive interests." Lastly, Foucha's confinement could not be justified in the interest of protecting others or the community from danger, as detention for such a purpose is constitutionally permissible absent criminal conviction only if "strictly limited in duration," which was not the case here.

In most jurisdictions the burden of proof is on the patient, in habeas corpus or other statutory proceedings for release, to persuade the court that he meets the statutory criteria and is thus entitled to release. Sometimes the burden is a preponderance of the evidence, and sometimes it is clear and convincing evidence. But in either event the burden will often be an insurmountable one. This is particularly so when his petition for release is opposed by the authoritative judgment of the hospital staff. He may be no more successful, however, even when his application has the full support of the hospital authorities, for courts are often skeptical of the ability of mental health professionals to determine whether the individual is no longer dangerous.

Chapter 8

EXCUSES AND OTHER CONDITIONS

Table of Sections

For additional analysis of the above topics and citations to authorities supporting their discussion in this Book, consult the author's 3-volume *Substantive Criminal Law* treatise, also available as Westlaw database SUBCRL. See the Table of Cross-References in this Book.

---

§ 8.1 Defenses Generally

The preceding two chapters have to do with the substantive and procedural aspects, respectively, of one of the best known (albeit probably the least invoked) of all the defenses known in the criminal law: the insanity defense. The present chapter and the following chapter explore a great many other criminal law defenses. It is therefore appropriate at this point, before looking at the particulars of these other defenses, to examine in more general terms just what criminal law defenses are all about.

(a) Classification of Defenses. As discussed earlier (see § 1.2(a)), the substantive criminal law is made up in part of the definitions of the various specific crimes, and in part by many general principles that have application well beyond the confines of any particular offense. Some of these general principles are of the affirmative-liability type, as is the case with those concerning inchoate offenses and parties to crime. The other general principles each have to do with some defense, a term "commonly used, at least in a casual sense, to mean any set of identifiable conditions or circumstances that may prevent conviction for an offense."

One leading criminal law theorist who has given particular and close attention to the subject of defenses, Professor Paul Robinson, has on the basis of his study of the functions and rationales of the various defenses placed them in five general categories. These categories, described seriatim below, are: (i) failure of proof defenses; (ii) offense modification defenses; (iii) justifications; (iv) excuses; and (v) nonexculpatory defenses.

(1) Failure of Proof Defenses. A failure of proof defense is one in which the defendant has introduced evidence at his criminal trial showing that some essential element of the crime charged has not been proved beyond a reasonable doubt. As Robinson explains, such a defense is "in essence no more than the negation of an element required by the definition of the offense," and the "characterization of a given failure of proof as a defense rather than as a defect in proving the offense depends, for the most part, upon common language usage." However, whether or not it is customary to use the defense terminology is not determinative on the question of burden of proof, for as a constitutional matter the prosecution must bear the burden of proving all the elements of the offense beyond a reasonable doubt (see § 1.8(b),(c)). When a defendant invokes this type of "defense," therefore, he is not doing so because he has a burden of proof to meet on the matter at issue, but only because the evidence received in the prosecution's case-in-chief, if left unanswered, might well result in the defendant's conviction.

One illustration of a failure of proof defense would be a mistake of fact or law by virtue of which the defendant lacks the mental state required for the crime charged, discussed earlier in connection with the broader consideration of the mental element part of crime definitions (see § 4.6). The classic case is where a man takes another's umbrella out of a restaurant because he mistakenly believes that the umbrella is his. As was concluded in that earlier context, notwithstanding the longstanding practice of referring to this situation as one involving a "defense," it could just as easily (and more correctly) be said that in light of this mistake of fact it is not possible to convict the defendant because the prosecution is unable to establish the mental state, i.e., the intent to steal the property of another, required for the crime of larceny or its modern equivalent of theft. For purposes of distinction, it was also noted in that earlier discussion that a mistaken belief that one's conduct is not proscribed by the criminal law is ordinarily *not* a defense, although in many jurisdictions the rule is otherwise where such belief is attributable to reasonable reliance upon certain government action (e.g., an assurance from the prosecutor that the contemplated conduct would not be a crime). Except in the rare instances in which knowledge-of-unlawfulness is actually an element of the crime, this kind of mistake would not negate a mental state or any other element of the crime, and thus it would not constitute a failure of proof defense, but rather would more appropriately be placed in the excuses category.

(2) Offense Modification Defenses. Offense modification defenses are different from the failure of proof defenses because they do more than simply negate an element of the offense charged. Rather, they come into play, Professor Robinson explains, when "the actor has apparently satisfied all elements of the offense charged," but yet "has not in fact caused the harm or evil sought to be prevented by the statute defining the offense." An overarching defense broadly defined in those terms would not likely afford sufficient guidance to prosecutors, judges and juries, and consequently it is generally the case that these offense modification defenses identify just what it is on an offense-by-offense basis that would make the defendant's conduct nonproductive of the harm or evil the statute is intended to prevent. Consequently, offense modification defenses typically are defined in terms of a single crime or small group of related crimes. Illustrations would be the so-called Wharton's rule defense to conspiracy in those cases involving two conspirators and an underlying offense requiring the participation of more than one person (see § 11.4(c)(4)), and the abandonment or renunciation defense sometimes recognized as to inchoate offenses (see §§ 10.5(b)(2), 11.4(b)).

Depending upon the form that the statute defining the offense charged takes, a particular defense may fall either into the failure of proof category or the offense modification category. The concept of consent (see § 5.5(a)) provides a useful illustration of this point. Sometimes the absence of consent is included in the definition of the crime charged as one of the elements, as sometimes is the case with the crime of rape (see § 15.4), in which case the defendant's proof of consent by the purported victim would constitute a failure of proof type of defense. On other occasions, however, the crime charged does not have a nonconsent element, in which case it is true as a general proposition that consent is no defense at all. However, in those jurisdictions following the principle in Model Penal Code § 2.11(1) that consent, even when it does not negative an element, is a defense if it "precludes the infliction of the harm or evil sought to be prevented by the law defining the offense," a defendant who established the existence of this kind of consent would have made out an offense modification defense.

(3) Justifications. In contrast to the failure of proof and offense modification defenses discussed above, justification defenses are not grounded in the proposition that the harm caused by the defendant is not of the type sought to be prevented by the offense charged. Rather, as Professor Robinson has explained, the "harm caused by the justified behavior remains a legally recognized harm that is to be avoided whenever possible. Under the special justifying circumstances, however, that harm is outweighed by the need to avoid an even greater harm or to further a greater societal interest." In other words, a justification defense is one that defines conduct "otherwise criminal, which under the circumstances is socially acceptable and which deserves neither criminal liability nor even censure." It is this characteristic that distinguishes justifications from other similar-appearing defenses that are instead properly classified as of the offense modification variety. Thus, burning a field in order to create a firebreak preventing a raging fire from reaching nearby homes is a justification, for the legally recognized harm of destroying another's property by fire is justified as a means of preventing a greater harm. By contrast, when there is consent to a slight battery this is merely offense modification because the conduct was thereby made harmless.

Under the Robinson formulation, justification defenses all have the same internal structure: "triggering conditions permit a necessary and proportional response." Triggering conditions, the circumstances that must exist before the defendant can be deemed to have been eligible to act under a particular justification, typically consist of an event putting at risk some legally-protected interest. With respect to the justification of self-defense, for example, the triggering condition would be a threat of physical harm to the defendant's person. But for the defendant to be justified in responding with defensive force, it is first essential that such a response be necessary, which means that the defendant may "act only when and to the extent necessary to protect or further the interest at stake." Thus if the threat to the defendant is only that of harm to his person on some future occasion, so that there is no need for an immediate response and, indeed, some opportunity to seek less drastic means of avoiding that harm, an immediate use of force in self-defense would not be justified. As for the proportionality requirement, it "places a limit on the maxim harm that may be used in protection or furtherance of an interest." Again using self-defense as an example, our defendant would not be justified in using deadly force just to prevent a bloody nose.

(4) Excuses. Excuses are in some respects like justifications; they apply in the case of a particular offense even though all of the elements of that offense are fully established, and they typically apply to offenses generally instead of only with respect to a particular crime. The principle distinction, however, is that in the case of an excuse conviction is deemed inappropriate because of a lack of responsibility on the part of the defendant. An excuse defense, under the Robinson scheme, has this internal structure: "a *disability* causing an *excusing condition*." The example usually given is a defense that has already been discussed herein in some detail: the insanity defense (see ch. 6 & 7).

The requisite disability may be permanent (subnormality) or temporary (intoxication), internal (insanity) or external (duress). Generally speaking, it may be said that for the disability to have caused an excusing condition it must appear that the condition has one of the following consequences: (i) the defendant's conduct was not a product of his voluntary effort; (ii) the foregoing is not the case, but the defendant failed to perceive the nature or consequences of his conduct; (iii) the foregoing are not the case, but the defendant does not know that his conduct or its results are wrong or criminal; or (iv) the foregoing are not the case, but the defendant is so lacking in control over his conduct that it would not be proper to hold him accountable for it.

At early common law, the distinction between justification and excuse was a critical one, for an acquittal on the basis of justification provided a complete defense, while a finding of excuse merely gave the Crown an opportunity to grant a pardon. The distinction later fell into disuse, however, when both kinds of defenses came to provide a basis for acquittal. Even the Model Penal Code relies very little upon the distinction; as the draftsmen explained: "If it is clear that conduct will not be subject to criminal sanctions, the effort to establish precisely in each case whether that conduct is actually justified or only excused does not seem worthwhile, especially since, in regard to the difficult cases, members of society may disagree over the appropriate characterization." But criminal law theorists, in the main, see value in maintaining and, indeed, clarifying, the distinctions between these two categories of defenses. As Robinson puts it:

> The conceptual distinction remains an important one, however. Justified conduct is correct behavior that is encouraged or at least tolerated. In determining whether conduct is justified, the focus is on the *act*, not the actor. An excuse represents a legal conclusion that the conduct is wrong, undesirable, but that criminal liability is inappropriate because some characteristic of the actor vitiates society's desire to punish him. Excuses do not destroy blame, as do the three groups of defenses previously discussed; rather, they shift it from the actor to the excusing conditions. The focus in excuses is on the *actor*. Acts are justified; actors are excused.

(5) Nonexculpatory Defenses. The final category under Robinson's scheme is that of nonexculpatory defenses, by which is meant those defenses that (unlike the foregoing) are not at all grounded in a lack of culpability of the defendant. Rather, a nonexculpatory defense is supported by some other important public policy consideration. A balancing of interests is involved, but the balancing is different from that which occurs with respect to those defenses falling into the justifications category. In the latter instance, the harm that the defendant has done is deemed to be outweighed by the benefit flowing from his otherwise criminal conduct, but in the case of nonexculpatory defenses the outweighing benefit comes from foregoing conviction of the defendant. Perhaps the best example is the various statutes of limitations, legislative time limits on the commencement of criminal prosecutions, which are "designed to protect individuals from having to defense themselves against charges when the basic facts may have become obscured by the passage of time and to minimize the danger of official punishment because of acts in the far-distant past."

(b) Particular Defenses Classified. What remains to be considered is just where the defenses considered in this and the following chapter fit into the scheme outlined above. Perhaps easiest to deal with are the various defenses included in chapter 9: necessity; public duty; domestic authority; self defense; defense of another; and law enforcement. It is generally accepted that these defenses are, for the most part, properly viewed as justifications, and they are all so classified herein. As to each of them, it may generally be said of the conduct falling within these justifications that the harm done is justified by the fact that the action taken either accomplished a greater good or prevented a greater harm.

Of course, the extent to which the above is true beyond dispute and also without exception will depend to some degree on exactly how the aforementioned defenses are defined and perceived, as may be seen via a couple of illustrations. The first has to do with the defense of necessity (see § 9.1). The necessity defense has sometimes been viewed as analogous to the defense of coercion, the essential difference between the two being that the former has to do with the pressure of natural physical forces (e.g., a fire) while the latter has to do with a threat from a human agent. Under this approach, necessity (as is true of duress) might well be viewed as a defense belonging in the excuses category. On the other hand, if this defense is recast (as it is under Model Penal Code § 2.09) so as to clearly encompass various choice-of-evils situations, no matter what the source of threatened harm, it then becomes clearer that it belongs in the justifications category. The second illustration also has to do with the Model Penal Code, this time with the fact that the Code (e.g., in §§ 3.04(1), 3.05(1)(c), 3.07(1)) broadly defines many justifications as including the situation where the defendant actually (whether reasonably or unreasonably) believes there exists a threatened harm that would, if it really exists, make the defensive response both necessary and proportional. In those instances in which the defendant is mistaken in his belief, what is called a justification would seem more properly characterized as an excuse, for his "conduct has not, in fact, avoided a greater harm or furthered a greater good; it has not caused a net benefit, but rather a net harm."

The actual or proposed defenses in the present chapter are more of a mixed bag, and thus are best considered individually. As for partial responsibility (see § 8.2), a line of California cases treated certain mental illness which did not support an insanity defense as a type of partial insanity that mitigated murder to manslaughter notwithstanding the fact that the defendant had the mental state required for a murder conviction. That variety of partial responsibility, best classified in the excuses category, was adopted in no other American jurisdiction and was ultimately rejected by the legislature in California, and so today it may be said without qualification that the partial responsibility defense is of the failure of proof type, for what is involved is using mental illness to negate a required mental state.

No state has recognized the so-called XYY chromosome defense (see § 8.3); suffice it to note that if a defense of this type is recognized in the future, it will doubtless be properly characterized as being of the excuse variety. As for automatism (see § 8.4), which results in the conduct not being a product of the defendant's determination or else causes a defect in the defendant's perception or knowledge of the nature of his conduct or the consequences thereof, it has been argued that this defense in its entirely is best treated as an excuse because "it is not qualitatively different from other excusing conditions." But since modern criminal codes treat the voluntary act requirement as a necessary element of each offense (see 5.1(c)), it might well be concluded that the more common automatism case in which the defendant's condition has caused him to act involuntarily is a defense of the failure of proof variety.

Regarding intoxication (see § 8.5), it falls into either of two categories, depending upon the circumstances. Intoxication is sometimes recognized as a reason why the defendant may be deemed to lack a necessary mental state for the crime charged, and when that is so and in addition it is determined the intoxication actually had that effect, then obviously the defense is of the failure of proof variety. On the other hand, when the state of intoxication is not the fault of the defendant and has produced certain defects in the defendant's understanding of the nature of his conduct or in his capacity for self control, any defense recognized because of those circumstances is clearly an excuse.

The infancy defense (see § 8.6) also falls into the excuses category. Although it is common to rely upon chronological age limits below which irresponsibility is conclusively presumed, the expectation is that, for the most part, the defense will exclude from criminal liability those whose immaturity renders them blameless because of their diminished capacity to appreciate the physical or moral consequences of their conduct. As for the duress defense (see § 8.7), it is likewise properly classified as an excuse. The notion here is that there are circumstances in which a defendant should not be held accountable for his conduct because of an insufficient ability to control it, brought on by a threat of a harm too severe to be resisted.

Finally, regarding the entrapment defense (see § 8.8), it might at first blush appear very similar to the duress defense, in that again the defendant is being excused because he is not fully responsible for his actions. Such an approach is suggested by the traditional view of entrapment, developed by the Supreme Court in *Sorrells v. U.S.* (1932), where the defense is said to turn upon whether the defendant was predisposed or "otherwise innocent." But *Sorrells* also says that the entrapment defense only applies when "officials of the Government" (directly or through their agents) "induce [a crime's] commission in order that they may prosecute," which strongly suggests that entrapment is better viewed as a nonexculpatory defense. Such a characterization of the defense is unquestionably the correct one in those jurisdictions which have adopted the theory of entrapment expressed in the *Sorrells* concurrence, i.e., that courts must refuse to convict an entrapped defendant not because he lacked culpability, but rather because the methods employed on behalf of the government to bring about the crime cannot be countenanced.

§ 8.2 Partial Responsibility

A defendant in a criminal case, at the time he engaged in the conduct giving rise to the charges against him, may have been suffering from an abnormal mental condition that was not of a kind or character to afford him a successful insanity defense under the right-wrong test or other standard applicable in that jurisdiction. But, while this defendant is therefore ineligible for a finding of not guilty by reason of insanity, his mental abnormality may nonetheless be a most relevant consideration in the determination of whether he is guilty of the crime charged. Under the doctrine referred to as partial responsibility, diminished responsibility, or (somewhat less accurately) partial insanity, recognized in some but not all jurisdictions, evidence concerning the defendant's mental condition is admissible on the question of whether the defendant had the mental state that is an element of the offense with which he is charged.

Such evidence has been most frequently received in cases requiring a determination whether the defendant acted with the premeditation and deliberation required for first degree murder. In at least some jurisdictions, however, this evidence has been held admissible on the issue of whether the defendant's crime is murder or manslaughter and the issue of whether the defendant had the requisite mental state for other lesser offenses.

(a) Distinguished From Insanity Defense. It must be emphasized that the notion of partial responsibility is quite separate and distinct from the defense of insanity. If a successful insanity defense is interposed, the result is a finding of not guilty by reason of insanity (see § 7.3(d)) and, usually, commitment of the defendant (see § 7.4). By contrast, an appropriate showing of partial responsibility will result in a finding of not guilty of the offense charged, although the circumstances will usually be such that conviction of some lesser offense is still possible. The ultimate result, then, is not commitment but rather a sentence of imprisonment following conviction of an offense carrying lesser penalties than the crime originally charged.

The distinction between partial responsibility and the defense of insanity is sometimes important for other reasons as well. Thus, for example, failure to give advance notice, to enter a special plea, or to take other steps required only to preserve an insanity defense (see § 7.2(b)) would not bar the introduction of evidence to show partial responsibility. And, in those jurisdictions utilizing the bifurcated trial procedure, where the insanity defense is held in abeyance until the second stage of the trial following determination of the general guilt of the defendant (see § 7.3(c)), evidence of partial responsibility is admissible at the first stage of the trial and only the first stage.

In those jurisdictions which have rejected the doctrine of partial responsibility, the rejection has usually occurred as a result of a mistaken assumption that the doctrine does not involve considerations separate and distinct from established law concerning the defense of insanity. Insanity is viewed as an all-or-nothing proposition, so that the defendant must either establish his insanity as a complete defense or else be held fully responsible for the crime charged. The insanity defense is considered to be the only means by which evidence of defendant's abnormal mental condition may be admitted, apparently on the erroneous conclusion that a defendant who did know right from wrong (or, who otherwise fails to establish a complete defense of insanity) must thereby have possessed the requisite mental state for the crime charged.

On the other hand, those jurisdictions which have accepted the notion that evidence of an abnormal mental condition may be considered on the issue whether the defendant had the mental state required for the offense charged have typically done so by emphasizing the difference between partial responsibility and the insanity defense. Because the various tests for insanity as a defense do not of necessity require a determination of defendant's ability to have the specific mental state defined for the offense charged, there is no inconsistency in the conclusion that a defendant undeserving of a finding of not guilty by reason of insanity might nonetheless have lacked that mental state. For example, if such a defendant is charged with first degree murder, thus calling for the prosecution to prove that the killing was committed with premeditation and deliberation (see § 13.7(a)), evidence tending to show that the defendant did not premeditate or deliberate because of a mental abnormality remains most relevant. Or, if such a defendant is charged with manslaughter of the recklessness type, thus calling for the prosecution to show defendant was consciously aware of the risk of death (see § 14.4(a)), evidence tending to show that defendant was unaware because of some mental abnormality would again be most relevant.

(b) Specific Applications. The majority of the courts that have held evidence of an abnormal mental condition admissible on the issue of mental state have been concerned with the admission of this evidence for the purpose of negating the premeditation or deliberation requisite to first degree murder. A considerably lesser number have held the evidence admissible to negate the existence of malice aforethought and thereby reduce a charge of murder to manslaughter, undoubtedly because there exists much doubt about the relevancy of subjective factors in drawing the line between those two crimes. Finally, in a few instances the doctrine of partial responsibility has also been applied where the question was whether the defendant had the requisite mental state to be convicted of any crime.

(1) First or Second Degree Murder. In many states murder is divided into two degrees, the purpose being to limit the applicability of the more severe sanction (usually the death penalty) to only certain kinds of murder. One form of first degree murder is intent-to-kill murder accompanied by premeditation and deliberation. In the absence of premeditation and deliberation, intent-to-kill murder constitutes murder in the second degree (see § 13.7). Deliberation requires a cool mind that is capable of reflection, while premeditation requires that the one with the cool mind did reflect—at least briefly—before his act of killing.

Given the obviously subjective character of the premeditation and deliberation requirements, it is perhaps not surprising that many courts have adopted the partial responsibility doctrine in cases involving a prosecution for first degree murder. It has been noted, for example, that it would be grossly inconsistent to receive evidence of voluntary intoxication to disprove premeditation and deliberation, and then not accept evidence of an involuntary mental condition for the same purpose.

Moreover, given the fact that the premeditation and deliberation requirements are usually relevant to the critical question of which murderers may be subjected to the death penalty, it is clear that the doctrine of partial responsibility is particularly applicable here.

A heavier sanction accompanies premeditated murder, not because of the act of murder but because of the mental processes which accompany it. If the objective of this heavier sanction be deterrence, it is doubtful that a person *incapable* of premeditation and deliberation will be dissuaded from committing a premeditated murder by the higher penalty imposed for murder accompanied by these mental processes. Nor is a "fully responsible" person likely to be deterred because those who are incapable of premeditation also face the same punishment. If this differential treatment reflects a community attitude that "cold-blooded" murder is somehow more culpable than killing which springs from momentary impulses, these traditional notions are actually undermined by inflicting the penalty reserved for the "cold-blooded" on those capable only of the impulse.

(2) Murder or Manslaughter. In most jurisdictions, voluntary manslaughter consists of an intentional homicide committed under certain extenuating circumstances, namely, that the defendant, when he killed the victim, was in a state of passion engendered in him by an adequate provocation (i.e., a provocation which would cause a reasonable man to lose his normal self-control; see § 14.2). It is important to note, for purposes of comparison with the preceding discussion, that "the murder-manslaughter distinction has a wholly different history and is based on wholly different criteria from those involved in distinguishing degrees of murder. The former is of common law origin, the latter statutory; the former involves an objective test, the latter subjective."

Under the traditional doctrine, then, heat-of-passion voluntary manslaughter is distinguishable from murder by resort to objective criteria. True, the defendant must have in fact been provoked and his passion must have in fact not "cooled" at the time of the killing, but in addition the circumstances must have been such that a reasonable man would have been provoked and would not have cooled (see § 14.2). This being the case, it is apparent that the concept of partial responsibility has no place in the decision whether what has been charged as murder is actually heat-of-passion voluntary manslaughter. To hold otherwise would conflict with the reasonable man standard, which by its very nature presumes a person without serious mental and emotional defects.

There is a modern tendency, not yet far advanced, to add other extenuating circumstances in the category of voluntary manslaughter. For example, while a reasonable belief in the existence of circumstances requiring the use of deadly force is necessary for complete exoneration under an affirmative defense such as self-defense (see § 9.4), there is some authority that an "imperfect" defense (in the sense that the belief was not reasonable) will downgrade what would otherwise be murder to voluntary manslaughter (see § 14.3). In those jurisdictions recognizing the "imperfect" defense type of voluntary manslaughter, it would be appropriate to introduce evidence of the defendant's abnormal mental condition as bearing on the question of whether he unreasonably believed that defensive measures involving deadly force were called for.

It is well to keep in mind that we are here concerned with the dividing line between murder and manslaughter and that the traditional distinction between the two crimes is that murder is a killing "with malice aforethought." That phrase, however, has not been given its literal meaning (see § 13.1(a)). Thus, it is more meaningful to say that a killing is murder if done (1) with intent to kill, (2) with intent to do serious bodily harm, (3) with a depraved heart (i.e., extremely negligent conduct), or (4) in the commission or attempted commission of a felony (see §§ 13.2, 13.3, 13.4, 13.5, respectively), subject to the qualification that an intentional homicide is only manslaughter if the killing occurred in a heat of passion (objective test) or, perhaps, in an "imperfect" defense. If this prevailing meaning of "malice aforethought" is accepted, then, as noted above, the only occasion for receiving evidence of the defendant's abnormal mental condition on the issue of malice aforethought will be when the evidence relates to a claim that the defendant believed (albeit unreasonably) that defensive deadly force was required.

At one time, evidence of the defendant's mental condition as it relates to the murder versus manslaughter issue was not so limited in California, but this can only be explained on the ground that the California courts had adopted a somewhat unusual definition of malice aforethought. In *People v. Conley* (1966), Conley was charged with murder because he shot and killed both a woman with whom he had been romantically involved and her husband. A defense psychiatrist testified that the defendant "was in a dissociative state at the time of the killings and because of personality fragmentation did not function with his normal personality." The trial judge refused to instruct on manslaughter, and on appeal it was held that this was prejudicial error because that testimony raised a doubt as to whether the defendant killed with malice aforethought.

Noting that manslaughter was defined by statute as "the unlawful killing of a human being without malice," the *Conley* court first concluded that the language of the statute did not require the conclusion that malice could be negated only by the usual provocation formula. The court then proceeded to identify another kind of mitigating circumstance that would make the defendant's crime only manslaughter: "If because of mental defect, disease, or intoxication, * * * the defendant is unable to comprehend his duty to govern his actions in accord with the duty imposed by law, he does not act with malice aforethought and cannot be guilty of murder * * *."

As is made even more apparent by the *Conley* court's repeated references to their earlier decision in *People v. Gorshen* (1959), this added mitigating circumstance concerns an absence of self-control such as would likely afford a complete insanity defense under any of the extant insanity tests except *M'Naghten*. The one-time *Conley* rule, then, can best be understood as a limited measure for taking account of a defendant's inability to conform his conduct to the requirements of law, adopted in a jurisdiction where *M'Naghten* was the sole test for insanity, and where departure from *M'Naghten* was believed to be a matter for the legislature.

(3) Crime or No Crime. The term partial responsibility may be misleading, for it suggests that it involves a doctrine under which a defendant is partially responsible for the commission of some offense. This, of course, is not true. If the defendant's mental condition was such that he did not premeditate and deliberate, then there is *no* responsibility for first degree murder but *full* responsibility for second degree murder. Likewise, if it was such that he killed without malice aforethought, then there is *no* responsibility for murder but *full* responsibility for manslaughter. This suggests, of course, that there may be instances in which the doctrine of partial responsibility might be applied so as to result in a complete acquittal, in that there is no lesser offense as to which the defendant possesses the requisite mental state.

This might even occur on a charge of murder. In *People v. Gorshen* (1959), for example, the defense psychiatrist testified that the defendant's abnormal mental condition was such that his act of killing was not intentional. The trial judge acknowledged that if he accepted the psychiatrist's testimony in toto he should acquit the defendant, and the defendant claimed on appeal from the judge's finding of guilty of murder in the second degree that he should have been acquitted. Certainly conviction of voluntary manslaughter would not have been appropriate if the psychiatrist's testimony had been accepted, for voluntary manslaughter has always been defined as an *intentional* homicide under certain extenuating circumstances (see §§ 14.2, 14.3).

The possibility of complete acquittal may be even greater as to charges outside the homicide area, for there will often be no lesser offense which remains proved in the face of evidence of defendant's abnormal mental condition. Such a result could be anticipated, for example, if the evidence raised a reasonable doubt of defendant's intent to steal in a larceny case or robbery case, intent to commit a crime within the dwelling in a burglary case, intent to escape in a felonious escape case, or the requisite knowledge in an income tax evasion case. Some courts have nonetheless applied the partial responsibility doctrine to offenses other than homicide, at least if the offense is of the specific intent variety.

(c) Policy Considerations. The logic of the partial responsibility doctrine would seem to be unassailable. The reception of evidence of the defendant's abnormal mental condition, totally apart from the defense of insanity, is certainly appropriate whenever that evidence is relevant to the issue of whether he had the mental state constituting a necessary element of the crime charged. Were it otherwise, major crimes specifically requiring a certain bad state of mind would, in effect, be strict liability offenses as applied to abnormal defendants.

Opposition to the doctrine has been based more upon what are thought to be practical difficulties in its use. It is claimed, for example, that juries are ill equipped to handle psychiatric testimony which makes subtle distinctions, such as that a defendant's mental impairment prevented him from premeditating and deliberating but not from having an intent to kill. This difficulty, some say, stems not from the partial responsibility doctrine but rather from the fact that in some jurisdictions the distinction between first and second degree murder has not been made sufficiently clear. But others seriously question the trustworthiness and reliability of psychiatric testimony on the mental state issue, especially in light of the "marked propensity of those who purport to have psychiatric expertise to tailor their testimony to the particular client whom they represent." It has been suggested, however, that this problem may be solved through "careful administration by the trial judge," who should ordinarily "require counsel first to make a proffer of the proof to be adduced outside the presence of the jury" and "then determine whether the testimony is grounded in sufficient scientific support to warrant use in the courtroom, and whether it would aid the jury in reaching a decision on the ultimate issues."

Another argument is that the doctrine will result in compromise verdicts—that a jury divided on the sufficiency of an insanity defense may agree upon the middle ground of partial responsibility and conviction for a lesser offense. In response, it has been noted that many opportunities for compromise already exist and that compromise is not necessarily wrong when it is the only way to the quantum of punishment appropriate under the circumstances.

Finally, concern has been expressed that application of the partial responsibility doctrine will result in inadequate protection for the public. Individuals who theretofore would have been convicted of the offense charged and subjected to a long prison term or else found not guilty by reason of insanity and committed indefinitely, it is feared, will now serve shorter sentences for lesser offenses or else be completely acquitted at trial. To the extent that the doctrine is utilized only to reduce what otherwise would be murder in the first degree to either murder in the second degree or voluntary manslaughter, the risks are probably not great. The sentences for these lesser offenses are "usually long enough to keep the offender in custody until he is cured or has reached an age when the criminal tendencies of even the most dangerous are likely to have disappeared." But the danger is a real one when the result will be complete acquittal or conviction of a relatively minor offense, at least until such time as commitment procedures equivalent to those following a finding of not guilty by reason of insanity are made applicable.

Doubtless underlying all of these concerns is the fear that recognition of the partial responsibility doctrine will, as a practical matter, often result in the prosecution being unable to meet its burden of proof. While the burden of proof as to the insanity defense may be placed on the defendant (see § 7.3(a)), this is not so as to the matter of partial responsibility. "Since the purpose of the diminished-capacity doctrine is to establish the absence of an essential element of the crime, the state still has the burden of overcoming this effort by proof of all the essential elements beyond a reasonable doubt."

(d) Constitutional Considerations. As several cases rejecting the partial responsibility doctrine have acknowledged, the significance of such a rejection is that psychiatric evidence is inadmissible on the issue of whether the defendant in fact possessed the requisite mental state. This evidentiary consequence prompts the question of whether such exclusion of psychiatric evidence violates the defendant's constitutional right to present evidence in his own behalf. Some state court decisions embracing the partial responsibility doctrine have suggested that because of this due process right they could hardly reach any other result, but federal courts have generally been unreceptive to the claim that nonrecognition of the partial responsibility doctrine is unconstitutional.

In *Chambers v. Miss.* (1973), holding that strict application of the state's evidentiary rules to exclude the defendant's evidence violated due process, the Court declared: "The right of an accused in a criminal trial to due process is, in essence, the right to a fair opportunity to defend against the state's accusations. The rights to confront and cross-examine witnesses and to call witnesses in one's own behalf have long been recognized as essential to due process." As explained in Justice Harlan's concurring opinion, this right of a defendant is violated where "the State has recognized as relevant and competent the testimony of this type of witness, but has arbitrarily barred its use by the defendant." Thus, if psychiatric testimony is relevant and competent on the mental state issue and there is no good reason for barring it, then, as some have concluded, exclusion of this evidence is constitutionally impermissible.

This question was confronted in *Hughes v. Mathews* (1978), holding that petitioner's rights were violated when he was not allowed to introduce psychiatric testimony to show that he lacked the specific intent required for the charged crime of first-degree murder. Noting that evidence is relevant "when it pertains to a fact in issue and has a tendency to prove or disprove that fact," the federal court concluded that most certainly psychiatric evidence would be relevant on the issue of the defendant's capacity to form an intent to kill. As for the matter of competency, that is, whether psychiatric testimony is "trustworthy evidence of mental state," the court concluded the "best indication that Wisconsin views psychiatric testimony as competent evidence is its use in other parts of the criminal proceeding," that is, with respect to competency to stand trial and the insanity defense. Whether that must be so is perhaps the heart of the matter. Significantly, another panel of the same court later upheld a similar exclusion of psychiatric evidence, doubtless influenced by the intervening state court decision in *Steele v. State* (1980). In *Steele,* the court concluded that psychiatric testimony was relevant and competent to make the "gross evaluation" of whether or not a defendant is criminally responsible under the insanity defense, but that such testimony was not relevant or competent for the "fine tuning" necessary to assess capacity to form an intent of the sort demanded by the criminal law.

This issue was finally resolved by the Supreme Court in *Clark v. Arizona* (2006), where the defendant, on trial for murder of a police officer, undertook to introduce evidence of his mental illness for two purposes: (i) in connection with his affirmative defense of insanity; and (ii) to rebut the prosecution's evidence of the requisite *mens rea* (which was, in this case, intent or knowledge, alternatively, re killing a police officer). The state, which had declined to adopt a diminished capacity defense, prohibited the defendant from introducing such evidence for the latter purpose. The defendant's claim that this limitation violated due process, which the *Clark* majority rejected, was seen as "turn[ing] on the application of [i] the presumption of innocence in criminal cases, [ii] the presumption of sanity, and [iii] the principle that a criminal defendant is entitled to present relevant and favorable evidence on an element of the offense charged against him."

The first presumption, the Court noted, is "that a defendant is innocent unless and until the government proves beyond a reasonable doubt each element of the offense charged," which was not violated in the instant case because the prosecution was required to submit "proof beyond a reasonable doubt that a defendant's state of mind was in fact what the charge states." As for the presumption of sanity, the Court emphasized that it may be placed in issue at two points: (i) relating to the government's burden to show *mens rea* (where "the strength of the presumption of sanity is no greater than the strength of the evidence of abnormal mental state that the factfinder thinks is enough to raise a reasonable doubt"); and (ii) relating to the insanity defense (where the state is constitutionally free to provide that the presumption remains unless the defendant proves insanity "by a preponderance of the evidence or to some more convincing degree"). From this, concluded the *Clark* majority, there flows the "first reason" supporting the Arizona rule: for a state to have such authority re the insanity defense "in practice as well as in theory, it must be able to deny a defendant the opportunity to displace the presumption of sanity more easily when addressing a different issue in the course of the criminal trial." But this, the Court acknowledged "cannot be the sole reason," "for it fails to answer an objection the dissent makes," namely, that "if the same evidence that affirmatively shows he was not guilty by reason of insanity * * * also shows it was at least doubtful that he could form *mens rea*, then he should not be found guilty in the first place."

The *Clark* Court thus turned to proposition [iii] above, concerning a defendant's constitutional right to introduce relevant evidence, noting that (as it had just declared in *Holmes v. South Carolina* (2006)) "well-established rules of evidence permit trial judges to exclude evidence if its probative value is outweighed by certain other factors such as unfair prejudice, confusion of the issues, or potential to mislead the jury." Three such adverse factors were deemed to be present in the instant case, "risks that may reasonably be hedged by channeling the consideration of such evidence to the insanity issue [in states where] a defendant has the burden of persuasion." First of all, there is "the controversial character of some categories of mental disease," that is, the fact that "the diagnosis may mask vigorous debate within the [psychiatric] profession about the very contours of the mental disease itself." Second, there is "the potential of mental-disease evidence to mislead jurors * * * through the power of this kind of evidence to suggest that a defendant suffering from a recognized mental disease lacks cognitive, moral, volitional, or other capacity, when that may not be a sound conclusion at all." And third, there is "the danger of according greater certainty to capacity evidence than experts claim for it," as such evidence "consists of judgment, and judgment fraught with multiple perils," as "a defendant's state of mind at the crucial moment can be elusive no matter how conscientious the enquiry, and the law's categories that set the terms of the capacity judgment are not the categories of psychology that govern the expert's professional thinking."

§ 8.3   The XYY Chromosome Defense

Women normally have two special sex chromosomes (gonosomes) called X chromosomes (XX), while most men have an X chromosome paired with a Y chromosome (XY). Some individuals are born with chromosomal abnormalities, in that they have either too few or too many chromosomes. One of these abnormalities is the so-called "super-male" or XYY, who has an extra Y chromosome. There is evidence that XYY males are more likely than others to engage in antisocial or criminal conduct that will result in their confinement in an institution. However, the behavioral impact of this genetic abnormality has not been precisely determined, and thus an XYY defendant is unlikely to be recognized as having an insanity defense.

(a) Chromosomal Abnormalities. Chromosomes are thread-like structures of complex molecules that transmit the genetic information arranged and ordered in the cell and determine the heredity of all plant and animal life. In human beings, the characteristic number of chromosomes found in the nucleus of each cell is 46. Egg and sperm cells contain 23 chromosomes each, but upon uniting the chromosomes are pooled so that the new individual has 46 chromosomes arranged in 23 pairs. As the fertilized ovum grows, the chromosomes divide so that each normal cell of the human body contains this same number of chromosomes. Twenty-two of the 23 pairs of chromosomes in each cell are called autosomes, while the remaining pair are referred to as gonosomes. The autosomes contain genes that determine most of the biological characteristics of the individual, but the gonosomes contain those genes that determine the person's primary sexual characteristics.

The normal female possesses two X-type gonosomes, or an XX complement, and the normal male possesses one X-type and a much smaller Y-type gonosome, or an XY structure. (The structure may be determined by a process known as karotyping, which involves culturing the cells, photographing the stained chromosomes, and rearranging the photographed chromosomes to fit a standard pattern.) It is thus obvious that it is the sperm of the father that determines the sex of the child. Because the mother's sex chromosomes are both X, each ovum must contain an X chromosome. But the father's XY pair of chromosomes divides in the formation of sperm; one sperm cell contains an X chromosome and the other a Y chromosome. The child will be male (XY) or female (XX), depending upon which sperm cell fertilizes the egg.

This process does not always work properly, and thus some individuals are born with more or less than the normal complement of two gonosomes. Some women, for example, have only one X chromosome (referred to as XO or Turner's Syndrome); others are the so-called "super females" who possess one extra X chromosome (XXX); and even XXXX and XXXXX complements have been reported. As for males (i.e., whenever at least one Y chromosome is present), the most common chromosomal abnormality—occurring in about one of every 400 male births—is the XXY (the Klinefelter Syndrome). Others that have been described and confirmed include the XYY, XXYY, and XXXXY. Of particular interest here are those with an extra Y chromosome, the XYY's or so-called "super males."

(b) The XYY Syndrome. The first report of an XYY male occurred in 1961, but it was not until 1965 that an investigation was conducted into the possible relationship between chromosome abnormalities and antisocial behavior. That year, a team of researchers at the maximum security State Hospital at Carstairs in Kanarkshire, Scotland (for patients who require treatment in conditions of special security on account of their dangerous, violent or criminal propensities), determined that about three per cent of the 315 males tested there were XYY. A year later, other researchers in England examined the chromosome complement of detained males six feet and over in height (XYY's are significantly taller than XY's) and found XYY's in 24% of those mentally subnormal and detained because of antisocial behavior, 8% of those mentally ill and detained because of antisocial behavior, and 8% of those sentenced to imprisonment for 6 months to 5 years. More recent studies in the United States, Australia, and Denmark have also revealed the presence of gross chromosomal errors among criminal or delinquent males in numbers that could not be accounted for by chance alone. There are presently no accurate figures on the proportion of XYY constitutions in the general noncriminal male population, but the best estimates are that the figure would be about one in a thousand (0.1%) and certainly not more than two in a thousand (0.2%).

While some students of the XYY male question whether enough evidence has been collected to warrant use of the term "XYY syndrome," some tentative conclusions about the XYY male have been reached on the basis of the research conducted to date. He is very likely to be extremely tall, with long limbs and facial acne. Contrary to early expectations, he is not predisposed to unusually aggressive behavior; he is much more likely to have committed a crime against property than a crime against the person. However, he is likely to begin his criminal activities at a very early age, although he is not likely to have a significant family history of crime or mental illness. He is much more resistant to conventional corrective training and treatment than other prisoners or patients.

But, while it is now possible to identify some characteristics of the XYY male and to conclude that this type of chromosomal abnormality is found in small but consistent numbers of antisocial males who have been institutionalized for criminal or abnormal behavior, presently available medical evidence is unable to establish a reasonably certain causal connection between the XYY defect and criminal conduct. That is, we know that there exists a strong statistical correlation between the genetic condition and antisocial behavior, but confirmation of the causal link through the demonstration of a physiological mechanism is not yet possible. One theory, as yet unproven, is that the XYY condition causes a certain hormone (plasma testosterone) to be present in abnormal amounts, which in turn brings about a greater degree of "maleness" and thus aggressive behavior. Others reject this theory and instead suggest that the causal connection may ultimately be made on the basis of the known fact that chromosomes are the ultimate source of the biochemical substances called enzymes which regulate all biochemical processes, which in turn are known to have an effect upon behavior. Support for this theory is found in the widespread physical and mental abnormalities observable in persons affected by other chromosomal defects, such as mongolism.

(c) XYY and the Insanity Defense. In view of the limitations on existing knowledge concerning the XYY male, an insanity defense based upon the defendant's XYY condition is unlikely to succeed. The difficulties in presenting this kind of defense are illustrated by *Millard v. State* (1970), where the defendant, on trial for robbery with a deadly weapon, interposed the insanity defense. The basis for his insanity plea, as later developed at trial, was that he had an extra Y chromosome, resulting in his lacking substantial capacity either to appreciate the criminality of his conduct or to conform his conduct to the requirements of law (Maryland follows the A.L.I. test).

The defendant's only medical witness was a professor who had engaged in considerable research in the field of genetics. He testified that he had examined the defendant and found him to be an XYY and that he had studied published reports showing that such a person is likely to have marked antisocial aggressive reactions. In response to a question, the witness stated that the defendant did have a mental defect, but when asked if the defendant lacked substantial capacity either to appreciate the criminality of his conduct or to conform his conduct to the requirement of law, he answered that he could not say because he had not examined him as a psychiatrist and had no competence in that area. Upon further questioning, he asserted the defendant had a propensity toward crime because of his genetic abnormality. On behalf of the state, a psychiatrist testified that in his opinion the defendant was not insane. He added that he had not made any study of the defendant with respect to the extra Y chromosome because, in his judgment, if such a genetic defect existed it was not a mental defect. Upon this evidence, the trial judge declined to submit the issue of the defendant's sanity to the jury, and the defendant was convicted.

The conviction was affirmed on appeal:

[T]o simply state that persons having the extra Y chromosome are prone to aggressiveness, are antisocial, and continually run afoul of the criminal laws, is hardly sufficient to rebut the presumption of sanity and show the requisite lack of "substantial capacity" under § 9(a). Moreover, we think it entirely plain from the record that in testifying that appellant had a "mental defect," Dr. Jacobson did so only in a most general sense, without full appreciation for the meaning of the term as used in § 9(a), and particularly without an understanding that such term expressly excludes "an abnormality manifested only by repeated criminal or otherwise antisocial conduct." But even if it were accepted that appellant had a "mental defect" within the contemplation of § 9(a), Dr. Jacobson, by his own testimony, indicated an inability to meaningfully relate the effect of such defect to the "substantial capacity" requirements of the subsection. * * * In so concluding, we do not intend to hold, as a matter of law, that a defense of insanity based upon the so-called XYY genetic defect is beyond the pale of proof under § 9(a).

As one commentator has suggested, the *Millard* decision illustrates the fact that "an attorney defending an XYY individual will be required to call upon both a geneticist and a psychiatrist to give expert testimony. The geneticist's role would be to testify with respect to the individual's genetic structure, any distinguishing characteristics which are relevant to an insanity defense, and the result of family studies designated to determine the influence of genetics and environment on the development of this individual. The psychiatrist's testimony would focus upon the defendant's mental capacity or condition." But in the absence of sound medical support for an XYY defense, courts are understandably unsympathetic to defense efforts to obtain such expert testimony.

(d) XYY and the Insanity Tests. Assuming such testimony, and perhaps some added knowledge about the XYY in confirmation of existing theories, how will the XYY defendant fare under the various insanity tests? One problem, as illustrated by the testimony in the *Millard* case, is whether an XYY chromosomal abnormality can be said to be a mental disease or defect or, at least, evidence of such a disease or defect. Beyond that, there are questions of whether an XYY condition does have a bearing upon the cognition or control tests.

The initial question is whether an individual with an XYY chromosomal abnormality can be said to be suffering from a "disease of the mind" (under the *M'Naghten* or irresistible impulse tests) or a "mental disease or defect" (under the A.L.I. test). A precise answer cannot be given, for these terms have not been adequately defined by the courts. But if these phrases are given a liberal interpretation, as many have proposed, then this initial difficulty may be overcome. It has been pursuasively argued that it should be sufficient that "the accused suffers from a disorder or disturbance of his mental functioning which goes considerably beyond the usual range of variations in excitability, impulsiveness, obtuseness or lack of self control found in ordinary persons," and that such a showing may be possible as to a defendant with an XYY chromosomal abnormality.

There are also those who state flatly that the XYY individual is suffering only from "physical compulsion or physical abnormality," but they nonetheless believe that the defendant's XYY condition may be admissible as evidence of his mental condition, particularly if some evidence is forthcoming that the physical malady may cause a mental disturbance. Thus, it has been suggested that developments here may parallel those that occurred earlier concerning proof of epilepsy to show mental condition. Courts first insisted upon proof of a link between the malady and mental disturbance, but later they merely required proof of the malady and took judicial notice of the medical fact that epilepsy could have a serious effect on the defendant's mentality.

There is general agreement that it is highly unlikely that a successful insanity defense can be predicated upon an XYY abnormality where the test of criminal responsibility is determined under the *M'Naghten* rules. *M'Naghten* is generally assumed to be restricted to the cognitive element (see § 6.2(b)(2)), and existing knowledge about the XYY individual does not suggest that possession of the extra Y chromosome of itself affects a person's ability to appreciate either the nature and quality of his acts or whether they are wrong.

The chances are somewhat greater that an XYY condition may serve as the foundation for an insanity defense under the irresistible impulse test. Problems exist because of the "unwillingness of geneticists to mechanistically attribute compulsive or aggressive behavior to any single genetic defect" and also because of the uncertainty over the exact meaning of this test (see § 6.3(a)). If the word "impulse" is taken literally, as it probably should not be, to require a sudden loss of control, then it seems unlikely that the XYY defendant can qualify. But a more serious hurdle exists because of the common assumption that this test requires "a complete impairment of ability to * * * control," for it is unlikely that future research will find that the XYY individual has a total lack of control.

In jurisdictions that follow the A.L.I. insanity test (see § 6.5(a)), the XYY syndrome might well be significant in establishing that the defendant lacked substantial capacity to conform his conduct to the requirements of law. Certainly the defendant's chances would be better than under the irresistible impulse test, for the A.L.I. test "does not demand *complete* impairment of capacity. It asks instead for *substantial* impairment." But even here the changes are not substantial, as the A.L.I. test "calls for a more complete lack of mental control over one's acts than is commonly associated with XYY offenders or unusually aggressive individuals generally."

Finally, it is well to note that even if insanity standards were modified so as to encompass the XYY defendant, the defense is not likely to be an attractive one to the defendant. There presently exists no treatment or cure for the XYY anomaly. Thus, an XYY defendant who successfully pleaded insanity "would find himself in a compulsory criminal commitment proceeding," and "once the disease for which he was committed is established as 'in his genes,' he can expect never to be released."

§ 8.4 Automatism

A defense related to but different from the defense of insanity is that of unconsciousness, often referred to as automatism: one who engages in what would otherwise be criminal conduct is not guilty of a crime if he does so in a state of unconsciousness or semi-consciousness. Although this is sometimes explained on the ground that such a person could not have the requisite mental state for commission of the crime, the better rationale is that the individual has not engaged in a voluntary act.

(a) Meaning of "Automatism." The term "automatism," which has appeared in the legal literature with some frequency in recent years, has been defined as connoting the state of a person who, though capable of action, is not conscious of what he is doing. It is to be equated with unconsciousness, involuntary action [and] implies that there must be some attendant disturbance of conscious awareness. Undoubtedly automatic states exist and medically they may be defined as conditions in which the patient may perform simple or complex actions in a more or less skilled or uncoordinated fashion without having full awareness of what he is doing. * * * Clinically, automatism has been described in a wide variety of conditions. These include epileptic and post-epileptic states, clouded states of consciousness associated with organic brain disease, concussional states following head injuries and, less commonly, in some types of schizophrenic and acute emotional disturbance. Metabolic disorders such as anoxia and hypoglycemia as well as drug-induced impairment of consciousness can be manifested by automatic behavior. Finally, as is well known, automatic acts can occur during sleepwalking and hypnagogic states.

(b) The Automatism Defense. Although the cases in the United States are not substantial in number, they support the proposition that automatism is a defense. Thus it has been held that one who kills another when in a clouded state somewhere between sleep and wakefulness is not guilty of a crime. Likewise, one who, while driving a car, suddenly and without warning "blacks out" so that his car runs upon the sidewalk and kills a pedestrian, is not guilty of any crime—unless, of course, because of previous blackouts he is on notice that it may happen again, in which case his conduct in driving may amount to criminal negligence. (So too, there can be other circumstances in which the defense will be unavailable because of defendant's prior awareness of the risk of unconsciousness.)

Consistent with the definition of automatism set out above, American courts have recognized that an automatism defense might be made out when the defendant's condition is brought about by any one of a variety of circumstances, including epilepsy, a stroke, somnambulism, extended lack of sleep, hypnotism, a concussion or some other physical trauma, or even an emotional trauma. While case authority is generally lacking, it has been argued that an automatism defense might be made out by a defendant who, at the time of his or her acts, was suffering from PMS (the premenstrual syndrome), PPP (postpartum psychosis), or PTSD (post-traumatic stress disorder). But it is not enough that the defendant suffers from amnesia and thus cannot remember the events in question, or that he was suffering from a multiple personality disorder. Also, a person who has been "brainwashed" does not have an automatism defense, nor does a person whose unconsciousness is attributable to "voluntary ingestion of alcohol or drugs."

The basis of the automatism defense is seldom made clear in the cases. One may, of course, note some similarities between the insanity defense and the automatism defense, although it is clear that the latter is not merely a facet of the former; the automatism defense may be present notwithstanding the defendant's lack of the "mental disease or defect" that insanity requires. Another explanation is that the automaton-defendant is not criminally liable because he lacks the mental state which the crime requires, and this appears to be the rationale most commonly hinted at in the cases. However, it is undoubtedly more correct to say that such a person is not guilty of a crime because he has not engaged in an "act" (defined as a voluntary bodily movement), and without an act there can be no crime (see § 5.1). This rationale, which is employed in Model Penal Code § 2.01, goes well beyond the no-mental-state reasoning, for it would support an automatism defense to a charge of a strict-liability offense. But under either of the latter two theories the defense, if successful, results in outright acquittal.

Some authority is to be found to the effect that the defendant has the burden of proving the defense of automatism. The prevailing view, however, is that the defendant need only produce evidence raising a doubt as to his consciousness at the time of the alleged crime. If the defense really is concerned with whether the defendant engaged in a voluntary act, an essential element of the crime, then it would seem that the burden of proof must as a constitutional matter be on the prosecution.

(c) Automatism vs. Insanity. As noted earlier (see § 6.1(b)), one of the purposes served by the insanity defense is that it makes possible the commitment of some persons, not as an alternative to conviction and imprisonment, but rather as an alternative to outright acquittal. That is, if the defendant did not commit the acts with the mental state required for conviction of the crime charged, but this is because he was suffering from a mental disease or defect, the result is likely to be a finding of not guilty by reason of insanity followed by commitment rather than a mere finding of not guilty followed by release. In this way, so the argument goes, society is protected from persons who might present a continuing danger to the public.

If, as just noted, the insanity defense has been utilized as if it "superceded" a no-mental-state defense for those who might pose a continuing danger because of their mental illness, it might logically be asked whether there has developed a comparable relationship between the insanity defense and the no-voluntary-act automatism defense. That is, is there here as well pressure to "make the insanity defense the exclusive avenue for bringing subjective evidence into the trial," to the end that those who did not act voluntarily might be committed if there is some chance that they are still dangerous?

The American cases in this area are not particularly helpful in this regard, although they do reflect that what has been described herein as automatism has more often than not been instead labelled insanity, perhaps for the reason suggested above. Consider, for example, the sleepwalking cases. The leading case, *Fain v. Commonwealth* (1879), makes no mention at all of insanity, although the Kentucky court in a subsequent case asserted that it could not see "how these facts [evidence of somnambulism] would constitute any defense other than that embraced in a plea of insanity." Similarly, another court characterized somnambulism as "a species of insanity." To the same effect are the epilepsy cases; sometimes epilepsy has been held to present an insanity defense, sometimes an automatism defense.

The experience in Britain, where the automatism defense has been raised with much greater frequency, is instructive. There are three cases worthy of brief note here: *Regina v. Charlson* (1955); *Regina v. Kemp* (1956); and *Bratty v. Attorney–General for Northern Ireland* (1961). Charlson, who struck his ten-year-old son with a mallet and then threw him out of a window, was charged with (1) causing grievous bodily harm with intent to murder; (2) causing grievous bodily harm with intent to cause such harm; and (3) causing grievous bodily harm (a strict-liability offense). There was evidence that Charlson had a cerebral tumor, because of which he would be subject to outbursts of impulsive violence over which he would have no control. He did not plead insanity, and testimony was offered that he was not suffering from any mental disease. Charlson was acquitted of all three charges by a jury that had been instructed in part as follows:

> No specific intention need be proved by the prosecution before the accused can be found guilty of the third charge * * *. You must, however, be satisfied that he was acting consciously * * *. Therefore, in considering this third charge you have to ask yourself "was the accused knowingly striking his son, or was he acting as an automaton without any control or knowledge of the act which he was committing?" * * * If you are left in doubt about the matter, and you think he might well have been acting as an automaton without any real knowledge of what he was doing, then the proper verdict would be not guilty, even on the third and least serious of these alternatives.

The commentators have uniformly expressed concern over the result in *Charlson*. As one writer put it, "it is difficult to accept with equanimity a state of the criminal law in which it is more than possible, it is proper, to set free someone who on his own showing is likely to be suffering from a condition which may make him repeat an irrational and savage attack on a child with whose welfare he is entrusted by law." A similar concern appears to have influenced the judge in *Kemp,* where the defendant was charged with causing grievous bodily harm to his wife by striking her with a hammer. It was agreed that Kemp was suffering from arteriosclerosis and had not known what he was doing at the time. One doctor, called by the prosecution, gave as his opinion that this was due to melancholia, a disease of the mind induced by the arteriosclerosis. Two other doctors, one called by the defense and one by the prosecution, testified that the defendant's condition did not constitute a disease of the mind.

Although it was Kemp's position that he was entitled to outright acquittal on the basis of *Charlson,* the trial court instructed only on insanity on the ground that the facts of the case fit within *M'Naghten* whether one accepted the evidence of the prosecution or defense: "The hardening of the arteries is a disease which is shown on the evidence to be capable of affecting the mind in such a way as to cause a defect, temporarily or permanently, of its reasoning and understanding, and is thus a disease of the mind within the meaning of the rule." Most significant, the court made it apparent that this conclusion was not based upon any medical definition of the term "mental disease or defect" but rather upon the policy "that people who committed crimes of violence, even though they were not responsible for their actions, ought not be allowed to go free because they might commit an act of violence again."

In *Kemp,* unlike *Charlson,* there was at least some expert testimony of mental disease, but it is generally agreed that the two cases may not be reconciled on this basis. It was noted, for example, that both cases "involved organic interference with the brain," and that it "is difficult to understand why arteriosclerosis can be said to affect the powers of 'reasoning, understanding, and so on,' when a cerebral tumor cannot." *Kemp* was viewed as a way of "meeting what has been accepted as a defect in the law," namely, an avenue of outright release for dangerous defendants.

The matter reached the House of Lords in the *Bratty* case, an appeal from a conviction in a murder case in which both automatism and insanity were raised as defenses. The only evidence on both defenses was Bratty's testimony that he "had some terrible feeling and then a sort of blackness" before the killing, and expert testimony that he was suffering from psychomotor epilepsy at the time he strangled his victim. The trial judge refused to instruct on automatism, and the insanity defense was rejected by the jury. The House of Lords upheld the conviction, explaining that the defendant's own testimony had not provided a basis for an automatism instruction because there was no medical evidence to support the claim of blackout, and that the evidence of psychomotor epilepsy did not provide a basis because the doctors who testified "agreed that psychomotor epilepsy * * * is a defect of reason due to disease of the mind." As stated by Lord Kilmuir, "where the only cause alleged for the unconsciousness is a defect of reason from disease of the mind, and that cause is rejected by the jury, there can be no room for the alternative defense of automatism."

Lord Denning's opinion in *Bratty* has received more attention. He noted that the question of whether the evidence concerning the cause of the defective consciousness establishes a disease of the mind is a policy matter to be decided by the courts rather than the medical experts. As to the policy, he stated: "It seems to me that any mental disorder which has manifested itself in violence and is prone to recur is a disease of the mind. At any rate it is the sort of disease for which a person should be detained in hospital rather than be given an unqualified acquittal." Lord Denning, therefore, quite frankly acknowledged that the need for protective custody of the defendant is a major consideration in determining whether the defendant has an automatism-disease or an insanity-disease.

While *Kemp* and *Bratty* have received a sympathetic reception on the ground that it is desirable to avoid the result reached in *Charlson,* it has been questioned whether "the broadening of the definition of the phrase 'disease of the mind' may not be a cure worse than the ill it is intended to remedy." By this extension of the insanity defense into an area which might otherwise be occupied by the defense of automatism, medical experts are "forced into the position of making statements in court they would not make in the clinic," while a defendant who "has acted unconsciously due to a physical or organic disorder [is] faced with a verdict of insanity and committal" to an institution intended only for the treatment of mental illness. It has been suggested that it would be preferable if provision were made whereby one who interposed a successful automatism defense could be detained or conditionally discharged for the purpose of his receiving the surgical or medical treatment which might be necessary to prevent a recurrence of the unconsciousness.

§ 8.5 Intoxication

One who is charged with having committed a crime may claim in his defense that, at the time, he was intoxicated (by alcohol or by narcotic drugs) and so is not guilty. If the crime in question is that of driving while intoxicated, or of being drunk in a public place, he will not get very far with the defense, for with such crimes intoxication, far from being a defense, is an element of the crime.

With crimes of which intoxication is not an element, the defendant's defense may be: I committed, while intoxicated, an act that I would not have committed when sober, so that my conduct was the result of my intoxication. His claim that he would not have committed the crime had he been sober is no defense, however, any more than one's claim that he would not have committed a crime of violence had he been a less excitable or pugnacious person, or a crime of theft had he been of a less acquisitive nature.

His claim, however, may be the stronger one that, as a result of his intoxication, he possessed a state of mind like that of an insane person—so that he did not know that what he was doing was wrong (in a jurisdiction applying the *M'Naghten* test) or that he was unable to resist what he knew to be wrong (in a jurisdiction adding the irresistible impulse test)—and so he should have the same defense that an insane person would have. He is not, however, insane just because he is intoxicated, for insanity requires a "disease of the mind" (or, in modern terminology, "mental disease or defect"), a requirement that mere drunkenness cannot satisfy; and therefore, being sane, he is not eligible for the defense of insanity.

Nevertheless, though intoxication is not insanity, it does have an effect upon criminal liability in some circumstances. Where the intoxication was "involuntary," it may be a defense in the same circumstances as would insanity. Or, the intoxication may negate the existence of an element of the crime.

(a) Intoxication Negativing Intention or Knowledge. Intoxication is a defense to crime if it negatives a required element of the crime; and this is so whether the intoxication is voluntary or involuntary. Perhaps the defendant is too intoxicated to accomplish the physical act that the crime requires, as where, in a burglary situation, he is so drunk that he cannot move, much less break and enter the building in question. But generally intoxication, when it negatives an element of the crime, does so by negativing some mental element (intent or knowledge) that the crime requires.

Thus one who takes and carries away another person's property by stealth or at gunpoint is not guilty of larceny or of robbery if he is too intoxicated to be able to entertain the necessary intent to steal. One cannot be guilty of burglary when, although he breaks and enters another's house, his intoxication deprives him of the capacity to intend to commit a felony therein. One is not guilty of rape, or of assault with intent to rape, if he is intoxicated to such an extent that he is unable to entertain the intent to have sexual intercourse. Assault with intent to murder is not committed by one too drunk to have an intent to kill. The same result obtains as to all crimes with the mental state of "intent." A crime defined as "knowingly" (and sometimes a crime defined as "wilfully," when "wilfully" means "knowingly") doing some act may be negatived by intoxication which negatives the required knowledge. A crime (like forgery or false pretenses) that requires an intent to defraud is not committed by one too drunk to have such an intent.

On the same basis, intoxication that negatives the underlying felony is a defense to a charge of felony murder. Thus, a defendant, charged with first degree murder on account of a killing during the commission of a robbery, may properly defend himself from the first degree murder charge on the ground that, being too intoxicated to entertain the intent to rob, he was not guilty of the underlying felony of robbery.

It is sometimes stated that intoxication can negative a "specific intent" which the crime in question may require (meaning some intent in addition to the intent to do the physical act which the crime requires), but it cannot negative a crime's "general intent" (meaning an intent to do the physical act—or, perhaps, recklessly doing the physical act—which the crime requires). Some cases therefore have held that voluntary intoxication cannot be a defense to rape even though it blots out the intent to have intercourse, since that intent is a general intent and not a specific intent. But this is wrong on principle, for if intoxication does in fact negative an intention that is a required element of the crime (whether it be called specific intent or general intent), the crime has not been committed. Some cases have held that intoxication cannot be a defense to battery, a crime sometimes said to require only a general intent. This, however, is correct on principle, since battery can be committed not only with an intent to do the physical act of striking the other person (which intoxication can negative) but also, without any such intent to strike, by recklessly striking; and recklessness cannot, by the weight of authority, be negatived by intoxication (see § 8.5(c)).

A few jurisdictions, going even further astray, have held that voluntary intoxication is no defense even when it negatives the "specific intent" or knowledge that a crime requires. This view is clearly wrong.

By way of conclusion, it may be said that it is better, when considering the effect of the defendant's voluntary intoxication upon his criminal liability, to stay away from those misleading concepts of general intent and specific intent. Instead one should ask, first, what intent (or knowledge) if any does the crime in question require; and then, if the crime requires some intent (knowledge), did the defendant in fact entertain such an intent (or, did he in fact know what the crime requires him to know).

In order for intoxication to serve as a defense to a crime by blotting out some intent or knowledge which the crime requires, it is enough that the defendant, because of his intoxication, actually lacked the requisite intent or knowledge. (Some of the factors pertinent to that determination are "the quantity of intoxicant consumed, the period of time involved, the actor's conduct as perceived by others (what he said, how he said it, how he appeared, how he acted, how his coordination or lack thereof manifested itself), any odor of alcohol or other intoxicating substance, the results of any tests to determine blood-alcohol content, and the actor's ability to recall significant events.") He need not be insane or so intoxicated as to be unconscious or to be incapable of distinguishing between right and wrong. One who, having already formed the intention to commit a crime, drinks in order to work up his nerve to commit the crime, cannot avail himself of the defense of intoxication even though, by the time he does commit the crime, he has become too intoxicated to entertain the intent that the crime requires.

(b) Intoxication Negativing Premeditation and Deliberation. Just as intoxication may negative some required intention or knowledge, so too it may negative the premeditation and deliberation that a common type of first degree murder statute requires. Just as one may be so emotionally upset, or in such a panic, or so mentally abnormal (though not insane), as to be incapable of premeditation and deliberation (see § 13.7(a)), so intoxication may rob him of his capacity to premeditate and deliberate and thus reduce his crime from first degree to second degree murder. It is generally, held, however, that intoxication cannot further reduce the homicide from second degree murder down to manslaughter. This is because one may be guilty of second degree murder, in most jurisdictions which divide murder into two degrees, by killing without any intent to kill or injure but with a high degree of recklessness (the "depraved heart" type of murder, see § 13.4), and, as we shall see below, although intoxication can negative a required intention, it cannot (by the majority view) negative recklessness. Nevertheless, there is some authority for the proposition that intoxication which blots out not only the premeditation and deliberation but also the intent to kill or do serious injury will reduce a homicide down to manslaughter.

Once again, for intoxication to negative premeditation and deliberation it must be so severe as to rob the defendant of his ability to premeditate and deliberate, although it need not in addition be so great as to render him unconscious or to deprive him of his normal ability to know right from wrong. Once again, too, he must not, before becoming intoxicated, have premeditated and deliberated and formed an intent to kill, then drinking to get up his nerve; he is eligible for a first degree murder conviction even though by the time of the killing he may have become so intoxicated that he was no longer capable of premeditation and deliberation.

(c) Intoxication and Recklessness or Negligence. Some crimes may be committed without any sort of intention or knowledge but with some degree of criminal negligence or recklessness. As we have seen (see § 4.4), the word "negligence" is often used in different ways, although under the better view negligence (in the tort sense) must be distinguished from criminal negligence or a high degree of negligence (conduct, measured by an objective standard, which creates a high degree of risk) and from recklessness (also requiring a subjective awareness of the risk).

When the defendant's actions are judged by an objective standard—whether a reasonable man would be aware of the risk—then it is beyond dispute that the defendant's intoxication is no defense. Just as in the law of torts, the defendant is held to the standard of the reasonable man of ordinary prudence, so that his ignorance of the risk because of his intoxication is not relevant. Thus, when one is charged with assault upon a police officer under a statute requiring a showing that he "knows or reasonably should know that such victim is a peace officer," his intoxication may be considered by the jury in determining whether he actually knew the victim was an officer but not in determining whether he reasonably should have known.

But if the crime requires what is most properly called recklessness, in that the defendant must be aware of the risk which his conduct creates, then what is the effect of his unawareness because of intoxication? There is some authority for the proposition that, where awareness is required for criminal liability, lack of awareness because of intoxication negatives the crime; that so long as he is actually unaware of the risk, it makes no difference how he came to be unaware. On principle, this view might seem correct. However, the majority of cases in America support the creation of a special rule relating to intoxication, so that, if the only reason why the defendant does not realize the riskiness of his conduct is that he is too intoxicated to realize it, he is guilty of the recklessness which the crime requires. Model Penal Code § 2.08(2) adopts the latter view on the ground "that awareness of the potential consequences of excessive drinking on the capacity of human beings to gauge the risks incident to their conduct is by now so dispersed in our culture that it is not unfair to postulate a general equivalence between the risks created by the conduct of the drunken actor and the risks created by his conduct in becoming drunk." Many of the modern recodifications follow the Model Penal Code in this respect.

(d) Intoxication and Self Defense. In order for one who kills or injures another to avail himself of the defense of self defense, it is necessary that he reasonably believe that his adversary intends to kill or injure him and that the only way to prevent this result is to kill or injure the adversary first. It may be that an intoxicated defendant actually believes these matters, but had he been sober he would have not believed them. At least where his intoxication is voluntary, he does not have the defense of self defense, which requires that the defendant appraise the situation as would a reasonable *sober* man.

(e) Intoxication and Voluntary Manslaughter. One of the requirements for the reduction of an intentional homicide from murder down to voluntary manslaughter is the requirement that the defendant must have been provoked into a reasonable loss of self control by his victim's conduct (see § 14.2(b)). It may be that a defendant, while intoxicated, is actually provoked by the other's conduct into killing him, although, had he been sober, he would not have been so provoked. Thus intoxication may make the defendant more pugnacious or excitable than he is when he is sober. Since the provocation that will do for voluntary manslaughter must be sufficient to arouse a heat of passion in a reasonable *sober* man, the defendant's voluntary intoxication which unreasonably provokes him will not do to reduce his homicide to manslaughter. But, if the provocation would be adequate with respect to a sober man, then the fact of defendant's intoxication is relevant in determining whether he was in fact acting in the heat of passion.

(f) Prohibiting Evidence of Voluntary Intoxication. In *Mont. v. Egelhoff* (1996), the plurality had occasion to present an historical perspective with regard to the receipt of evidence of voluntary intoxication to disprove the existence of the defendant's mental state at the time of his alleged crime. As the plurality noted, the "stern rejection of inebriation as a defense" in the English common law that "became a fixture of early American law as well" did not "permit the defendant to show that intoxication prevented the requisite *mens rea*." However, "by the end of the 19th century, in most American jurisdictions, intoxication could be considered in determining whether a defendant was capable of forming the specific intent necessary to commit the crime charged," though "fully one-fifth of the States either never adopted the 'new common-law rule' * * * or have recently abandoned it." This latter position, the *Egelhoff* plurality opined, "has considerable justification" because it "deters drunkenness or irresponsible behavior while drunk" and "comports with and implements society's moral perception that one who has voluntarily impaired his own faculties should be responsible for the consequences."

Montana is one of the states where, by statute, voluntary intoxication "may not be taken into consideration in determining the existence of a mental state." At Egelhoff's trial there for deliberate homicide, evidence of his intoxication was admitted in an effort to show he lacked the coordination to have physically accomplished the killings, but the trial court instructed the jury it could not consider that intoxication in determining whether the defendant had the statutory mental state of "knowingly" or "purposefully." The state supreme court held that the statutory prohibition on so using evidence of voluntary intoxication violated due process, but in *Egelhoff* the Supreme Court disagreed, albeit in a manner that leaves the governing principles in some doubt.

The four-Justice plurality in *Egelhoff* started with the premise that there is not an absolute right to present all relevant evidence, but only a due process right not to have evidence excluded when such exclusion "offends some principle of justice so rooted in the traditions and conscience of our people as to be ranked as fundamental." Given the history described above, they concluded the defendant had not made a showing of such a fundamental principle. "Although the rule allowing a jury to consider evidence of a defendant's voluntary intoxication where relevant to *mens rea* has gained considerable acceptance, it is of too recent vintage, and has not received sufficiently uniform and permanent allegiance to qualify as fundamental, especially since it displaces a lengthy common-law tradition which remains supported by valid justifications today."

The four dissenting Justices, on the other hand, began their analysis with the "simple principle" that "due process demands that a criminal defendant be afforded a fair opportunity to defend against the State's accusations." The challenged statute denied the defendant in *Egelhoff* that opportunity, the dissenters rightly concluded, for it "forestalls the defendant's ability to raise an effective defense by placing a blanket exclusion on the presentation of a type of evidence that directly negates an element of the crime, and by doing so, it lightens the prosecution's burden to prove that mental-state element beyond a reasonable doubt."

A fifth vote for either position was not forthcoming, however, as the remaining Justice (Ginsburg) characterized the Montana statute differently, namely, "as a measure redefining *mens rea*" and not "merely an evidentiary prescription." With the statute so characterized, she then concluded that "it is within the legislature's province to instruct courts to treat a sober person and a voluntarily intoxicated person as equally responsible for conduct." If such characterization is appropriate, there is much to be said for this conclusion, though two members of the Court expressly reserved judgment on that question. However, while Justice Ginsburg supported her characterization of the statute with the cogent observation that it appears in the "Crimes" title of the Montana Code rather than in the title containing evidentiary rules, the four dissenters stressed that such a "reading of Montana law is plainly inconsistent with that given by the Montana Supreme Court."

(g) Involuntary Intoxication as a Defense. Thus far we have been considering the usual case where the defendant is "voluntarily" intoxicated (where his intoxication is "self-induced," as it is sometimes expressed). We have seen that such intoxication is a defense only if it negatives some required element of the crime in question. It is not enough that it puts the defendant in a state of mind which resembles insanity. Involuntary intoxication, on the other hand, does constitute a defense if it puts the defendant in such a state of mind, e.g., so that he does not know the nature and quality of his act or know that his act is wrong, in a jurisdiction which has adopted the *M'Naghten* test for insanity. It is akin to insanity because there is no immoral or blameworthy stigma attached to the condition.

When is intoxication, through alcohol or drugs, properly characterized as involuntary? One such case is when the intoxication has resulted from an innocent mistake by the defendant as to the character of the substance taken, as when another person has tricked him into taking the liquor or drugs. Another, recognized by dicta in some cases, is intoxication under duress, although the courts have been quite restrictive in determining what pressures are required to overcome the will of the actor. Yet another instance of involuntary intoxication is when the substance was taken pursuant to medical advice. Finally, there is pathological intoxication, which is self-induced in the sense that the defendant knew what substance he was taking, but which was "grossly excessive in degree, given the amount of the intoxicant." In the latter case, the intoxication is involuntary only if the defendant was unaware that he is susceptible to an atypical reaction to the substance taken. Moreover, there is a disinclination to recognize the intoxication as involuntary if the alleged pathological intoxication resulted only from the combined effects of a lawfully or involuntarily ingested substance *and* "voluntary ingestion of illegal intoxicants, or of legal intoxicants from which a person should reasonably expect an adverse reaction." The mere fact the defendant is an alcoholic or addict is not sufficient to put his intoxicated or drugged condition into the involuntary category.

(h) Intoxication and Insanity. While, as we have seen, the defense of intoxication is quite different from the defense of insanity, yet excessive drinking may bring on actual insanity (delirium tremens); in such a case, if a defendant does not know right from wrong (in a *M'Naghten* test jurisdiction), he is not guilty of a crime because of his otherwise criminal conduct. However, a temporary mental condition brought about by use of alcohol or drugs, as compared to a "settled" or "established" form of insanity, is not sufficient for a defense of insanity. Conversely, excessive drinking may be behavior that results from some forms of insanity. One who is thus actually insane does not lose the defense of insanity just because, at the time he committed the act in question, he was also intoxicated.

(i) Narcotics Addiction and Chronic Alcoholism. The traditional defense of intoxication, discussed above, must be distinguished from the more recent concern over whether the narcotics addict and chronic alcoholic may be convicted and punished for their status or for certain acts attributable to their condition. The latter problem has often been dealt with in terms of the constitutional prohibition on cruel and unusual punishment, although courts have not infrequently referred (at least for purposes of analogy) to the voluntary act requirement and to such defenses as automatism, compulsion, and involuntary intoxication.

One of the leading cases is *Robinson v. Cal.* (1962), in which the Supreme Court held unconstitutional, on cruel and unusual punishment grounds, a statute making it a criminal offense for a person to "be addicted to the use of narcotics." The basis for this holding is somewhat obscure in the *Robinson* opinion, for the Court emphasized all of these factors: (1) under the statute, conviction was possible for the mere "status" of being an addict, for it was not necessary to prove any use of narcotics or other irregular behavior within the state; (2) addiction is an illness; and (3) addiction may be contracted innocently or involuntarily (e.g., from the use of medically prescribed narcotics, or at the time of birth because of maternal addiction).

Relying in part upon the *Robinson* decision, some courts then held that it would be cruel and usual punishment to convict a chronic alcoholic—a "person who is powerless to stop drinking and whose drinking seriously alters his normal living pattern"—of the crime of public drunkenness. This offense, of course, involves more than status, so *Robinson* clearly was broadly interpreted as barring conviction for a disease or for acts "which are compulsive as symptomatic of the disease." Some reliance was also placed upon traditional criminal law concepts; it was said that "a chronic alcoholic cannot have the *mens rea* necessary to be held responsible criminally for being drunk in public," and that he has not engaged in any voluntary act.

But in *Powell v. Tex.* (1968), the Supreme Court refused to adopt such a "wide-ranging new constitutional principle." One reason was the state of the record in that case; the medical testimony was that when appellant was sober, the act of taking the first drink was a "voluntary exercise of his will," but that this exercise of will was undertaken under the "exceedingly strong influence" of a "compulsion" which was "not completely overpowering." Noting that these "concepts, when juxtaposed in this fashion, have little meaning," the Court found this testimony illustrative of the fact that medical knowledge in this area had not progressed to the point where it could support "a constitutional doctrine of criminal responsibility." Moreover, the Court indicated its reluctance to "constitutionalize" the whole area of criminal responsibility, and thus gave *Robinson* a narrow reading. *Robinson* was interpreted as only barring punishment of status on the ground that unless so viewed "it is difficult to see any limiting principle that would serve to prevent this Court from becoming, under the aegis of the Cruel and Unusual Punishment Clause, the ultimate arbiter of the standards of criminal responsibility, in diverse areas of the criminal law, throughout the country." This means an addict may constitutionally be convicted of possession of the drugs intended for his own use, though the actual practice in some jurisdictions is to channel such offenders into a pretrial diversion program.

Running through all of the decisions in this area is a concern for some limiting principle whereby application of the cruel and unusual punishment prohibition in some circumstances would not ultimately result in the exoneration of narcotics addicts and chronic alcoholics for all conduct (e.g., taking of property, killing or injuring people) somehow related to their condition. In *Robinson,* the Court emphasized that states were free to punish such crimes as the sale, purchase, or possession of narcotics. In the pre-*Powell* cases holding that a chronic alcoholic could not be convicted of public intoxication, it was likewise noted that such a person "would be judged as would any person not so afflicted" with respect to other behavior. Clearly, neither narcotics addiction nor chronic alcoholism is per se a defense.

Following *Powell,* lower courts rather consistently have held that alcoholism is no defense to a charge of drunkenness. What conceivably could occur, however, in the event of somewhat greater medical knowledge about alcoholism than was displayed in *Powell,* is a broadening of the involuntary intoxication classification— heretofore limited to intoxication by mistake, duress, or medical advice (see § 8.5(g)). If the medical evidence is not merely that the defendant is an alcoholic, or a chronic alcoholic, but that he has reached the stage where even the taking of the first drink is not a matter of choice, his intoxication may be viewed as involuntary rather than voluntary so that the broader defense comparable to that for insanity would apply. But to date most courts have been disinclined to equate alcoholism with involuntariness. (The issue is confronted less often today, for most states have decriminalized drunkenness.)

What then of the narcotics addict who resorts to crime in order to obtain funds for drugs to prevent withdrawal symptoms? This is a more serious problem, in the sense that a great many crimes are committed under precisely these circumstances. Although it certainly could be argued that such a person is in need of treatment for his addiction rather than punishment for the crime committed to support it, there is no discernible trend toward recognizing a defense in such a case. Moreover, some have argued there should be no defense here because "there is no medical foundation for adopting the general proposition at the crux of the exculpatory legal arguments, the proposition that addictive conduct is involuntary."

(j) Procedure for Intoxication Defense. Where voluntary or involuntary intoxication negatives an element of the crime charged, or where involuntary intoxication puts the defendant in a state of mind resembling insanity, there is no special plea that raises the defense of intoxication; the defendant simply pleads not guilty. Nevertheless, the defense of intoxication is an "affirmative" defense in the sense that the defendant has the burden of going forward, so that he must put on some evidence of his intoxication, unless the prosecution's own proof shows the defendant's intoxication.

Once the defendant has thus introduced some evidence of his intoxication, who has the burden of persuasion? Where the claim is that involuntary intoxication put the defendant into a state of mind resembling insanity, the burden of proof (as with the insanity defense itself, see § 7.3(a)) may constitutionally be placed upon the defendant. But the same is not true when the intoxication negatives an element of the crime.

§ 8.6 Infancy

At common law, children under the age of seven are conclusively presumed to be without criminal capacity, those who have reached the age of fourteen are treated as fully responsible, while as to those between the ages of seven and fourteen there is a rebuttable presumption of criminal incapacity. Several states have made some change by statute in the age of criminal responsibility for minors. In addition, all jurisdictions have adopted juvenile court legislation providing that some or all criminal conduct by those persons under a certain age must or may be adjudicated in the juvenile court rather than in a criminal prosecution.

(a) Common Law. At the early common law infancy apparently was not a defense to a criminal prosecution, although a youthful defendant usually received a pardon. In the tenth century, by statute no one under the age of fifteen could be subjected to capital punishment unless he attempted to escape or refused to give himself up. Finally, by the beginning of the fourteenth century it was established that children under the age of seven were without criminal capacity. Seven was the age of responsibility under the Roman Civil Law, and this probably influenced the common law through Canon Law.

By 1338 infants over seven were presumed to lack the capacity to commit crime, but the presumption could be rebutted by proof of malice, which in turn could be shown by concealment of the crime. At this time the age at which the presumption of incapacity no longer was applicable had not been precisely fixed, but by the seventeenth century the age of discretion had been established at fourteen. The common law had thus developed to its present form: (1) children under seven had no criminal capacity; (2) children at age fourteen and over had the same criminal capacity as adults; and (3) children over seven and under fourteen were presumed to be without capacity, but this presumption could be rebutted in an individual case.

The early common law infancy defense was based upon an unwillingness to punish those thought to be incapable of forming criminal intent and not of an age where the threat of punishment could serve as a deterrent. The rebuttable presumption was explained on the ground that failure to punish particularly atrocious acts committed by those between the ages of seven and fourteen would encourage other children to commit them with impunity. The early commentators emphasized that the presumption of incapacity could be rebutted by proof of the youthful defendant's ability to distinguish between good and evil. Moreover, the weight of the presumption was said to decrease as the child approached the age of discretion, and this view has also been followed in the United States.

The burden of proof in overcoming the presumption is on the prosecution, although there is not complete agreement on what exactly must be proved. Various phrases have been used to describe what is required: guilty knowledge of wrongdoing, a mischievous inclination, an "intelligent design and malice in the execution of the act," a consciousness of the wrongfulness of the act, and knowledge of good from evil. However, "the most modern definition of the test is simply that the surrounding circumstances must demonstrate * * * that the individual knew what he was doing and that it was wrong." Some courts have taken the position that an inference of such knowledge may arise from proof of the child's general knowledge of the difference between good and evil, while elsewhere proof of this general knowledge has not been deemed sufficient to show knowledge of the consequences of the particular acts engaged in.

Conduct of the defendant relating to the acts charged may be most relevant in overcoming the presumption. Thus hiding the body, inquiry as to the detection of poison, bribery of a witness, or false accusation of others have all been relied upon in finding capacity. In other instances, however, the gruesome nature of the crime, the attempt to silence a witness, and the disposal of evidence have been found insufficient to rebut the presumption. The factors most often looked to are the cunning and shrewdness of the child.

It is the defendant's age at the time of the alleged conduct and not at the time of the proceedings that controls. Also, it is the defendant's physical age rather than his "mental age" that is used to determine capacity, although some have viewed this as illogical.

(b) Legislation on Capacity or Lack of Jurisdiction. The question of when young persons can be convicted of crimes is now typically addressed by a statute of one kind or another. One type of statute is that which is expressed in terms of lack of capacity, to be found in a minority of the modern criminal codes. A very few of these statutes follow the common law format by utilizing, as to a specified age group, a presumption of incapacity that can be overcome only by a showing that the juvenile knew the wrongfulness of what he was doing. The other simply specify an age—usually 14 but in some instances 10, 12, 13, 15, or 16—below which capacity is conclusively presumed to be lacking. Where the absolute minimum age is below 14, the question may arise as to whether the common law presumption of incapacity is still operative as to those between the statutory age and the common law age of 14.

Even in states with modern criminal codes, the problem is more frequently addressed in terms of the allocation of jurisdiction between the criminal and juvenile courts. A typical provision of this type declares that juveniles under 14—or, under some other age, such as 10, 15, or 16—may not be subjected to criminal prosecution but only to delinquency proceedings in juvenile court. Some other statutes give exclusive jurisdiction to the juvenile court unless the juvenile was of a certain age, such as 15, 16 or 17, but with exceptions for certain serious offenses. Still others merely declare more generally that juvenile court jurisdiction is not exclusive. Except for those instances in which the juvenile ends up in criminal court instead of juvenile court because of a legislative, judicial or prosecutorial waiver of juvenile court jurisdiction, these jurisdiction statutes eliminate any question concerning the applicability of the common law rules in a criminal prosecution context.

(c) Juvenile Court Jurisdiction. All jurisdictions have by statute or constitutional provision established a juvenile court system (see § 1.7(a)). Juvenile courts typically deal with juvenile delinquents, juveniles otherwise in need of supervision, and neglected and dependent children. The most common statutory definition of delinquency is conduct which transgresses penal law, and it is only that aspect of juvenile court jurisdiction which is of concern here, for the following discussion is intended only to reflect the extent to which that jurisdiction has diminished the practical significance of common law and statutory provisions on the criminal capacity of children.

Most juvenile court acts place no lower age limit on juvenile court jurisdiction. Thus, unless the common law immunity for infants under seven is incorporated into juvenile law, children under seven may be adjudged delinquent for conduct for which they lacked criminal responsibility. This issue seems not to have been confronted in the cases (perhaps indicating that it is not the practice to adjudicate as delinquent children under seven), and the commentators are not in agreement on the point. On the one hand, it is claimed that "the traditional concept of incapacity has no application" in juvenile court, presumably on the ground that juvenile courts are not intended to deal with moral responsibility and are concerned only with the welfare of children. On the other, it is contended that the common law immunity should be applicable because the juvenile court serves to vindicate the public interest in the enforcement of the criminal law. Even if that is so, it does not follow that a significantly higher minimum age of criminal responsibility set by statute should be deemed equally applicable to delinquency proceedings in juvenile court.

A related question is whether the common law presumption of incapacity may be asserted as a defense to juvenile court proceedings by alleged delinquents between the age of seven and fourteen. The majority view is that no such defense is available. In support of this position, it is contended that "the purpose of treatment of immature offenders is solely rehabilitation" and that "rebuttable presumptions of incapacity become superfluous in the light of this treatment purpose." But some courts have held that the common law defense, as codified in the state penal code, is equally applicable to delinquency proceedings in juvenile court. That result has been praised on the ground "that the recent switch from treatment back to blameworthiness as the hallmark of juvenile offender law lays the basis for recognizing the infancy defense's crucial role in the new juvenile justice court." (Similar arguments are made regarding whether the insanity defense should be available in juvenile court, as to which the practice varies.)

All juvenile court acts set an upper age limit upon juvenile court jurisdiction. In almost all states the age is eighteen, and the fact the person before the court is not older must be established by the state. Laws setting the age limit for girls higher than for boys were at one time upheld against attacks made on equal protection grounds, but the more recent cases have found these provisions unconstitutional.

Assuming an age limit of eighteen, what if the youth was seventeen at the time of the alleged delinquent acts but has passed his eighteenth birthday prior to the time that juvenile court proceedings are begun? Some statutes expressly provide that the juvenile court still has jurisdiction because it is the age at the time of the conduct which is determinative, although many of the juvenile court acts are silent on this point. In the face of this ambiguity, most courts which have considered this issue have held that it is the age at the time of the proceedings which controls, while some others have taken the position that it is the age at the time of the conduct which governs.

(d) Waiver to Criminal Court. The preceding discussion is not intended to suggest that every case involving a juvenile within the age limit for juvenile court jurisdiction will be dealt with by the juvenile court instead of the criminal court. Lawmakers, "responding to public outrage and fears about increasing juvenile crime, are [pursuing] 'get tough' polices in an apparent attempt to incapacitate specific juvenile criminals and to deter violent juvenile crime. The most popular form of legislation is designed to 'waive' juveniles charged with serious crimes to criminal court." Every state now has a transfer statute allowing for transfer of some juveniles to adult court in at least one of the following ways, discussed below: judicial waiver, prosecutorial waiver, or legislative waiver. And, while it may be true that "even the most aggressive attacks on the juvenile court * * * leave a large majority of cases traditionally handled by juveniles courts within the courts' jurisdiction," this increased reliance upon waiver has resulted in more and younger juveniles being subjected to criminal prosecution than was once the case.

The most traditional and common form of waiver is judicial waiver, which occurs when a juvenile court judge uses his discretionary authority to transfer a juvenile case to an adult court. This form of waiver is utilized in almost all jurisdictions. Certain procedures are required for an effective waiver of juvenile court jurisdiction. The Supreme Court in *Kent v. U.S.* (1966), construing the District of Columbia waiver statute, held that the juvenile court must afford a hearing on waiver and state reasons or considerations for the transfer sufficient to demonstrate that there has been a full investigation, and specific enough to permit meaningful review. Subsequent decisions have often viewed *Kent* as constitutionally based. As for the criteria to be used in making the judicial waiver decision, the great majority of states have adopted, either by statute or case law, some or all of the D.C. criteria helpfully set out in an appendix to the *Kent* opinion:

1. The seriousness of the alleged offense to the community and whether the protection of the community requires waiver.

2. Whether the alleged offense was committed in an aggressive, violent, premeditated or willful manner.

3. Whether the alleged offense was against persons or against property, greater weight being given to offenses against persons especially if personal injury resulted.

4. The prosecutive merit of the complaint, i.e., whether there is evidence upon which a Grand Jury may be expected to return an indictment (to be determined by consultation with the United States Attorney).

5. The desirability of trial and disposition of the entire offense in one court when the juvenile's associates in the alleged offense are adults who will be charged with a crime in the U.S. District Court for the District of Columbia.

6. The sophistication and maturity of the juvenile as determined by consideration of his home, environmental situation, emotional attitude and pattern of living.

7. The record and previous history of the juvenile, including previous contacts with the Youth Aid Division, other law enforcement agencies, juvenile courts and other jurisdictions, prior periods of probation to this Court, or prior commitments to juvenile institutions.

8. The prospects for adequate protection of the public and the likelihood of reasonable rehabilitation of the juvenile (if he is found to have committed the alleged offense) by the use of procedures, services and facilities currently available to the Juvenile Court.

The second type of waiver is prosecutorial waiver, sometimes called "direct filing" because the governing statutes provide that both the criminal court and juvenile court have jurisdiction as to offenders under a certain age but that the prosecuting attorney has the power to determine in which forum the case will be filed. These statutes usually confer virtually total discretion upon the prosecutor; the juvenile is not entitled to a hearing on the issue of where the case should be filed, and the prosecutor's decision is not ordinarily subject to judicial review. About a quarter of the states utilize prosecutorial waiver in at least some circumstances. "While such a process may offer the attraction of speed and finality, opponents of this waiver system argue that its use may be arbitrary, and that in some jurisdictions political pressures are likely to influence the prosecutor's decision." The direct filing approach, consequently, is seen by some to "represent a total repudiation of the philosophy of the parens patriae juvenile court."

The third and final variety of waiver is legislative waiver, distinguishable from the other two in that no discretion by either the prosecutor or the juvenile court judge is involved in the determination of whether the juvenile is to be dealt with instead by the criminal courts. Rather, the legislature merely declares that *all* cases involving juveniles (or juveniles above a certain age) alleged to have committed certain specified offenses are to be automatically transferred to juvenile court. At one time this variety of waiver was exceedingly rare, but today it is to be found in about two-thirds of the states. Moreover, the "almost irreversible legislative tendency * * * is for lists of excluded offenses to expand." Because the legislative waiver is determined exclusively by the nature of the offense and not at all by the needs of the individual offender, it is apparent that the focus of such waiver statutes is upon retribution rather than rehabilitation. This is the basis upon which the legislative waiver device is most often criticized. (However, due process and equal protection challenges to these statutes have not met with success.) Some favor legislative waivers over the other types because then unpredictability is no longer a factor and the delays caused by individual transfer hearings can be avoided.

An alternative to waiver to criminal court is now available in about a third of the states, where the legislature has adopted the concept of extended juvenile jurisdiction, and its corollary, blended sentencing, which allows the juvenile court judge to impose both a juvenile disposition and an adult sentence when a juvenile is found to have committed a serious offense. The adult sentence is stayed until the completion of the terms of the juvenile disposition. Juveniles tried under extended juvenile jurisdiction are provided the same procedural rights as adults tried in criminal court, including the right to a jury trial. Because the adult sentence is only imposed after the juvenile disposition, rehabilitation which occurs before that point makes release from custody possible. On the other hand, if the juvenile violates the terms of the disposition or commits another offense, the adult sentence is implemented without the need for additional court proceedings.

§ 8.7 Duress

A person's unlawful threat (1) which causes the defendant reasonably to believe that the only way to avoid imminent death or serious bodily injury to himself or to another is to engage in conduct which violates the literal terms of the criminal law, and (2) which causes the defendant to engage in that conduct, gives the defendant the defense of duress (sometimes called compulsion or coercion) to the crime in question unless that crime consists of intentionally killing an innocent third person. The rationale of the defense of duress is that the defendant ought to be excused when he "is a victim of a threat that a person of reasonable moral strength could not fairly be expected to resist."

(a) **Nature of the Defense of Duress.** One who, under the pressure of an unlawful threat from another human being to harm him (or to harm a third person), commits what would otherwise be a crime may, under some circumstances, be excused for doing what he did and thus not be guilty of the crime in question. The requirement for this defense of duress is that of a threat of a human being which operates upon the defendant's mind, rather than of the pressure of a human being which operates upon his body (as where A pushes B against C, causing C to fall over the cliff where the three are standing, admiring the view). The rationale of the defense is not that the defendant, faced with the unnerving threat of harm unless he does an act violating the literal language of the criminal law, somehow loses his mental capacity to commit the crime in question. Nor is it that the defendant has not engaged in a voluntary act. Rather it is that, even though he has done the act the crime requires and has the mental state which the crime requires, his conduct violating the literal language of the criminal law is excused because he "lacked a fair opportunity to avoid acting unlawfully." That is, the notion is that there are circumstances in which a defendant should not be held accountable for his conduct because of an insufficient ability to control it, brought on by a threat of a harm too severe to be resisted.

Some modern writers have thus argued concerning the defense of duress that it should apply even when the harm done by the defendant is greater than or equal to the threatened harm which he avoids by doing it. It has been suggested that it ought to apply, without regard to any balancing of harms done and avoided, where the unlawfully threatened harm is such that the threat of criminal punishment for doing the harmful conduct does not serve to deter the defendant; so that, if A holds an axe over B's head, threatening to kill B unless B holds C's hands so that A can kill C, B would be justified in aiding A to kill C when the threat of criminal punishment for murder in the distant future does not in B's mind offset the certainty of immediate death by means of A's axe if he refuses. The Model Penal Code, however, while agreeing that there is little use in punishing when punishment cannot deter, rejects as too subjective the contention that, where the threat of punishment does not deter, one is not to be blamed for what he must choose to do. Code § 2.09(1) instead proposes a more objective test—that one unlawfully threatened by another is excused for committing what would otherwise be a crime if the threat which compels him to commit it is such that a person of reasonable firmness in his situation would have been unable to resist it. To apply this test to the above example concerning the axe killing: *B* would be excused for helping *A* kill *C* if men of ordinary firmness (and most men are not heroes, as they are not cowards) would have done so too, to save their own lives. A majority of the modern codes contain such an extension of the duress defense.

(b) Authorities on Duress as a Defense. The defense of duress is a common law defense, applicable in appropriate cases although no statute makes it so. But the case law in the absence of statute has generally held that duress cannot excuse murder—or, as it is better expressed (since duress may excuse the underlying felony for what would otherwise be a felony murder), duress cannot excuse the intentional killing of (or attempt to kill) an innocent third person. It has been recognized, however, that duress can excuse treason, though treason like murder is a capital offense—an explanation of the difference between treason and murder being that treason is a continuing crime from which there may be an opportunity to escape and repair the damage done; but murder is a consummated act as to which no repairs can be effective. Duress has been held a good defense to such lesser crimes as robbery, burglary, and malicious mischief. It has been recognized that duress may be a defense to kidnaping, arson, prison escape, and possession of a weapon. When an employee hands over his employer's money to a threatening gunman who demands it, he commits what would be embezzlement (fraudulent conversion of his employer's property in his possession) but for the defense of duress.

As stated above, duress is no defense to the intentional taking of life by the threatened person; but it is a defense to a killing done by another in the commission of some lesser felony participated in by the defendant under duress. Thus, if *A* compels *B* at gunpoint to drive him to the bank that *A* intends to rob, and during the ensuing robbery *A* kills a bank customer *C*, *B* is not guilty of the robbery (for he was excused by duress) and so is not guilty of felony murder of *C* in the commission of robbery. The law properly recognizes that one may aid in a robbery if he is forced by threats to do so to save his life; he should not lose the defense because his threateners unexpectedly kill someone in the course of the robbery and thus convert a mere robbery into a murder.

It is generally held that, as to those crimes which are excused by duress, the duress must consist of threatening conduct which produces in the defendant (1) a reasonable fear of (2) immediate (or imminent) (3) death or serious bodily harm. (Threatened *future* death or serious bodily harm, or threatened immediate *nonserious* bodily harm or property damage, or a threat that produces an *unreasonable* fear of immediate death or serious bodily harm, will therefore not suffice.) Doubtless a reasonable fear of immediate death or serious bodily injury to someone other than the defendant, such as a member of his family, will do. Doubtless too, the danger need not be real; it is enough if the defendant reasonably believes it to be real. One threatened with immediate death or serious bodily injury may lose his defense of duress if he does not take advantage of a reasonable opportunity to escape, where that can be done without exposing himself unduly to death or serious bodily injury. And where the offense is a continuing one, the defendant will lose his defense of duress if he fails to terminate his conduct "as soon as the claimed duress * * * had lost its coercive force."

Although the great majority of the modern criminal codes provide for a duress defense, there is no uniformity in the statutory definition of this defense. Most of these statutes appear to require that there have been actual coercion which caused the defendant's conduct, for it is typically stated that the defendant must have acted "because of" the coercion or compulsion. But other provisions seem somewhat broader by declaring it sufficient that the defendant "reasonably believed" that otherwise the threatened harm would occur. As for the nature of the threatened harm, in one state only a threat of death will do, but in several others a threat of either death or serious bodily harm is sufficient. A considerable number of the statutes move beyond the common law rule in this regard by providing that threats of lesser bodily harm can sometimes suffice. Most of the duress defense statutes state that the threatened harm must be "imminent," "immediate" or "instant," but some include no such limitation. The overwhelming majority of these provisions extend to threats of harm to third parties, though a few are expressly limited to threats to injure the defendant himself. A very distinct majority of the modern recodifications follow Model Penal Code § 2.09(1) by requiring only that the threat be such that a person of reasonable firmness would have been unable to resist it. (Significantly, all of the statutes that extend to threats of more remote injury and to injury short of serious bodily injury are of this type.)

While a significant number of the modern provisions make the duress defense available whatever the charge against the defendant, about half of them do not allow the defense if the defendant has been charged with murder. In a few jurisdictions, the exceptions are stated considerably broader. It is also generally recognized that a defendant can lose this defense by his own fault in getting into the difficulty. Thus, close to all of these statutes declare that the duress defense is unavailable if the defendant recklessly placed himself in a situation in which it was probable that he would be subjected to duress. A few go on to state that mere negligence in this regard is a bar if the defendant is charged with an offense for which negligence suffices to establish culpability.

(c) Duress as a Defense: On Principle. The case law and statutory law of duress as a defense has tended to jell into fixed rules that depart somewhat from the rationale underlying the rule stated above (see § 8.7(a)). Even assuming that B is not justified in intentionally killing an innocent third person C, who would otherwise be safe, in order to avoid being killed himself at the hands of an armed threatener A, if by killing C, B avoids death to two or more (as where A, with power to carry out the threat, threatens to kill B and Mrs. B, whom he holds as a hostage), his act ought on principle to be excused. So too, if B's act played a minor rather than a necessary part in bringing about C's death (as where A would have been able to kill C even if B had not helped), it would seem that B should be excused for doing what he did.

It is not necessarily true that all acts of treason are excused by duress; some acts may be, but others are clearly not. If a prisoner of war, to save his own life, disclosed to his country's enemies military plans, which disclosure was likely to cost his country a thousand casualties, he would not be excused.

It is not proper, on principle, to limit the defense of duress to situations where the instrument of coercion is a threat of death or serious bodily injury. A threat to do bodily harm less than serious bodily harm, or a threat to destroy property or reputation, ought to do where the act the defendant does to avoid the threatened harm is relatively minor—as where A threatens to strike B with a nondeadly weapon capable of inflicting great pain unless B drives somewhat over the speed limit.

On principle, the threatened harm, though perhaps it need not be "immediate," ought not to be remote in time, for until the threatened disaster is pretty close to happening, there may arise a chance both to refuse to do the criminal act and also to avoid the threatened harm—the opportunity to escape without undue danger which the cases recognize as enough to deprive the defendant of his defense. So too, as a matter of principle, the threatened harm need not be directed at the defendant himself; it may be aimed at a member of his family or a friend (or, it would seem, even a stranger).

The present law may be right in requiring that the threat of harm produce in the defendant a reasonable ("well grounded," as the cases sometimes say) fear that the harm will be inflicted if the defendant refuses to obey. A reasonable fear is generally required as to such defenses as self-defense, defense of others and necessity; and there is no reason for a different rule with duress.

The present law is right in requiring, for the defense, that the defendant be actually coerced by the threat into violating the terms of the criminal law. A taxi driver would not have the defense, for instance, if he voluntarily drove over the speed limit, only to learn later, to his surprise, that his passenger in the back seat was holding a gun pointed at the driver's head ready to order the driver to speed had he not voluntarily done so.

(d) Mitigation of Punishment. One who commits a crime while subject to coercion, but whose situation does not come under the rules which permit him to be excused (perhaps his crime was murder of the intent-to-kill sort; or his fear of death or serious bodily injury was not reasonable; or his fear was one of future harm), may nevertheless properly urge that his punishment, within the permissible limits of punishment for the crime in question, should be lower than it would have been if he had not been coerced.

In addition, where the defendant, coerced by another into killing a third person, is charged with murder but is not excused for doing so, nevertheless he might successfully argue that he is not guilty of first-degree murder consisting of a deliberate and premeditated killing, since the fear generated in him by the other's threatening conduct made him incapable of premeditating and deliberating; his crime thus was only murder in the second degree. The further suggestion that this fear might even render him incapable of entertaining an intent to kill, and so serve to reduce his crime to manslaughter, was rejected in one of the leading duress cases. Nevertheless, a few states by statute have provided that what is otherwise murder except for duress is reduced to manslaughter; and there is something rather reasonable about the view that such a crime, though not excused, at least should not be murder (see § 14.3(c)).

(e) Guilt of the Coercer. Where A by threats coerces B to engage in criminal conduct, A is guilty of the crime in question although B may, because of the coercion, be excused and so not be guilty. In one case, where A, armed with a gun, forced B, another man, to attempt to have sexual intercourse with Mrs. A (B's fright preventing him from being able to effect a penetration), A argued, on appeal from his conviction for assault with intent to rape, that he could not be guilty of the crime since B, because of the duress, was not guilty. The court affirmed A's conviction on the erroneous ground that attempted rape cannot be justified by duress. It would have been better law to affirm the conviction on the ground that, even though *B* was justified, *A* is nevertheless guilty, for one can commit a crime through means of an innocent agent, such as an underage child or an insane person (see § 12.1(a)).

(f) Coercion of Wife by Husband. The common law rule was that, except for murder and treason, a married woman was not punishable for crime if she acted under the coercion of her husband; and, if she committed the criminal act in her husband's presence, there was a rebuttable presumption that he had coerced her. Something less in the way of pressure was required for a wife to be coerced than for an ordinary person to meet the requirements of the defense of duress; one early English case held that the husband's mere command would do.

This special defense for wives arose at a time when married women were actually much under their husband's control; it doubtless continued because of the courts' desire to avoid the death penalty for women (who were not, until 1692, eligible for benefit of clergy) at a time when many crimes were punishable by death. Today the position of married women is quite different: they may own their separate property; they may vote and serve on juries; their husbands may no longer enforce obedience with a stick the thickness of the husband's thumb; in short, their "independence * * * in political, social and economic matters rightly places upon them an increased responsibility." Many of the recent state criminal codes abolish any special rule about coercion of wives by husbands and the presumption of such coercion. A number of courts, without the aid of any special statute (other than the statutes that have revolutionized the position of married women), have abolished the special common law rule and its accompanying presumption, leaving married women to the protection of the ordinary defense of duress. A dwindling number of states probably still adhere to the old doctrine.

(g) Orders of a Superior. It is no defense to a crime committed by an employee that he was only carrying out his employer's unlawful orders. It is likewise no defense to a crime that it was committed by a military subordinate pursuant to an unlawful military order, as where he is ordered by his superior to shoot prisoners of war. On the other hand, if he believed the unlawful order to be legal, or perhaps if he reasonably believed it to be legal, he is not guilty of the crime in question.

§ 8.8   Entrapment

Certain criminal offenses present the police with unique and difficult detection problems because they are committed privately between individuals who are willing participants. Consequently, in addition to employing search and seizure techniques, routine and electronic surveillance, and informants to expose such consensual crime, law enforcement officers resort to the use of encouragement. "Encouragement" is a word used to describe the activity of a police officer or agent "(a) who acts as a victim; (b) who intends, by his actions, to encourage the suspect to commit a crime; (c) who actually communicates this encouragement to the suspect; and (d) who thereby has some influence upon the commission of a crime."

At the heart of the encouragement practice is the need to simulate reality. An environment is created in which the suspect is presented with an opportunity to commit a crime. The simulation of reality must be accurate enough to induce the criminal activity at the point in time when the agents are in a position to gather evidence of the crime. The tactics used vary from case to case. Some solicitations are innocuous, but since persons engaged in criminal activity are generally suspicious of strangers, government agents typically do more than simply approach a target and request the commission of a crime. Multiple requests or the formation of personal relationships with a subject may be necessary to overcome that suspicion. In addition, appeals to personal considerations, representations of benefits to be derived from the offense, and actual assistance in obtaining contraband or planning the details of the crime are frequently employed.

(a) Development and Scope of the Defense. The more extreme forms of encouragement activity are a matter of legitimate concern for a variety of reasons. Of central concern is the possibility that the encouragement might induce a person who otherwise would be law-abiding to engage in criminal conduct. Yet, as a historical matter, the traditional response of the law was that there were no limits upon the degree of temptation to which law enforcement officers and their agents could subject those under investigation. The attitude was that the courts would "not look to see who held out the bait, but [rather] who took it."

Even today, neither courts nor legislatures have affirmatively developed detailed guidelines for police and their agents to follow when engaging in encouragement activity. However, there did ultimately develop, originally in the state courts, a defense called "entrapment" that may be interposed in a criminal prosecution. Beginning with the decision in *Sorrells v. U.S.* (1932), the development of the law of entrapment became largely an activity of the federal courts, with the states then adopting the doctrine thereby created. The classic definition of entrapment is that articulated by Justice Roberts in *Sorrells,* the first Supreme Court decision to acknowledge the defense: "Entrapment is the conception and planning of an offense by an officer, and his procurement of its commission by one who would not have perpetrated it except for the trickery, persuasion, or fraud of the officer."

The defense of entrapment has been asserted in the context of a wide variety of criminal activity, including prostitution, alcohol offenses, counterfeiting, price controlling, and, probably most spectacularly, bribery of public officials. However, the great majority of the cases in which an entrapment defense is interposed involve a charge of some drug offense. There is a dearth of case authority on the question of whether the entrapment defense is available no matter what the nature of the charge brought against the defendant. But in *Sorrells* there appears a caution that the defense might be unavailable where the defendant is charged with a "heinous" or "revolting" crime, and the Model Penal Code § 2.13 formulation of the defense expressly makes it "unavailable when causing or threatening bodily injury is an element of the offense charged and the prosecution is based on conduct causing or threatening such injury to a person other than the person perpetrating the entrapment." In support of this latter limitation, it is explained that one "who can be persuaded to cause such injury presents a danger that the public cannot safely disregard," and that the impropriety of the inducement will likely be dealt with by other means because the public will, "in all probability, demand the punishment of the conniving or cooperating officers."

The defense of entrapment does not extend to *all* inducements, and thus another important issue concerning the scope of the defense is that of "whose inducements may result in entrapment." As the Supreme Court cases themselves illustrate, "entrapment can occur through an undercover agent, a confidential informant or a private citizen knowingly acting under the direction of government agents." This is not to suggest, however, that any sort of relationship between the police and a private citizen will suffice; for example, it is not enough that the police had earlier made "an informal request for potential future information" to the person who made the inducements. But on the other hand, a sufficient agency relationship can exist even when the police did not expressly request the particular inducement techniques later challenged via an entrapment defense. As it was put in *Sherman v. U.S.* (1958), the government "cannot make such use of an informer and then claim disassociation through ignorance."

A more troublesome question is whether "entrapment can occur through a third party who is not knowingly furthering a government scheme." Perhaps at least in certain circumstances, but to appreciate precisely when this might occur, it is necessary to distinguish between three different situations. The first, what might be called "private entrapment" in the purest sense, involves an instance in which a private individual, of his own will and without any official involvement, induces another person to commit a crime. Illustrative is *U.S. v. Maddox* (1974), where private investigators acting without police involvement ensnared several other persons in a sting operation. The court in *Maddox* declared that "the entrapment defense does not extend to inducement by private individuals." As another court put it, "private entrapment is just another term for criminal solicitation, and outside the narrow haven created by the defense of necessity or compulsion, the person who yields to the solicitation and commits the solicited crime is guilty of that crime." If the entrapment defense was conceived of as being based upon the notion that a person is not culpable whenever he engages in what would otherwise be criminal conduct because of the strong inducement of another person, this limitation would be open to serious question. What this limitation reflects, then, is that the "purpose of the defense is to deter misconduct in enforcing the law."

This leaves two other situations, "vicarious entrapment" and "derivative entrapment," where again the inducement is by a third party who is not knowingly furthering a government scheme, although now there is a relationship of sorts between the government and the third party. In the case of vicarious entrapment, a private individual, who himself has been induced by an undercover law enforcement officer or agent, now in turn induces someone else to join in the scheme. Illustrative is *U.S. v. Valencia* (1981), where government agents solicited the defendant's wife and she in turn solicited her husband, in the process informing him of the inducements that had been directed at her, after which both of them engaged in a drug buy. The *Valencia* court ruled that in such circumstances the husband could raise the entrapment defense: "If a person is brought into a criminal scheme after being informed indirectly of conduct or statements by a government agent which could amount to inducement, then that person should be able to avail himself of the defense of entrapment just as may the person who received the inducement directly." Some have expressed broad approval for the *Valencia* approach; indeed, one commentator declared that "even when the government has no reason to expect that a target of an investigation will induce a nonessential collaborator to join in criminal activity, the third party should still be able to plead entrapment if it is found that the initial target was himself entrapped," as in such a case the third party is another "victim of the same misconduct." And another court, though insisting that the middleman must have passed on the inducement offered by the government in an unaltered form, pointed to the "absurdity" of acquitting the one defendant but not the other in such circumstances. But other courts deem it inappropriate to confer an entrapment defense upon individuals never targeted by the government in the first place. One commentator has expressed agreement with that conclusion, asserting that "although vicarious entrapment may serve the purpose of the predisposition (or subjective) prong of the entrapment defense—protecting the 'unwary innocent'—it ignores the purpose of the inducement (or objective) prong of the defense—discouraging certain government conduct."

Consistent with the latter view but going further are those decisions which assert, in effect, that the entrapment defense is *never* available to a defendant who was not directly induced by a law enforcement officer or an agent knowingly acting on the officer's behalf. Such a broad rule would, of course, extend even to the third situation, "derivative entrapment," by which is meant the case in which the undercover government officer or agent uses the unsuspecting middleman as a means of passing on an inducement to a distant target. Some other federal and state courts, however, have taken the view that the entrapment defense should be available to the distant target under these circumstances. As explained in *U.S. v. Washington* (1997), in the case of derivative entrapment it should make no difference that the intermediary is unwitting because

> the purpose behind allowing such a defense is to prevent the government from circumventing rules against entrapment merely by deploying intermediaries, only one degree removed from the officials themselves, who carry out the government's instructions to persuade a particular individual to commit a particular crime using a particular type of inducement.

The *Washington* court placed great stress upon the limitations of its rule: "the derivative entrapment defense may only be raised if the alleged inducement communicated by the unwitting intermediary is the *same* inducement, directed at the *same* target, as the inducement that the government agent directs the intermediary to communicate." This highlights the tough question of just where, from the standpoint of both policy and practicality, the line between vicarious and derivative entrapment should be drawn. It has been argued that the more sensible line would be one drawn between (a) those cases in which "a mere friend or acquaintance of the primary target of an undercover investigation is drawn into a nonessential criminal role in the enterprise," where it should be concluded "the entrapment defense is unavailable," and (b) those cases in which "involvement by third persons is inherent in the design of a government investigation," where the entrapment defense should be available without regard to "whether the middleman adheres to the inducements offered by the agent or alters them to suit the target he has chosen" or "whether the secondary target was selected by the agent or by the middleman."

or judicial decision. A few other jurisdictions have adopted a combination of the objective and subjective tests.

The objective approach focuses upon the inducements used by the government agents. This means that entrapment has been established if the offense was induced or encouraged by "employing methods of persuasion or inducement which create a substantial risk that such an offense will be committed by persons other than those who are ready to commit it." In applying this test, it is necessary to consider the surrounding circumstances, such as evidence of the manner in which the particular criminal business is usually carried on. Though such practices as appeals to sympathy or friendship, offers of inordinate gain, or persistent offers to overcome hesitancy are suspect, courts in jurisdictions using the objective test have been reluctant to lay down absolutes. Though such temptations may be impermissible in some instances, each case must be judged on its own facts. Thus, it would seem that this "objective" focus upon the propriety of the police conduct leaves as much room for value judgments to be made as does the "subjective" focus upon the defendant's state of mind.

The rationale behind the objective approach is grounded in public policy considerations. Proponents of this approach reject the legislative intent argument. They believe that courts must refuse to convict an entrapped defendant not because his conduct falls outside the proscription of the statute, but rather because, even if his guilt has been established, the methods employed on behalf of the government to bring about the crime "cannot be countenanced." To some extent, this reflects the notion that the courts should not become tainted by condoning law enforcement improprieties. If government agents have instigated the commission of a crime, then the courts should not in effect approve that "abhorrent transaction" by permitting the induced individual to be convicted. But the primary consideration is that an affirmative duty resides in the courts to control police excesses in inducing criminal behavior, and that this duty should not be limited to instances in which the defendant is otherwise "innocent." So viewed, the entrapment defense appears to be a procedural device (somewhat like the Fourth Amendment and *Miranda* exclusionary rules) for deterring undesirable governmental intrusions into the lives of citizens.

As currently applied, the two approaches differ more than merely at the theoretical level. True, in *Sorrells* and *Sherman* the majority (subjective approach) and minority (objective approach) opinions agreed as to the result on the facts there presented. But the concurring justices in *Sherman* were the dissenters in *Masciale v. U.S.* (1958), decided the same day. And in *U.S. v. Russell* (1973), the result would certainly have been different had the objective test been utilized. However, neither of the two approaches is uniformly more favorable to defendants, as is reflected by this brief comparison:

> Under the [subjective approach], if *A*, an informer, makes overreaching appeals to compassion and friendship and thus moves *D* to sell narcotics, *D* has no defense if he is predisposed to narcotics peddling. Under the [objective approach] a defense would be established because the police conduct, not *D*'s predisposition, determines the issue. Under the [subjective approach], *A*'s mere offer to purchase narcotics from *D* may give rise to the defense provided *D* is not predisposed to sell. A contrary result is reached under the [objective approach]. A mere offer to buy hardly creates a serious risk of offending by the innocent.

(d) Objections to the Subjective Approach. Proponents of the objective approach raise three main arguments against the subjective approach. First of all, the "legislative intent" theory is attacked as "sheer fiction." It is argued that the Congress or state legislature intended to proscribe precisely the conduct in which the defendant engaged, as is reflected by the fact that the conduct is unquestionably criminal if the temptor was a private person rather than a government agent. Because the prior innocence of the defendant will not sustain the defense of entrapment, then, so the argument proceeds, the public policies of deterring unlawful police conduct and preserving the purity of the courts must be controlling. Those policies, it is concluded, are not effectuated by looking to the defendant's predisposition.

A second criticism of the subjective approach is that it creates, in effect, an "anything goes" rule for use against persons who can be shown by their prior convictions or otherwise to have been predisposed to engage in criminal behavior. This is because if the trier of fact determines that a defendant was predisposed to commit the type of crime charged, then no level of police deceit, badgering or other unsavory practices will be deemed impermissible. Such a result is unsound, it is argued, because it ignores "the possibility that no matter what his past crimes and general disposition the defendant might not have committed the particular crime unless confronted with inordinate inducements." Moreover, so this reasoning proceeds, this notion that the permissible police conduct may vary according to the particular defendant is inconsistent with the objective of equality under the law.

Yet a third objection to the subjective approach is that delving into the defendant's character and predisposition not only "has often obscured the important task of judging the quality of the police behavior," but also has prejudiced the defendant more generally. This is because once the entrapment defense is raised, certain usual evidentiary rules are discarded, and the defendant will be subjected to an "appropriate and searching inquiry into his own conduct and predisposition as bearing upon that issue." This means a prosecutor may admit evidence of a prior criminal record, reputation evidence, acts of prior misconduct, and other information generally barred as hearsay or as being more prejudicial than probative.

(e) Objections to the Objective Approach. Proponents of the subjective approach have likewise raised various criticisms concerning the objective approach. One of them is that defendant's predisposition, at least if known by the police when the investigation in question was conducted, has an important bearing upon the question of whether the conduct of the police and their agents was proper. For example, if it is known that a particular suspect has sold drugs in the past, then it is proper to subject that person to more persuasive inducements than would be permissible as to an individual about whose predisposition the authorities knew nothing. By like token, knowledge that a target has a weakness for a vice crime but is currently abstaining is also a fact that merits consideration when assessing an agent's conduct. Thus, the objective approach is said to be inherently defective because it eliminates entirely the need for considering a particular defendant's criminal predisposition. So the argument goes, "evidence of criminal proclivity ought to be taken into account when it bears on the question of whether the agent should have known that his inducement would create a substantial risk of corrupting a person not otherwise disposed to commit the offense."

A second major criticism of the objective approach is that the "wrong" people end up in jail if a dangerous, chronic offender may only be offered those inducements which might have tempted a hypothetical, law-abiding person. This is because, for example, the fact that the defendant in a particular case has been a shrewd, active member of a narcotics ring prior to and continuing through the incident in question is irrelevant under the objective test to a determination of the propriety of the inducements used. So the argument continues, to avoid this acquittal of "wary criminals," courts are likely to allow agents substantial leeway in determining the limits of permissible inducement, with the result that this same freedom will allow the police to lead astray the "unwary innocent."

Still another criticism directed at the objective approach to entrapment is that it will foster inaccuracy in the factfinding process. It is argued that the nature of the inducement offered in secret is a factual issue less susceptible to reliable proof than the issue of predisposition. This is because if a defendant claims that an inducement was improper, the agent can take the stand and rebut

the allegations, resulting in a swearing match. Especially because
the defense of entrapment ordinarily assumes an admission of guilt
(unless inconsistent defenses are permitted), this means the factfinder will often have to make the "imponderable choice" between the
testimony of an informer, often with a criminal record, and that of
a defendant who has admittedly committed the criminal act.

A fourth objection relates to the public policy justifications of
the objective approach. It is questioned whether the "purity" of the
courts is itself a sufficient justification, and whether the objective
approach can be expected to serve the deterrence objective in a
meaningful way. Because courts are disinclined to adopt per se
rules regarding what are impermissible police inducements, it is
doubted whether there will actually result significant restrictions
upon the types of inducements that police are entitled to utilize.
Moreover, so the argument continues, even if such limitations are
developed the police will still be left with the discretion to decide
upon the context or target of encouragement activity. To this are
added the familiar arguments against other attempts to deter the
police, such as that they can be thwarted by police perjury or that
they will be totally ineffective when the police are acting for
objectives other than conviction. For all these reasons, this line of
argument concludes, the deterrence objective should be dismissed
in favor of an effort to do justice to the individual defendant in the
particular case.

(f) Procedural Considerations. Entrapment, it has been
said, is a "dangerous and judicially unpopular defense that should
only be used in a few cases with ideal fact situations or in desperate
circumstances where no other defense is possible." This perceived
danger is largely attributable to various procedural consequences
that attend interposition of an entrapment defense where the
majority, subjective approach is followed.

**(1) Admissibility of Evidence of Defendant's Past Con-
duct.** As the Supreme Court put it in *Sherman v. U.S.* (1958),
under the subjective approach the prosecution may engage in a
" 'searching inquiry into [defendant's] own conduct and predisposition' as bearing on his claim of innocence." In most jurisdictions
this means that once entrapment has been raised as a defense, the
usual evidentiary rules are no longer followed. For the purported
purpose of allowing the factfinder access to all information bearing
upon the "predisposition" issue, courts have allowed the receipt
into evidence of defendant's prior convictions, prior arrests, and
information about his "reputation" and even concerning "suspicious conduct" on his part. The result, as Justice Stewart objected
in *U.S. v. Russell* (1973), is that otherwise inadmissible "hearsay,
suspicion and rumor" is brought into the case to the detriment of

the defendant. The defendant, in effect, is "put on trial for his past offenses and character."

Although it has quite correctly been said that the "greatest fault" of the subjective approach as it developed in the federal courts "lies in the permissiveness of its ancillary rules of evidence," it is important to note that this "indiscriminate attitude toward predisposition evidence is by no means a necessary feature of the subjective test." This is because less prejudicial means of determining the readiness and willingness of a defendant to engage in the criminal conduct will often be available. The most promising alternative is testimony about the defendant's actions during the negotiations leading to the charged offense, such as his ready acquiescence, his expert knowledge about such criminal activity, his admissions of past deeds or future plans, and his ready access to the contraband. Another possibility is evidence obtained in a subsequent search or otherwise which shows that the defendant was involved in a course of ongoing criminal activity.

(2) Triable by Court or Jury. Traditionally, the entrapment defense has been regarded as a matter for the jury rather than for determination by the judge. (Even where this is unquestionably the case, the judge may rule on the sufficiency of the proof to raise the issue in the first place, and where uncontradicted evidence supports the conclusion that the defendant was entrapped the issue may of course be decided as a matter of law by the court.) Under the majority, subjective approach to entrapment, grounded upon the implied exception theory, it is apparent that "the issue of whether a defendant has been entrapped is for the jury as part of its function of determining the guilt or innocence of the accused."

In support of this state of affairs, it has been argued that determining matters of credibility and assessing the subjective response to the stimulus of police encouragement are peculiarly within the ken of the jury. Also, it has been observed that if the matter is placed in the hands of the jury there is an opportunity for jury nullification, meaning that "the jury, if it wishes, can acquit because of the moral revulsion which the police conduct evokes in them, notwithstanding any amount of convincing evidence of the defendant's predisposition." On the other hand, the argument has been made that the case for putting the matter in the hands of the court is especially strong under the subjective approach. This is because where the rules of evidence on proving predisposition are very loose, which is usually the case, "the defense can be raised only at a great price to the defendant" if that evidence becomes known to the jury.

Under the objective approach to entrapment, the judge-versus-jury issue "is more evenly balanced." In favor of having the matter decided by the judge is the notion that it is the function of the court to preserve the purity of the court. Similarly, it may be said that to the extent the objective approach rests upon a deterrence-of-police rationale this function also is the proper responsibility of the court, just as it is when the court rules on suppression motions. And there is the added point made by Justice Frankfurter in *Sherman*, namely,

> that a jury verdict, although it may settle the issue of entrapment in the particular case, cannot give significant guidance for official conduct for the future. Only the court, through the gradual evolution of explicit standards in accumulated precedents, can do this with the degree of certainty that the wise administration of criminal justice demands.

Also, there is a sense in which trial of the issue before the judge would be to the state's advantage; the defendant "would no longer be able to divert a jury's attention from his crime by attacking the sins of the police."

However, not all of the states that have adopted the objective approach submit the issue to the judge instead of the jury. In light of the above considerations, it is not entirely clear why this is so. Perhaps there is concern that taking the issue from the jury might give rise to constitutional questions about the breadth of the right to jury trial. More likely, however, is the explanation that the issue is deemed an appropriate one for the jury because the jury has "a special claim to competence" on the question of what temptations would be too great for an ordinary law-abiding citizen.

(3) Inconsistent Defenses. The traditional view has been that the defense of entrapment is not available to one who denies commission of the criminal act with which he is charged, for the reason that the denial is inconsistent with the assertion of such a defense. However, a trend in the opposite direction appears to be developing, and there is much to be said in favor of this latter position. For one thing, it avoids serious constitutional questions concerning whether a defendant may be required, in effect, to surrender his presumption of innocence and his privilege against self-incrimination in order to plead entrapment. Also, it would seem that the adversary process is itself a sufficient restraint upon resort to positions which are truly inconsistent. In a case where two positions are unquestionably logically inconsistent, a defendant who pursued both positions would certainly be found to be lacking credibility.

In any event, where the circumstances are such that there is no inherent inconsistency between claiming entrapment and yet not admitting commission of the criminal acts, certainly the defendant must be allowed to raise the defense of entrapment without admitting the crime. Thus, the inconsistency rule does not apply when the government in its own case in chief has interjected the issue of entrapment into the case. And if a defendant testifies that a government agent encouraged him to commit a crime which he had never contemplated before that time and that he resisted the temptation nonetheless, there is nothing internally inconsistent in thereby claiming entrapment and that the crime did not occur. Asserting the entrapment defense is not necessarily inconsistent with denial of the crime even when it is admitted that the requisite acts occurred, for the defendant might nonetheless claim that he lacked the requisite bad state of mind.

The matter was settled in the federal courts by *Mathews v. U.S.* (1988), where the Supreme Court held that even if a defendant denies one or more elements of the crime, he is entitled to an entrapment instruction whenever there is sufficient evidence from which a reasonable jury could find entrapment. Such a result, the Court noted, squares with the fact that federal defendants are allowed to raise inconsistent defenses in other contexts. The Court found unpersuasive the government's claim "that allowing a defendant to rely on inconsistent defenses will encourage perjury, lead to jury confusion, and subvert the truthfinding function of the trial."

(4) Burden of Proof. In those jurisdictions which follow the majority, subjective approach to entrapment, it is generally accepted that the defendant has the burden of establishing the fact of inducement by a government agent. The extent of this burden is less than clear. Some courts require a defendant to sustain a burden of persuasion by proving government inducement by a preponderance of the evidence. Many courts, however, indicate that the defendant only has the burden of production, which can be met by coming forward with "some evidence" of government conduct which created a risk of persuading a nondisposed person to commit a crime (sometimes said to include *both* inducement and nonpredisposition). In any event, once the defendant's threshold responsibility is satisfied (even if by evidence introduced during the prosecution's case-in-chief), the burden is then on the government to negate the defense by showing beyond a reasonable doubt defendant's predisposition or an absence of inducement.

In states where the objective approach is followed, the entire burden of production and persuasion is on the defendant, who must establish the impropriety of the police conduct by a preponderance of the evidence. This is a consequence of the entrapment defense under this approach being an "affirmative defense" rather than something that negatives the existence of an element of the crime charged. Such an allocation of the burden of proof might be questioned on the ground that as a general matter the government is in a much better position than the defendant to obtain and preserve evidence on the question of what kinds of government inducements were utilized in the particular case. This has led to the suggestion that perhaps the real basis for placing the burden of persuasion on the defendant is that entrapment is a disfavored defense, so that factual doubts should be resolved against it.

(g) Due Process: Government "Overinvolvement" in a Criminal Enterprise. In *Sorrells* and *Sherman* the entrapment doctrine was explained in terms of the presumed intention of Congress rather than as a matter of constitutional law. This means, of course, that Congress may depart from the *Sorrells–Sherman* test if it wishes, and that state courts and legislatures may do likewise. In short, the law of entrapment is not itself of constitutional dimension. But there remains for consideration the question of whether certain kinds of government involvement in a criminal enterprise would warrant the conclusion that the due process rights of the person induced had been violated.

In *U.S. v. Russell* (1973), an undercover agent supplied the defendant and his associates with 100 grams of propanone, an essential but difficult to obtain ingredient in the manufacture of methamphetamine ("speed"); the defendants used it to produce two batches of "speed," which pursuant to agreement the agent received half of in return. The defendant, convicted of unlawfully manufacturing and selling the substance, conceded on appeal that the jury could have found him predisposed, but claimed that the agent's involvement in the enterprise was so substantial that the prosecution violated due process. In particular, he contended that prosecution should be precluded when it is shown that the criminal conduct would not have been possible had not the agent "supplied an indispensable means to the commission of the crime that could not have been obtained otherwise, through legal or illegal channels." The Court in *Russell* found it unnecessary to pass on that contention because the record showed that propanone "was by no means impossible" to obtain by other sources. Though acknowledging that "we may some day be presented with a situation in which the conduct of law enforcement agents is so outrageous that due process principles would absolutely bar the government from invoking judicial processes to obtain a conviction," the majority concluded "the instant case is distinctly not of that breed" because the agent had simply supplied a legal and harmless substance to a person who had theretofore been "an active participant in an illegal drug manufacturing enterprise." Three dissenters urged adoption of the objective approach to entrapment and asserted that if propanone "had been wholly unobtainable from other sources" the agent's actions would be "conduct that constitutes entrapment under any definition."

Then came *Hampton v. U.S.* (1976), where petitioner, convicted of distributing heroin, objected to the denial of his requested jury instruction that he must be acquitted if the narcotics he sold to government agents had earlier been supplied to him by a government informant. Three members of the Court concluded that the difference between the instant case and *Russell* was "one of degree, not of kind," in that here the government supplied an illegal substance which was the corpus delicti of petitioner's crime and thus "played a more significant role" in enabling the crime to occur. But such conduct as to a predisposed defendant was deemed not to violate due process. Significantly, two concurring Justices, while agreeing that "this case is controlled completely by *Russell*," expressed their unwillingness "to join the plurality in concluding that, no matter what the circumstances, neither due process principles nor our supervisory power could support a bar to conviction in any case where the Government is able to prove disposition." The three dissenters in *Hampton* urged that conviction be "barred as a matter of law where the subject of the criminal charge is the sale of contraband provided to the defendant by a Government agent." The instant case, they contended, was different from *Russell* because (i) here the supplied substance was contraband and (ii) here the "beginning and end of this crime" coincided with the government's involvement. "The Government," they protested, "is doing nothing less than buying contraband from itself through an intermediary and jailing the intermediary."

Russell and *Hampton,* then, indicate that a majority of the Court accepts the notion that there may well be *some* circumstances in which a due process defense would be available even to a defendant found to be predisposed. However, those two cases do not provide clear guidance as to how the police conduct is to be assessed in making this judgment, though they do justify the conclusion that instances of government conduct outrageous enough to violate due process will be exceedingly rare. One possibility would be an instance in which government agents induce others to engage in violence or threat of violence against innocent parties. Another would be "where concern for overreaching government inducement overlaps with concern for first amendment freedoms, as where the government sends provocateurs into political organizations to suggest the commission of crimes." And then of course there is the situation put by the *Russell* dissenters—supplying contraband "wholly unobtainable from other sources" so as to "make possible the commission of an otherwise totally impossible crime." Other possibilities are where the government initiated or exploited a sexual relationship to bring about the crime or offered such extraordinarily large financial inducements as to bring about a coercive situation.

Special note must be taken of *U.S. v. Twigg* (1978), apparently the first case since *Hampton* in which a defendant has prevailed on a due process defense. Neville and Twigg were convicted of conspiracy to manufacture "speed." A government informer proposed to Neville that the laboratory be established, and Neville assumed responsibility for raising the capital and arranging for distribution, while the informer supplied the equipment, raw materials and laboratory site and was in complete charge of the lab because he alone had the expertise to manufacture the drug. Distinguishing *Russell* as a case in which the defendant was an active participant before the government agent appeared on the scene, and *Hampton* as concerned with "a much more fleeting and elusive crime to detect," the majority in *Twigg* concluded that the government involvement had reached "a demonstrable level of outrageousness." In reaching that conclusion, the court stressed (i) that "the illicit plan did not originate with the criminal defendants"; (ii) that the informer's expertise was "an indispensable requisite to this criminal enterprise"; and (iii) that, "as far as the record reveals, [Neville] was lawfully and peaceably minding his own affairs" until approached by the informant.

Twigg thus suggests that a "reasonable suspicion" prerequisite may on occasion emerge as an aspect of the due process limits upon encouragement activity. The point seems to be that overinvolvement by the government to the extent reflected in *Twigg* is permissible, if at all, only against a person who is "reasonably suspected of criminal conduct or design." The other important principle recognized in *Twigg* is that "the practicalities of combating" a certain type of criminal activity must be taken into account in determining whether "more extreme methods of investigation" are constitutionally permissible. However, there is reason to question the application of that sound principle in the *Twigg* case to conclude that more extreme methods are needed to detect drug distribution than drug manufacture. It has been persuasively argued that precisely the opposite conclusion is called for, that is, that "there usually will be a greater justification for government involvement in drug manufacturing schemes than in drug sales."

Chapter 9

JUSTIFICATION

Table of Sections

For additional analysis of the above topics and citations to authorities supporting their discussion in this Book, consult the author's 3-volume *Substantive Criminal Law* treatise, also available as Westlaw database SUBCRL. See the Table of Cross-References in this Book.

§ 9.1 Necessity

The pressure of natural physical forces sometimes confronts a person in an emergency with a choice of two evils: either he may violate the literal terms of the criminal law and thus produce a harmful result, or he may comply with those terms and thus produce a greater or equal or lesser amount of harm. For reasons of social policy, if the harm which will result from compliance with the law is greater than that which will result from violation of it, he is by virtue of the defense of necessity justified in violating it.

(a) Nature of the Defense of Necessity. One who, under the pressure of circumstances, commits what would otherwise be a crime may be justified by "necessity" in doing as he did and so not be guilty of the crime in question. With the defense of necessity, the traditional view has been that the pressure must come from the physical forces of nature (storms, privations) rather than from other human beings. (When the pressure is from human beings, the defense, if applicable, is called duress rather than necessity.) However, the "modern cases have tended to blur the distinction between duress and necessity." More significantly, most but not all of the modern recodifications (following Model Penal Code § 3.02 in this respect) contain a broader choice-of-evils defense that is not limited to any particular source of danger.

In any event, for a defense of necessity or choice-of-evils, the pressure must operate upon the mind of the defendant rather than upon his body. (When A and B are standing atop a precipice, and an earthquake causes A to stumble against B, throwing B over the cliff to his death, A's defense to a homicide charge is not that of necessity, for A's mind did not will his body against B's; instead, his defense is that he did no "act" (a willed movement), and one cannot be guilty of a crime of action without an act.) But when A, starving to death, takes and eats B's food to save his own life, or when A in an emergency intentionally kills B to save C and D, he may be eligible for the defense of necessity.

The rationale of the necessity defense is not that a person, when faced with the pressure of circumstances of nature, lacks the mental element that the crime in question requires. Rather, it is this reason of public policy: the law ought to promote the achievement of higher values at the expense of lesser values, and sometimes the greater good for society will be accomplished by violating the literal language of the criminal law. The law forbids stealing and murder, for there are positive values in the right to property and the right to life; but (as in the case of the starving man) it is better to save a life than to save the property, and (in the case of the killing of B to save C and D) it is better that two lives be saved and one lost than that two be lost and one saved.

The matter is often expressed in terms of choice of evils: When the pressure of circumstances presents one with a choice of evils, the law prefers that he avoid the greater evil by bringing about the lesser evil. Thus the evil involved in violating the terms of the criminal law (taking another's property; even taking another's life) may be less than that which would result from literal compliance with the law (starving to death; two lives lost).

The defense of necessity is available only in situations wherein the legislature has not itself, in its criminal statute, made a determination of values. The mere fact that the statute under which defendant is charged has *some* exceptions from liability not covering the situation at hand does not inevitably mean there has been a legislative determination contrary to defendant's position. But if the legislature *has* made a determination on this matter one way or another, then its decision governs. Thus the legislature might, in its abortion statute, expressly provide that the crime is not committed if the abortion is performed to save the mother's life; under such a statute there would be no need for courts to speculate about the relative value of preserving the fetus and safeguarding the mother's life. Conversely the abortion statute might expressly (or by its legislative history) provide that the crime is committed even when the abortion is performed to save the mother's life; here too the legislature has made a determination of values and by its decision thereon foreclosed the possibility of the defense that the abortion was necessary to save life. But if the abortion statute (even when read in the light of its legislative history) is silent upon the matter, then the question of the defense of necessity is open, and courts can properly consider the relative merits of preserving the fetus and saving the mother. The latter two situations, of course, have been described purely from an intent-of-the-legislature perspective. In light of *Roe v. Wade* (1973), however, the analysis cannot stop there, and thus such situations would in the final analysis be governed by the immutable proposition that a necessity defense may not be invoked as to conduct undertaken to prevent another person from exercising a constitutionally protected right.

When the necessity defense applies, it justifies the defendant's conduct in violating the literal language of the criminal law and so the defendant is not guilty of the crime in question. Where the defense does not apply, and yet the defendant did act with the good motive of preserving some value, his good motive, though not a defense, may be considered in mitigation of punishment for the crime committed (see § 4.3).

One may thus be justified by necessity in violating the law and causing harm in order to avoid a greater harm by complying with the law. Perhaps he has not only a power to violate the law but a duty to do so (much as a trustee, in appropriate circumstances, has a duty, and not simply a power, to deviate from the terms of a trust). If A is confronted with a choice between (1) intentionally killing B and thus saving the population of a city and (2) letting nature run its course, thus saving B but destroying the city, he ought to be criminally liable for murder of the city population if he does nothing. The difficulty, of course, lies in the fact that only in limited circumstances has the law imposed an affirmative duty to act as a basis of criminal liability (see § 5.2).

(b) Related Defenses. The defense of necessity is, of course, clearly related to that of duress (or coercion), where the pressure on the defendant's will comes from human beings rather than from physical circumstances. Duress is generally regarded as a separate defense (see § 8.7), but it would doubtless be possible to treat it as a branch of the law of necessity.

The defenses of self-defense and defense of others (see §§ 9.4, 9.5) are also related to the defense of necessity, justifying intentional homicide or the intentional infliction of bodily injury in cases where it is necessary to save the life of, or to prevent bodily injury to, the defendant or another. It has been said that self-defense and defense of others constitute a part of the law of necessity which has attained relatively fixed rules.

(c) Examples of the Defense. Although the cases are not numerous, the defense of necessity has been held applicable in a number of situations. The master of a ship forced by a storm to take refuge in a port in order to save the lives of those on board is not guilty of violating an embargo law forbidding entry into that port. Sailors who on the high seas refuse to obey the captain's orders are not guilty of mutiny when their object is to force the captain to return the unseaworthy vessel to port for necessary repairs. A doctor who performs an abortion upon a young-girl rape victim in order to prevent her from becoming a physical and metal wreck has been held not guilty of the crime of abortion under a statute punishing one who "unlawfully" produces a miscarriage. A parent who withdraws his child from school because of the child's feeble health is not guilty of violating the school law that provides for compulsory attendance unless excused by the school board. A police officer speeding after a fleeing criminal, or an ambulance driver on the way to the hospital with an emergency case, is not guilty of violating the speed laws. A police officer who plays a hand at cards in order, by disarming suspicion, to catch and arrest a gambler is not guilty of violating the gambling laws. An intoxicated person may operate a vehicle in which she was a passenger after the driver abandoned the vehicle when it stalled on railroad tracks. A glaucoma victim who shows that smoking marijuana is medically beneficial to his eye condition is not guilty of using and possessing marijuana. A prisoner who departs from prison is not guilty of the crime of prison-escape if the prison, through no fault of the prisoner, is afire—"for he is not to be hanged because he would not stay to be burnt." A person is not guilty of unlawful possession of a handgun when he wrestled the weapon from his attacker and then held it to ward off other assailants.

In addition to these decided cases, the Model Penal Code § 3.02 commentaries suggest that the defense is available in these situations: a person intentionally kills one person in order to save two or more; a firefighter destroys some property to prevent the spread of fire to other property; a mountain climber lost in a storm takes refuge in a house and appropriates provisions; a ship (or airplane) captain jettisons cargo to preserve the ship or plane and its passengers; a druggist dispenses a drug without the required prescription to alleviate suffering in an emergency.

On the other hand, the defense of necessity has been rejected in other circumstances. One who, unemployed and in great want, but not actually starving, helps himself to groceries from a grocery store is nevertheless guilty of larceny; "economic necessity" is no defense to crime, the court says. A prisoner who escapes from a prison camp where the conditions are unsanitary and the treatment brutal is nonetheless guilty of the crime of escaping from an officer. One who brings whiskey to church as a precautionary measure against the possibility of a sudden heart attack is guilty of the crime of bringing intoxicating liquor to church.

So too, in the area of homicide committed under the pressure of circumstances, one who intentionally kills another to save himself (as where two dying men are together without food or water or hope of timely rescue) may be guilty of murder. Two famous lifeboat cases, one English and the other American, have reached the courts. In the English case of *Regina v. Dudley & Stephens* (1884), three sailors and a cabin boy, as a result of shipwreck, were adrift in an open lifeboat more than a thousand miles from land; on the twentieth day, having been nine days without food and seven days without water, two of the men killed the cabin boy with a knife; the three men fed upon his body and drank his blood; four days later the three survivors were rescued by a passing ship, although in this time they and the boy (who was in the weakest condition) would probably have died had not one of them been killed and eaten. The court held this to be murder by the two killers, not justified by the circumstances. The American case, *U.S. v. Holmes* (1842), involved an overloaded lifeboat after a shipwreck, with nine seamen and thirty-two passengers aboard the boat. A storm came up which threatened to sink the boat; to lighten the boat so that she might ride out the storm, some of the crew members, including the defendant, threw fourteen male passengers overboard to their certain deaths. Thus lightened the boat remained afloat. But after arrival in port, the defendant was tried for manslaughter. The court instructed the jury that some of the crew members are necessary to navigate the boat; that any supernumerary seamen should be sacrificed before the passengers; and that as between people in an equal situation the determination of who are to be sacrificed for the safety of the whole group is to be determined by lot. The jury's guilty verdict was upheld by the court. (It has been argued, however, that a "state of nature" defense should be recognized in circumstances such as these.)

(d) Requirements of the Defense. The rationale of the defense, as stated above, lies in the social advantage gained when the defendant chooses the lesser of two evils and thus, by bringing about the lesser harm, avoids the greater harm.

(1) The Harm Avoided. The harm avoided need not be physical harm (death or bodily injury). It may, for instance, be harm to property, as where a firefighter destroys some property to prevent the spread of fire that threatens to consume other property of greater value. It may be harm to the defendant himself, as where he takes another's food to save his own life; or it may be harm to others, as where *A*, in no personal danger, intentionally runs his car over *B* in order to avoid hitting *C* and *D*.

(2) The Harm Done. On the other side of the equation, too, the harm done is not limited to any particular type of harm. It includes intentional homicide (as where *A*, faced with an emergency situation wherein he must either kill *B* or kill *C* and *D*, kills *B* to save the others) as well as lesser types of harm, like intentional battery or property damage (e.g., the plane commander jettisons cargo into the sea when one engine becomes disabled on an ocean passage). No doubt, in cases where there is a difference between the harm that his conduct actually causes and the harm that was necessarily to be expected from his conduct—as where *A*, driving a car, suddenly finds himself in a predicament where he must either run down *B* or hit *C*'s house and he reasonably chooses the latter, unfortunately killing two people in the house who by bad luck happened to be just at that place inside the house where A's car struck—it is the harm-reasonably-expected, rather than the harm-actually-caused, that governs.

(3) Intention to Avoid Harm. To have the defense of necessity, the defendant must have acted with the intention of avoiding the greater harm. Actual necessity, without the intention, is not enough. If A kills his enemy B for revenge, and he later learns to his happy surprise that by killing B he saved the lives of C and D, A has no defense to murder. In other words, he must believe that his act is necessary to avoid the greater harm. An honest (and, doubtless, reasonable) belief in the necessity of his action is all that is required, however, so that he has the defense even if, unknown to him, the situation did not in fact call for the drastic action taken. Thus if A kills B reasonably believing it to be necessary to save C and D, he is not guilty of murder even though, unknown to A, C and D could have been rescued without the necessity of killing B.

(4) Relative Value of Harm Avoided and Harm Done. The defendant's belief as to the relative harmfulness of the harm avoided and the harm done does not control, however. It is for the court, not the defendant, to weigh the relative harmfulness of the two alternatives; to allow the defense the court must conclude that the harm done by the defendant in choosing the one alternative was less than the harm which would have been done if he had chosen the other. A person with unusual values might think it more important to preserve a valuable painting than to save a human life; but if, faced in an emergency with a choice of saving one of the two, he should choose to destroy the life to save the painting, the court would disagree as to his choice of values and so reject his defense of necessity.

Sometimes, in necessity cases, the choice of values as to both alternatives concerns human lives: if some are sacrificed, the rest can be saved. Although it would perhaps be possible to assign a higher value to the life of a young person than to that of an older one, and to the life of a virtuous person than to that of an immoral one—so that A might be justified in killing old bad B in order to save young innocent C—yet the law doubtless considers one person's life equal to that of another (as one man's vote is the equal of another's), without regard to the age, character, health or good looks of the persons involved. Thus, in the example above, if the pressure of circumstances puts virtuous C in the pathway of death, and the only way to prevent C's death is for A to kill immoral B, A would not be justified in doing so.

Sometimes, but not always, the situation is such that the harm threatened by the pressure of circumstances cannot be avoided by the defendant; the harm will occur whatever choice he makes. If two men in mid-ocean are on a plank that can hold only one, either one can be saved if the other is sacrificed, so that if one kills the other he is not justified (unless, perhaps, they have drawn lots). But if a mountain climber, one of two roped together on a mountain, falls over a ledge and dangles in space, and the other, unable to pull his companion to safety, is slowly losing his grip on the mountainside, and if the inevitable consequence, unless the rope parts, is that both will plunge to their deaths, it is not a question of which one of the two shall die to save the other; for the dangling mountaineer is doomed in any event. If the other should cut the rope (no doubt in violation of the moral code of mountaineers), the law would consider that he has killed (accelerated death by a few moments) justifiably, for it is better that one be saved than that both should die.

(5) Optional Courses of Action; Imminence of Disaster. The defense of necessity applies when the defendant is faced with this choice of two evils: he may either do something that violates the literal terms of the criminal law and thus produce some harm, or not do it and so produce a greater harm. If, however, there is open to him a third alternative, which will cause less harm than will be caused by violating the law, he is not justified in violating the law. So in the case of the criminal statute that forbade taking intoxicating liquor to church, wherein the defendant took whiskey there for medicinal purposes, the court, rejecting his defense of necessity, pointed out the alternative of staying at home or of bringing some other kind of medicine. A starving man is not justified in stealing food from a grocery if he can obtain food by presenting himself at a soup kitchen. A prisoner subjected to inhumane treatment by his jailors is not justified in breaking prison if he can bring about an improvement in conditions by other means. One man in a lifeboat facing death by starvation cannot justifiably kill another to save himself (unless perhaps lots are first drawn); a fortiori he cannot do so if he can, without starving to death, wait a while longer, with a possibility of rescue during the interval of waiting. And in those cases of trespass on government property or similar criminal protest activity purportedly undertaken to terminate some dangerous governmental action, "a defendant's legal alternatives will rarely, if ever, be deemed exhausted when the harm of which he complains can be palliated by political action." (By similar reasoning, a citizen who engages in criminal conduct in an effort to cause the government to terminate action he believes is in violation of international law cannot invoke an international law or Nuremberg defense, as "an individual cannot assert a privilege to disregard domestic law in order to escape liability under international law unless domestic law forces that person to violate international law.")

It is sometimes said that the defense of necessity does not apply except in an emergency—when the threatened harm is immediate, the threatened disaster imminent. Perhaps this is but a way of saying that, until the time comes when the threatened harm is immediate, there are generally options open to the defendant, to avoid the harm, other than the option of disobeying the literal terms of the law—the rescue ship may appear, the storm may pass; and so the defendant must wait until that hope of survival disappears.

(6) No Fault in Bringing About the Situation. So far we have assumed that the defendant was not personally at fault in creating the situation calling for the necessity of his choosing between two evils. Thus, in the lifeboat cases, he did not cause the shipwreck or produce the shortage of sustenance or bring on the storm. If, however, he was at fault in creating the situation, he may be criminally liable in some circumstances.

One approach, taken in Model Penal Code § 3.02(2) and followed in some of the modern codes, is to determine the level of liability on the basis of the defendant's culpability in creating the danger. Thus, if he intentionally brings on the situation, he may be guilty of a crime of intention; if he was reckless, of a crime of recklessness; if negligent, of a crime of negligence. Thus if *A* drives recklessly and thereby creates a situation where he must either stay in the roadway and run down *B* and *C* or go on the sidewalk and strike *D,* and he chooses the lesser harm and hence strike and kills *D,* he is guilty of the recklessness type of manslaughter of *D* (on account of his reckless conduct in creating the situation) but not, it would seem, for the intentional murder of *D*. These provisions also apply when the defendant was at fault in appraising the necessity for his conduct.

A few jurisdictions go farther than this, providing that the defense of necessity or choice-of-evils simply is unavailable to one who was at fault in occasioning or developing the situation requiring choice of a lesser harm. This approach is objectionable because it does not distinguish between levels of fault. "The person who negligently starts the forest fire is not distinguished from the person who does so intentionally. Both would be convicted of the intentional offense of arson for burning the firebreak." Even more objectionable, however, is the provision found in one state that permits the defense only if the "situation occasioned or developed through no conduct of the actor."

§ 9.2 Public Duty

A public officer is justified in using reasonable force against the person of another, or in taking his property, when he acts pursuant to a valid law, or court order or process, requiring or authorizing him so to act. By the better view, he is justified in so acting, even if the law turns out to be unconstitutional or the process defective, if he reasonably believes the law or process to be valid.

(a) Executing a Court Order. A public officer is justified in detaining an individual, in using a reasonable amount of force against the person of another, or in taking or destroying another's property, when he is acting pursuant to a valid court order requiring him or authorizing him so to act. Thus, the public executioner is not guilty of murder, though he intentionally brings about another's death, when he is carrying out the death penalty imposed by a court of competent jurisdiction that condemned the defendant to death. So too an officer, executing a valid civil process, is justified in taking another's property on a writ of attachment or execution; or, executing a valid arrest warrant, in using force against another in effecting the arrest. A person who is required or authorized to assist a public officer is likewise justified in so acting.

There is a question whether the justification is lost when it turns out that the legal process executed by the public officer was defective or was issued by a court lacking jurisdiction. Various positions are to be found in the modern codes: some extend the defense to situations in which the officer actually believed his conduct was authorized or required by the court order; some others go not so far by requiring that the belief be reasonable; and a few others define the defense in such a way that the particular public officer's belief appears to be irrelevant, either in the sense that the defense extends even to instances in which that officer knows the process is invalid, or in the sense that actual validity of the court order is essential to the defense.

Similarly, there is also a split of authority as to the extent of the public duty defense as to a private person who was assisting a public official. Many statutes declare it is sufficient that this person actually believed his assistance was required or authorized by law, while others require that the belief be a reasonable one. A few other provisions appear to make the private person's state of mind concerning the validity of the order or the lawfulness of the officer's conduct in carrying it out irrelevant in terms of narrowing or expanding the defense.

(b) Other Actions of Public Officials. Statutes in the modern codes dealing with the public duty defense are not limited to official action pursuant to court order, but rather extend to other exercises of public duty as well. Usually this is indicated by a broad provision covering any instance in which the actor's conduct is "required or authorized by law," though sometimes these statutes make specific mention of the performance of official duties by a public servant. These statutes do not themselves recognize any room for error (even reasonable mistake) concerning what the law actually authorizes with respect to these duties, nor do they typically require that the public official's conduct be limited to the least intrusive step needed under the circumstances.

(c) Military Duties. Yet another aspect of the public duty defense is where the conduct was required or authorized by "the law governing the armed services or the lawful conduct of war." Several modern codes specify that situation within a more general public duty statute. This means, for example, that if a soldier intentionally kills an enemy combatant in time of war and within the rules of warfare, he is not guilty of murder; but if he intentionally kills a prisoner of war, then he commits murder.

§ 9.3　Domestic Authority; Other Special Relationships

The parent of a minor child, or one "in loco parentis" with respect to such child, is justified in using reasonable force upon the child for the purpose of promoting the child's welfare. Similarly, a schoolteacher is justified in using reasonable force upon a pupil for the purpose of enforcing school discipline. Other persons with responsibility for the care, discipline or safety of others (e.g., an asylum superintendent, prison warden, ship captain) are justified in using reasonable force upon others for the purpose of carrying out their responsibilities.

(a) Parents of a Minor Child. The parent of a minor child is justified in using a reasonable amount of force upon the child for the purpose of safeguarding or promoting the child's welfare. Thus the parent may punish the child for wrongdoing and not be guilty of a battery or of a violation of a statute punishing cruelty to children if the punishment is inflicted for this beneficent purpose, and if the punishment thus inflicted is not excessive in view of all the circumstances (including the child's age, sex, health, his misconduct on the present occasion and in the past, the kind of punishment inflicted, and the degree of harm done to the child thereby). Indeed, it has been said that a parent has a constitutional right, "a fundamental liberty interest in maintaining a familiar relationship with his or her child," which "includes the right of parents 'to direct the upbringing and education of children,' including the use of reasonable or moderate physical force to control behavior."

There is a dispute as to whether the test of liability in the case of a parent should be (1) an objective one, concerned with whether a reasonable man would consider the punishment excessive, or (2) a subjective one, concerned with whether the punisher acted with "malice," i.e., a purpose other than that of promoting the child's welfare. The courts that adopt the latter view say, however, that such "malice" may be inferred from the infliction of excessive punishment, or punishment which results in serious injury to the child.

Model Penal Code § 3.08 combines these two views, as do virtually all the statutes on this subject appearing in the recent recodifications. On the matter of the reasonableness of the force, some statutes merely say it must be reasonable, reasonable and moderate, reasonable and necessary, reasonable and appropriate, or other than deadly force. Others more wisely essentially follow the Model Penal Code formulation, requiring the force be "not designed to cause or known to create a substantial risk of causing death, serious bodily harm, disfigurement, extreme pain or mental distress or gross degradation." As for the proper purpose, these provisions state that the parent must be acting to maintain discipline, to restrain or correct, to prevent or punish misconduct, or to promote or safeguard and promote the welfare of the child.

The parent's right to use reasonable force has been extended to those, not parents, who are "in loco parentis"—such as a stepfather or even a paramour living with the child's mother without benefit of matrimony, a guardian, or the director of an orphanage. Modern statutes seldom employ the "in loco parentis" term. Rather, they typically refer to other persons responsible for or entrusted with the general care and supervision of the child, and, less frequently, to persons acting at the request of a parent. Such formulations may extend somewhat beyond the traditional "in loco parentis" test.

(b) School Teacher. A schoolteacher may use reasonable force upon his pupil for the purpose of either promoting the child's education or of maintaining reasonable discipline in the school. Thus he may punish the pupil for wrongdoing, without criminal liability for battery or for violating a special statute punishing cruelty to children, if he does so to maintain discipline and does not inflict punishment that is excessive under the circumstances. The privilege is not a delegation to the teacher of the parent's right to punish the child; therefore, the teacher can exercise the power to punish even if the parent disapproves or even if the parent has no such power himself. The privilege of a teacher applies to the pupil's misconduct affecting school discipline that takes place off the school grounds—as where, on their way from home to school, one pupil commits a battery upon another.

Here, as with punishment by parents, courts have taken two different views of the test of liability. Under the "malice" rule, the teacher is deemed to act in a quasi-judicial capacity and thus is not criminally liable because of an error in judgment or because the punishment was disproportionate, so long as the purpose was to promote discipline rather than the "malicious" purpose to inflict pain. Under the reasonableness test, on the other hand, the punishment must not exceed what is reasonable under the circumstances. This latter view has been characterized as "the more enlightened" one because it "refuses to make the teacher the sole arbiter" of whether the punishment inflicted was called for.

Model Penal Code § 3.08(2) focuses upon both the reasonableness of the punishment and the purpose underlying its use, as is generally the case in the statutes on this subject appearing in the modern criminal codes. The amount of force which may be used is equivalent to that authorized for parents. As for the permissible purpose, it is variously stated in this legislation in terms of maintaining discipline, maintaining discipline or promoting the welfare of the child, maintaining discipline consistent with the welfare of the child, maintaining order, quelling a disturbance and removing the offending student, or restraining or correcting the student.

(c) Other Relationships. Many of the modern codes deal not only with the parent-child and teacher-student relationships, but also with other situations in which there is a special responsibility for certain persons to see to the care, discipline or safety of others. Most often addressed in this legislation is the authority of those responsible for incompetent persons. These provisions typically follow Model Penal Code § 3.08(3) by recognizing that nondeadly force may be used to promote the welfare of an incompetent person (including the prevention of his misconduct) or to maintain discipline within an institution. Similarly, it is frequently provided that correctional officials are justified in using reasonable force to maintain order in and enforce the rules of a prison or jail.

Even prior to the drafting of the Model Penal Code, legislation allowing those responsible for maintaining order and decorum on trains or other carriers to expel disorderly passengers was not uncommon. Legislation on this subject is typically found in the modern recodifications, usually following Model Penal Code § 3.08(7) in extending the justification to persons authorized or required to maintain order in other public places (e.g., a theatre). But only a few states have adopted Model Penal Code § 3.08(6), expressly recognizing that a person responsible for the safety of a vessel or aircraft may use force (even deadly force if necessary) to prevent interference with operation of the vessel or aircraft.

Several of the modern codes also declare that the use of force by a doctor is justified in specified circumstances. Many follow Model Penal Code § 3.08(4), providing that the force must be used as part of a recognized form of treatment and with consent of the patient or one authorized to consent on the patient's behalf, except that consent is unnecessary in an emergency. Even if the rules concerning civil liability are not this broad, it is important that medical personnel be allowed to administer unconsented medical treatment in emergencies without fear of criminal liability. This "good Samaritan" notion doubtless accounts for yet another common statutory provision, namely, that one is justified in using force upon another to the extent reasonably believed necessary to thwart a suicide attempt.

§ 9.4 Self Defense

One who is not the aggressor in an encounter is justified in using a reasonable amount of force against his adversary when he reasonably believes (a) that he is in immediate danger of unlawful bodily harm from his adversary and (b) that the use of such force is necessary to avoid this danger. It is never reasonable to use deadly force against his nondeadly attack. There is a dispute as to whether one threatened with a deadly attack must retreat, if he can safely do so, before resorting to deadly force, except that it is agreed that ordinarily he need not retreat from his home or place of business.

(a) Generally. It is only just that one who is unlawfully attacked by another, and who has no opportunity to resort to the law for his defense, should be able to take reasonable steps to defend himself from physical harm. When the steps he takes are reasonable, he has a complete defense to such crimes against the person as murder and manslaughter, attempted murder, assault and battery and the aggravated forms of assault and battery, and perhaps other offenses as well. His intentional infliction of (or, if he misses, his attempt to inflict) physical harm upon the other, or his threat to inflict such harm, is said to be justified when he acts in proper self-defense, so that he is not guilty of any crime.

In order that one be entitled to use force in self-defense (or in defense of others) to oppose the force of his adversary, it is necessary that the adversary's force be, or at least that the defendant reasonably believe it to be, "unlawful" force—meaning, in general, that it be a crime or tort (generally assault and battery) for the adversary to use the force. Thus one cannot properly defend himself against known lawful force or against the use of force to which he has consented.

The law of self-defense (and of defense of others) makes a distinction between "deadly" force and "nondeadly" (or "moderate") force, holding that there are situations wherein it is reasonable to use nondeadly force but not to use deadly force. "Deadly force" may be defined as force (a) that its user uses with the intent to cause death or serious bodily injury to another or (b) that he knows creates a substantial risk of death or serious bodily injury to the other. One thus uses deadly force if he fires at another with intent to kill him or do him serious bodily harm, though actually he misses him completely or causes him only minor bodily injury. But merely to threaten death or serious bodily harm, without any intention to carry out the threat, is not to use deadly force, so that one may be justified in pointing a gun at his attacker when he would not be justified in pulling the trigger.

(b) Amount of Force. In determining how much force one may use in self-defense, the law recognizes that the amount of force which he may justifiably use must be reasonably related to the threatened harm which he seeks to avoid. One may justifiably use *nondeadly* force against another in self-defense if he reasonably believes that the other is about to inflict unlawful bodily harm (it need not be death or serious bodily harm) upon him (and also believes that it is necessary to use such force to prevent it). That is, under such circumstances he is not guilty of assault (if he merely threatens to use the nondeadly force or if he aims that force at the other but misses) or battery (if he injuries the other by use of that force). He may justifiably use *deadly* force against the other in self-defense, however, only if he reasonably believes that the other is about to inflict unlawful death or serious bodily harm upon him (and also that it is necessary to use deadly force to prevent it). Such use of deadly force is authorized in the modern codes, which typically go on to permit this amount of force in defense of serious offenses against the person.

As for the rule that deadly force may only be used against what is reasonably believed to be deadly force, it may generally be said that "this requirement precludes the use of a deadly weapon against an *unarmed* assailant." But this is not inevitably the case; account must be taken of the respective sizes and sex and health of the assailant and defendant, of the presence of multiple assailants, and of the especially violent nature of the unarmed attack. Past violent conduct of the assailant known by the defendant is also relevant in assessing what the defendant reasonably believed was the quantum of risk to him.

(c) Reasonable Belief in Necessity for Force. As indicated in the above statements, the case law and statutory law on self-defense generally require that the defendant's belief in the necessity of using force to prevent harm to himself be a reasonable one, so that one who honestly though unreasonably believes in the necessity of using force in self-protection loses the defense. This is an objective requirement, though it has sometimes been held that certain "circumstances" relating to the particular defendant are relevant thereto, such as that defendant is a battered woman.

When his belief is reasonable, however, he may be mistaken in his belief and still have the defense. Thus one may be justified in shooting to death an adversary who, having threatened to kill him, reaches for his pocket as if for a gun, though it later appears that he had no gun and that he was only reaching for his handkerchief. In appraising the situation one may, under the circumstances, be reasonable though mistaken since, as Mr. Justice Holmes put it in *Brown v. U.S.* (1921): "Detached reflection cannot be demanded in the presence of an uplifted knife." One who because of voluntary intoxication thinks that he is in danger of imminent attack, though a sober man would not have thought so, does not have the reasonable belief that the law requires.

There is a little authority that an honest belief in the necessity of self-defense will do; it need not in addition be a reasonable belief. Model Penal Code § 3.04(1) supports this view, on the theory that there should be no conviction of a crime requiring intentional misconduct of one who is guilty only of negligence in making the unreasonable mistake. Only a few of the modern codes have adopted this position.

Of course, whether a reasonable belief is required or not, the defendant must *actually* believe in the necessity for force. He has no defense when he intentionally kills his enemy in complete ignorance of the fact that his enemy, when killed, was about to launch a deadly attack upon him. Nevertheless, if he acts in proper self-defense, he does not lose the defense because he acts with some less admirable motive in addition to that of defending himself, as where he enjoys using force upon his adversary because he hates him.

(d) Imminence of Attack. Case law and legislation concerning self-defense require that the defendant reasonably believe his adversary's unlawful violence to be almost immediately forthcoming. Most of the modern codes require that the defendant reasonably perceive an "imminent" use of force, although other language making the same point is sometimes to be found. Very few of the self-defense provisions in the modern codes fail to address this point explicitly.

As a general matter, the requirement that the attack reasonably appear to be imminent is a sensible one. If the threatened violence is scheduled to arrive in the more distant future, there may be avenues open to the defendant to prevent it other than to kill or injure the prospective attacker; but this is not so where the attack is imminent. But the application of this requirement in some contexts has been questioned. "Suppose *A* kidnaps and confines *D* with the announced intention of killing him one week later. *D* has an opportunity to kill *A* and escape each morning as *A* brings him his daily ration. Taken literally, the *imminent* requirement would prevent *D* from using deadly force in self-defense until *A* is standing over him with a knife, but that outcome seems inappropriate. * * * The proper inquiry is not the immediacy of the threat but the immediacy of the response necessary in defense. If a threatened harm is such that it cannot be avoided if the intended victim waits until the last moment, the principle of self-defense must permit him to act earlier—as early as is required to defend himself effectively."

However, the question of whether there should be an imminence-of-attack requirement and, if so, how it should be characterized, is most dramatically presented in the context of a homicide by a battered wife. It sometimes occurs that a wife who has repeatedly been subjected to serious bodily harm by her husband will take his life on a particular occasion when there was not, strictly speaking, any immediate threat of repetition of the husband's conduct, though the wife knew with virtual certainty that more severe beatings were in the offing. Such a state of affairs often comes about, experts have testified, because of what is known as the "battered woman syndrome": "a man physically and psychologically abuses a wife or loved one, gains her forgiveness, seeks her love and reconciliation and then repeats the cycle over and over so many times that the woman, at all times hoping the relationship will last, is reduced to a state of learned helplessness." Some have argued that the "battered wife thus is literally faced with the dilemma of either waiting for her husband to kill her or striking out at him first," and that consequently the "imminency" requirement should be abolished or loosely construed so that on such facts the battered wife's self-defense claim will prevail. Others just as fervently contend that the battered wife case shows just how essential the "imminency" requirement really is, as especially in such circumstances the law must encourage resort to alternatives other than the taking of human life.

(e) The Aggressor's Right to Self–Defense. It is generally said that one who is the aggressor in an encounter with another— i.e., one who brings about the difficulty with the other—may not avail himself of the defense of self-defense. Ordinarily, this is certainly a correct statement, since the aggressor's victim, defending himself against the aggressor, is using lawful, not unlawful, force; and the force defended against must be unlawful force, for self-defense. Nevertheless, there are two situations in which an aggressor may justifiably defend himself. (1) A nondeadly aggressor (i.e., one who begins an encounter, using only his fists or some nondeadly weapon) who is met with deadly force in defense may justifiably defend himself against the deadly attack. This is so because the aggressor's victim, by using deadly force against non-deadly aggression, uses unlawful force. (2) So too, an aggressor who in good faith effectively withdraws from any further encounter with his victim (and to make an effective withdrawal he must notify the victim, or at least take reasonable steps to notify him) is restored to his right of self-defense.

Some modern codes specify still other circumstances in which a person, by virtue of his own prior conduct, has lost the right of self-defense he would otherwise have. Most common is a provision that one who provokes the use of force against himself for the purpose of causing serious bodily harm may not defend against the force he has provoked. Some statutes expressly disallow defense against force that was the product of combat by agreement, and some declare that those involved in certain criminal activities do not during such time have any right of self-defense. A few states have provisions generally not permitting defensive force against one who is an occupier or possessor of property and is defending that property under a claim of right.

(f) Necessity for Retreat. We have already noted that one may not, in self-defense, use more force than reasonably appears to be necessary to avoid his adversary's threatened harm. A difficulty arises, however, when there is one way open to avoid the threatened harm other than by injuring or killing the adversary: what if, instead of standing his ground and using force, the defender can safely (though ignominiously) run away? There is a strong policy against the unnecessary taking of human life (and a somewhat weaker policy against causing unnecessary bodily injury). On the other hand, there is a policy against making one act a cowardly and humiliating role.

It seems everywhere agreed that one who can safely retreat need not do so before using nondeadly force. "If he does not resort to a deadly force, one who is assailed may hold his ground whether the attack upon him be of a deadly or some lessor [sic] character. Although it might be argued that a safe retreat should be taken if thereby the use of *any* force could be avoided, yet * * * the logic of this position never has been accepted when moderate force is used in self-defense."

Thus the question of the duty to retreat is a problem only when deadly force is used in self-defense. The majority of American jurisdictions holds that the defender (who was not the original aggressor) need not retreat, even though he can do so safely, before using deadly force upon an assailant whom he reasonably believes will kill him or do him serious bodily harm. A strong minority, however, taking what might be regarded as a more civilized view, holds that he must retreat ("retreat to the wall," it is sometimes said), before using deadly force, if he can do so in safety. But even in those jurisdictions that require retreat, the defender need not retreat unless he knows he can do so in complete safety; and he need not retreat from his home or place of business, except perhaps when the defender was the original aggressor or the assailant is a co-occupant of those premises. Moreover, the retreat requirement does not apply to a police officer or a private person assisting him.

If retreat is to be preferred over use of deadly force, then it might be argued that certain other alternative steps which would terminate the dangerous encounter should likewise be required in lieu of self-defense with deadly force. Thus, Model Penal Code § 3.04(2)(b)(ii) expressly provides that deadly force is not permissible if the actor knows he can avoid the necessity for its use "by surrendering possession of a thing to a person asserting a claim of right thereto or by complying with a demand that he abstain from any action which he has no duty to take." A few modern codes contain such surrender-possession and comply-with-demand limits on deadly force.

Since 2005, more than forty states have passed or proposed new legislation intended to expand the right to use deadly force in self-defense. These statutes, advocated by the National Rifle Association, purport to change existing self-defense law in one or both of the following ways: first, they permit a home resident to kill an intruder by presuming rather than requiring proof of reasonable fear of death or serious bodily harm; second, they reject a general duty to retreat from attack, even when retreat is possible, not only in the home, but also in public space.

(g) Accidental Injury to Third Person. If A in proper self-defense aims at his adversary B but misses B and unintentionally strikes innocent bystander C, he is not liable for C's injury or death. But the result is otherwise if under all the circumstances (including the need to defend himself) A was reckless with regard to C. In such a case he would be liable for battery if he merely injures, involuntary manslaughter if he kills, C.

(h) Resisting Unlawful Arrest. A problem much like that of self-defense against unlawful aggression is that concerning the right to use force to resist an unlawful arrest. Here the threatened harm is not, as with self-defense, that of bodily injury or death but rather the indignity and inconvenience of undergoing arrest and its accompanying detention. In most jurisdictions the arrested person is justified in using nondeadly force, but not in using deadly force, to resist the arrest. (If he uses deadly force, intentionally killing the arresting person, he may, by a view, have his crime mitigated from murder to voluntary manslaughter, on the theory that the unlawful arrest is the sort of provocation which causes reasonable men to lose their self-control; see § 14.2(b)(4).)

It is arguable, however, that it is not justifiable to use any force to resist an unlawful arrest by one whom the arrested person knows to be a police officer. There are remedies for release available to one unlawfully arrested, and the indignity of the arrest and the inconvenience of the detention until release are relatively minor matters, goes the argument; the remedies should be used rather than force. Model Penal Code § 3.04(2)(a)(i) adopts a rule outlawing the use of force against a known police officer, though the arrest is unlawful. Many of the modern codes include such a provision, and even in the absence of such an enactment some courts have abandoned the common law view or have declined to apply it in the case of police intrusions short of arrest. This rule, of course, does not bar use of force in self-defense if the officer uses excessive force in making the arrest.

(i) "Imperfect" Self–Defense. We have noted that one who uses force against another with an honest but unreasonable belief that he must use force to defend himself from an imminent attack by his adversary is not, in most jurisdictions, justified in his use of force, for proper self-defense requires that the belief in the necessity for the force he uses be reasonable. Although in many jurisdictions such a person is guilty of murder when he uses deadly force in such circumstances, some courts and legislatures have taken the more humane view that, while he is not innocent of crime, he is nevertheless not guilty of murder; rather, he is guilty of the in-between crime of manslaughter. "Outside of homicide law, the concept [of imperfect self-defense] doesn't exist. * * * With respect to all other crimes, the defendant is either guilty or not guilty. * * * There is no 'in between.' "

§ 9.5 Defense of Another

The prevailing rule is that one is justified in using reasonable force in defense of another person, even a stranger, when he reasonably believes that the other is in immediate danger of unlawful bodily harm from his adversary and that the use of such force is necessary to avoid this danger. Deadly force is reasonable force only when the attack of the adversary upon the other person reasonably appears to the defender to be a deadly attack.

(a) Relationship to Person Defended. Some early English cases suggested that force may not be used in defense of another unless the defender stands in some personal relationship to the one in need of protection (e.g., husband, wife, child, parent, relative, or employee or employer), and some American statutes still on the books purport to limit the use of force in defense of others to the defense of those who bear some designated relationship to the defender. Yet the modern and better rule is that there need be no such relationship, so that one is entitled in an appropriate case to use force to protect a friend or acquaintance or even a stranger from threatened harm by a third person. The modern codes rather consistently take this view. Whether this defense extends to protection of an unborn child by preventing an unlawful termination of a pregnancy will likely turn on the wording of the applicable defense-of-others statute and whether the jurisdiction otherwise recognizes such an interest.

(b) Reasonable Belief in Necessity for Force. As with self-defense, so too with the defense of another, one is not justified in using force to protect the other unless he reasonably believes that the other is in immediate danger of unlawful bodily harm and that force is necessary to prevent that harm; and even when he entertains these reasonable beliefs, he may not use more force than he reasonably believes necessary to relieve the risk of harm.

The courts have experienced some difficulty in the case where the defender goes to the aid of another reasonably believing the other is in danger of unlawful bodily harm, but in fact the bodily harm directed at him is lawful. Thus B unlawfully attacks C and C defends himself in proper self-defense (or plainclothes policeman C tries lawfully to arrest B and properly uses force against B in making the arrest). A arrives on the scene and, not knowing the true facts, reasonably concludes that B is the innocent victim of an unlawful attack by C; so A goes to B's rescue and uses force against C.

One set of cases adopts what is sometimes called the "alter ego" rule, which holds that the right to defend another is coextensive with the other's right to defend himself; thus the defender A who intervenes to protect B against C takes the risk that B is not in fact privileged to defend himself in the manner he employs; so that, where B is not privileged, A is guilty of assault and battery or murder of B in spite of his reasonable belief that B is privileged. It has been argued that, at least in the case of the policeman in civilian clothes, such a rule is necessary to prevent the hampering of law enforcement.

The other view is that, so long as the defendant reasonably believes that the other is being unlawfully attacked, he is justified in using reasonable force to defend him. This view, which has been adopted in the new state criminal codes, is surely the preferable view. As the New Jersey court expressed it in *State v. Fair* (1965): not only, as a matter of justice, should one "not be convicted of a crime if he selflessly attempts to protect the victim of an apparently unjustified assault, but how else can we encourage bystanders to go to the aid of another who is being subject to assault?" To impose liability upon the defender in these circumstances is to impose upon him liability without fault; and yet the assault and homicide crimes are crimes that require fault.

The defense of defending of others overlaps somewhat with the defense of crime prevention (see § 9.7(c)). Thus one may be justified in defending another person in order to prevent the commission of a felony (e.g., murder, assault with intent to kill or do serious bodily injury) upon him. There may be some situations where the defense of others may be justified only on the grounds of crime prevention.

(c) Necessity for Retreat. Because many jurisdictions have adopted a retreat rule with respect to the defense of self defense (see § 9.4(f)), often in statutory provisions that also extend to defense of third parties, this rule is frequently applicable in the present context as well. It is apparent, however, that the retreat alternative must be assessed somewhat differently here. To take the most obvious case, surely the ability of the defendant to retreat without risk to himself should not control when the force is being used to protect another party who cannot retreat.

A few of the modern codes substantially follow Model Penal Code § 3.05(2) by giving special attention to when retreat is and is not required in a defense-of-another situation. Under the Code, the defender who would be required to retreat if defending himself need not do so here unless he knows he can thereby secure the complete safety of the person being defended. If the person being defended would be required to retreat, then the defender must try to cause him to do so if the defender knows he could obtain complete safety in that way. Finally, the dwelling-workplace exception to the retreat rule applies here if the place is the dwelling or place of work of either the defender or the person defended.

§ 9.6 Defense of Property

One is justified in using reasonable force to protect his property from trespass or theft, when he reasonably believes that his property is in immediate danger of such an unlawful interference and that the use of such force is necessary to avoid that danger. Under the better view, deadly force is never reasonable except where the unlawful interference with property is accompanied by a threat of deadly force (in which case it is proper to use deadly force in self-defense), or where the unlawful interference involves an invasion of an occupied dwelling house under circumstances causing the defender reasonably to believe that the invader intends to commit a felony therein or to do serious bodily harm to its occupants.

(a) Generally. One whose lawful possession of property is threatened by the unlawful conduct of another, and who has no time to resort to the law for its protection, may take reasonable steps, including the use of force, to "prevent or terminate" such interference with the property. The defender of property, to justify the use of force, must reasonably believe (a) that his real property is in immediate danger of unlawful entry or trespass, or that his personal property is in immediate danger of an unlawful trespass or carrying away, and (b) that the use of force is necessary to avoid this danger. However, some courts, by analogy to the modern rule disallowing force to resist an unlawful arrest (see § 9.4(h)), have held force is inappropriate against a police officer's seizure or unlawful entry of property.

Even when he entertains these reasonable beliefs, however, he may not use more than reasonable force—the amount of force that reasonably appears necessary to prevent the threatened interference with the property or by seeking assistance of police on the scene. It is not reasonable to use any force at all if the threatened danger to property can be avoided by a request to the other to desist from interfering with the property or by seeking assistance of police on the scene. And even when it is reasonable to use some force, it is not reasonable to use deadly force to prevent threatened harm to property, such as a mere trespass or theft, even though the harm cannot otherwise be prevented. This is because the preservation of human life is more important to society than the protection of property. Of course, if the defender's reasonable force in protection of his property is met with an attack upon his person, he may then respond by defending himself and then may be entitled to use deadly force.

(b) Defense of Dwelling. In the case of a mere civil trespass upon a dwelling, the rule stated above also applies, so that once again deadly force may not be used. Yet, it has long been recognized that the limitations on the use of force to protect other property are not always applicable when defense of a dwelling is involved, although the courts are not in agreement as to when deadly force may be used.

An early view, based upon the English notion that defense of the home that sheltered life was just as important as defense of life itself, permitted the householder to use deadly force if it reasonably appeared necessary to prevent forcible entry against his will after a warning to the intruder not to enter and to desist from the use of force. Subsequent decisions have for the most part rejected this rule as too broad. Some courts now say that deadly force is permissible only when the defender reasonably believes that the trespasser intends to commit a felony or do harm to him or another within the house. This rule, incorporated into some statutes, also attaches special importance to the dwelling as a place of security, for it permits the use of deadly force even when the anticipated attack would not result in the killing or serious injury of someone within. Other courts have adopted a still narrower view, more in keeping with the right of self-defense and crime prevention (see §§ 9.4, 9.7(c)), by holding that deadly force may be used only against an entry of a dwelling reasonably believed to be for the purpose of committing a felony (including killing or doing great bodily harm therein). In any event, the right to protect the home by use of deadly force is not limited by a requirement that the person instead retreat if reasonably possible.

Modern statutes on protection of dwellings (or, of premises generally) state that necessary deadly force may be used to prevent or terminate some specific felony, such as arson or burglary or robbery, or all forcible felonies, or all felonies. By contrast, the Model Penal Code § 3.06(3)(d)(ii) approach, adopted in a few states, is more specific in its requirement that deadly force be limited to instances in which there is a substantial risk to the person. Deadly force may be used if the defender believes that the other person is attempting to commit or consummate arson, burglary, robbery or other felonious theft or property destruction and either (1) has employed or threatened deadly force against or in the presence of the defender, or (2) the use of force other than deadly force would expose the defender or another to substantial danger of serious bodily harm.

A separate question is that of whether the householder is entitled to use deadly force to resist dispossession of a dwelling. While the old common law view on use of force in defense of a dwelling was broad enough to permit deadly force under these circumstances, the same is not true of the more limited rules on deadly force that have developed in recent years. Consideration of the dispossession case as a separate issue seems not to have occurred in this country, except by the draftsmen of the Model Penal Code. Noting the difficult question of policy involved, they have taken the position in Code § 3.06(3)(d)(i) that deadly force may only be used when "the person against whom the force is used is attempting to dispossess him of his dwelling otherwise than under a claim of right to its possession."

(c) Use of Mechanical Devices. Just as one cannot use deadly force to protect his property from trespass or theft, so too he cannot use a deadly spring gun or other mechanical device as a protection against trespass or theft. A killing by such a device is justifiable only if the one who employs the device would in fact have been justified in taking the life of the trespasser had he been present, as where the trespasser tries to enter an occupied dwelling to do great violence to the occupants or to commit a burglary therein.

Model Penal Code § 3.06(5) rejects the latter justification, taking the view that use of a deadly mantrap is never justifiable. The common law rule was properly rejected on the ground that it does not prescribe a workable standard of conduct, in that liability depends upon fortuitous circumstances—the intentions of the trespasser who happens to be killed or seriously injured by the mechanical device. Under the Code, nondeadly mechanical devices such as spiked fences may justifiably be used to protect one's property.

(d) Re-entry and Recaption. If a person reasonably believes that he has been illegally dispossessed of real or personal property by another, he may resort to reasonable nondeadly force to repossess the property if he acts immediately after the dispossession or upon hot pursuit. Thus, a momentary advantage obtained by the supposed wrongdoer does not alter the rules on defense of property; where force is allowed to defend property, similar force may be used to regain possession promptly after its loss.

Assume, however, that an attempt at recapture of a chattel is made only after some interval has elapsed since the dispossession. The common law rule is that the use of force in recaption is then not justified; the victim of the original dispossession is left to his remedy in the courts. Model Penal Code § 3.06(1)(b)(ii), however, permits recaption of personal property at any time if the actor believes that the person against whom he uses force has no claim of right to possession of the property in question. This is based upon the notion that the rules of the criminal law in this area, which are not likely to be known to the general public, should correspond to the privileges that "a well-conducted person would expect to have."

Almost all states have legislation making it a crime for one entitled to the possession of land to recover it by force, and thus the courts have held that forcible re-entry is not justified unless made immediately upon the wrongful dispossession. The theory is that because land is indestructible and buildings immovable, no harm is likely to result during the delay while the matter is determined in the courts. Again, Model Penal Code § 3.06(1)(b)(ii) takes a broader view consistent with what is expected of the "well-conducted person": force may be used to re-enter, other than immediately after dispossession, if the actor believes (a) that the person against whom the force is used has no claim of right to possession, and (b) that the circumstances are of such urgency that it would be an exceptional hardship to postpone action until a court order could be obtained.

(e) Property of Another. Although, as we have seen, virtually all the modern codes have recognized the right to come to the defense of third parties who are threatened with bodily harm (see § 9.5(a)), the situation is different as to defense of another's property. Some of the statutes dealing with all forms of property allow defense by anyone; others permit defense only by the person whose property is threatened or who is "in lawful possession" of the property, and still others recognize specific third-party relationships justifying property defense: where there is a legal duty to protect the property, where the owner has requested assistance, or where there is a family or similar relationship. There are also statutes dealing with certain types of property, such as dwellings or non-premises, which permit defense by any third party. But many other special-category statutes are much more limited. There are protection-of-premises provisions allowing defense only by a "person in lawful possession or control" or a "person who is licensed or privileged to be therein." Some statutes dealing only with defense of dwellings permit defense only by the person whose dwelling it is or by anyone within the dwelling, and some statutes on non-premises are also limited to property of the defender. And then there are a group of non-dwelling provisions which require that the property be lawfully in the possession of the defender or a member of his immediate family or belong to a person whose property he has a legal duty to protect. Though the common law rule on defense of property was apparently limited to the person in possession, some broadening of that position by court decision has sometimes occurred.

The Model Penal Code § 3.06(1) approach is grounded in the conclusion that there is "no adequate reason for limiting the privilege to protect property of others." The narrower approach taken in the many statutes referred to above appears to be based upon two policy judgments. One is that a mistake as to the respective legal rights of the disputants is more likely when property interests are involved. The other is that property interests are somewhat less deserving of protection and that consequently violence by strangers for the purpose of protecting such interests should not be encouraged.

§ 9.7 Law Enforcement (Arrest, Escape Prevention, Crime Prevention)

A police officer, or a person aiding him, is justified in using reasonable force to make a lawful arrest or to prevent the escape from custody of one already arrested. However, deadly force by an officer is constitutionally permissible only upon probable cause to believe that the person to be arrested poses a threat of serious physical harm, either to the officer or to others.

One, not necessarily a police officer, is justified in using reasonable force to prevent or terminate what he reasonably believes to be the commission of a misdemeanor amounting to a breach of the peace or of a felony, but it is not reasonable to use deadly force except in the case of a "dangerous" felony.

(a) Effecting an Arrest. At common law a police officer or private person may arrest without an arrest warrant for a felony or breach of the peace committed in his presence. In addition, an officer may arrest without a warrant for a felony not in his presence if he has reasonable grounds to believe (a) that a felony has been committed, and (b) that the person to be arrested committed it. A private person, however, is privileged to make such an arrest only if the felony has in fact been committed.

The authority to arrest is now governed by statute in most jurisdictions. The prevailing view is that an officer may arrest under authority of an arrest warrant, without a warrant on reasonable grounds to believe that a felony has been committed by the person arrested, or without a warrant for any offense committed in his presence. The requirement of a warrant for misdemeanors out of the presence is sometimes too strict, and thus in recent years some jurisdictions have allowed officers to arrest without warrant for misdemeanors on reasonable grounds to believe under some or any circumstances. By statute, the power of private persons to arrest without warrant has typically been extended to all offenses occurring in the presence.

Sometimes a police officer making a lawful arrest, with or without a warrant, for a felony or misdemeanor, meets with such resistance as to make him reasonably believe that the person he is trying to arrest will immediately inflict on the officer bodily harm (or serious bodily harm or death), and that the only way to prevent it is to use moderate (or deadly) force upon the arrestee. In such a situation, the officer's use of reasonable force is justifiable under the rules concerning the defense of self-defense, except that, even in a jurisdiction which ordinarily requires a retreat, if it can be safely done, before using deadly force (see § 9.4(f)), the officer making the arrest is not obliged to retreat.

A different problem is presented when the person to be arrested, instead of resisting, flees, so that the officer is in no danger of any bodily harm. The general rule, as now commonly expressed by statute, is that the officer may utilize that degree of physical force which he reasonably believes necessary to make the arrest. This is not to suggest, however, that the use of deadly force is generally permissible whenever necessary. The common law view was that an officer may use deadly force, if he reasonably believes it necessary, to prevent the escape of a person fleeing from an arrest for a felony;

but he may not use such force in the case of one fleeing from arrest for a misdemeanor, though the misdemeanant will otherwise escape. This means an officer is not justified in shooting at a speeding automobile driver who does not heed his signal to stop: if he aims at the driver, he is guilty of murder when he kills; if he aims at the tires, this criminally negligent conduct should make him guilty of manslaughter for the resulting death to a motorist.

The felony portion of the above rule may have made some sense in the days when all felonies were punishable by death; but it is too harsh a rule in these days of many felonies that are not subject to any such penalty. Thus, while a significant minority of the modern codes follow the common law rule, most do not. Instead, they limit the use of deadly force to arrests for offenses in the forcible felony category, or for those felonies reasonably (or actually) believed to involve the use or threat of deadly force. Several of the codes add that deadly force may also be used, if necessary, where the person to be arrested is armed with a gun or it is believed that, if the arrest is delayed, there is a substantial risk that the person to be arrested will cause death or serious bodily harm. But even if the officer might otherwise employ deadly force, he may not do so if it would create a substantial danger to innocent bystanders. Only rarely is it specifically required that a warning, if feasible, be given before deadly force is employed.

These statutory provisions must now be construed in light of *Tenn. v. Garner* (1985), where the Court held that apprehension by the use of deadly force is a seizure subject to the reasonableness requirement of the Fourth Amendment, and that "use of deadly force to prevent the escape of all felony suspects, whatever the circumstances, is constitutionally unreasonable." Utilizing the Fourth Amendment "balancing process," the Court declared it had not been persuaded "that shooting nondangerous fleeing suspects" effectively served law enforcement interests which were "so vital as to outweigh the suspect's interest in his own life." As for the argument that the common law rule, "the prevailing rule at the time of the adoption of the Fourth Amendment," could hardly be unconstitutional under that Amendment, the *Garner* majority responded that this was not so in light of "sweeping change in the legal and technological context": the common law rule arose when virtually all felonies were punishable by death, when all felons were relatively dangerous, and when deadly force required hand-to-hand combat and consequently risk to the arresting officer, but none of this was true today. Thus the Tennessee statute, which followed the common law approach, was deemed unconstitutional "insofar as it authorizes the use of deadly force against" an "unarmed, nondangerous suspect," such as the suspected fleeing and apparently unarmed burglar in the instant case.

As for when deadly force would be permissible, the Court explained:

> Where the officer has probable cause to believe that the suspect poses a threat of serious physical harm, either to the officer or to others, it is not constitutionally unreasonable to prevent escape by using deadly force. Thus, if the suspect threatens the officer with a weapon or there is probable cause to believe that he has committed a crime involving the infliction or threatened infliction of serious physical harm, deadly force may be used if necessary to prevent escape, and if, where feasible, some warning has been given.

Although this certainly means that a statute following the Model Penal Code § 3.07(2)(b) formulation will pass muster, it must be emphasized that the Supreme Court did *not* expressly state (as did the court of appeals) that the Model Penal Code declares the "Fourth Amendment limitations on the use of deadly force against fleeing felons." Moreover, the Court asserted it was not adopting a rule that "requires the police to make impossible, split-second evaluations of unknowable facts." This suggests that certain types of statutes referred to earlier, such as those permitting deadly force against an *armed* felon or against a person who committed a type of felony defined in terms of actual or potential serious harm to a *person,* may also pass the *Garner* test, though they would permit use of deadly force when additional facts about the degree of actual danger in the particular case were yet lacking. Significantly, the Court refused to recognize such a general category with respect to the offense of burglary because it is only a crime against property and is rarely attended by physical violence.

In *Scott v. Harris* (2007), the Court had occasion to apply *Garner* in the context of a high-speed chase. A deputy signaled Harris to stop for traveling 73 m.p.h. in a 55 m.p.h. zone, but Harris sped away at speeds exceeding 85 m.p.h.; other officers joined the chase, and six minutes and 10 miles later deputy Scott applied his push bumper to the rear of the vehicle, causing it to crash and rendering Harris a quadriplegic. A videotape of the chase showed a scenario that "closely resembles a Hollywood-style car chase of the most frightening sort, placing police officers and innocent bystanders alike at great risk of serious injury." In holding the police use of force reasonable, the Court emphasized (1) that Harris "posed an actual and imminent threat to the lives of any pedestrians who might have been present, to other civilian motorists, and to the officers involved in the chase"; (2) that "Scott's actions posed a high likelihood of serious injury or death to respondent"; and (3) that in "weighing the perhaps lesser probability of injuring or killing numerous bystanders against the perhaps larger probability of injuring or killing a single person," it is "appropriate * * * to take into account not only the number of lives at risk but also their relative culpability," particularly the fact that it was Harris "who intentionally placed himself and the public in danger by unlawfully engaging in the reckless, high-speed flight that ultimately produced the choice between two evils that Scott confronted." As for Harris's contention that "the innocent public [could] equally have been protected, and the tragic accident entirely avoided, if the police had simply ceased their pursuit," the Court responded that "there would have been no way to convey convincingly to respondent that the chase was off," and that in any event "we are loath to lay down a rule requiring the police to allow fleeing suspects to get away whenever they drive so recklessly that they put other people's lives in danger."

A police officer is authorized to summon bystanders to assist him in effecting a lawful arrest. Because the private citizen is required by law to respond to such a request, he not only has the same authority as the officer to use force in making the arrest, but may also be justified when the officer is not. Since the person summoned may not delay to inquire into the officer's authority to make that particular arrest, his good faith assistance is justified even if it turns out that the officer was exceeding his authority.

As to the comparatively rare situation in which a private person makes an arrest on his own, he acts at his peril in using deadly force. He is not privileged if it turns out that the person against whom the deadly force was used actually did not commit a dangerous felony. Model Penal Code § 3.07(2)(b)(ii) takes the next logical step and bars the use of deadly force by a private person in making arrests except when that person believes he is assisting a peace officer.

(b) Preventing Escape From Custody by Arrested Person. One is justified in using force to prevent the escape of an already-arrested person to the same extent that he would be justified in using force to effect that person's arrest for the crime for which he is in custody. Thus, since an officer is not justified in using deadly force to arrest a misdemeanant who is fleeing from arrest, so he is not justified in using such force to prevent the escape of one already arrested for a misdemeanor, though without the employment of such force the misdemeanant is sure to escape.

However, most modern codes also permit a guard or policeman employed at a prison or jail to use any force, including deadly force, when reasonably believed necessary to prevent the escape of a person. This is because of the greater public interest in preventing escape by persons in institutions who are in the custody of the law and not merely of individuals. The previously-discussed Fourth Amendment *Garner* rule is probably not applicable in the present context, so that the relevant constitutional limitations on use of deadly force in the escape situations are the less strict requirements of the due process clause for pretrial detainees and the Eighth Amendment's cruel and unusual punishment prohibition for post-conviction detainees.

(c) Crime Prevention and Termination. The privilege to use force to prevent the commission of a crime about to be committed, or to prevent the consummation of a crime already underway, overlaps somewhat with two other privileges already discussed: (1) the privilege of the defense of property (in the case of a crime against property, like burglary and larceny), and (2) the privilege of self-defense or defense of another (in the case of a crime against the person, like murder, mayhem, assault and battery). On the other hand, there are crimes that do not involve a threat of harm to property or to bodily security (e.g., treason, perjury, statutory rape), so that the justification, if any, for the use of force must come solely under the defense of crime prevention, which is not limited to police officers or those aiding them.

One who reasonably believes that a felony, or a misdemeanor amounting to a breach of the peace, is being committed, or is about to be committed, in his presence may use reasonable force to terminate or prevent it. Thus moderate force may justifiably be used in such cases. But, as with self-defense, the law has jelled somewhat on the reasonableness of using deadly force in crime prevention.

Originally, the law was that deadly force was justifiable to prevent or terminate a felony, but was not justifiable to prevent or terminate a misdemeanor. This rule made some sense in the days when the relatively few felonies were all punishable by death anyway; but with the expansion of the felony concept to many new types of conduct, and the lowering of the penalties for many felonies, it will not do today. It is a felony to file a false income tax return; but one is not justified in shooting the filer on his way to the mailbox, even though the filing cannot otherwise be prevented.

The modern rule limits the right to use deadly force to "dangerous" felonies (those felonies of the type that involve a substantial risk of death or serious bodily harm) or, as it is sometimes said, to "atrocious" felonies involving "violence or surprise." Thus it is not justifiable to kill to prevent grand larceny or adultery, though these crimes cannot otherwise be prevented. It ought not to be justifiable to shoot to kill to prevent some modern statutory forms of burglary not involving the house, such as "burglary" of a hen house or telephone booth. As to the dangerous (atrocious) felonies (e.g., murder, voluntary manslaughter, mayhem, kidnaping, arson, burglary of a dwelling, robbery, forcible sodomy, forcible rape), one is, of course, not justified in killing except when it reasonably appears necessary to kill to prevent the commission, or bring about the termination of the felony. When neither self-defense or defense of property would justify resort to deadly force, there is good reason to limit the termination-of-felony aspect of this rule to instances in which the force was "being used to repel force." And the commission of the felony must appear to be imminent, rather than in the more distant future, to justify the use of such force.

There is a question, as to the dangerous felonies, whether the justification for killing should depend upon the type of felony involved, or whether it should depend on the risk encountered in the particular felony involved. Thus arson is a type of felony that generally involves a substantial risk of death or serious bodily harm; but in a particular case of arson there may be no such risk because of the arsonist's careful planning. If one kills to prevent this particular arson, is he justified because it is justifiable to kill to prevent arson, or is he not justified because this particular arson did not involve a substantial risk of death or serious bodily harm? Doubtless, the matter is generally treated in the former fashion, but it would seem that the latter method is more just.

In order to have the benefit of the defense of crime prevention, it is necessary that the actor act with the purpose (motive) of crime prevention. Thus he is not justified in shooting to death his enemy, though he later discovers, to his agreeable surprise, that the enemy was on the point of committing, or was in the process of committing, a dangerous felony.

(d) Other Law Enforcement Activity. Although the matter has seldom been litigated or made the subject of legislation, it would appear that in certain other circumstances the otherwise criminal conduct of a police officer, or a private person acting on behalf of an officer, may be privileged because the person was pursuing law enforcement purposes at the time. Illustrative is *Lilly v. W.Va.* (1928), overturning an involuntary manslaughter conviction for a death caused by a federal agent's violation of the speeding laws while pursuing a violator. The court reasoned, in effect, that the applicable speeding prohibition contained an implied exception for "public officials engaged in the performance of a public duty where speed and the right of way are a necessity."

The question of how far this privilege extends, however, is most starkly presented as to undercover law enforcement activity by police and their agents. This undercover activity may include dealing in contraband substances or false representations, and often involves providing inducement to others to engage in criminal activity. As to the latter, the inducements in some circumstances will constitute a defense, called entrapment (see § 8.8), for the person induced, and the common assumption is that when this is the case the encouraging police may be convicted of the crime in question. Thus, it has been held that if game wardens, posing as fur buyers, induce some boys who would not otherwise have done so to engage in forbidden beaver trapping, the boys are not to be punished, but the game wardens are guilty of illegal trapping. It is doubtful, however, whether it makes sense to conclude that the officer is guilty in any instance in which the "target" was entrapped. Why should the officer's otherwise legitimate activity be punishable merely because, under the prevailing subjective theory of entrapment, it turns out that the object of the investigation was not predisposed? But the question has not received careful attention from the courts, as excessive zeal in law enforcement rarely leads to a criminal prosecution of the police.

Presumably there are certain kinds of criminal conduct so serious that any law enforcement exception will not extend to them. "It would be unthinkable, for example, to permit government agents to instigate robberies and beatings merely to gather evidence to convict other members of a gang of hoodlums." But once some other illegal activity is sanctioned for law enforcement purposes, "problems may be anticipated as to where to draw the line."

Finally, it is well to note that in some circumstances the action taken for a law enforcement purpose will not be criminal simply because the required mental state was not present. Thus, as to the crime of "feloniously" (i.e., with an evil purpose) receiving stolen property, this element is not present where the purchaser obtained the property so that it could be turned over to the authorities. And one who helps another enter a store to take whiskey is not an accomplice to larceny and burglary where he intended to and immediately did summon the police, for the requisite intent to permanently deprive was not present.

Chapter 10

SOLICITATION AND ATTEMPT

Table of Sections

For additional analysis of the above topics and citations to authorities supporting their discussion in this Book, consult the author's 3-volume *Substantive Criminal Law* treatise, also available as Westlaw database SUBCRL. See the Table of Cross-References in this Book.

---

§ 10.1 Solicitation

Assume that A wishes to have his enemy B killed, and thus—perhaps because he lacks the nerve to do the deed himself—A asks C to kill B. If C acts upon A's request and fatally shoots B, then both A and C are guilty of murder. If, again, C proceeds with the plan to kill B, but he is unsuccessful, then both A and C are guilty of attempted murder. If *C* agrees to *A*'s plan to kill *B* but the killing is not accomplished or even attempted, *A* and *C* are nonetheless guilty of the crime of conspiracy. But what if *C* immediately rejects *A*'s homicidal scheme, so that there is never even any agreement between *A* and *C* with respect to the intended crime? Quite obviously, *C* has committed no crime at all. *A,* however, because of his bad state of mind in intending that *B* be killed and his bad conduct in importuning *C* to do the killing, is guilty of the crime of solicitation. For the crime of solicitation to be completed, it is only necessary that the actor with intent that another person commit a crime, have enticed, advised, incited, ordered or otherwise encouraged that person to commit a crime. The crime solicited need not be committed.

(a) Common Law and Statutes. Whether the offense of solicitation was known to the common law before the nineteenth century is uncertain. In one early case it was held that a man could not be indicted for simply requesting a servant to leave his master's service, although the opinion states that enticing a servant to embezzle his master's goods would be indictable. Shortly thereafter, however, it was held in another case that no offense was charged where it was not alleged that the servant actually took the goods. Only two special types of solicitation were clearly indictable under the early cases: a solicitation to commit a forgery to be used in trial or perjury; and the offering of a bribe to a public official.

The case of *Rex v. Higgins* (1801) was based upon an indictment charging the defendant with soliciting a servant to steal his master's goods, although the servant had ignored the request. Defense counsel examined the prior cases and concluded, except with respect to the unique situation concerning perjury, forgery, and bribery: "In none of the books is there any case or precedent to be found of an indictment for bare solicitation to commit an offense without an act in pursuance of it, and the silence of all writers on Crown law on this subject is of itself a strong argument that no such offense is known to the law." The judges unanimously ruled that the common law misdemeanor of solicitation had been charged. However, the only cases cited in their opinions as precedent were those which had dealt with bribery, perjury, or forgery. Indeed, the opinions of the judges rest more upon the policy of finding the acts to be an offense than upon whether the offense had previously existed in the common law.

Since the *Higgins* case the offense of solicitation has been recognized as a common law offense both in England and the United States with few exceptions. The solicitation of another to commit a felony is uniformly held indictable as a misdemeanor under the common law and, when the issue has presented itself, the same result has been reached as to the soliciting of another to commit a misdemeanor that would breach the peace, obstruct justice or otherwise be injurious to the public welfare. There is no reported decision in this country that holds the solicitation of *any* type of misdemeanor is a common law offense.

Even in those jurisdictions with modern recodifications, it is not uncommon for there to be no statute making solicitation a crime. In those states with solicitation statutes, there is considerable variation in their coverage. Some extend to the solicitation of all crimes, some only the solicitation of felonies, particular classes of felonies, or all felonies plus particular classes of misdemeanors, and one only the solicitation of certain specified offenses. These solicitation statutes typically provide that the solicitation constitutes a grade of crime one level below the offense which was solicited. Some, however, generally authorize punishment equivalent to that which is provided for the solicited crime.

Model Penal Code § 5.02 defines solicitation broadly to include requesting another to commit any offense, and would generally make solicitation punishable to the same degree as authorized for the offense solicited. The theory is that "to the extent that sentencing depends upon the antisocial disposition of the actor and the demonstrated need for a corrective sanction, there is likely to be little difference in the gravity of the required measures depending on the consummation or the failure of the plan."

(b) Policy Considerations. As already noted, the solicitation of crimes has received varied statutory treatment in this country. In some jurisdictions, all common law crimes (including solicitation) have been abolished but no general solicitation statute has been enacted. Elsewhere the statutes cover only the solicitation of certain crimes, while other jurisdictions have made no statutory additions to the limited common law offense. This suggests, as does language in some of the reported cases, that there is not a uniformity of opinion on the necessity of declaring criminal the soliciting of others to commit offenses.

One view is that a mere solicitation to commit a crime, not accompanied by agreement or action by the person solicited, presents no significant social danger. It is argued, for example, that solicitation is not dangerous because the resisting will of an independent agent is interposed between the solicitor and commission of the crime which is his object. Similarly, it is claimed that the solicitor does not constitute a menace in view of the fact that he has manifested an unwillingness to carry out the criminal scheme himself. There is not the dangerous proximity to success that exists when the crime is actually attempted, for, "despite the earnestness of the solicitation, the actor is merely engaging in talk which may never be taken seriously.''

On the other hand, it is argued ''that a solicitation is, if anything, more dangerous than a direct attempt, because it may give rise to that cooperation among criminals which is a special hazard. Solicitation may, indeed, be thought of as an attempt to conspire. Moreover, the solicitor, working his will through one or more agents, manifests an approach to crime more intelligent and masterful than the efforts of his hireling.'' It is noted, for example, that the imposition of liability for criminal solicitation has proved to be an important means by which the leadership of criminal movements may be suppressed.

Without regard to whether it is correct to say that solicitations are more dangerous than attempts, it is fair to conclude that the purposes of the criminal law (see § 1.5) are well served by inclusion of the crime of solicitation within the substantive criminal law. Providing punishment for solicitation aids in the prevention of the harm that would result should the inducements prove successful, and also aids in protecting the public from being exposed to inducements to commit or join in the commission of crimes. As is true of the law of attempts, the crime of solicitation (a) provides a basis for timely law enforcement intervention to prevent the intended crime, (b) permits the criminal justice process to deal with individuals who have indicated their dangerousness, and (c) avoids inequality of treatment based upon a fortuity (here, withholding of the desired response by the person solicited) beyond the control of the actor.

Objections to making solicitation a crime or to extending it to such minor crimes as adultery are sometimes based upon the fear that false charges may readily be brought, either out of a misunderstanding as to what the defendant said or for purposes of harassment. This risk is inherent in the punishment of almost all inchoate crimes, although it is perhaps somewhat greater as to the crime of solicitation in that the crime may be committed merely by speaking. In an attempt to deal with this problem, some state statutes require corroboration of the testimony of the person allegedly solicited that the solicitation was made. On occasion, even in the absence of such a statute, courts have refused to uphold convictions for solicitation-type offenses when corroboration was lacking. Another statutory approach, found in one state, is to require that the solicitation take place ''under circumstances which indicate unequivocally'' the defendant's intent that a crime be committed. Yet another state requires that the person solicited commit an overt act in response to the solicitation.

When, as is usually the case, a solicitation-type statute covers only inducements to engage in criminal conduct, then it can hardly be claimed that the statute unconstitutionally proscribes free speech. As one court put it, "if consummated crimes themselves are constitutional in terms of their criminality * * *, then constitutionality follows as to their incipient or inchoate phases." Sometimes the converse has also been held to be true, namely, that a statute making it illegal to solicit conduct which is not itself criminal intrudes upon protected free speech interests. The contrary argument is that the criminal law may be used to protect the public from solicitations to do that which they could lawfully do—or, indeed, that which they have a constitutional right to do. Thus, it has been held that even if the constitutional right of privacy allows consenting adults to engage in sodomy in private, a statute may nonetheless proscribe "public solicitations of strangers for sodomy."

(c) Required Mental State and Act. Although the crime of solicitation might be defined quite simply as asking another person to commit an offense, this does not adequately reflect either the mental element or act that must exist in order for the crime to be completed.

As to the required mental state, none is explicitly stated in the usual common law definition of solicitation, and likewise none is expressly set forth in several solicitation statutes. However, the acts of commanding or requesting another to engage in conduct that is criminal would seem of necessity to require an accompanying intent that such conduct occur, and there is nothing in the decided cases suggesting otherwise. Virtually all of the more recently enacted solicitation statutes avoid any doubt by setting forth in specific terms the intent requirement. Some state the solicitor must intend that an offense be committed, some that he must intend to promote or facilitate its commission, and some others that he must intend that the person solicited engage in criminal conduct.

Thus, as to those crimes defined in terms of certain prohibited results, it is necessary that the solicitor intend to achieve that result through the participation of another. If he does not intend such a result, then the crime has not been solicited, and this is true even though the person solicited will have committed the crime if he proceeds with the requested conduct and thereby causes the prohibited result. For example, if B were to engage in criminally negligent conduct that caused the death of C, then B would be guilty of manslaughter (see § 14.4); but it would not be a criminal solicitation to commit murder or manslaughter for A to request B to engage in such conduct *unless* A did so for the purpose of causing C's death.

Likewise, where the prohibited result involves special circumstances as to which a *mens rea* requirement is imposed, the solicitor cannot be said to have intended that result unless he personally had this added mental state. For example, assume a jurisdiction with the usual misdemeanor of battery and also a felony of aggravated battery, defined in part as inflicting bodily harm upon a person known to be a peace officer. If *A*, not knowing that *C* was an officer, asked *B* to do bodily harm to *C*, then *A* has solicited a battery rather than an aggravated battery.

In the usual solicitation case, it is the solicitor's intention that the criminal result be directly brought about by the person he has solicited; that is, it is his intention that the crime be committed and that the other commit it as a principal in the first degree, as where *A* asks *B* to kill *C*. However, it would seem sufficient that *A* requested *B* to get involved in the scheme to kill *C* in any way which would establish *B*'s complicity in the killing of *C* were that to occur. Thus it would be criminal for one person to solicit another to in turn solicit a third party, to solicit another to join a conspiracy, or to solicit another to aid and abet the commission of a crime.

An evil intent cannot alone constitute a crime; there must also be an act (see § 5.1). However, the mere speaking of words is an act, and that is the kind of act which most often completes the crime of solicitation, although the crime may also be committed through the written word or even by nonverbal conduct. Courts, legislatures and commentators have utilized a great variety of words to describe the required acts for solicitation, including the following and variants thereof; advises, commands, counsels, encourages, entices, entreats, importunes, incites, induces, procures, requests, solicits, and urges. Some of these words are doubtlessly more appropriate than others, in that the crime of solicitation should not be extended to persons who merely express general approval of criminal acts or who are otherwise legitimately exercising their rights to free speech. But because the essence of the crime of solicitation is "asking a person to commit a crime," it "requires neither a direction to proceed nor the fulfillment of any conditions" nor, for that matter, a *quid pro quo*.

It is not necessary that the act of solicitation be a personal communication to a particular individual. Thus an information charging one with soliciting from a public platform a number of persons to commit the crimes of murder and robbery is sufficient. However, there is some authority to the effect that it is not a criminal solicitation to make a general solicitation by publication to a large indefinable group.

What if the solicitor's message never reaches the person intended to be solicited, as where an intermediary fails to pass on the communication or the solicitor's letter is intercepted before it reaches the addressee? The act is nonetheless criminal, although it may be that the solicitor must be prosecuted for an attempt to solicit on such facts. Liability properly attaches under these circumstances, as the solicitor has manifested his dangerousness and should not escape punishment because of a fortuitous event beyond his control.

(d) Defenses. As noted earlier, the crime of solicitation requires no agreement or action by the person solicited, and thus the solicitation is complete when the solicitor, acting with the requisite intent, makes the command or request. What then of the case in which the solicitor thereafter has a change of heart and persuades the person solicited not to commit the crime or otherwise prevents the crime from being committed? It might be argued that such a renunciation of criminal purpose should be no defense. Given the fact that a solicitation is punishable although immediately rejected by the other party, it might be thought illogical for it to be otherwise when the other party accepted the solicitation and only later was stopped from acting on it. In the latter situation the solicitation came even closer to bringing about the antisocial conduct originally intended. Also, it could be maintained that "the solicitor has engaged in irreparably harmful conduct in implanting the suggestion of criminality in the mind of another."

On the other hand, it might well be argued that a voluntary renunciation of criminal purpose by the solicitor should be a defense to the crime of solicitation. One basis for the defense is that the solicitor, by his act of renunciation, has shown that he is not sufficiently dangerous to require application of the corrective processes of the law to him. Another is that by allowing the defense solicitors will be encouraged to prevent the solicited crimes from occurring because they will thereby escape liability altogether.

Apparently the question of whether voluntary renunciation is a defense to a solicitation charge has never been decided one way or another by an appellate court. However, voluntary renunciation is currently a statutory defense in several of the modern recodifications, and is also a defense to solicitation under Model Penal Code § 5.02(3).

It is not uncommon for law enforcement officers and others acting on their behalf to encourage suspects to engage in criminal conduct as a means of identifying persons who are willing to engage in certain forms of criminal activity. This practice is most prevalent as to such crimes as prostitution, gambling, and sale of narcotics, which (because they involve only "willing victims") would otherwise go undetected. If the inducements are not so extreme as to constitute entrapment (see § 8.8), then the practice is a permissible one. It does not constitute the crime of solicitation for a person, having reason to believe another is willing to commit a crime, to furnish an opportunity for the commission of the offense, if the purpose is, in good faith, to secure evidence against a guilty person and not to induce an innocent person to commit a crime.

As noted at the outset of this section, it is generally true that if *A* solicits *B* to commit a crime and *B* then proceeds to commit the crime in response to *A*'s solicitation, then *A* is liable as an accomplice for the crime which *B* has committed. However, there are exceptions (see § 12.3(e)). For example, if *A* solicited *B* to commit the crime with *A,* and the nature of the crime is such that *A*'s participation is inevitably incident to its commission, then it may be concluded that the legislature—by defining the offense solely in terms of one of the two necessary parties' participation—did not intend to impose liability on a person in *A*'s position. So too, *A* should not be considered an accomplice to *B*'s crime if the legislative purpose in enacting the statute violated by *B* was to protect persons such as *A*.

In situations such as these, where the soliciting party would not be held guilty of the completed crime if it were committed as a result of the solicitation, the act of soliciting is itself not criminal. Or, to state it another way, it is a defense to a charge of solicitation to commit a crime that if the criminal object were achieved, the solicitor would not be guilty of a crime under the law defining the offense or the law concerning accomplice liability. Were the rule otherwise, the law of criminal solicitation would conflict with the policies expressed in the definitions of the substantive criminal law. This does not mean, of course, that the mere fact the solicitor was legally incapable of committing the crime directly provides him with a defense when he solicits another to do it.

On the other hand, it is *not* a defense to a solicitation charge that, unknown to the solicitor, the person solicited could not commit the crime. The defendant's culpability is to be measured by the circumstances as he believes them to be. Nor is it a defense that the person solicited is irresponsible or would have an immunity to prosecution or conviction for commission of the crime solicited.

(e) The Scope of the Solicitation. In the law of conspiracy, the question has frequently arisen as to whether an agreement reached by several persons on a single occasion as to several objective crimes is but one conspiracy or is as many conspiracies as there were criminal objectives (see § 11.3(b)(1)). The generally accepted answer is that because the requisite act for conspiracy is agreement, one agreement amounts to but one conspiracy regardless of the number of objectives. By analogy to that rule, it certainly might be argued that a solicitation on one occasion concerning several criminal objectives likewise involves but a single instance of the requisite act for the crime of solicitation, and consequently but one solicitation offense. Indeed, given the result where the solicitation is accepted and a conspiracy is thus formed, it would be illogical to obtain a different result where the conspiracy fails and the only crime committed is solicitation.

However, in what is apparently the only reported decision on this question, a different result was reached. In *Meyer v. State* (1981) the court rejected "the notion that merely because there is but one solicitor, one solicitee, and one conversation, only one solicitation can arise." Rather, the court concluded, the number of incitements depends upon the number of separate events that were solicited, which is not inevitably determined by the number of intended victims or intended crimes. Thus, the *Meyer* court stated, "an entreaty made by a solicitor to blow up a building in the hope that two or more particular persons may be killed in the blast could be characterized as one solicitation, notwithstanding that implementation of the scheme might violate several different laws or, because of multiple victims, constitute separate violations of the same law." But in the instant case, where defendant in one conversation solicited three murders to occur on separate occasions and for separate fees, the court concluded there were multiple solicitation offenses.

(f) Solicitation as an Attempt. Whether a solicitation constitutes an attempt was the subject of debate in the late nineteenth and early twentieth centuries, primarily between two scholars of the criminal law. Bishop held to the view that any solicitation to commit an offense was an attempt to commit that offense. Wharton, on the other hand, asserted that a solicitation was not indictable as an attempt. Of the cases cited by Bishop to support his position, only one holds a solicitor guilty of an attempt, and it involved something more than a bare solicitation.

Some of the reported decisions seem to say that a solicitation constitutes a specific type of attempt, although in these cases the facts usually indicate that something more than a bare solicitation was involved. Another group of cases supports the position that a mere solicitation is not an attempt, but that a solicitation accompanied by other overt acts, such as the furnishing of materials, is an attempt. Yet another view is that a solicitation may become an attempt only if the overt acts have proceeded beyond what would constitute preparation if the solicitor himself planned to commit the offense. Finally, there are also cases holding that the solicitor cannot be guilty of an attempt no matter what he does because it is not his purpose personally to commit the offense. The trend is toward the latter two positions.

Although the issue has seldom been raised in the recent appellate decisions, it continues to be of some importance. This is particularly true in those jurisdictions where there is no crime of solicitation or where the crime of solicitation does not extend to as many offenses as does the crime of attempt. And, even where the solicitation of any type of crime is covered, the defendant may not be convicted of what is only a solicitation upon a charge of an attempt.

§ 10.2   Attempt—Introduction

The crime of attempt is a relatively recent development of the common law. The primary purpose in punishing attempts is not to deter the commission of completed crimes, but rather to subject to corrective action those individuals who have sufficiently manifested their dangerousness.

(a) Development of the Crime of Attempt. Although the crime of attempt did not exist in early English law, in the fourteenth century courts occasionally convicted of a felony those who were guilty only of an unsuccessful attempt to commit that felony. These convictions apparently were rested upon the doctrine that *voluntas reputabitur pro facto*—the intention is to be taken for the deed. However, even at that time a mere intention alone would not suffice. Coke pointed out that to be liable to punishment the defendant must have manifested his intent "by some open deed tending to the execution of his intent. * * * So as if a man had compassed the death of another, and had uttered the same by words or writing, yet he should not have died for it, for there wanted an overt deed tending to the execution of his compassing. But if a man had imagined to murder, or rob another, and to that intent had become *insidiator viarum* [one who lies in wait to commit an offense], and assaulted him though he killed him not, nor took anything from him, yet was it felony, for there was an overt deed." Thus, even in medieval law there was an insistence on conduct.

Instances of convictions based upon the doctrine *voluntas reputabitur pro facto* were quite rare and were confined to attempts to commit the more heinous felonies; there did not exist a general conception that an attempt to commit a crime was criminal as such. However, there existed other means for checking criminal conduct, including the system of frankpledge and surety for the peace, and such crimes as vagrancy, unlawful assembly, and going armed.

The modern doctrine of criminal attempts is said to have had its origin in the Court of Star Chamber, which had as one of its functions the correction of the manifest defects and shortcomings of the common law courts. The Chamber did deal with many cases of what we would today call attempts, and the word "attempt" was occasionally used loosely in describing these situations. However, the Court of Star Chamber never formulated a general theory of criminal attempts, although the principle was developed that an attempt to commit the offense of dueling was itself a distinct offense.

The Court of Star Chamber was abolished in 1640, and its influence upon subsequent common law courts is a matter of dispute. But it is clear that many years elapsed after its abolition before a doctrine of criminal attempt was actually formulated. "[T]he language of the common law courts after 1640 continues to reflect the early common law views and statements antedating the Star Chamber; there is not a ripple in the calm surface to indicate that a new doctrine of criminal attempts had been suggested." Most likely the development of the crime of attempt was retarded by the fact that other means often existed for dealing with unsuccessful or incompleted criminal schemes. Of particular significance is the accelerated growth of the aggravated assault type of crime during this period.

The modern doctrine of attempt may actually be traced back to the case of *Rex v. Scofield* (1784). The defendant was charged with having put a lighted candle and combustible material in a house he was renting with intention of setting fire to it, but there was no allegation or proof that the house was burned. On his behalf it was contended that an attempt to commit a misdemeanor was not a misdemeanor, but the court rejected that argument: "The intent may make an act, innocent in itself, criminal; nor is the completion of an act, criminal in itself, necessary to constitute criminality."

The doctrine that an attempt to commit a crime was itself a crime was thereafter crystalized in the case of *Rex v. Higgins* (1801). The defendant was indicted for soliciting a servant to steal his master's goods, but the indictment contained no charge that the servant stole the goods. The court, relying upon *Scofield,* affirmed the conviction: "All offenses of a public nature, that is, all such acts or attempts as tend to the prejudice of the community, are indictable." This statement was soon accepted and repeated by the commentators, and the courts thereafter made it clear that it was a misdemeanor indictable at common law to attempt to commit any felony or misdemeanor, whether such felony or misdemeanor was an offense at common law or was created by statute. Such is the common law rule in the United States, subject to the qualification that some decisions support the view that it is not criminal to attempt to commit a statutory misdemeanor of the *malum prohibitum* variety. It has been questioned, however, whether those decisions represent the law today.

Most American jurisdictions have enacted some form of general attempt statute, and with few exceptions these statutes cover an attempt to commit any felony or misdemeanor. In addition, some states have adopted legislation making it an offense to attempt certain specific crimes. (Omission of an offense from both the general and the specific attempt statutes provides immunity for one who attempts that offense only if the jurisdiction has abolished common law crimes.) Except in the more modern recodifications, these statutes usually do not elaborate upon the term attempt, and thus courts have interpreted them by following the principles of attempt liability developed at common law.

It is important to keep in mind that even with this full development of the crime of attempt, prosecution for attempt is only one of several ways in which the criminal law can reach conduct merely tending toward the doing of some harm otherwise proscribed by law. The crimes of assault and burglary, which served as a means of dealing with the most common forms of attempt prior to recognition of attempt as a distinct crime, are still very much with us. In addition, even the most modern codes include crimes defined in terms of conduct that is arguably of itself harmless but which has been made criminal because it is (or is very likely to be) a step toward the doing of harm. For example, one modern code includes not only a host of possession-type crimes (e.g., possession of obscene material with intent to disseminate it, possession of a forged instrument with intent to issue or deliver same, possession of burglary tools with intent to commit a burglary, possession of explosives or incendiary devices with intent to use them in committing an offense, possession of any instrument adapted for the use of narcotics by subcutaneous injection, possession of weapons with intent to use same against another unlawfully, possession of a gambling device), but also other substantive offenses defined in terms of using certain items for a particular purpose, offering to do something, or even being in a certain place for a bad purpose. As will become more apparent later, many (but not all) of these statutes reach conduct that is merely preparatory in nature and thus would not be encompassed within the general law of attempts.

Defendants prosecuted for attempting to violate such statutes have with some frequency interposed the objection that these statutes themselves define a particular kind of attempt, from which it is argued that there may be no such thing as an attempt to attempt. Thus, to take the most common case, it is claimed that one cannot be said to have attempted an assault of the attempted-battery type. Although it has been noted that a charge of attempted assault might more logically be characterized as an attempted battery, the courts have upheld convictions for attempted assault on the ground that the crime of assault—with its usual requirement of present ability to inflict injury—is more limited than attempted battery. Similarly, courts have consistently held that it is permissible to charge and convict for an attempt to commit a crime, such as burglary, which is defined in terms of doing an act with intent to commit some other crime. This is a proper result, for "if a preliminary act is prominent enough to serve as the basis of substantive liability, it should also provide a sufficient foundation for attempt liability." By contrast, where a certain crime is actually defined in terms of either doing or attempting a certain crime, then the argument that there is no crime of attempting this attempt is persuasive.

(b) The Rationale of Attempt. It has been noted "that the main rationale behind the practice of punishing attempts to commit serious felonies in the Star Chamber and later in the seventeenth century common law courts was preventive and that the all-embracing doctrine was formulated in the eighteenth century simply to extend this to attempts to commit any crime. * * * More bluntly, the law of attempts exists because there is just as much need to stop, deter and reform a person who has unsuccessfully attempted or is attempting to commit a crime than one who has already committed such an offense."

Thus, one important function served by the crime of attempt is to provide a basis whereby law enforcement officers may intervene in time to prevent a completed crime. More precisely, attempt law makes possible preventive action by the police *before* the defendant has come dangerously close to committing the intended crime; as one court put it, the police must be allowed "a reasonable margin of safety after the intent to commit the crime was sufficiently apparent to them." Of course, law enforcement agencies could be given authority to take preventive action in other ways, including ways that do not at all involve the substantive law of crimes. Illustrative is the stop-and-frisk legislation, which permits an officer to stop, frisk and question a person he suspects is "about to" commit an offense. Such laws may serve a useful purpose by permitting a limited form of preventive action in ambiguous situations, but it does not follow from this that stronger preventive measures (which may include prosecution and conviction) are unnecessary when the defendant's criminal purpose is apparent.

The objectives of the criminal law (see § 1.5) would not be sufficiently served if the only action that could be taken against an attempt were on-the-spot prevention of the crime on that particular occasion. An attempt "yields an indication that the actor is disposed toward such activity, not alone on this occasion but on others." Indeed, in some circumstances a person whose criminal scheme has miscarried on a particular occasion may present a greater continuing danger than the person who succeeded. Prosecution and conviction are thus appropriate, for the individual who has engaged in an attempt should be subjected to rehabilitative measures and to restraints that adequately protect the public.

Indeed, exculpation of those who fail due to a fortuity "would involve inequality of treatment that would shock the common sense of justice." Assume that *A, B, C,* and *D* all set out to murder their respective enemies. *A* succeeds, but the others fail: *B*'s aim is bad; *C*'s gun misfires; and *D* is intercepted by the police just as he is about to fire. Although there was a day when only *A* would be punished on the ground that the others had done no harm, it is now accepted that "criminal attempts are harmful in a substantive sense" and that consequently it would be unthinkable to consider *B, C,* and *D* immune from punishment.

Finally, it is important to note that "general deterrence is at most a minor function" of the law of attempt. There may be instances in which the actor has planned what he perceives to be almost the "perfect crime," so that the chance of discovery is thought to be very slight unless the plan miscarries in some way. In such a case the threat of punishment for the attempt may serve as a deterrent. However, as a general proposition it may be said that such a threat is unlikely to deter a person who is willing to risk the sanction provided for the crime which is his object.

In considering the dimensions of attempt law, the purposes served by this crime must constantly be kept in mind. These purposes have a bearing upon such questions as what mental state and what acts are required, whether either impossibility of success or abandonment should be a defense, and what degree of punishment should be permitted.

§ 10.3   Attempt—The Mental State

The crime of attempt consists of (1) an intent to do an act or to bring about a certain consequence that would in law amount to a crime; and (2) an act in furtherance of that intent. Under the prevailing view, an attempt thus cannot be committed by recklessness or negligence or on a strict liability basis, even if the underlying crime can be so committed.

(a) Intent to Commit a Crime. The mental state required for the crime of attempt, as it is customarily stated in the cases, is an intent to commit some other crime. Some attempt statutes do not specify the requisite mental state, although in the modern recodifications an intent to commit some offense is usually set forth as an element of the crime of attempt. Especially precise is the language of the Wisconsin statute, which requires "that the actor have an intent to perform acts and attain a result which, if accomplished, would constitute such crime." This makes it more apparent that it is the intent to do certain proscribed acts or to bring about a certain proscribed result, rather than an intent to engage in criminality, which is required. Thus, if the defendant intended to do something which he believed was against the law but which in fact was not unlawful, then he cannot be said to have engaged in a criminal attempt. So too, ignorance of the applicable criminal law is no more of an excuse here than as to completed crimes, and thus it would make no difference that the defendant engaged in the attempt without knowledge that his intended result would be a crime.

Some crimes, such as murder, are defined in terms of acts causing a particular result plus some mental state that need not be an intent to bring about that result. Thus, if *A, B, C* and *D* have each taken the life of another, *A* acting with intent to kill, *B* with an intent to do serious bodily injury, *C* with a reckless disregard of human life, and *D* in the course of a dangerous felony, all three are guilty of murder because the crime of murder is defined in such a way that any one of these mental states will suffice (see §§ 13.2, 13.3, 13.4, 13.5). However, if the victims do not die from their injuries, then only *A* is guilty of attempted murder; on a charge of attempted murder it is not sufficient to show that the defendant intended to do serious bodily harm, that he acted in reckless disregard for human life, or that he was committing a dangerous felony. Again, this is because intent is needed for the crime of attempt, so that attempted murder requires an intent to bring about that result described by the crime of murder (i.e., the death of another). While there is disagreement in the cases as to whether there can logically be such a crime as attempted second degree murder, this is largely attributable to variations in the way that the crime of murder is divided into degrees; where second degree murder is defined so as to include an intentional killing without the premeditation and deliberation that would make it first degree murder, then an attempt to kill with such a mental state is attempted second degree murder, but there is no such thing as attempted second degree murder in those jurisdictions where the types of malice sufficient for second degree murder do not include intent to kill.

As is true generally of anticipatory offenses (see §§ 10.1(c) and 11.2(c)), a clear understanding of the requisite mental state in a particular case necessitates an analysis of the elements of the crime to which the anticipatory offense relates. The crime of attempt does not exist in the abstract, but rather exists only in relation to other offenses; a defendant must be charged with an attempt to commit a specifically designated crime, and it is to that crime one must look in identifying the kind of intent required. For example, if the charge is attempted theft and theft is defined as requiring an intent to permanently deprive the owner of his property, then that same intent must be established to prove the attempt. It is not enough to show that the defendant intended to do some unspecified criminal act.

The Model Penal Code draftsmen put the case of a defendant who intends to demolish a building and proceeds with his plan to do so notwithstanding knowledge that it is virtually inevitable that persons within the building will be killed by the explosion. If the plan does not succeed, is he guilty of attempted murder? In view of the intent requirement, it would seem not, for his intent was to destroy the building rather than to kill the inhabitants, although some doubt exists because the concept of "intent" has sometimes been thought to include consequences that the defendant knows are substantially certain to result (see § 4.2(a)). Under Code § 5.01, the defendant would be deemed guilty of attempted murder, a result that is "based on the conclusion that the manifestation of the actor's dangerousness is just as great—or very nearly as great— as in the case of purposive conduct."

(b) Recklessness and Negligence. May a defendant be convicted of an attempt to commit a crime that is defined only in terms of reckless or negligent conduct? In theory at least, it is conceivable that conviction might be possible if the completed crime consists simply of reckless or negligent creation of danger *and* it was shown that the defendant actually intended to engage in conduct creating that danger. Thus, it has been suggested that if one attempts to start his car in order to drive it, knowing it has no brakes, this would warrant a conviction for attempting to drive negligently. Such a result could be reached without holding that an attempt may be committed through negligence, and therefore could be distinguished from the case in which the defendant had merely been negligent in failing to discover the condition of his brakes.

The above analysis, it should be noted, cannot be applied when the completed crime consists of recklessly or negligently causing a certain result, for if there were an intent to cause such a result then the attempt would not be to commit that crime but rather the greater crime of intentionally causing such result. For example, so long as the crime of attempt is deemed to require an intent-type of mental state, there can be no such thing as an attempt to commit criminal-negligence involuntary manslaughter. "The consequence involved in that crime is the death of the victim and an act done with intent to achieve this, if an attempt at all, is attempted murder."

It has been strongly urged, however, that recklessness or negligence should suffice for attempt liability and that therefore it *should* be possible to attempt such a crime as involuntary manslaughter. "If a pharmacist is grossly negligent in making up a prescription and the patient dies as a result of taking the dosage on the bottle, the pharmacist is clearly guilty of manslaughter. Surely the policy considerations which dictate such a conviction apply equally if, through chance, the negligent error is discovered before any damage is done. There seems to be every reason for a verdict of attempted manslaughter." It may well be that the purposes of the criminal law would be properly served by conviction of the pharmacist for his grossly negligent conduct even though it did not in fact cause harm, but it might be questioned whether this result should be reached by a redefinition of attempt law as opposed to merely making it an offense to engage in negligent or reckless conduct that endangers others.

(c) Liability Without Fault. Although the issue has seldom reached the courts, it would seem to follow from the generally accepted notion that intent is required for an attempt that there is no such thing as strict liability attempt. That is, even if the completed crime may be committed without intent, knowledge, recklessness or even negligence, the same is not true of an attempt to commit that crime. An attempt to commit a strict liability offense is thus possible only if it is shown that the defendant acted with an intent to bring about the proscribed result.

It has been argued that "if crimes of * * * strict liability are necessary and valid instruments of policy, then there is no reason for not applying this same policy in the case of attempts." Thus, so the argument goes, "if it is right and necessary in the public interest that *D* should be held liable for selling adulterated milk although he did not know and had no reasonable means of knowing that the milk was adulterated, why is it not right that he should be guilty of an attempt if he tries unsuccessfully to sell the same milk in similar circumstances." Others, however, have contended that there is "no reason of policy to extend the dubious notion of strict liability to the law of attempts." Taking into account the rather shaky justification for strict-liability crimes, the latter view is a more appealing one.

It must be noted that the above comments are applicable to the true strict-liability offense, which must be distinguished from those crimes that do require proof of an intent to bring about some result but yet do not require a showing of any state of mind as to certain attendant circumstances. As to the latter offenses, the question is whether one may likewise be said to have attempted to commit such a crime when no intent (or even knowledge) is established concerning those attendant circumstances. It has been noted that authority on this issue is lacking and that it is consequently difficult to say what the result would be under prevailing principles of attempt liability. However, a persuasive argument has been made "that an attempt is so essentially connected with consequences—with that event or series of events which is the principal constituent of the crime—that the only essential intention is an intention to bring about those consequences; and that if recklessness, or negligence, or even blameless inadvertence with respect to the remaining constituents of the crime (the pure circumstances) will suffice for the substantive crime, it will suffice also for the attempt." Under this view, if the crime of burglary may be committed without regard to the defendant's knowledge that he was actually acting in the nighttime, then the same is true of attempted burglary. Likewise, assuming it is a federal offense to kill or injure an FBI agent and that recklessness or even negligence with respect to the victim's status will suffice, an attempt to commit that offense would also only require recklessness or negligence as to the victim's position. So too, a defendant may be convicted of attempted statutory rape notwithstanding lack of knowledge that the intended victim was under age.

§ 10.4 Attempt—The Act

One of the basic premises of the criminal law is that bad thoughts alone cannot constitute a crime (see § 5.1). This is no less true as to an attempt, and thus it is not enough that the defendant have intended to commit a crime. There must also be an act, and not any act will suffice.

(a) The Confusion. Precisely what kind of act is required is not made very clear by the language traditionally used by courts and legislatures. It is commonly stated that more than an act of preparation must occur, which perhaps is of some help, although the situation is confused somewhat because courts occasionally say that preparatory acts will be enough under certain circumstances. The traditional attempt statute requires an "act toward the commission of" some offense, although slightly different wording is also to be found: "conduct which tends to effect the commission of" a crime; an act "in furtherance of" or "tending directly toward" or which "constitutes a substantial step toward" the commission of an offense. Similarly, the courts use a wide variety of phrases: "a step toward the commission of the crime"; an "act in part execution of the intent"; "a direct movement toward the commission of the offense"; "the commencement of the consummation"; or "some appreciable fragment of the crime."

The situation is further complicated by the fact that the acts in question may be committed in so many different ways because of the great number of offenses on which the crime of attempt may be overlaid. An infinite variety of situations can arise. If *A*, with a gun in his pocket, checks in at the airline ticket counter and takes a seat in the departure lounge, has he attempted to commit the offense of boarding an aircraft while carrying a concealed weapon? If *B*, planning to rob a bank messenger, drives around to the places where it is expected that the messenger will make deliveries but fails to locate him, has he attempted to commit the crime of robbery? If *C* proceeds with a bunco scheme which requires that he display a large roll of fake money to another, convince the other person to withdraw his own money from the bank to prove that the bank is a safe place to keep one's funds, and then make a sleight of hand switch of the victim's money for the fake money, has he attempted to commit the crime of theft if the intended victim procures his bank book and goes to the bank but does not draw out his money? The result reached in any one of these cases is unlikely to afford a clear indication of how the other two should be resolved.

A closer look at the decided cases on the law of attempt, however, affords some guidance as to what types of acts will be sufficient. In many instances the cases cannot be reconciled with one another, but this is because different courts have utilized somewhat different tests on this issue. This is not to say that every jurisdiction has expressly opted for one of these theories over the other. It is to these tests that we now look.

(b) The Proximity Approach. Under one approach, the question is whether the defendant's act was sufficiently proximate to the intended crime. But, how proximate must the act be? The strictest approach, at least in one sense, would be to require that the defendant have engaged in the "last proximate act," that is, that he have done everything which he believes necessary to bring about the intended result. If this approach were taken, then it would be attempted murder if *A* shot at *B* and missed or *B* were hit but did not die, but not if *A* were just about to fire but had not done so. Similarly, an attempt at false pretenses would exist only if the defendant had done everything he needed to do prior to actual receipt of the money. And any crime planned to be committed through an innocent agent would be attempted as soon as the agent were briefed on what he was to do, even though considerable time was still to elapse before the agent was to act. It is generally accepted that where the actor has engaged in the "last proximate act" he has committed an attempt. However, "no jurisdiction operating within the framework of Anglo–American law requires that the last proximate act occur before an attempt can be charged." Although it was intimated in the famous English case of *Reg. v. Eagleton* (1855) that the last proximate act was necessary, that view was very promptly rejected by the same court. Thus the first administration of poison in a case of intended slow poisoning by repeated doses would amount to attempted murder even though it quite obviously was not the last proximate act.

Because the last act is not required, some courts have instead tried to identify an aspect of the criminal scheme which is indispensable—the notion being that there is not a proximity to success until the defendant has obtained control over that indispensable element. This approach has been followed most frequently as to those schemes requiring that the defendant induce someone else to take certain action. Thus, in the bunco scheme case described earlier, it could be said that indispensable to the scheme was the victim's withdrawal of his money from the bank, so that the theft was not attempted unless the intended victim did draw out his funds. Similarly, if the scheme is to defraud an insurance company by having the named beneficiary file a false claim, it would be indispensable that the beneficiary file the claim or at least agree to file it. (Consistent with this view is the generally accepted notion that a bare solicitation is not an attempt because completion of the crime requires action by the person solicited; see § 10.1(f).) The indispensable element approach has also been used when the scheme is such that the defendant cannot undertake the crime until he obtains some item; for example, it has been held that one cannot attempt to vote illegally until he gets a ballot and that one cannot attempt an assault with a deadly weapon until he acquires the weapon.

Yet another variation of the proximity approach is that which focuses upon whether the defendant's acts may be said to be physically proximate to the intended crime. The emphasis is not so much upon what the defendant has done as upon what remains to be done, and the time and place at which the intended crime is supposed to occur take on considerable importance. Thus, in the case described earlier in which the defendant unsuccessfully sought out the bank messenger, *People v. Rizzo* (1927), it was held that the robbery had not been attempted:

> [T]hese defendants had planned to commit a crime, and were looking around the city for an opportunity to commit it, but the opportunity fortunately never came. Men would not be guilty of an attempt at burglary if they had planned to break into a building and were arrested while they were hunting about the streets for the building not knowing where it was. Neither would a man be guilty of an attempt to commit murder if he armed himself and started out to find the person whom he had planned to kill but could not find him. So here these defen-

dants were not guilty of an attempt to commit robbery in the first degree when they had not found or reached the presence of the person they intended to rob.

There are other situations, however, in which determining where to draw the dangerous proximity line is much more difficult.

The physical proximity test may be viewed as but a part of a broader notion that, as put by Justice Holmes, there "must be a dangerous proximity to success." Under this approach, account must be taken of "the gravity of the crime, the uncertainty of the result, and the seriousness of the apprehension, coupled with the great harm likely to result." Thus the "potentially and immediately dangerous circumstances" presented by the defendant's entry of a company's premises carrying dynamite with intent to destroy one of the company's buildings make that act sufficient for the crime of attempting to destroy premises by dynamite. "While it might be argued that the accused should have been allowed to actually place the dynamite or even prepare to ignite it before being apprehended, again, this would be a dangerous requirement. Even if there might exist an opportunity to prevent the ignition of the explosive there still would be a chance that the perpetrator might instead ignite it and hurl it toward or into the building in which case preventive measures would virtually be precluded."

What are the merits of the proximity approach? In support of it, it has been argued that an act should not be punished except "to prevent some harm which is foreseen as likely to follow that act under the circumstances in which it is done." Under this view, deterrence of the completed crime is assumed to be the function of attempt law, so that conduct does not constitute an attempt until the defendant has come dangerously close to accomplishing the completed crime. The proximity test has been questioned on the ground that it is inconsistent with the rule that impossibility of success is not necessarily a defense, and on the broader principle that "the primary purpose of punishing attempts is to neutralize dangerous individuals and not to deter dangerous acts." So the argument goes, whether one should be subjected to the corrective processes of the law for his actions tending toward the commission of a substantive crime is not an issue that should necessarily be determined by the extent to which that person's conduct actually created a danger.

(c) The Probable Desistance Approach. Some courts have taken the view that the act required to establish a criminal attempt must be one which in the ordinary course of events would result in the commission of the target crime except for the intervention of some extraneous factor. This, it would seem, necessitates a determination of whether one who had gone that far with a criminal scheme would thereafter voluntarily desist from his efforts to commit the crime. One commentator has stated the test somewhat differently:

> The defendant's conduct must pass that point where most men, holding such an intention as the defendant holds, would think better of their conduct and desist. All of us, or most of us, at some time or other harbor what may be described as a criminal intent to effect unlawful consequences. Many of us take some steps—often slight enough in character—to bring the consequences about; but most of us, when we reach a certain point, desist, and return to our roles as law-abiding citizens. The few who do not and pass beyond that point are, if the object of their conduct is not achieved, guilty of a criminal attempt.

An inquiry into whether there exists a probability of desistance or whether a normal person would thereafter desist has something to commend it, at least as compared with the proximity approach, for it does square with the function of attempt law in identifying dangerous persons. However, the probable or normal desistance approach has been criticized as a "highly artificial device" in that there exists no basis for making such judgments as when desistance is no longer probable or when the normal citizen would stop. Because of the lack of an empirical basis for making such predictions, this approach as applied does not differ from the proximity test.

(d) The Equivocality Approach. A totally different approach is that which is referred to as the equivocality theory or the *res ipsa loquitur* test. As stated by Salmond: "An attempt is an act of such a nature that it is itself evidence of the criminal intent with which it is done. A criminal attempt bears criminal intent upon its face." Or, as put by Turner: "The actus reus of an attempt to commit a specific crime is constituted when the accused person does an act which is a step towards the commission of the specific crime, and the doing of such act can have no other purpose than the commission of that specific crime." This is not merely a restatement in somewhat different form of the necessity to prove the mental state, for, unlike proof of the intent itself, the defendant's confession or other representations about his intentions may not be taken into consideration. Rather, "it is as though a cinematograph film, which had so far depicted merely the accused person's acts without stating what was his intention, had been suddenly stopped, and the audience were asked to say to what end those acts were directed. If there is only one reasonable answer to this question then the accused has done what amounts to an 'attempt' to attain that end. If there is more than one reasonably possible answer, then the accused has not yet done enough."

A well-known example of this approach is the New Zealand case of *Campbell & Bradley v. Ward* (1955), where the court held the evidence did not establish the necessary act for attempted theft. A car in which the two defendants and another were riding stopped and the defendants' companion got out of the car and entered a parked car, but he left and returned to the defendants when the owner of the parked car approached. Nothing in the parked car had been taken or disturbed. The defendants fled but they were later arrested and each of them confessed that they were participants in a plan whereby their companion was going to steal a battery and radio from the parked car. The court somewhat reluctantly concluded that the act of entering the car was too equivocal.

It is not at all uncommon for courts in this country to refer explicitly to the necessity for unequivocal behavior in order to prove an attempt. However, it is not entirely clear to what extent these statements reflect an acceptance of the equivocality theory as applied in *Campbell & Bradley*, as opposed to a concern with the need for adequate proof of criminal intent *in addition to* proof of the act. The situation is further confounded because a number of courts have asserted that equivocal conduct will not suffice, but then seem to qualify that somewhat with the statement that if "the design of a person to commit a crime is clearly shown, slight acts done in furtherance thereof will constitute an attempt."

What can be said for the equivocality approach? In contrast to the proximity theory, it is arguably consistent with the major purpose of the crime of attempt in that equivocal acts may well reflect an equivocal purpose. Statements of intent made prior to equivocal acts or a confession of intent made subsequent thereto give no assurance of that firmness of purpose that manifests the actor's dangerousness. "But once the actor must desist or perform acts that he realizes would incriminate him if all external facts were known, in all probability a firmer state of mind exists."

Yet, most commentators have been critical of the equivocality approach. It is said to restrict unduly the value of confessions in attempt cases. Moreover, if strictly followed it would bar conviction for attempt even when the defendant, whose intent was otherwise established, had engaged in virtually the last act required for the carrying out of his intent. Putting other evidence to one side in assessing the act itself would also lead to unfortunate results when the defendant's conduct shows *some* criminal purpose but is equivocal in the sense that it does not establish beyond a reasonable doubt the particular offense being attempted.

(e) The Model Penal Code Approach. Model Penal Code § 5.01(1)(c) requires "an act or omission constituting a substantial step in a course of conduct planned to culminate in [the actor's] commission of the crime." Moreover, under Code § 5.01(2), conduct cannot constitute a substantial step "unless it is strongly corroborative of the actor's criminal purpose." This, the draftsmen note, will broaden the scope of attempt liability in a way that is consistent with the purpose of restraining dangerous persons, as: (1) the emphasis is upon what the actor has already done rather than what remains to be done; (2) liability will be imposed only if some firmness of criminal purpose is shown; and (3) the conduct may be assessed in light of the defendant's statements.

The Model Penal Code's "substantial step" language is to be found in the great majority of the attempt statutes in the modern recodifications. Even in the absence of such a statute, the courts in several jurisdictions have adopted the Model Penal Code "substantial step" approach. The "substantial step" statutes referred to above more often than not also include the Model Penal Code requirement that the step must be "strongly corroborative" of the defendant's criminal purpose.

Model Penal Code § 5.01(2) is also unique in that it sets forth several categories of conduct which are not to be held insufficient as a matter of law if strongly corroborative of the actor's criminal purpose. Although states that have followed the Code approach in other respects have for the most part declined to enumerate these categories by statute, the categories are worthy of brief note here because they illustrate how the Code approach would achieve results different from the other tests:

"(a) lying in wait, searching for or following the contemplated victim of the crime." By contrast, cases taking the proximity approach have sometimes found the act insufficient where the victim had not arrived at the intended crime scene or where the defendant was still searching out the victim.

"(b) enticing or seeking to entice the contemplated victim of the crime to go to the place contemplated for its commission." Cases utilizing other theories have sometimes found insufficient the defendant's acts of offering the intended victim a reward for going to the place where the crime was to be committed.

"(c) reconnoitering the place contemplated for the commission of the crime." Whether this would suffice at common law is unclear because the cases have usually emphasized other factors as well, such as the possession of necessary equipment. However, reconnoitering in advance of the time for the crime probably would not suffice where the physical proximity test is employed.

"(d) unlawful entry of a structure, vehicle or enclosure in which it is contemplated that the crime will be committed." As *Campbell & Bradley* illustrates, this well might not suffice under the equivocality approach. However, such entry could be expected to be sufficient under the proximity approach, although there is some questionable authority to the contrary.

"(e) possession of materials to be employed in the commission of the crime, which are specially designed for such unlawful use or which serve no lawful purpose of the actor under the circumstances." Some decisions in accord are to be found. Illustrative is the holding that possession of a still and mash are sufficient for an attempt illegally to manufacture intoxicating beverages.

"(f) possession, collection or fabrication of materials to be employed in the commission of the crime, at or near the place contemplated for its commission, where such possession, collection or fabrication serves no lawful purpose of the actor under the circumstances." Again, decisions in accord are to be found, such as that the defendant's arrival with inflammables at the premises to be burned is enough, although it would be otherwise under the proximity theory if the crime was to be completed later.

"(g) soliciting an innocent agent to engage in conduct constituting an element of the crime." Doubtless this would also be sufficient at common law because the defendant has even taken his last step.

§ 10.5 Attempt—The Limits of Liability

Under the traditional approach, legal impossibility but not factual impossibility is a defense to a charge of attempt. Legal impossibility is the situation in which the defendant did everything he intended to do but yet had not committed the completed crime, while factual impossibility is that in which the defendant is unable to accomplish what he intends because of some facts unknown to him. The modern and better view is that impossibility is not a defense when the defendant's actual intent (not limited by the true facts unknown to him) was to do an act or bring about a result proscribed by law. Considerable uncertainty exists in the cases as to whether voluntary abandonment is a defense to a charge of attempt, but the better view is that it is. As with the modern view of impossibility, this follows from the fact that the purpose of the crime of attempt is to subject dangerous persons to the corrective processes of the law.

Although the crime of attempt is sometimes defined as if failure were an essential element, the modern view is that a defendant may be convicted on a charge of attempt even if it is shown that the crime was completed. Taking into account the rationale of attempt, a person who attempts a crime should be amenable to the same punishment as a person who completed the crime, subject to the qualification that extreme sanctions intended only for general deterrence should not be permitted.

(a) Impossibility. Judging from the volume of literature in this area, scholars in the field of substantive criminal law appear to be more fascinated with the subject of impossibility in attempts than with any other subject. Perhaps this is not surprising, for the question of whether we should punish a person who has attempted what was not possible under the surrounding circumstances requires careful consideration of many of the fundamental notions concerning the theory and purposes of a system of substantive criminal law.

Moreover, the cases on the subject are often intriguing, as is illustrated by these fact situations, all from reported decisions. *A* was dancing with a girl when she collapsed in his arms, after which he took her out to his car and engaged in sexual intercourse with her; *A* believed the girl was drunk but she had actually died. *B* broke into a coin box with intent to take money from the box, but it turned out that the box did not contain any money. *C* received certain property that he believed to be stolen, but the property had not been stolen but was only represented as such to *C* by undercover law enforcement officers. *D* was smoking what he believed to be marijuana, but he was in fact puffing on an innocuous weed. *E* put a gun to his wife's head and pulled the trigger twice, but the weapon did not fire, for, unknown to *E*, the gun was not loaded. Query whether *A*, *B*, *C*, *D*, and *E* are all guilty of attempt, whether they are all not guilty, or whether on some basis only some of them are guilty.

The traditional approach in dealing with such fact situations has been to distinguish what is called "legal impossibility" from what is termed "factual impossibility." If the case is one of legal impossibility, in the sense that what the defendant set out to do is not criminal, then the defendant is not guilty of attempt. On the other hand, factual impossibility, where the intended substantive crime is impossible of accomplishment merely because of some physical impossibility unknown to the defendant, is not a defense. This in itself may appear to be a rather simple distinction, but courts have frequently experienced considerable difficulty with it. Account must also be taken of what some view as a third category, perhaps best termed "inherent impossibility," where any reasonable person would have known from the outset that the means being employed could not accomplish the ends sought. In addition, the impossibility of success may sometimes be relevant in a more limited sense, for it might cast doubt upon whether the defendant was acting with the requisite mental state for the crime of attempt.

(1) Mental State. It is important to keep in mind that impossibility will sometimes have a bearing upon the issue of whether the defendant acted with the necessary mental state. This is because the impossibility may sometimes establish the lack of the requisite intent even when it is of the factual variety and thus would not otherwise be a defense. For example, impotence is not a defense to a charge of attempted rape because it merely constitutes a factual impossibility of success. However, if the defendant has known for some time that he is impotent, then that evidence is certainly relevant to show a lack of intent to rape. Similarly, a defendant's declared intent to kill another person may be put in doubt if he only attacks with a small switch.

Of course, if the defendant is unaware of the facts that show he cannot succeed, then it would seem those facts do not relate to his intent. There nonetheless may be cases in which it appears on the surface that the defendant was unaware of those facts, yet a more careful inquiry may show that he in fact was aware and proceeded as he did because he really did not want to do any harm. For example, consider the case of *State v. Damms* (1960), referred to earlier. The defendant, while driving with his estranged wife, pulled a gun from under the car seat while engaged in an argument with her. He threatened her life but also spoke of reconciliation. When the car stopped she fled; he pursued her, overtook her, placed the gun against her head and pulled the trigger twice, but the gun was not loaded. These acts occurred in the presence of two policemen, who arrested the defendant. The Wisconsin Supreme Court affirmed the defendant's conviction for attempted murder, concluding that it was an "extraneous factor" that the gun was unloaded, while a dissenting justice concluded that the cause of failure was not extraneous because it resulted from the defendant's own conduct in not loading the gun. One commentator has pointed out that neither opinion took account of the unloaded gun as it bears upon "the potential dangerousness of the offender. The dissent, by ignoring defendant's state of mind, failed to consider the possibility that the act of omission, although directly traceable to the actor, may have been caused by a factor other than the exercise of internal control. Likewise, the majority's definition, by focusing solely upon defendant's awareness at the conscious level of the omission, did not consider the possibility that failure to load the gun might have resulted from internal control at the unconscious level."

Some commentators, however, have gone well beyond that point by asserting, in effect, that a person's intent is to do what he was actually doing rather than what he thought he was doing. One of the most famous impossibility cases is *People v. Jaffe* (1906), where the defendant purchased certain goods on the mistaken belief that they were stolen. As will be discussed later, the court of appeals reversed the defendant's conviction of an attempt to receive stolen goods. It has been asserted, however, that the *Jaffe* decision is "easily explainable, without reference to any conception of 'legal

impossibility' " in that "the necessary intent * * * was lacking."
So the argument goes, the defendant's intent was to receive the
very goods received, and since those goods were in fact not stolen
he cannot be said to have intended to receive stolen goods. On the
same basis, it has been claimed that there is no intent to kill if one
strikes at a block of wood believing it to be his deadly enemy, and
no intent to steal if one carries away his own umbrella believing it
to belong to someone else. The "primary intent" is said to be that
of dealing with the object at hand.

Surely there is nothing about the concept of intent (see § 4.2)
that justifies such conclusions. It has been aptly noted that such
analysis "must at the least be supported by argument before we
can accept it, for it certainly is not supported by the conventions of
ordinary language, which would not in the least be strained by
saying, for example, that a man who forcibly has intercourse with
his wife believing her to be her own twin sister intends to commit
rape." However, no arguments in support of that curious position
have been offered. Indeed, considerations of policy lead to the
contrary conclusion, for certainly one who strikes at an inanimate
object thinking it to be a man is more comparable, in terms of
dangerousness, to a person who actually strikes at a human being
than one who is chopping wood.

(2) Factual Impossibility. All courts are in agreement that
what is usually referred to as "factual impossibility" is no defense
to a charge of attempt. That is, if what the defendant intends to
accomplish is proscribed by the criminal law, but he is unable to
bring about that result because of some circumstances unknown to
him when he engaged in the attempt, then he may be convicted. On
this basis, attempt convictions have been affirmed in such circumstances as these: where the defendant attempted to steal from an
empty pocket, an empty receptacle, or an empty house; where the
defendant entered a room to molest two girls a police sting operation falsely led him to believe did exist and were in that room;
where the defendant shot a decoy believing it was a deer; where the
defendant attempted sexual exploitation of a minor by communicating via the Internet with a person he mistakenly believed was
under age; where the defendant shot with intent to kill a certain
person but failed because the intended victim was not where the
defendant believed he was or because the victim was too far away
to be killed by the weapon employed; where the defendant attempted to kill with an unloaded or defective gun or by use of poison or a
bomb that was incapable of producing death; where the defendant
attempted rape but was impotent; where the defendant attempted
an abortion but the woman was not pregnant or the drugs or
instruments were incapable of producing an abortion; where the
intended sale of an illegal drug actually involved a different sub-

stance; where the intended victim of false pretenses had no money or was not deceived; where the intended victim of extortion was not put in fear; and where an attempt at bribery was unsuccessful because the employee who was to offer the bribe instead went to the police or because the other party was unwilling to take a bribe.

In all of the above situations, it is clear as a matter of policy that no reason exists for exonerating the defendant because of facts unknown to him which made it impossible for him to succeed. In each instance the defendant's mental state was the same as that of a person guilty of the completed crime, and by committing the acts in question he has demonstrated his readiness to carry out his illegal venture. He is therefore deserving of conviction and is just as much in need of restraint and corrective treatment as the defendant who did not meet with the unanticipated events that barred successful completion of the crime.

One commentator, however, has suggested a test for impossibility cases that would afford a defense in at least some of the fact situations set forth above. Under his approach, "an attempt at a particular crime, to be punishable as a relative criminal attempt, must create a substantial impairment of some interest protected by the involved prohibitions against the crime or its related attempt." The assumption is that the law of attempts is intended to prevent certain lesser harms than the completed crime, so that no conviction should be permitted unless that identifiable harm has occurred. Thus, he concluded, the impotent defendant *is* guilty of attempted rape because the crime of attempted rape is intended to protect women from being put in fear of a sexual attack, and the defendant who puts an unloaded gun to his intended victim's head likewise *is* guilty of attempted murder because the crime of attempted murder is intended to protect against the fear of violence, but it would be otherwise when the intended victim was not even aware of the unsuccessful attempt to take his life. Apart from the obvious difficulty in identifying what the interests are which are invaded by various sorts of attempts, that approach is clearly inconsistent with the modern rationale of attempt law (see § 10.2(b)). A person whose acts and accompanying mental state show him to be dangerous is deserving of conviction of attempt without regard to whether he encroached upon some lesser interest of the victim than intended.

(3) **Legal Impossibility.** The case of *Wilson v. State* (1905) deserves consideration here because it is a case that quite clearly calls for a result different from those in the cases of factual impossibility described above. The defendant was convicted of attempt to commit forgery, in that he had tampered with a draft for two dollars and fifty cents by writing in the figure 1 so as to make what read \$2 $^{50}/_{100}$ appear instead as \$12 $^{50}/_{100}$. No change was made in the written out sum of "two and $^{50}/_{100}$ dollars," nor was any

attempt made to obliterate the words "Ten Dollars or Less" stamped on the document. Noting that the completed crime of forgery requires the alteration of a material part of the document, which the figures themselves were not, the Mississippi Supreme Court concluded that the defendant had not committed the crime of attempted forgery. The court held, in effect, that since the defendant had done everything which he had meant to do and had thereby not committed a completed crime, he could hardly be considered guilty of an attempt.

Despite all of the disagreement between the commentators on the subject of impossibility, it is uniformly agreed that the result in *Wilson* was correct. "It may be true that the layman and perhaps Wilson himself would be very surprised to be told that what he had done did not amount to forgery or an attempt to commit forgery, but an immoral motive to inflict some injury on one's fellows coupled with a misapprehension about the content of the criminal law are not good reasons for conviction." The important point to keep in mind here is that one would not have to invent a doctrine called legal impossibility to dispose of the *Wilson* case. Rather, all that is involved is an application of the principle of legality; the defendant did not intend to do anything which had been made criminal, and what is not criminal may not be turned into a crime after the fact by characterizing his acts as an attempt. "The reason for not convicting him has nothing to do with the failure of the enterprise, but rather with the absence of any prohibition of the conduct whether completed or not."

If *Wilson* marked the boundaries of the legal impossibility doctrine as it has been applied by the courts, then there would be no basis for criticism of it. But that has not been the case, as is illustrated by the famous case of *People v. Jaffe* (1906). The defendant there was convicted of an attempt to violate a section of the criminal code making it an offense for a person to buy or receive any stolen property knowing the same to have been stolen. Unknown to the defendant, the property in question had been restored to the owners and was within their control when he purchased it, and thus no longer had the character of stolen goods. The prosecution relied upon the "empty pocket" and other factual impossibility cases, but the court reversed Jaffe's conviction on the ground that "if the accused had completed the act which he attempted to do, he would not be guilty of a criminal offense." In other words, since Jaffe had done everything he had intended to do—in the sense that he had already received the goods in question—and had not thereby committed the crime of receiving stolen property, he could not be found guilty of attempting to commit that crime.

Although this sounds very much like the reasoning used in *Wilson,* it is apparent that *Jaffe* and *Wilson* are not precisely the same kind of case. In *Wilson* the defendant may have thought he was committing a crime, but if he did it was not because he intended to do something that the criminal law prohibited but rather because he was ignorant of the material alteration requirement of the crime of forgery. In *Jaffe,* on the other hand, what the defendant intended to do was a crime, and if the facts had been as the defendant believed them to be he would have been guilty of the completed crime.

Jaffe is not an aberration in the law, for defendants have prevailed with a legal impossibility type of defense in many other cases where the defendant would have been guilty if the actual facts were consistent with his belief. Thus, there are other decisions holding that one has not attempted to receive stolen property if the defendant's belief that the goods were stolen is in error. In addition, it has been held: that the defendant had not attempted to take deer out of season when he shot a stuffed deer believing it to be alive; that the defendant had not attempted to bribe a juror when he offered a bribe to a person he mistakenly believed to be a juror; that the defendant had not attempted to illegally contract a valid debt when he believed the debt to be valid but it was unauthorized and a nullity. But the *Jaffe* analysis has been rejected on other occasions in which the defendant was held properly convicted of an attempt although, in one sense, he had done everything intended but had not committed the completed crime. Attempt convictions have been affirmed where the defendant mistakenly believed that the property received was stolen, that the items stolen was a trade secret, that the substance sold or received was heroin or other illegal drugs, that the cigarette smoked contained marijuana, that the girl with whom he had sexual intercourse was alive, and that the man he shot was alive. (Hence the objection that the difficulty in these types of cases is that the distinction between factual and legal impossibility is essentially a matter of semantics, for every case of legal impossibility can reasonably be characterized as a factual impossibility.)

These latter decisions represent the better view as to the impossibility defense, which has been criticized by many commentators and rejected in Model Penal Code § 5.01(1)(a) and in virtually all of the recent recodifications. The *Jaffe* approach, concluded the Code draftsmen,

> is unsound in that it seeks to evaluate a mental attitude—"intent" or "purpose"—not by looking to the actor's mental frame of reference, but to a situation wholly at variance with the actor's beliefs. In so doing, the courts exonerate defendants in situations where attempt liability most certainly should be

imposed. In all of these cases the actor's criminal purpose has been clearly demonstrated; he went as far as he could in implementing that purpose; and, as a result, his "dangerousness" is plainly manifested.

This rejection of the impossibility defense, it must be emphasized, has no effect upon such cases as *Wilson,* which may still be disposed of upon the ground that the requisite intent was lacking. As noted earlier, decisions such as *Wilson* rest upon the principle of legality, and it is "perfectly consistent with the legality principle to treat, as criminal attempts, those situations in which the actor intends to violate the statute and performs an act he thinks is in furtherance of that intent."

However, some commentators, while rejecting the kind of reasoning employed in *Jaffe,* have taken the position that the defense of impossibility is not totally without merit. Part of the concern is simply with sufficient proof of the defendant's mental state, and it has been pointed out that cases of either factual or legal impossibility can arise in which doubts are raised about whether the defendant had the requisite intent. *Jaffe,* for example, is said to be a case where the defendant's purchase of property that in fact was not stolen is equivocal, so that further inquiry is called for to determine if the goods were purchased at a very low price or were received under generally suspicious circumstances. Likewise, it is said that similar close scrutiny on the intent issue is required when the prosecution contends that the defendant intended to kill when giving the victim a nonpoisonous substance or that the defendant intended to possess narcotics when he in fact possessed an innocuous substance. The perceived risk is that without an impossibility defense a much broader class of persons are potentially subject to prosecution, so that the chances of an erroneous conviction are enhanced.

A slightly different objection begins with the premise that criminal conduct should be clearly defined by the legislature in advance whenever possible, with the courts being delegated rather limited power to fill in the details. Thus, while "a crucial factor justifying legislative delegation of the power to define the act element of attempts in the preparation-attempt cases was the inability of the legislature to provide for the infinitely varying acts in advance," there are some instances in which "the legislature is perfectly capable of deciding in advance whether or not to require the particular element." Put in terms of the *Jaffe* case, the impossibility issue arose in the first instance because the receiving statute required the person *know* the property to have been stolen, a problem that the legislature could very easily have avoided by instead providing that *belief* that the property was stolen is sufficient. That being the case, "analytic tools are lacking" whereby a court could decide whether, on an attempt theory, belief may suffice for conviction without doing violence to the legislature's wishes. So the argument goes, the proper solution to *Jaffe* is to "attend to the statute defining the substantive crime."

(4) Inherent Impossibility. Yet another type of impossibility, which understandably has seldom confronted the courts, is what might be called inherent impossibility—the situation in which the defendant employs means that a reasonable man would view as totally inappropriate to the objective sought. The matter has been frequently discussed by the commentators in relation to this example put by one judge in *Commonwealth v. Johnson* (1933):

> Even though a "voodoo doctor" just arrived here from Haiti actually believed that his malediction would surely bring death to the person on whom he was invoking it, I cannot conceive of an American court upholding a conviction of such a maledicting "doctor" for attempted murder or even attempted assault and battery. Murderous maledictions might have to be punished by the law as disorderly conduct, but they could not be classed as attempted crimes unless the courts so far departed from the law of criminal attempts as to engage in legislation. A malediction arising out of a murderous intent is not such a substantial overt act that it would support a charge of attempted murder.

Why should this be so? Because, some commentators have argued, the inherent impossibility of success shows that the defendant is not dangerous. "If in the point of view of a reasonable man in the same circumstances as the defendant the desired criminal consequence could not be expected to result from the defendant's acts, it cannot endanger social interests to allow the defendant to go unpunished, no matter how evil may have been his intentions." Others, however, have contended that acquittal of such a defendant could be explained only on the ground that his acts do not seem to call for retribution, in that he *has* manifested sufficient dangerousness to warrant corrective treatment. "When a man makes a harmless attempt to commit a crime, he may well try again, perhaps more effectively. The voodoo witch doctor may use a gun next time. Thus the purposes of special deterrence and neutralization can be served by punishing even the marginal cases." It has also been suggested that the "reasonable man" test is an inappropriate one because it would extend to the case in which the defendant pursued "an extremely marginal chance of successfully committing a harm."

On the ground that even those who make unreasonable mistakes may be dangerous, the Model Penal Code eliminates the defense of impossibility even in cases of inherent impossibility. However, under Code § 5.05(2) the court would be empowered to dismiss the prosecution or impose a lower sentence than generally permitted for the crime attempted if the defendant's conduct was "so inherently unlikely to result or culminate in the commission of a crime that neither such conduct nor the actor presents a public danger." Because of the absence of cases in point, it is difficult to generalize about the existing state of the law concerning inherent impossibility. The Model Penal Code approach was expressly rejected by one legislature, which recognizes impossibility as a defense when "such impossibility would have been clearly evident to a person of normal understanding." Elsewhere, inherent impossibility may also continue to be a defense even in the face of statutory language that seemingly abolishes all impossibility defenses.

(b) **Abandonment.** In *People v. Staples* (1970), the facts were as follows: In October 1967, while his wife was away on a trip, one Staples, under an assumed name, rented an office on the second floor of a building directly over the mezzanine of a bank. Staples was aware of the layout of the building, and specifically of the relation of the office he rented to the bank vault. He paid rent for the period October 23–November 23, and the landlord had the 10 days before the start of that period to finish some interior repairs and painting. During the prerental period Staples brought into the office certain equipment, including drilling tools, two acetylene gas tanks, a blow torch, a blanket and a linoleum rug. Learning that no one was in the building on Saturdays, he drilled several holes part way through the floor on Saturday, October 14. He covered the holes with the rug, and at some point he locked his tools in a closet, although he left the key on the premises. Around the end of November, the landlord notified the police and turned the equipment over to them. Some time later Staples was arrested, after which he voluntarily gave a statement to the police that read in part as follows: "The actual commencement of my plan made me begin to realize that even if I were to succeed a fugitive life of living off of stolen money would not give the enjoyment of the life of a mathematician however humble a job I might have. * * * My wife came back and my life as bank robber seemed more and more absurd."

Is Staples guilty of attempted burglary, or is his apparent abandonment of the criminal scheme under these circumstances a valid defense? One way to approach this issue is *not* to think about the possibility of some unique doctrine that an attempt, unlike most other crimes, may be abandoned after it has been committed, but rather to ask whether upon the available facts it may be said that the essential elements of an attempt are present. That is, looking at all of the facts may it be said that there existed both (1) the requisite mental state of an intent to commit a burglary (see

§ 10.3), and (2) an act in furtherance of that intent beyond mere preparation (see § 10.4), or on the other hand does it appear that at least one of these elements is missing so that the crime of attempt was never committed? If it is concluded that the necessary mental state and act are present, then a different approach is required; it then must be asked whether abandonment can ever be a defense to what would otherwise be a completed attempt and, if so, whether the circumstances of the abandonment in this case bring it within that defense.

(1) Mental State and Act. As to the bearing of Staples' abandonment on the question of whether he had the requisite intent, it has been suggested that "where the accused has changed his mind, it would be only just to interpret his previous intention where possible as only half-formed or provisional, and hold it to be insufficient mens rea." It is undoubtedly true that under some circumstances the defendant's abandonment will create a reasonable doubt as to whether he ever actually had the criminal intent. For example, proof of voluntary abandonment is rather strong evidence of lack of intent by a defendant, charged with attempted rape, who did not commit the rape notwithstanding the ability to do so. Likewise, the failure to carry out what appears to be an attempt at suicide may show that it was not seriously intended or was subconsciously desired to fail. In the *Staples* case, one might expect the defense to contend that the totality of the evidence shows that Staples was a Walter Mitty type who fantasized about the perfect crime but never really formed an intent to burglarize the bank. However, the court—properly it would seem—concluded that the defendant's intent was clearly established. "Defendant admitted in his written confession that he rented the office fully intending to burglarize the bank, that he brought in tools and equipment to accomplish this purpose, and that he began drilling into the floor with the intent of making an entry into the bank."

What is the relevance of the abandonment on the issue of whether the requisite act occurred? It has been observed that "anywhere between the conception of the intent and the overt act toward its commission, there is room for repentance; and the law in its beneficence extends the hand of forgiveness." However, that language should not be taken too seriously, for if the overt act has not yet occurred there is nothing to forgive. That is, in such a case the law is not taking account of the defendant's repentance, and thus it makes no difference whether the absence of the requisite act is attributable to the defendant's change of heart or to the fact that he became aware of an increased risk of apprehension. Yet, it is undoubtedly true that courts are sometimes influenced by the fact of voluntary withdrawal to the extent that they characterize the defendant's prior acts as mere preparation upon facts which would certainly justify a contrary conclusion. The *Staples* case, however, does not lend itself to such a result, for, as the court noted, the defendant had quite clearly passed the stage of preparation when he commenced the drilling, for it was an unequivocal act that actually constituted a fragment of the contemplated crime. As the court put it, the drilling was "the beginning of the 'breaking' element."

(2) As a Defense. Assuming now that both the mental state and act required for the crime of attempt are found to exist, how will Staples fare if he claims to have a defense because of his abandonment? At this point we may find it useful to look more closely at all of the facts in order to determine precisely why he did not proceed with his scheme. One possibility (indeed, the possibility the court in *Staples* found to be supported by the evidence) is that his self-serving statement to the police implying repentance was false and that instead the defendant ceased his efforts because he "became aware that the landlord had resumed control over the office and had turned defendant's equipment and tools over to the police." If this conclusion is correct, then quite clearly the purposes of the criminal law would be ill-served by requiring acquittal. Withdrawal by one who thought his plan had been detected or who encountered more resistance than he anticipated does not negative his dangerousness, and it is totally consistent with the rationale of attempt law (see § 10.2(b)) to subject such a person to the corrective processes of the law.

The cases are in agreement that what is usually referred to as involuntary abandonment is no defense. Thus, if the defendant fails because of unanticipated difficulties in carrying out the criminal plan at the precise time and place intended and then decides not to pursue the victim under these less advantageous circumstances, he is still guilty of attempt. The same is true when the defendant withdraws because of a belief that the intended victim has become aware of his plans, or because he thinks that his scheme has been discovered or would be thwarted by police observed in the area of the intended crime.

What then if Staples' abandonment were truly voluntary in character, in that he was in no sense influenced by extrinsic circumstances but rather underwent a real change of heart? Model Penal Code § 5.01(4) recognizes a defense under these circumstances, and that view has been adopted in some of the modern criminal codes and by some courts. However, it is impossible to generalize about the current status of such a defense; one survey concluded that the issue remains an open question in most jurisdictions, and in some states the cases in point cannot be reconciled.

The traditional view as expressed by most commentators is that abandonment is *never* a defense to a charge of attempt if the defendant has gone so far as to engage in the requisite acts with criminal intent. The assumption seems to be that because a completed crime may not thereafter be abandoned it follows that the same must be true as to the crime of attempt. "A criminal attempt is a 'complete offense' in the sense that one who has carried a criminal effort to such a point that it is punishable, can no more wipe out his criminal guilt by an abandonment of his plan than a thief can obliterate the larceny by a restoration of the stolen chattel." Many of the cases denying the defense are in fact assault cases, and it has been correctly noted that they are distinguishable because something in the way of a completed offense has been committed. In the attempt cases stating without reservation that abandonment, even due to a stricken conscience, is not a defense, a close examination of the facts before the court will usually disclose that the defendant would not have had a defense in any event because he involuntarily withdrew.

The language frequently used to define the crime of attempt lends itself to the interpretation that voluntary abandonment *is* a defense. A common statutory definition of attempt is stated in terms of one who engages in acts toward the commission of a crime "but fails in the perpetration thereof or is prevented or intercepted in executing such crime." Some courts have said that an attempt requires conduct which in the ordinary course of events would result in commission of the target crime except for the intervention of some extraneous factor (see § 10.4(b)). Yet, the broad judicial pronouncement that no kind of abandonment is a defense has been made notwithstanding such language in the applicable statute and precedents. And while the Model Penal Code draftsmen state that the "prevailing view" is in favor of allowing voluntary desistance as a defense, the American cases cited in support for the most part contain such statements in dictum or in concurring or dissenting opinions. Cases in which the defendant's claim of voluntary withdrawal was plausible enough to make failure to instruct on the defense reversible error are extremely rare.

On balance, the arguments in favor of recognizing voluntary abandonment as a defense to a charge of attempt are more persuasive than the arguments against the defense. For one thing, recognition of the defense is consistent with the rationale of attempt, as a complete and voluntary renunciation of criminal purpose "tends to negative dangerousness." In addition, if the defense is allowed, then those who have crossed the threshold of attempt will still be encouraged to desist and thereby escape any penalty. The counter-argument is that the defense may actually embolden those considering some criminal endeavor because they will be more willing to take the first steps toward the crime when they know they can withdraw with impunity. This risk, however, seems slight, as does the risk that recognition of the defense will result in the acceptance of false claims of repentance.

Although this subject is often discussed in terms of voluntary versus involuntary abandonment, Model Penal Code § 5.01(4) requires that the defendant's abandonment occur "under circumstances manifesting a complete and voluntary renunciation of his criminal purpose." The renunciation is not voluntary if "motivated, in whole or in part, by circumstances, not present or apparent at the inception of the actor's course of conduct, which increase the probability of detection or apprehension or which make more difficult the accomplishment of the criminal purpose," and is not complete if "motivated by a decision to postpone the criminal conduct until a more advantageous time or to transfer the criminal effort to another but similar objective or victim." This definition of the defense appears to be somewhat broader than the usual statement (e.g., that there must be "no outside cause" or "extraneous factor"), a difference that may be of some importance in those cases where the defendant is dissuaded from completing the crime by the intended victim or where the defendant changes his mind upon learning that the fruits of the crime would not be as great as previously expected.

Assuming a defense of voluntary abandonment, does there come a point at which it is too late for the defendant to withdraw? Obviously there must be, for it would hardly do to excuse the defendant from attempted murder after he had wounded the intended victim or, indeed, after he had fired and missed. It might even be argued that it is too late whenever the defendant has taken the last proximate step, for at that point his dangerousness is not rebutted by the withdrawal. On the other hand, as the Model Penal Code draftsmen point out, recognizing withdrawal, even after the last proximate act has occurred will encourage desistance at a time when such encouragement is most important.

(c) Prosecution and Punishment. Assume that *A* has been charged with and is on trial for the offense of burglary, but during the course of the trial the evidence develops in such a way that it appears *A* may have only attempted the offense of burglary. May *A* be convicted of attempted burglary? At one time the answer was no, for while it was generally recognized that when a charge of an offense included within it a lesser offense the defendant could be convicted of that lesser crime, this rule was subject to one important qualification: "upon an indictment for a felony, the defendant could not be convicted of a misdemeanor." Thus a conviction for the common law misdemeanor of attempt could not be had upon an indictment charging the felony of burglary.

Insofar as can be determined, that exception was based upon the fact that under early English criminal procedure a defendant in a felony trial had fewer rights than a defendant on trial for a misdemeanor. That quite clearly is not the case in the United States, and thus there has been no reason to honor this exception in this country. The courts are in general agreement that an attempt conviction may be had on a charge of the completed crime, and statutes to this effect exist in some jurisdictions.

This is not to say, however, that upon any charge of a completed crime the trier of fact will inevitably be confronted with the possibility of returning a verdict or finding of only an attempt. The judge may give an instruction on the attempt alternative only if the evidence would support such a verdict. For example, if on *A*'s trial for burglary *A* merely interposes an alibi defense or admits to being within the dwelling but claims to have been acting with an innocent intent, then the only logical alternatives are guilty of burglary or not guilty. On the other hand, if *A* asserts that he had not yet entered at the time of his apprehension, then the third alternative of guilt of attempted burglary exists. In such a case the attempt alternative may go to the jury even over the defendant's objection.

Quite obviously the reverse is not true. That is, if *A* had been on trial only for attempted burglary but it was shown at trial that he had actually entered the dwelling, clearly *A* may not be convicted of the greater uncharged offense of burglary. But, under those facts may he even be convicted of attempted burglary? The crime of attempt is often defined as if failure were an essential element, and on this basis it has sometimes been held that proof of the completed crime requires reversal of an attempt to commit it. The assumption that failure is required may be derived from the old common law rule of merger, whereby if an act resulted in both a felony and a misdemeanor the misdemeanor was said to be absorbed into the felony. (Taking that as the basis of the rule, then the problem would not arise if the completed crime would also be only a misdemeanor or, in the alternative, if the completed crime would be a felony but an attempt to commit it had by statute also been made a felony.)

The English merger rule was laid to rest by statute in 1851, and there seems no reason to follow it in this country. As one court observed, a defendant can hardly complain "where the determination of his case was more favorable to him than the evidence warranted." Thus, many recent cases have held that a defendant may be convicted of the attempt even if the completed crime is proved, and many jurisdictions expressly so provide by statute.

Considerable variation is to be found across the country concerning the authorized penalties for attempt. As to statutory provisions concerning the sentences that may be imposed for all or a broad class of attempts, the most common in the modern recodifications is that which declares the attempt to be a crime one degree below the object crime. Another common provision establishes categories according to the severity of the penalty for the completed crime and specifies a range of penalties for attempts to commit crimes within each category. Some merely provide that the penalty for attempt may be as great as for the completed crime. As to statutes dealing with attempts to commit particular crimes, the authorized punishment is usually lower than for the completed crime, but in some instances the same or even a higher punishment is possible.

Taking into account the rationale of the crime of attempt (see § 10.2(b)), the Model Penal Code § 5.05(1) penalty provisions are most sensible. An attempt may be punished to the same extent as the completed crime, except that a lower punishment is provided for attempts to commit capital crimes or the most serious felonies. "To the extent that sentencing depends upon the antisocial disposition of the actor and the demonstrated need for a corrective sanction, there is likely to be little difference in the gravity of the required measures depending on the consummation or the failure of the plan." The more severe penalties designed for general deterrence are withheld because the threat of punishment for the attempt would not add significantly to the deterrent efficacy of the sanction threatened for the completed crime.

Chapter 11

CONSPIRACY

Table of Sections

For additional analysis of the above topics and citations to authorities supporting their discussion in this Book, consult the author's 3-volume *Substantive Criminal Law* treatise, also available as Westlaw database SUBCRL. See the Table of Cross-References in this Book.

---

§ 11.1 Introduction

Although the crime of conspiracy is somewhat vague, this is but one of many reasons why it is often asserted that the prosecution has a distinct advantage in conspiracy cases. The crime of conspiracy serves as a device for acting against the special and continuing dangers incident to group activity, and also (like other anticipatory offenses) as a means to proceed against persons who have sufficiently manifested their disposition to criminality.

(a) Development of the Crime of Conspiracy. The crime of conspiracy, unknown to the early common law, emerged from the enactment of three statutes during the reign of Edward I. These

486

statutes were intended to correct the abuses of ancient criminal procedure, and conspiracy was accordingly defined narrowly. "Combinations only to procure false indictments or to bring false appeals or to maintain vexatious suits could constitute conspiracies." Moreover, the crime of conspiracy was not complete unless the person falsely accused had been actually indicted and acquitted.

The first significant expansion of conspiracy occurred with the decision by the Court of Star Chamber in *Poulterer's Case* (1611). The defendants had confederated to bring a false accusation against one Stone, but Stone was so clearly innocent that the grand jury refused to indict him. This being so, it was the contention of the defendants that no conspiracy had occurred, but the court decided to the contrary. Thus, *Poulterer's Case* gave rise to a doctrine that survives to this day: the gist of conspiracy is the agreement, and so the agreement is punishable even if its purpose was not achieved.

Later in the seventeenth century the courts took a second step toward broadening the crime of conspiracy: an agreement to commit any offense became a punishable conspiracy. During this same period, the tendency of the courts was in the direction of undertaking to punish acts that were immoral even if not in violation of express law, and thus it was not surprising that in arguments of counsel it was claimed a combination could be criminal even if the object thereof was not criminal. With apparently but one exception, this suggestion was rejected by the courts.

Nonetheless, Hawkins asserted in 1716 that "there can be no doubt, but that all confederacies whatsoever, wrongfully to prejudice a third person, are highly criminal at common law," and just a few years thereafter a case supporting the Hawkins doctrine was decided. The vast majority of the decisions, however, continued to adhere to the long-established law that the object of the conspiracy or the means used must in fact be criminal.

Then in 1832 came Lord Denman's famous epigram that a conspiracy indictment must "charge a conspiracy either to do an unlawful act or a lawful act by unlawful means," which was "seized upon by judges laboring bewildered through the mazes of the conspiracy cases as a ready solution for all their difficulties." Although Lord Denman's statement was somewhat ambiguous, in that the word "unlawful" might be interpreted to mean criminal, courts in England and the United States gave it a broad reading. Illustrative is *State v. Burnham* (1844): "When it is said in the books that the means must be unlawful, it is not to be understood that those means must amount to indictable offenses, in order to make the offense of conspiracy complete. It will be enough if they are corrupt, dishonest, fraudulent, immoral, and in that sense illegal, and it is in the combination to make use of such practices that the dangers of this offense consist."

Thus the definition which persists in those jurisdictions retaining common law crimes is that conspiracy is a combination between two or more persons formed for the purpose of doing either an unlawful act or a lawful act by unlawful means. (Where conspiracy is defined by statute, the common law definition is sometimes followed, elsewhere other language is used that makes it apparent some noncriminal objectives are also covered, while some states have now limited conspiracy to criminal objectives.) Although a more precise definition of conspiracy may be difficult, it is useful to keep in mind that conspiracy, like most other offenses, requires both an act and an accompanying mental state (see §§ 4.1, 5.1). The agreement constitutes the act, while the intention to thereby achieve the objective is the mental state; it is not necessary that the objective have been realized. The practical consequences and theoretical justification of conspiracy prosecutions are considered in this section. Subsequent sections in this chapter consider the requisite act and mental state, the dimensions of a conspiracy, and then other limits on conspiracy liability.

(b) The Prosecution's Advantage. Some years ago, Judge Learned Hand called conspiracy "the darling of the modern prosecutor's nursery," and this characterization certainly is not without justification. Wherever one might think the "balance of advantage" generally lies in the criminal process, it is clear that a conspiracy charge gives the prosecution certain unique advantages and that one who must defend against such a charge bears a particularly heavy burden. This is attributable not only to the elusive quality of conspiracy as a legal concept, but also to various rules of procedure and evidence that have special application in a conspiracy context.

Conspiracy has been and certainly continues to be a most controversial subject for a variety of reasons. Prosecutors continue to rely heavily upon this particular weapon in their arsenal, and this has heightened concern about the dangers of unfairness to conspiracy defendants. The controversy has been intensified because of the activities against which the law of conspiracy has been invoked. There is, of course, that sad chapter in our history when labor unions were condemned and suppressed as criminal conspiracies. More recently, we have witnessed several instances in which conspiracy law has been used against those who are called "political" defendants, and here as well many see the conspiracy device as posing a serious threat to the freedom of speech and association.

Although these matters cannot be fully explored here, it will be useful to take note of the principal reasons why it is so often said that conspiracy prosecutions afford the prosecution undue advantage. Some appreciation of these factors is essential to a full understanding of the significance of the remaining discussion concerning the bases of and limitations upon liability for criminal conspiracy.

(1) Vagueness. The criticism commentators have voiced most often and most strongly is that there is an inherent vagueness in the crime of conspiracy. "In the long category of crimes there is none," wrote Dean Harno, "not excepting criminal attempt, more difficult to confine within the boundaries of definitive statement than conspiracy." Professor Sayre, in his classic article on the subject, noted: "A doctrine so vague in its outlines and uncertain in its fundamental nature as criminal conspiracy lends no strength or glory to the law; it is a veritable quicksand of shifting opinion and ill-considered thought." And Justice Jackson, in his oft-quoted concurring opinion in *Krulewitch v. U.S.* (1949), referred to conspiracy as an "elastic, sprawling and pervasive offense, * * * so vague that it almost defies definition [and also] chameleon-like [because it] takes on a special coloration from each of the many independent offenses on which it may be overlaid."

Undoubtedly the main reason for this criticism is the fact that the law of conspiracy developed in such a way that certain objectives not in themselves criminal will suffice (see § 11.3(a)). However, the vagueness stems from other aspects of the crime as well, including the uncertainty over what is sufficient to constitute the agreement (see § 11.2(a)) and what attendant mental state must be shown (see § 11.2(c)). These ambiguities compound the difficulties of defending against a conspiracy charge, for "it is hard to find an antidote for the poison you cannot identify."

(2) Venue. The Sixth Amendment provides that in "all criminal prosecutions, the accused shall enjoy the right to a speedy and public trial, by an impartial jury of the State and district wherein the crime shall have been committed." Similarly, most state constitutions also provide that a defendant in a criminal case is entitled to be tried in the county, parish, or district where the crime occurred. These venue provisions constitute an important constitutional guarantee, for they "safeguard against the unfairness and hardship involved when an accused is prosecuted in a remote place."

Given the common reference to the agreement in conspiracy as the "gist" of the offense, it might be thought that the place of trial for conspiracy prosecutions must be the place where the agreement was made. But, while it has long been settled that a conspiracy prosecution may be brought at the place of agreement, it is clear that the prosecution may also elect to have the trial in any locale where any overt act by any of the conspirators took place. Although it is argued in support of this rule that if it were otherwise conspiracy prosecutions would often be impossible because of the frequent difficulty of proving the place of agreement, the rule makes it possible for the prosecution to select a district inconvenient to the defendant or one in which a jury may be more disposed to convict. As Justice Jackson observed In *Krulewitch*:

> The leverage of a conspiracy charge lifts [the constitutional venue] limitation from the prosecution and reduces its protection to a phantom, for the crime is considered so vagrant as to have been committed in any district where any one of the conspirators did any one of the acts, however innocent, intended to accomplish its object. The Government may, and often does, compel one to defend at a great distance from any place he ever did any act because some accused confederate did some trivial and by itself innocent act in the chosen district.

The prosecutor's options in this regard are enhanced by the fact that, under the prevailing view, venue need be established only by a preponderance of the evidence and need only be submitted to the jury when the matter of venue is in issue.

(3) Hearsay Exception. The general rule that hearsay is not admissible in a criminal prosecution is marked by many exceptions. One of these is the co-conspirator exception: any act or declaration by one co-conspirator committed during and in furtherance of the conspiracy is admissible against each co-conspirator. For example, Fed.R.Evid. 801(d)(2)(E) "allows introduction of the admissions of a confederate as if they were the defendant's own upon a showing 1) that a conspiracy existed and that the defendant participated in it, 2) that an identified hearsay declarant and the defendant were involved in the same conspiracy, 3) that the statement was made in the course of the conspiracy, and 4) that the statement was made in furtherance of the conspiracy. The rationale most often given for this exception is that each of the conspirators is the agent of all the others."

However, the co-conspirator hearsay exception as applied often extends beyond that rationale. The requirement that the act or statement be in furtherance of the conspiracy is often applied broadly, with the result that any evidence somehow relating to the conspiracy comes in. Occasionally statements have been held properly admitted into evidence notwithstanding the fact that they were made prior to the formation of the conspiracy or after its termination. And frequently, on the ground that the addition of a new member does not create a new conspiracy, statements by one conspirator are held admissible against others who joined the group after they were made. Indeed, as one court elaborated: "As long as it is shown that a party, having joined a conspiracy, is aware of the conspiracy's features and general aims, statements pertaining to the details of the plans to further the conspiracy can be admitted against the party even if the party does not have specific knowledge of the acts spoken of."

The procedures typically followed regarding admission of a co-conspirator's statements tend to favor the prosecutor, who need establish the preliminary facts of the existence of a conspiracy and defendant's involvement in it only by a preponderance of the evidence. For one thing, while courts have sometimes declared that the statement by one conspirator is not admissible against the others unless the existence of the conspiracy has been independently established, the Supreme Court ruled in *Bourjaily v. U.S.* (1987) that the government need not prove the existence of the conspiracy through extrinsic evidence alone, but may use the co-conspirator's statement itself in meeting its burden. Moreover, courts have been sympathetic to the problems of the prosecution in presenting evidence in a vast conspiracy case, and thus have admitted evidence falling under the exception, subject to an instruction to the jury that such evidence is not to be considered against the other defendants if independent proof of the conspiracy is not thereafter presented. As Justice Jackson saw it, "In other words, a conspiracy often is proved by evidence that is admissible only upon assumption that conspiracy existed. The naive assumption that prejudicial effects can be overcome by instructions to the jury * * * all practicing lawyers know to be unmitigated fiction."

(4) Circumstantial Evidence. Most conspiracy convictions are based upon circumstantial evidence, and this evidence is often admitted under rather loose standards of relevance. As one court put it, "Wide latitude is allowed [the prosecution] in presenting evidence, and it is within the discretion of the trial court to admit evidence which even remotely tends to establish the conspiracy charged." The Supreme Court offered this explanation in *Blumenthal v. U.S.* (1947):

> Secrecy and concealment are essential features of successful conspiracy. The more completely they are achieved, the more successful the crime. Hence the law rightly gives room for allowing the conviction of those discovered upon showing sufficiently the essential nature of the plan and their connections with it, without requiring evidence of knowledge of all its details or of the participation of others. Otherwise the difficulties, not only of discovery, but of certainty in proof and of correlating proof with pleading would become insuperable, and conspirators would go free by their very ingenuity.

There is, to be sure, something to the point that the prosecution confronts particularly difficult problems in proving conspiracy because persons who join together for a criminal purpose resort to methods that are "devious, hidden, secret and clandestine." However, it may well be that in some respects the courts are "overcompensating for the difficulties faced by the prosecution." Courts are particularly vulnerable to this criticism when they confuse the agreement requirement with the evidence from which it may be inferred, and when upon proof of agreement other defendants are connected with the conspiracy upon slight additional evidence.

(5) Joint Trial. When several defendants have been charged as participants in a single conspiracy, they may be required to defend against the charges in a single trial. Given the inherent nature of most conspiracies, this is understandable. "Only by prosecuting all the members together and by culling the sum total of their knowledge is it possible to obtain a detailed mosaic of the whole undertaking." However, a joint trial may present added disadvantages for the several defendants.

For one thing, what would otherwise be rights individual to each defendant may become, in effect, group rights that must be exercised jointly by all of the defendants. The most obvious example of this is the statutory right to challenge peremptorily prospective jurors; it is not uncommon for the several joined defendants to have in toto no more peremptory challenges than a single defendant would have if tried alone. Also, certain rights that are individual in nature and remain so even in a joint trial may be diminished in the joint-trial setting. Such is the case as to the right to counsel.

The greatest danger, however, is that the probability of an individual defendant being convicted may be greatly enhanced by his association through joinder with the others. This is particularly true when there is a long, complicated trial involving many defendants, where the jury may have great difficulty in keeping the evidence and jury instructions straight as they apply to particular defendants. But even when the alleged conspirators are few in number, the individual defendant "occupies an uneasy seat. There generally will be evidence of wrongdoing by somebody. It is difficult for the individual to make his own case stand on its own merits in the minds of jurors who are ready to believe that birds of a feather are flocked together. If he is silent, he is taken to admit it and if, as often happens, codefendants can be prodded into accusing or contradicting each other, they convict each other."

(c) The Rationale of Conspiracy. However, even those who have voiced such criticisms have acknowledged that "the basic conspiracy principle has some place in modern criminal law." The crime of conspiracy, which exists in virtually all jurisdictions, serves two important but different functions: (1) as with solicitation and attempt, it is a means for preventive intervention against persons who manifest a disposition to criminality; and (2) it is also a means of striking against the special danger incident to group activity.

Viewing conspiracy solely as an anticipatory offense, it is useful to compare conspiracy with attempt. As we have seen (see § 10.4(d)), under attempt law it must be shown that the defendant has taken what is sometimes referred to as a "substantial step" toward commission of the crime; earlier acts of preparation will not suffice. Conspiracy law, however, attacks inchoate crime at a far more incipient stage—the crime of conspiracy is complete at the time of the agreement or (in some jurisdictions) at the time of the first overt act in pursuance of the conspiracy by any party thereto (see § 11.2(b)). How can this earlier legal intervention be justified?

This question can best be answered by noting once again two significant considerations that are properly taken into account in marking the boundaries of inchoate offenses: (a) the need to permit law enforcement intervention before the defendant's activities come dangerously close to bringing about the criminal result; and (b) the need to subject to corrective treatment those who have clearly indicated their criminal disposition. Thus, the attempt cases on what constitutes a "substantial step" reflect a concern with whether the actor was close to success and whether the actor's conduct is so unequivocal as to make certain his intentions.

These points are reached earlier when the defendant has chosen to combine with others. In theory at least, the act of reaching agreement with one or more other persons on an unlawful purpose is a clearer manifestation of intent than, say, such acts by one person as purchasing a gun. It is less likely that the defendant will turn back, for "a conspirator who has committed himself to support his associates may be less likely to violate this commitment than he would be to revise a purely private decision." Even if the defendant does have a change of heart, he no longer has control of the situation; his fellow conspirators may finish what he started. The agreement also increases the danger to society, for by a division of labor the group is more likely to be able to bring about the criminal result. This is particularly true when the objects of the conspiracy are ambitious and elaborate.

But, as suggested above, conspiracy cannot be viewed solely as an inchoate crime. If it were, then it would hardly make sense to say that it "is an offense of the gravest character, sometimes quite outweighing, in injury to the public, the mere commission of the contemplated crime," nor would it be sensible to allow punishment for both the conspiracy and its criminal object (see § 11.4(d)). The other function of conspiracy is as a sanction against group activity. "The antisocial potentialities of a conspiracy, unlike those of an attempt, are not confined to the objects specifically contemplated at any given time. The existence of a grouping for criminal purposes provides a continuing focal point for further crimes either related or unrelated to those immediately envisaged."

§ 11.2   Acts and Mental State

As with other crimes, conspiracy requires certain acts and in addition a certain mental state. In the case of conspiracy, there must be: (1) an agreement between two or more persons, which constitutes the act; and (2) an intent thereby to achieve a certain objective, which, under the common law definition, is the doing of either an unlawful act or a lawful act by unlawful means. Many jurisdictions also require an overt act in furtherance of the conspiracy, but this is usually viewed as an evidentiary requirement rather than yet another element of the offense.

(a) **The Agreement.** As noted earlier (see § 5.1), an essential element of every crime is an act (or omission). The crime of conspiracy might appear to be an exception to this general rule, however, in that a conspiracy may be found to exist by virtue of the fact that the parties thereto have entered into an agreement. But conspiracy is not an exception, for the agreement itself is the requisite act. As one court observed: "When two agree to carry [an unlawful design] into effect, the very plot is an act in itself * * *. The agreement is an advancement of the intention which each has conceived in his mind; the mind proceeds from a secret intention to the overt act of mutual consultation and agreement."

The agreement is all-important in conspiracy, for one must look to the nature of the agreement to decide several critical issues, such as whether the requisite mental state is also present (see § 11.2(c)), whether the requisite plurality is present (see § 11.4(c)), and whether there is more than one conspiracy (see § 11.3(b)). As courts have so often said, the agreement is the "essence" or "gist" of the crime of conspiracy.

One might suppose that the agreement necessary for conspiracy is essentially like the agreement or "meeting of the minds" which is critical to a contract, but this is not the case. Although there continues to exist some uncertainty as to the precise meaning of the word in the context of conspiracy, it is clear that the definition in this setting is somewhat more lax than elsewhere. A mere tacit understanding will suffice, and there need not be any written statement or even a speaking of words that expressly communicates agreement. As the Supreme Court has put it in *Iannelli v. U.S.* (1975): "The agreement need not be shown to have been explicit. It can instead be inferred from the facts and circumstances of the case." It is possible for various persons to be parties to a single agreement (and thus one conspiracy) even though they have no direct dealings with one another or do not know the identify of one another, and even though they are not all aware of the details of the plan of operation or were not all in on the scheme from the beginning.

Because most conspiracies are clandestine in nature, the prosecution is seldom able to present direct evidence of the agreement. Courts have been sympathetic to this problem, and it is thus well established that the prosecution may "rely on inferences drawn from the course of conduct of the alleged conspirators." This notion has been traced back to an oft-quoted instruction in an English case, *Regina v. Murphy* (1837), where the judge told the jury: "If you find that these two persons pursued by their acts the same object, often by the same means, one performing one part of an act and the other another part of the same act, so as to complete it, with a view to the attainment of the object which they were pursuing, you will be at liberty to draw the conclusion that they have been engaged in a conspiracy to effect that object." Such language, it has been noted, might be erroneously interpreted as meaning that there need be only a concurrence of wills rather than concurrence resulting from agreement, and may in practice have resulted in "neglect of the fundamental fact that there is an agreement to be proved."

Assume that *A* wants to burglarize a store and thus approaches *B* to solicit his assistance in the commission of the crime, that upon hearing *A*'s plan *B* manifests his complete concurrence in the scheme and expresses his willingness to participate, but that *B* secretly intends not to go through with the plan and has merely feigned agreement because he wishes to trap *A*. Is there a conspiracy under these circumstances? No is the answer traditionally given by the courts. *B* quite clearly is not guilty of conspiracy, if for no other reason because he does not have the intent-to-burglarize mental state (see § 11.2(c)); *A* does have the requisite mental state, but yet may not be convicted of conspiracy because there has been no agreement and thus no criminal act. Although it has been suggested that *A* might appropriately be convicted of attempted conspiracy on those facts, the Model Penal Code § 5.03(1) unilateral approach to conspiracy (generally followed in modern recodifications) instead makes it possible for *A* to be convicted of conspiracy. There is something to be said for that result: *A*'s culpability is hardly decreased by *B*'s secret intention, and, while the chances of the scheme succeeding may be minimal under these circumstances, *A* has nonetheless engaged in conduct that provides unequivocal evidence of his firm purpose to commit a crime.

Although it is generally true that an act is not required when there is instead an omission which constitutes the failure to perform a legal duty (see § 5.2), there would not appear to be any set of circumstances in which a failure to agree instead of an agreement would suffice for the crime of conspiracy. For example, a conspiracy not to pay certain taxes is not established by the absence of any agreement to pay those taxes. However, conduct of an individual that constitutes a failure to perform a legal duty, such as the failure of a law enforcement official to enforce the law against a certain group, is relevant as some evidence that the individual had entered into an agreement with the group.

Is it possible for a person to become a party to the crime of conspiracy even in the absence of any agreement on his part? The question is deliberately stated in this way, for the inquiry is whether the principles applicable in determining whether one is a party to a substantive crime (see §§ 12.1–12.3) are also applicable to conspiracy. As we shall see (see § 12.2(a)), it is possible for one to become a party to a crime directly committed by another without there being any agreement or communication of any kind between the two persons. For example, A is an accomplice to murder if, knowing that B and C have set out to kill D, he prevents a warning from reaching D, and this is so even though A's actions were not by preconcert with B and C and did not become known to B and C prior to the killing. This is because A has actually aided in the murder of D and rendered the aid with the intent that D be killed. But, on these facts may it be concluded by like analysis that A is a member of a conspiracy with B and C because A knew of the conspiracy and intentionally gave aid to the conspiratorial objective?

The Supreme Court has assumed without deciding the issue that the answer is yes, and other courts have taken the position that aiding a conspiracy with knowledge of its purposes suffices to make one a party to the conspiracy. In support of that view, it has been argued that one who aids what is known to be a conspiracy is deserving of punishment, for he has the requisite evil intent and also has taken some action to bring that intent to fruition. Although he has not increased the danger to the community in the same way as other conspirators by enhancing the chances of the objective being achieved through mutual support and encouragement, he has added to the danger by giving aid that makes it more probable that the criminal objective will be achieved. Moreover, if giving aid to a known conspiracy is recognized as an independent ground for conviction of conspiracy, then "the impetus to derive a fictional consensus to support the liability would be diminished."

On the other hand, it has been objected that the aiding and abetting theory is not applicable in the circumstances stated above. "A person does not aid and abet a conspiracy by helping the 'conspiracy' to commit a substantive offense, for the crime of conspiracy is separate from the offense which is its object. It is necessary to help the 'conspiracy' in the commission of the crime of conspiracy, that is, in the commission of the act of agreement." Thus, so the argument goes, one may become a conspirator without agreement by giving aid only if the assistance is that of bringing two or more persons together with the intention that they reach an agreement to commit a crime. On a more practical level, taking into account the several disadvantages that may flow from being a conspiracy defendant (see § 11.1(b)), there is the contention that one who aids a conspiracy should be subjected to prosecution and punishment on some theory other than that he has become a member of the conspiracy. On this basis, Model Penal Code § 5.01(3) characterizes such activity as an attempt.

(b) The Overt Act Requirement. At common law a conspiracy was punishable even though no act was done beyond the mere making of the agreement. This is still the rule in the absence of a statute providing otherwise, but most of the states now require that an overt act in furtherance of the plan be proven for all or specified conspiratorial objectives. In a few states this overt act must be a "substantial step" toward commission of the crime. On the federal level, an overt act is specifically required by the general conspiracy statute, and thus the absence of such a requirement in subsequently enacted federal conspiracy statutes dealing with specific subjects have been taken to reflect an intent by Congress to instead follow the common law as to those other provisions.

The statutes uniformly require an overt act by only one of the conspirators, and the act need not be criminal or unlawful in itself. If the defendant charged with committing the only overt act is acquitted, then the other alleged members of the conspiracy must also be acquitted.

The overt act provisions in the conspiracy statutes raise the issue whether the act is a part of the offense or merely an element of proof. A few statutes make this clear, but most are open to both constructions. The Supreme Court currently regards the overt act merely as evidence of the offense, but this has not always been the rule. The problem is rarely important except for purposes of the statute of limitations, jurisdiction or venue.

"The function of the overt act in a conspiracy prosecution is simply to manifest 'that the conspiracy is at work,' * * * and is neither a project still resting solely in the minds of the conspirators nor a fully completed operation no longer in existence." Thus the overt act may be the substantive offense that was the object of the conspiracy, but may not be simply a part of the act of agreement.

Courts have said that the overt act must be a step towards the execution of the conspiracy, an act that tends to carry out the conspiracy, an act to effect the object of the conspiracy, or a step in preparation for effecting the object. However, these definitions have sometimes led to confusion of the overt act with the object of the conspiracy. Thus it has sometimes been required that the overt act be the commencement of the consummation, criminal, or an element of the offense that is the object of the conspiracy. These decisions are incorrect, for they are inconsistent with the function of the overt act requirement as stated above.

If the agreement has been established but the object has not been attained, virtually any act will satisfy the overt act requirement. Thus unexplained possession of a large quantity of dynamite, an interview with a lawyer, attending a lawful meeting, picking a lock, making a phone call, delivering goods without the proper invoices, distributing handbills in violation of an injunction, and giving a co-conspirator money to deliver to another have all been held to be overt acts in the context of the criminal object alleged. The overt act requirement may be satisfied by an omission, and it may be the commission of some crime other than the object of the conspiracy.

The overt act requirement may be said to be a legislative determination that mere agreement to commit the offense is insufficient to warrant criminal prosecution. It has been suggested, however, that an overt act should not be required if the contemplated crime is serious, likely of completion, or likely to encourage future criminal activity. Model Penal Code § 5.03(5) excepts conspiracies to commit felonies of the first or second degree from the overt act requirement on the ground that in such instances "the importance of preventive intervention is *pro tanto* greater than in dealing with less serious offenses." However, this exception has not been generally adopted in the recent codes, including those that in other respects have tended to follow the Model Penal Code approach.

(c) The Mental State. Although the crime of conspiracy is "predominantly mental in composition," there has nonetheless always existed considerable confusion and uncertainty about precisely what mental state is required for this crime. The traditional definition of conspiracy does not focus upon the requisite state of mind, and the matter has often been dealt with ambiguously by the courts and has been largely ignored by the commentators. As we shall see, this is undoubtedly attributable to two factors: (1) it is conceptually difficult to separate the mental state requirement from the agreement constituting the act (see § 11.2(a)); and (2) as with all inchoate crimes, it is necessary to take into account the elements of the crime that is the objective.

(1) Intent to Agree Distinguished. At the outset, it is useful to note that there are really two intents required for the crime of conspiracy. Every conspiracy involves an agreement, so it must be established that the several parties intended to agree. But such an intent is "without moral content," and thus it is also necessary to determine what objective the parties intended to achieve by their agreement. Only if there is a common purpose to attain an objective covered by the law of conspiracy (see § 11.3(a)) is there liability.

One of these intents may exist without the other. Quite clearly there may be an intent to agree without there also being a common intent to achieve an unlawful objective, as where A and B agree to burn certain property and A knows the property belongs to C but B (perhaps because he has been misled by A) believes that the property belongs to A. On the other hand, two persons may share an unlawful objective without having reached an agreement; A and B might both want C's property burned and yet have reached no agreement in that regard—even if they had communicated their intentions to one another.

The intent to agree is so intimately tied up with the agreement (the act part of the crime) that it is best dealt with in that context. Indeed, it may even be said that such intent is not really part of the *mens rea* of conspiracy; as one court put it, the state of mind in conspiracy "does not refer to the act of conspiring, but to the fruits of the conspiracy." Thus, the concern in what follows is not with the intent to agree but rather with the additional mental state that is required in order to make the agreement a criminal conspiracy.

(2) Intent to Achieve Objective. Although there may be some uncertainty in existing law on the requisite state of mind because of the varied phrases used by the courts and the occasional assertion that liability is based upon "joining" or "adhering" to a group, it may generally be said that the mental state required is an intent to achieve a particular result which is criminal or which though noncriminal is nonetheless covered by the law of conspiracy. (As is considered in more detail later, see § 11.3, certain noncriminal objectives are included within the common law definition and also in some statutory formulations of the crime.) This has been characterized as a specific intent, although it has also been said that it would be difficult "to conceive of any crime in which the intent is less specific" because of the many different objectives that might be intended. Doubtless we would be better off if the phrase "specific intent" were abandoned because of the confusion it has caused (see § 4.2(e)), but to the extent that it has meaning it is fair to say that conspiracy is a specific intent crime.

Confusion is most likely to arise in those cases where the objective of the conspiracy, if achieved, is itself a crime, for under such circumstances the mental state for that crime must also be taken into account. Clearly, a "conspiracy to commit a particular substantive offense cannot exist without *at least* the degree of criminal intent necessary for the substantive offense itself." If *A* and *B* agree to take *C*'s property, for example, this is not a conspiracy to commit the crime of larceny unless *A* and *B* had the intent to permanently deprive required for commission of larceny. Likewise, where *D* and *E* agree to conceal *F,* this is not a conspiracy to violate the statute making it an offense to conceal a person against whom it is known a federal warrant has issued unless *D* and *E* had that knowledge.

On the other hand, the fact that conspiracy requires an intent to achieve a certain objective means that individuals who have together committed a certain crime have not necessarily participated in a conspiracy to commit that crime. To take the example given by the Model Penal Code draftsmen, assume that two persons plan to destroy a building by detonating a bomb, though they know and believe that there are inhabitants in the building who will be killed by the explosion. If they do destroy the building and persons are killed, they are guilty of murder, but this is because murder may be committed other than with an intent-to-kill mental state (see § 13.4). Their plan constitutes a conspiracy to destroy the building, but not a conspiracy to kill the inhabitants, for they did not intend the latter result. It follows, therefore, that there is no such thing as a conspiracy to commit a crime which is defined in terms of recklessly or negligently causing a result.

A somewhat different problem is that presented in *People v. Horn* (1974), where the defendants were convicted of conspiracy to commit murder. There was evidence that the defendants had been so intoxicated as to lack the capacity to entertain malice aforethought, meaning their scheme, if carried out, would have been only voluntary manslaughter. The trial judge's refusal to instruct on the lesser offense of conspiracy to commit voluntary manslaughter was held to be reversible error. A dissent in *Horn* cogently pointed out that concepts of diminished capacity and the like, applicable to determine the level of a criminal homicide, did not carry over to conspiracy, where only an intent mental state (unadorned by further malice aforethought or premeditation-deliberation distinctions) need be proved. The failure of the *Horn* majority to accept that reasoning is doubtless attributable to a desire to afford conspiracy defendants the same sentence-mitigating benefits they would have as to the object crime. Such a concern is especially legitimate in *Horn,* where, as the majority emphasized, "the punishment for conspiracy to commit a homicide is the same as the punishment for the conspired felony."

Horn was later disapproved in *People v. Cortez* (1998), largely because of two intervening legislative actions regarding two of the linchpins in the *Horn* analysis: the legislature had (i) abolished the diminished capacity defense, and (ii) amended the murder statute by adding the declaration that "to prove the killing was 'deliberate and premeditated,' it shall not be necessary to prove the defendant maturely and meaningfully reflected upon the gravity of his or her act." The court in *Cortez* thus concluded that "all conspiracy to commit murder is necessarily conspiracy to commit premeditated and deliberated first-degree murder, and that all murder conspiracies are punishable in the same manner as murder in the first degree." As one member of the court had explained on an earlier occasion, conspiracy to commit murder "does not require, as a factual matter, a premeditated and deliberate intent to kill unlawfully. But an intent of such character is present in the context of a conspiracy, practically by definition, because it does not arise all of a sudden within a single person but is necessarily formed and then shared by at least two persons." Other courts agree with the *Cortez* view that conspiracy to murder is necessarily a conspiracy to commit murder in the first degree, but there is also contrary authority.

(3) Providing Goods or Services. While one "can be a conspirator by agreeing to facilitate only some of the acts leading to the substantive offense," what mental state must exist regarding such contemplated facilitation? One problem in this area which has continued to perplex the courts is that of determining under what circumstances the supplier of goods or services to a known criminal undertaking becomes a party to the conspiracy. If the notion "that a conspiracy is a partnership in criminal purposes and that all are guilty who join it with knowledge of such purposes" was generally accepted as the basis of conspiracy liability, then it might be said that all such suppliers are conspirators. But, as we have seen, it is intent rather than knowledge that is usually required, and thus the question is when the circumstances will suffice to show that the supplier shared the intent to achieve the criminal objective. The two leading cases on this point are *U.S. v. Falcone* (1940) and *Direct Sales Co. v. U.S.* (1943).

In *Falcone,* a group of distillers and others who supplied them with sugar, yeast and cans were convicted of a conspiracy to operate illicit stills. The Court of Appeals reversed as to the suppliers, holding that the seller of innocent goods does not become a conspirator merely because of his knowledge that the buyer plans to use them in the commission of a crime. "[I]n prosecutions for conspiracy * * * his attitude towards the forbidden undertaking must be more positive. It is not enough that he does not forego a normally lawful activity, of the fruits of which he knows that others will make an unlawful use; he must in some sense promote their venture himself, make it his own, have a stake in its outcome." Before the Supreme Court, the government attempted to avoid that result by shifting to a theory that the suppliers had aided and abetted a conspiracy, but they did not succeed because the evidence did not show the suppliers knew that a conspiracy existed between others.

In *Direct Sales,* the defendant company, a registered drug manufacturer and wholesaler, was convicted of conspiracy to violate the narcotics laws upon a showing that the corporation "sold morphine sulphate to Dr. Tate in such quantities, so frequently and over so long a period it must have known he could not dispense the amounts received in lawful practice and was therefore distributing the drug illegally." The defendant contended that such a result was inconsistent with the rationale of *Falcone,* but the Supreme Court held that *Falcone* was not controlling because the "commodities sold there were articles of free commerce" while in the instant case they were "restricted commodities, incapable of further legal use except by compliance with rigid regulations." The Court noted that the character of the goods in the present case was important for two reasons: (1) to show that the defendant knew the illegal use to which they were being put by the buyer; and (2) to show that the defendant had taken "the step from knowledge to intent and agreement." Although declining to state that a "stake in the venture" would be essential, the Court found sufficient evidence of the defendant's intent from the fact that it actively stimulated repeated sales of unlimited quantities of a restricted commodity and thus received profits which it was known could only come from its encouragement of the illegal operation.

Lower courts have also placed reliance upon the factors stressed in *Direct Sales:* the quantity of the sales; the continuity of the relationship between seller and buyer; the seller's initiative or encouragement; and the nature of the goods. The failure of the seller to submit sales reports required by government regulations has also been considered relevant, as has the failure to keep the usual business records or other secretive techniques. Intent may also be inferred from the fact that the seller has made inflated charges, that he has supplied goods or services which have no legitimate use, or that the sales to the illegal operation have become the dominant proportion of the seller's business.

Dictum in *People v. Lauria* (1967) suggests that

a supplier who furnishes equipment which he *knows* will be used to commit a serious crime may be deemed from that

knowledge alone to have intended to produce the result. * * *
For instance, we think the operator of a telephone answering
service with positive knowledge that his service was being used
to facilitate the extortion of ransom, the distribution of heroin,
or the passing of counterfeit money who continued to furnish
the service with knowledge of its use, might be chargeable on
knowledge alone with participation in a scheme to extort
money, to distribute narcotics, or to pass counterfeit money.
The same result would follow the seller of gasoline who knew
the buyer was using his product to make Molotov cocktails for
terroristic use.

There do not appear to be any decisions reaching such a result,
although it certainly could be argued that taking account of the
seriousness of the criminal objective is appropriate in striking a
balance between the "conflicting interests * * * of the vendors in
freedom to engage in gainful and otherwise lawful activities without policing their vendees, and that of the community in preventing
behavior that facilitates the commission of crimes."

(4) Liability Without Fault. Although the question has seldom been confronted in the cases, it seems clear that there is no
such thing as liability without fault conspiracy. "While one may, for
instance, be guilty of running past a traffic light of whose existence
one is ignorant, one cannot be guilty of conspiring to run past such
a light, for one cannot agree to run past a light unless one supposes
that there is a light to run past." Thus, even if what was done
under an agreement has been made unlawful on a liability without
fault basis, there can be no conviction for conspiracy unless it is
shown that the parties actually intended to achieve what was done.
This is as it should be, for the fact that a statute has made the
doing of a certain act an offense without regard to mental fault can
hardly be said to have a worked a change in the mental element of
the distinct crime of conspiracy.

The offense that is a liability without fault crime in all respects
must be distinguished from the offense requiring a certain mental
state as to some elements of the crime but not as to others. This is
the case as to several federal statutes in which the attendant
circumstances affording a basis for federal jurisdiction are made an
element of the crime. Although strict liability is often imposed as to
these circumstance elements, for a time some federal courts held
that knowledge of those circumstances was essential for a conspiracy to violate such statutes. The better view, however, is that when
one "sets out with the purpose of engaging in the proscribed
conduct or producing the undesirable result with the lesser culpability concerning attendant circumstances that suffices for commission of the crime, and his preparation progresses to the point of a
conspiracy or attempt, the reasons for reaching his behavior as an

inchoate crime are in no way decreased by such lesser culpability concerning the circumstances." The Supreme Court adopted this position as to the federal conspiracy statute in *U.S. v. Feola* (1975). The Court explained that a contrary result, requiring that the conspirators be aware of the facts giving rise to federal jurisdiction, would not serve the policies underlying the crime of conspiracy. This means, for example, that a conspiracy to transport stolen goods in interstate commerce does not require knowledge by the conspirators that the stolen goods are to be transported across state lines, for such awareness would be unnecessary on a transportation charge.

(5) The "Corrupt Motive" Doctrine. In *People v. Powell* (1875), the defendants were prosecuted for conspiracy to violate a statute requiring municipal officers to advertise for bids before purchasing supplies, and they asserted as a defense that they had acted in good faith because they were unaware of the existence of the statute. The court ruled in their favor, holding it was "implied in the meaning of the word conspiracy" that the agreement "must have been entered into with an evil purpose, as distinguished from a purpose to do the act prohibited, in ignorance of the prohibition." Under what has since become known as the corrupt motive doctrine, it has similarly been held, for example, that election officials may defend against a charge of conspiracy to violate the election laws by showing they were ignorant of those laws, and that druggists could defend against a charge of conspiracy to violate the prohibition laws by establishing that they had erroneously interpreted those laws as not being applicable to their selling methods.

Some courts have rejected the corrupt motive doctrine, usually by resort to the general rule that ignorance of the criminality of one's conduct is no defense (see § 4.6(d)). Several other courts that have considered the issue have accepted the *Powell* rule in one form or another. Because it was noted in *Powell* that the offense was "innocent in itself," many jurisdictions utilize the *malum in se–malum prohibitum* distinction (see § 1.6(b)) here and thus recognize a claim of good faith only if the criminal objective of the conspiracy was not inherently wrong. Assuming circumstances in which the defense may be presented, some courts have taken the view that it is sufficient that the defendants were unaware of the statute prohibiting their objective, while others require the absence of a corrupt or evil motive in a more general sense.

The decisions accepting the corrupt motive doctrine usually give no explanation for it beyond the notion expressed in *Powell* that such a result is implied by the word conspiracy. That reasoning is hardly convincing, and it has been questioned whether any other reason exists for making an exception to the general principle that ignorance of the law is no excuse. Some commentators have suggested, however, that the corrupt motive doctrine is consistent with the rationale underlying the crime of conspiracy (see § 11.1(c)). Thus, taking note of the fact that conspiracy reaches farther back than attempt to a point where immediate achievement of the objective is less likely, it is argued that "the danger arising from the mere act of agreement is less when the defendants are actuated by no 'criminal intent,' and so may be expected to desist if, before committing the act, they discover its illegality." Similarly, it has been suggested that a group which combines to achieve an objective not inherently wrong and not known by them to be illegal poses no threat of continued wrongdoing because they are unlikely to undertake similar schemes after learning that the objective is against the law. On the other hand, it has been observed that the corrupt motive doctrine has created much confusion concerning the *mens rea* requirements of conspiracy, and that the question of whether unawareness of regulatory offenses should be a defense is better resolved without regard to whether there was group activity.

(6) **Plurality of Intent.** Although some of the decisions seem to suggest that when a person joins a group enterprise he is by that fact alone shown to have the same intention as the others, it must be remembered that the question of whether the requisite intent was present must be separately considered as to each individual who is alleged to be a member of the conspiracy. If, for example, *A, B,* and *C* agree to take *D*'s property, and *A* and *B* thereby intend to permanently deprive *D* of the property but *C* does not have that intent, then it is not correct to conclude that *C* is part of a conspiracy to commit larceny. Likewise, where the corrupt motive doctrine prevails, if *E, F,* and *G* agree to do a certain act not inherently wrong that is proscribed by a statute of which only *E* and *F* are aware, then it may not be said that *G* was a member of a conspiracy to violate that statute.

Moreover, because of the plurality requirement (see § 11.4(c)) it must be shown that the requisite intent existed as to at least two persons. That is, there must be a common design, so that if only one party to the agreement has the necessary mental state then even that person may not be convicted of conspiracy. This result has been questioned on the ground that there still exists a need to proceed against that person because of his criminal disposition, and under the unilateral approach of Model Penal Code § 5.03(1) the one party to the agreement with the necessary mental state could be convicted.

§ 11.3   Dimensions

Under the modern view, conspiracy statutes are limited to criminal objectives. An agreement to commit several crimes is but one conspiracy. Several persons may be parties to a single conspiracy even if they have never directly communicated with one another; the question is whether they are aware of each other's participation in a general way and have a community of interest. Conspiracy is an offense that continues up to the point of abandonment or success.

(a) The Conspiratorial Objective. The generally accepted common law definition of conspiracy is "a combination of two or more persons * * * to accomplish some criminal or unlawful purpose, or to accomplish some purpose, not in itself criminal or unlawful, by criminal or unlawful means." Not every unlawful purpose is criminal and thus acts lawful when performed by an individual may become criminal when the object of an agreement by many to perform them. Although the common law rule is based on what is probably an incorrect reading of the early cases, it has survived except when changed by statute. Most states provide that the object of a criminal conspiracy must be some crime or some felony.

Only conspiracies to falsely accuse others of felonies were criminal in the early seventeenth century. A loosely reasoned assertion by Hawkins that "there can be no doubt, but that all confederacies whatsoever, wrongfully to prejudice a third person, are highly criminal at common law" helped extend the law of conspiracy to cover non-criminal objects. This extension is usually justified on the grounds that the means to perpetrate the wrong are particularly dangerous to the public, because the conspirators will draw new courage and be less likely to refrain from the act than an individual, or that the moral fibre of the community is weakened by concerted wrongdoing. As stated in an early case: "An unlawful act may not prove injurious * * * when attempted by an individual, and may be readily prevented; the same act attempted by the confederation of two or more may become dangerous to the public peace and to the security of persons and property, and harmful to public morals by the very weight and power of numbers."

Thus in England it was held to be a criminal conspiracy to combine to falsely accuse one of fathering a bastard, to indenture a girl at prostitution, to marry off a pauper so as to charge another parish with his support, or to raise workmen's wages. Lord Edenborough refused to extend the doctrine to civil trespass, but was later overruled.

Conspiracies to defraud by acts not criminal by one person have been consistently held to be punishable. Beginning with a conspiracy by London hewers to deprive the tax men of their revenue, combinations to defraud the government have been declared criminal conspiracies. Today practically any scheme to affect the government may be indicted as a conspiracy to defraud.

Schemes to defraud individuals or corporations are generally held to be criminal conspiracies, and were punishable as conspiracies before the fraud became a substantive crime.

In the United States the cases have occasionally held that no indictment for criminal conspiracy lies if the object is merely *malum prohibitum.* Generally, however, combinations are prohibited where either the object or means are mischievous to the public or oppressive to individuals. Thus combinations to commit fornication, to interfere with the "social intercourse" of a picnic, or to use a car without the owner's permission have been punished as conspiracies. Most states require only a nominal showing of harm to the public from conspiracies, but others require a strong probability of public injury or that the object benefit the conspirators to the necessary prejudice of the public. The wide sweep of the present substantive criminal law, however, has made criminal many acts formerly only unlawful, and thus most combinations today are to commit crimes or to defraud.

The breadth of the law of conspiracy makes it subject to prosecutorial and judicial abuse. Statutes that make criminal combinations to commit acts injurious to the public health or morals or to trade or commerce or for the perversion or obstruction of justice or the due administration of the laws are particularly objectionable. The Supreme Court has recognized this possible abuse and has held that such conspiracy statutes may be unconstitutionally vague because they do not give adequate notice of what conduct will be considered criminal. Specifically, the Court held in *Musser v. Utah* (1948) that a statute proscribing conspiracies to commit acts injurious to the public morals would be vague unless the state court construed it narrowly. On remand, the Utah Supreme Court held the provision vague and violative of due process.

However, other state courts have upheld their rather broad conspiracy statutes in the face of similar due process objections. Statutes making combinations "to pervert or obstruct justice, or the due administration of the laws" have been upheld because such acts were defined at common law and in the statutes. Similarly, a statute prohibiting conspiracies to injure trade or commerce has been held not to be vague, and the same result has been reached as to legislation proscribing conspiracies to perform any act injurious to the public health and conspiracies to commit acts injurious to public health, morals or to obstruct justice.

Notwithstanding such decisions, it is undoubtedly a fair conclusion that "most such provisions failed to provide a sufficiently definite standard of conduct to have any place in a penal code." It is far better to limit the general conspiracy statute to objectives that are themselves criminal, as has been done in the most recent recodifications. To the extent that broader conspiracy statutes and common law conspiracy made it possible to reach group activity directed toward acts which one person could do with impunity because of the "frustrating technicalities" of certain areas of substantive criminal law, the solution is reform in those areas. And if it is true that there are some activities which should be criminal only if engaged in by groups, these should be specifically identified in special conspiracy provisions "no less precise than penal provisions generally."

(b) The Scope of the Conspiracy. The agreement, which is an essential element of every conspiracy (see § 11.2(a)), has two dimensions: the persons privy thereto, and the objectives encompassed therein. Even when it is clear that every defendant is a conspirator, it may be extremely important to determine precisely what the object dimension and party dimension of the agreement are, for that in turn will decide the critical question of whether more than one conspiracy exists.

This question may be an extremely important one for a variety of reasons. Assume, for example, that A agrees with B that A will retail for B any narcotics delivered to him by B, and that some time later B makes contact with wholesaler C in another part of the country and enters into an arrangement to obtain narcotics from C, after which C takes some steps toward making the delivery but is apprehended by police who heard C make some statements about the plan. If it is concluded that A, B, and C are all parties to a single conspiracy, then: A, B and C may be tried in a single prosecution; A may be required to stand trial across the country at the place of C's acts; C's statements will be admissible against A; C's recent acts will foreclose any claim by A that the statute of limitations had run; if there is a statutory overt act requirement (see § 11.2(b)), C's act will suffice as against A; and middleman B will be subject to prosecution and punishment for one conspiracy instead of two.

(1) The Object Dimension. One way in which the problem can arise is when the same group has planned or committed several crimes, simultaneous or successive violations of either the same statute or several different statutes. At one time, there was a split of authority in the federal courts on the approach to be taken in analyzing such a situation. Some courts applied the "same evidence" test, which meant that it was very easy to establish the existence of more than one conspiracy by showing that if the various objectives were accomplished their proof would be based upon different facts. Others focused upon the agreement rather than the acts done or to be done in pursuance of it, holding that there was but one conspiracy if the several objectives were part of a single agreement.

The issue was finally resolved in *Braverman v. U.S.* (1942). The defendants there were engaged in the illegal manufacture, transportation and distribution of liquor in violation of a number of internal revenue laws, for which they were charged and convicted on seven counts. Each count charged a conspiracy to violate a different internal revenue law, although the government conceded that only a single agreement had been proved. The Court reversed on this analysis:

> [T]he precise nature and extent of the conspiracy must be determined by reference to the agreement which embraces and defines its objects. Whether the object of a single agreement is to commit one or many crimes, it is in either case that agreement which constitutes the conspiracy which the statute punishes. The one agreement cannot be taken to be several agreements and hence several conspiracies because it envisages the violation of several statutes rather than one.

The Court emphasized that the same evidence test, an appropriate guide in other circumstances, was not applicable to conspiracy: "Since the single continuing agreement, which is the conspiracy here, thus embraces its criminal objects, it differs from successive acts which violate a single penal statute and from a single act which violates two statutes." Other courts have reached the same result where the conspiracy was to violate the same statute on successive occasions or to violate more than one statute by a single course of action. But *Braverman* is not applicable to a single agreement to violate separate conspiracy statutes.

Although *Braverman* might be objected to on the ground that an agreement to commit several crimes should be treated as a number of anticipatory offenses in the same way as an attempt to commit several crimes, this objection is not convincing. There are at least two reasons for dealing with the conspiracy situation differently: (1) conspiracy, unlike attempt, is defined in terms of agreement; and (2) conspiracy, in contrast to attempt, reaches farther back into preparatory conduct. However, *Braverman* has also been criticized on other grounds. It has been noted that "inquiry into the precise time at which each objective was conceived * * * is unrealistic" because of the difficulty in making that determination, and that, in any event, the *Braverman* rule "tends to place a premium upon foresight in crime." So the argument goes, if the second object was agreed to before attainment of the first, then no new grouping has been created and thus there does not exist an added danger justifying a finding of more than one conspiracy. Thus, Model Penal Code § 5.03(3) provides that there is but one conspiracy if the multiple crimes are the object of the same agreement *or* continuous conspiratorial relationship. This view has been adopted by statute in some states, and it has been suggested that courts elsewhere are inclined to reach the same result by "finding that the original agreement subsequently came to 'embrace' additional objects."

(2) The Party Dimension. Somewhat more difficult is the situation in which there is a question as to the number of parties in a particular conspiracy because of the absence of evidence showing direct communication or cooperation between all of the defendants. In dealing with this issue, it is useful to distinguish two different structures: (1) the so-called "wheel" or "circle" conspiracy, in which there is a single person or group (the "hub") dealing individually with two or more other persons or groups (the "spokes"); and (2) the "chain" conspiracy, usually involving the distribution of narcotics or other contraband, in which there is successive communication and cooperation in much the same way as with legitimate business operations between manufacturer and wholesaler, then wholesaler and retailer, and then retailer and consumer.

U.S. v. Bruno (1939) involved both types of relationships, although the concern presently is solely with the chain relationship. Some 88 defendants were indicted for a conspiracy to import, sell and possess narcotics, and the proof established the existence of a vast and continuing operation involving smugglers who brought the narcotics into New York, middlemen who paid the smugglers and distributed to retailers, a group of retailers operating in New York, and another group of retailers operating in Texas and Louisiana. The evidence did not show any cooperation or communication between the smugglers and either group of retailers, yet the court held there was a smuggler-middleman-retailer "chain" conspiracy because the parties' knowledge of the existence and importance of the remote links could be inferred from the nature of the enterprise: "the smugglers knew that the middlemen must sell to retailers, and the retailers knew that the middlemen must buy of importers of one sort or another. Thus the conspirators at one end of the chain knew that the unlawful business would not, and could not, stop with their buyers; and those at the other end knew that it had not begun with their sellers." Thus, the court concluded, the evidence was sufficient to show that community of interest between all of the defendants which makes for but one conspiracy, as each member knew "that the success of that part with which he was immediately concerned, was dependent upon the success of the whole."

The *Bruno* court distinguished the case of *U.S. v. Peoni* (1938), also involving a "chain." Peoni sold counterfeit money to Regno, Regno sold it to Dorsey, and Dorsey then passed it on to innocent persons. Peoni was held not to be a co-conspirator with Dorsey because the evidence did not establish "a concert of purpose" between the two; Peoni knew that Regno *might* turn the bills over to another person for ultimate disposal, but it really made no difference to him whether Regno passed the bills himself or sold them to a second passer. This conclusion appears justified, for it was not shown that Peoni planned further sales or that the one sale was of such a large amount that Regno could not have disposed of the entire amount himself. *Peoni* is thus different from the usual one-conspiracy "chain" involving an ongoing scheme from which it may be concluded that the defendants had "knowledge of its essential features and broad scope."

A "wheel" or "circle" arrangement, on the other hand, is by its nature less likely to support the conclusion that the parties had a community of interest. For example, reconsider the *Bruno* case, this time focusing upon the "wheel" part of the organization. Granting the existence of a single smuggler-middleman-retailer "chain" conspiracy because of the clear interdependence of the parties, may it also be said that the New York group of retailers are in the *same* conspiracy as the Texas–Louisiana retailers, between whom there was no cooperation or communication? It would seem doubtful, at least in the absence of any evidence showing some form of interdependence between the two groups, but the *Bruno* court answered in the affirmative. Any retailer, said the court, "knew that he was a necessary link in a scheme of distribution, and the others, whom he knew to be convenient to its execution, were as much parts of a single undertaking or enterprise as two salesmen in the same shop." The notion seems to be that if the hub views his dealings with each spoke as a part of a single large enterprise, but each spoke is concerned only with his own transactions with the hub, the knowledge of the spoke that there are other spokes will nonetheless justify the conclusion that the spoke was aware of and consented to the plan as envisaged by the hub.

Compare the Supreme Court's treatment of the issue in *Kotteakos v. U.S.* (1946), where Brown, the hub, made fraudulent applications for loans under the National Housing Act at different times on behalf of several persons, many of whom had no connection with one another. The Court held this was not one conspiracy—that the similarity of purpose by the various spokes was not the same as a common purpose—and later elaborated upon the rationale of *Kotteakos* in these terms:

> Each loan was an end in itself, separate from all others, although all were alike in having similar illegal objects. Except for Brown, the common figure, no conspirator was interested in whether any loan except his own went through. And none aided in any way, by agreement or otherwise, in procuring

another's loan. The conspiracies therefore were distinct and disconnected, not parts of a larger general scheme, both in the phase of agreement with Brown and also in the absence of any aid given to others as well as in specific object and result. There was no drawing of all together in a single, over-all, comprehensive plan.

Even under this reasoning, however, some wheel arrangements, may properly be found to be a single conspiracy. For example, where the feasibility of an illegal horse racing wire service depends upon there being several customers paying high rates, subscribers aware of this situation are properly considered co-conspirators. So too, a state-wide attempt to unionize coal fields, centered in three separate areas but directed from a central headquarters, constitutes but one conspiracy because the effectiveness of the strike would depend upon the activities undertaken at all three locations. As with the chain arrangement, a wheel is more likely to be characterized as a single conspiracy if continuing relationships are involved.

Some courts have taken to examining the "totality of the circumstances" in determining whether a particular course of conduct constitutes one or several conspiracies. The factors usually considered in this connection are: (1) the number of alleged overt acts in common; (2) the overlap in personnel; (3) the time period during which the alleged acts took place; (4) the similarity in the methods of operation; (5) the locations in which the alleged acts took place; (6) the extent to which purported conspiracies share a common objective; and (7) the degree of interdependence needed for the overall operation to succeed. What would otherwise be a single conspiracy does not become more than one conspiracy simply because of some change in the membership by way of exiting and/or entering participants during an otherwise ongoing scheme.

(3) RICO Conspiracies. Under the Racketeer Influence and Corrupt Organizations Act of 1970 (RICO), it is "unlawful for any person employed by or associated with any enterprise engaged in, or the activities of which affect, interstate or foreign commerce, to conduct or participate, directly or indirectly, in the conduct of such enterprise's affairs through a pattern of racketeering activity or collection of unlawful debt." ("Racketeering activity" includes a great variety of serious criminal conduct, including murder, kidnaping, arson, robbery, bribery, extortion and drug dealing, and for there to be a "pattern" there must be at least two such acts within a 10 year span.) This RICO statute has its own conspiracy provision.

In *U.S. v. Elliott* (1978), it was held that a single conspiracy may exist under this conspiracy statute even when, applying pre-

RICO concepts applicable to the general federal conspiracy statute, the circumstances would indicate there were multiple conspiracies. The latter conclusion would otherwise be reached because a single agreement or common objective could not be inferred from the commission of highly diverse crimes by apparently unrelated individuals. But, as stated in *Elliott,*

> RICO helps to eliminate this problem by creating a substantive offense which ties together these diverse parties and crimes. Thus, the object of a RICO conspiracy is to violate a substantive RICO provision—here, to conduct or participate in the affairs of an enterprise through a pattern of racketeering activity—and not merely to commit each of the predicate crimes necessary to demonstrate a pattern of racketeering activity. The gravamen of the conspiracy charge in this case is not that each defendant agreed to commit arson, to steal goods from interstate commerce, to obstruct justice, and to sell narcotics; rather, it is that each agreed to participate, directly and indirectly, in the affairs of the enterprise by committing two or more predicate crimes.

That is, under the *Elliott* interpretation of the RICO statute it is irrelevant that each defendant participated in the enterprise's affairs through different, even unrelated crimes, if each crime was intended to further the enterprise's affairs.

The *Elliott* approach has been sharply criticized by legal commentators, and understandably so. "RICO did not change conspiracy law; it merely made conducting the affairs of an enterprise in certain ways that Congress judges harmful a new substantive offense, separate from and in addition to the underlying illegal racketeering activity. The requirement remains that the activities making up a multiple criminal conspiracy must be connected, and the term 'enterprise' as applied by *Elliott* does not supply that connection." Although some other courts have accepted the *Elliott* approach, another group "rejects the ideas espoused in *Elliott* and returns to traditional conspiracy principles in determining complicity in multi-defendant RICO prosecutions."

(c) The Duration of the Conspiracy. The temporal dimensions of a conspiracy is a matter of considerable importance for a number of reasons. The longer a conspiracy is deemed to continue, the greater the chances that additional persons will be found to have joined it. Also, as the conspiracy continues there may occur new overt acts at different locations that will afford the prosecution new choices for the place of trial. If the conspiracy has not yet ended, then the hearsay acts and declarations of one conspirator will be admissible against the other conspirators, and one conspirator may be held liable for substantive crimes committed by other members of the conspiracy. Most important, however, is the fact that the statute of limitations for the crime of conspiracy does not begin to run at the time of the agreement or (when required by statute) the overt act, but only from the point at which the conspiracy is terminated. For this purpose, "the conspiracy continues up to the abandonment or success."

As to abandonment by all the parties, the generally accepted view is that abandonment is presumed if no party to the conspiracy has done any overt act to further its objective during the applicable period of limitations. For example, where the applicable statute of limitations specified three years, and the indictment was returned on October 25, 1954, it must be shown that "at least one overt act in furtherance of the conspiracy was performed after" October 25, 1951. Arrest of some of the co-conspirators does not automatically terminate the conspiracy.

As to the success of the conspiracy, it is important to keep in mind that "success" has not necessarily been accomplished at the point in time when the crime which was the objective of the conspiracy has been completed, in the sense that enough has been done to support a conviction for that crime. For example, a conspiracy to commit a theft, a burglary, or a robbery is not ended upon the completion of those crimes if the fruits thereof are still to be divided among the conspirators. "Kidnappers in hiding, waiting for ransom, commit acts of concealment in furtherance of the objectives of the conspiracy itself, just as repainting a stolen car would be in furtherance of a conspiracy to steal; in both cases the successful accomplishment of the crime necessitates concealment." But it is at precisely this point that the problem becomes complicated; as reflected in a series of Supreme Court decisions, it is not easy to determine what acts of concealment will suffice to establish a continuation of the conspiracy.

In *Krulewitch v. U.S.* (1949), Krulewitch and another were convicted of conspiracy to transport a woman in interstate commerce for purposes of prostitution. A month and a half after the trip in question, Krulewitch's female co-conspirator made a statement attempting to conceal his role in the crime, and this conversation was admitted at trial on the ground that it fell within an exception to the hearsay rule because it was made in furtherance of the conspiracy. Before the Supreme Court, the petitioners contended that the conspiracy was at an end when the transportation was completed, while the government, relying upon lower court cases, asserted that the declarations were admissible as being in furtherance of an "implied but uncharged conspiracy aimed at preventing detection and punishment." Justice Jackson, in his oft-quoted concurring opinion, noted that acceptance of the government's position would "result in an indeterminate extension of the statute of limitations," for if "the law implies an agreement to cooperate in defeating prosecution, it must imply that it continues as long as prosecution is a possibility, and prosecution is a possibility as long as the conspiracy to defeat it is implied to continue." The majority, however, rejected the government's contention by merely noting that hearsay statements, to be admissible against the other conspirators, "must be made in furtherance of the conspiracy charged."

Apparently with *Krulewitch* in mind, the government proceeded more cautiously in *Lutwak v. U.S.* (1953), a prosecution for conspiring to violate those statutes making it a crime for an alien to obtain entry by misrepresentation or concealment of a material fact. Again the question was the admissibility against other conspirators of acts and statements occurring after the date of the substantive offenses, but this time the government had expressly charged in the indictment that integral to the conspiracy were concealment and other acts extending beyond that date. Notwithstanding "the government's seemingly well-founded contention that the [subsequent acts] were not a mere retrospective concealment of a consummated scheme to obtain entry, but an integral part of the plan Lutwak originally devised," the Court ruled in favor of the defendants. The holding was rested upon the questionable conclusion that there was "no statement in the indictment of a single overt act of concealment that was committed after [the date of entry], and no substantial evidence of any," and thus the ultimate question of whether acts of concealment could ever extend the life of a conspiracy remained unanswered.

Then came *Grunewald v. U.S.* (1957), a case involving convictions for conspiracy to defraud the government by fixing income tax cases. The defendants had used improper influence to obtain "no prosecution" rulings for certain taxpayers in 1948 and 1949, dates outside the three-year statute of limitations, but had engaged in acts of concealment up to 1954, the time of indictment. In response to the defense claim that the prosecution was barred by the statute of limitations, the government contended that an actual rather than an implied agreement to conceal existed and had been an express part of the original conspiracy. This attempt to distinguish *Krulewitch* and *Lutwak* was unsuccessful, for the Court found on the record before it that "the distinction between 'actual' and 'implied' conspiracies to conceal, as urged upon us by the Government, is no more than a verbal tour de force":

> The crucial teaching of *Krulewitch* and *Lutwak* is that after the central criminal purposes of a conspiracy have been attained, a subsidiary conspiracy to conceal may not be implied from circumstantial evidence showing merely that the conspiracy was kept a secret and that the conspirators took care to cover up their crime in order to escape detection and punish-

ment. As was there stated, allowing such a conspiracy to conceal to be inferred or implied from mere overt acts of concealment would result in a great widening of the scope of conspiracy prosecutions, since it would extend the life of a conspiracy indefinitely. Acts of covering up, even though done in the context of a mutually understood need for secrecy, cannot themselves constitute proof that concealment of the crime after its commission was part of the initial agreement among the conspirators. For every conspiracy is by its very nature secret; a case can hardly be supposed where men concert together for crime and advertise their purpose to the world. And again, every conspiracy will inevitably be followed by actions taken to cover the conspirators' traces.

The Court in *Grunewald,* therefore, appears to have accepted the notion that a subsidiary agreement to conceal may be a basis for finding that a conspiracy continues beyond commission of the substantive offenses which are its object. However, the Court made it clear that the prosecution bears a heavy burden in proving such a subsidiary agreement, much more than has been "demanded to infer conspiratorial agreements for non-concealment objectives." Mere proof of the "elements which will be present in virtually every conspiracy case, that is, secrecy plus overt acts of concealment," will not suffice. Rather, what appears to be required is that which the Court found lacking in *Grunewald:* "direct evidence [of] an express original agreement among the conspirators to continue to act in concert in order to cover up, for their own self-protection, traces of the crime after its commission." This test, it has been aptly noted, makes proof of a subsidiary conspiracy to conceal virtually impossible, for it will be the most unusual case in which the prosecution will be able to obtain direct evidence of an explicit agreement to conceal.

However, there remains another avenue open to the prosecution: it may be shown that the conspiracy was to commit a crime of such a nature that acts of concealment were actually part of the commission of the substantive crime. This was the alternate argument urged by the government in *Grunewald.* The conspiracy's objective, it was contended, was not merely to obtain the "no prosecution" rulings for the taxpayers in 1948 and 1949, but rather to assure them complete immunity from tax prosecution, an objective that could not be realized until 1952, when the six-year statute of limitations would run out as against the taxpayers. The Supreme Court accepted this theory, but remanded the case for a new trial because the jury had not been instructed that it could convict only upon this basis. To the same effect is *Forman v. U.S.* (1960), holding that the defendants could be tried on the theory that the conspiracy did not end with the filing of tax returns concealing certain income, but rather continued "until action thereon is barred and the evasion permanently effected."

For a time, there was some federal case law to the effect that a conspiracy terminates with "the defeat of the object of the conspiracy." As applied, this was taken to mean "that the conspiracy ends through 'defeat' when the Government intervenes, making the conspiracy's goals impossible to achieve, even if the conspirators do not know that the Government has intervened and are totally unaware that the conspiracy is bound to fail." But in *U.S. v. Jimenez Recio* (2003), the Supreme Court summarily rejected that position as contrary to "the view of almost all courts and commentators" and inconsistent with the well-established notion that a conspiratorial agreement is a distinct evil, whether or not the substantive crime ensues.

§ 11.4   Other Limits

Impossibility of success is not a defense to a conspiracy charge, as criminal combinations are dangerous apart from the danger of attaining the particular objective. The traditional rule is that withdrawal by one conspirator after the conspiracy has been formed does not give him a defense to a charge of conspiracy, although there is good reason to question that rule. In most jurisdictions an acquittal or similar disposition of one conspirator bars conviction of a single remaining co-conspirator. A person may be guilty of a conspiracy to commit a crime he could not personally commit (e.g., a woman may conspire to rape), but one who is in a legislatively protected class and thus could not even be guilty as an accessory of the crime that is the objective is likewise not guilty of conspiracy to commit that crime. That must be distinguished from the oft-criticized Wharton rule, whereby a conspiracy is said to require the participation of more persons than are logically necessary to commit the completed crime. If the conspiracy is successful, under the prevailing rule a conspirator may be subject to conviction for both the conspiracy and the completed crime. Cumulative sentences are permissible in most jurisdictions, though this has been criticized when the conspiracy is to do no more than that crime.

(a) **Impossibility.** Is it a defense to a charge of conspiracy that it is impossible for the conspirators to achieve their objective? For example, in a jurisdiction where an essential element of the crime of abortion is that the woman be pregnant, are A and B guilty of a conspiracy to commit abortion if their plan was to commit an abortion on C, a police agent who falsely represented to A and B that she was pregnant?

Before discussing that question, it is useful to review briefly how the issue of impossibility has been dealt with in the law of attempts, where it has arisen with much greater frequency (see § 10.5(a)). As to attempts, the traditional approach has been to distinguish between factual and legal impossibility. Factual impossibility is not a defense, and thus, to take the classic case, one is guilty if he attempted to steal from an empty pocket. On the other hand, what is called legal impossibility *is* a defense, so that one who received goods believed to have been stolen but which were not then stolen goods is not guilty of an attempt to receive stolen goods. It is often not a simple matter to determine whether a given set of facts should be characterized as factual or legal impossibility, as is reflected in the many decided cases on the subject.

Although the defense of impossibility in the law of attempts serves several functions, one important consideration has been "the view that the criminal law need not take notice of conduct that is innocuous, the element of impossibility preventing any dangerous proximity to the completed crime." Courts have tended to assume that the sole purpose of the law of attempts is to deal with conduct which creates a risk of immediate harmful consequences, and on that assumption have concluded that there is no need for the law to intervene if the actor's conduct presented no such risk because it was legally impossible for him to complete the crime. (Only recently has this assumption been challenged; the modern view, in contrast to the traditional view, is that the law of attempts also serves as a means for proceeding against those who have sufficiently manifested their dangerousness, so that legal impossibility is not a defense because it is not a useful guide in determining whether the actor "is disposed toward such activity, not alone on this occasion but on others.")

Courts have generally taken a broader view of the purposes of the law of conspiracy. "The antisocial potentialities of a conspiracy, unlike those of an attempt, are not confined to the objects specifically contemplated at any given time. The existence of a grouping for criminal purposes provides a continuing focal point for further crimes either related or unrelated to those immediately envisaged. Moreover, the uneasiness produced by the consciousness that such groupings exist is in itself an important antisocial effect. Consequently, the state has an interest in stamping out conspiracy above and beyond its interest in preventing the commission of any specific substantive offense."

It is not surprising, therefore, that courts have not been as receptive to the impossibility defense when the charge is conspiracy rather than attempt. As noted in *State v. Moretti* (1968):

> The case has been argued as though, for purposes of the defense of impossibility, a conspiracy charge is the same as a charge of attempting to commit a crime. It seems that such an

equation could not be sustained, however, because * * * a conspiracy charge focuses primarily on the *intent* of the defendants, while in an attempt case the primary inquiry centers on the defendants' *conduct* tending toward the commission of the substantive crime. The crime of conspiracy is complete once the conspirators, having formed the intent to commit a crime, take any step in preparation; mere preparation, however, is an inadequate basis for an attempt conviction regardless of the intent. * * * Thus, the impossibility that the defendants' conduct will result in the consummation of the contemplated crime is not as pertinent in a conspiracy case as it might be in an attempt prosecution.

As a result, while the attempt cases are notable for their lengthy explorations of the distinction between factual and legal impossibility, the conspiracy cases have usually gone the simple route of holding that impossibility of any kind is not a defense. (The Supreme Court in *U.S. v. Jimenez Recio* (2003) indicated its agreement with this position in the course of holding impossibility does not terminate an existing conspiracy; see § 11.3(c).) It has been held, for example: that there may be a conspiracy to commit abortion even when, unknown to the conspirators, the woman was not pregnant; that there may be a conspiracy to commit rape on a woman believed to be unconscious although she was in fact dead; that there may be a conspiracy to defraud the United States notwithstanding the fact that the fraud was impossible of commission because the government was aware of the scheme or because the forged bonds were not witnessed by the proper official; that there may be a conspiracy to murder even though the one person the others believe will carry out the deed is actually a government agent; that there may be a conspiracy to steal trade secrets even if the objects of the theft are mistakenly believed to be such; that there may be a conspiracy to smuggle liquor in violation of the customs law even though, unknown to the conspirators, the liquor was of domestic origin; and that there may be a conspiracy to obstruct justice even if the scheme of having certain individuals called as jurors could not have been accomplished by the conspirators.

A few decisions are to be found holding that impossibility is a defense upon a charge of conspiracy. In one instance the result is attributable in part to the erroneous premise that the impossibility-in-attempt cases are controlling, while in another the holding appears to have been influenced by the fact that the alleged conspirators were entrapped. By comparison, what is sometimes called "pure legal impossibility is always a defense," but this only means, as discussed earlier (see § 11.3(a)), that the requisite conspiratorial objective is lacking.

(b) Withdrawal. Whether a particular individual has withdrawn from a conspiracy may be an important issue for several reasons. For one thing, a defendant may attempt to establish his withdrawal as a defense in a prosecution for substantive crimes subsequently committed by the other conspirators (see § 12.3(d)). Or, the defendant, if charged only with conspiracy, may want to prove his withdrawal so as to show that as to him the statute of limitations has run. Another possibility is that the defendant will rely upon his withdrawal as a means of limiting the admissibility against him of the subsequent acts and declarations of the other conspirators. It may also be significant whether a person other than the defendant has withdrawn from the conspiracy. The defendant, on the one hand, may wish to show that an overt act or a substantive crime was committed by a former co-conspirator only after that conspirator had withdrawn, or, on the other, may try to show that a fellow conspirator did not withdraw so as to gain the benefit of the rule in some jurisdictions that testimony of one co-conspirator against another must be corroborated.

In all of the above contexts, virtually all courts have dealt with the issue in the same way, applying exactly the same test as to whether an effective withdrawal occurred. What is required is an "affirmative act bringing home the fact of his withdrawal to his confederates," made in time for his companions to effectively abandon the conspiracy and in a way that would be sufficient to inform a reasonable man of the withdrawal. The notice is insufficient unless it is given to all of the other conspirators. One court has used a more stringent test, requiring that the defendant also successfully persuade his co-conspirators not to pursue the conspiracy any further, arguably a proper result upon the unique facts there presented. Another stricter approach is that mere resignation from the enterprise is alone insufficient, that a total severing of ties may suffice, but that even such severing will not suffice if the defendant "continues to do acts in furtherance of the conspiracy and continues to receive benefits from the conspiracy's operations." Model Penal Code § 5.03(7)(c), on the other hand, provides that withdrawal by an individual occurs "only if and when he advises those with whom he conspired of his abandonment or he informs the law enforcement authorities of the existence of the conspiracy and of his participation therein."

A quite different matter is the question of whether withdrawal is an affirmative defense to the crime of conspiracy (similar to the questions whether withdrawal is a defense to solicitation or attempt; see §§ 10.1, 10.5). The traditional rule here "is strict and inflexible: since the crime is complete with the agreement, no subsequent action can exonerate the conspirator of that crime." In those jurisdictions that have added by statute an overt act requirement (see § 11.2(b)), the defendant is not punishable as a member of the conspiracy only if he withdraws before the overt act has been committed, but as a practical matter this is not significantly different from the common law rule.

Some commentators have expressed disagreement with the rule that withdrawal is not an affirmative defense to conspiracy, although there is no agreement on what would be a better rule. It has been suggested, for example, that withdrawal should be permitted, except when the "agreement is dangerous enough at its formation to warrant punishment," until "a significant act has taken place betraying the positive disposition of the group to accomplish its object." It has also been argued that both prevention of the ultimate crime and permanent renunciation are called for, to be accomplished by requiring "the withdrawer to seasonably notify and assist police officials in the arrest of the co-conspirators before the ultimate crime is committed."

Model Penal Code § 5.03(6) recognizes withdrawal as an affirmative defense to a conspiracy charge, but requires that the defendant must have "thwarted the success of the conspiracy, under circumstances manifesting a complete and voluntary renunciation of his criminal purpose." This provision is based upon two most sensible propositions: (1) the act of agreement is not of itself sufficiently undesirable and indicative of the defendant's dangerousness to warrant punishment in spite of subsequent withdrawal; and (2) it is proper to require a thwarting of the conspiracy because the objective of a conspiracy will generally be pursued in spite of renunciation by one conspirator. Most of the modern recodifications take this position, though some instead provide that it is sufficient the defendant gave a timely warning to the authorities or otherwise made a substantial effort to prevent the crime. (In each event the renunciation must be complete and voluntary; some of the statutes elaborate that it must not have been motivated by a presumed increased difficulty in committing the crime or increased likelihood of detection or apprehension, or by a decision to postpone the crime to another time or transfer the effort to another victim or place or similar objective.) A few of these statutes permit renunciation only prior to the occurrence of an overt act.

(c) The Plurality Requirement. To constitute a conspiracy, there "must be a combination of two or more persons." This plurality requirement has given rise to several issues, including the following: (1) whether one conspirator may lawfully be convicted if his sole alleged co-conspirator has been acquitted; (2) whether there may be a conspiracy consisting solely of a man and his wife; (3) whether there may be a conspiracy consisting solely of a corporation and a corporate agent; and (4) whether there may be a conspiracy when no more persons are involved than are necessary to commit the offense that is the objective of the conspiracy.

(1) Acquittal or Similar Disposition of Co-conspirator. The requirement of two or more persons referred to above might be restated in terms of at least two guilty parties, for the traditional view is that acquittal of all persons with whom the defendant is alleged to have conspired precludes his conviction. Thus, if A and B are jointly charged with a conspiracy not alleged to involve any other parties and the jury returns a verdict of guilty as to A and not guilty as to B, A's conviction may not stand under this traditional view (since abandoned in some jurisdictions). This, of course, might be explained on the ground that internal consistency should be required in the verdicts returned by a single jury. However, the rule in conspiracy cases sometimes is extended beyond this, so that if A had been tried alone and convicted, after which B was separately tried and acquitted, it would still be true that A's conviction will be overturned. This rule, it has been suggested, "rather than based solely on logic, reflects the community sense of a just outcome." But it is not constitutionally compelled, and a growing number of courts treat the rule as limited to inconsistent verdicts and thus inapplicable where the acquittal was in a separate trial.

It has similarly been held that the grant of a new trial to one of only two conspirators requires similar action as to the other, although this result has been questioned when the reversal is based upon error prejudicial to only one of them. As to the entry of a *nolle prosequi* as to all except one of the defendants to a charge of conspiracy, some courts view the *nolle prosequi* as equivalent to an acquittal and thus consider it a bar to conviction of the remaining conspirator. The better view, however, based upon the fact that a *nolle* is merely a declaration by the prosecution that it will not presently pursue the charge further, is that entry of a *nolle prosequi* as to all except one conspiracy defendant will not vitiate his conviction. There is actually no inconsistency in result in such a case, and this is also true when the only other conspirator has been granted immunity in exchange for his testimony, is otherwise immune from prosecution on some basis unrelated to his alleged involvement in the conspiracy, or simply has never been charged.

Although this might not seem to square completely with the above, it is clear that one conspirator may be convicted even if his sole co-conspirator has not been brought to justice. Thus, if it is alleged that the conspiracy involved only A and B, A may be tried and convicted even though B is dead, has not been apprehended, or even if B is only a "person unknown." In all such cases, of course, it remains a part of the prosecution's case at A's trial to establish A's agreement with another.

It must be emphasized that an acquittal or similar disposition of a co-conspirator is a bar *only* if there then remains but one conspirator. Where two or more defendants have been lawfully convicted, for example, it makes no difference that others also alleged to be a part of the conspiracy have not been convicted, and this is so even when the person alleged to be the "head" of the conspiracy has not been convicted. However, in a jurisdiction that has adopted the overt act requirement, acquittal of the one defendant who allegedly engaged in the requisite overt act is a bar to conviction of the others.

The general rule that conviction of only one defendant in a conspiracy prosecution will not be upheld when all the other alleged conspirators have been acquitted or similarly disposed of, even in separate trials, has not escaped criticism. It has been said to be "founded upon a false premise, for a not guilty verdict is not necessarily a declaration of innocence by the jury, but simply an indication of lack of proof of guilt beyond reasonable doubt." And it has been noted that there are circumstances in which there clearly is no basis for finding an inconsistency in the verdicts, as where conspirator A is tried and acquitted for lack of evidence, after which conspirator B is apprehended and convicted in part on the basis of A's testimony, or where A is convicted on the basis of the testimony of a certain witness who dies before the trial of B.

The Model Penal Code departs from the traditional view of conspiracy as an entirely bilateral or multilateral relationship in favor of a unilateral approach. That is, the Code § 5.03(1) definition of conspiracy requires agreement by the defendant but not agreement between two or more persons, and one consequence of this is that an inconsistent disposition or verdict in a different trial will not affect a defendant's liability. "This result * * * recognizes that inequalities in the administration of the law are, to some extent, inevitable, that they may reflect unavoidable differences in proof, and that, in any event, they are a lesser evil than granting immunity to one criminal because justice may have miscarried in dealing with another."

A substantial minority of the modern recodifications expressly provide that it is no defense that the co-conspirators have been either acquitted or convicted of a different offense. A greater number instead or in addition state that it is not a defense that the co-conspirator lacked capacity. A few others specify it is not a defense that the co-conspirator lacked certain requisite characteristics, that he only feigned agreement, or that he was unaware of the criminal intent or criminal nature of the conduct.

(2) Husband and Wife. It was established at early common law that a husband and wife could not make up the two parties necessary to constitute a conspiracy, and this rule was accepted in the United States as a part of the common law. It was based primarily on the old notion that husband and wife became by marriage one person, although occasionally a court would also suggest that the rule was merely an extension of the ancient doctrine that the wife was not liable for the substantive offenses committed jointly with her husband because she was presumably under his control. In any event, the rule was always limited to instances in which husband and wife were the sole conspirators; a husband and wife could be convicted as co-conspirators if there were one or more other parties to the conspiracy.

In recent years, virtually every jurisdiction that has had occasion to consider the issue has rejected the common law rule. Taking into account the fact that husband and wife are no longer considered one in other fields of law and also that the old presumption of coercion no longer obtains (see § 8.7(f)), it has been concluded that there remains no valid reason for the rule. A husband-wife combination results in the same mutual encouragement as other conspiratorial combinations, thereby increasing the likelihood that the unlawful object will be achieved, and also manifests at least the same degree of continuing danger as do other groups.

However, there is not complete agreement that the old common law rule should be abolished merely because the reasons originally given for it are no longer applicable. In *U.S. v. Dege* (1960), four Justices of the Supreme Court took the contrary view:

It is not necessary to be wedded to fictions to approve the husband-wife conspiracy doctrine, for one of the dangers which that doctrine averts is the prosecution and conviction of persons for "conspiracies" which Congress never meant to be included within the statute. A wife, simply by virtue of the intimate life she shares with her husband, might easily perform acts that would technically be sufficient to involve her in a criminal conspiracy with him, but which might be far removed from the arms-length agreement typical of that crime. It is not a medieval mental quirk or an attitude "unnourished by sense" to believe that husbands and wives should not be subjected to such a risk, or that such a possibility should not be permitted to endanger the confidentiality of the marriage relationship.

(3) Corporations. Although it is clear that a corporation may be indicted as a conspirator, problems may arise in determining the existence of the plurality necessary for a conspiracy. No problem exists when two corporations and an officer of each are indicted, or when a corporation is indicted with one of its officers and a third party, for in such situations it is clear (without regard to whether the corporation and its agent are one) that there are at least two distinct participants in the conspiracy. However, plurality has been found to be lacking when the corporate entity and a single agent are the only parties, and also when two corporations and one person acting as the agent of both were the only alleged conspirators. This is a logical result, for if only one human actor is involved then mutual encouragement is lacking and the risk of the object of the scheme being attained has not been enhanced.

Some courts have gone one step farther by holding that the requisite plurality does not exist when two or more agents of the same corporation have conspired together. The premise apparently is that such collective action for a corporate principal produces no greater antisocial effects than similar action taken by a single corporate agent. Other cases have reached a contrary result, and it may be significant that in these cases the agents were acting chiefly for their own benefit. It has been cogently argued, however, that the necessary plurality is present whenever two or more agents of the same corporation are involved: "When a corporation acts through more than one person to accomplish an antisocial end, the increased likelihood of success, potentially more serious effects of the contemplated offense, and the danger of further unlawful conduct which are the essence of conspiracy rationales are present to the same extent as if the same persons combined their resources without incorporation."

(4) The Wharton Rule and Related Problems. Crimes are often defined in such a way that they may be directly committed only by a person who has a particular characteristic or occupies a particular position, as with adultery, which can be committed only by a married person. This, however, has not prevented courts from concluding that others outside the legislative class may be guilty of these crimes on an accomplice theory (see § 12.3(e)), or that other persons may likewise be guilty of a conspiracy to commit such crimes. Thus, for example, an unmarried man may be convicted of conspiring with a married man that the latter commit adultery; a person not bankrupt may be convicted of conspiring with a bankrupt to conceal the latter's property from the trustee, an offense defined only in terms of a bankrupt's actions; and the giver of a bribe may be convicted of conspiring with a public official to commit the crime of receiving a bribe, defined as receiving by a public officer. This is as it should be. "The substantive offense seems more likely to be accomplished once the agreement is made, and in any event, a combination dangerous in itself, no matter who is liable for the substantive offense, introduces the normal general dangers of conspiracy."

The above situation must be distinguished from that in which the person is a member of a legislatively protected class. Again the situation is comparable to that which obtains as to accomplice liability (see § 12.3(e)); one who may not be deemed an accomplice to a crime because a contrary holding would conflict with the legislative purpose may likewise not be found to be a member of a conspiracy to commit that crime. The leading case is *Gebardi v. U.S.* (1932), where a man and a woman were convicted of a conspiracy to violate the Mann Act in that the man transported the woman from one state to another for immoral purposes. Both convictions were reversed:

> [W]e perceive in the failure of the Mann Act to condemn the woman's participation in those transportations which are effected with her mere consent, evidence of an affirmative legislative policy to leave her acquiescence unpunished. We think it a necessary implication of that policy that when the Mann Act and the conspiracy statute came to be construed together, as they necessarily would be, the same participation which the former contemplates as an inseparable incident of all cases in which the woman is a voluntary agent at all, but does not punish, was not automatically to be made punishable under the latter. It would contravene that policy to hold that the very passage of the Mann Act effected a withdrawal by the conspiracy statute of that immunity which the Mann Act itself confers.

This kind of legislative-intent reasoning must in turn be distinguished from what has come to be known as the Wharton rule. As stated by the commentator whose name it bears, "when to the idea of an offense plurality of agents is logically necessary, conspiracy, which assumes the voluntary accession of a person to a crime of such a nature that it is aggravated by a plurality of agents, cannot be maintained." The classic cases are dueling, bigamy, adultery, and incest, to which may be added such other offenses as pandering, gambling, the buying and selling of contraband goods, and the giving and receiving of bribes. The rule does not apply when the offense could be committed by one of the conspirators alone, nor even when cooperation was a practical but not logical necessity.

Although there is some authority to the contrary, the prevailing view is that the Wharton rule does not apply when the number of conspirators exceeds the essential participants in the contemplated crime. Thus, while it is not a conspiracy for *A* and *B* to agree to the commission of adultery involving only themselves, if *C* conspires with *A* and *B* for the commission of adultery by the latter two then all three are guilty of conspiracy. So too, there is no conspiracy if *D* agrees with *F* to give *F* a bribe, but it is otherwise if *D* and *E* agreed to bribe *F*.

A somewhat different limitation on the Wharton rule is this: if the law defining the substantive offense does not specify any punishment for one of the necessary participants, then it is no bar to a conspiracy conviction that only the essential participants were involved. That is, the rule applies only if the statute defining the criminal objective "requires the culpable participation of two persons for its violation." For example, if *A* agrees with *B* to give him an illegal rebate, but the applicable statute imposes a penalty only on the giver of the rebate, then *A* and *B* may be convicted of conspiracy. Or, if *C* agrees to make an illegal sale of liquor to *D,* but the statute penalizes only the seller, *C* and *D* are guilty of conspiracy.

By taking into account these two limitations, the apparent rationale of the Wharton rule may be seen more clearly. The notion seems to be that if all the necessary participants would be subject to punishment for the completed substantive crime and if only the necessary participants are parties to the agreement, then the agreement presents no danger beyond that inherent in the crime planned. Put somewhat differently, under the circumstances just stated it may be said that the legislature took into account the dangers of the combination in setting the penalties for the substantive offense, so that it would be inconsistent to permit a separate punishment for the same combination on a conspiracy theory.

As the Supreme Court emphasized in *Iannelli v. U.S.* (1975), "the broadly formulated Wharton's Rule does not rest on principles of double jeopardy," but instead "has current vitality only as a judicial presumption, to be applied in the absence of legislative intent to the contrary." The issue in *Iannelli* was whether the rule applied so as to bar prosecution for conspiracy to violate a federal statute making it a crime for five or more persons to conduct, finance, manage, supervise, direct, or own a gambling business prohibited by state law. In answering in the negative, the Court noted that the classic Wharton's Rule offenses listed above are those in which the consequences of the crime "rest on the parties themselves rather than society at large" and in which the agreement poses no distinct threat in the sense that it is likely to lead to "agreements to engage in a more general pattern of criminal conduct." By contrast, the criminal objective of the conspiracy charge in the instant case both involved "the participation of additional persons—the bettors—who are parties neither to the conspiracy nor to the substantive offense that resulted from it," and was "likely to generate additional agreements to engage in other criminal endeavors." Those distinctions and the legislative history of the statute all supported the conclusion reached by the Court, namely, that Congress did not intend to foreclose prosecution for conspiracy to violate that statute. Employing similar reasoning, lower courts have held the Wharton rule inapplicable as to various other criminal objectives that threaten the interests of those other than the immediate participants in the conspiracy.

To the extent that it avoids cumulative punishment for conspiracy and the completed offense (see § 11.4(d)), the Wharton rule makes sense. However, when it is applied in circumstances where the object of the conspiratorial agreement has not been achieved, the rule and its rationale are then properly subject to the criticism that they "completely overlook the functions of conspiracy as an inchoate crime. That an offense inevitably requires concert is no reason to immunize criminal preparation to commit it," for even in such a case there should exist "a basis for preventive intervention by the agencies of law enforcement and for the corrective treatment of persons who reveal that they are disposed to criminality." For this reason, the Wharton rule is rejected in Model Penal Code § 5.04(2), which instead provides only that a person who could not be convicted of the substantive offense as an accomplice may likewise not be convicted of conspiracy to commit that offense. Consistent with the unilateral approach of the Code, such person's immunity does not bar a conspiracy conviction of the other party to the agreement.

(d) Punishment. At common law, all conspiracies—except conspiracy to commit treason—were misdemeanors. Because of the significant procedural differences between the trial of felonies and the trial of misdemeanors, if a felony was committed in furtherance of the conspiracy the misdemeanor of conspiracy was said to merge into that felony. This, of course, meant that in such a case punishment could not be imposed for both the conspiracy and the felony, but it also meant that proof of the felony would bar conviction even for the conspiracy. The problem did not exist if the completed offense was a misdemeanor or conspiracy was by statute made a felony.

Because the original justification for the merger doctrine no longer exists, it has now been abandoned. It is thus clear that the conspiracy and the crime that was its object are separate and distinct offenses. This means that a conspiracy conviction may not be obtained on a charge of the completed crime, and that acquittal of the crime which was the object of the conspiracy is no bar to conviction for the conspiracy to commit it. Most significant, however, is the fact that with rejection of the merger doctrine it is now possible for a defendant to be convicted and punished for both the conspiracy and the substantive offense.

The rationale behind permitting cumulative sentences was stated this way in *Callanan v. U.S.* (1961):

This settled principle derives from the reason of things in dealing with socially reprehensible conduct: collective criminal agreement—partnership in crime—presents a greater potential threat to the public than individual delicts. Concerted action both increases the likelihood that the criminal object will be successfully attained and decreased the probability that the individuals involved will depart from their path of criminality. Group association for criminal purposes often, if not normally, makes possible the attainment of ends more complex than those which one criminal could accomplish. Nor is the danger of a conspiratorial group limited to the particular end toward which it has embarked. Combination in crime makes more likely the commission of crimes unrelated to the original purpose for which the group was formed. In sum, the danger which a conspiracy generates is not confined to the substantive offense which is the immediate aim of the enterprise.

This reasoning was rejected by the draftsmen of the Model Penal Code: "When a conspiracy is declared criminal because its object is a crime, it is entirely meaningless to say that the preliminary combination is more dangerous than the forbidden consummation; the measure of its danger is the risk of such a culmination. On the other hand, the combination may and often does have criminal objectives that transcend any particular offenses that have been committed in pursuance of its goals. In the latter case, cumulative sentences for conspiracy and substantive offenses ought to be permissible." Code § 1.07(1)(b) so provides, but this view is taken only in a minority of the modern recodifications.

Most jurisdictions have now enacted general conspiracy statutes with express penalty provisions, but these provisions vary considerably from state to state. Some statutes provide that conspiracy is a misdemeanor regardless of its object, some that the permissible maximum sentence is the same regardless of the objective, and some provide different maxima depending upon whether the objective was a felony or misdemeanor. If the statute does not set the maximum sentence in terms of an equivalent or fraction of the maximum permitted for the criminal objective, it may happen that the penalty for the conspiracy is greater than the permissible penalty for the crime which was its object. Model Penal Code § 5.05(1) authorizes penalties for conspiracy equivalent to those permitted for the most serious offense that was an object of the conspiracy. The theory is that the rehabilitative needs of the defendant will be essentially the same whether or not the plan is consummated, and that no added general deterrence would be gained by permitting punishment beyond that authorized for the crime which was his object. Many of the modern recodifications take that position, though about as many provide that the conspiracy crime is one class lower than the object crime.

Chapter 12

PARTIES; LIABILITY FOR CONDUCT OF ANOTHER

Table of Sections

> For additional analysis of the above topics and citations to authorities supporting their discussion in this Book, consult the author's 3-volume *Substantive Criminal Law* treatise, also available as Westlaw database SUBCRL. See the Table of Cross-References in this Book.

§ 12.1   Parties to Crime

In the commission of each criminal offense there may be several persons or groups that play distinct roles before, during and after the offense. Collectively these persons or groups are termed the parties to the crime. The common law classification of parties to a felony consisted of four categories: (1) principal in the first degree; (2) principal in the second degree; (3) accessory before the fact; and (4) accessory after the fact.

This classification scheme gave rise to many procedural difficulties (see § 12.1(d)), but if they were overcome a person in any one of the four categories could be convicted and subjected to the penalties authorized for commission of the felony. It was later recognized that the accessory after the fact, by virtue of his involvement only after the felony was completed, was not truly an accomplice in the felony. This category has thus remained distinct from the others, and today the accessory after the fact is not deemed a participant in the felony but rather one who has obstructed justice, subjecting him to different and lesser penalties. The distinctions between the other three categories, however, have now been largely abrogated, although some statutes resort to the common law terminology in defining the scope of complicity. It thus remains important to understand what is collectively encompassed within these three categories.

The common law classification scheme described above existed only as to felonies. When treason was committed, those who would be included within any of the four felony categories were all classified as principals. As to misdemeanors, all parties were again held to be principals, although conduct that would constitute one an accessory after the fact to a felony was not criminal when the post-crime aid was to a misdemeanant.

In this section, the principal in the first degree, principal in the second degree, and accessory before the fact classifications will be described, with emphasis upon the distinctions between them. (Because the accessory after the fact is not truly a "party" to the crime, this category will be discussed later with related forms of post-crime aid; see § 12.6(a).) Note will be taken of the procedural technicalities that developed out of this classification scheme, and of the ways in which these difficulties have now been largely overcome by statute. A closer look at accomplice liability will be undertaken in a later section (see § 12.2), where more specific treatment is given to the questions of what acts or omissions with what mental state are required to establish complicity in an offense directly committed by another.

(a) Principal in the First Degree. A principal in the first degree may simply be defined as the criminal actor. He is the one who, with the requisite mental state (see §§ 4.1–4.4), engages in the act or omission (see §§ 5.1, 5.2) concurring with the mental state (see § 5.3) that causes the criminal result (see § 5.4). In each section of this book dealing with a substantive offense, the elements are defined in terms of what an actor, or first degree principal, must do to be guilty of that offense.

One who uses an intermediary to commit a crime is not ordinarily a principal in the first degree. It is otherwise, however, when the crime is accomplished by the use of an innocent or irresponsible agent, as where the defendant causes a child or mentally incompetent or one without a criminal state of mind (most likely because the defendant has misled or withheld facts from him) to engage in conduct. In such a case the intermediary is regarded as a mere instrument and the originating actor is the principal in the first degree. The principal is accountable for the acts or omissions of the innocent or irresponsible person, and the principal's liability is determined on the basis of that conduct and the principal's own mental state. Thus, if *A,* with intent to bring about *B*'s death, causes *C* (a child) to take *B*'s life, *A* is guilty of intent-to-kill murder. But because the crime of obtaining property by false pretenses requires an actual intent to defraud (see § 16.7(f)), *A* has not committed that crime by negligently causing *B* to make false statements to *C.*

There can be more than one principal in the first degree. This occurs when more than one actor participates in the actual commission of the offense. Thus, when one man beats a victim and another shoots him, both may be principals in first degree to murder. And when two persons forge separate parts of the same instrument, they are both principals in the first degree to the forgery. While there may be more than one principal in the first degree, there must always be at least one for a crime to have taken place.

Although it has been said that a principal in the first degree must be present at the commission of the offense, this is not literally so. He may be "constructively" present when some instrument that he left or guided caused the criminal result. Thus, when an actor leaves poison for another who later drinks it, he is a first degree principal, as is the person whose unwitting agent acts for him in his absence.

(b) Principal in the Second Degree. To be a principal in the second degree, one must be present at the commission of a criminal offense and aid, counsel, command, or encourage the principal in the first degree in the commission of that offense. This requirement of presence may be fulfilled by constructive presence. A person is constructively present when he is physically absent from the situs of the crime but aids and abets the principal in the first degree at the time of the offense from some distance. This may happen when one stands watch for the primary actor, signals to the principal from a distance that the victim is coming, or stands ready (though out of sight or hearing) to render aid to the principal if needed. While close physical proximity to the scene of the crime is not necessary, one must be close enough to render aid if needed.

The assistance rendered by the principal in the second degree has traditionally been referred to as "aiding and abetting." The term "abet" is an appropriate one, for it contemplates aid combined with *mens rea,* while the term "aid" standing alone is insufficient in that it does not suggest the necessity for a mental state in addition to conduct. As is true in the criminal law generally, one can be guilty as a principal in the second degree only if the requisite acts (or omissions) and accompanying mental state are both present. These requirements will be discussed later (see § 12.2).

(c) Accessory Before the Fact. An accessory before the fact is one who orders, counsels, encourages, or otherwise aids and abets another to commit a felony and who is not present at the commission of the offense. The primary distinction between the accessory before the fact and the principal in the second degree is presence. If a person was actually or constructively present at the offense, due to his participation he is a principal in the second degree; if he was not present, he is an accessory before the fact. Through prior counseling followed by appearance at the scene of the crime to aid the primary actor, one may become both an accessory before the fact and also a principal in the second degree.

The aid or counsel may be far removed in time from the commission of the offense, although it must be shown to have retained some relationship to it by causing, encouraging, or assisting the offense. If one contributes specific material aid, he will still be an accessory though it is not used in the offense. The exact time of the commission of the offense is also immaterial. One may intend to aid a crime that is to occur on a certain date but which in fact occurs later, and he will still be an accessory before the fact to the crime. The quantity of the aid is immaterial, and it may come through some intermediary. More will be said later about precisely what conduct and mental state are required (see § 12.2).

Although the accessory before the fact is often the originator of the offense, this need not be the case. Indeed, if one is enlisted by another to lend aid toward the commission of the offense and the aid is given, the person giving the assistance may thereby become an accessory before the fact.

(d) Problems of Procedure. The common law distinction between principals and accessories in felony cases gave rise to several procedural difficulties. There developed several technical and not altogether logical rules that tended to shield accessories from punishment notwithstanding overwhelming evidence of their criminal assistance. This is undoubtedly another instance of resort to procedural niceties in order to limit the application of the death penalty, which at early common law was the penalty for all parties to any felony.

(1) Criminal Jurisdiction. Under the common law territorial theory of jurisdiction, a state's criminal law reaches only those wrongs deemed to have their situs in that state. Generally, it may be said that the situs of a crime is the place of the act (or omission) if the crime is defined only in these terms, and the place of the result if the definition of the crime includes such a result. The crime of murder, which is quite obviously defined in the terms of a result, thus has its situs where the fatal force impinges upon the body of the victim. For example, if A fires a shot at B and hits and kills B, and A was then standing in state X but B was standing over the border in state Y, state Y would have jurisdiction over this crime.

What if, in the above example, A had as his accessory one C, who, at all times in state X, commanded or encouraged A to commit the crime or perhaps assisted A before the crime by supplying him with the gun or ammunition? As a matter of logic, one might well conclude that C is likewise subject to prosecution in state Y, for C is a party to a crime which had its result in that state. However, the common law rule was otherwise; an accessory could only be tried where the acts of accessoryship occurred, rather than where the ultimate crime took place. Therefore C would be punishable only in state X and not in state Y, the jurisdiction that might well be most interested in his prosecution.

No comparable difficulty existed if the aid was given under circumstances that placed the accomplice in the category of principal in the second degree. If, in the example given above, C had been present at the time of the shooting giving aid or encouragement to

A as they both stood in state *X*, then state *Y* would have jurisdiction over both *A* and *C*. One court will have jurisdiction over all principals, for by definition a principal in the second degree abets the crime at the time and place that it is committed by the principal in the first degree.

(2) Variance Between Charge and Proof. Under the common law rules of pleading, it was not necessary for the defendant to be charged specifically as a principal in the first degree or principal in the second degree; a general allegation that the defendant was a principal would suffice. If the indictment did specify either that the defendant actually committed the felony or that he was present aiding and abetting, it did not matter that the proof placed the defendant in the other principal category. Thus, where *A* was charged as a principal in the first degree and *B* as a principal in the second degree, both *A* and *B* could be convicted notwithstanding proof that their roles were reversed.

The same was not true, however, when the variance between charge and proof was spread over the principal and accessory categories. If the defendant were charged as a principal, he could not be convicted upon proof that he was an accessory. Likewise, one charged only as an accessory could not be convicted if the evidence established that he was instead a principal. As a result, it was possible for an accomplice to escape altogether because of uncertainty as to whether he had been actually or constructively present at the time the offense was committed by the principal in the first degree.

(3) Conviction of Principal Required. The most significant procedural limitation on conviction of an accessory at common law was that conviction of the principal was an absolute prerequisite. An accessory could not be placed on trial in advance of the principal, and this was so even if the principal was not amenable to prosecution because he could not be apprehended or had died. A principal and accessory could be jointly charged and tried, although in such a case the finder of fact was required first to determine the guilt of the principal. The accessory could not be convicted unless the principal was found guilty, and this was also the case when the accessory was tried separately at a later time. If the principal's conviction was later reversed on appeal or he was pardoned, then the conviction of the accessory could not stand.

Once again, the same limitations did not apply with respect to the prosecution of one who was a principal in the second degree. A second degree principal could be tried and convicted even though the person who actually committed the crime had not yet been tried. Indeed, the principal in the second degree could be convicted notwithstanding the prior acquittal of the principal in the first degree.

(e) Legislative Reform. The problems discussed above have been largely overcome by legislation. In 1861, for example, an English statute provided that an accessory before the fact could be "indicted, tried, convicted and punished as if he were a principal felon" and that he may be "indicted and convicted of a substantive felony, whether the principal felon shall or shall not have been previously convicted, or shall or shall not be amenable to justice."

All states have now expressly abrogated the distinction between principals and accessories before the fact. One form of legislation declares that accessories before the fact are now principals, although substantially the same result has been reached by providing that those who would have been accessories before the fact may be prosecuted, tried and punished as if they were principals. Some statutes, following the English model, declare that an accessory before the fact may be punished for a "substantive felony" whether or not the principal has been convicted, while others maintain the common law classifications but provide that conviction of the principal is not a pre-condition to the prosecution of an accessory before the fact.

Indeed, whether or not the common law terminology is retained, the modern codes usually address specifically the troublesome question of whether nonconviction of the principal for one reason or another bars conviction of an accomplice. Most common are those provisions declaring that the accomplice may be convicted even if the principal has not been prosecuted, has not been convicted, has immunity to prosecution or conviction, has been acquitted, or has been convicted of a different offense or degree of offense. Some statutes also state that it is no barrier to conviction of an accomplice that the principal has not been charged or is not amenable to justice. Certain other provisions, by contrast, appear to be directed at the "innocent agent" situation.

By virtue of such legislation, the procedural problems discussed earlier have been obviated in most jurisdictions. Relying upon these statutes, courts have held that an accessory acting elsewhere may be tried in the jurisdiction where the felony occurred, that the charge need not specify whether the defendant was an accessory or principal, that if the charge does specify it is not a fatal variance if the proof puts the case in the other category, and that an accessory may be prosecuted even though the principal has not yet been convicted, or has been previously acquitted, or has been previously convicted only of a lesser offense. However, the rule requiring internal consistency in a verdict may bar acquittal of the principal and conviction of an accessory in a single trial.

Although it is now generally true that conviction of the principal is no longer a prerequisite to prosecution and conviction of an accessory, it is of course still necessary for the prosecution to show on trial of the accessory that the crime was committed, as well as whom and how the defendant aided in its commission. It is generally accepted, however, that the prior conviction of the principal is *not* admissible at the accessory's trial to establish that the crime was committed. This is because of "the right of every defendant to stand or fall with the proof of the charge made against him, not somebody else." Indeed, it may well be that admission of the conviction is a denial of the accessory's constitutional right to confront the witnesses against him.

A much more modern approach to the entire subject of parties to crime is to abandon completely the old common law terminology and simply provide that a person is legally accountable for the conduct of another when he is an accomplice of the other person in the commission of the crime. Such is the view taken in Model Penal Code § 2.06(2)(c), which provides that a person is an accomplice of another person in the commission of an offense if, with the purpose of promoting or facilitating the commission of the offense, he solicits the other person to commit it, or aids or agrees or attempts to aid the other person in planning or committing it, or (having a legal duty to prevent the crime) fails to make proper effort to prevent it. A similar approach has been taken in many of the recent recodifications. Under this approach, "a person guilty by accountability is guilty of the substantive crime itself" and punishable accordingly.

§ 12.2 Accomplice Liability—Acts and Mental State

This and the following section are concerned with the general principles governing accomplice liability. Because these principles are applicable to those who come within the common law classifications of principal in the second degree and accessory before the fact, no attempt will be made to distinguish between these two classifications or to identify the accomplices in those terms. Rather, consistent with the modern approach, the word "accomplice" is used herein to describe all persons who are accountable for crimes committed by another, without regard to whether they were or were not actually or constructively present at the time the crimes were committed.

As we have seen (see §§ 4.1–4.4, 5.1, 5.2), in the process of determining whether a person has committed a crime it is useful to give separate consideration to whether that person engaged in the requisite acts (or omissions) and to whether he had the requisite mental state. This same approach is used herein in determining the limits of accomplice liability. It may generally be said that one is liable as an accomplice to the crime of another if he (a) gave assistance or encouragement or failed to perform a legal duty to prevent it (b) with the intent thereby to promote or facilitate commission of the crime. There is a split of authority as to whether some lesser mental state will suffice for accomplice liability, such as mere knowledge that one is aiding a crime or knowledge that one is aiding reckless or negligent conduct which may produce a criminal result.

(a) Acts or Omissions. Several terms have been employed by courts and legislatures in describing the kinds of acts that will suffice for accomplice liability. The most common are "aid," "abet," "advise," "assist," "cause," "command," "counsel," "encourage," "hire," "induce," and "procure." Although there is very little difference between the meaning of several of these words, the following comments must be read with the caveat that the results in some cases may depend upon the precise combination of terms included within the applicable accessory statute.

Such terms as "advise," "command," "counsel," "encourage," "induce," and "procure" suggest that one may become an accomplice without actually rendering physical aid to the endeavor. This is the case. One may become an accomplice by acting to induce another through threats or promises, by words or gestures of encouragement, or by providing others with the plan for the crime. The encouragement may come long before the time the crime was committed, and may be communicated to the principal through an intermediary. It is sufficient encouragement that the accomplice is standing by at the scene of the crime ready to give some aid if needed, although in such a case it is necessary that the principal actually be aware of the accomplice's intentions. An undisclosed intention to render aid if needed will not suffice, for it cannot encourage the principal in his commission of the crime. Quite clearly, mere presence at the scene of the crime is not enough, nor is mental approval of the actor's conduct. Also, in the absence of unique circumstances giving rise to a duty to do so, one does not become an accomplice by refusing to intervene in the commission of a crime. But it is not the case "that passive behavior can never be the basis of a finding of accessory liability," absent violation of a duty to act, "where that behavior is accompanied by a communicated assurance of passivity," which of course constitutes the requisite act.

Because this is so, courts have experienced considerable difficulty in cases where the defendant was present at the time of the crime and the circumstances of his presence suggest that he might be there pursuant to a prior agreement to give aid if needed. Depending upon the facts, the circumstantial evidence may be sufficient to permit the jury to find that such an agreement did exist. The mere fact that the alleged accomplice was a prior acquaintance of the actor will not support an inference of guilt, although silence in the face of a friend's crime will sometimes suffice when the immediate proximity of the bystander is such that he could be expected to voice some opposition or surprise if he were not a party to the crime. Mere presence plus flight has often been held insufficient, the reasoning being that this is equivocal conduct because an innocent man may flee out of a fear of being wrongfully accused of guilt or from an unwillingness to appear as a witness. Flight may be taken into account with other facts, however, such as that the bystander positioned himself very close to the victim, or failed to make any effort to disassociate himself from ongoing criminal activity until it was completed.

Somewhat easier, as a class, are those cases in which the liability of the accomplice is based upon the fact that he actually did "aid," "abet," or "assist" in the commission of the crime. The assistance may be rendered in a variety of ways. The accomplice may furnish guns, money, supplies or instrumentalities to be used in committing the crime, or he may act as a lookout or man the getaway car while the crime is committed. He might signal the approach of the victim, send the victim to the actor, prevent a warning from reaching the victim, prevent escape by the victim, or facilitate the crime by getting the victim or possible witness away from the scene. The aid may be supplied through an intermediary, and it is not necessary that the principal actor be aware of the assistance that was given.

As noted earlier, it is generally true that liability will not flow merely from a failure to intervene. But, under the general principle that an omission in violation of a legal duty will suffice (see § 5.2(a)), one may become an accomplice by not preventing a crime which he has a duty to prevent. Thus, a conductor on a train might become an accomplice in the knowing transportation of liquor on his train for his failure to take steps to prevent the offense. Or, even in the absence of positive encouragement, the owner of a car who sat beside the driver might become an accomplice to the driver's crime of driving at a dangerous speed. Or, a parent might become an accomplice to a crime because of the parent's failure to intervene to prevent that crime from being committed on the parent's offspring.

To what extent is it necessary that the aid or encouragement have played a part in the commission of the crime? For example, if A prevented the delivery to B of a warning that C was seeking to kill him and B is thereafter killed by C, must it be shown that the murder would not have been accomplished but for A's aid? No, said one court confronted with these facts, *State ex rel. Martin v. Tally* (1894):

> The assistance given * * * need not contribute to the criminal result in the sense that but for it the result would not have ensued. It is quite sufficient if it facilitated a result that would have transpired without it. It is quite enough if the aid merely renders it easier for the principal actor to accomplish the end intended by him and the aider and abetter, though in all human probability the end would have been attained without it. If the aid in homicide can be shown to have put the deceased at a disadvantage, to have deprived him of a single chance of life, which but for it he would have had, he who furnished such aid is guilty though it can not be known or shown that the dead man, in the absence thereof, would have availed himself of that chance. As where one counsels murder he is guilty as an accessory before the fact, though it appears to be probable that murder would have been done without his counsel.

What, then, of attempted aid? For instance, in the example given above, what if *A* had been unsuccessful in his efforts to stop the delivery of the warning to *B* but *B* was killed nonetheless? At least where the attempted aid is known to the actor, it may make no difference that the aid was unsuccessful or was not utilized, as it may qualify as an encouragement. On this basis it is correct to conclude that an accessory who provides instrumentalities to a burglar for use in a particular burglary should not escape liability as an accomplice merely because the burglar found and used other instrumentalities at the crime scene. On the other hand, where preconcert is lacking and there was only an attempt to aid, it might be argued that this is analogous to the uncommunicated intent to give aid if needed, so that there would be no liability. Model Penal Code § 2.06(3)(a)(ii), however, covers all attempts to aid on the ground that "attempted complicity ought to be criminal, and to distinguish it from effective complicity appears unnecessary where the crime has been committed." Several modern codes have adopted this innovation.

(b) Mental State Generally. Considerable confusion exists as to what the accomplice's mental state must be in order to hold him accountable for an offense committed by another. In part, this may be attributable to some uncertainty as to whether the law should be concerned with the mental state relating to his own acts of assistance or encouragement, to his awareness of the principal's mental state, to the fault requirements for the substantive offense involved, or some combination of the above.

This uncertainty is reflected in the considerable variation in the language used by courts and legislatures on this point. Some cases speak in terms of the accomplice's knowledge or reason to know of the principal's mental state, some as to the accomplice's sharing the criminal intent of the actor, and some about the accomplice's intent to aid or encourage. Likewise, the statutes on accomplice liability (putting aside those which do not specify what mental state is required to be convicted as an aider or abettor) may require that one "intentionally" or "knowingly" assist or encourage a crime, that one assist or encourage a crime "with the intent to promote or facilitate such commission," or that the aid and encouragement be given by one "acting with the mental state required for commission of an offense." Although to some extent these may represent different ways of stating the same mental state requirement, it is undoubtedly true that some rather subtle differences exist between them and that therefore what follows is not in all respects applicable in every jurisdiction.

Generally, it may be said that accomplice liability exists when the accomplice intentionally encourages or assists, in the sense that his purpose is to encourage or assist another in the commission of a crime as to which the accomplice has the requisite mental state. Beyond this, the situation is much less certain. There is some authority to the effect that one may become an accomplice by giving encouragement or assistance with knowledge that it will promote or facilitate a crime, although liability has seldom been imposed on this basis. Also, there is considerable diversity in the cases on the subject of whether accomplice liability may rest upon knowing aid to reckless or negligent conduct if that conduct produces a criminal result. It does seem clear, however, that liability without fault does not obtain in this area.

(c) Intentional Assistance or Encouragement. Under the usual requirement that the accomplice must intentionally assist or encourage, it is not sufficient that he intentionally engaged in acts which, as it turned out, did give assistance or encouragement to the principal. Rather, the accomplice must intend that his acts have the effect of assisting or encouraging another. For example, assume that A shoots and kills B while C was standing by shouting and gesturing. Is it sufficient, for purposes of accomplice liability to the crime of murder, to show that A took C's words and actions to be a manifestation of encouragement, if in fact C was attempting to dissuade A from killing B? Quite obviously not. Thus, even if knowledge of the actor's intent (as opposed to sharing that intent) is otherwise sufficient, the accomplice must have intended to give the aid or encouragement.

In other instances, it may be clear that the alleged accomplice intended to give aid or encouragement to another, but he will still not be liable as an accomplice. For example, assume that A and B go to C's house, that A removes the screen so as to permit B to enter, that B enters through the window and comes back out with several items of C's personal property, which A then helps B carry away from the scene. Is A an accomplice with B in the crimes of burglary and larceny if B misled A into believing that C had given B permission to borrow the property taken? Clearly not, for these facts show that A was unaware that he was aiding criminal conduct. (This is not to suggest, however, that an accomplice can escape liability by showing he did not intend to aid a crime in the sense that he was unaware that the criminal law covered the conduct of the person he aided. Such is not the case, for here as well the general principle that ignorance of the law is no excuse prevails; see § 4.6(d).)

Although one might conclude from the above example that what the law *does* require is that the accomplice intend to aid or encourage what he knows is criminal conduct by another, this is an overstatement. The prevailing view is that the accomplice must also have the mental state required for the crime of which he is to be convicted on an accomplice theory. Thus, if A and B go to C's store pursuant to their prior discussion about stealing liquor from the store and A boosts B through the transom and thereafter receives the liquor as it is handed out by B, all of which was done by A to settle a score with B, and A notifies the police while B is inside, A is not an accomplice to B's crimes of burglary and larceny, for A did not intend to permanently deprive C of his goods.

The notion that the accomplice may be convicted, on an accomplice liability theory, only for those crimes as to which he personally has the requisite mental state, is applicable in a variety of circumstances. It means, for example, that one may not be held as an accomplice to the crime of assault with intent to kill if that intent was not shared by the accomplice. But this limitation has proved most significant in the homicide area, where the precise state of mind of the defendant has great significance in determining the degree of the offense. To determine the kind of homicide of which the accomplice is guilty, it is necessary to look to his state of mind; it may have been different from the state of mind of the principal and they thus may be guilty of different offenses. Thus, because first degree murder requires a deliberate and premeditated killing (see § 13.7(a)), an accomplice is not guilty of this degree of murder unless he acted with premeditation and deliberation. And, because a killing in a heat of passion is manslaughter and not murder (see § 14.2), an accomplice who aids while in such a state is guilty only of manslaughter even though the killer is himself guilty of murder. Likewise, it is equally possible that the killer is guilty only of manslaughter because of his heat of passion but that the accomplice, aiding in a state of cool blood, is guilty of murder.

Brief mention should also be made here of the somewhat unique results as to accomplice liability that may flow from application of the felony-murder and misdemeanor-manslaughter rules (see §§ 13.5, 14.5). Under these doctrines, the actor in committing a felony or dangerous misdemeanor is liable for a killing that occurs in the execution of such crimes, and there is no requirement that he have intended the homicide or have even negligently brought it about. This being the case, it is not surprising that one who intentionally aids or encourages the actor in the underlying crime may likewise be convicted of felony-murder or misdemeanor-manslaughter notwithstanding his lack of intent that death result.

(d) Knowing Assistance or Encouragement. In many cases the facts will make it clear that the accessory actually intended to promote the criminal venture, in the sense that he was personally interested in its success. Such is the case, for example, when one supplies guns for use in a bank robbery on the understanding that he will receive part of proceeds of the illegal venture, or when one induces a public official to take unlawful fees so that he may also be paid for the benefit to be granted in exchange. The accomplice's interest, of course, need not be financial; there may be many reasons why he shares in the hope for success.

But there are many other instances in which the alleged accomplice's actions will qualify only as knowing assistance, in that he is lending assistance or encouragement to a criminal scheme toward which he is indifferent.

> A lessor rents with knowledge that the premises will be used to establish a bordello. A vendor sells with knowledge that the subject of the sale will be used in commission of a crime. A doctor counsels against an abortion during the third trimester but, at the patient's insistence, refers her to a competent abortionist. A utility provides telephone or telegraph service, knowing it is used for bookmaking. An employee puts through a shipment in the course of his employment though he knows the shipment is illegal. A farm boy clears the ground for setting up a still, knowing that the venture is illicit.

Should such knowing assistance or encouragement suffice as a basis for accomplice liability?

The earlier decisions generally held that aid with knowledge was enough, and it has been forcefully argued that such a view is consistent with the preventive objectives of the criminal law. As stated in *Backun v. U.S.* (1940):

> The seller may not ignore the purpose for which the purchase is made if he is advised of that purpose, or wash his hands of the aid that he has given the perpetrator of a felony by the plea

that he has merely made a sale of merchandise. One who sells a gun to another knowing that he is buying it to commit a murder, would hardly escape conviction as an accessory to the murder by showing that he received full price for the gun.

Under this approach, even "wilful blindness" would suffice as a mental state for accomplice liability (see § 4.2(b)).

The leading case to the contrary is *U.S. v. Peoni* (1938), where the court took the position that the traditional definitions of accomplice liability "have nothing whatever to do with the probability that the forbidden result would follow upon the accessory's conduct; and that they all demand that he in some sort associate himself with the venture, that he participate in it as something that he wishes to bring about, that he seek by his action to make it succeed. All the words used—even the most colorless, 'abet'—carry an implication of purposive attitude towards it." Other courts have tended to accept the *Peoni* limitation on accomplice liability, although dictum to the contrary still persists.

Various compromises between the views expressed in *Backun* and *Peoni* have been suggested. One is that knowing aid should be deemed sufficient when the criminal scheme is serious in nature. Some of the decided cases may be reconciled on this basis; this would explain, for example, why liability has been imposed for knowing aid to a group planning the overthrow of the government or to one planning to burglarize a bank, but not for knowing aid to such crimes as gambling, prostitution, and unlawful sale of liquor. Taking into account the seriousness of the crime aided makes some sense, for it may be argued that in such a case the "inconvenience to legitimate trade of requiring a merchant to concern himself with the affairs of his customers" is a lesser consideration than the prevention of major crimes.

Another approach is to take into account the degree to which the accomplice knowingly aided in the criminal scheme. This was the recommendation of the draftsmen of the Model Penal Code, who proposed accomplice liability for a person if, "acting with knowledge that such other person was committing or had the purpose of committing the crime, he knowingly, substantially facilitated its commission." This, they explained, would avoid the imposition of liability upon the vendor who supplies materials readily available on the open market and the minor employee who minds his own business to keep his job, but at the same time provide a basis for conviction of those who were aware that they were giving substantial aid. The conflicting interests would be balanced by subordinating the "freedom to forego concern about the criminal purposes of others" to the interest in crime prevention when the supplier is aware that his contribution to the criminal enterprise would be a substantial one. However, this recommendation was voted down by the American Law Institute, perhaps because of its vagueness, and Code § 2.06(3)(a) thus limits accomplice liability to instances in which there exists "the purpose of promoting or facilitating the commission of an offense."

A somewhat different solution is to deal with knowing assistance or encouragement as a distinct criminal offense rather than as a basis for accomplice liability for the crime aided. This would have the advantage of providing means whereby such persons, clearly less culpable than those directly participating in the crime, could be subjected to lesser and different penalties, just has long been the case for the accessory after the fact. This is the solution adopted in a few of the modern codes by adding "criminal facilitation" to the usual list of anticipatory crimes.

(e) Assistance or Encouragement to Reckless or Negligent Conduct. Assume that A, the owner of a car, permits B, who A knows is intoxicated, to operate his car on the public highways, and that as a consequence B is involved in an accident which causes the death of C. Under principles of accomplice liability, may A be viewed as an accomplice to B's criminal-negligence involuntary manslaughter? In considering this question, it is useful to take account once again of the teaching of *U.S. v. Peoni* (1938) that the traditional definitions of accomplice liability "have nothing whatever to do with the probability that the forbidden result would follow upon the accessory's conduct; and that they all demand that he in some sort associate himself with the venture, that he participate in it as something that he wishes to bring about, that he seek by his action to make it succeed."

As we have seen, the *Peoni* rule is today generally accepted to mean that one does not become an accomplice by an intentional act of assistance or encouragement merely because he knows that such act will facilitate a crime. If this is so, then does it not follow that one also does not become an accomplice by an intentional act of assistance or encouragement merely because he knows that such act *might* facilitate a crime? That is, in the example given above, how can A be an accomplice as to C's death when A did not give the aid or encouragement with an intent that such a result ensue?

The cases in this area are generally in a state of confusion, and the matter is further confounded by the fact that the problem just stated does not exist when the involuntary manslaughter is of the unlawful-act type (see § 14.5) rather than the criminal-negligence type (see § 14.4). However, it has been held with some frequency that accomplice liability exists under the circumstances stated. The most common case has been like the example given above in that a car owner has permitted a person known to be intoxicated to operate his vehicle, but the same result has been reached on quite different facts. Although the rationale of these decisions is seldom made explicit, the assumption apparently is that giving assistance or encouragement to one it is known will thereby engage in conduct dangerous to life should suffice for accomplice liability as to crimes defined in terms of recklessness or negligence. This conclusion, permitted under some accomplice liability statutes, it might be argued, is not inconsistent with the *Peoni* rule holding knowing facilitation insufficient, for *Peoni* has been applied so as to avoid holding one as an accomplice upon a lesser mental state than would be required for conviction of the principal in the first degree.

This theory of accomplice liability has been rejected by some courts, and it would seem inapplicable under many of the modern accomplice statutes requiring an actual intent to assist the commission of a crime, although the courts in some of these states have in effect decided to judicially amend their statutes to add on what their legislatures decided to leave out. But even if this has not occurred, this is not to say, however, to return to the example of *A* permitting intoxicated *B* to drive his car, that *A* will necessarily escape liability. *A* could well be found guilty of criminal-negligence involuntary manslaughter without being declared an accomplice of *B*.

To understand how this might be so, it is important to reconsider why and when accomplice liability is needed. It is required to establish liability as to one who did not himself engage in the conduct required for commission of the crime, and this becomes most critical when the relevant statute speaks of a specific kind of conduct. For example, the crime of burglary requires (among other things) a breaking and entering, and thus if *A* breaks and enters by using a ladder supplied by *B* and held by *C* while *D* keeps a lookout, *B, C* and *D* are accountable for the crime of burglary only if they are accomplices of *A*, for only *A* has done the requisite breaking and entering. But certain crimes are defined quite differently, in that specific acts are not enumerated; rather, it is only required that the unspecified conduct cause a certain specified result. Such is the case as to criminal-negligence involuntary manslaughter (see § 14.4). And this is why, if *A* gives his car to intoxicated *B* and *B* runs down and kills *C*, it is not necessary to find that *A* is an accomplice to *B*'s crime; if *A*'s own conduct in turning over the car to one known to be intoxicated is itself criminally negligent and if that conduct is found to be the legal cause of the death, then *A* is guilty of manslaughter on that basis. Indeed, this approach is to be much preferred over the accomplice liability theory, for the latter is not limited by the legal cause requirement and thus could easily be extended to all forms of assistance or encouragement to negligent or reckless conduct.

(f) Liability Without Fault. Under the general principles applicable to accomplice liability, there is no such thing as liability without fault. Thus, it is not enough that the alleged accomplice's acts in fact assisted or encouraged the person who committed the crime. One does not become an accomplice to a murder merely because the murderer misinterpreted his words and gestures as encouragement.

A somewhat different situation is that in which the alleged accomplice is aiding another with intent to do so, but the aid is given without knowledge of the facts making the principal's conduct a crime. It has been argued that in such a case the accomplice may be held on a liability-without-fault basis if the crime committed by the principal is of the strict liability variety, but this argument has been rejected. The argument is not sound, for the special circumstances that justify the imposition of liability without fault on certain persons who themselves engage in the proscribed conduct (see § 4.5(c)) are not likely to exist as to those rendering aid. For example, as a matter of policy it may be sound to make the filing of a false financial statement with a state official a strict liability offense, so that the person filing the statement may not defend on the ground that he believed the statement to be true. It does not follow from this, however, that one who assists in the filing should likewise be held liable on this basis. (This is to be distinguished from the situation where the crime is *not* totally of a strict liability type, but no awareness is required as to some attendant circumstance to convict either the principal or an accomplice.)

The above comments, it must be emphasized, refer only to accomplice liability as it exists under common law and statutes, where mental fault is an absolute requirement. One who is not truly an accomplice may nonetheless be held responsible for the conduct of another by virtue of special statutory provisions, and such legislation may indeed impose that variety of liability without fault referred to as vicarious liability (see § 12.4).

§ 12.3   The Limits of Accomplice Liability

Under the better view, one is not an accomplice to a crime merely because that crime was committed in furtherance of a conspiracy of which he is a member, or because that crime was a natural and probable consequence of another offense as to which he is an accomplice. While guilt of the principal is ordinarily a prerequisite to accomplice liability, it may be otherwise when the principal has a defense that is personal to him or when the accomplice has attempted to aid or encourage another.

One may be an accomplice in a crime that, by its definition, he could not commit personally. However, one is not an accomplice to a crime if (a) he is a victim of the crime; (b) the offense is defined so as to make his conduct inevitably incident thereto; or (c) he takes sufficient steps to make a timely withdrawal of his aid or encouragement.

(a) Complicity and Conspiracy Distinguished. One source of continuing confusion in this area is whether the doctrines concerning complicity and conspiracy are essentially the same, so that liability as a conspirator and as an accomplice may be based upon essentially the same facts. Is one who is a member of a conspiracy of necessity a party to any crime committed in the course of the conspiracy? Is one who qualifies as an accomplice to a crime of necessity part of a conspiracy to commit that crime? Under the better view, both of these questions must be answered in the negative.

The leading case for the proposition that membership in a conspiracy is sufficient for criminal liability not only as a conspirator but also for all specified offenses committed in furtherance of the conspiracy is *Pinkerton v. U.S.* (1946). Pinkerton was indicted both for conspiring with his brother to evade taxes and also for specific tax evasions committed by his brother while Pinkerton was in jail. Although the evidence in the case tended to show that Pinkerton actually played a part in the planning of the specific offenses notwithstanding his incarceration, the trial court instructed the jury that it could convict on the substantive counts if it found that the defendant had been engaged in a conspiracy and that the offenses charged were in furtherance of the conspiracy. The Supreme Court affirmed, holding in effect that evidence of direct participation in the commission of the substantive offenses was not necessary, although it was indicated that the result might be otherwise if the crimes were not reasonably foreseeable as a natural consequence of the unlawful agreement.

The notion that one is responsible for the substantive crimes of fellow conspirators in furtherance of the conspiracy has often been expressed in the cases, although such statements have been most frequently made in decisions involving only a conspiracy charge. When this "rule" has been relied upon in connection with a charge of specific offenses, the facts have often shown sufficient counseling or aiding of those offenses to make unnecessary reliance upon the conspiracy as a basis for establishing complicity. But this is not to suggest that what might be called the *Pinkerton* rule has not had an impact upon the law of accomplice liability. The *Pinkerton* approach has been used from time to time by courts in establishing a basis for finding that the defendant was accountable for crimes directly committed by another. For example, in one case the defendant's conduct in referring women to an abortionist was held to make her a part of a larger conspiracy whereby she might be convicted of twenty-six individual abortions, including many performed on women not known by this defendant and referred to the abortionist by others. And in another case the defendant's acts in introducing the head of the conspiracy to check-cashing agencies was deemed sufficient to make him a member of the general conspiracy and thereby liable for 131 separate forging and uttering offenses. The *Pinkerton* rule also appears to have been included within some statutes defining accomplice liability.

Any assessment of the *Pinkerton* rule involves a reconsideration of the question considered at the outset of the preceding section: to what extent must the defendant's acts have played a part in inducing or aiding the crime in order to justify holding him accountable for it as an accomplice? In support of the *Pinkerton* rule, this question might be answered in this way:

> Criminal acts done in furtherance of a conspiracy may be sufficiently dependent upon the encouragement and material support of the group as a whole to warrant treating each member as a causal agent to each act. Under this view, which of the conspirators committed the substantive offense would be less significant in determining the defendant's liability than the fact that the crime was performed as a part of a larger division of labor to which the defendant had also contributed his efforts. * * * If a defendant can be convicted as an accomplice for advising or counseling the perpetrator, it likewise seems fair to impose vicarious liability upon one who, in alliance with others, has declared his allegiance to a particular common object, has implicitly assented to the commission of foreseeable crimes in furtherance of this object, and has himself collaborated or agreed to collaborate with his associates, since these acts necessarily give support to the other members of the conspiracy. Perhaps the underlying theme of this argument is that the strict concepts of causality and intent embodied in the traditional doctrine of complicity are inadequate to cope with the phenomenon of modern-day organized crime.

The better view, however, is that "aiding should mean something more than the attenuated connection resulting solely from membership in a conspiracy and the objective standard of what is reasonably foreseeable." As the draftsmen of the Model Penal Code have pointed out, "law would lose all sense of just proportion" if one might, by virtue of his one crime of conspiracy, be "held accountable for thousands of additional offenses of which he was completely unaware and which he did not influence at all." If the *Pinkerton* rule were adhered to, each prostitute or runner in a large commercialized vice ring could be held liable for an untold number of acts of prostitution by persons unknown to them and not directly aided by them. Each retailer in an extensive narcotics ring could be held accountable as an accomplice to every sale of narcotics made by every other retailer in that vast conspiracy. Such liability might be justified for those who are at the top directing and controlling the entire operation, but it is clearly inappropriate to visit the same results upon the lesser participants in the conspiracy.

Although the *Pinkerton* rule never gained broad acceptance, the opposition to it has grown significantly in recent years. It was rejected by the draftsmen of the Model Penal Code and of the proposed new federal criminal code. Most of the state statutes on accomplice liability require more than membership in the conspiracy, and the language in these statutes has been relied upon by courts in rejecting the conclusion that complicity is coextensive with conspiracy. The rule continues to exist in the federal system, though the courts "are mindful of the potential due process limitations on the *Pinkerton* doctrine in cases involving attenuated relationships between the conspirator and the substantive crime." The same may be said of at least some of the states that still utilize the *Pinkerton* principle.

A much simpler question is whether one must be guilty of engaging in a conspiracy with the principal in the first degree in order to be his accomplice. The answer is no, for while an agreement is an essential element of the crime of conspiracy (see § 11.2(a)), aid sufficient for accomplice liability may be given without any agreement between the parties. Indeed, it is even possible for *A* to encourage *B* to commit a crime so as to be liable as an accomplice without the facts also supporting the conclusion that *A* and *B* were co-conspirators.

(b) Foreseeability of Other Crimes. The question considered above as to whether liability for the conspiracy also suffices for accomplice liability with regard to any crimes committed in pursuance of the conspiracy is, as was suggested, a means for testing the outer limits of the act requirement for accomplice liability. A somewhat similar question is whether, on an accomplice liability theory, one may be held accountable for a crime because it was a natural and probable consequence of the crime which that person intended to aid or encourage. This tests the outer limits of the mental state requirement for accomplice liability, for it asks, in effect, whether an intent with respect to one offense should suffice as to another offense that was the consequence of the one intended.

The established rule, as it is usually stated by courts and commentators, is that accomplice liability extends to acts of the principal in the first degree which were a "natural and probable consequence" of the criminal scheme the accomplice encouraged or aided. Some accomplice liability statutes, even in recent recodifications, expressly adopt this position. Under this approach, if A counsels or aids B in the commission of a burglary or a robbery of C, and B encounters resistance from C and thus shoots at him in the course of the burglary or robbery, A is an accomplice to attempted murder. On the other hand, if A is an accomplice in a scheme to steal a safe from a building, and one of the other parties, B, takes it upon himself while alone to also rob the watchman in the building, A is not an accomplice to the robbery.

The "natural and probable consequence" rule of accomplice liability, if viewed as a broad generalization, is inconsistent with more fundamental principles of our system of criminal law. It would permit liability to be predicated upon negligence even when the crime involved requires a different state of mind. Such is not possible as to one who has personally committed a crime, and should likewise not be the case as to those who have given aid or counsel.

For example, we have already established that an intent to commit one crime cannot be substituted for an intent to commit another, nor can the commission of one offense be the basis of guilt for another crime requiring a different mental state merely because the harm required for the latter offense flowed from the first crime (see § 5.3(d)). Thus, if A steals a gas meter and as a result B is harmed by the escaping gas, A's intent to steal is not of itself a basis for holding him liable for the harm to B; rather A is liable for the harm to B only upon a finding that he had the mental state (intent, recklessness, or whatever) required under the applicable statute on causing physical harm to a person. Similarly, if C lights a candle to aid in a theft, resulting in a burning of the premises, C's intent to steal does not justify his conviction for arson; again, C must also be shown to have the mental state required for the crime of arson. Were it otherwise, the legislative classification of offenses and punishments would lose all meaning.

For the same reason, general application of the "natural and probable consequence" rule of accomplice liability is unwarranted. A's guilt as an accomplice to one crime should not per se be a basis for holding A accountable for a related crime merely because the latter offense was carried out by A's principal, for this as well would result in A's guilt of a crime as to which he did not have the requisite mental state. Some courts have recognized this point. A, an accomplice in B's crime of falsifying corporate books, is not for that reason also accountable for B's related crime of filing a false tax return based upon the false entries. Similarly, C, by virtue of his accomplice liability in D's embezzlement of city funds, is not necessarily also guilty of *D*'s related crime of filing false reports concerning those funds.

Indeed, the most that can be said for the "natural and probable consequence" rule of accomplice liability is that it has usually been applied to unique situations in which unusual principles of liability obtain. Two striking exceptions to the general rules discussed above are felony-murder and misdemeanor-manslaughter (see §§ 13.5, 14.5), for they do permit conviction for a homicide occurring in the execution of a felony or dangerous misdemeanor without any showing that the defendant intentionally, knowingly, recklessly, or even negligently caused the death. If *A* commits a felony or dangerous misdemeanor and in the process even accidentally causes *B*'s death, *A* is guilty of murder or manslaughter because of his commission of the felony or misdemeanor. This being the case, it is appropriate that complicity in the underlying felony or misdemeanor should likewise suffice to establish guilt of the murder or manslaughter. That is, if, in the above example, *C* was an accomplice to *A* in his commission of the felony or misdemeanor, *C* is equally guilty with *A* of the homicide of *B*. If the "natural and probable consequence" rule of accomplice liability is limited to such cases it is not objectionable—or, at least is no more objectionable than other applications of the felony-murder and misdemeanor-manslaughter rules.

(c) Crime by the Principal. Subject to the inconsistent verdict problem when the principal in the first degree and an accomplice are jointly tried, it is now generally accepted that an accomplice may be convicted notwithstanding the fact that the principal in the first degree has been acquitted or has not yet been tried (see § 12.1(e)). But in such situations, or even when the principal has theretofore been convicted, the guilt of the principal must be established at the trial of the accomplice as a part of the proof on the charge against the accomplice. If the acts of the principal in the first degree are found not to be criminal, then the accomplice may not be convicted. Ordinarily, the proof will be of completed criminal conduct by the principal, although it would seem theoretically possible for one to be an accomplice to an attempt or a conspiracy.

One question which has not been resolved is whether the various defenses available to the principal in the first degree are likewise available to the accomplice in the sense that the accomplice may establish the defense and thus show that no crime was committed by the principal. For example, what if *A* shot and killed *B* upon a reasonable but mistaken belief that such deadly force was necessary in his own defense. This is clearly a defense to *A* (see § 9.4), but should accomplice *C*, who aids *A* without such a belief, thereby go free? If, as we are assuming, *C* gave aid with the intent that A kill B, it would seem that C should not escape liability. Just as an accomplice may not benefit from a principal's heat of passion so as to downgrade his own liability to voluntary manslaughter, it would seem equally true that the accomplice may not defend upon the basis of the principal's own beliefs. But, on this notion that "the liability of each is measured by his or her own degree of culpability," an accomplice might well have a defense (e.g., self-defense) because of his or her own beliefs, without regard to whether the principal likewise has such a defense.

A similar problem was dealt with in *U.S. v. Azadian* (1971), where the defendant was charged with having aided and abetted a draft board employee in soliciting the receipt of money in return for using her influence in her official capacity. He was convicted, although in the same action the employee was found not guilty because of entrapment by a government informant. On appeal, the court concluded that because the defendant had not been entrapped he could not escape conviction because of the entrapment of the principal. This result was rested upon the following characterization of the entrapment defense: "It is made available not because inducement negatives criminal intent and thus establishes the fact of innocence; but because Government agents should not be permitted to act in such a fashion. The defense does not so much establish innocence as grant immunity from prosecution for criminal acts concededly committed." If this is a proper characterization of entrapment, then the result may be correct.

Another question deserving consideration is whether one acting in the role of an accomplice should escape liability because, unknown to him, the individual in the role of principal in the first degree is not really committing a crime because he (unlike the accomplice) does not have the mental state required for commission of the offense. An excellent example is afforded by the case of *State v. Hayes* (1891). A proposed to B that they burglarize C's store, and B feigned agreement in order to obtain A's arrest. They arrived at the store together, and A raised the window and assisted B in climbing into the window. B handed out some food to A. On these facts it was held that A could not be convicted of burglary. A was not the principal in the first degree, as he did not himself enter the premises, and thus he could be held for the burglary only as an accessory to B. B, however, did not commit a burglary, for he lacked the intent to permanently deprive C of the food. Thus, concluded the court, A could not be held as an accessory to B's burglary, for B committed no burglary. If the roles of A and B had been reversed, then A would quite clearly be guilty of burglary, which raises the question of whether the fortuitous event of who entered the premises should actually have a bearing on A's criminality. Perhaps A

should be subject to conviction on the ground that he attempted to aid another in the commission of a crime.

(d) Withdrawal From the Crime. One who has given aid or counsel to a criminal scheme sufficient to otherwise be liable for the offense as an accomplice may sometimes escape liability by withdrawing from the crime. A mere change of heart, flight from the crime scene, apprehension by the police, or an uncommunicated decision not to carry out his part of the scheme will not suffice. Rather, it is necessary that he (1) repudiate his prior aid, or (2) do all that is possible to countermand his prior aid or counsel, and (3) do so before the chain of events has become unstoppable. If the prior aid consisted of supplying materials to be used in commission of the offense, effective withdrawal may require that these materials be reacquired so as to prevent their use by the principal. On the other hand, if one's prior efforts were limited to requesting or encouraging commission of the crime, then an intention to withdraw communicated to the others will be sufficient. In the alternative, in either case an effective withdrawal might also be possible by timely warning to the police or similar actions directed toward preventing the others from committing the crime. It is not necessary that the crime actually have been prevented.

The issue of when withdrawal is a bar to accomplice liability is dealt with in most of the recent recodifications. Some of these statutes impose added requirements, such as that the withdrawal must not be motivated by a belief that the circumstances increase the probability of detection or apprehension or render accomplishment of the crime more difficult, or by a decision to postpone the crime to another time or transfer the effort to another victim or objective.

Permitting withdrawal under the circumstances stated above so as to avert liability is certainly appropriate. One of the objectives of the criminal law is to prevent crime, and thus it is desirable to provide an inducement to those who have counseled and aided a criminal scheme to take steps to deprive their complicity of effectiveness. Whether the added requirements imposed by some statutes concerning the person's motives are desirable is debatable. In support, it may certainly be contended that one who withdraws merely because of a belief that the chances of apprehension have increased has not truly reformed and that he is still a proper object of criminal sanctions. On the other hand, it may be argued that even one acting under such a motive should be induced to take action directed toward prevention of the crime.

One who has participated in a criminal scheme to a degree sufficient for accomplice liability may also have engaged in conduct that brings him within the definition of conspiracy or solicitation.

Whether his withdrawal is a defense to those crimes is a separate matter (see §§ 10.1(d), 11.4(b)).

(e) Exceptions to Accomplice Liability. Some crimes are so defined by statute or common law that they may be committed only by certain persons or classes of persons. For example, the statutory offense of concealing the death of a bastard typically refers specifically to concealment only by the mother. By definition, the crime of incest covers only those related to the victim in certain ways. And the crime of rape as traditionally defined requires that the unconsented sexual intercourse be by a male, excluding the woman's husband and (in some jurisdictions) any boy under the age of fourteen. As to such crimes, may a person who could not directly commit the offense become criminally liable by acting as an accomplice to another who is within the scope of the definition? The courts have consistently answered this in the affirmative.

Thus, as to the crimes mentioned above, liability as an accomplice will extend to the individual who aids the mother in concealing a bastard's death, to one not related to any other party who lends encouragement to an act of incest, and to another woman or a boy under fourteen or the victim's husband who procures or assists another to commit rape. Many other illustrations are to be found in the cases. For example, on an accomplice theory: one not the owner of the destroyed premises may be guilty under a statute making it an offense for the owner of property to burn it with intent to defraud the insurer; one not a public officer may be guilty of improperly keeping state records or of misconduct in public office; one not a fiduciary or public officer may be guilty of the crime of embezzlement by such persons; one not the mortgagor may be guilty of the unlawful disposition of mortgaged property; one not a minor may be guilty of illegal possession of alcoholic beverages by a minor; one not a prisoner may be guilty of engaging in oral copulation by a jail inmate; and one not the driver of the car may be guilty of a traffic violation concerning operation of the vehicle.

Such results as these are in no sense inconsistent with the terms of the offenses involved. While the applicable statutes state that these crimes may be committed only by certain persons or classes of persons, it must be remembered that an individual within the scope of the definition *did* commit the crime as a principal in the first degree. The evil or harm with which the legislature was concerned has thus occurred, and the purposes of the criminal law (see § 1.5) are well served by also holding accountable those persons not covered by the statute who assisted in bringing about the proscribed result.

There are, however, some exceptions to the general principle that a person who assists or encourages a crime is also guilty as an accomplice. For one, the victim of the crime may not be held as an accomplice even though his conduct in a significant sense has assisted in the commission of the crime. "The businessman who yields to the extortion of a racketeer, the parent who pays ransom to the kidnapper, may be unwise or even may be thought immoral; to view them as involved in the commission of the crime confounds the policy embodied in the prohibition." Where the statute in question was enacted for the protection of certain defined persons thought to be in need of special protection, it would clearly be contrary to the legislative purpose to impose accomplice liability upon such a person. Thus the consenting victim may not become a party to statutory rape or a violation of the Mann Act.

Another exception is where the crime is so defined that participation by another is inevitably incident to its commission. It is justified on the ground that the legislature, by specifying the kind of individual who was guilty when involved in a transaction necessarily involving two or more parties, must have intended to leave the participation by the others unpunished. A secondary consideration, equally applicable to the victim exception, is that if the law were otherwise convictions would be more difficult to obtain in those jurisdictions requiring corroboration of an accomplice's testimony. Thus, under this exception one having intercourse with a prostitute is not liable as a party to the crime of prostitution, a purchaser is not a party to the crime of illegal sale, an unmarried man is not guilty as a party to the crime of adultery where the legislature has only specified punishment for the married participant, and a female welfare recipient is not guilty as a party to a male's offense of receiving subsistence from such a person.

Model Penal Code § 2.06(6) gives express recognition to these two exceptions to accomplice liability, as do many of the recent recodifications.

§ 12.4 Vicarious Liability

We now consider another type of criminal liability, called vicarious liability, whereby the defendant, generally one conducting a business, is made liable, though without personal fault, for the bad conduct of someone else, generally his employee. Vicarious liability must be distinguished from accomplice liability, discussed in the previous sections (see §§ 12.1–12.3), for the latter requires that the defendant must have aided or abetted the crime and that such action be accompanied by appropriate mental fault. Vicarious liability must also be distinguished from strict liability, for there is a clear and important difference between these two types of liability without fault, although courts have not always distinguished carefully between the two. With strict liability (see § 4.5), there must be a showing that the defendant personally engaged in the necessary acts or omissions; only the requirement of mental fault is dispensed with altogether. By contrast, with vicarious liability it is the need for a personal *actus reus* that is dispensed with, and there remains the need for whatever mental fault the law requires on the part of the employee. It is common, however, for a vicarious liability statute to also impose strict liability; in such an instance, there is no need to prove an act or omission by the defendant-employer (one by his employee will do), and there is no need to prove mental fault by anyone.

In the area of the civil law we are quite used to vicarious responsibility (the doctrine of respondeat superior), although in criminal law it is a departure from the basic premise of criminal justice that crime requires personal fault (once again, *actus facit reum nisi mens sit rea*). Said one court: "The distinction between respondeat superior in tort law and its application to the criminal law is obvious. In tort law, the doctrine is employed for the purpose of settling the incidence of loss upon the party who can best bear such loss. But the criminal law is supported by totally different concepts. We impose penal treatment upon those who injure or menace social interest, partly in order to reform, partly to prevent the continuation of the anti-social activity and partly to deter others. If a defendant has personally lived up to the social standards of the criminal law and has not menaced or injured anyone, why impose penal treatment?" The answer, as given by the court itself, is that some crimes represent a use of the machinery of criminal justice to impose strict standards of performance on certain business activities which, if improperly conducted, pose a danger to the public. However, it is one thing to hold that the faultless employer ought to pay for the damage which his employee (often impecunious) inflicts upon third persons in the course of furthering his employer's business; it is much more drastic to visit criminal punishment and moral condemnation upon the employer who is innocent of any personal fault.

(a) Common Law Crimes. The common law did not impose criminal liability upon a faultless employer for the unauthorized criminal conduct of his employee except in two isolated instances: nuisance and libel. An employer was criminally liable for the criminal nuisances and libels of his employees though he did not know of or authorize the conduct and may have even forbidden it. In other areas of conduct constituting common law crimes the employer is not liable for what the employee did without his knowledge or authorization, and even the two exceptions of nuisance and libel have seldom received recognition in this country.

(b) Statutory Crimes—Interpretation. Because vicarious liability "cannot be created by the courts" but can only "be delineated by statute," the question as to statutory offenses is whether the language of the statute manifests a legislative intent to impose such liability. Some criminal statutes, generally containing no language of fault, specifically impose criminal liability upon the employer for the bad conduct of his employee—e.g., "whoever, by himself or by his agent, sells articles at short weight shall be punished by * * *," or "whoever sells liquor to a minor is punishable by * * * and any sale by an employee shall be deemed the act of the employer as well as the act of the employee." Such statutes (generally carrying a misdemeanor penalty) are naturally construed to impose vicarious liability upon the employer though he expressly forbade his employee to engage in the forbidden conduct.

Although virtually all of the statutes expressly imposing vicarious liability do so only in the context of an employer-employee relationship, this is not inevitably the case. There are, for example, statutes that hold the registered owners of vehicles vicariously liable for parking and similar violations involving their vehicles. Occasionally a statute has attempted to impose vicarious liability upon parents for the conduct of their children.

Often statutes are not that specific as to whether or not they impose vicarious liability. In such a case, if the statutory crime is worded in language requiring some type of fault ("knowingly," "wilfully," "with intent to," etc.), then it is the rule that the employer must personally know or be wilful or have the requisite intention to be liable for the criminal conduct of his employee; even though the latter is acting to further his employer's business, the employer is not criminally liable unless he knew of or authorized that action. That is, if the statute requires mental fault, it will not be presumed that the legislature intended that the fault of the employee should suffice for conviction of the employer.

In between the statutes specifically requiring fault and others specifically imposing criminal liability on the employer for his employee's conduct fall those statutes that neither contain fault-words nor contain any expression that the conduct of the employee makes the employer liable. Thus a statute may simply state that "whoever employs children under 14 in a factory is guilty of a misdemeanor." The factory owner instructs his manager not to employ children under 14, but the manager disregards the instruction and does so. Is the owner liable? The question is one of construction of the statute, and is likely to be approached in much the same way as the question of whether statutes empty of language of fault are to be construed to impose strict liability (see § 4.5). If the authorized punishment is light—a fine or perhaps a short imprisonment—the statute is likely to be construed to impose vicarious liability on a faultless employer. But if the permitted punishment is severe—a felony or a serious misdemeanor—the statute is not apt to be so construed in the absence of an express provision for vicarious responsibility. A possible intermediate view is to construe the statute as requiring the employer's fault, but to impose upon him the burden of showing lack of fault rather than to impose upon the prosecution the burden of showing the employer's knowledge or approval of the employee's conduct.

In construing statutes of this type, courts often jump to the unwarranted conclusion that a statute which imposes strict liability must of necessity also impose vicarious liability. A particularly outrageous example is afforded by the Supreme Court's decision in *U.S. v. Dotterweich* (1943), which upheld the conviction of the president of a company that shipped misbranded or adulterated products in interstate commerce notwithstanding the fact that he had nothing to do with the shipment. The case presented two distinct issues as to the meaning of the applicable statute, the Food, Drug, and Cosmetic Act: (1) whether whoever was responsible for the shipment could be held criminally liable even without mental fault (the issue of strict liability); and (2) whether the president of the company could be held criminally liable, notwithstanding his own lack of connection with the shipment (the issue of vicarious liability). The Court assumed an affirmative answer on the first issue without careful examination of this premise, and then merely concluded that because the liability was strict it was also vicarious.

There is no basis for assuming that vicarious liability necessarily follows from strict liability. That is, even when it is correctly decided that the legislature has intended to permit conviction of the actor even when he is without mental fault, this result does not compel the conclusion that the legislature must have also intended that it be possible to convict someone else (the actor's employer) as well. It is true, of course, that when strict liability is imposed upon the employee, there is no greater severity in holding the employer liable than in holding the employee liable, but this is hardly conclusive on the issue of legislative intent, which may vary depending upon the subject matter. For example, in enacting a child labor law the legislature might well impose strict liability on hiring agents in the hope of inducing them to obtain clear proof of a person's age prior to hiring that person, but yet might not wish to hold absent employers for all mistakes by their hiring agents. On the other hand, when the legislature enacts criminal statutes dealing with the sale of dangerous articles, it might well wish to impose strict liability and also to bar those engaged in such hazardous enterprises from escaping liability by doing business through others.

There is likewise no basis for assuming that vicarious liability upon individuals follows from the fact that enterprise liability (see § 12.5) exists with respect to the offense in question. Instructive is

People v. Byrne (1991), where defendant and his brother were the president and secretary-treasurer, respectively, of a corporation in which each owned 50% of the shares. The defendant, as an individual, was prosecuted on a vicarious liability theory because his brother sold alcoholic beverages to a minor at the tavern operated by the corporation. The prosecution claimed the applicable law should be interpreted as imposing such vicarious liability because it clearly authorized prosecution of the corporation, but the court rejected this contention:

> It is true that when a corporation is prosecuted, the factual predicate for its liability is, invariably, the conduct of someone else, namely its agents or employees. However, since corporations, which are legal fictions, can operate only through their designated agents and employees, the acts of the latter are, in a sense, the acts of the corporation as well. Thus, when a corporation is held criminally liable because it is a "person" under Alcoholic Beverage Control Law § 3(22), it is, in reality, being made to answer for its *own* acts. Such a theory of liability is a far cry from one involving *true* vicarious liability, in which, by virtue of the parties' relationship, the conduct of one individual is artificially imputed to another who "has played no part in it [and] has done nothing whatever to aid or encourage it."

A final type of statute punishes those who "permit" or "allow" or "suffer" some forbidden thing to be done—e.g., "one who sells or permits to be sold intoxicating liquors to a minor is punishable by * * *." The better view is that an employer does not "allow" or "permit" his employee to do an act unless he knows of or authorizes it, or at least is reckless in failing to know of it, but some courts have construed such language so as to impose upon the employer liability without fault on account of the act of the employee.

(c) Constitutionality. Statutes imposing criminal liability upon the innocent employer for the illegal conduct of his employee are generally upheld as constitutional. The assumption is that it "is not too onerous a burden" to require the employer to "control and supervise his employees." The Supreme Court has never passed directly upon the constitutional limits of vicarious liability, but it is noteworthy that in *U.S. v. Park* (1975) the Court upheld the imposition of liability upon a corporation president who had a "responsible relation" to the corporate conduct that was criminal and who did not show he was "powerless" to prevent the violation.

Park has been viewed by lower courts as relevant to the constitutional issue. Consistent with *Park* are those cases that uphold the vicarious liability provision by reading in an "escape valve" regarding certain violations clearly beyond the defendant's control, as where a statute making the owner of a car liable for all parking violations involving that vehicle is construed as not applicable if the car was stolen. By the same token, cases holding the imposition of vicarious liability unconstitutional typically stress that liability is imposed even as to persons over whom the defendant has no control or even if the defendant had done everything within his power to prevent the violation. Apparently a "responsible relation" can be grounded in an employment or bailment relationship, and perhaps a parent-child relationship.

The Pennsylvania case of *Commonwealth v. Koczwara* (1959) imposes another quite proper limitation even when vicarious liability is imposed for conduct by the defendant's employee. Koczwara, a tavern owner, was convicted of violating the liquor code on the basis of acts committed by his bartender that occurred in his absence and without his knowledge or consent. As a second offender, he received the mandatory penalty of a $500 fine and three months in jail. The court held that punishment by imprisonment in such circumstances would be a denial of due process under the state constitution. "It would be unthinkable to impose vicarious criminal responsibility in cases involving true crimes. Although to hold a principal criminally liable might possibly be an effective means of enforcing law and order, it would do violence to our more sophisticated modern-day concepts of justice. * * * A man's *liberty* cannot rest on so frail a reed as whether his employee will commit a mistake in judgment."

The distinction drawn by the court between a fine and imprisonment is an appropriate one. To the extent that vicarious liability can be justified in the criminal law, it should not be utilized to bring about the type of moral condemnation that is implicit when a sentence of imprisonment is imposed. On the other hand, imposition of a fine is consistent with the rationale behind vicarious criminal liability. Vicarious liability is imposed because of the nature and inherent danger of certain business activities and the difficulties of establishing actual fault in the operation of such businesses. A fine, unlike imprisonment, is less personal and is more properly viewed as a penalty on the business enterprise.

(d) Pros and Cons of Vicarious–Liability Crimes. The reasons for enacting vicarious-liability statutory crimes, imposing liability upon innocent and careful employers for the conduct of their employees acting within the scope of their employers' business, are the same as those underlying strict-liability crimes (see § 4.5(c)). That the employer knew of or authorized the employee's conduct is sometimes difficult to prove, so the legislature makes the matters of knowledge and authorization irrelevant. The number of prosecutions to be expected may be such that the legislature undertakes to relieve the prosecution of the time-consuming task of proving the employer's knowledge or authority. Perhaps the legislature hopes that the prosecuting officials will use the statute only against persons who probably did know of or authorize the employee's conduct in question. Perhaps too vicarious-liability crimes tend to make employers more careful in the selection and supervision of their employees than they otherwise would be.

Yet, it must be recognized that the imposition of criminal liability for faultless conduct is contrary to the basic Anglo–American premise of criminal justice that crime requires personal fault on the part of the accused. Perhaps the answer should be the same as the answer proposed in the case of strict-liability crimes: it is proper for the legislature to single out some special areas of human activity and impose vicarious liability on employers who are without personal fault, but the matter should not be called a "crime" and the punishment should not include more than a fine or forfeiture or other civil penalty; that is, it should not include imprisonment. As the law now stands, however, in almost all jurisdictions imprisonment and the word "criminal" may be visited upon perfectly innocent employers for the sins of their employees.

If the problem is essentially one of the difficulty in proving actual fault by the person being held vicariously liable, then any assessment of the vicarious liability solution must take into account alternative means of dealing with that problem. One that has sometimes been utilized is adoption of a statutory inference or presumption which has the effect of imposing some kind of burden on the defendant to prove lack of knowledge or authorization regarding the other person's conduct. Of course, there are constitutional limits upon what may be done along these lines (see § 3.4), and some but not all of these statutes have been held unconstitutional. Indeed, it is sometimes said that imposition of vicarious liability is the "safe" alternative, to be preferred over burden-shifting statutes. But even if this is so, the vicarious liability need not be unlimited. Consistent with the constitutional power to characterize certain matters as affirmative defenses to be proved by the defendant (see § 1.8(c)), a vicarious liability statute might allow a defendant to avoid conviction by proving that he had exercised due diligence to prevent the crime.

§ 12.5 Enterprise Liability

Contrary to the early common law view, it is now generally conceded that a corporation may be held criminally liable for conduct performed by an agent of the corporation acting in its behalf within the scope of his employment. Under the better view, called the "superior agent" rule, corporate criminal liability for

other than strict-liability regulatory offenses is limited to situations
in which the conduct is performed or participated in by the board of
directors or a high managerial agent. Partnerships and unincorporated associations may also be held criminally liable when so
provided by statute, which is frequently the case as to regulatory
offenses.

Enterprise officers and employees are not ordinarily held personally liable for crimes of the enterprise or of their subordinates
except under usual principles of accountability. If the individual
personally engaged in the criminal conduct or directed or permitted
its commission, it is no defense that the offense was performed on
behalf of the enterprise.

(a) Corporations. The early common law view was that a
corporation could not be guilty of a crime: it had no mind, and thus
was incapable of the criminal intent then required for all crimes; it
had no body, and thus could not be imprisoned. This view has
changed with the growth and development of the corporate entity
in the modern business world, and today it is almost universally
conceded that a corporation may be criminally liable for actions or
omissions of its agents in its behalf. It is still true, of course, that a
corporation cannot be imprisoned, but a variety of other sanctions
have been developed.

Movement away from the old common law view began, as
might be expected, with strict liability welfare offenses, for there no
mental state was required and the penalty (a fine) was such that it
could be imposed upon a corporation. Initially, corporations were
prosecuted only for acts of nonfeasance. The case for corporate
criminal liability was strongest in such instances, for the public
duty imposed by law (e.g., to keep a railroad bridge in repair)
seemed just as applicable to corporations as to others, and no
individual corporate employee could be said to be in breach of this
duty. This reasoning led some courts to rule that a corporation
could not be convicted for misfeasance, but this view has not
prevailed. Rather, courts abandoned the nonfeasance-misfeasance
distinction on two grounds: (1) the distinction often proved to be
more a matter of form than of substance, in that the same offense
often could be just as easily characterized as a failure to act (e.g.,
failure to construct a safe bridge) as an act (e.g., construction of a
bridge in an unsafe manner); and (2) it seemed appropriate to
punish for misfeasance when the mischief aimed at by the penal
statute could just as easily be produced by a corporation.

Once corporations were subjected to criminal prosecution for
the *acts* of their agents, it became apparent that a form of vicarious
liability was involved. But the Supreme Court decided in *New York
Cent. & H.R.R. v. U.S.* (1909) that constitutionally "the act of

agent, while exercising the authority delegated to him * * * may be controlled, in the interest of public policy, by imputing his act to his employer and imposing penalties upon the corporation for which he is acting." This language has been frequently relied upon in both federal and state cases, so that now it is said to be "familiar law that a substantive offense committed by a corporate employee in the scope of his employment will be imputed to the corporation." That language, it should be noted, makes no distinction between imputing acts and mental state, reflecting the fact that courts have now concluded that a corporate agent may also supply the intent or other mental state needed for conviction of a corporation. As one court noted, it is "as easy and logical to ascribe to a corporation an evil mind as it is to impute to it a sense of contractual obligation."

It does not necessarily follow, of course, that vicarious corporate liability exists with respect to all crimes. For one thing, if the statute only provides for the punishment of death or imprisonment, then a corporation is not subject to prosecution under it because of the impossibility of imposing such a sentence upon a corporation. This problem is often obviated in modern codes by a special provision that permits fines on corporations in fixed amounts for offenses not otherwise carrying such a penalty, and such statutes are not invalid as discriminatory where part of the punishment provided for individuals could not be applied to corporations. Another limitation expressed in dicta in earlier cases is that some crimes, such as bigamy, perjury, rape or murder, are inherently human and thus not subject to commission by a corporation. It is now established that a corporation may be guilty of manslaughter, and it has been persuasively argued that there "is no logical reason why a corporation should not equally be able to incur criminal liability for murder."

Sometimes the language of the statute must be examined in order to determine whether the legislature intended the statute also to apply to corporations. For example, it has occasionally been held that a statutory definition of homicide as "the killing of one human being by the act, procurement or omission of another" is inapplicable to a corporation because the word "another" clearly means another human being, although it seems more logical to say that a corporation can (indeed, only can) kill one human by the act of another human. The word "person" is common in criminal statutes, and is sometimes defined in a general provision as including corporations unless a contrary legislative intention clearly appears in the statute. In the absence of such a statutory definition, the general rule followed today by courts is that "the word 'person' in a penal statute which is intended to inhibit an act, means 'person in law' (that is, an artificial as well as a natural person), and therefore includes corporations, if they are within the spirit and purpose of the statute." The same approach has been utilized in finding that the words "any tenant," "everyone," "whoever," and "every owner" may, in the proper context, include corporations. (However, it is generally assumed that corporate liability does not extent to governmental entities absent quite specific legislative language indicating otherwise.)

(b) Corporate Liability: Policy Considerations. It must be emphasized again that corporate criminal liability is a form of vicarious liability. Indeed, it sometimes involves what has been termed "vicarious liability twice removed," in that the shareholders may suffer for the criminal acts of the corporate management (without regard to the shareholders' opportunity to control the management) and also for those of lesser employees (without regard to the nature of the management's efforts to control these employees). This is a substantial departure from the ordinary rule that a principal is not answerable criminally for the acts of his agent without the principal's authorization, consent or knowledge, and thus corporate criminal liability continues to be a matter of vigorous debate.

The following arguments have been made in favor of corporate criminal liability: (1) that the corporate business entity is so common that such liability is necessary to effectuate regulatory policy; (2) that the imposition of sanctions upon the stockholders will prompt them to "see that the corporate business is so conducted as not to injure others or infringe upon public right and good order"; (3) that often no one other than the corporation could be convicted, either because the offense is an omission of a duty imposed only on the corporation, or because "the division of responsibility within a corporation is so great that it is difficult to fix on an individual"; (4) that, even when an individual agent could be convicted, it may be unjust to single out one person for substantial punishment when the offense resulted from habits common to the organization as a whole; (5) that the fines should be borne by those who received the fruits of the illegal enterprise so as to prevent unjust enrichment; (6) that proceeding against the corporation (rather than merely against an individual) serves to link the offense with the corporation in the public mind; and (7) that vicarious liability is less severe here than if imposed upon a human principal, as the individual shareholders escape the opprobrium and incidental disabilities of a personal indictment or conviction and their loss is limited to the equity held in the corporation.

A number of the above contentions have been challenged with these counter-arguments: (1) that the imposition of a criminal fine on the corporation is often ineffective as a profit-diminishing sanction, in that the economic cost of the fine may be "passed on" to the consumer by means of higher prices or rates; (2) that in the "endocratic" corporation (the large publicly-held corporation whose stock is scattered in small fractions among thousands of stockholders) the stockholders simply cannot control the management, and thus should not be penalized for their failure to do so; (3) that the availability of the corporation as a defendant provides a convenient "scapegoat" whereby corporate agents engaged in the wrongdoing escape the personal criminal liability which would be a greater deterrent; (4) that depriving wrongdoers of their ill-gotten gains is not a function of the criminal law, and that in any event fines are usually unrelated to the gains and may penalize stockholders other than those who profited from the illegal activity; and (5) that the criminal prosecutions of corporations are not adequately reported to the public to result in damage to the "corporate image."

Unfortunately, most of the court decisions concerning vicarious corporate criminal liability do not involve an assessment of these arguments. Rather, the tort principle of *respondeat superior* is applied without question, so that the crimes of any employee—no matter what his position in the corporate hierarchy—become the crimes of the corporation. And if the crimes require "intent," "knowledge," or some other mental state, it is often said that such a mental state by "subordinate, even menial, employees" suffices.

(c) Corporate Liability: Limitations. Although it is unwise to assume that vicarious liability always automatically follows from strict liability (see § 12.4), it is fair to say that generally the imposition of criminal liability on corporations for acts of any and all employees that constitute violations of strict-liability regulatory offenses is sound. For the most part, these statutes may be said to impose a duty upon the corporation not to act in such a way as to endanger the health, safety or welfare of the general public, and thus the corporation is quite properly held for such acts by any employee. But, if the crime is one for which mens rea is required, should the mental state of any corporate employee suffice? No, it has been forcefully argued; the mind or brain of the corporation consists only of "those officers, whether elected or appointed, who direct, supervise and manage the corporation within its business sphere and policy-wise, the 'inner circle.' " Under this approach, for example, the intent to steal by a minor corporate employee in taking another's property within the scope of his employment and in behalf of the corporation would not constitute the requisite corporate mens rea, and thus the corporation would not be guilty of larceny.

This is essentially the position taken in the Model Penal Code and reflected (to some degree at least) in several modern recodifications. Except when the offense consists of an omission to discharge a specific duty of affirmative performance imposed on the corporation by law, or the offense is a violation or is defined by a statute outside the Code in which a legislative purpose to impose liability on corporations plainly appears, under Model Penal Code § 2.07(1)(c) a corporation may be convicted of the commission of an offense only if it was "authorized, requested, commanded, performed or recklessly tolerated by the board of directors or by a high managerial agent acting in behalf of the corporation within the scope of his office or employment." Many modern recodifications contain a provision along these lines. "High managerial agent" is defined in Code § 2.07(4)(c) as "an officer of a corporation or * * * any other agent of a corporation * * * having duties of such responsibility that his conduct may fairly be assumed to represent the policy of the corporation." Some modern codes contain such a definition, while others include a broader definition encompassing both those who have responsibility as to the formulation of policy and those who supervise in a managerial capacity. Absent such legislation, courts sometimes take a somewhat broader approach encompassing at least some corporate employees below the supervisory level.

When corporate liability is possible because the offense is a violation or is defined by a statute plainly so providing, then under Model Penal Code § 2.07(5) "it shall be a defense if the defendant proves by a preponderance of evidence that the high managerial agent having supervisory responsibility over the subject matter of the offense employed due diligence to prevent its commission." This latter provision, to be found in only a small number of modern recodifications, shifts the presumption of *mens rea,* but may be justified on the ground that the prosecution's normal burden of proof would frustrate enforcement of laws specifically applicable to corporations.

The Model Penal Code provision is generally consistent with those cases adopting the so-called "superior agent" rule. Under this rule, corporate criminal liability (except for strict liability offenses) is limited to situations in which the criminal conduct is performed or participated in by corporate agents sufficiently high in the hierarchy to make it reasonable to assume that their acts reflect the policy of the corporate body. Most of these cases assume it would not be necessary for the prosecution to prove the necessary corporate *mens rea;* rather the corporation could rebut the presumption of responsibility by showing it had taken adequate precautions against its commission.

Another limitation on vicarious corporate criminal liability should be re-emphasized here, for (unlike the "superior agent" rule) it is universally accepted: except where the law defining the offense specifically provides otherwise, the conduct giving rise to corporate liability must be "performed by an agent of the corporation acting in behalf of the corporation within the scope of his office or employment." However, this does not mean that a corporation can escape liability merely by contending that criminal acts are "ultra vires" (beyond the power of the corporation, as defined by its charter or act of incorporation), that the agents acts were not expressly authorized, or that the agent acted contrary to instructions. The criminal act must be directly related to the performance of the duties that the officer or agent has the broad authority to perform, and must be done with the "intention to perform it as a part of or incident to a service on account of which he is employed." It is not necessary that the criminal acts actually benefit the corporation, but an agent's acts are not "in behalf of the corporation" if undertaken solely to advance the agent's own interests or interests of parties other than the corporate employer. "Thus the taking in or paying out of money by a bank teller, while certainly one of his regular functions, would hardly cast the corporation for criminal liability if in such 'handling' the faithless employee was pocketing the funds as an embezzler or handing them over to a confederate under some ruse."

(d) Partnerships and Other Unincorporated Associations. Generally, it may be said that the fact that the defendant is a partner in a business enterprise has no bearing on the question of whether he is accountable for the criminal conduct of others. The usual rules of accountability apply (see §§ 12.1–12.3), and thus a partner is not by virtue of his status liable for the crimes of his co-partners or employees of the partnership, although he is liable for such crimes when he has authorized or participated in them.

Of course, a particular criminal statute may be construed to impose vicarious liability on a partner, as an individual, for crimes committed by his co-partners or partnership employees. When the statute in question does not do so explicitly, the problem of determining the actual meaning of the statute is not unlike that discussed earlier (see § 12.4(b)). Once again, courts have a tendency to find that a statute imposes vicarious liability because it imposes strict liability, so that it is sometimes said that partners are liable for those crimes committed in the operation of the business which do not require proof of any mental state. However, for the reasons stated earlier (see § 12.4), vicarious liability should not automatically follow from strict liability; determination of legislative intent requires that the two questions (i.e., does the statute impose liability on the actor without requiring mental fault; does the statute impose liability on others) be separately considered. Under this approach, it may nonetheless be concluded that a given strict liability statute also makes partners vicariously liable, as where it imposes a nondelegable duty on the business or where it appears that a contrary result would frustrate the policy behind the statute.

What, then, of criminal liability of the *partnership* as a business enterprise, as distinguished from the several partners as individuals? In the absence of a statute imposing vicarious liability, it is clear that the partnership is not criminally liable for the crimes of individual partners or employees of the partnership. Even with a statute that does impose vicarious liability, the liability is usually said to be that of the partners as individuals rather than the partnership as an entity. This is because of the traditional view that a partnership has no legal existence apart from its several individual partners, so that only the partners as individuals are subject to criminal proceedings. There is, however, a movement away from this view, called the aggregate theory of partnership, toward the entity theory, under which the partnership can sue and be sued in its own name. In a jurisdiction that has adopted the entity theory, a court might rule that under a statute providing for vicarious liability for certain business crimes (but making no specific reference to liability of partnerships), prosecution could be brought against the partnership.

Even where the entity theory has not been adopted, there are two situations in which prosecution of the partnership is possible. One is where the offense consists of an omission to perform some act that the partnership (as opposed to the partners, as individuals) is required by law to perform. The other is where the statute in question expressly provides for liability of the partnership for conduct performed in its behalf, although whether the legislature intended such a result in face of the prevailing aggregate theory may present a difficult issue. The leading case is *U.S. v. A & P Trucking Co.* (1958), involving prosecution of partnerships for "knowingly" violating certain Interstate Commerce Commission regulations and "knowingly and willfully" violating provisions of the Motor Carrier Act. The latter Act refers to "any person," but "person" is defined therein to mean "any individual, firm, copartnership, corporation, company, association, or joint-stock association." The statute concerning the violation of ICC regulations refers to "whoever," but a separate enactment dealing with the construction of statutes provides that "in determining the meaning of any Act of Congress, unless the context indicates otherwise— * * * the words 'person' and 'whoever' include corporations, companies, associations, firms, partnerships, societies, and joint stock companies, as well as individuals." On the basis of these provisions, a majority of the Court concluded that partnerships could be prosecuted for the violations in question. Congress could hardly have intended otherwise, the majority argued, as both enactments have as their purpose compliance by motor carriers with safety and other requirements, and in effectuating this policy it could hardly make any difference what kind of business form is used by the carrier. Moreover, the words "knowingly" and "willfully" in the statutes do not indicate to the contrary; partnerships cannot so act, but neither can corporations, and as to both Congress must have intended to deter such violations by providing for the imposition of monetary sanctions on the business enterprise.

As a matter of policy, it would appear that the kind of vicarious liability involved in the *A & P Trucking* case is generally preferable to vicarious liability of the partners as individuals. For one thing, it ensures that vicarious liability will not be utilized to impose the sanction of imprisonment, for the partnership can only be fined even if the statute in question also includes imprisonment as a sanction generally available. For another, prosecution of the partnership instead of the partners protects the partners, as individuals, from acquiring criminal status and the disabilities or legal disadvantages that might flow from conviction of a crime.

Given the reasoning in *A & P Trucking*, should that case be deemed equally applicable to all kinds of partnerships? One question that has arisen is whether the case also extends to limited partnerships, which the courts have answered in the affirmative, reasoning that otherwise limited partnerships could profit from criminality and yet violate the law with impunity. Another question is whether criminal prosecution of professional partnerships (e.g., of doctors or lawyers) is also justified on the same basis. Such partnerships are sometimes criminally prosecuted, and in support it is contended (i) that even "assuming that various partners may go about their professions in an independent fashion, that does not make general oversight impossible or any more difficult than in any other business," (ii) that "the fact that certain professions are governed by a code of ethics enforced by a board of overseers" is not "sufficient to distinguish a professional partnership from a strictly commercial partnership," and (iii) that, indeed, "the factors underlying traditional corporate and partnership criminal liability appear particularly applicable in the professional setting." The contrary argument is that in *A & P Trucking* and similar cases "the enterprises were hierarchical in structure and their members were focused on a single business purpose," neither of which is true of professional partnerships, meaning that "it is unlikely that the goals sought through extension of criminal liability to businesses can be achieved" by criminal prosecution of such partnerships.

Generally, what has been said above about partnerships is true of the other forms of unincorporated associations. Vicarious liability on the individual members thereof or on the business entity does not exist in the absence of a statute providing to the contrary. However, as illustrated by the statutes in the *A & P Trucking* case, it is quite common for regulatory legislation on both the federal and state level to provide for the application of criminal penalties to a variety of unincorporated groups. Where the offense in question is not of the strict liability variety, the better view is that the unincorporated association (as well as the corporation) should ordinarily be entitled to prove by way of defense that the appropriate supervisory official exercised due diligence to prevent its commission. Finally, it should be kept in mind that the fact vicarious liability has been imposed upon an unincorporated association in no way affects the liability of the individual who actually performed the criminal acts with any required mental fault.

(e) Corporate Officers and Employees. A corporate agent who engages in criminal conduct is personally liable notwithstanding the fact that he acted in behalf of the corporation within the scope of his office. Certain problems in holding the corporate employee liable have sometimes arisen, but these can be easily solved by sound drafting. For example, when the circumstances are such that the employee is an accessory to the crime committed by the corporation as a principal, it has been held that the accessory may not be subjected to greater liability than the principal. This means that if the offense does not allow for imposition of a fine, then the corporation cannot be held criminally liable and the employee-accessory cannot either. And if the offense does allow for a fine and imprisonment, the employee-accessory may only be fined because that is the only sanction which may be imposed upon the corporation. Model Penal Code § 2.07(6) overcomes these difficulties, as do most of the modern recodifications.

An officer of a corporation is not personally liable for the crimes of the corporation or of corporate employees merely by virtue of the fact that he is an officer. Rather, the usual principles of accountability ordinarily apply, so that it must be shown that the criminal acts were done by his direction or with his permission. The question of who, if anyone, should be held personally liable for the strict-liability criminal omissions of the corporation has been particularly troublesome. Under existing law, the corporate officer generally escapes individual liability even though he is under an affirmative obligation to perform the duty in behalf of the corporation. The Model Penal Code § 2.07(6)(b) position is that the corporate agent having "primary responsibility for the discharge of the duty" imposed by law on the corporation is accountable for "a reckless omission to perform the required act to the same extent as if the duty were imposed by law directly upon himself." A few of the modern recodifications contain such a provision.

The Supreme Court has on two occasions confronted the question of when a corporate officer may be held criminally liable because of the commission of a public welfare type of offense by the corporation. *U.S. v. Dotterweich* (1943) involved a prosecution of a corporation and defendant, its president and general manager, for two interstate shipments of misbranded and adulterated drugs. Company employees had merely repackaged drugs received from the manufacturer and sent them out in response to an order from a doctor, and defendant had no personal connection with either shipment. The Supreme Court affirmed Dotterweich's conviction, holding that all persons having a "responsible share in the furtherance of the transaction which the statute outlaws" violate the Federal Food, Drug and Cosmetic Act. Stressing that the statute was enacted as a regulatory measure to protect public health and welfare and was of the strict liability type, the *Dotterweich* majority concluded it "puts the burden of acting at hazard upon a person otherwise innocent but standing in responsible relation to a public danger." Despite the criticism of the four dissenters "that guilt is personal and that it ought not lightly be imputed to a citizen who, like the respondent, has no evil intention or consciousness of wrongdoing," the majority concluded there was sufficient evidence to hold Dotterweich responsible for the shipment. But the precise meaning of *Dotterweich* was, at best, unclear; the Court never specified what evidence was decisive and declined to elaborate upon the "responsible relation" test, which was simply left to "the good sense of prosecutors, the wise guidance of trial judges, and the ultimate judgment of juries." Notwithstanding reference in *Dotterweich* to an aiding-and-abetting theory, lower courts found the requisite "responsible relation" to be present absent any evidence the charged official participated in the illegal transaction or was even present at the time it occurred.

In *U.S. v. Park* (1975), arising under the same Act, the corporation, a national retail food chain, and Park, president and chief executive officer of the corporation, were charged with causing food to be held in a warehouse where it was exposed to rodents and thereby became contaminated. Although the three dissenters in *Park* found the trial judge's instruction to the jury to find Park guilty if he "had a responsible relation to the situation" to be "nothing more than a tautology," the majority deemed this *Dotterweich*-style instruction sufficient. But once again the Court did not indicate just what evidence sufficed to show the requisite "responsible relation." At trial there had been testimony that Park was "responsible for the entire operation of the company," including providing sanitary conditions, but that he had delegated "normal operating duties," including sanitation, to trusted subordinates. Park had earlier received notice of unsanitary conditions at another warehouse, but had been assured his subordinates had taken corrective action. The majority asserted that the prosecution "establishes a prima facie case when it introduces evidence sufficient to warrant a finding by the trier of the facts that the defendant had, by reason of his position in the corporation, responsibility and authority either to prevent in the first instance, or promptly to correct, the violation complained of, and that he failed to do so."

Does this mean that the *Dotterweich-Park* standard is one of absolute, strict liability upon the responsible corporate officials so that, for example, Park would be guilty of any contamination occurring at any of the corporation's 874 retail outlets or 16 warehouses? Apparently not. Though the *Park* majority did not agree with the view of the three dissenters that *Dotterweich* requires a showing the official "engaged in wrongful conduct amounting at least to common law negligence," the majority significantly did say that the "concept of 'responsible relationship' * * * imports some measure of blameworthiness." Moreover, the Court in *Park* also declared:

> The duty imposed by Congress on responsible corporate agents is, we emphasize, one that requires the highest standard of foresight and vigilance, but the Act, in its criminal aspect, does not require that which is objectively impossible. The theory upon which responsible corporate agents are held criminally accountable for "causing" violations of the Act permits a claim that a defendant was "powerless" to prevent or correct the violation to "be raised defensively at a trial on the merits." If such a claim is made, the defendant has the burden of coming forward with evidence, but this does not alter the Government's ultimate burden of proving beyond a reasonable doubt the defendant's guilt, including his power, in light of the duty imposed by the Act, to prevent or correct the prohibited condition.

Though this language is susceptible to various interpretations, it appears that "with the impossibility defense, the strict liability standard as applied to indirect actors becomes in practice a standard of extraordinary care." "Under this view, all that must be proved by the government is a deviation from that standard—something certainly less than common law negligence; it can be characterized as 'very slight' or 'slight' negligence, to be distinguished from 'ordinary' negligence." Application of *Park* by the lower courts generally squares with this standard-of-care interpretation of the case.

§ 12.6 Post–Crime Aid: Accessory After the Fact, Misprision and Compounding

At common law, one not himself a principal in the commission of a felony was an accessory after the fact if a completed felony had theretofore been committed by another; he knew of the commission of the felony by the other person; and he gave aid to the felon personally for the purpose of hindering the felon's apprehension, conviction, or punishment. Unlike the principal in the second degree and accessory before the fact, the accessory after the fact is generally not treated as a party to the felony nor subject to the same punishment prescribed for the felony.

Misprision of felony, consisting of concealment of a known felony by one who was not a principal or accessory before the fact to the felony, is no longer an offense in most jurisdictions. The offense of compounding crime consists of the receipt of some consideration in return for an agreement not to prosecute or inform on another who is known to have committed an offense.

(a) Accessory After the Fact. At common law accessories after the fact existed only in relation to felonies. When treason was committed, all such accessories were considered to be principals, although the situation may be otherwise in the United States because of the constitutional description of the elements of treason. In the absence of a specific statutory provision to the contrary, one does not become an accessory after the fact by giving aid to a misdemeanant.

There are three basic requirements that must be met to constitute one an accessory after the fact. The first of these is that a completed felony must have been committed. It is not enough that the aider had a mistaken belief that the other person committed a felony, nor is it sufficient that the person assisted had theretofore been accused of a felony. But if the felony has been committed prior to the aid, it is not also necessary that the felon have been already charged with the crime. Because the felony must be complete at the time the assistance is rendered, a person cannot be convicted as an accessory after the fact to a murder because of aid given after the murderer's acts but before the victim's death.

The second requirement is that the person giving aid must have known of the perpetration of the felony by the one he aids. Mere suspicion is not enough.

Finally, the aid must have been given to the felon personally for the purpose of hindering the felon's apprehension, conviction or punishment. Because the aid must be to the felon personally, one does not become an accessory after the fact by, for example, receiving and concealing what are known to be stolen goods. There must be, in the mind of the aider, the objective of impeding law enforcement, and thus it is not sufficient that the felon was actually aided if the assistance was given out of charity or for some similar motive.

As to what acts constitute the prohibited aid, some early writers seem to have assumed that any assistance would suffice. Blackstone, for example, asserted that "any assistance whatever given to the felon, to hinder his being apprehended, tried or suffering punishment, makes the assister an accessory." However, the mere failure to report the felony or to arrest the felon will not suffice. Illustrative of the acts that qualify, assuming the presence of the other requirements, are harboring and concealing the felon, aiding the felon in making his escape, concealing, destroying or altering evidence, inducing a witness to absent himself or to remain silent, giving false testimony at an official inquiry into the crime, and giving false information to the police in order to divert suspicion away from the felon. (Where, as is often true in modern legislation, certain types of aid are specified by statute, all of the foregoing may not suffice.)

A principal in either the first or second degree may not also become an accessory after the fact by his subsequent acts. However, it has been held that one who was only an accessory before the fact may also be an accessory after the fact. If one does not render aid or encouragement before or during the offense, although he was present at the offense, and later gives aid, he will be liable only as an accessory after the fact.

At common law, only one class was excused from liability for being accessories after the fact. Wives did not become accessories by aiding their husbands. No other relationship, including that of husband to wife, would suffice. But many states broadened the exemption to cover other close relatives. The exemption provisions range from those exculpating husbands, wives, parents, and children to broad exclusions of ascendants, descendants and even servants. Such broadening of the exemption is grounded in the assumption that it is unrealistic to expect persons to be deterred from giving aid to their close relations.

Originally, all principals and accessories were felons and thus all were punishable with death, although this was soon modified by granting accessories after the fact the benefit of clergy. Accessories after the fact were again subject to the same punishment as their principals when benefit of clergy became obsolete. This was later changed by statute in England so that one who renders aid after a crime is guilty of a separate, lesser offense. Almost all American jurisdictions prescribed penalties for the accessory after the fact without reference to the penalty attached to the principal offense.

This development whereby the accessory after the fact is dealt with in a distinct way is a most appropriate one and does not conflict at all with the modern tendency to abolish the distinctions between principals in the first degree, principals in the second degree, and accessories before the fact. The latter three types of offenders have all played a part in the commission of the crime and are quite appropriately held accountable for its commission. The accessory after the fact, on the other hand, had no part in causing the crime; his offense is instead that of interfering with the processes of justice and is best dealt with in those terms.

Because the original view was that one who helped a felon avoid justice was an accomplice in the felony (see § 12.1(d)), the procedural problems described earlier concerning the accessory before the fact also existed with respect to the accessory after the fact. Most significant of these problems was that an accessory after the fact could not be tried until after the principal was found guilty. This meant that the accessory was immune from prosecution if the principal had been acquitted or had not been prosecuted because of his death or escape. But most jurisdictions now only require that the fact of the completed felony be proved in the trial of the accessory after the fact.

This is not to suggest that all of the procedural reforms concerning the law of parties to crime are or should be equally applicable to the accessory after the fact. Unlike the principals in the first and second degree and the accessory before the fact, he has not actually had a part in causing the crime. Thus, while it is now generally accepted that a defendant may be charged as if a principal and convicted on proof that he aided another, a conviction as an accessory after the fact cannot be sustained upon an indictment charging the principal crime. This is as it should be, for a charge alleging the defendant's guilt of the principal crime only places him on notice that he must defend against accountability for the crime as a principal or accessory before the fact, not that he must be prepared to meet evidence that he aided the perpetrator after the crime had been committed.

Today, the accessory after the fact situation is dealt with by statute in most jurisdictions. Even in states with modern recodifications, the "accessory after the fact" terminology is still occasionally used. But in the great majority of these states the offense is characterized as "hindering" apprehension or prosecution, or is otherwise described to reflect its true character as a crime involving interference with the processes of government. Most of these statutes cover aid to both felons and misdemeanants, although several are limited to those who aid felons.

As for the required mental state, virtually all of the statutes in the modern recodifications substantially conform to the Model Penal Code § 242.3 approach by requiring an intent or purpose to hinder apprehension, prosecution, conviction or punishment. In a few states, however, the mental element has been broadened to include the situation in which the intent is "to assist a person in profiting or benefitting from the commission" of a felony or any crime. One significant aspect of the common intent-to-hinder formulation is that it can usually be construed to "have dispensed with the necessity that it be shown that the putative offender actually committed a crime and that the person rendering assistance was aware of that fact." But some of these statutes adhere to the common law approach by requiring that the defendant have known of the guilt of the person aided, and some others appear to require that such guilt in fact exist. In contrast to these are a few other provisions expressly stating that it is sufficient the defendant believed or reasonably believed the person aided was guilty.

The great majority of the provisions in the modern codes specify the kinds of aid that are proscribed. This is as it should be, for experience has shown that a "general prohibition of any 'aid' is likely to lead courts to haphazardly narrowing interpretations or perhaps to excess coverage." Although the description of the specifics varies somewhat from state to state, it is nonetheless possible to generalize about the kinds of aid that will often or sometimes suffice. Five kinds of aid usually are proscribed: (1) harboring or concealing the criminal; (2) providing him with certain means (e.g., a weapon, transportation, a disguise) of avoiding apprehension; (3) concealing, destroying or tampering with evidence; (4) warning the criminal of his impending discovery or apprehension; and (5) using force, deception or intimidation to prevent or obstruct the criminal's discovery or apprehension. To this list, a few jurisdictions have added the giving of false information in certain circumstances. Some other states include aid in the nature of securing the proceeds of the crime, while several other states instead follow the Model Penal Code § 242.4 approach by making activity of that general type the separate offense of aiding consummation of crime.

The great majority of these statutes do not give special attention to aid given to a family member. Some, however, recognize an exception in the case of aid given to a relative. A few others strike a compromise by providing that the fact the person aided was a relative reduces the grade of the aider's offense. One court has suggested that "basing [an] accessory conviction on normal and expected spousal conduct might well violate" *Griswold v. Conn.* (1965), declaring that the marital relationship lies "within the zone of privacy created by several fundamental constitutional guarantees."

(b) Misprision of Felony. Misprision of felony consisted of a failure to report or prosecute a known felon. It was sometimes said also to include a failure to prevent the commission of a felony, although this view appears to be erroneous. One was not guilty of this common law misdemeanor if he was accountable for the felony as either a principal or accessory before the fact.

It is doubtful whether this offense ever had a meaningful existence beyond the textbook writers. The offense was said to be "practically obsolete" in England almost a century ago, and the few prosecutions in that country in recent years have been limited to the most extreme situations. Doubt has been expressed as to whether this offense was ever inherited by the United States as a part of the common law. While "it may be the duty of a citizen to accuse every offender, and to proclaim every offense which comes to his knowledge, * * * the law which would punish him in every case for not performing this duty is too harsh for man."

In virtually all of the modern recodifications, a misprision statute has not been included. There is a misprision of felony statute in the United States Code, but it is not a true misprision statute in that it requires an act of concealment in addition to failure to disclose. Even this statute has fallen into disuse, and the proposed new federal criminal code would have eliminated it in favor of the more common hindering of law enforcement offense.

(c) Compounding Crime. Compounding crime consists of the receipt of some property or other consideration in return for an agreement not to prosecute or inform on one who has committed a crime. There are three elements to this offense at common law and under the typical compounding statute: (1) the agreement not to prosecute; (2) knowledge of the actual commission of a crime; and (3) the receipt of some consideration.

The agreement is essential. Thus, if a criminal returns or gives property to the victim or another merely in the hope that the other person will not commence prosecution, there is no compounding. Modern statutes vary as to what kind of agreement is necessary. An agreement not to seek or initiate prosecution will usually suffice, but some of the statutes in the modern recodifications recognize other possibilities as well. Among them are agreements to abandon a prosecution, to delay a prosecution, to refrain from aiding a prosecution, to withhold evidence, abstain from testifying, or procure the absence of witnesses, to conceal the offense, or to not report the crime.

That a crime has actually been committed is usually held to be an element of the offense. However, some courts, under the language of individual statutes, have held that the showing of an actual offense is not required.

There must also be some consideration. This includes money or anything of value or advantage. The consideration may pass to another, as in a third-party beneficiary contract.

Only the party who receives the consideration is criminally liable; the former criminal is not guilty of compounding by virtue of his act in giving the consideration. But some modern statutes also cover the person who pays or offers to pay the consideration. A compounder need not, however, be the victim of the former criminal act. At common law the compounding of any crime was itself an offense, and this also is true of the compounding statutes found in most modern codes. But some states limit the offense to the compounding of felonies. This is a questionable basis for distinction, however, in that the more logical basis for barring compromise is "the likelihood that [the offender] will repeat his aggressions against others." Some statutes even allow the compromise of felonies by victims, although this often is permitted only with judicial approval (see § 5.5(d)).

It certainly makes sense to exclude from the crime of compounding the receipt of a benefit that the victim of the crime "believes to be due as restitution or indemnification for harm caused by the offense," as some states do. As explained by the draftsmen of the Model Penal Code:

> In general, our society does not use penal sanctions to compel reporting of crime. [A] victim of crime who refrains from reporting the offense because his loss has been made good is no more derelict in his societal duty than one who, out of indifference or affection for the offender, fails to report known criminal conduct.
>
> * * * In a variety of ways, current practice impugns the application of penal sanctions to the victim who agrees to forego prosecution in return for restitution. First, liability for compounding is easily evaded by accepting indemnification without explicit agreement to prosecution in return for restitution. * * *
>
> Furthermore, many laws and practices of enforcement openly tolerate and sometimes actively encourage private compromise of criminal liability. [P]rosecutors themselves are often content to drop criminal proceedings when the alleged offender agrees to make appropriate restitution to the victim.

Judicial approval, it has been argued, should not be a requirement under such circumstances. It seldom is under modern compounding statutes.

Chapter 13

MURDER

Table of Sections

For additional analysis of the above topics and citations to authorities supporting their discussion in this Book, consult the author's 3-volume *Substantive Criminal Law* treatise, also available as Westlaw database SUBCRL. See the Table of Cross-References in this Book.

§ 13.1   "Malice Aforethought" and "Living Human Being"

Murder is a common law crime whose complete development required several centuries. Though murder is frequently defined as the unlawful killing of another "living human being" with "malice aforethought," in modern times the latter phrase does not even approximate its literal meaning. Hence it is preferable not to rely upon that misleading expression for an understanding of murder but rather to consider the various types of murder (typed according to the mental element) which the common law came to recognize and which exist today in most jurisdictions: (1) intent-to-kill murder; (2) intent-to-do-serious-bodily-injury murder; (3) depraved-heart murder; and (4) felony murder. A comparatively modern statutory innovation divides murder into degrees of murder for purposes of awarding punishment.

(a) **"Malice Aforethought, Express or Implied."** Murder is a common law crime—that is, it was created by the English judges rather than by the English legislature. Though it was first recognized many centuries ago, its exact boundaries were not determined all at once, but rather were worked out by the judges over several centuries of time as a parade of cases, involving different fact situations, came before the judges for decision. At first the judges thought in terms of two broad categories—felonious homicide (without as yet any subdivision into murder and manslaughter) and non-felonious homicide. As time went on, felonious homicide was divided (with some help from the legislature) into murder and manslaughter, and murder was defined as the unlawful killing of another human being "with malice aforethought." What, in these early days, did "malice aforethought" mean? Literally, "malice" in the murder setting required at least an intent to kill, plus perhaps an element of hatred, spite or ill-will; "aforethought" required that the intent to kill be thought out in advance of the killing. At first the judges in fact did require for murder that the defendant actually have a previously thought-out (i.e., premeditated) intent to kill, though probably the spite, etc., was never actually necessary. Later (about 1550), English statutes made it murder intentionally to kill another by poisoning or by lying in wait; but these two situations would seem to be no more than typical cases involving a premeditated intent to kill, the almost literal meaning of "malice aforethought." So at this time in the history of criminal homicide there was only one type of murder: unlawfully killing another with a premeditated intent to kill.

Thereafter the judges started to invent some new types of murder where there existed no premeditated intent to kill. First of all, when the defendant intentionally killed his victim in a heat of passion aroused in him by the conduct of the victim—the issue being whether the defendant should be guilty of murder or of voluntary manslaughter—the judges decided that manslaughter required that the defendant's passion be reasonable. If he was unreasonably provoked, or if a reasonable man would have cooled off in the interval between the provocation and the defendant's fatal blow, then the defendant, though actually in a passion and hence unable to premeditate, would be guilty of murder. No longer then did murder require malice aforethought in the literal sense of premeditated intent to kill. Moreover, as time went by the requirement of premeditation, in situations other than that involving unreasonable passion, was dropped, so that in all situations an unpremeditated intent to kill would do for murder.

Secondly, when the defendant unintentionally killed another person in the commission of a felony—as where A set fire to B's house (arson) and accidentally B or a member of his family was burned to death—the judges held this to be murder ("felony murder"), though the defendant did not intend to kill at all and a fortiori did not premeditate a killing.

Thirdly, when the defendant unintentionally killed another person while conducting himself in an extremely negligent way ("evincing a depraved heart," as this sort of conduct was generally described)—as where A, a workman constructing a tall building, without looking tossed a large stone from the roof onto the busy roadway below, thereby killing B, a pedestrian—the judges held such conduct to be murder ("depraved-heart murder"), though the stone-thrower did not intend to kill anyone.

Lastly, the judges took one more step toward the destruction of the idea that premeditated-intent-to-kill murder is the sole type of murder: it was decided that an intent to do serious bodily injury short of death would do for murder.

The judges still continued to say that murder is committed by one who unlawfully kills another "with malice aforethought," now however adding the phrase "express or implied," the word "implied" covering the four situations just described wherein literally there exists no premeditated intent to kill. Modern courts and legislatures occasionally define murder in terms of "malice aforethought, express or implied," by which they mean the same types of murder as those the English judges ultimately recognized, including felony murder, depraved-heart murder, intent-to-do-serious-bodily-injury murder and murder committed in an unreasonable passion.

The moral to be drawn from this short history of murder is that it will not solve modern homicide cases to say simply that murder is the unlawful killing of another with malice aforethought, that manslaughter is the unlawful killing of another without malice aforethought, and that no crime is committed if the killing is lawful. For an understanding of the crime of murder, it is necessary to consider, one by one, the various types of murder the judges created and that, in general, remain to this day, and to note those statutory or case-law changes to these types legislatures or courts have made in modern times.

To sum up these various modern types of murder, they are: (1) intent-to-kill murder; (2) intent-to-do-serious-bodily-injury murder; (3) felony murder; (4) depraved-heart murder. We shall also consider whether there is a fifth type: (5) resisting-lawful-arrest murder. In addition to the problem of what constitutes murder—a matter developed by the common law with very little statutory intervention—there is the problem in many jurisdictions in America of how murder is divided into degrees of murder—an entirely statutory matter, since the judges themselves never undertook to divide murder into degrees. This book will deal first with murder in general, then with the ways in which murder is divided into degrees.

(b) Statutory Definitions of Murder. Several states have statutes that punish murder but do not undertake to define murder and thus adopt the common law definition of murder, including its various types. A typical statute of this type provides that "murder" committed in this way or that way constitutes first-degree murder; all other "murder" is second-degree murder. Most of the modern recodifications, however, contain statutes defining murder in terms of "killing" or "causing death," which therefore do not necessarily come out with the same types of murder as common-law murder. The following sections, which discuss the common-law types of murder, must be read with this fact in mind.

(c) When Does Life Begin? It is a general requirement of the law of homicide that the victim be a living human being. Shooting a dead body is not homicide, although it may be another crime. The question of life arises most frequently in the cases involving destruction of the human fetus. At early common law the fetus was considered alive thirty to eighty days after conception. By the mid-seventeenth century, however, it was no crime to abort, with the consent of the mother, a fetus which had not "quickened," an event that occurs four to five months after conception. Even then, the killing of a fetus was not homicide unless the fetus had been "born alive." Being "born alive" required that the fetus be totally expelled from the mother and show a clear sign of independent vitality, such as respiration, although respiration was not strictly required.

In the United States the "born alive" requirement has come to mean that the fetus must be fully brought forth and establish an "independent circulation" before it can be considered a human being. Proof of live birth and death by criminal agency are required beyond a reasonable doubt to sustain a homicide conviction. "Independent circulation" can be established by evidence of the fetus having breathed, but such proof usually is not conclusive in the absence of the evidence of life, such as crying. Some courts have required that the umbilical cord be severed before an independent circulation can be established. Severance of the cord probably is no longer required if the fetus is brought forth fully. Through the efforts of doctors and technology, a fetus can now be delivered with no heartbeat, no breathing, and no brain function, yet have those functions artificially resuscitated and maintained some time later. Because of these advances, states employing the born alive doctrine have required that the child show some spontaneous sign of life, as well as the ability to exist independent of artificial support at some point in the future.

A pathologist's opinion on live birth usually is not conclusive, but it will sustain a conviction when corroborated by other evidence. Where respiration alone is sufficient to establish a live birth, a pathologist's opinion on live birth will sustain a conviction even in the absence of other evidence. The grossness of the crime and circumstantial evidence such as preparation for the care of the baby are irrelevant factors that are sometimes considered in the determination of live birth.

People v. Chavez (1947) rejected the "born alive" test of earlier infanticide cases. The court in *Chavez* held that since it was the typical human experience that babies are born alive, it was a legal fiction to say a fetus was not human until completely born. Although a baby is dependent on its mother before birth, in another sense it has reached a state of independent existence when it reaches a stage from which it will normally grow into a living human being given the proper care. The court then held that a fetus killed during the course of birth would be considered a human being under the homicide statute if in the natural course of events the birth would be successfully completed. Nonfeasance by the mother immediately following childbirth in the care for her child might not, however, support a conviction under the *Chavez* theory.

In *Keeler v. Superior Court* (1970) the Supreme Court of California refused to extend the *Chavez* rule to the assault of a pregnant woman resulting in the killing of an unborn but viable fetus not in the process of birth. The court held that the common law homicide requirement that the fetus be in the process of birth was not changed by medical advances which might keep a fetus alive upon premature birth. Furthermore, any civil law remedies available to a fetus are based on different considerations than criminal liability and are inapplicable. A similar conclusion was reached by the Ohio Court of Appeals in *State v. Dickinson* (1970), a homicide by vehicle situation. The defendant's car collided with a vehicle in which a seven-month pregnant woman was riding. Before the collision the baby was viable and capable of sustaining life outside the womb. The mother aborted shortly thereafter and the injuries received by the fetus in the crash were the cause of death. In reversing the conviction, the court held that civil remedies afforded the fetus and medical advances did not justify changing the common law homicide requirement of live birth. But some jurisdictions, while maintaining the "born alive" rule, have taken the position that the infliction of injury upon a fetus before birth may be homicide if the fetus dies after being born alive.

Even greater protection for the fetus is provided by legislation passed in about half of the states which either amends existing homicide statutes so that a fetus is an additional possible victim or else enacts totally new feticide statutes. These statutes criminalizing certain actions taken against the fetus vary considerably as to the threshold at which criminal culpability attaches. Some say it is viability, some quickening, some state a specified length of fetal development in terms of weeks, some go so far as to say it is fertilization or conception, and the others provide no specification on this point whatever. That legislation must be distinguished from yet other laws which give protection to the fetus more indirectly by providing that under specified circumstances action directed at a pregnant woman and resulting in a miscarriage is criminal.

(d) When Does Life End? As noted in *In re Bowman* (1980): "Until recently, the definition of death was both medically and legally a relatively simple matter. When the heart stopped beating and the lungs stopped breathing, the individual was dead according to physicians and according to the law. The traditional definition did not include the criterion of lack of brain activity because no method existed for diagnosing brain death. Moreover, until recently, no mechanical means have been available to maintain heart and lung action; and respiration, heart action, and brain function are so closely related that without artificial support, the cessation of any one of them will bring the other two to a halt within a very few minutes." But the situation has now changed dramatically. By resort to modern resuscitative and supportive measures, it is possible to "restore life as judged by the ancient standards of persistent respiration and continuing heart beat. This can be the case even when there is not the remotest possibility of an individual recovering consciousness following massive brain damage."

In tandem with this development has come the virtually universal acceptance in the medical profession of the concept of "brain death," the permanent cessation of all brain functions that, absent mechanical support, would result in the cessation of other body functions as well. As for the criteria utilized in the medical community to determine brain death, they are: (1) a total lack of responsivity to externally applied stimuli (e.g., pinching) and inner need; (2) no spontaneous muscular movements or respiration; and (3) no reflexes, as measured by a fixed, dilated pupil and lack of ocular, pharyngeal, and muscle-tendon reflexes. It has also been emphasized that a flat or isoelectric electroencephalogram (EEG) reading has great confirmatory value, although more recent studies have deemphasized reliance upon the EEG and emphasized the absence of spinal reflexes.

The traditional legal definition of death was just like the traditional medical definition: so long as the heart remains beating and there is breathing, death has not occurred. But in light of the developments in medical science noted above, should this continue to be the legal definition in homicide cases? This is an issue of some importance, as can be seen from a recitation of the facts of one case. The defendant shot the victim in the head, and the victim was then taken to the hospital where it was preliminarily determined that he had suffered brain death. The victim was maintained on life support systems for the next three days, during which time follow-up studies confirmed that conclusion. A doctor then terminated the support measures, and defendant was thereafter charged with murder. Given the fact that certain forms of improper medical treatment constitute an intervening and supervening cause barring a homicide conviction of the person who inflicted the original injury (see § 5.4(f)(5), (g)(2)), it is important to know just when the victim's death occurred. If as a legal matter brain death is sufficient, then the victim's death occurred before the doctor "pulled the plug," meaning no cause intervened between the defendant's conduct and the victim's death; if, on the other hand, brain death is not a proper legal test, then there is at least a chance the doctor's conduct would bar conviction.

On the above facts and in similar situations there also exists the question of the criminal liability of the doctor. The time of death as a legal matter is, if anything, even more important here, for it has long been accepted that it is homicide to kill one already dying, to accelerate one's death, to kill one condemned to be executed the next day, or to kill a "worthless" victim. Thus, a doctor who "pulls the plug" or removes an organ from the victim could find himself subject to criminal liability if the traditional heart-lungs legal test of death were utilized.

As a policy matter, use of the brain death test as a sufficient legal definition of death in homicide cases makes great sense if, as would seem to be the case, "the harm associated with the loss of psyche is seen as the equivalent to, or even greater than, the harm associated with 'death' itself." On this and like reasoning, the commentators have rather consistently concluded that the brain death test should be applied in fact situations like that described above to ensure that the person causing the original harm can be held accountable for the homicide and to ensure also that the doctor's conduct is not a basis for a homicide prosecution. It appears that all jurisdictions would reach that conclusion today. Many states have by statute adopted brain death as an acceptable (though perhaps not the exclusive) legal standard. In cases arising in states lacking any statutory definition of death clearly applicable to homicide cases, the courts have consistently opted for the brain death test as the applicable legal standard, and hence it may now be concluded that all fifty states accept brain death as a legal definition of death.

It remains to be seen whether the brain death test will continue unaltered as advances in medical science bring to the fore new and difficult issues for consideration. Illustrative is the very difficult and much-disputed question of whether it should be legally permissible to remove organs for transplantation from anencephalic infants. While there is "no doubt that a need exists for infant organs for transplantation" and that "anencephalics make good organ donors because they are almost always born normally except that they are missing most of their brain and skull," the problem arises because "anencephalics usually have ceased to be suitable organ donors by the time they meet all the criteria for 'whole brain death,' i.e., the complete absence of brain-stem function," as "the process of dying involves deprivation of oxygen that, for the most part, renders the organs unusable." While the American Medical Association in 1994 reversed its longstanding position that an anencephalic infant must be declared dead in order to be treated as an organ donor, the new policy was soon suspended because of strong opposition from many quarters and the realization that "if physicians followed [it], they would face criminal prosecution for murder." Efforts to resolve the problem by amending state statutes defining death to say, for example, that "an individual born with the condition of anencephaly is dead" have failed. Opponents of such legislation are fearful that it "could be the first step * * * down a slippery slope of obtaining organs from others in similar situations," while the proponents claim that "the anencephalic newborn is physically unique and the limited exception to brain death cannot be broadened if anencephaly is specifically defined."

(e) Year-and-a-Day Rule. We have already noted, in discussing the topic of causation (a vital subject in the case of those crimes, including murder, defined so as to require both conduct and a specified result of conduct), that the English judges centuries ago required for murder (and later required for manslaughter) that the victim's death must occur within a year and a day after the fatal blow was delivered. In a sense, the judges were saying that, in the case of a longer interval, the blow could not have caused the death. The year-and-a-day rule made some sense in the days of its birth, when there was little medical knowledge; but it seems strange that it should exist today. Yet the year-and-a-day rule crossed the Atlantic with the colonists and still exists in some states today, although most have abrogated the rule judicially or legislatively.

(f) Elements of Murder. It may be useful to summarize briefly here the required elements of murder: (1) There must be some conduct (affirmative act, or omission to act where there is a duty to act) on the part of the defendant. (2) He must have an accompanying "malicious" state of mind (intent to kill or do serious bodily injury; a depraved heart; an intent to commit a felony). (3) His conduct must "legally cause" the death of a living-human-being victim. And (4), in many jurisdictions, this death must occur within a year and a day after the defendant's conduct thus caused the victim's fatal injury.

§ 13.2 Intent–To–Kill Murder

Conduct, accompanied by an intent to kill, which is the legal cause of another's death constitutes murder, unless the circumstances surrounding the homicide are such that the crime is reduced to voluntary manslaughter (see § 14.2) or such that the intentional killing is justifiable or excusable and so constitutes no crime at all (see chs. 8 & 9). Intentional death may be produced by affirmative action involving a variety of possible weapons, or even without weapons, as by hands or feet or simply spoken words. Intended death may likewise be produced by omission to act; but for murder liability the omission to act must be accompanied by a duty to act.

(a) Intention. The commonest type of murder, of course, is the intent-to-kill type, where *A,* with an intent to kill *B,* by his conduct succeeds in killing *B.* Usually where *A*'s conduct causes a death his aim is good: he aims his deadly missile at *B* with intent to kill *B,* and hits *B* and kills *B.* But sometimes his aim is bad, and he misses B but hits and kills C. He is, of course, nonetheless guilty of murdering C (see § 5.4(d)).

Under the traditional view, one intends to cause a certain result under two different circumstances: (1) when he desires that result, whatever the likelihood of that result occurring; and (2) when he knows that such a result is substantially certain to occur, whatever his desire concerning that result (see § 4.2(a)). Thus (1) A has an intent to kill B when he fires his gun at B desiring to cause his death, though A's hand may be so unsteady or B so far away that A's chances of hitting B are small. And (2) A has an intent to kill B when he fires a bullet from a high-powered rifle at his enemy C, who is holding B in front of him as a human shield; for, though he may not desire B's death (he may even be fond of B, though of course his actions demonstrate that he does not like B as much as he hates C), he knows that B is substantially certain to be killed. (So in either case, if B is actually killed, we would say that, since A intended to kill him, A is guilty of intent-to-kill murder.)

The modern view is to limit "intent" to instances where it is the actor's purpose to cause the harmful result, and the word "knowledge" is used to cover instances in which the actor knows that the harmful result is substantially certain to occur (see § 4.2(b)). In a criminal code utilizing such definitions, what is here called intent-to-kill murder may be described as intentionally or knowingly killing another. Apart from the question of when capital punishment should be permitted, there is "no basis in principle for separating purposeful from knowing homicide." Many of the American codes do not distinguish between them, although a majority do appear to require intent rather than knowledge or, at least, to classify intentional and knowing killings differently.

We have seen that, historically, in the beginning an intent to kill was not of itself enough of a bad intent for murder; the intent to kill had to be "aforethought"—i.e., thought-out in advance, premeditated. But as time went on, the premeditation requirement was dropped, so that an unpremeditated intent to kill would do. So today an unpremeditated intent to kill is enough for the intent-to-kill type of murder.

(b) Deadly–Weapon Doctrine. One who intentionally kills another does not often announce to bystanders, "I have in my mind an intent to kill" at the moment, or just before or after, he kills. If there are witnesses to the killing, he often acts without speaking at all or at least without speaking so specifically about his intent; and of course he often kills in secret, so that there are no witnesses. How then can the prosecution prove beyond a reasonable doubt that when he killed he intended to kill? Obviously this intent must be gathered from all the circumstances of the killing—the killer's actions and his words (if any) in the light of the surrounding circumstances.

It is commonly said in civil and in criminal cases (not just murder cases) that one is presumed to intend the natural and probable consequences of his acts. Thus if one carefully aims a gun at his enemy and pulls the trigger, and the bullet strikes the enemy in the heart and kills him, we ought logically to conclude, in the absence of some other facts, that he intended to kill, though he spoke no words of intent at the time. A special application of the presumption that one intends to produce the natural results of his actions is found in the deadly-weapon doctrine applicable to homicide cases: one who intentionally uses a deadly weapon on another human being and thereby kills him presumably intends to kill him.

As a constitutional matter, it is necessary to express the idea, not in terms of a mandatory presumption, but in terms of a permissive inference: it may properly be inferred (i.e., the conclusion *may* be drawn, rather than *must* be drawn, in the absence of counter proof) from the fact that the killer intentionally used a deadly weapon upon the deceased that he intended to kill the deceased. Note that the deadly-weapon doctrine is not a category of murder separate from the intent-to-kill category; there must be an intent to kill, but the intentional use of a deadly weapon authorizes the drawing of an inference that the user intends to kill. It cannot be said that the intentional use of a deadly weapon producing death is necessarily murder; we still allow the user a chance to convince the trier-of-fact (generally the jury) that in spite of his intentional use of a deadly weapon he actually did not intend to kill—as where he intentionally shot toward his victim intending merely to scare or to inflict a non-fatal wound.

What weapon is a "deadly weapon" for purposes of the deadly-weapon doctrine in homicide cases? "[A] deadly weapon [is] one which, from the manner used, is calculated or likely to produce death or serious bodily injury." Thus whether a weapon is deadly depends upon two factors: (1) what it intrinsically is and (2) how it is used. If almost anyone can kill with it, it is a deadly weapon when used in a manner calculated to kill. Thus the following items have been held to be deadly weapons in view of the circumstances of their use: loaded guns, daggers, swords, axes, iron bars, baseball bats, bricks, rocks, ice picks, automobiles, and pistols used as bludgeons. Some cases have spoken of loaded guns, daggers, axes and heavy iron bars as deadly weapons *per se,* without regard to their use, perhaps with the thought that they are of such a nature that they cannot be used gently. However, while it is true that almost anyone can kill with a heavy iron bar, yet if the defendant actually used it to tap the victim lightly on the head, the deadly-weapon doctrine ought not to apply so as to authorize an inference that he intended to kill, even though the victim unfortunately had such an uncommonly thin skull that he died from the tap.

There are some weapons with which the ordinary person could not kill; it takes something of an expert to kill another with a pen knife or a pin. Yet such weapons, intentionally used in an artistic way by an expert, do constitute deadly weapons.

Lastly, there is the problem of death produced solely by the intentional use of the hands or feet, where there is no "weapon" at all to serve as a basis for a finding of a "deadly weapon," and where, of course, it would often be ridiculous to infer an intent to kill from their use. Yet in appropriate cases, generally involving big men attacking small, frail men or women or children, and generally involving the repeated use of hands and feet, an inference of an intent to kill may properly be drawn.

In order to get the benefit of the inference, the prosecution must show not only that a weapon actually killed but also that the weapon used was a deadly weapon. With those weapons (guns, swords, axes, iron bars, daggers) with which anyone can kill, there is probably no need to introduce the weapon into evidence or to describe the weapon to the jury; but with rocks (which may be large or small) and walking canes (which may be thick or thin) a verdict of murder may not be supportable without evidence of the weapon or a description of its size and shape.

(c) Means of Producing Intentional Death. While the method of producing an intentional death is usually some weapon in the hands of the murderer, and less frequently his hands and feet without a weapon, sometimes more subtle means are used. Thus the act of opening, on a cold winter day, a window next to the bed of a helpless sick person, who must remain warm to recover, would be murderous conduct by one who intended thereby to kill. One ingenious fellow with a flair for the picturesque caused his wife to be bitten by a rattlesnake and then, to make doubly sure, placed her face down in a fish pond. Words alone may be used to produce an intentional death, as where one perjures an innocent man into the electric chair; or nags another, whom he knows to have heart trouble, into some death-producing exertion; or, seeing a blind man at the edge of a precipice, advises him that it is all clear ahead. Words may be used intentionally to produce death through fright or shock, as when one shouts "boo" at a person leaning precariously over the rim of the Grand Canyon or the balustrade atop the Empire State Building; or where he falsely shouts, "Your son is dead" into the ears of a woman he knows to have a heart condition.

So far, we have discussed deaths intentionally produced by affirmative action, including that mild form of affirmative action involved in speaking words (see § 5.2). We have already noted, however, that intentional death may be effectively brought about by an omission to act. One is not guilty of murder for intentionally killing by failure to act, however, unless the circumstances are such that there is a duty to act.

(d) Causation. For one to be guilty of murder of the intent-to-kill (or any other) variety, his conduct (act or omission) must be the "legal cause" of the death of the person killed. In the realm of murder, this means (1) that his conduct must be a substantial factor in bringing about the death; and (2) that in addition the actual result (death of the victim) cannot be brought about in a manner too greatly different from the intended manner. These matters have been discussed elsewhere in this book (see § 5.4(b), (f)).

§ 13.3 Intent–To–Do–Serious–Bodily–Injury Murder

We have already seen that the English judges came to hold that one who intended to do serious bodily injury short of death, but who actually succeeded in killing, was guilty of murder in spite of his lack of an intent to kill, in the absence of circumstances which mitigated the offense to voluntary manslaughter or which justified or excused it. This type of common-law murder became a part of the law of murder in America.

On principle, it may seem quite proper to make it murder for one to kill another with an intent to do serious bodily injury though not to kill. Such conduct may appear at least as dangerous to life as that required for depraved-heart murder; so that if the latter conduct constitutes murder (as is almost everywhere recognized), so should the conduct here under discussion. It has been suggested, however, that there is no need for the separate category of intent-to-do-serious-bodily-injury murder, and that such cases are properly encompassed within the depraved-heart murder and recklessness manslaughter categories, depending upon the facts of the particular case. Most modern codes define murder as not including the intent-to-do-serious-bodily-injury type.

"Serious bodily injury" (or "great" or "grievous bodily harm," as it is often called) is something more than plain "bodily injury"; it means something close to, though of course less than, death. As with intent-to-kill murder, the intent to do serious bodily harm must be gathered from the defendant's conduct (including his words, if any) in the light of the surrounding circumstances; and, once again, his intentional use of a deadly weapon (one which, from the manner used, is calculated to cause death or serious bodily injury) upon another human being will properly give rise to an inference of an intent to kill or at least to do serious bodily injury.

And such an inference can also be properly drawn where the only "weapon" used is the defendant's hands or feet, in an appropriate case.

Just as murder may be committed by an omission to act, in violation of a duty to act, when accompanied by an intent to kill, so also may it be committed where the omission is accompanied by an intent to do serious bodily injury. Thus if *A* fails to warn or rescue *B,* to whom he owes a duty, desiring to cause him serious bodily injury, or (without such a desire) knowing that such an injury is substantially sure to follow, and death to *B* results, *A* is guilty of the murder of *B.*

The same problems of causation arise here as with intent-to-kill murder, as where *A* aims at *B* with intent to do him serious bodily harm short of death but, missing *B,* strikes and kills *C* (i.e., an unintended victim); or where *A* strikes *B* with intent to do serious bodily harm but he inflicts only a plain bodily injury, which, however, is so negligently treated by the doctor that *B* dies (i.e., an unintended manner of producing the forbidden harm).

It would doubtless be quite possible to combine the two types of murder treated so far—(1) intent-to-kill murder and (2) intent-to-do-serious-bodily-injury murder—into a single type of murder called intent-to-kill-or-do-serious-bodily-injury murder. For historical reasons, and because most modern statutory treatments of murder do not seem to recognize intent-to-do-serious-bodily-injury murder, the two notions have been treated separately in this book.

§ 13.4   Depraved–Heart Murder

Extremely negligent conduct, which creates what a reasonable man would realize to be not only an unjustifiable but also a very high degree of risk of death or serious bodily injury to another or to others—though unaccompanied by any intent to kill or do serious bodily injury—and which actually causes the death of another, may constitute murder. There is a dispute as to whether, in addition to creating this great risk, the defendant himself must subjectively be aware of the great risk that his conduct creates, in order to be guilty of murder.

(a) **Creation of Risk.** Conduct that creates an unreasonable risk of injury to other persons or to their property is generally termed "ordinary negligence," a type of fault which will generally serve as the basis for tort liability and occasionally for criminal liability (see § 4.4(a)). Conduct that creates not only an unreasonable risk but also a "high degree" of risk (something more than mere "unreasonable" risk) may be termed "gross negligence," and if in addition the one who creates such a risk realizes that he does so, his conduct may be called "recklessness" (see § 4.4(b)) Grossly negligent conduct, or reckless conduct, which results in death may serve as the basis for manslaughter liability (see § 14.4), but it will not do for murder.

For murder the degree of risk of death or serious bodily injury must be more than a mere unreasonable risk, more even than a high degree of risk. Perhaps the required danger may be designated a "very high degree" of risk to distinguish it from those lesser degrees of risk that will suffice for other crimes. Such a designation of conduct at all events is more accurately descriptive than that flowery expression found in the old cases and occasionally incorporated into some modern statutes—i.e., conduct "evincing a depraved heart, devoid of social duty, and fatally bent on mischief." Although "very high degree of risk" means something quite substantial, it is still something far less than certainty or substantial certainty.

The distinctions between an unreasonable risk and a high degree of risk and a very high degree of risk are, of course, matters of degree, and there is no exact boundary line between each category; they shade gradually like a spectrum from one group to another. Some have thus questioned whether this is a sound basis upon which to make the important distinction between murder and manslaughter. More appealing is the Model Penal Code § 210.2(1)(b) approach, whereunder a reckless killing is murder only if done "under circumstances manifesting extreme indifference to the value of human life." This language, which better serves the "purpose of communicating to jurors in ordinary language the task expected of them," has been substantially followed in several of the American codes. Some codes use the old "abandoned and malignant heart" language or else refer more generally to conduct evincing either a "depraved mind" or "depraved heart," while a substantial number attempt no definition at all. (A very significant minority of American jurisdictions do not recognize this type of murder at all.)

It should be noted, however, that for depraved-heart murder it is not a great amount of risk in the abstract which is decisive. The risk is exactly the same when one fires his rifle into the window of what appears to be an abandoned cabin in a deserted mining town as when one shoots the same bullet into the window of a well-kept city home, when in fact in each case one person occupies the room into which the shot is fired. In the deserted cabin situation it may not be, while in the occupied home situation it may be, murder when the occupant is killed. This illustrates that it is what the defendant should realize to be the degree of risk, in the light of the surrounding circumstances which he knows, that is important, rather than the amount of risk as an abstract proposition of the mathematics of chance.

Another matter to be noted is that the risk must not only be very high, as the defendant ought to realize in the light of what he knows; it must also under the circumstances be unjustifiable for him to take the risk. The motives for the defendant's risky conduct thus become relevant; or, to express the thought in another way, the social utility of his conduct is a factor to be considered. If he speeds through crowded streets, thereby endangering other motorists and pedestrians, in order to rush a passenger to the hospital for an emergency operation, he may not be guilty of murder if he unintentionally kills, though the same conduct done solely for the purpose of experiencing the thrill of fast driving may be enough for murder. Since the amount of risk that will do for depraved-heart murder varies with these two variable factors—the extent of the defendant's knowledge of the surrounding circumstances and the social utility of his conduct (see § 4.4(a)(1))—the mathematical chances of producing death required for murder cannot be measured in terms of percentages.

The following types of conduct have been held, under the circumstances, to involve the very high degree of unjustifiable homicidal danger that will do for depraved-heart murder: firing a bullet into a room occupied, as the defendant knows, by several people; starting a fire at the front door of an occupied dwelling; shooting into the caboose of a passing train or into a moving automobile, necessarily occupied by human beings; throwing a beer glass at one who is carrying a lighted oil lamp; playing a game of "Russian roulette" with another person; shooting at a point near, but not aiming directly at, another person; driving a car at very high speeds along a main street; shaking an infant so long and so vigorously that it cannot breathe; selling "pure" (i.e., undiluted) heroin. Other sorts of extremely risky conduct may be imagined: throwing stones from the roof of a tall building onto the busy street below; piloting a speedboat through a group of swimmers; swooping an airplane so low over a traveling automobile as to risk the decapitation of the motorist. A very risky omission will suffice where there is a duty to act. In any such case, if death actually results to an endangered person and occurs in a foreseeable way, the defendant's conduct makes him an eligible candidate for a murder conviction.

For murder of the depraved-heart type the above cases show that the required risk may be risk to a group of persons, as in the case of the shots fired into the caboose or into the room containing several persons; or it may be risk only to a single person, as in the case of the thrown beer glass or the shaken baby. Of course, the situation may be such that the risk of death is too slight for murder where only one person is endangered by defendant's conduct, whereas the risk is sufficient where several are thus hazarded; thus it may not be murder for a hunter to shoot at a deer with one lone hunting companion nearby, though unluckily the companion is killed; whereas the same conduct in a wooded area filled with hunters (one of whom is killed) may amount to murder.

(b) Realization of the Risk. Assuming that the defendant's conduct creates what a reasonable man would know to be an unreasonable and very high degree of risk of death or serious bodily injury to another person or to several others, there remains the question of whether he is guilty of murder if he is not aware of the risk created by his conduct. He may, for instance, be too absent-minded or to feeble-minded (though not insane) or too drunk to realize the seriousness of the risk.

Most of the cases are ambiguous on the matter; they tend to speak of conduct that "evinces" or "manifests" or "shows" a depraved heart, without spelling out whether he must actually possess this depraved heart (i.e., have a subjective realization of the risk) or whether it is enough that a reasonable man would have realized the risk and so would have had a depraved heart. The same is true of many statutes, even those found in modern codes. But some of the recent recodifications follow Model Penal Code § 210.2(1)(b) in expressly stating that the subjective state of mind of recklessness is required, while a few others express some other mental state.

The English judge and criminal law historian Stephen took the view that one should not be guilty of murder of this type unless he was subjectively aware of the risk. Justice Holmes, on the other hand, thought that he should be guilty of murder if a reasonable man would have realized the risk, regardless of whether he himself actually realized it. A few cases have specifically taken sides on the issue. Thus an English case, following the Holmes view, approved the trial court's instruction to the jury that if the defendant's conduct (shaking a baby, thus suffocating it to death) was such that a reasonable man would have realized that death or serious bodily injury was likely to result, the defendant would be guilty of murder. On the other hand, some cases have considered the defendant's conduct after the fatal blow as relevant on the issue of liability for murder, thus in effect recognizing the Stephen view of the subjective nature of depraved-heart murder. So when the defendant, by driving his car in a way that created great risk, struck and fatally injured a pedestrian, his conduct in stopping and taking the victim to the hospital was held to "negative the idea of wickedness of disposition and hardness of heart" required for depraved-heart murder.

No doubt most depraved-heart murder cases do not require a determination of the issue of whether the defendant actually was aware of the risk entailed by his conduct; his conduct was very risky and he himself was reasonable enough to know it to be so. It is only the unusual case that raises the issue—where the defendant is more absent-minded, stupid or intoxicated than the reasonable man.

In the unusual case where the defendant is not aware of the risk, which view is preferable, Holmes' objective view or Stephen's subjective one? It is a question of how much fault should be required for murder; for one who consciously creates risk is morally a worse person than one who unconsciously does so, though each of the two persons may constitute an equal danger to his fellow man. On balance, it would seem that, to convict of murder, with its drastic penal consequences, subjective realization should be required. One who is too absent-minded or feeble-minded to think of the risk ought not to be held guilty of murder, though it does not follow that he should escape all criminal liability, such as a conviction of manslaughter or of some other crime of negligent homicide.

The real difficulty concerns the intoxicated person who conducts himself in a very risky way but, because of his drunkenness, fails to realize it. If his conduct causes death, should he escape murder liability? The person who unconsciously creates risk because he is voluntarily drunk is perhaps morally worse than one who does so because he is sober but mentally deficient. At all events, the cases generally hold that drunkenness does not negative a depraved heart by blotting out consciousness of risk, and the Model Penal Code, which generally requires awareness of the risk for depraved-heart murder (and for recklessness manslaughter), so provides.

§ 13.5   Felony Murder

At the early common law one whose conduct brought about an unintended death in the commission or attempted commission of a felony was guilty of murder. Today the law of felony murder varies substantially throughout the country, largely as a result of efforts to limit the scope of the felony-murder rule. American jurisdictions have limited the rule in one or more of the following ways: (1) by permitting its use only as to certain types of felonies; (2) by more strict interpretation of the requirement of proximate or legal cause; (3) by a narrower construction of the time period during which the felony is in the process of commission; (4) by requiring that the underlying felony be independent of the homicide.

(a) History of the Felony–Murder Doctrine. At one time the English common law felony-murder rule was that one who, in the commission or attempted commission of a felony, caused another's death, was guilty of murder, without regard to the dangerous nature of the felony involved or to the likelihood that death might result from the defendant's manner of committing or attempting the felony. Later, as the number of felonies multiplied so as to include a great number of relatively minor offenses, many of which involved no great danger to life or limb, it became necessary, in order to alleviate the harshness of the rule, to limit it in some fashion. Thus, suppose a statute makes it a felony to sell intoxicating liquor; yet if the purchaser should drink so much as to fall asleep in a blizzard on the way home and die of exposure, the seller ought not to be deemed a murderer, even though the felony actually caused the death in the sense that, but for the felony, the death would not have occurred. It is a felony to make a false tax return; but if the revenue agent investigating the taxpayer's return should slip on the taxpayer's front steps and break his neck, the taxpayer ought not to be guilty of murder, though his act in filing a false return may have been an actual cause of death.

In England the courts came to limit the felony-murder doctrine in one of two ways: (1) by requiring that the defendant's conduct in committing the felony involve an act of violence in carrying out a felony of violence, or (2) by requiring that the death be the natural and probable consequence of the defendant's conduct in committing the felony. In America some cases state the felony-murder rule in the language of the unlimited common law statement, although in fact the felony involved is generally a dangerous kind of felony and the manner of its commission generally involves a risk that in the normal course of events someone might be killed. The better cases, however, expressly add some limitation to the rule, most often requiring that the defendant's conduct be the proximate or legal cause of the victim's death or that the felony attempted or committed be dangerous to life. Some jurisdictions have limited the rule in other ways, such as by requiring that the felony be independent of the homicide or by a strict interpretation of the requirement that the death occur in the commission or attempted commission of a felony.

(b) Limitation to Certain Felonies. In many states, the felony-murder rule has been limited in scope by a requirement that the felony attempted or committed by the defendant must be dangerous to life. Similarly, other courts have required that the felony be one of the few which were felonies at common law (i.e., rape, sodomy, robbery, burglary, arson, mayhem, larceny), or that the felony in question be *malum in se* rather than *malum prohibitum*. The latter two limitations are quite similar to the first: with the exceptions of larceny and consensual sodomy, all the common-law felonies (and especially robbery, arson and rape) involve a danger to life; and generally the felonies that are designated *malum* *in se* as distinguished from those *malum prohibitum* likewise involve this danger to life. The limitation is best worded, however, in language of dangerousness rather than in terms of common-law felonies or of felonies that are *mala in se.*

The requirement that the felony be dangerous to life has been stated in two different ways. Under one approach, the question is whether on the facts of the particular case, including the circumstances under which the felony was committed, there was a foreseeable danger to human life. Thus, while it may be said as an abstract proposition that the theft felonies (larceny, embezzlement and false pretenses) do not involve danger to life, a thief may commit his theft crime in a way which does create a foreseeable danger to life; under this first view it would be felony murder if death did result under these circumstances. The other approach limits the felony-murder doctrine to those felonies which are "inherently dangerous," that is, the peril to human life must be determined from the elements of the felony in the abstract rather than from the facts of the particular case. Under this view, false pretenses is not a dangerous felony even when committed by inducing a person to forego a life-prolonging operation.

On principle, the latter approach is incorrect, for if the purpose of the felony-murder doctrine is to hold felons accountable for unintended deaths caused by their dangerous conduct, then it would seem to make little difference whether the felony committed was dangerous by its very nature or merely dangerous as committed in the particular case. If the armed robber is to be held guilty of felony murder because of a death occurring from the accidental firing of his gun, it seems no more harsh to apply the felony-murder doctrine to the thief whose fraudulent scheme includes inducing the victim to forego a life-prolonging operation. The requirement that the felony be "inherently dangerous" is more understandable, however, if viewed as an attempt by some courts to limit what they believe to be "a highly artificial concept that deserves no extension beyond its required application."

In the modern criminal codes, the question of what kind of felony will suffice is ordinarily addressed in the felony murder statute. Some of these statutes state without qualification that any felony will do, but it is always possible a court will conclude this language must be construed in light of the history of felony murder rather than literally, so that one of the limitations previously discussed will be read into the statute. Some other of the modern statutes describe a general category of felonies that will suffice; these categories in one way or another relate to the dangerousness of the felony and, depending upon the exact language used, might give rise to the inherent-vs.-in-this-case question previously discussed. But most modern felony murder statutes limit the crime to a list of specific felonies—usually rape, robbery, kidnaping, arson and burglary—which involve a significant prospect of violence. Where these lists are found in a statute called first-degree murder and another statute of some lesser degree states it encompasses "all other murder," then it is possible that unlisted felonies will be held to suffice for felony murder of that lesser degree. But a court that views the felony murder rule with some disfavor may hold that the "all other" language is not sufficient to preserve otherwise-abolished common law crimes.

(c) Vicarious Responsibility of Co-felons. Many of the felony-murder cases involve co-felons, only one of whom accidentally or intentionally fires the fatal shot. That person is of course liable for intent-to-kill murder if the shot is fired with intent to kill or of felony murder if it is fired accidentally in the commission of the felony and death is foreseeable. Are his co-felons also liable? This is not so much a matter of felony murder as a matter of parties to crime (see § 12.1)—the problem of the responsibility of one criminal (A) for the conduct of a fellow-criminal (B) who, in the process of committing or attempting the agreed-upon crime, commits another crime.

If A and B have agreed to rob X by killing him, or by killing him if he resists or if he recognizes his robbers or if necessary to effect an escape, A is of course guilty though B is the one who actually fires the fatal shot. Even though the two have made no such agreement, if in the process of robbing or attempting to rob X B's gun goes off accidentally, killing X, A would be guilty of the felony murder of X as much as B would be, under the rule concerning parties to crime that all parties are guilty for deviations from the common plan that are the foreseeable consequences of carrying out the plan (an accidental shooting during an armed robbery being a typical example of a foreseeable deviation from the plan to rob). Doubtless too if A, B and C undertake to rob X and B accidentally shoots C to death during the robbery, A is as guilty as B of the felony murder of C.

What if B, angry perhaps at C's inept manner of assisting in the robbery of X, should intentionally shoot C; B would be liable for C's murder, of course, of the intent-to-kill type; but would A be liable for intent-to-kill murder or felony murder? B's intentional shooting of C is so far removed from the common plan as not to make A responsible for B's intent-to-kill murder; and B's act should not be considered a felony-murder by A because B's conduct had nothing to do with furthering the robbery, the only connection between the robbery and the shooting being a mere coincidence of time and place. The result would be otherwise, therefore, if B killed co-felon C so as to eliminate him as a possible witness.

There may be instances, however, in which the killing by B is more closely related to the felony but yet was not a reasonably foreseeable consequence of the plan of A and B because, for example, the plan as conceived did not contemplate the use or even the carrying of a weapon or other dangerous instrument. In such a case, it is less apparent that unqualified application of parties-to-crime principles, making A guilty of the murder by B merely because he is a party to the felony by B, is just. Because of the realization that rigid application of the felony-murder doctrine in such circumstances can be unduly harsh, a substantial minority of the modern codes provide that if the defendant was not the only participant in the underlying crime, then it is an affirmative defense that the defendant: (a) did not commit the homicidal act or in any way solicit, request, command, importune, cause or aid the commission thereof; and (b) was not armed with a deadly weapon or dangerous instrument; and (c) had no reasonable ground to believe any other participant was armed with such a weapon or instrument; and (d) had no reasonable ground to believe that any other participant intended to engage in conduct likely to result in death or serious physical injury.

(d) The "Proximate" or "Legal" Cause Limitation. The requirement in some jurisdictions that the felony be inherently dangerous to life (that is, that death be a foreseeable consequence of the felony), must be distinguished from the additional requirement of "proximate" or "legal" cause. A given category of felony may be inherently dangerous, but it may still be that the death which actually occurred has come about in such an extraordinary way that as a matter of causation the defendant should not be held accountable for the death. For example, as an abstract proposition arson is a crime that involves danger to life, for death sometimes results from arson. In a given case, however, the victim's conduct in exposing himself to the danger of the fire may be so abnormal and unforeseeable that it cannot be said that his death was legally caused by the defendant's felonious conduct.

The requirement of causation, as applicable to felony-murder cases as well as other cases, is discussed in detail elsewhere in this book (see § 5.4). The subject of causation is briefly reconsidered here for the purpose of showing how it has sometimes been used to limit the harshness of the felony-murder rule.

In felony-murder cases as well as other homicide cases, it is often said that the death must have been the "natural and probable consequence" of the defendant's conduct. When death has occurred only as a consequence of some intervening act following the defendant's conduct (as is frequently the case in the felony-murder context), the issue is frequently put in terms of whether the intervening cause was "foreseeable" (as distinguished from actually "foreseen").

As noted earlier (see § 5.4), however, courts have drawn the perimeters of legal cause more closely when the intervening cause was a mere *coincidence* (i.e., where the defendant's act merely put the victim at a certain place at a certain time, and because the victim was so located it was possible for him to be acted upon by the intervening cause) than when it was a *response* to the defendant's prior actions (i.e., a reaction to conditions created by the defendant). Foreseeability is required as to the former, but in the latter instance the question is whether the intervening act was abnormal—that is, whether, looking at the matter with hindsight, it seems extraordinary.

On the basis of these principles, it is clear that if *A* sets fire to *B*'s occupied house it is felony-murder if *B* or a member of his household or a fireman fighting the blaze is burned to death. While the chances may be all in favor of no one's death by fire, these deaths are neither unforeseeable nor the result of abnormal happenings. Firemen usually put out house fires without getting killed, but the death of a fireman fighting such a blaze happens often enough that its occurrence does not greatly surprise us. So too we would not view it as abnormal if a brave stranger were to rush into the house in an attempt to save a trapped member of *B*'s household crying for help at an upstairs window, and if the stranger died in the fire this would also be felony murder. On the other hand, it seems unlikely that the arsonist would be held guilty of felony murder if a looter entered the blazing building to steal whatever he could find or if a fireman were to fall off the fire truck on its way back to the fire station after putting out the conflagration.

Robberies by armed robbers no doubt are even more likely to result in unintended deaths than are arsons. Often it is the victim of the robbery who is accidentally killed. The armed robber committing or attempting a robbery whose loaded gun, pointed at his victim, goes off accidentally, or is discharged accidentally when the robber and his victim are struggling for the gun, is guilty of felony murder when the robbery victim is thus killed. And if the robber should hit his victim hard with a bludgeon, not intending to kill him but only to facilitate the robbery by disabling him temporarily, but thereby crushing his skull and causing death, the robber again would be guilty of felony murder.

In the robbery situation it sometimes happens that someone other than the robbery victim is killed by the robber's gun. If the robber, in the commission or attempted commission of the crime, should, even accidentally, kill an interfering policeman or bystander at whom the robber points his gun or with whom the robber struggles, this is felony-murder. The same may sometimes be true even when a confederate robber is accidentally killed by the robber's gun. Thus in one case A and B attempted to rob X, a pedestrian, on the street; while B, in front of X, held a knife in X's ribs, A, behind X, struck him over the head with the butt of his loaded pistol; the shock of the blow discharged the gun; and the bullet killed B. A was held guilty of the felony murder of B.

In the robbery cases it may also happen that someone (the robbery victim, an interceding policeman, an innocent bystander, a fellow robber) is killed by a bullet fired from the gun of someone other than the robber. A series of cases from Pennsylvania raises the issue of the robber's liability under various alternative circumstances: In *Commonwealth v. Moyer* (1947), A attempted to rob X and Y; X reached for his gun to frustrate the robbery; A shot at X; X returned the fire, aiming at A but accidentally killing Y. Under these circumstances A was held guilty of the murder of Y, because his actions in attempting the robbery set in motion "a chain of events which were or should have been within his contemplation." In *Commonwealth v. Almeida* (1949), three robbers were preparing to flee after a robbery when two policemen, X and Y, appeared on the scene; the robbers fired at the policemen, who fired back; X's bullet struck and killed Y. It was held that the robbers were guilty of murdering Y, since their conduct in firing at the policemen, knowing that their fire would be returned, was the "proximate cause" of Y's death. In *Commonwealth v. Thomas* (1955), A and B, after robbing X, started to flee; X grabbed his gun and fired at the robbers, his bullet killing B. A was held guilty of the murder of B on the theory that the death of B, though unintended by A, was the foreseeable consequence of A's conduct in joining in the robbery of X. Three years later, in *Commonwealth v. Redline* (1958), involving substantially the same facts (the only difference being that an interceding policeman, rather than the robbery victim, shot one of the two robbers to death), the last of the above cases was overruled. The court stated that murder cannot be based upon a shooting which constitutes a justifiable homicide (e.g., where the policeman or felony victim shoots the felon to prevent the commission of the felony or to prevent the felon's escape).

Although it is now generally accepted that there is no felony-murder liability when one of the felons is shot and killed by the victim, a police officer, or a bystander, it is not easy to explain why this is so. It cannot be correct, as the *Redline* court at one point indicated, that the felon is never liable where the death in question constitutes lawful homicide. Nor can it be correct to say, as the court at another point says, rather apologetically, that the felon is never liable when the death is lawful because "justifiable," though he can be when it is lawful because "excusable." It has been suggested that, though it may be foreseeable that someone (robbery victim, policeman, bystander) might be killed by a robber's gun during the robbery, it is not foreseeable that anyone would be slain by another's gun. It would seem, however, that robbery triggers armed resistance from robbery victims and policemen often enough that it is neither unforeseeable nor abnormal that lethal bullets might fly from guns other than those of the robbers.

A more plausible explanation, it is submitted, is the feeling that it is not justice (though it may be poetic justice) to hold the felon liable for murder on account of the death, which the felon did not intend, of a co-felon willingly participating in the risky venture. It is true that it is no defense to intentional homicide crimes that the victim voluntarily placed himself in danger of death at the hands of the defendant, or even that he consented to his own death: a mercy killing constitutes murder; and aiding suicide is murder unless special legislation reduces it to manslaughter (see § 14.6(c)). But with unintended killings it would seem proper to take the victim's willing participation into account, especially if one is not altogether enamored of the felony-murder doctrine. That notion is quite clearly reflected in the provision to be found in several of the modern criminal codes: felony murder liability is expressly limited to the killing of one other than a participant in the underlying felony.

It occasionally happens that one of several co-felons accidentally kills himself while committing or attempting the felony, and the question arises as to the murder liability of his fellow-criminals for the death. Thus A and B together commit arson, or A hires B to commit an arson, and B, who starts the blaze, accidentally burns himself to death; is A guilty of the arson-murder of B? It would seem that the death of B, caused in such a way, is no more unforeseeable or abnormal than a fireman's death would be, so that A might be held liable for the felony murder of B. On the other hand, if one accepts the *Redline* limitation on murder liability for a co-felon's death, on the theory that it is not right to hold him for the death of a willing participant in the risky criminal venture, there should be a similar limitation for the death of a co-felon who manages accidentally to kill himself while voluntarily engaging in the risky criminal enterprise.

Most of the more recent cases involving the killing of a co-felon, however, do not purport to rest upon this latter theory. Rather, it is more generally said that whenever a death is caused by a shot fired by someone other than one of the felons, the killing "can hardly be considered to be 'in furtherance' of the commission or attempted commission of a felony," and does not satisfy "the 'agency' theory of felony murder." Liability in any such case is declared to be "discordant with rational and enlightened views of criminal culpability and liability," especially inasmuch as "the purpose of deterring felons from killing by holding them strictly responsible for killings they or their co-felons commit is not effectuated by punishing them for killings committed by persons not acting in furtherance of the felony." Such reasoning logically leads to the conclusion, which several courts have reached, that the felony-murder rule is equally inapplicable when the killing by another is of the victim, a police officer, or a bystander.

As the cases rejecting that conclusion emphasize, such results cannot be explained on the ground that proximate cause is lacking. Sometimes this is forthrightly acknowledged. When the California Supreme Court in *People v. Gilbert* (1965) narrowed the felony-murder rule in that state so that it did not extend to shootings by non-felons, the court did not purport to rest its position upon principles of causation at all; rather, it forthrightly explained that its limitation of the felony-murder doctrine was based upon a dissatisfaction with its strict liability aspect. The court thus made it clear that if a felon initiates a gun battle "the victim's self-defensive killing or the police officer's killing in the performance of his duty cannot be considered an independent intervening cause for which the defendant is not liable." Causation is thus established, but malice will not be implied under the felony-murder doctrine. Rather malice must be proved under the depraved-heart theory of murder. Reliance upon that theory, of course, increases the prosecution's problems of proof, and in most jurisdictions reduces the penalty which may be imposed upon conviction.

Special mention must be made of one circumstance in which courts *have* generally been willing to impose felony-murder liability even though the shooting was by a person other than one of the felons. This is in the so-called "shield" situation, where courts have reasoned "that a felon's act in using a victim as a shield or in compelling a victim to occupy a place or position of danger constitutes a direct lethal act against the victim." This direct lethal act is deemed to establish a sufficiently close and direct causal connection to justify felony-murder liability.

(e) Felony Murder vs. Depraved–Heart Murder. Both depraved-heart murder and felony murder (with its dangerous felony and causation limitations) may convict a defendant for an unintended death; both require that the defendant's conduct involve a risk of death to another or to others. That being so, does the fact that the defendant causes the accidental death in the commission of a felony, rather than causing it while not committing any felony, add anything to his liability? It does do so in one, perhaps two, ways. First, the risk of death may be much less for felony murder than is required for depraved-heart murder, just as less risk is needed for ordinary negligence than is needed for recklessness-manslaughter and less for manslaughter than for that great amount of negligence which "evinces a depraved heart" as is required for murder. Perhaps an arson that creates a 1% chance of killing some fireman will do for murder if a fireman is in fact killed; but if the defendant, instead of committing arson, merely burns his trash in such a careless way as to create the same danger to firemen, he would not have created enough risk for depraved-heart murder or perhaps even recklessness-manslaughter. Secondly, we saw that some authorities require for depraved-heart murder that the defendant be subjectively aware of the (great) risk he creates, but that for felony murder he need not subjectively foresee the (lesser) risk he creates.

All this points up the fact that the somewhat primitive rationale of the felony-murder doctrine is that the defendant, because he is committing a felony, is by hypothesis a bad person, so that we should not worry too much about the difference between the bad results he intends and the bad results he brings about.

(f) "In the Commission or Attempted Commission of" the Felony. The common law felony-murder rule requires that the killing occur "in the commission or attempted commission of" the felony. The typical modern statute make it murder to cause a death, accidentally or intentionally, "in the commission [or perpetration] or attempted commission [perpetration] of" certain named felonies. Another common type of felony-murder statute says the killing must happen "in the course of and in furtherance of" specified felonies, and yet another declares the killing must occur "while" specified felonies are being committed or attempted. What is the scope of these rather vague expressions?

First of all, it is not enough that a killing occur "during" the felony or its attempt or "while" it is committed or attempted; something more is required than mere coincidence of time and place. Thus if, while the defendant was robbing the teller at the bank, a customer standing in the lobby but unaware of the robbery should, from natural causes, suffer a fatal heart attack, the mere fact that a death occurred at the time of and at the place of the robbery would not make the defendant a murderer. There must be some causal relationship between the felony and the death, a factor that would doubtless be present if the customer, with a weak heart, died of a heart seizure brought on by fright at witnessing the robbery.

Secondly, if this causal connection does exist, the killing may take place at some time before or after, as distinguished from during, the felony, and nevertheless qualify for a killing "in the commission or attempted commission of" the felony. How long before or after the felony? Consider the following hypothetical situations. A conceives the idea of robbing X's gasoline station, five miles away. He gets into his car to drive toward X's station. Four miles (or one mile or one block) from the station, his mind so taken up with his thoughts concerning the robbery that he fails to notice a pedestrian Y, he accidentally runs over Y and kills him. Is Y's death "in the commission or attempted commission of" a robbery? Suppose he runs over pedestrian Y when turning into the station? A good deal depends upon the question concerning the point at which mere preparation for a crime becomes an attempt to commit it (see § 10.4), since for felony murder A must commit or at least attempt to commit the felony. Suppose A does get close enough for an attempt (or else actually commits the crime)—as where he pulls out his gun and tells X to stick up his hands, at which point the gun goes off (accidentally or on purpose) killing X. Here the homicide is actually accomplished "during" the commission or attempted commission of the robbery; such a homicide is surely "in the commission or attempted commission of" the felony.

Suppose A, however, does not thus shoot X; he either takes X's money at gunpoint (i.e., commits robbery) or is frightened away without the money after saying "stick 'em up," by X's armed resistance or by the arrival of a policeman P at the scene (i.e., A commits only attempted robbery); he accidentally or intentionally shoots X or P to death on the gas station premises while making good his escape. Or suppose X or P pursues him for two blocks (or two miles), at which point A, to elude pursuit, shoots X or P to death. Or suppose, after his robbery or attempted robbery, he succeeds in effecting his escape; but two weeks later, driving his car and thinking about the robbery instead of the road, he accidentally runs down Y, a pedestrian. In all these various situations is the death "in the commission or attempted commission of" the robbery? The same sort of problems arise in connection with the other felonies commonly involved in felony-murder cases, e.g., arson, rape, burglary. The difficulty in giving exact answers lies in the inherent vagueness of the term "in the commission of."

It is sometimes said that the killing must occur in the *res gestae* of the felony or attempted felony; but that, without some further explanation, is not particularly helpful. In *State v. Adams* (1936), a leading case on the scope of the term "in the commission of," A and B were in the process of burglarizing X's gas station at night when a policeman P arrived at the scene. The burglars dropped their booty and took to the near-by woods. P followed them for a distance from the station of several hundred feet, B then shot P to death, no doubt intentionally. B, and A as well on the basis of general principles relating to parties to crime, were guilty of intent-to-kill murder (not necessarily constituting first degree murder), but were they guilty of first degree murder (murder "in the commission of" the burglary)? The court held that they were. The homicide must be within the *res gestae* of the burglary; this means that the homicide and the burglary must be "closely connected in point of time, place and causal relation." Applying these factors to the case, the court found the homicide to be in the commission of the burglary, the time between the burglary and the fatal shot being a few minutes, the place being a few hundred feet distant, and the causal connection being that *B* fired the shot to prevent arrest on account of the burglary. At least the case tells us what to look for in construing the scope of the expression "in the commission of": (1) time, (2) place, (3) causal connection.

(1) Time. For purposes of comparing the time of the commission of the felony with the time of the homicide, when is the time of the felony? Robbery is first committed when the defendant takes possession of and moves (i.e., the caption and the asportation of) the victim's property, but it continues as long as he continues to carry it. Burglary is committed when the defendant breaks and enters the building with the appropriate intent; nothing further, like the caption and asportation necessary for robbery, is required for burglary. Arson is committed when the building first catches fire; the further consumption of the building by fire adds nothing further to the arson already committed. Rape is committed upon the first penetration; further sexual activity by the defendant after this initial connection adds nothing to the crime of rape already committed.

Yet for purposes of the time connection implicit in the expression "in the commission of," the crimes of arson, burglary and rape may be considered to continue while the building burns, while the burglars search the building and while the sexual connection is maintained. Thus in the case of the drug store arson which killed the fireman the defendant argued that, even if the death was the foreseeable consequence of the defendant's conduct in committing arson, yet the death did not occur "in the perpetration of" the arson; the arson was complete the moment the fire he set was communicated to the building, and the death occurred much later. The court, however, took the view that the arson continued while the building burned, for purposes of construing the phrase "in the perpetration of" the arson.

But even if it is clear beyond question that the crime was completed before the killing, the felony-murder rule might still apply. The most common case is that in which the killing occurs during the defendant's flight. A great many of the modern statutes contain language—typically the phrase "or in immediate flight therefrom"—making this absolutely clear. But even statutes without such language have rather consistently been construed to extend to immediate flight situations. In assessing what flight is sufficiently immediate, courts require that there have been "no break in the chain of events," as to which a most important consideration is whether the fleeing felon has reached a "place of temporary safety."

Because an attempted felony will also suffice for felony murder, it is likewise true that the felony-murder rule might apply even after the attempt has ended. Illustrative is *State v. Kaesontae* (1996), where defendant called a late-night pedestrian over to his car and then attempted to rob him at gunpoint. The intended victim then moved away from the car without incident and the judge (the trier of fact) found that the attempted robbery then "stopped." When the intended victim then saw another car with three men who "seemed to be affiliated with the would-be robber and the driver of the lead car," he returned to and leaned into the lead car and then was shot by defendant. The court, in accepting the prosecution's argument "that a victim's resistance to an underlying felony may extend the duration of the criminal transaction beyond the time when the felony is technically complete," stressed the matter next discussed below: there was a "causal connection" between the death and the attempted robbery, as the intended victim reasonably assumed that the danger had not passed, and thus his return to the lead car was a part of "the train of events set in motion" by the attempted felony.

(2) Causal Connection. We have seen that the homicide must have some causal connection with the felony in order to qualify for felony murder; more than a mere coincidence of time and place is necessary. In most jurisdictions even more than a but-for causal relationship is required, the usual rule being that the death must be the foreseeable or natural result of the felony (see § 13.5(d)). Aside from these matters, however, the term "in the commission of" implies a more or less close causal connection between felony and homicide. A robber who, in flight from the scene, shoots a policeman who threatens to capture him may easily be found to have caused a death in the commission of the robbery; but if, during his flight, he should happen to spot his enemy and shoot him, this death, though equal to the policeman's death in point of time and place, would lack the causal connection that existed in the policeman's case.

So too of accidental, rather than intentional, killings. A robber fleeing at high speed in his getaway car from the scene of his crime who accidentally runs over and kills a pedestrian stands on a different footing from the robber who, after his robbery and successful flight, speeds (and accidentally runs over the pedestrian) from other motives. The fact that the defendant, having committed a robbery or burglary, is carrying away the booty at the time of the homicide is not so much relevant as to the matter of time (see § 13.5(f)(1)) as it is as a matter of causal relation. One who carries booty is often more in need of a homicide to effect an escape than one who does not. Thus where a robber, carrying in his car the fruits of his robbery, is stopped by a policeman for speeding some time after and some distance away from the place of robbery and he shoots the policeman to death to prevent his discovery of the stolen goods, the causal connection between the robbery and the homicide is quite close. A similar shooting by a robber without booty would lack the causal connection necessary to place the homicide "in the commission of" the robbery.

In short, whether there is a sufficient causal connection between the felony and the homicide depends on whether the defendant's felony dictated his conduct leading to the homicide. If it did, and the matters of time and place are not too remote, the homicide may be "in the commission of" the felony; but if it did not, it may not be.

(3) Differing Views on Scope. Though the scope of the phrase "in the commission or attempted commission of" is properly a matter of time, place and causal connection, the question remains how much time, how much space, how much causal connection is close enough, how much too remote? The cases from different jurisdictions differ considerably in this regard. At one extreme are cases like the following: A and B attempted to rob X at his store but were interrupted by a passerby and ran out the door. X grabbed B on the sidewalk in front of the next store; A shot X dead. Though time (a few moments), place (a few feet) and causal relation (A shot X to prevent his arrest for the attempted robbery) were all very close, they were held to be not close enough for the killing to be considered in the attempt to commit robbery, because A and B had desisted from the attempt and were running away. At the other extreme is the case wherein A and B robbed X in Philadelphia at 2 a.m., stole a car, drove to New Jersey, stopped for something to eat at a diner, sped on their way, were stopped in New Brunswick, N.J., by a policeman P for speeding, whereupon A shot P to death at 4 a.m. Though time (two hours), place (many miles away) and causal relation (perhaps the robbers feared that P was stopping them for the robbery, perhaps they feared P might notice the booty in the car) were rather remote, the court held that the jury could properly find that the killing occurred in the commission of the robbery. Most of the cases take a view somewhere between these extremes.

Is it preferable to take a narrow or broad or in-between view of the scope of the expression "in the commission or attempted commission of"? No doubt the narrow view indicates an antipathy to the whole notion of the felony-murder doctrine.

(4) Homicide Followed by Felony. A problem arises concerning felony murder if the death-blow precedes the felony or the attempt, after which the defendant continues on and commits the felony or its attempt. Of course, if the defendant knocks his intended robbery victim on the head to disable him from resistance, thereby intentionally or accidentally injuring him fatally, and thereafter he takes his victim's money, the homicide occurs in the commission of the felony and so constitutes murder (and under most statutes first-degree murder). But what if the robber thus injures him in a fight, with no thoughts of robbing him, and only later seeing his adversary helpless, decides to rob him? There is a split of authority as to whether this constitutes a homicide in the commission of robbery. It would seem that the homicide, done without thought of a felony, could not be "in the commission of" the felony.

(g) Manslaughter and Aggravated Batteries as Felonies. Voluntary and involuntary manslaughter are generally felonies; and though simple battery is generally only a misdemeanor, aggravated batteries (e.g., battery with a deadly weapon, battery to prevent arrest, battery that causes great bodily harm) usually constitute felonies. What if A commits an act that constitutes the felony of manslaughter or aggravated battery toward B, from which act B dies; is A guilty of the felony-murder of B?

(1) Manslaughter. Suppose A recklessly operates his car, unintentionally killing B, and thus committing involuntary manslaughter, a felony. Has not A committed a foreseeable homicide in the commission of a felony, and therefore is he not guilty of murder rather than of manslaughter? If so, manslaughter has ceased to exist as a separate crime; all manslaughters automatically ride up an escalator to become felony-murders. This is not so, of course; manslaughter will not thus serve as a felony for purposes of the felony-murder doctrine.

(2) Aggravated Battery. Suppose A commits a battery on B with a deadly weapon but not intending to kill, and B unforeseeably dies therefrom, e.g., A, with a knife, cuts B in the arm and B, a hemophiliac, bleeds to death. This constitutes manslaughter, not murder (see § 14.5(d)). But is it not death in the commission of the felony of aggravated battery and hence murder after all? Some cases have held that the collateral felony must be a felony that is "independent" of the conduct which kills; it must involve conduct separate from the acts of personal violence that constitute a necessary part of the homicide itself. Thus, although rape, arson, robbery and burglary are sufficiently independent of the homicide, manslaughter and aggravated battery toward the deceased will not do for felony murder.

What about mayhem, a special type of aggravated battery, as where *A* intentionally cuts off *B*'s arm, not intending to kill, and *B* bleeds to death? Under the rule that requires the collateral felony to be independent, perhaps mayhem will not qualify for felony-murder. It would seem, however, that many jurisdictions would consider this to be felony murder. Where the aggravated-battery felony in question is battery with intent to rape or maim, and the battery causes death, there would be little difficulty in applying the felony-murder rule. Where it is battery with intent to kill or do serious bodily harm, and death results from the battery, the homicide constitutes murder of the intent-to-kill or intent-to-do-serious-bodily-harm types, with no need to resort to felony murder.

What then of a burglary committed with intent to engage in an aggravated battery? One court has concluded that such a felony will not suffice either, reasoning that "the same bootstrapping" is involved here because the offense—practically speaking, a battery occurring inside a dwelling—was still "an integral part of the homicide." But the majority view is to the contrary. As one court explained, the rationale of felony murder, "to reduce the disproportionate number of accidental homicides which occur during the commission" of felonies, applies more forcefully in the burglary case than in the aggravated battery case because the fact the battery takes place inside a dwelling significantly increases the likelihood that death will result from the battery.

(3) Double Jeopardy Distinguished. The principles discussed above should not be confused with the broader double jeopardy doctrine concerning whether a defendant may be prosecuted and punished for both felony murder and the underlying felony. One double jeopardy issue concerns when multiple prosecutions may be undertaken, as to which the Supreme Court in *Brown v. Ohio* (1977) adopted the longstanding *Blockburger* test, which originated as a device for determining congressional intent as to cumulative sentencing: "The applicable rule is that where the same act or transaction constitutes a violation of two distinct statutory provisions, the test to be applied to determine whether there are two offenses or only one, is whether each provision requires proof of an additional fact which the other does not." This means, as the Supreme Court later held in *Harris v. Oklahoma* (1977), that except in extraordinary circumstances a defendant may not constitutionally be separately tried for felony murder and the underlying felony.

What then of prosecution, conviction and cumulative punishment for both felony murder and the underlying felony in a single prosecution? Here, the Supreme Court held in *Albernaz v. U.S.* (1981), *Blockburger* is merely a method for ascertaining legislative intent when nothing more concrete is available. Once the legislative intent is ascertained by that or other means, that is the end of the matter, for "the question of what punishments are constitutionally permissible is not different from the question of what punishment the Legislative Branch intended to be imposed." Thus, as the Court later made clear in *Mo. v. Hunter* (1983), where "a legislature specifically authorizes cumulative punishment under two statutes, regardless of whether those two statutes proscribe the 'same' conduct under *Blockburger,* a court's task of statutory construction is at an end and the prosecutor may seek and the trial court or jury may impose cumulative punishment under such statutes in a single trial." In some states, the courts have concluded that the legislature has authorized cumulative punishments for the felony murder and underlying felony. More frequently, however, such authority has been held to be lacking.

(h) The Future of the Felony–Murder Doctrine. Although most jurisdictions accept the felony-murder doctrine, generally with one or more of the limitations discussed above, it is arguable that there should be no such separate category of murder. The rationale of the doctrine is that one who commits a felony is a bad person with a bad state of mind, and he has caused a bad result, so that we should not worry too much about the fact that the fatal result he accomplished was quite different and a good deal worse than the bad result he intended. Yet it is a general principle of criminal law that one is not ordinarily criminally liable for bad results which differ greatly from intended results (see § 5.3). Nor, as suggested earlier (see § 13.5(e)), can the felony-murder doctrine be justified as the approximate equivalent of depraved-heart murder, where the defendant's conduct carries with it a very high risk of death (see § 13.4). What statistics are available demonstrate that accidental killings do not occur disproportionately often even in connection with the so-called "inherently dangerous" felonies.

Long ago Holmes, in his book *The Common Law,* discussing the felony-murder doctrine, supposed the case of one who, to steal some chickens, shoots at them, accidentally killing a man in the chicken-house whose presence could not have been suspected. Holmes suggests that the fact that the defendant happened to be committing a felony when he shot is an illogical thing to fasten onto to make the accidental killing a murder, for the fact that the shooting is felonious does not increase the likelihood of killing people. "If the object of the [felony-murder] rule is to prevent such accidents, it should make accidental killing with firearms murder, not accidental killing in the effort to steal; while if its object is to prevent stealing, it would do better to hang one thief in every thousand by lot."

Such criticisms have, as we have seen, resulted in the narrowing of the felony-murder doctrine in various ways in many jurisdictions. This has often been accomplished by legislative action in the context of recodification, though courts have often played an important role as well by recognizing that "the felony-murder doctrine expresses a highly artificial concept that deserves no extension beyond its required application."

In other respects, however, the felony-murder doctrine is well entrenched in American law. In England, where for some years felony murder was disparagingly referred to as "constructive murder," the doctrine was abolished in 1957. But in this country, despite the fact that two-thirds of the states have adopted modern codes, only two of those jurisdictions have totally abolished the felony-murder rule. (In one other state, abolition was accomplished by court decision.) A few others have accomplished essentially the same result by requiring that some additional mental state be proved, such as that the death have occurred "under circumstances manifesting extreme indifference to the value of human life" or as a result of recklessness or criminal negligence. Only one state has adopted the Model Penal Code § 210.2(1)(b) rebuttable presumption formulation, whereunder "recklessness and indifference are presumed" if the killing occurred in the commission of certain specified felonies, facilitating conviction for murder of the grossly reckless type.

This experience stands in sharp contrast to what has occurred with respect to the somewhat analogous misdemeanor-manslaughter rule, which very frequently has been abolished in the recodification process (see § 14.5(e)). Consequently, there is reason to believe that the felony-murder doctrine will continue to exist (albeit in a somewhat limited form) for many years to come.

§ 13.6   Resisting–Lawful–Arrest Murder

The old writers—e.g., Hale and Blackstone—announced the flat rule that a homicide caused by conduct in resisting a lawful arrest is murder, without regard to whether the resister had an intent to kill or do serious bodily harm, or did an act in a depraved-heart manner, or by such resistance he was committing a felony so as to come under the felony-murder rule. In other words, these writers stated there was a separate type of murder, in addition to the several types discussed in the preceding sections of this book. Some cases have faithfully reiterated this old rule, but in fact these cases could have been decided on the basis of one of the other types of murder.

In the few cases that actually have raised the issue of whether this separate category of murder exists, the courts have held that it does not. Thus in one case an officer, with a warrant for the defendant's arrest, jumped on the running board of the defendant's car (in which he and his children were riding) to arrest him. The defendant, to prevent arrest by crossing the state line, drove toward the bridge that spanned the river constituting the boundary. The officer grabbed the steering wheel; the car, out of control, hit the bridge; and the officer was killed. It was quite obvious that the defendant did not intentionally crash into the bridge and thus endanger himself and his children as well as the officer. The trial judge, however, charged the jury that it was murder for the defendant to kill while resisting a lawful arrest, even though he did not intend to kill or do violent injury.

On appeal the conviction for murder was reversed, the court stating that it could find no case holding that death while resisting lawful arrest constituted murder where the defendant did not intentionally kill or do serious injury or do an act inherently dangerous. The holding thus negatives the existence of homicide-while-resisting-lawful-arrest murder as a separate kind of murder. And on principle there should not be this separate category.

There remains the possibility that an unintended death caused by resisting lawful arrest might come under the felony-murder rule, if it is a statutory felony to resist lawful arrest and (in most jurisdictions) if death is the foreseeable result of the resister's manner of resisting arrest. In most jurisdictions the crime of resisting arrest is a misdemeanor only. In one state, where it was a statutory felony to resist lawful arrest, the defendant was held guilty of murder on the felony-murder theory; but another state held that the crime of battery-to-prevent-arrest, though a felony, was not a felony independent of the homicide and so could not support a felony-murder conviction.

Finally, there is also the possibility that a murder statute will expressly cover the resisting-lawful-arrest situation. Although such provisions are not common, they are to be found even in a few of the modern recodifications.

§ 13.7   Degrees of Murder

Although the English judges created the crime of murder, including the four separate types of murder discussed in the preceding sections, they never divided murder into degrees. That development has come about through legislation. In England and in a minority of American states there is no division of murder into degrees. But in most states murder is thus divided, usually into two (sometimes into three) degrees. The purpose of doing so is to limit the more severe punishments (usually but not always including the death penalty) to first degree murder, with less severe penalties (generally including life imprisonment, but not the death penalty) for second degree murder.

Almost all American jurisdictions that divide murder into degrees include the following two murder situations in the category of first degree murder: (1) intent-to-kill murder where there exists (in addition to the intent to kill) the elements of premeditation and deliberation, and (2) felony murder where the felony in question is one of five or six listed felonies, generally including rape, robbery, kidnaping, arson and burglary. Some states instead or in addition have other kinds of first degree murder.

(a) Premeditated, Deliberate, Intentional Killing. To be guilty of this form of first degree murder the defendant must not only intend to kill but in addition he must premeditate the killing and deliberate about it. It is not easy to give a meaningful definition of the words "premeditate" and "deliberate" as they are used in connection with first degree murder. Perhaps the best that can be said of "deliberation" is that it requires a cool mind that is capable of reflection, and of "premeditation" that it requires that the one with the cool mind did in fact reflect, at least for a short period of time before his act of killing.

It is often said that premeditation and deliberation require only a "brief moment of thought" or a "matter of seconds," and convictions for first degree murder have frequently been affirmed where such short periods of time were involved. The better view, however, is that to "speak of premeditation and deliberation which are instantaneous, or which take no appreciable time, * * * destroys the statutory distinction between first and second degree murder," and (in much the same fashion that the felony-murder rule is being increasingly limited) this view is growing in popularity. This is not to say, however, that premeditation and deliberation cannot exist when the act of killing follows immediately after the formation of the intent. The intention may be finally formed only as a conclusion of prior premeditation and deliberation, while in other cases the intention may be formed without prior thought so that premeditation and deliberation occurs only with the passage of additional time for "further thought, and a turning over in the mind."

It is not enough that the defendant is shown to have had time to premeditate and deliberate. One must actually premeditate and deliberate, as well as actually intend to kill, to be guilty of this sort of first degree murder. A killer may, in a particular situation, be incapable of that cool reflection called for by the requirement of premeditation and deliberation, as where his capacity to premeditate and deliberate is prevented by emotional upset, by intoxication, by feebleness of intellect short of insanity, or by terror. In such cases he can generally be held guilty of second degree murder, however, on the theory that, though he could not premeditate and deliberate, he could and did at least have an intent to kill (as shown, in most cases, by his intentional use of a deadly weapon upon the victim).

Premeditation and deliberation, like intent to kill, are subjective states of mind. Often there is no witness to the killing; and even if there is a witness, the killer does not always speak aloud what is in his mind. So existence of the facts of premeditation and deliberation must be determined from the defendant's conduct (so far as we can learn of it, usually from circumstantial evidence) in the light of the surrounding circumstances. There is no presumption that the murder is first degree murder; for the higher degree there must be some affirmative evidence to support a finding that the defendant in fact did premeditate and deliberate.

On the basis of events before and at the time of the killing, the trier of fact will sometimes be entitled to infer that the defendant actually premeditated and deliberated his intentional killing. Three categories of evidence are important for this purpose: (1) facts about how and what the defendant did prior to the actual killing which show he was engaged in activity directed toward the killing, that is, *planning activity;* (2) facts about the defendant's prior relationship and conduct with the victim from which *motive* may be inferred; and (3) facts about the *nature of the killing* from which it may be inferred that the manner of killing was so particular and exacting that the defendant must have intentionally killed according to a preconceived design. Illustrative of the first category are such acts by the defendant as prior possession of the murder weapon, surreptitious approach of the victim, or taking the prospective victim to a place where others are unlikely to intrude. In the second category are prior threats by the defendant to do violence to the victim, plans or desires of the defendant that would be facilitated by the death of the victim, and prior conduct of the victim known to have angered the defendant. As to the third category, the manner of killing, what is required is evidence (usually based upon examination of the victim's body) showing that the wounds were deliberately placed at vital areas of the body. The mere fact that the killing was attended by much violence or that a great many wounds were inflicted is not relevant in this regard, as such a killing is just as likely (or perhaps more likely) to have been on impulse. Conduct by the defendant *after* the killing in an effort to avoid detection and punishment is obviously not relevant for purposes of showing premeditation and deliberation, as it only goes to show the defendant's state of mind at the time and not before or during the killing.

In dealing with the subject of causation in the criminal law, and in particular the problem of the bad aim, we noted that where A unjustifiably aims a lethal blow at B with intent to kill B, but the blow misses B and kills C, A is guilty of the murder of C though he never intended harm to C. On the same principle, if A without justification aims at B with a premeditated and deliberate intent to kill B (so that if he should kill B he would be guilty of first degree murder) but, missing B, he accidentally hits and kills C, A is, by the great weight of authority, guilty of the first degree murder of C (see § 5.4(d)).

Judge (later Justice) Cardozo suggested that the distinction between first and second degree murder based upon the existence or nonexistence of premeditation and deliberation is too vague and obscure for any jury to understand, and that it should not be continued in the law. The Model Penal Code does not utilize the degree device, but instead lists in § 210.6 several mitigating and aggravating factors that are to be taken into account at the time of sentencing. As the draftsmen point out, the premeditation-deliberation formula is not a sound basis upon which to determine the severity of the sanction to be imposed upon the murder defendant; there are cases in which extreme depravity is revealed by a murder on impulse, just as there are so-called premeditated murders (e.g., mercy killings, suicide pacts) that are "far more the product of extraordinary circumstances than a true reflection of the actor's normal character." But most of the recent state criminal codes have retained the distinction, and thus it still must be grappled with.

(b) In the Commission of Listed Felonies. A killing (even an unintended killing) in the commission or attempted commission of a felony may be murder (see § 13.5); if it is, and if the felony in question is one listed in the first degree murder statute (e.g., rape, robbery, kidnaping, arson and burglary) then the murder will be murder in the first degree.

Often we find an intentional killing committed during one of these listed felonies dealt with as a first degree murder of the felony-murder sort, rather than of the deliberate and premeditated intent-to-kill sort. This is because the prosecuting attorney may, in a particular case, find it easier to obtain a first degree murder conviction in the felony murder situation—for here he need not prove those vague concepts premeditation and deliberation in addition to the intent to kill.

(c) Lying in Wait; Poison; Torture. Although such language is almost never found in the modern codes, at one time it was common for first degree murder statutes also to cover those murders done by poison, lying in wait, or torture. "Lying in wait" is generally held to require a watching and waiting in a concealed position with an intent to kill or do serious bodily injury to another; it does not, of course, require that the one "lying" in wait be in a prone, rather than a sitting or standing, position. Thus it is not lying in wait to wait for the victim, at the invitation of his family, in his living room, or to follow close behind the victim on the street, approaching him when the victim pauses; for in each case the element of concealment is missing.

It is not necessarily murder by poison to kill another person with poison, as where one administered poison innocently and for a lawful purpose and yet produces a death. The homicide must first amount to murder, either because the defendant had an intent to kill or do serious bodily injury, or because his conduct evinced a depraved heart, or because the death by poison resulted from the defendant's commission or attempted commission of a felony. A poison is not necessarily something administered internally; it may be inhaled or injected.

Murder by torture requires something in the way of pain endured over a period of time. It is not enough, however, that the defendant, in murdering his victim, cause him such pain; the defendant must intend to inflict the pain. The following forms of killing, among others, have been held to constitute torture when accompanied by the necessary intent to cause pain: burning, beating, and failure to call medical aid after inflicting a beating. It has been held that the act causing the pain must be the act that causes the death.

On occasion, the legislature of a particular state has added to the traditional three forms of murder just discussed, in which case it is even less likely that any killing by such means will be deemed to suffice. Illustrative is a statute including within the definition of murder in the first degree that murder "perpetrated by means of poison, lying in wait, torture or child abuse or by any other kind of willful, deliberate or premeditated killing." A court construing such a statute understandably concluded that because child abuse "more clearly diverges from the other three enumerated means in that it does not strongly correlate with deliberate, premeditated action since it can be and often is committed in a rash, impulsive manner," it is necessary to prove that malice aforethought is otherwise present (i.e., by showing intent to kill or an abandoned and malignant heart).

(d) Other First Degree Murder. Even in the modern codes, certain other types of murder are sometimes put into the first degree category. On occasion this is done by reference to some other manner of killing, such as by bombing or by procuring execution by perjury. More common are statutes putting a murder into the first degree bracket because of the status of the victim. A few statutes identify certain other aggravating characteristics, such as that the murder was committed for pay, that it involved the killing of more than one person, or that it was committed by a person with a prior murder conviction or a person in prison. As a consequence of rejecting the oft-criticized premeditation-deliberation distinction (see § 13.7(a)), some jurisdictions have put all intentional killings into the first degree murder category. Less defensible is placing even depraved heart murder into this category, as a few states have done.

(e) Second Degree Murder. At one time, the typical statute dividing murder into degrees provided that a premeditated, deliberate, intentional killing, and murder in the perpetration or attempted perpetration of five or six named felonies, was first degree murder (often adding murder by lying in wait, by poison, or by torture); and that all other murder was second degree murder. Under such a statute, still to be found in some states, what murder is left over for second degree murder to encompass?

First, intent-to-kill murder without the added ingredients of premeditation and deliberation is second degree murder. Second, intent-to-do-serious-bodily-injury murder (whether this intent is premeditated and deliberated or not) is second degree murder. Third, depraved-heart murder falls into the second degree murder category. Lastly, felony-murder, where the felony in question is not a listed one (e.g., abortion, larceny), comes under the second degree category, unless the defendant's conduct is covered by some other part of the first degree murder statute, as where in the felony's commission he intentionally kills with premeditation and deliberation. Thus where a statute makes it a felony to destroy or remove a navigational marker, if a defendant should cut adrift the bell buoy marking the Inchcape Rock, as a consequence of which a vessel should strike the rock and a sailor drown, the defendant would be guilty of felony murder, for death to a mariner is the foreseeable consequence of such conduct; but the murder would be that of the second degree, for malicious mischief is not a listed felony.

Although the kind of statute just discussed does not undertake to define the crime of murder it thus divides into degrees ("murder" committed in certain ways is first degree murder; all other "murder" is second degree murder), most murder statutes in the recent criminal codes define murder and its various degrees in terms of "killing" or "causing death" under certain described conditions. Such statutes often make changes in the scope of the common law crime of murder; and, not fitting into the pattern of the statute above described, the particular statute must be consulted as to the degree of murder as well as referred to as to the scope of murder.

Chapter 14

MANSLAUGHTER; SUICIDE ASSISTANCE

Table of Sections

> For additional analysis of the above topics and citations to authorities supporting their discussion in this Book, consult the author's 3-volume *Substantive Criminal Law* treatise, also available as Westlaw database SUBCRL. See the Table of Cross-References in this Book.

§ 14.1 Manslaughter—Classification

It is sometimes stated in statutes and judicial decisions which undertake to define manslaughter that manslaughter is "the unlawful killing of another human being without malice aforethought." But as "malice aforethought" in connection with the law of homicide is not to be taken literally (see § 13.1(a)), this definition is of small help in solving particular cases. It is more helpful to recognize at the outset that manslaughter is an intermediate crime which lies half-way between the more serious crime of murder, at the one extreme, and, at the other extreme, justifiable or excusable homicide, which is not criminal at all (see chs. 8 & 9). Thus manslaughter constitutes a sort of catch-all category that includes homicides which are not bad enough to be murder but which are too bad to be no crime whatever.

Although the common law drew a distinction between voluntary manslaughter and involuntary manslaughter on the basis of the different types of conduct involved, it did not do so for any purpose of providing different punishments. Today many American jurisdictions maintain the old distinction between voluntary and involuntary manslaughter, usually awarding a less severe punishment for involuntary than for voluntary manslaughter. Some modern American statutes, however, have discarded the adjectives (voluntary and involuntary) and instead divide manslaughter into degrees, reserving a higher penalty for first degree manslaughter. But the modern trend, reflected in a majority of recent recodifications, is for these to be but one single manslaughter crime.

A few modern statutes place within the manslaughter category certain homicides that constituted murder rather than manslaughter at common law. Thus, in some jurisdictions the crime of manslaughter is defined to include killings of the intent-to-do-serious-bodily-injury, depraved heart, and felony murder varieties. But whether or not that is so, manslaughter is a crime which is separate and distinct from, rather than merely a degree of, the crime of murder.

§ 14.2 Heat–Of–Passion Voluntary Manslaughter

Voluntary manslaughter in most jurisdictions consists of an intentional homicide committed under extenuating circumstances that mitigate, though they do not justify or excuse, the killing. The principal extenuating circumstance is the fact that the defendant, when he killed the victim, was in a state of passion engendered in him by an adequate provocation (i.e., a provocation that would cause a reasonable man to lose his normal self-control).

(a) The State of Mind. Although the killing of another person—when accompanied by an intent to kill, or by an intent to do serious bodily injury short of death, or when resulting from such unreasonable and highly reckless conduct as to "evince a depraved heart"—often amounts to murder, yet it may under certain circumstances amount only to voluntary manslaughter. Most killings that constitute voluntary manslaughter are of the intent-to-kill sort—so much so that voluntary manslaughter is often defined in the cases (and, sometimes, by statute) as if intent to kill were a required ingredient. But, theoretically at least, they might be of the intent-to-do-serious-bodily-injury, or of the depraved-heart, types. Thus—to take the most common sort of voluntary manslaughter, a killing while in a reasonable "heat of passion"—in most cases the defendant intentionally kills the one who has aroused this passion in him. But if, in the throes of such a passion, he should intend instead to do his tormentor serious bodily injury short of death, or if he should, without intending to kill him, endanger his life by very reckless (depraved heart) conduct, the resulting death ought equally to be voluntary manslaughter rather than murder or no crime. Thus, the great majority of modern statutes, either by a reference to all cases that would otherwise be murder or by similar general language, take this broad view.

The usual view of voluntary manslaughter thus presupposes an intent to kill (or perhaps an intent to do serious injury or to engage in very reckless conduct), holding that in spite of the existence of this bad intent the circumstances may reduce the homicide to manslaughter. But there is a minority view, expressed in an occasional case and in a few manslaughter statutes, to the effect that the passion must be so great as to destroy the intent to kill, in order to accomplish the reduction of the homicide to voluntary manslaughter. Such a stringent view doubtless makes it more difficult for a defendant to obtain a reduction of his homicide to voluntary manslaughter; for he must show that his passion went so far as to rob him of his normal capacity to entertain murderous thoughts, rather than that it merely made him lose the normal self-control which enables him to resist any temptation to slay another person.

The usual type of voluntary manslaughter involves the intentional killing of another while under the influence of a reasonably-induced emotional disturbance (in earlier terminology, while in a "heat of passion") causing a temporary loss of normal self-control. Except for this reasonable emotional condition, the intentional killing would be murder. The term traditionally used to describe that condition—"heat of passion"—is very often used in modern manslaughter statutes, either alone or with some additional language. (But some modern statutes seek to define this mitigating circumstance more broadly and thus do not utilize the "heat of passion" term; see § 14.2(b).) The "passion" (emotional disturbance) involved in the crime of voluntary manslaughter is generally rage (great anger); but some cases have pointed out that other intense emotions—such as fright or terror or "wild desperation"—will do. A "passion for revenge," of course, will not do.

There are four obstacles for the defendant to overcome before he can have his intentional killing reduced from murder to voluntary manslaughter: (1) There must have been a reasonable provocation. (2) The defendant must have been in fact provoked. (3) A reasonable man so provoked would not have cooled off in the interval of time between the provocation and the delivery of the fatal blow. And (4), the defendant must not in fact have cooled off during that interval.

(b) Reasonable Provocation. It is sometimes stated that, in order to reduce an intentional killing to voluntary manslaughter, the provocation involved must be such as to cause a reasonable man to kill. Yet the reasonable man, however greatly provoked he may be, does not kill. The law recognizes this fact, by holding that the one who thus kills is guilty of the crime of voluntary manslaughter, while at the same time, the law considers that one who really acts reasonably in killing another (as in proper self-defense) is guilty of no crime. What is really meant by "reasonable provocation" is provocation that causes a reasonable man to lose his normal self-control; and, although a reasonable man who has thus lost control over himself would not kill, yet his homicidal reaction to the provocation is at least understandable. Therefore, one who reacts to the provocation by killing his provoker should not be guilty of murder. But neither should he be guilty of no crime at all. So his conduct falls into the intermediate category of voluntary manslaughter.

There has been a tendency for the law to jell concerning what conduct does or does not constitute a reasonable provocation for purposes of voluntary manslaughter. Thus it is often held that a reasonable man may be provoked into a passion when he (or a close relative) is hurt by violent physical blows, or is unlawfully arrested or discovers his spouse in the act of adultery; but that he can never be provoked by mere words or by trespasses to his property. In modern times, however, there seems to be a growing realization that what might or might not cause a loss of self-control in a reasonable Englishman of a century ago might not necessarily produce the same reaction in the reasonable Anglo–American of today. As a consequence of this realization there may be a future trend away from the usual practice of placing the various types of provocatory conduct into pigeon-holes. At all events the following is a list of provocations which have traditionally been considered, almost as a matter of law, to be reasonable or unreasonable and which, in general, influence our legal thinking today.

(1) **Battery.** A light blow, though it may constitute a battery, can not constitute a reasonable provocation; but a violent, painful blow, with fist or weapon, ordinarily will do so. Even in the case where the defendant kills in response to a violent blow, however, he may not have his homicide reduced to voluntary manslaughter if he himself by his own prior conduct (as by vigorously starting the fracas) was responsible for that violent blow. Something too may depend upon a comparison of the weapon used by the victim to inflict the blow upon the killer and the weapon the latter "used in retort," as where a dagger is used in retaliation for a blow with a fist, or five lethal slashes with a straight razor for one wifely blow on the head with a small fireplace poker.

(2) **Mutual Combat.** Where two persons willingly engage in mutual combat, and during the fight one kills the other as the result of an intention to do so formed during the struggle, the homicide has long been held to be manslaughter, and not murder, the notion being that the suddenness of the occasion, rather than some provocation by the victim, mitigates the intentional killing to something less than murder. A study of this type of voluntary manslaughter concludes that cases of intentional killings in mutual combat are generally treated on the basis of provocation involved in batteries, the type of provocation discussed immediately above.

(3) **Assault.** Where one attempts but fails to commit a violent battery upon another (thereby committing a criminal assault), there is a disagreement in the cases as to whether the assault can arouse in a reasonable man that passion which will mitigate to manslaughter an intentional killing of the assaulter by the one assaulted. The better view, however, is that an attack upon the defendant which was unsuccessful may constitute adequate provocation in extreme cases, as where the attacker fires a pistol at him.

(4) **Illegal Arrest.** The cases are in dispute concerning the effect of an illegal arrest upon the passions of a reasonable man— some taking the view that such an arrest might reasonably arouse a heat of passion in him, others the view that a reasonable man could not be so aroused. If an illegal arrest may be a reasonable provocation in some circumstances, it would seem that these circumstances

should include the fact that the defendant knew or at least believed that his arrest was illegal; and perhaps that the defendant knew or believed he was innocent of the crime for which he was arrested, since an innocent man would more reasonably be provoked by an illegal arrest than a guilty one. In any event, a *lawful* arrest cannot constitute sufficient provocation.

(5) Adultery. It is the law practically everywhere that a husband who discovers his wife in the act of committing adultery is reasonably provoked, so that when, in his passion, he intentionally kills either his wife or her lover (or both), his crime is voluntary manslaughter rather than murder. So too a wife may be reasonably provoked into a heat of passion upon finding her husband in the act of adultery with another woman. The modern tendency is to extend the rule of mitigation beyond the narrow situation where one spouse actually catches the other in the act of committing adultery. Thus it has been held that a reasonable though erroneous belief on the part of the husband that his wife is committing adultery will do. Some cases have held that a reasonable man may be provoked upon suddenly being told of his wife's infidelity (see § 14.2(b)(6)). One case holds that the sudden sight of his wife's paramour in his mother-in-law's home might reasonably cause the husband, who knew his wife had been having an affair with the man, to lose his ordinary self-control, mitigating his killing to manslaughter.

The rule of mitigation does not, however, extend beyond the marital relationship so as to include engaged persons, divorced couples and unmarried lovers—as where a man is enraged at the discovery of his mistress in the sexual embrace of another man. This limitation seems questionable, however, at least in cases where there existed a longstanding relationship comparable to that of husband and wife.

In the adultery situation there is a popular belief that it is not the crime of voluntary manslaughter, but rather no crime at all, for the enraged husband to kill his wife's paramour. A few states by statute and one by court decision once made this conduct a form of justifiable homicide, but this is no longer the case. The criminal law does not recognize the existence of the so-called "unwritten law" by which a man who finds his wife in adultery becomes temporarily "insane" just long enough to enable him to kill her lover. Nevertheless, juries no doubt sometimes disregard the judge's instructions in these cases and take the law into their own hands, finding the husband not guilty of any crime when, legally speaking, they ought to find him guilty of voluntary manslaughter.

(6) Words. The formerly well-established rule that words alone (or words plus gestures) will never do for reducing an intentional killing to voluntary manslaughter has in many jurisdictions changed into a rule that words alone will sometimes do, at least if the words are informational (conveying information of a fact which constitutes a reasonable provocation when that fact is observed) rather than merely insulting or abusive words. Thus a sudden confession of adultery by a wife, or information from a third person that a wife has been unfaithful, has sometimes been held to constitute a provocation to the husband of the same sort as if he had made an "ocular observation" of his wife's adultery.

Words have also been relied upon in an effort to reduce an intentional killing to voluntary manslaughter when the defendant makes a claim of homosexual panic, "premised on the theory that a person with latent homosexual tendencies will have an extreme and uncontrollably violent reaction when confronted with a homosexual proposition." However, there is not agreement on whether a non-violent homosexual advance (NHA) should ever qualify as reasonable provocation. On the one hand, it is claimed that the answer must be no because the defendant must have "acted in the heat of passion caused by provocation sufficient to cause a reasonable person in similar circumstances to lose his or her normal self-control," while merely "experiencing fear or hatred of gay people in response to a homosexual overture should not suffice to provoke a reasonable person to lose his or her self-control and resort to deadly force." On the other hand, it has been forcefully argued that when provocation is properly viewed in terms of "a person who possesses ordinary human weaknesses," it becomes apparent that there is no compelling reason why "a homicide motivated by a NHA [should] be treated any differently" than other "out-of-control homicides in responses to provocations" that the criminal justice system "punishe[s] less severely than ordinary intentional killings." The latter view apparently prevails in the trial courts, for the appellate reports reveal a number of NHA cases in which the trial judge gave the jury a provocation instruction (sometimes, but usually not, resulting in a jury verdict of voluntary manslaughter). However, those cases in which the trial judge *refused* to so instruct have been affirmed on appeal. Some of these decisions might be explained away on the notion that "a defendant is not entitled to an instruction on any defense, including provocation, unless he presents some credible evidence in support of his claim," but others cannot be disposed of so readily.

(7) Injuries to Third Persons. Just as a reasonable man may be provoked by some sorts of conduct that inflict injury upon himself, so too he may be provoked by the same sorts of conduct that causes injury to his close relatives. It has been held that the rule does not extend beyond close relatives to more distant relatives and friends, but in view of the modern tendency to leave questions of the reasonableness of a provocation to the jury, there ought not to be any absolute rule that injuries, however grievous, to friends, however close, can never constitute a reasonable provocation.

(8) Miscellaneous. Aside from the commonly-urged provocations discussed above, various defendants have from time to time tried out novel ones, generally without success—e.g., the fact that the wife, in a property settlement, actually made off with more property than had been agreed upon with her husband; that another person had attempted to steal the defendant's vehicle; that a police officer was illegally searching the defendant's residence; that a loved one was suffering greatly and was killed by defendant to end his misery; that a judge, in a non-support case instituted by a wife against her husband, may have erroneously ruled against the husband; that defendant has lost custody of his grandson to his son-in-law, who he viewed as abusive; that the defendant and his victim "had minutes earlier been enmeshed in a fit of 'road rage' spurred by each other's aggressive driving"; that an infant had been persistently crying; or that a job supervisor gave an unfavorable rating likely to result in termination of employment. Yet, courts have on occasion extended the notion of reasonable provocation to other situations.

(9) Mistake as to Provocation. Sometimes the defendant intentionally kills another in a reasonable, but erroneous, belief that the victim has injured him—as where the circumstances of the provocation are such that the defendant reasonably concludes that his wife is committing adultery, when in fact she is not. It would seem that the provocation is adequate to reduce the homicide to voluntary manslaughter if the killer reasonably believes that the injury to him exists, though actually he has not been injured. In other words, a man's passion directed against another person suffices for manslaughter if (1) he reasonably believes that he has been injured by the other, and (2) a reasonable man who actually has suffered such an injury would be put in a passion directed against the other. But this issue is rarely addressed even in modern manslaughter statutes.

(10) The Reasonable Man. Some cases have considered whether the law should take into account, in measuring the adequacy of the provocation, the fact that the defendant possesses some peculiar mental or physical characteristic, not possessed by the ordinary person, which caused him, in the particular case, to lose his self-control. It is quite uniformly held that the defendant's special mental qualities—as where, because of a sunstroke or head injury, he is particularly excitable—are not to be considered. Even more clearly, he does not qualify for the voluntary manslaughter treatment where, because of intoxication, he easily loses his self-control; that is to say, he is to be judged by the standard of the reasonable sober man. In a case involving a defendant who killed a prostitute, the fact that the defendant, who was sexually impotent, was jeered at by the prostitute for his impotency was held not to constitute a reasonable provocation, the defendant's physical abnormality being irrelevant; the test is how the victim's conduct affects a reasonable man, not how it affects a man with the defendant's physical characteristics.

There has, however, been some discussion of the fairness of the strictly objective reasonable-man test for determining the adequacy of the provocation. It has been persuasively argued that at least some individual peculiarities should be taken into account "because they bear upon the inference as to the actor's character that it is fair to draw upon the basis of his act." In some recent decisions courts have shown a greater willingness to consider subjective factors while still giving lip service to the reasonable man requirement.

Model Penal Code § 210.3 introduces a certain amount of subjectivity in its proposed test, under which a homicide otherwise murder is only manslaughter if "committed under the influence of extreme mental or emotional disturbance for which there is reasonable explanation or excuse," the reasonableness of which is to be "determined from the viewpoint of a person in the actor's situation under the circumstances as he believes them to be." This provision states a middle ground between a standard ignoring all individual peculiarities and one making emotional distress decisive regardless of the nature of its cause. The actor's "situation" takes into account his "personal handicaps and some external circumstances," such as "blindness, shock from traumatic injury, and extreme grief," but not his "idiosyncratic moral values." The ultimate question is "whether the actor's loss of self-control can be understood in terms that arouse sympathy in the ordinary citizen."

A substantial minority of the modern criminal codes contain a provision along these lines. Some of them, however, either by leaving out the language about the actor's situation or by use of certain other language seem less subjective than the Model Penal Code provision. A few also require that the defendant not have been at fault in bringing about the provoking events.

(c) Actual Provocation. Assuming that the provocation was such as to cause a reasonable man to lose his self-control, there remains the question of whether the defendant was in fact provoked by the victim's conduct. If, because he is of a cooler temperament than the reasonable man, he was not actually provoked (and therefore he killed his victim in cold blood), he is guilty of murder and cannot have his intentional killing reduced to voluntary manslaughter.

(d) Reasonable Time to Cool Off. Assuming that the victim's conduct actually provokes, and reasonably provokes, the defendant into a passion which robs him of his normal capacity for self-control, there still remains a problem of reasonable time for the passion to subside whenever there is a time lag between provocation and infliction of the fatal wound. By the majority view, a provoked defendant cannot have his homicide reduced to voluntary manslaughter where the time elapsing between the provocation and the death blow is such that a reasonable man thus provoked would have cooled; and this is so even though the defendant, being slower to cool off than the ordinary person, has not in fact cooled off by the time he delivers the lethal blow. A minority view, however, eliminates the reasonable-time test, stating that if there is a reasonable and actual provocation, the defendant's crime is manslaughter if in fact, because of his peculiar temperament, he has not cooled off, though a reasonable man's passion would have subsided.

What constitutes a reasonable cooling time in a particular case depends upon the nature of the provocation and the circumstances surrounding its occurrence—a matter to be determined by the jury as a question of fact, unless the time is so short or so long that the court may hold that, as a matter of law, it was reasonable or unreasonable.

Not infrequently there is a considerable time interval between the victim's act of provocation and the defendant's fatal conduct— time enough for passion to subside. In the meantime, however, some event occurs that rekindles the defendant's passion. If this new occurrence is such as to trigger the passion of a reasonable man, the cooling-off period should start with the new occurrence—a fact the cases have not always recognized.

The typical heat-of-passion manslaughter case is that in which one specific event (of one of the kinds previously discussed) immediately produces a rage in the defendant. This may account for the fact that modern codes usually state that defendant's passion must be "sudden." However, a more realistic appraisal of how human emotions work compels the conclusion—which some courts have reached—that a reasonable provocation can be produced by a series of events occurring over a considerable span of time. When that is the case, then of course the measurement of the cooling time should commence with the occurrence of the last provocative event.

(e) Actual Cooling Off. One more bridge remains for the defendant to cross: although (1) he is reasonably provoked and (2) he is actually provoked and (3) a reasonable man would not have cooled off, yet he cannot have his homicide reduced to voluntary manslaughter if, because his passions subside more quickly than those of the ordinary person, he has actually cooled off by the time he commits his deadly act. One who, in full possession of his faculties, kills another without justification or excuse commits murder; and it is no help to his cause that an ordinary man would not have held his emotions under control.

(f) Classification. Thus it may be seen that there are three intent-to-kill homicide situations, each calling for a different conclusion: (1) One who successfully surmounts all four hurdles—i.e., one who is reasonably and actually provoked and who reasonably and actually does not cool off—is guilty of voluntary manslaughter. (2) One who stumbles on hurdles 1 or 3—i.e., one who, though actually in a passion when he kills, is unreasonably so, either because a reasonable men would not have been provoked in the first place or because a reasonable man so provoked would have cooled—is a candidate for second-degree murder in most jurisdictions, for though he intended to kill he lacked the premeditation and deliberation that distinguishes first from second degree murder in most jurisdictions. (3) One who trips up on hurdles 2 or 4—i.e., one who, although he receives a reasonable provocation and although a reasonable man would not have cooled off, either is not provoked or actually cools off—kills in cold blood, with time and capacity to premeditate and deliberate, and so may be convicted of first-degree murder.

(g) Provocation From One Other Than Person Killed. It sometimes happens that the source of the provocation is a person other than the individual killed by the defendant while in a heat of passion. This may happen (1) because the defendant is mistaken as to the person responsible for the acts of provocation; (2) because the defendant attempts to kill his provoker but instead kills an innocent bystander; or (3) because the defendant strikes out in a rage at a third party.

If *A* has been reasonably provoked and believes that *B* is the person (or, one of the persons) responsible for the provoking conduct, then his killing of *B* in a heat of passion is manslaughter even if it turns out that *C* and not *B* was actually the provoking party. Likewise, if *A*, who has been reasonably and actually provoked by *B* into a passion to kill *B*, shoots at *B* but instead hits and kills innocent-bystander *C*, *A*'s crime is voluntary manslaughter. In each instance *A*'s purpose has been to act against the individual thought to be responsible for his outrage, and thus there are mitigating circumstances that should be taken into account even if *A* was negligent in determining the source of the provocation or in causing danger to bystanders. But a few of the modern codes appear to foreclose such a result.

More difficult is the situation in which *A*, actually and reasonably provoked by *B*, in his passion strikes out at and kills *C*, known by *A* to be only an innocent bystander. The courts have quite consistently held that the killing of *C* does not qualify as manslaughter, apparently upon the assumption that a reasonable man would never be so greatly provoked as to strike out in blind anger at an innocent person. The Model Penal Code, however, does not so limit provocation, on the ground that there may be some such cases in which "the cause and the intensity of the actor's emotion * * * [are] less indicative of moral depravity than would be a homicidal response to a blow to one's person."

(h) Rationale of Voluntary Manslaughter. Why is it that there exists such a crime as voluntary manslaughter to aid one who kills when provoked into a passion, yet there is no crime like, say, voluntary theft or voluntary mayhem to aid others who, reasonably provoked into a passion, steal from or maim their tormentors? The answer is historical. With most crimes other than murder the English court came to have discretion as to the punishment and so could take extenuating circumstances into account in the sentencing process; but with murder the penalty remained fixed at death, without the possibility of making any allowance for the extenuating fact that the victim provoked the defendant into a reasonable passion. "The rule of law that provocation may, within narrow bounds, reduce murder to manslaughter, represents an attempt by the courts to reconcile the preservation of the fixed penalty for murder with a limited concession to natural human weakness."

This, of course, "fails to explain the doctrine's continued viability," and courts have by and large failed to articulate a modern rationale. It has been suggested, however, that the present rationale for heat-of-passion manslaughter is that when

> the provocation is so great that the ordinary law abiding person would be expected to lose self-control so that he could not help but act violently, yet he would still have sufficient self-control so that he could avoid using force likely to cause death or great bodily harm in response to the provocation, then * * * the actor's moral blameworthiness is found not in his violent response, but in his *homicidal* violent response. He did not control himself as much as he *should* have, or as much as common experience tells us he *could* have, nor as much as the ordinary law abiding person *would* have.

§ 14.3 Other–Extenuating–Circumstances Voluntary Manslaughter

The reasoning set forth at the conclusion of the last section leads to the question of whether the crime of voluntary manslaughter is a big enough receptacle to include other intentional homicides that, by reason of other extenuating features (i.e., other than the one feature of passion induced by reasonable provocation), ought to be less than murder yet more than no crime at all. In some states such a view, however desirable, is made difficult (though apparently not impossible) by narrowly-drawn statutes defining voluntary manslaughter solely in terms of heat of passion. In those states that do not define voluntary manslaughter by statute, however, it has been easier to open up the crime to include other homicides. But in recent years, such expansion of the concept of voluntary manslaughter has often occurred by legislation.

(a) "Imperfect" Right of Self–Defense. In order for a killer to have a "perfect" defense of self-defense to homicide, (1) he must be free from fault in bringing on the difficulty with his adversary; and (2) he must reasonably believe (though he need not correctly believe) both (a) that his adversary will, unless forcibly prevented, immediately inflict upon him a fatal or serious bodily injury, and (b) that he must use deadly force upon the adversary to prevent him from inflicting such an injury. If one who is not the aggressor kills his adversary with these two actual and reasonable beliefs in his mind, his homicide is justified, and he is guilty of no crime—not murder, not manslaughter, but no crime (see § 9.4).

What if a defendant who did not initiate the difficulty honestly but unreasonably believes either that he is in danger of the injury or that killing is the only way to prevent it; or, even though he reasonably believes these things, he was at fault in bringing about the difficulty? He cannot have the defense of self-defense, for that requires both freedom from fault in the inception of the difficulty and the entertainment of beliefs which are reasonable. But is murder the only alternative? Or should the matter fall into the category of manslaughter, consisting of those homicides which lie in between murder and no crime. Some cases so hold, whether the reason for the "imperfection" of the defense is the defendant's own fault in bringing on the difficulty or the unreasonableness of the honest but erroneous beliefs he entertains. On principle, the same rule should apply to a killing done in the case of a homicide under an "imperfect" right to defend others, as applies in the case of the homicide under an "imperfect" right of self-defense. The manslaughter provisions of some of the modern comprehensive criminal codes recognize the existence of this imperfect-right-of-self-defense or defense-of-others type of voluntary manslaughter.

Where this "imperfect" right of self-defense is recognized, it is generally the case that whenever the facts would entitle the defendant to an instruction on self-defense regarding a murder charge, an instruction on this variety of manslaughter should also be given. Indeed, even if a jury could not find defendant's belief reasonable (so that no self-defense instruction is necessary), the facts might still support a manslaughter instruction because the jury could find there was an actual but unreasonable belief.

(b) "Imperfect" Right to Prevent Felony. Under some circumstances one has a right intentionally to kill another person to prevent or terminate the commission of a felony or to prevent the escape or effect the arrest of the felon; the tendency today is to apply this rule of justifiable homicide not to all felonies but only to dangerous or violent felonies. As with the justification of self-defense, the defendant need not be correct in his beliefs that the other is committing such a felony or that he is such a felon; once again reasonable beliefs are all he needs (see § 9.7).

What if the defendant has an unreasonable, though honest, incorrect belief that the other is committing or attempting a felony or that the other is a felon trying to escape? Or, though the defendant is correct in his belief that the other is committing a crime or trying to escape, what if the crime in question being of a peaceful sort (like larceny) or being a mere misdemeanor, does not amount to a dangerous or violent felony? Here again, the defendant's intentional killing is not justifiable; but should it not be manslaughter rather than murder, even though it does not involve the "heat of passion" that one ordinarily associates with voluntary manslaughter? Some cases so hold; and some of the most recent state criminal codes agree.

(c) "Imperfect" Defense of Coercion or Necessity. One who is coerced by another person, or forced by the pressure of natural physical circumstances (e.g., thirst, starvation) into committing what is otherwise a crime, may have in some circumstances a complete defense to the crime, but not if the crime in question consists of intentionally killing another human being (see §§ 9.6, 10.1). Thus one who, not in self-defense or defense of another, kills an innocent third person to save himself or to save another is guilty of a crime. But it is arguable that his crime should be manslaughter rather than murder, on the theory that the pressure upon him, although not enough to justify his act, should serve at least to mitigate it to something less than murder. Some of the latest state criminal codes so provide.

(d) Miscellaneous Intentional Killings. There are other situations too in which an intentional killing might be thought to be bad enough to be criminal yet not bad enough to be murder. It has been suggested that mental disorder not amounting to insanity might reduce the killing to manslaughter. Most cases, however, have rejected this position; they go only so far as to reduce the homicide from first-degree murder to second-degree murder, the theory being that the mental defect may serve to negative the killer's capacity to deliberate and premeditate but not his malice. A few cases have rejected even this moderate reduction, holding the crime to be first-degree murder.

So too, a few cases have held that voluntary intoxication may reduce a homicide to manslaughter if the intoxication is so extreme as to negative the defendant's intent to kill. Most of the cases, however, hold that, while voluntary intoxication may be so great as to negative premeditation and deliberation, this fact serves only to reduce the homicide from first degree to second degree murder. We have already noted, in discussing voluntary manslaughter of the "heat of passion" type, that one who, because of his intoxication, is more easily provoked or slower to cool off than the reasonable man, is not eligible for voluntary manslaughter treatment, which serves to benefit only the reasonable sober man (see § 14.2(b)(10)).

Although the usual Anglo–American view is that one who commits a mercy killing, either by directly causing the other's death (as by poisoning the food of an unsuspecting victim) or by assisting him to commit suicide (as by placing poison within the suicide's reach, at his request) is guilty of murder rather than manslaughter, yet several modern codes provide by statute that assisting a successful suicide is manslaughter or is a separate crime less than murder.

§ 14.4 Criminal–Negligence Involuntary Manslaughter

Manslaughter, like murder, originated as a common law crime, created by the judges rather than by the legislature. At first the courts did not distinguish between murder and manslaughter. Later murder and manslaughter became separate crimes, and manslaughter itself was subdivided into two branches—voluntary manslaughter (intended homicide in a heat of passion upon adequate provocation) and involuntary manslaughter (unintended homicide under certain circumstances discussed below). Involuntary manslaughter itself may be divided into two separate types, whose scope has been and is still undergoing slow change, and which may be labeled (1) "criminal-negligence" manslaughter and (2) "unlawful-act" manslaughter.

All American jurisdictions undertake to punish involuntary manslaughter, though some of them either do not define it or define it rather vaguely in common law terms. A statute of the latter sort, used in some states, defines involuntary manslaughter as an unlawful killing in the commission of an unlawful act not amounting to a felony (the "unlawful-act" type of manslaughter mentioned above) or in the commission of a lawful act without due caution or circumspection (the "criminal-negligence" type). Another type of statute found in some other states uses the terms "culpable negligence" or "criminal negligence" or "gross negligence" in setting out the negligence branch of involuntary manslaughter, without, however, defining those terms. But modern statutes, to be discussed below, undertake to spell out with some particularity the requirements for involuntary manslaughter.

Statutes in a number of states divide manslaughter into two or more degrees, utilizing the common-law concepts of voluntary and involuntary manslaughter, though not using those terms. In many states, but not all, voluntary manslaughter is considered a more serious crime than involuntary manslaughter, carrying a heavier punishment (see § 14.1).

(a) Criminal Negligence. Although a few states have held that ordinary (tort) negligence (see § 4.4) will suffice for involuntary manslaughter, the great weight of authority requires something more in the way of negligence than ordinary negligence. Most of the cases which state that more than ordinary negligence is needed for manslaughter do not clearly articulate what the extra something is; but on principle it must be either one or both of these two things: (1) the defendant's conduct, under the circumstances known to him, must involve a high degree of risk of death or serious bodily injury, in addition to the unreasonable risk required for ordinary negligence; and (2) whatever the degree of risk required (merely unreasonable, or both unreasonable and high), the defendant must be aware of the fact that his conduct creates this risk (see § 4.4). (If both are required, then "recklessness" is a more appropriate term than negligence.)

A few cases have made it plain that manslaughter is committed when the defendant's death-producing conduct involves an unreasonable and high degree of risk of death, though the defendant does not realize it. On the other hand, a few other cases have made it clear that manslaughter is not committed, even though the defendant's death-inflicting conduct involves such a risk, unless the defendant in fact was conscious of the danger. Doubtless in most cases one whose conduct is highly risky is actually aware of that fact; but occasionally a particular defendant may be so absent-minded or stupid or intoxicated as not to realize the risk. One who consciously takes a chance with other people's lives—whose attitude is, I may kill someone but I'll risk it—is, of course, morally much worse than one who unconsciously does so.

It would seem that with the quite serious crime of involuntary manslaughter, a felony in most jurisdictions, actual awareness of risk should be required (see § 4.4), excepting perhaps, for reasons of policy, in the case where the defendant's only reason for not being aware of the risk is his state of voluntary intoxication. In the converse case of the person who is more perceptive or knowledgeable than a reasonable man and who conducts himself in a risky manner, with full realization of the risk, although a reasonable man would not have realized it, such a person is guilty of manslaughter for the resulting death in all jurisdictions, even those not requiring realization.

The modern view, evidenced by the position taken in most of the recent comprehensive criminal codes, is to require for involuntary manslaughter a consciousness of risk—i.e., "recklessness," as does Model Penal Code § 210.3. But some of these codes provide no clear definition of the standard or else utilize a standard which at least appears to be somewhat different than that in the Model Penal Code. The modern codes sometimes single out special situations for criminal condemnation where no such consciousness exists. And then there are the negligent homicide statutes to be found in many states, which do not require realization of the risk.

There is a question of manslaughter law as to whether the conduct of a person with mental or physical defects is to be judged by the standard of the hypothetical reasonable man (who is without such defects) or by the standard of a reasonable man who is endowed with the defendant's peculiar characteristics. So far as a physical deficiency—e.g., nearsightedness, deafness, epilepsy—is concerned, the defect is generally considered a "circumstance" to be considered when asking whether the defendant, "under the circumstances," acted as a reasonable man would have acted. The law makes less allowance for a mental defect not amounting to insanity—e.g., absent-mindedness or stupidity—although, as we have seen, the defect may operate to negative awareness of the risk where awareness is required for manslaughter.

The factual situations that have given rise to involuntary manslaughter liability on account of deaths resulting from criminal negligence or recklessness are, of course, very numerous, though those involving the operation of motor vehicles and the handling of firearms lead the list. A number of reported cases have concerned criminal negligence or recklessness in omitting to furnish medical care for helpless, sick or injured persons to whom the defendant owes a duty of care. Other cases involve such diverse situations of criminal negligence or recklessness as: permitting overcrowded conditions in, and failing to provide adequate fire exits for, a place of entertainment; prescribing improper medical remedies for disease or injury; delivery of dangerous drugs; permitting one's baby to remain in an environment that endangered her life; conducting dangerous blasting operations; and taking up railroad tracks for repair just before a passenger train is due.

(b) Omission. Manslaughter liability has not infrequently been based upon criminal negligence or recklessness in omitting to act—for example, the failure of a parent to provide medical attention for his sick child or that of a railroad switchman to throw the switch. For omission to act to give rise to criminal liability for a homicide resulting from the omission, it must first be shown that the one who failed to act had a duty to act—as a parent has a duty, based upon the family relationship, to act to rescue his minor child (or as a railroad switchman has a duty, based upon his contract of employment, to act to save his railroad's crew and passengers) from the perils of serious illness (or of derailment, in the case of the switchman). Thus failure to act where there is a duty to act is the equivalent of affirmative action (see § 5.2).

But an omission to act where there is a duty to act, although death results, is not necessarily a crime at all, for murder and manslaughter liability require some sort of fault in addition to conduct causing death. If the defendant knows that death is certain (or substantially certain) to result from his omission, he intends to kill and so is guilty of murder. If under the circumstances his omission amounts to criminal negligence (or, where required, recklessness), or if his omission is an unlawful act, then he is guilty of involuntary manslaughter. If his omission is not accompanied by an intent to kill and does not amount either to criminal negligence or to an unlawful act, he is not guilty of either murder or manslaughter.

(c) Causation. With manslaughter, as with other crimes defined in terms of cause and result, the defendant's conduct (whether affirmative act, or omission to act when there is a duty to act) must be the "legal cause" of the death. As treated more fully in that part of this book which deals with the basic principle of causation in criminal law (see § 5.4), this means, in connection with crimes based upon some form of negligence, not only (1) that the defendant's negligent conduct must be the "cause in fact" of the victim's death; but also (2) that the victim be the person foreseeably endangered, or a member of the class of persons foreseeably endangered, by the defendant's negligent conduct; (3) that the victim be harmed in a manner which is foreseeable; and (4) that the type and degree of harm suffered by the victim be foreseeable. In this connection, "foreseeable" means something less than probable or likely but more than possible; perhaps it is best described as something that, as one looks back on the event, does not strike him as extraordinary. Applying these basic principles to a case of manslaughter from death arising out of criminally negligent conduct, the defendant's conduct (which, as we have seen, must entail an unjustifiable and high degree of risk of death or serious bodily injury to another or to others, a fact of which perhaps the defendant must be aware) must in fact cause the death of a person who is foreseeably endangered by the conduct and whose death occurs in a foreseeable way. If it seems quite extraordinary that this victim was killed in the way he was killed, the defendant is not liable for manslaughter.

However, a Pennsylvania case, *Commonwealth v. Root* (1961), suggests that a defendant whose criminally-negligent conduct causes a foreseeable death should not always be guilty of manslaughter. Here *A* and *B* were drag-racing at a reckless speed; *B*, trying to pass *A* on a hill, hit *C*'s truck head-on and was killed. Is *A* guilty of manslaughter on account of *B*'s death? *A*'s conduct in thus racing *B* was certainly conduct involving an unreasonable and high degree of deadly risk; *A* doubtless was conscious of the risk, if such consciousness is required; and surely it is foreseeable that one of the participants in the race be killed. Nevertheless, the court held that *A* was not guilty, saying, somewhat vaguely, that tort concepts of proximate cause are inapplicable to criminal cases, and that a more direct cause is required for criminal liability.

What the court really means, it appears, is that one whose criminally-negligent conduct kills another, justly should not be liable for the unintended death (even though it be a foreseeable death) of a willing participant in the same criminally-negligent conduct. If *C*, the truck driver, or *D*, a pedestrian walking along the road, had been killed, *A* (and *B*) would have been liable. Whether *A* would be liable, on this theory, for the death of *E*, a passenger in *B*'s car, would depend, it would seem, upon whether *E* was a willing participant in *B*'s conduct.

Although the Pennsylvania view, thus explained, has much to recommend it, a more recent Massachusetts case refused to follow it. In *Commonwealth v. Atencio* (1963), *A*, *B* and *C* played "Russian roulette"; as part of the game *A* and then *B* each aimed the pistol at his own head and pulled the trigger without ill effect; but when *C*'s turn came, he shot himself to death. *A* and *B* were prosecuted for manslaughter on the theory that the game involved an unreasonable and high degree of risk of death, so that the conduct of each participant, encouraging the others to endanger their lives, constituted criminal negligence. *A* and *B* urged the adoption of the Pennsylvania view: they should not be liable for the death of a willing participant in the highly risky conduct. The court nevertheless upheld their convictions of manslaughter.

(d) Contributory Negligence. Another part of this book contains a discussion of the effect upon the defendant's criminal liability of the victim's contributory negligence, in connection with those crimes (including involuntary manslaughter) in which some form of negligence constitutes the required element of fault (see § 4.4(a)). Contributory negligence is no defense to manslaughter of the criminal-negligence type. But the victim's unusual conduct is nevertheless relevant to the question of the defendant's liability for manslaughter, for it is a factor to be considered in determining whether the defendant's conduct, under all the circumstances, amounted to criminal negligence.

(e) Modern Statutory Variations. In many American jurisdictions the automobile has been singled out for special statutory treatment, in an endeavor to reduce the number of highway fatalities. Because of difficulties experienced in obtaining juries willing to convict the death driver of manslaughter (in this area juries are apt to think, "There, but for the grace of God, go I"), a number of states have enacted statutes creating the new crime of homicide by automobile (which is related to the crime of manslaughter but is not manslaughter proper), generally punishable less severely than manslaughter. These statutes often reduce the requirement from the criminal negligence or recklessness necessary for manslaughter liability to some lesser degree of negligence (although sometimes not so plainly as to avoid the need for judicial interpretation), differing, however, as to the degree of negligence necessary for guilt—sometimes requiring only ordinary negligence, sometimes negligence of a higher degree. Another type of statute inflicts punishment (generally more severely than for manslaughter proper) on one who causes a death while driving a car while under the influence.

A few states have separated out other limited homicide situations for special nonmanslaughter treatment, such as the negligent use of firearms or vicious animals. Model Penal Code § 210.4 creates a new crime, less severely punished than manslaughter (which in the Code is defined in terms of high risk of death or serious harm subjectively realized), called "negligent homicide," requiring only inadvertence to risk and not limited to motor vehicles or any other special situation of danger of death or serious bodily injury. Many modern codes treat negligent homicide as a criminal offense.

§ 14.5 Unlawful–Act Involuntary Manslaughter

Centuries ago it was stated to be the law that an unintended homicide in the commission of an unlawful act constituted criminal homicide; and later, when criminal homicide was subdivided into the separate crimes of murder and manslaughter, this type of criminal homicide was assigned to the (involuntary) manslaughter category. As time passed it came to be considered too harsh a rule, and the courts began to place limitations upon it.

The trend today is to abolish altogether this type of involuntary manslaughter, leaving the field of involuntary manslaughter occupied only by the criminal-negligence type already discussed. About half of the states no longer have manslaughter or comparable crime grounded in the defendant's death-causing unlawful act. The other states have retained the crime of unlawful-act manslaughter.

(a) Meaning of "Unlawful." "Unlawful act" is a vague expression, and literally it may be broad enough to include not only an act that is punishable as a crime (felony, misdemeanor, and perhaps ordinance violation) but also noncriminal conduct such as a trespass or other civil wrong, and in fact any conduct that the court making the determination does not like. Misdemeanors are certainly included, so much so that the unlawful-act type of manslaughter is often referred to, somewhat loosely, as the "misdemeanor-manslaughter doctrine," a sort of junior-grade counterpart of the "felony-murder doctrine." Although the misdemeanor involved is commonly a traffic offense (e.g., speeding, drunk driving), another common type of misdemeanor causing death is simple battery, as where the defendant hits the victim a light blow, intending to inflict only minor harm, but actually causing a quite unexpected death (see § 14.5(d)).

"Unlawful act" is a phrase, however, which also includes criminal acts other than misdemeanors. Thus a felony that for some reason will not suffice for felony-murder (see § 13.5) may do for unlawful-act manslaughter. Local ordinance violations (which in some jurisdictions are considered crimes, in others mere "civil wrongs"; see § 1.7(c)) may qualify as unlawful acts to the same extent as violation of state criminal laws. And going clearly outside the area of criminal conduct, it has been held that attempted suicide, though not a crime, is an unlawful act for manslaughter purposes; and the sale of liquor to one already intoxicated, and attempting to drive through a toll-gate without paying the toll, though not criminal offenses, were said to be unlawful acts for manslaughter purposes.

There is a dispute as to whether a reckless act that is not a crime is an unlawful act for purposes of manslaughter liability. On the other hand, in a case wherein the defendant picked up a box lying on a pier and threw it into the sea, hitting and killing a swimmer beneath the pier, it was held that the trespass to the box, a civil wrong against its owner, was not an unlawful act that would support a manslaughter conviction. The word "act" in the phrase "unlawful act," though somewhat vague, includes an omission to act where there is a duty to act. Thus "unlawful conduct" (the word "conduct" including omissions as well as affirmative acts) would be a more accurate term than "unlawful act," the more commonly used expression.

There remains the question of whether an innocent-minded violation can be an "unlawful act," as where the criminal statute that punishes certain conduct is of the strict-liability sort. Thus suppose it is a misdemeanor to drive at night without lights or at any time without brakes; suddenly, without any fault on the defendant's part, the lights go out or the brakes fail; and, before the car can be brought to a stop, a pedestrian or motorist is struck and killed. On principle, this sort of violation should not aid in any way in establishing the defendant's guilt of manslaughter, as some cases have recognized. On the other hand, for the defendant's conduct to be "unlawful" for purposes of manslaughter liability it is not necessary that he know that some law forbids it (in the case of an act) or commands it (in the case of an omission); in other words, there is no requirement of a specific intent to violate the law which makes his conduct unlawful.

(b) Required Causal Connection. Assuming that, while the defendant is committing an "unlawful act," a death occurs near the defendant, still the defendant is not guilty of manslaughter unless the unlawful act causes the death. Mere coincidence of time and place will not do. Yet closeness of time and place does have relevance, for it seems clear that, in addition to the necessary causal connection, the requirement that the homicide be committed "in the commission of" the unlawful act necessitates, on analogy to felony-murder (see § 13.5(f)), a somewhat close connection in point of time and place, as well as causal relation, between the unlawful act and the infliction of the death-causing injury.

(c) Limitations Upon Unlawful–Act Manslaughter. Just as the felony-murder doctrine has been circumscribed by limitations (and perhaps in the end will be abolished), so too the counterpart misdemeanor-manslaughter doctrine has been subjected to limitations. "Unlawful acts" are in many (but not all) jurisdictions divided into those which are *mala in se* and those which are only *mala prohibita* (see § 1.6(b)). As to unlawful conduct *malum in se,* the usual rule is that where a defendant, in the commission or attempted commission of such conduct, unintentionally causes another's death, he is guilty of involuntary manslaughter, without regard either to the foreseeability of the victim's death or to the existence of any causal connection between the "unlawful excess" portion of the defendant's conduct and the victim's death. But if the defendant unintentionally kills another in the commission or attempted commission of an unlawful act that is *malum prohibitum,* he is not necessarily guilty of manslaughter. In this situation three different views have been taken by the courts:

View (1): He is not guilty unless the death that occurs is the foreseeable or natural consequence of the defendant's unlawful conduct. It is unnecessary under this view that the defendant himself subjectively foresee the possibility of death; the word "foreseeable" itself implies that it is enough that a reasonable man would have foreseen. Again, as with criminal-negligence manslaughter, it is not necessary that death to this particular victim, occurring in this particular manner, be foreseeable; it is enough that the victim be a member of an endangered class, and that his death come about in a foreseeable, rather than an extraordinary, way. And, once again, though contributory negligence is no defense to unlawful-act manslaughter where foreseeability of death is a requirement for guilt, the victim's careless conduct may be considered in dealing with the question whether a reasonable man would foresee that death might result from the defendant's unlawful conduct.

Finally, comparing criminal-negligence manslaughter, on the one hand, with unlawful-act manslaughter with the foreseeability limitation, on the other: (a) Where one, not doing any unlawful act, unintentionally kills another, his conduct must involve not only an unreasonable but also a high degree of risk of death or serious bodily injury (and perhaps in addition he must be conscious of this risk); whereas (b) where he is already doing an unlawful act, his conduct need involve only an unreasonable risk of death or serious bodily injury, and he need not subjectively realize the risk. The notion (illogical though it may be) seems to be: if he is doing something bad (other than creating risk) at the time he unintentionally inflicts the fatal injury, it should be easier to attach manslaughter liability to him than if he is not doing something bad.

It has already been noted that, for manslaughter liability of the criminal-negligence sort, perhaps one is not liable for an unintended death which happens to a willing participant in the defendant's criminally negligent conduct. If this limitation upon liability is valid as to the criminal negligence sort of manslaughter, it is, on principle, equally so as to the unlawful-act-causing-foreseeable-death type of manslaughter; if it is unjust to punish a person for the death of his willingly participating colleague in the one situation, it is equally unjust to do so in the other.

View (2): He is not guilty unless the death that occurs is in fact caused by his conduct's "unlawful excess," i.e., that portion of the defendant's whole conduct which makes the conduct unlawful. The defendant's whole unlawful conduct can be in most cases divided up into two portions: the lawful part and the unlawful excess. Thus where the defendant drives at 35 m.p.h. in a zone in which the speed limit is 25 m.p.h., the first 25 m.p.h. is lawful, and only the excess 10 m.p.h. is unlawful. With the crime of driving under the influence of liquor, the driving portion of his act is lawful, but the fact that the driver is under the influence constitutes the unlawful excess. So too of hunting on Sunday, or without permission of the landowner, or without a license, where such conduct is unlawful: hunting is the lawful part; it is only the Sunday or the no-permission or the no-license feature that is unlawful.

Where the defendant, while committing an unlawful act *malum prohibitum,* unintentionally kills another, the question, under this view, is: did the unlawful excess cause the death, or would it have happened even if the defendant had been acting lawfully? Thus if the defendant, hunting without permission, in violation of a statute forbidding hunting without permission of the landowner, shoots and kills another person by accident, the question is whether the fact that he had no permission caused the death, or would the death have occurred even if he had had permission. If the defendant, speeding at 35 miles per hour in a 25 mile zone, strikes and kills a pedestrian, the question is whether the death would have occurred even if the driver had been going only 25: if he could not have stopped in time at 25 m.p.h., the unlawful excess 10 m.p.h. did not cause the death; if he could have, the extra 10 m.p.h. did cause the death.

Comparing these two views, both of which serve to limit manslaughter liability for a death resulting from the defendant's unlawful conduct: under view (1) we look at the defendant's whole conduct (e.g., driving at 35 m.p.h.) and ask whether, under all the circumstances, the victim's death was the foreseeable result of this conduct; whereas under view (2) we divide his whole conduct into its two parts, the lawful portion (the first 25 m.p.h.) and the unlawful excess (the 10 m.p.h. from 25 to 35), and ask whether the extra 10 m.p.h. in fact caused the death. Often the answer will be the same under either view, but under some circumstances the answer may differ depending upon which view is taken. Suppose, for instance, that while the defendant is driving at 35 m.p.h. in a 25–mile zone, his car strikes and kills a pedestrian who suddenly steps off the curb in the middle of the block, although the defendant instantly applies the brakes. It may be that, under all the circumstances (including the victim's careless act), the death was the unforeseeable result of the defendant's conduct in driving as he did. Yet it may also be that, if the defendant had been traveling at 25 m.p.h., he could have stopped in time to avoid hitting the careless pedestrian; if so the extra 10 m.p.h. in fact caused the death.

View (3): He is not guilty unless his unlawful conduct *malum prohibitum* amounts to criminal negligence. In other words, the fact that the defendant commits a misdemeanor (or other unlawful act) *malum prohibitum* adds nothing to the defendant's liability for manslaughter; if he is to be found guilty of manslaughter, it must be under the criminal-negligence branch. Of course, the fact that the defendant violated a criminal statute (or ordinance) may be some evidence of criminal negligence, especially in the case of a statute (e.g., punishing driving under the influence, or firing a gun in a public place) aimed at protecting the general public from the possibility of death or serious bodily injury; but the violation is not conclusive evidence (or evidence *per se*) of criminal negligence.

(d) Assault or Battery Causing Death. An intentional battery is an unlawful act and one which is assignable to the *malum in se* category of unlawful acts. Therefore, it is almost universally held, as a specific instance of unlawful-act manslaughter, that one is guilty of involuntary manslaughter who intentionally inflicts bodily harm upon another person, as by a moderate blow with his fist, thereby causing an unintended and unforeseeable death to the victim (who, unknown to his attacker, may have a weak heart or a thin skull or a blood deficiency). A criminal assault, like a criminal battery, is an unlawful act *malum in se.* Therefore, if the defendant approaches close to another person intending to strike him but not to kill him, and the latter, who unknown to the defendant possesses a weak heart, has a heart seizure and dies as a result of fright produced by the threatened attack, the defendant is guilty of manslaughter, though he never touched the victim.

The assault-and-battery kind of unlawful-act manslaughter has been singled out for criticism on the ground of its harshness and on the ground of the lack of any rational theory-of-punishment basis for it. If the modern trend away from "constructive crime" (including unlawful-act manslaughter as well as felony murder) continues, it should eventually sweep away this type of manslaughter from the Anglo–American criminal law.

(e) The Future of Unlawful–Act Manslaughter. As pointed out earlier in this book (see § 1.6(b)), the traditional but vague distinction between an unlawful act *malum in se* and one *malum prohibitum,* with quite different criminal-law consequences flowing from this distinction, ought to be abandoned. Some courts, in fact, seem to get on very well without making the distinction. Some cases, as noted above, while recognizing the existence of a separate branch of involuntary manslaughter in the commission of an unlawful act, seem to apply the same rule in the case of all unlawful acts without regard to whether they are in the one category or the other. Other cases, while acknowledging the existence of unlawful-act manslaughter, suggest making the more specific distinction between an unlawful act in violation of a criminal law designed to protect persons against death or serious injury, on the one hand, and designed for other purposes (e.g., to protect property), on the other, rather than drawing the uncertain line between an act *malum in se* and one *malum prohibitum*. The unlawful-act manslaughter statutes themselves sometimes draw a distinction along these lines. But even where the distinction is made between criminal statutes (or ordinances) that are designed to protect against death or serious bodily injury and statutes (ordinances) with other purposes, still the question ought to be not whether the crime is generally dangerous, but whether the defendant's conduct in the particular death-causing situation was under the circumstances dangerous.

A modern tendency, however, is to go further and, by statute, to abandon the whole concept of involuntary manslaughter based upon unlawful conduct alone, leaving the field occupied solely by involuntary manslaughter based upon criminal negligence or recklessness (although of course the fact of the defendant's unlawful conduct may generally be looked to as evidence of criminal negligence). There is no logical reason for inflicting manslaughter punishment on one who unintentionally kills another simply because he is committing a traffic violation, unless it makes sense to punish the one-in-a-thousand traffic violation, which by bad luck produces an unexpected death, far more severely than the nine hundred and ninety-nine violations that happily do not produce any such devastating result. As Holmes suggested in discussing an analogous hypothetical case involving felony-murder (a one-in-a-thousand death resulting from a shot fired at another's chickens in an endeavor to steal them): the act of shooting at chickens knowing them to belong to another is no more or less blameworthy because an unexpected accident (the bullet hits and kills a person whose presence could not have been suspected) results, and if the object of the felony-murder rule in a larceny case "is to prevent stealing, it would do better to hang one thief in every thousand by lot."

It is true that, in the case of crimes defined in terms of bad results, it is often something of an accident whether the specified result occurs or not. Where one seriously wounds another by shooting at him with intent to kill, or severely but unintentionally injures him by reckless driving, chance often takes a hand in deciding whether the victim dies or recovers, and thus whether the defendant receives a greater or lesser punishment. If the bad result that happens is actually intended, or if it is recklessly produced (especially by one conscious of the risk), it does not seem too harsh to make the severity of his punishment depend somewhat on the actual result, however accidental. Where, however, the result is both unintended and produced without any consciousness of the risk of producing it, it seems too harsh and illogical. Involuntary manslaughter, therefore, ought, on principle, to be limited to the situation of unintended homicide by criminal negligence. The modern trend is properly in this direction.

§ 14.6 Aiding and Attempting Suicide

Suicide—the intentional destruction of himself by one who is sane and who has reached the age of discretion—was a common law crime (a felony) in England, punishable by burial in the highway with a stake through the suicide's body and by forfeiture of all his goods to the crown. Though the matter is not entirely clear, probably suicide was considered a form of murder rather than a crime separate from murder. In America today the forfeiture-of-goods and ignominious-burial forms of punishment have been abolished, so that no penalty attaches to a successful suicide. When common law crimes have been retained, suicide has been characterized as a "criminal" or "unlawful" act though, not being punishable, not strictly-speaking a crime.

The modern criminal law problems relating to suicide concern the criminal liability of (1) one who unsuccessfully attempts to commit suicide, causing harm to no one else; (2) one whose unsuccessful attempt kills or injures someone else—a would-be rescuer or innocent bystander; and (3) one who persuades or aids or forces another to commit a successful suicide.

(a) Attempted Suicide. In some states attempted suicide, which was a common law misdemeanor, was at one time a crime, but the prevailing view has long been otherwise. None of the modern codifications treats attempted suicide as a crime. Attempted suicide that harmed no one but the attempter himself was rarely prosecuted.

Doubtless it is better policy not to make such conduct criminal. Certainly one bent upon a successful suicide will not be deterred by thoughts of possible punishment. Moreover, "intrusion of the criminal law into such tragedies is an abuse. There is a certain moral extravagance in imposing criminal punishment on a person who has sought his own self-destruction * * * and who more properly requires medical or psychiatric attention."

(b) Attempted Suicide Which Harms Another. One attempting suicide sometimes accidentally kills another while failing to kill himself; the other is usually a person who, seeing the defendant bent on self-destruction, acts to restrain him, perhaps by struggling with him for possession of his gun. Such conduct producing such a result has been held to be murder, manslaughter, and no crime at all in the absence of recklessness. In most cases the proper solution is probably involuntary manslaughter: if the suicide attempt is made with bystanders and potential rescuers nearby, the suicide's conduct can generally be found to be reckless as to one or more persons' lives so as to support a conviction of involuntary manslaughter of the recklessness type.

(c) Inducing, Aiding, Forcing Another to Commit Suicide. If *A*, by resort to force or duress, were purposely to cause *B* to commit suicide, then there is no doubt that in all jurisdictions *A* would be held to have committed the crime of murder. Likewise, *A* is guilty of murder if he is actually the agent of *B*'s death, notwithstanding the fact that he acted at *B*'s request—as where *A* shoots and kills *B* upon *B*'s insistence that he wants to die now rather than continue to suffer from a serious illness.

Under appropriate circumstances, one who causes another to commit suicide may be guilty of murder even though he did not intend for the other person to take his own life. Thus if *A*, with intent to kill *B*, mortally wounds *B* and inflicts so much grief or pain upon *B* that *B* commits suicide, *A* is guilty of murder of the intent-to-kill sort. Or, if *A*, in raping *B*, inflicts such serious wounds that *B*, overcome by pain and shame, kills herself, *A* is guilty of murder of the felony-murder type.

There are three different views about the criminal liability of one who, whether pursuant to a suicide pact or not, solicits (by talk) or aids (as by providing the means of self-destruction) another to commit suicide. Occasionally aiding or soliciting suicide has been held to be no crime at all on the ground that suicide is not criminal. That view is most certainly unsound. At one time many jurisdictions held it to be murder, but a great many states now deal specifically with causing or aiding suicide by statute, treating it either as a form of manslaughter or as a separate crime. Such statutes typically do "not contemplate active participation by one in the overt act directly causing death," and thus their existence is no barrier to a murder conviction in such circumstances. However, the "traditional rationale" for holding the survivor of a suicide pact guilty of murder if he engaged in such active participation is inapplicable when the parties to the pact, "because of the instrumentality chosen, necessarily were to commit their suicidal acts simultaneously and were subject to identical risks of death," as in such circumstances the "potential for fraud is thus absent." Where the defendant did not intend for the other person to commit suicide, the providing of dangerous instrumentalities to one foreseeably bent on suicide is, if suicide results, a basis for a negligent homicide conviction.

Is there a constitutional bar to making it a crime to assist another in committing or attempting suicide? No, the Supreme Court answered in *Wash. v. Glucksberg* (1997). On the issue of "whether the 'liberty' specially protected by the Due Process

Clause includes a right to commit suicide which itself includes a right to assistance in doing so," the Court responded that recognition of such a right would require reversal of "centuries of legal doctrine and practice, and strike down the considered policy choice of almost every State." The Court noted that most states had retained their bars on assisted suicide despite the fact that medical technology and rapid advances in treating chronic illness have led to increasing interest in and concern with end-of-life issues. Such statutes, the Court explained, are rationally related to legitimate state interests in preserving human life, preventing suicide, protecting the integrity and ethics of the medical profession, protecting such vulnerable groups as the poor, elderly and disabled, and avoiding the slippery slope toward euthanasia. *Glucksberg* thus leaves state legislatures free either to include or exclude physician-assisted suicide from criminal law prohibitions upon aiding suicide, thereby renewing the debate upon that provocative issue.

Chapter 15

RAPE

Table of Sections

For additional analysis of the above topics and citations to authorities supporting their discussion in this Book, consult the author's 3-volume *Substantive Criminal Law* treatise, also available as Westlaw database SUBCRL. See the Table of Cross-References in this Book.

---

§ 15.1 Overview

This chapter has to do with the controversial subject of rape, defined at common law as "the carnal knowledge of a woman forcibly and against her will." This definition suggests that a proper parsing of the crime of rape would be into (i) a specified act, i.e., "carnal knowledge," (ii) brought about by a specified means of imposition, i.e., "forcibly," and (iii) in circumstances where the woman had a particular state of mind concerning the perpetration of that act by those means, i.e., "against her will." But it is a bit more complicated than that. For one thing, there is the question of whether the *defendant*'s state of mind, not specifically addressed in that definition, is relevant, considering that some mental state is required for most offenses, especially those this serious. The present section provides an overview of the traditional approach to rape and then examines the aforementioned controversy and the legislative reforms that have occurred. The act and mental state requirements are then examined in section 15.2.

There is some dispute about whether force and nonconsent are separate and distinct elements of the crime of rape, or whether on the other hand force merely plays an evidentiary role with regard to the nonconsent element (see § 15.3(a)). In either event, there is some value in trying to assess nonconsent and imposition separately, and that is done herein. Section 15.3 inquires into what kind of imposition is and should be required for the crime of rape, and considers not only force and threat of force but also nonphysical coercion and fraud. Section 15.4 inquires into the matter of nonconsent, especially whether it needs to be manifested by forcible resistance or in some other way, and also discusses those instances in which the law conclusively presumes either consent or nonconsent.

While this book is about substantive criminal law and not criminal procedure or evidence, sometimes consideration of the latter cannot be ignored. Such is the case with respect to the crime of rape, which traditionally has been attended by unique and especially demanding procedural and evidentiary rules. They are examined in Section 15.5, along with the matter of punishment.

(a) The Traditional Approach. The purpose here is to provide only a brief overview of the traditional approach to the crime of rape in the United States. The traditional approach refers to the approach generally followed prior to the reforms undertaken in relatively recent years, and reflects primarily but not exclusively substantive and procedural principles received in this country as part of the common law. The most noteworthy features of this traditional approach (each of which is elaborated upon later at the point specified) are these: (1) The physical act necessary for rape, usually referred to as "carnal knowledge," was penetration of the female sex organ by the male organ (see § 15.2(a)). (2) With rare exception, the necessary manner of commission of this act was "forcibly," which ordinarily required resort to force or threat of force above and beyond that inherent in the penetration (see § 15.3(a)). (3) Limited alternatives to force were recognized, namely, resort to fraud so extreme that the woman either did not know she was engaging in intercourse or did not know the intercourse was not with her husband, or to administration of drugs or intoxicants depriving the woman of the ability to resist (see § 15.3(c)). (4) The penetration also had to be against the will of the victim, and the need to establish such nonconsent often necessitated proof of the victim's continued physical resistance to the man's advances or a showing of force or threats to such a degree as to make such resistance unavailing (see § 15.4(a)). (5) Consent was conclusively presumed when a man engaged in intercourse with his wife (see § 15.4(d)). (6) No manifestation of refusal of consent was necessary when the female was under ten years of age and thus deemed incapable of consent as a matter of law, or when she was so incapacitated as to be unable to give consent (see § 15.4(b)). (7) The defendant's mental state at the time of the intercourse was generally deemed irrelevant, so that inquiry into whether he mistakenly believed the woman consented and on that basis should be exonerated was typically foreclosed (see § 15.2(b)). (8) Absence of a prompt complaint about an alleged rape was admissible as evidence that the later complaint was not genuine (see § 15.5(a)). (9) Some jurisdictions required that the victim's testimony be corroborated by other evidence (see § 15.5(b)). (10) Prior sexual conduct of the complainant was admissible in a rape prosecution as evidence of consent and to impeach the complainant's credibility (see § 15.5(c)). (11) Many jurisdictions used cautionary jury instructions warning that the offense was easily charged but hard to disprove and that consequently the victim's testimony required especially close scrutiny (see § 15.5(d)). (12) The crime of rape was at one time punishable by death in about half the states, and by extended prison terms in the others, but the number authorizing capital punishment ultimately dropped to just a few, and later the Supreme Court held such punishment unconstitutional in rape cases (see § 15.5(e)).

(b) The Impetus for Reform. One of the most frequently encountered quotations on the subject of rape, indeed, "one of the most oft-quoted passages in our jurisprudence" on any subject, originated with Lord Chief Justice Matthew Hale of England back in the seventeenth century: "rape * * * is an accusation easily to be made and hard to be proved, and harder to be defended by the party accused, tho never so innocent." The longstanding prevalence of that attitude doubtless accounts not only for the narrow and curious fashion in which the crime of rape came to be defined, but also for the array of procedural and evidentiary rules that are both unique to and inimical to rape prosecutions. This concern with false accusations is manifested in a variety of ways, including the usual requirement that force or threat of force must be shown, that nonconsent must ordinarily be manifested by physical resistance, that the victim's testimony must be corroborated, and that the prior sexual conduct of the complainant may be inquired into fully.

In more recent times, many have seen the aforementioned requirements in a quite different light, as a result of which "rape has increasingly become a topic of controversy * * * captur[ing] the public imagination." Those seeking redefinition of the crime of rape and reform of evidentiary and procedural impediments have frequently and vigorously put forward another proposition sharply contradictory to Hale's assertion: "In a rape case it is the victim, not the defendant, who is on trial." Critics of the status quo "argued that this focus on the victim was unique to rape law," and

> contended that traditional rape law negatively affected both victims of rape and the outcome of rape cases. They charged that the rules of evidence unique to rape caused pervasive skepticism of rape victims' claims and allowed criminal justice officials to use legally irrelevant assessments of the victim's character, behavior, and relationship with the defendant in processing and disposing of rape cases. Critics further suggested that traditional rape law was at least partially responsible for the unwillingness of victims to report rape, as well as low rates of arrest, prosecution, and conviction for rape. They argued, in short, that traditional rape law made it "easy to commit rape and get away with it."

Those pragmatic concerns were the primary motivation of victims' rights and "law and order" groups, while some feminist groups instead saw the consequences of rape law reform as being "largely symbolic and ideological—to educate the public about the seriousness of all forms of sexual assault, to reduce the stigma experienced by victims of rape, and to neutralize rape myth stereotypes."

Certainly one basic concern by many feminists and others seeking law reform in this area was that distinctions drawn in the substantive and procedural law regarding the crime of rape reflected perspectives about the crime that had no contemporary legitimacy. Some of these distinctions, most especially the marital exemption rule, reflected the ancient notion that rape was a property crime and that violation was of the property rights of the woman's father or husband. Another take on the situation was that many rape doctrines reflected not so much a special hostility toward women by the law, but rather the law's hostility toward those seeking to be excused from criminal liability, which the rape complainant ordinarily was back when rape resided alongside adultery and fornication as criminal offenses. But that, of course, is another circumstance lacking contemporary relevance given the virtual disappearance of the latter offenses from the law. A variety of more modern justifications for the crime of rape were put forward, which explains why it is said that rape "is now viewed simultaneously as a crime of violence, a sex crime, and a privacy offense." It seems fair to say, however, that today the crime of rape is properly classified (as it is in this book) as a crime against the person, one which hopefully "protects the female's freedom of choice and punishes unwanted and coerced intimacy."

(c) **The Modern Approach.** As a consequence of reforms undertaken in recent years, what might be called the modern approach to the crime of rape looks considerably different from the traditional approach of years past. This is not to suggest that all needed reforms have been accomplished in all jurisdictions, for this is not the case. Nor is it to suggest that in those many states where a full range of reform legislation has been adopted that all of the problems previously identified have been fully solved. In part this is attributable to the fact that the problem has never been entirely "the words of the statutes," but has also involved the general understanding in our society regarding such concepts and "consent," "will" and "force," which doubtless is changing, albeit at a somewhat slower pace.

The modern approach to rape has these features (each of which is elaborated upon later at the point specified): (1) The newer statutes are often drawn in gender-neutral terms and cover not only genital copulation but also anal and oral copulation and, sometimes, digital and mechanical penetration as well (see § 15.2(a)). (2) There is a trend toward recognition of a broader range of impositions as a basis for finding coercive conduct by the defendant, including other types of fraud and also certain nonphysical coercion (see § 15.3(c),(d)). (3) The requirements regarding physical resistance manifesting nonconsent have been lessened in some jurisdictions, while elsewhere there is movement toward more ready recognition that verbal resistance (if not absence of affirmative consent) should suffice (see § 15.4(a)). (4) The marital exemption has been removed in most states and substantially limited in the others (see § 15.4.(d)). (5) Protection of younger females has been extended by raising the age for so-called "statutory rape," where no showing of nonconsent is necessary (see § 15.4(c)). (6) There is somewhat greater recognition that the defendant's mental state is not always irrelevant, and that some mistaken beliefs in consent are a basis for exoneration (see § 15.2(b)). (7) The concept of a "prompt" complaint has been considerably broadened, and the fact of such a complaint is now admissible in support of the prosecution's case (see § 15.4(a)). (8) Most jurisdictions have abolished any requirement that the victim's testimony be corroborated (see § 15.4(b)). (9) So-called rape shield laws have been enacted everywhere and bar admission of the complainant's prior sexual conduct in most instances (see § 15.4(c)). (10) Cautionary instructions calling upon the jury to give special scrutiny to the victim's testimony have been largely abandoned (see § 15.4(d)). (11) The great majority of states now divide the offense into degrees, taking into account the severity of the injury and the seriousness of the imposition employed (see § 15.5(e)).

§ 15.2 Act and Mental State

As with other offenses, it is necessary to think about the crime of rape in terms of the requisite act and mental state requirements. Although the act is most commonly referred to these days simply as "sexual intercourse," some issues have arisen as to the meaning of this phrase in this particular context. Even more problems exist regarding the requisite mental state, especially regarding the important question of whether a mistake by the defendant, reasonable or unreasonable, regarding whether the victim has consented is or should be relevant.

(a) **Carnal Knowledge.** The act required for the common law crime of rape was called "carnal knowledge," Nearly half of the contemporary rape statutes use the term "sexual intercourse," while another very common term is "sexual penetration." Elsewhere such terms as "penetration," "vaginal intercourse," "sexual act," "sexual battery," "sexual intrusion," "sexual conduct," and "sexual abuse" are employed, while but one state continues to use the common law "carnal knowledge" terminology. Because the terms "carnal knowledge" and "sexual intercourse" in their ordinary meanings are synonymous, it is unlikely that use of the latter term changes in any way what constitutes the required act, although it must be realized that on occasion the same term may be used and defined in a broader sexual misconduct statute to encompass a broader range of activities. As for use of the phrase "vaginal intercourse," despite what a literal reading of that term might suggest, it likewise appears to require no greater act, although there exists some confusion on this point.

"Carnal knowledge" or any equivalent term refers to conduct involving a male and female sex organ. Because a penis is the instrumentality that must be employed, the actor will be a man, although it should be noted that it is nonetheless true that a female can be convicted of the crime of rape by virtue of her activities as an accomplice to that man. Mere contact of the male and female organs is insufficient; there must be penetration (except for a very few states where the statutory definition of the requisite act appears to provide otherwise). It is commonly said that slight penetration is enough, and it is sometimes elaborated that penetration between the labia or of the vulva will suffice. Entry of the vagina or rupturing of the hymen is not necessary. Despite rare suggestions to the contrary, emission is not necessary for the requisite act to be completed. Moreover, proof of emission is not a substitute for showing penetration. The prevailing view is that the victim must be alive at the time of penetration, although some courts have recognized an exception in those instances where the victim was killed and sexually assaulted by the same person.

In light of the above requirements, can it be said that certain disabilities in the defendant will present a bar to his conviction for rape? Certainly not if the disability is the lack of capacity regarding emission or procreation, as such events are not a part of the definition of the crime. What then of impotency, that is, the man's inability to have an erection. Although it is sometimes said that a man in such circumstances may not be convicted of rape, the cases typically cited in support for the most part do not lend solid support to such an absolute proposition. While on one occasion a defendant has actually obtained a reversal because he did not receive a specific jury instruction about such a defense, some other cases merely assert the existence of such a defense but then note an absence of any supporting evidence in the instant case or that the instant case involves a different charge for which no such defense would obtain. Or else they make no mention of such a defense as such, but merely note that defendant's inconclusive medical testimony about such evidence did not trump the victim's testimony about penetration. The proposition is more directly put to the test in a case like *State v. Kidwell* (1976), where "it was not disputed that appellant was impotent, in that he did not have an erection at the time of the offense," but the victim testified about a slight penetration of one inch and defendant's medical witness admitted that "penetration as defined by our law could have taken place." The court upheld the conviction and opined that it had "little doubt that most, if not all jurisdictions would reach the same result as we have" on such facts. Essential to the *Kidwell* conclusion, of course, was the court's ruling about the penetration required for rape, namely, that it can be accomplished "by an erect or non-erect penis," a proposition finding support in some other cases.

With regard to youthful defendants, however, the English common law regarded a boy under the age of 14 to be incapable of committing the crime of rape. At least at an earlier time, some American jurisdictions followed that rule, but others did not, often upon the explanation that the English rule "was based upon the physiological fact that in the climate and among the population of England * * * puberty was so rarely attained under the age of 14 in males," contrary to the situation in this country. The latter reasoning has been characterized as "obviously unsound since it was recognized from early times that penetration without emission completes the crime of rape," meaning the English rule instead "resulted from the unwillingness of the early judges to hang one so young for this type of misconduct." That risk no longer exists in the United States, and this has provided another reason for abandoning the English approach. The question seldom arises any more. These problems have been rendered largely irrelevant by the widespread adoption of juvenile court legislation.

In recent years, revision of rape laws have often brought about coverage of a broader range of conduct than is encompassed within the common law term "carnal knowledge." One trend is for new statutes to be drafted in gender-neutral terms. As for the acts covered, the new statutes fall into three categories: those that continue the narrow notion that rape should punish only genital copulation; those that agree with the Model Code that rape laws should be expanded to include anal and oral copulation; and those that go beyond the Model Code to include digital or mechanical penetration as well as genital, anal, and oral sex.

(b) Mental State; Mistake. It has been aptly noted that "[i]n defining the crime of rape, most American courts have omitted mens rea altogether." Just as the common law crime of rape was a general intent crime, courts typically give this characterization as well to statutes that, however named, encompass what is commonly known as the offense of rape. Although the term general intent is used in various ways in the criminal law (see § 4.2(e)), in the present context what resort to this characterization usually means is that there exists no issue in the prosecution of the crime of rape regarding defendant's perception of the requisite attendant circumstances (e.g., whether or not the woman had given consent). Thus, courts explain that this general intent is sufficiently evidenced "by the doing of the acts constituting the offense," that the prosecution need only "prove that the defendant voluntarily committed an act of sexual intercourse," that the defendant has the requisite general intent if he "intended to place his penis in the victim's vagina," and that consequently whether the defendant "thought the victim consented * * * is irrelevant." (This conclusion would seem not to square with the position that has often been taken with respect to the significance of a "general intent" mental state, namely, that in such instance a mistake of fact must be reasonable to provide a basis for exoneration (see § 4.6(b)), unless that notion is trumped by another which was also relied upon at an earlier time: that any mistake by the defendant may be disregarded if, under the facts as he supposed them to be, he would still be guilty of some legal or moral wrong (see § 4.6(c)).) In other jurisdictions, courts have reached essentially the same result without resorting to a general intent characterization, often with such sweeping pronouncements as that the applicable statute "imports no culpable state of mind," that "[c]onviction of rape * * * is possible without proof of any mental state," or that the "element of force negates any possible mistake as to consent." Such interpretations are facilitated by the fact that the overwhelming majority of the rape statutes on the books do not expressly state any generally applicable mental state. Of those remaining, a few require a mental state in such a way as to make it appear that the requirement applies only to the fact of intercourse rather than the circumstances making it unlawful, and a few others at least appear to have a mental state requirement even as to the absence of consent. (Mental state issues also arise as to other conduct falling within the modern statutes encompassing a broader range of conduct, such as digital penetration.)

On the particular question of whether the defendant's mistaken belief that the woman had consented should ever have a bearing on guilt or innocence, two other positions are to be found—each represented by a rather well-known case: (i) that such belief bars conviction unless negligently held; and (ii) that such belief bars conviction unless recklessly held. The first American case to adopt the former position as a settled principle of law was *People v. Mayberry* (1975), where the complainant and the defendant testified to quite different accounts. She testified that defendant repeatedly resorted to force and threats of force prior to the intercourse, while his story was that there had been no force or threats and that she had voluntarily accompanied him to his apartment and then willingly engaged in intercourse with him. On appeal from his conviction, the California high court ruled that on these facts defendant was entitled to a mistake of fact jury instruction regarding the victim's consent. While the applicable statutory provisions said nothing one way or the other on this point, the court reasoned:

> The severe penalties imposed for those offenses * * * and the serious loss of reputation following conviction make it extremely unlikely that the Legislature intended to exclude as to those offenses the element of wrongful intent. If a defendant entertains a reasonable and bona fide belief that a prosecutrix voluntarily consented to accompany him and to engage in sexual intercourse, it is apparent he does not possess the wrongful intent that is a prerequisite * * * to a conviction of * * * rape by means of force or threat."

This position was later taken by courts in a few other jurisdictions as well.

The second case, a contemporary of *Mayberry*, is an English case, the decision by the House of Lords in *Director of Public*

Prosecutions v. Morgan (1975). With the assistance of the woman's husband, three men had forcible intercourse with a woman; according to the men, the husband had told them that she had "kinky" sex habits and would welcome their advances even though she might appear to resist and struggle. Following conviction of the men for rape, the certified question was: "Whether in rape the defendant can properly be convicted, notwithstanding that he in fact believed that the woman consented, if such belief was not based on reasonable grounds." A majority answered in the negative; as Lord Hailsham explained, because "the mental element in rape is not knowledge but intent, to insist that a belief must be reasonable to excuse it is to insist that either the accused is to be found guilty of intending to do that which in truth he did not intend to do, or that his state of mind, though innocent of evil intent, can convict him if it be honest but not rational." *Morgan* thus rejected a *Mayberry*-style objective negligence test in favor of a subjective test interpreted to mean "that recklessness regarding consent is the mens rea required to support a rape conviction," a position thereafter taken by a few American courts, and codified in England's Sex Offences Act of 1976 with a proviso that the presence or absence of reasonable grounds for the belief has evidentiary significance.

In assaying the three models identified above regarding mistake of fact as to consent (strict liability, recklessness, negligence), it is useful to begin with strict liability, which is not without its defenders. The essence of the argument in favor is that even if strict liability is generally disfavored in the criminal law, it is appropriate in this particular situation because those who fail to perceive the absence of consent even when the requisite force or threat of force has been utilized are sufficiently dangerous to justify their incapacitation, and in any event the situations in which such a mistake of fact would be even arguably justifiable are so rare that trying to identify them is not worth the candle, especially since the efforts to do so would have unfortunate side effects, not the least of which is the biased, inconsistent and unpredictable verdicts that would occur in light of the fact that men and women have such divergent views on the matters at issue. Standing against that position are the various arguments against strict liability discussed elsewhere herein (see § 4.5(c)), which have special force when discussing a crime of this magnitude, and also the powerful contention that so long as rape law is structured so as to hold "the man guilty of rape regardless of whether he (or anyone) would have recognized nonconsent in the circumstances," the crime will continue to be "so limited that it would be virtually impossible for any man to be convicted where he was truly unaware or mistaken as to nonconsent," meaning that such reforms as broadening the range of impositions that could be the basis of liability or not requiring physical resistance by the woman would go by the wayside.

What if the choice comes down to the *Mayberry* objective test or the *Morgan* subjective test? Although the commentators have not been kind to *Morgan* ("notorious," "shocking" and "shameful" are among the adjectives used in describing the case), certainly the subjective approach cannot be dismissed out of hand. Indeed, it is not inappropriate to suggest, given that the unreasonable risk/objective fault variety of liability is rare in the criminal law and for the most part is limited to minor crimes carrying relatively light penalties (see § 4.4), that the burden falls upon those preferring the *Mayberry* approach in this context to make out a special case for it. Essential to meeting that burden, it would seem, as some *Morgan* critics admit, is an acknowledgment that a *Mayberry*-style type of liability is, in any event, appropriate only with respect to a lesser degree of the crime carrying a lower penalty.

Even in such circumstances, the remaining question is what justification there is for utilizing this level of fault (ordinarily reserved for tort law), requiring neither an objective awareness of the risk of nonconsent nor a higher than unreasonable risk of nonconsent, in this particular cranny of the substantive criminal law. The answer given by the critics of *Morgan* is that objective liability in this particular setting does not reach the unfortunate individual who simply lacked the capacity to do better, but rather the man who could have paid attention to the woman's manifestations of nonconsent but failed to do so. "The 'negligent rapist' who is intent on intercourse without attending to the possibility that the woman does not consent, or who is prepared to take another's word, or his own preconceptions, as adequate grounds for his belief in her consent, displays what must be counted, on any proper moral view of the significance of her consent, as a serious disregard for her consent and her sexual interests." This kind of argument takes on considerable force when it is stated in terms of requiring men to honor "a rule that 'no means no,'" and thus it may be suggested that how one comes out on this mental state issue may depend on what kind of manifestation of nonconsent, if any, the law requires (see § 15.4(a)).

Indeed, just how workable the *Mayberry* objective standard would be if more widely utilized is itself a significant question, especially in light of the arguments stated earlier for the strict liability alternative, for the prospect of rape prosecutions generally being confounded by bogus claims of reasonably mistaken belief in consent is a troublesome one. Courts have shown concern for this problem, as is reflected in those cases not rejecting the objective negligence test but yet finding the instant case not to be one justifying a jury instruction about defendant's possible mistaken belief in consent. The hard question is just when juries should be permitted to consider the possibility of a reasonably mistaken belief in consent, as to which some courts and commentators have offered answers.

One approach, severely criticized by some, is the so-called rule of equivocality, which means that the defense of mistake as to consent is unavailable as a matter of law unless there is "substantial evidence of equivocal conduct that would have led a defendant to reasonably and in good faith believe consent existed where it did not." In other words, if at trial the defendant testified to a set of facts that, if accepted by the jury, would support a finding of actual consent, and the alleged victim testified to a different set of facts that, if believed, would preclude any reasonable belief of consent, there remains "no middle ground" which could serve as a basis for sending the reasonable belief issue to the jury. Another feature of this equivocality test is that there is only one recognized permissible source of the defendant's confusion: "the victim's equivocal conduct." In a similar fashion, some other courts, without specifically mentioning equivocality, have likewise held that defendant's mistaken belief must be grounded in the complainant's conduct. Some commentators have suggested one further step, namely, that certain specified conduct by the victim should give rise to either a conclusive or a rebuttable presumption that any belief by the defendant that the victim consented was unreasonable.

§ 15.3   Nature and Degree of Imposition

Rape, it has been noted, "is the only form of violent criminal assault in which the physical act accomplished by the offender * * * is an act which may, under other circumstances, be desirable to the victim." This is why the line-drawing necessary in determining the boundaries of the crime of rape is especially difficult, and may help explain why it is that efforts to define that offense have traditionally necessitated, in a somewhat curious way, examination of *both* the victim's nonconsent and also the manner of the perpetrator's imposition. These two matters, it has been aptly noted, are "conceptually distinct," but yet "in practice * * * are not neatly separable." One reason this is so, it would seem, is that thinking about the nature and degree of imposition by the defendant often helps in the effort to make a judgment about whether there was nonconsent by the purported victim (just as it may help in figuring out the often-neglected question, see § 15.2(b), of the defendant's mental state). Thus the question pursued in this section—what types and degrees of imposition should suffice to support a rape conviction?—takes on added importance precisely because "inquiry into the victim's subjective state of mind and the attacker's perception of her state of mind often will not yield a clear answer."

(a) Force. Certainly the use of force can qualify as an imposition sufficient to support a rape charge, as is apparent from the usual common law definition of the crime: "the carnal knowledge of a woman forcibly and against her will." There is disagreement, however, stemming in part from the fact that sometimes the common law crime was defined *without* mention of force, as to the proper characterization of the force ingredient. Some courts and commentators view force as a separate and distinct element of the crime of rape; under this approach, it is of course true that "no matter how much force is used to obtain it, consent can still occur," while by like token "no matter how nonconsensual the sex may be, there is no crime without force." The contrary view is that force "plays merely a supporting evidentiary rule, as necessary only to insure an act of intercourse has been undertaken against a victim's will." But in either event, as suggested above, the two concepts of force and nonconsent cannot be completely disentangled from one another; the nature and extent of physical force used by the defendant cannot be ignored in assaying the consent issue.

However, the extent to which the foregoing is true will depend upon the exact wording of the particular rape statute under consideration, for the fact of the matter is that contemporary rape statutes reflect considerable variation on this matter of force, nonconsent and their relationship. In eight states the statements resemble the usual common law definition of rape, for they set out as elements of the crime *both* force (sometimes, however, as only an alternative form of imposition) *and* absence of consent by the victim. At the other extreme, there is one state which expressly states that "by force" and "against the will" are *alternative* rather than cumulative requirements.

All of the remaining statutes focus to a greater or lesser degree *either* upon force (again, either exclusively, or as an alternate form of imposition) *or* upon the absence of consent. On the consent side, the statutes of seven states appear to focus exclusively upon the absence of consent by declaring that the intercourse *must* be without the consent or against the will of the victim, and by making no mention whatsoever of force. Another seven states, by comparison, also define the offense in those terms, but their statutes then go on to elaborate that such terms mean, inter alia, compelled by the use of force. On the force side are all the remaining statutes, which are alike in that they all mention force and do not mention nonconsent at all, but which vary so much in their language that at least sometimes there is a suggestion that the force must have been such as to produce an absence of consent. Such a suggestion exists not at all in those two states that merely define the offense in terms of "use of force" (with or without mention of other sufficient types of imposition), and only slightly in the six other states merely requiring that the intercourse be "accomplished" or "caused" by such use of force. On the other hand, the suggestion is much stronger in the remaining nineteen jurisdictions, where the states require that the victim "submit" because of force, be "overcome" or "compelled" by the force, or be subjected to "forcible compulsion."

It is apparent that even the statutes in the latter group, although specifying the necessary effect of the force, do not otherwise indicate the quantum of force required, and this is likewise true of those few statutes declaring that the force must prevent resistance, overcome resistance, or overcome earnest resistance. Because the statutes defining the crime of rape typically "do not establish an amount of physical coercion sufficient to demonstrate that sexual activity was accomplished 'by force,' " and consequently the requisite degree of force mandated by the courts has been "subject to considerable dispute and variation." For the most part, however, the treatment by the courts of the force issue reflects utilization of either of two standards, which have been usefully characterized as the intrinsic force standard and the extrinsic force standard. The latter approach reflects the more traditional view, which is that the force requirement ordinarily requires proof of use of force or threat of force (separately discussed in § 15.3(b)) above and beyond that inherent in the act of nonconsensual intercourse. The intrinsic force standard is the directly contrary proposition, namely, that such inherent force itself suffices.

It is interesting to take note of the circumstances in which courts have opted for the intrinsic force standard over the more common extrinsic force rule. In more recent times, intrinsic force has been deemed sufficient in applying that variety of rape statute which contains a force element but no nonconsent element, as in *State in Interest of M.T.S* (1992). And, as noted in *M.T.S.*, the older cases in which "the force incident to penetration was deemed sufficient" likewise involved situations in which there was no possible need to rely on force to show nonconsent, albeit for some different reason, such as that the victim was incapable of giving consent because of her age or mental incapacity (see § 15.4(b),(c)), or had no opportunity to even make a choice regarding sexual intercourse because the defendant's deception made her unaware that such activity (instead of, say, a medical examination) would occur (see § 15.3(c)). Collectively, these cases suggest this generalization: that intrinsic force is sufficient to prove force, but that extrinsic force must be established whenever the case is one in which consent by the victim is neither impossible nor legally irrelevant. This squares with the force-as-an-element, force-as–proof-of-nonconsent dichotomy noted earlier.

The extrinsic force standard is inherently more ambiguous than the intrinsic force standard, for it is a requirement of more evidence and thus naturally gives rise to the question of just how much more will suffice. Thus, because the "distinction between the 'force' incidental to the act of intercourse and the 'force' required to convict a man of rape is one commonly drawn by courts," it "would seem to require the courts to define what additional acts are needed to constitute prohibited rather than incidental force." In one sense the results are a muddle; as one assessment puts it, the "degree of force required varies from state to state and is generally a function of the facts and circumstances of each case." Yet, it is possible to discover an approach that accounts for most of the cases of this genre. As one perceptive commentator has put it:

> For many courts and jurisdictions, "force" triggers an inquiry identical to that which informs the understanding of consent. Both serve as substitutes for a mens rea requirement. Force is required to constitute rape, for force—even force that goes far beyond the physical contact necessary to accomplish penetration—is not itself prohibited. Rather, what is required, and prohibited, is force used to overcome female nonconsent. The prohibition is defined in terms of a woman's resistance. Thus, "forcible compulsion" becomes the force necessary to overcome reasonable resistance. When the woman does not physically resist, the question becomes then whether the force was sufficient to overcome a reasonable woman's will to resist. Prohibited force turns on the judge's evaluation of a reasonable woman's response.

This is an unfortunate state of affairs, and one that can be remedied only by a variety of reforms discussed elsewhere herein. To the extent that such extraordinary demands regarding force are attributable to concerns about convicting and imposing severe sanctions upon a man who innocently misperceived the coercive impact of his conduct, greater attention to the oft-neglected mental state issue is necessary (see § 15.2(b)). The interplay of the force requirement with the notion of physical resistance highlights the need for recognition that nonconsent can be sufficiently manifested in other ways (see § 15.4(a)). And surely the undue emphasis upon physical force reflects a need to recognize a broader range of impositions as a justifiable basis for rape prosecutions (see § 15.3(c),(d)).

(b) Threat of Force. Despite use of the term "forcibly" in most common law definitions of rape, even at common law it was not necessary that actual force, of the kind discussed above, be utilized. Rather, as one court explained, that term "does not necessarily imply the positive exertion of actual physical force in the act of compelling submission," and force that is "threatened" is "in all respects equivalent to force actually exerted for the same purpose." So too, where statutes follow closely the common law definition and thus seemingly mandate that the intercourse be "by force," it has been held that this phrase means "either actual physical force or constructive force," the latter being sufficiently "demonstrated by evidence of threats." Usually statutory definitions leave little or no doubt on the matter; the phrase "threat of force" is commonly used, and more expansive language, such as "coercion" or "fear" appear to encompass threat of force together with other possibilities.

As with actual force, there exists confusion as to what the exact significance of threat of force is in a rape prosecution. It is sometimes specifically referred to as an element of the crime distinct from the element of nonconsent, and on other occasions has been viewed primarily as a fact demonstrating the absence of consent. (Just as previously discussed regarding use of force, there is considerable variation in the state statutes, and thus either of the foregoing positions will be correct as to some of them but not as to others.) But there is one sense in which the presence of a threat of force has a close connection with the troublesome question (see § 15.4(a)) of what will constitute a sufficient manifestation of nonconsent. "At common law and under derivative statutes, the actor's threats were significant chiefly to show that the woman was excused from the duty of 'utmost resistance.'"

While it is true that "courts and legislatures have rarely, if ever, defined * * * 'threat of force' within the context of rape law," courts have been inclined to indicate that the standard is a demanding one, necessitating appraisal of "the character and intensity of fear induced in the victim." In *State v. Hoffman* (1938), for example, it was said that the defendant's threats must have put the woman in " 'fear of death or great bodily harm,' a 'fear of great personal injury' or 'serious personal injury,' a fear that 'so overpowers her that she dares not resist,' a 'fear and terror so extreme as to preclude resistance.'" This means that fear of death is not necessary, and that a threat of force with a weapon is likely to suffice, but beyond this there is considerable uncertainty. However, both statutes and cases sometimes add one further particularity, namely, that the threat must be of *immediate* bodily harm.

Courts have also required that the woman's "reaction be reasonable or, in indirect statement of the same idea, that the actor have present capacity to inflict the harm feared." Even today, some statutory formulations mandate an "apparent power of execution" of the threat or a "reasonable belief" on the part of the woman as to the defendant's "present ability" to execute the threats or as to the futility of resistance. Such limitations are particularly inappropriate, and hopefully their demise will be accelerated by the powerful criticism of the Model Penal Code draftsmen, namely, "that one who takes advantage of a woman's unreasonable fears of violence should not escape punishment any more than a swindler who cheats gullible people by false statements which they should have found incredible. Neither the blameworthiness of the actor nor the gravity of the insult to the victim is ameliorated by a finding that the threat was implausible or that the actor lacked capacity to carry it out."

Of course, not even a reasonable fear by the victim should, standing alone, be a basis of liability where the requisite threat is absent. But must the threat be express, or can it be implied from intimidating behavior by the defendant? Although there is some case authority supporting the proposition that the threats may be implicit, involving actions rather than words, the facts of some rather well-known cases at least suggest the contrary. Hence this objection: "That a woman feels genuinely afraid, that a man has created the situation that she finds frightening, even that he has done it intentionally in order to secure sexual satisfaction, may not be enough to constitute the necessary force or even implicit force which earns bodily integrity any protection under the law of rape." The chances of an implied threat being deemed sufficient seem the greatest when the victim and defendant are strangers, and, when they are not strangers, appear to be the slightest when the implication is grounded in events not immediately connected with the intercourse in a temporal sense.

Finally, there is the question of whether the requisite threat of force must be directed at the victim, or whether a threat of harm to a third party should suffice. This is a matter that has long been a matter of some uncertainty; "the law provided little guidance as to the kind of threat that could lead to a rape conviction, other than a threat of physical injury to the female herself. It was even doubtful whether rape was committed where, for example, the offender compelled a mother to submit by threatening to shoot her child or where a girl submitted to save here escort's life." Certainly such threats should suffice, as a few cases in more recent years have clearly recognized. Indeed, threats against any other person should suffice, as a solid majority of the rape statutes now make clear. Model Penal Code § 213.1(1)(a) also takes this position, and otherwise properly broadens and clarifies what kind of threat should suffice by including all compulsion "by threat of imminent death, serious bodily injury, extreme pain or kidnaping, to be inflicted on anyone." About half of the states specify the threats in the same or a similar fashion.

(c) **Fraud.** Despite the requirement of force under the traditional definition of rape, the common law crime came to embrace a few situations in which the defendant employed deception rather than force. One group of cases, which is especially useful in describing the limits ordinarily imposed upon the rape-by-fraud category, involve deception employed by some doctors in order to have sexual intercourse with their female patients. The deceptions practiced are of two kinds, and only one, under the traditional view, can serve as a basis for a rape conviction. One such case is that in which the doctor has had intercourse with the patient but has managed to conceal from her the fact that it occurred by representing the event as nothing more than a routine pelvic examination or some similar treatment with medical or surgical instruments. Another is where the doctor has achieved intercourse with his patient by fraudulently misrepresenting that such intercourse was a necessary medical treatment for some real or pretended malady. The former constitutes rape, while the latter does not.

The former is typically explained as a case of fraud in the factum, meaning that the fraud by the doctor has caused a misunderstanding by the woman as to the fundamental fact that sexual intercourse was occurring, and the resulting ignorance by the woman as to the very nature of the act that occurred means that she did not give meaningful consent. Such ignorance because of the defendant's fraud in other situations has likewise resulted in a rape conviction. As for the second of the two doctor cases, it is characterized as fraud in the inducement; the woman knew that she was engaging in sexual intercourse but merely misunderstood a collateral matter, and consequently she did consent and thus the event did not constitute a rape. Here as well, where only that kind of ignorance existed a rape conviction has been barred in various other situations as well.

However, there is one kind of case that has proved difficult to classify, and that is where the deception is such that the woman believes the man is her husband. When this has occurred as a result of mistaken identity, as where defendant entered the woman's darkened room posing as her husband, the case has sometimes been viewed as one of fraud in the inducement, in that the woman was aware she was engaging in sexual intercourse, while elsewhere it has been characterized as fraud in the factum, apparently on the ground that it should suffice that she perceived the situation as one of lawful intercourse with her husband rather than adultery. Sexual intercourse as a result of deception of the woman with a sham wedding has also been viewed as fraud in the inducement, barring conviction for rape, although here as well a plausible argument can be made that the belief dictates a different result because the intercourse would be lawful if the facts had been as the victim believed them to be.

Opinions differ as to whether the fraud in the factum-fraud in the inducement distinction draws the proper line between those frauds that should and should not, respectively, serve as a basis for rape prosecutions. One view is that the traditional dividing line is about the best that can be hoped for because what is customarily characterized as fraud in the inducement "is too difficult to distinguish * * * from many instances of ordinary seduction," where it is common to engage is false or misleading representations about a variety of matters, and where in addition the relationships are much more complex, making it difficult to say that a single misrepresentation was determinative.

Others would make a broader range of deceptions a basis for rape prosecutions, based upon either the coercive nature of the misrepresentation (whereby rape law would "subsume the actions of a wealthy man who falsely promises to financially assist the mother of a sick child in return for her sexual favors but not the actions of the same rich man who merely offers a desirable, but not desperately needed, alternative to the woman"); the materiality of the misrepresentation to the victim's decision-making process (under which rape law would be used to "punish actors using fraud to obtain sexual intercourse in the same manner as actors using fraud to obtain money"); or a totality of the circumstances assessment (involving "an examination of policies that govern the meaning of effective consent in other situations where one person violates another's safety and freedom of choice"). The difficulty, of course, is in drawing clear lines without giving protection to interests not worthy of being protected by criminal sanctions, such as "the cheated expectations of women who sought to sleep their way to the top but discovered, too late, that they were dealing with swindlers."

It should be noted, however, that several jurisdictions have gone beyond the traditional common law position with respect to fraudulent conduct as a basis for a rape prosecution, and thus have at least made an attempt at drawing some lines. One exhaustive study has identified four different approaches to the problem: (1) Some states have outlawed fraud in the context of certain professional relationships, such as those involving medical and health care professionals, psychotherapists and mental health professionals, or members of the clergy, so that in such a setting even a fraud in the inducement, utilized by one in a position of trust or authority against a person likely to be vulnerable, can support a rape prosecution. (2) Some states specify a few very precise varieties of fraud under which victim consent is not a defense; included here are older provisions outlawing husband impersonation or fraud as to the nature of the act, plus a few newer provisions more generally making consent obtained by fraud insufficient. (3) At least one state revised its rape statute to encompass, without limitation, sexual penetration "accomplished by fraud," which has been treated as abolishing the traditional factum-inducement distinction but provides no other basis for distinguishing effective and ineffective consent in the fraud context. (4) Some states have adopted a global consent definition in the criminal code declaring consent to be ineffective if obtained by "deception," which is also likely to be interpreted as superceding the factum-inducement distinction, again without other guidance to the courts.

(d) Coercion. As noted above, courts found it possible, notwithstanding the limiting language in the common law definition of rape or comparable statutory definitions, to encompass within the crime those few rape-by-fraud situations in which the woman was deceived as to a very fundamental matter (whether sexual intercourse was occurring, or whether the intercourse was with her husband). Expansion of the crime beyond force or threat of force to encompass other techniques of coercion has proved to be another matter. Here, the courts have in the main taken such words as "by force" or "forcibly" as barring any extension of the crime of rape to include other varieties of coercion, no matter how severe.

Illustrative is *State v. Thompson* (1990), holding that defendant, who allegedly used his position as high school principal to intimidate a high school student to submit to acts of sexual intercourse by threatening not to allow her to graduate, could not be convicted of sexual intercourse without consent. Although the crime charged was simply defined as intercourse "without consent," a related definitional statute said that term meant being "compelled to submit by force," and force was in turn defined as actual or threatened "infliction of bodily injury," and the court thus concluded that consequently the concept of force could not be stretched "to include intimidation, fear, or apprehension."

But courts less hemmed in than the court in *Thompson* have likewise ruled for the defendant. In *Commonwealth v. Mlinarich* (1988), for example, where a 14–year-old girl's guardian threatened her with return to a juvenile detention facility if she did not accede to his sexual demands, the court ruled this did not constitute a "threat of forcible compulsion that would prevent resistance by a person of reasonable resolution," as required under the state's rape statute, for notwithstanding the psychological duress she was "left with a choice." It has been stated in criticism that "upon closer analysis the force requirement is considerably more elastic than courts like to admit," and that in rape law as with other crimes involving force it should be possible to expand the scope of the prohibited conduct by utilizing the doctrine of constructive force.

Some courts have taken that route in recent years, which once again doubtless manifests the fact that there currently exist quite different perspectives about what the crime of rape is and should be all about.

One view is that rape is and should remain a crime of violence, and that dilution of rape law by including cases where sexual intercourse was by other forms of coercion (or, for that matter, by fraud) is inadvisable for several reasons, including that such expansion of the crime may ultimately trivialize even forcible rape and may even make juries more reluctant to convict in rape cases. The contrary position is that rape law is properly perceived as "designed to protect victims' sexual integrity as well as physical security," and thus should be expanded "to include a broader range of methods by which sexual predation is accomplished." If this is the correct perception, then unquestionably the "exclusive reliance on force or violence as the indispensable element of rape has the undesirable effect of insulating a broad range of blameworthy conduct from criminal condemnation."

Even if, as seems to be the case, the latter perception is the correct one, this is the beginning rather than the end of the inquiry, for there remains the daunting problem of drawing a line between legitimate and illegitimate inducements, of determining "which of our sexual practices are legitimate means of obtaining sex and which are not." As one commentator has elaborated: "In the rape context, we must grade the pressures to have sex according to their legitimacy—from those pressures to have sex that are perfectly moral, to those that are immoral but not criminal, to those that are criminal, to those that constitute crimes of the most serious sort."

Regarding criminalization of rape by coercion, one prominent proposal is that rape law should "prohibit extortion to secure sex to the same extent we prohibit extortion to secure money." Another commentator, in what has been aptly characterized as "the broadest, most well-developed categorization of coercive pressures * * *, without resort to concepts that are hopelessly open-ended," would focus on women's autonomy, "the right to protection from those interferences that our culture and our legal system already consider impermissible." He further identifies three illegitimate pressures of the coercive type: (i) extortionate behavior, which is "already understood to be unprivileged and illegitimate"; (ii) coercion arising out of institutional and professional relationships; and (iii) coercion via economic pressure, the latter two of which involve situations where "coercion results from altering the [person's] ordinary range of options in a legally impermissible way."

But it would seem necessary, in one way or another, to look not only at the illegitimacy of the pressures but also their magnitude, so as to foreclose rape convictions for "the policeman who persuades a woman to submit to intercourse rather than to accept a parking ticket" and "the man who threatens to destroy an inexpensive object unless its owner agrees to sexual relations." To deal with that problem, Model Penal Code § 213.1(2)(a) "breaks out" from the traditional rape categories by creating a lesser offense of "gross sexual imposition," one variety of which is committed when a man has intercourse with a woman not his wife and has "compel[led] her to submit by any threat that would prevent resistance by a woman of ordinary resolution." An alternative approach would have instead required a threat "reasonably calculated to prevent resistance," but it was ultimately rejected on the ground that it "would have raised problems of the actor's anticipation of the peculiar effect of a given threat on the individual in question." Some prefer the rejected alternative on the ground that conviction is also proper where the man "makes a 'trivial' threat which has an unusual effect on this particular woman," assuming it is also established that he was at least reckless with regard to that consequence.

Finally, it is necessary to take brief note of just how far legislative reforms have encompassed coercive impositions beyond the traditional force requirement. A recent and thorough inquiry into that matter notes that state legislatures have adopted three general approaches to the line-drawing problem in cases of rape by coercion: (1) Some states have criminalized sexual intercourse between victims and persons holding positions of trust or authority, as by making it a crime to use that position to cause submission, altering or removing the consent requirement with regard to certain relationships (e.g., psychotherapist-patient), or by prohibiting sexual extortion in employment. (2) Several states have more generally made certain nonphysical coercion to accomplish sexual intercourse criminal, either by enactment of statutes like or similar to the Model Penal Code provision quoted above, or by specifying certain impermissible means of coercion, such as threats to retaliate (including extortion) or to expose the victim to public humiliation and disgrace. (3) At least one other jurisdiction has enacted a special provision regarding sexual extortion, specifying such threats as exposing secrets or harming another in health, business or reputation.

(e) Drugs or Intoxicants. Yet another type of imposition specifically mentioned in the statutes of about a third of the states as a basis for a rape conviction is the defendant's conduct in administering drugs or intoxicants to the victim. There is considerable variation in these provisions, which of course will affect the breadth of the circumstances in which they will be applicable. The most common form of such a provision, following Model Penal Code § 213.1(1)(b), covers the situation in which the substance is administered without the woman's consent and with the purpose of preventing resistance and in addition thereby "has substantially impaired her power to appraise or control her conduct." Other variations describe the effects of the drug or intoxicant in terms of it "facilitating" the intercourse, making the woman "intoxicated," preventing resistance, incapacitating the woman, or making her incapable of informed consent.

Two observations are in order concerning provisions of this general type. First of all, it might be asked whether these provisions are not superfluous given the fact that it has been traditionally and commonly understood that rape can occur from the incapacity of the victim even if the defendant was *not* the party who caused the victim to take the substance causing such incapacity from occurring. The answer is no, for each of the statutes referenced above is fully justified by at least one of the following explanations: (1) Distinguishing those instances in which the drugs or intoxicants were administered by the defendant is useful in connection with the grading of the various types of rape, for "administration of an intoxicant by the defendant appears to be the more blameworthy because it requires planning or premeditation while the rape of an intoxicated victim may be an opportunistic crime committed without foresight." This rationale is revealed most clearly when the defendant's administration of the substance is expressly identified as an "enhancement factor" in sentencing, or when victims's impairment from drugs or intoxicants to the very same degree suffices for two levels of the crime but the higher level crime in addition requires administration by the defendant. (2) Those provisions summarized above that are based upon the Model Penal Code clearly are not superfluous, for the reason that under the rules governing incapacity generally the effect of the substance upon the woman must be more profound. Specifically, it is usually required that the woman have been rendered unconscious (see § 15.4(b)). Even if there is a solid basis for the unconsciousness requirement in other circumstances, surely the situation in which the defendant has caused the impairment for the very purpose of preventing resistance (as under the Model Penal Code approach) is one in which a lesser degree of impairment ought to suffice. Illustrative would be the use of so-called "date rape drugs," which do not necessarily cause unconsciousness but substantially dissipate one's inhibitions and ability to react. (Indeed, this second reason doubtless goes a long way toward explaining a somewhat different kind of statutory provision found in about another third of the states: one where again a condition short of unconsciousness brought on by a drug or narcotic being administered to the victim will suffice, provided that administration was without the victim's consent. While under these statutes the prosecutor does not have the burden of proving administration of the substance by the defendant, such will typically be the case when the administration has occurred without the victim's consent.)

Secondly, it is important to emphasize the significance in both of these scenarios of the fact that the administering of the drug or intoxicant occurs without the knowledge or consent of the woman (a requirement in all the statutes in the second group and most of those in the first group). While "it might be possible to condemn as rape intercourse with any female who lacks substantial capacity to appraise or control her conduct," which on "a wholly conceptual level * * * would accord with the underlying premise[] that the law of rape * * * should protect against nonconsensual intimacy," such a rule of law, it has been forcefully argued,

> would be unsatisfactory[, as] it fails to take into account the social context of romance and seduction. Liquor and drugs may be potent agents of incapacitation, but they are also common ingredients of the ritual of courtship. The traditional routine of soft music and wine or the modern variant of loud music and marijuana implies some relaxation of inhibition. With continued consumption, relaxation blurs into intoxication and insensibility. Where this progression occurs in a course of mutual and voluntary behavior, it would be unrealistic and unfair to assign to the male total responsibility for the end result.

But, as we shall see later (see § 15.4(b)), it appears that a few jurisdictions have moved at least slightly in the direction of such a rule of law by recognizing that something short of unconsciousness can suffice in the instance of self-administered drugs or intoxicants.

§ 15.4 Absence of Consent

The English common law rule was that for there to be rape it was necessary that the carnal knowledge of the woman be done not only "by force," but also "against her will." This also came to be the accepted rule in the United States, as was manifested by the courts' use of such phrases as "without her consent" or "against her will." As for contemporary statutes, slightly less than half of the states utilize either of these phrases in setting out the elements of the crime. Elsewhere the crime (whether now called rape, sexual assault, sexual battery, sexual abuse, or whatever) is defined in terms of prohibited intrusions, including force and sometimes some of the other possibilities heretofore discussed (see § 15.3). But, especially when these latter statutes refer to the necessity for there to be "compulsion" of the victim or that the victim be "compelled" or "overcome" (see § 15.3(a)), it is not surprising that questions of about consent may seem to be lurking just below the surface. As for those statutes stating or interpreted as meaning that the crime has the elements of force and lack of consent, these are cumulative rather than alternative requirements, and thus it is possible that the force element could be proved beyond any question but yet nonconsent would nonetheless not be established.

The matter of consent or its absence has been traditionally dealt with in special ways in certain categories of cases. Sometimes the consent/nonconsent issue is resolved on the basis of the incapacity of the victim, and sometimes nonconsent is conclusively presumed because of the victim's age, as with what is commonly called "statutory rape." On the other hand, sometimes consent is conclusively presumed; at least, that is one of the explanations given for the traditional "marital exemption" to the crime of rape. These matters are also discussed herein.

(a) Manifestation of Nonconsent. While "consent appears to be a conceptually simple issue," searching for it "in a particular case * * * may reveal depths of ambiguity and contradiction that are scarcely suspected when the question is put in the abstract." Because this is so, and also because of the refusal of courts, especially in earlier times, "to inquire into mens rea" in rape cases (see § 15.2(b)), those courts "demanded that the victim demonstrate her nonconsent by engaging in resistance that will leave no doubt as to nonconsent." And so it was that under traditional rape statutes, many courts insisted upon proof of the "utmost resistance" by the victim to show her nonconsent. This was a most demanding test, for it encompassed "two distinct requirements: first, that the intensity of the struggle must reflect the victim's physical capacity to oppose sexual aggression; and second, that her efforts must not have abated during the encounter."

The utmost resistance requirement was demanding to such an extreme that it eventually came under intense scrutiny, and as a result some states began to require only that women exert "earnest resistance," while others took the view that the rape complainant need only respond with "reasonable resistance." Each of the latter alternatives ameliorated the Draconian "utter resistance" requirement, but physical resistance nonetheless remained the norm for manifesting nonconsent. Further reforms were thereafter undertaken, and it is now the case that only a few states mention a resistance requirement in the statutory language describing rape, while it is likewise true that only a few states explicitly note in their criminal codes that physical resistance is not required to substantiate a rape charge. The former step, however, appears to have produced a difference only in degree: "Even in the absence of a formal resistance requirement, many courts continue to define force and nonconsent in terms of the woman's resistance, and often, resistance is still required."

Despite the slow pace of change on this matter of what manifestation of nonconsent should suffice, it is worth thinking about where the law should head on this point and how far. There are two questions worthy of consideration, the first of which is whether it should be clearly recognized that verbal resistance is sufficient (which is not the case under the traditional approach). The answer here is clearly yes. One sense in which this is so is because of the two reasons that make it inappropriate for the law to continue the requirement that the consent be manifested by physical resistance: "First, resistance may prove an invitation to danger of death or serious bodily harm. Second, it is wrong to excuse the male assailant on the ground that his victim failed to protect herself with the dedication and intensity that a court might expect of a reasonable person in her situation."

But the essential point here is that our society has surely reached the point "where it is legitimate to punish the man who ignores a woman's explicit words of protestation," so that "at the very least the criminal law ought to say clearly that women who actually say no must be respected as meaning it; that nonconsent means saying no; that men who proceed nonetheless, claiming that they thought no meant yes, have acted unreasonably and unlawfully." In short, verbal resistance "should be the legal equivalent of physical resistance," for it "puts the attacker on notice that the woman does not consent." Just what "on notice" should mean in this context, of course, is another matter.

With respect to the issue here under discussion, proof of the absence of consent, the assumption by the commentators is that a flat-out " 'no' means 'no' standard" would be employed, so that "[p]roof of verbal nonconsent would raise an irrebuttable presumption of nonconsent" leaving no room for further inquiry into the woman's sincerity. (But how this should play out on the troublesome issue of what mental state if any should be required of the defendant as to such consent, see § 15.2(b), is a separate issue as to which different views exist. One is that "verbal resistance during the encounter" should merely give rise to "a rebuttable presumption" that a reasonable belief in consent by the defendant is lacking, while the other is, essentially, that " 'no' means 'no' " also means any belief to the contrary should be deemed unreasonable as a matter of law.) Because courts often fail to "distinguish between physical and verbal resistance explicitly," the extent to which the latter alone will suffice on the consent issue is impossible to say, but at least some appellate courts have clearly manifested acceptance of the "no means no" principle.

The second question to be considered here is much more difficult: whether not even verbal resistance should be required, so that silence by the alleged victim on the matter of consent—that is, absence of even a verbal expression of nonconsent—should be deemed sufficient proof that consent was lacking. Under the traditional approach, of course, silence is not viewed as showing nonconsent; the notion is "that proof beyond a reasonable doubt mandates some type of renunciation of the legality of the intercourse by the victim beyond her mere statement, made with the benefit of hindsight, that she did not consent." But a contrary rule is strongly suggested by some of the contemporary statutory formulations, for they seemingly require that consent be shown by an affirmative act.

The choice, then, is between placing the burden of asking on the man and placing the burden of expressing refusal on the woman, and of course "gender prejudice is implicated by either choice." In favor of the former, it has been argued that the traditional approach is just one more illustration of the special rules that obtain only in rape cases, as "only in rape is proof of a lack of consent insufficient to prove nonconsent." That is, only in rape law can it be said that "the 'default' position is consent," and thus moving to the opposite position would merely reverse a rule grounded in sexual bias.

However, even those who "have no doubt that women's silence is sometimes the product not of passion and desire but of pressure and pain" have concluded that it would not be "appropriate for the law to presume nonconsent from silence." One reason this is so is because of the complex dynamics attending sexual activity between acquaintances, the circumstances most often giving rise to the issue of how silence should be interpreted. Thus, the second option stated above

> is superior, because sexual encounters ought not to be lived or analyzed as sequences of particular touchings. In practice couples do not discuss in advance each specific sex act that one or another might initiate, and there is no strong reason why the law should attempt to compel them to do so. * * * If uncertainty and spontaneity can enhance the pleasures of love-making, people of either sex might prefer not being asked—so long as they can be sure that behavior they don't like will be stopped on demand.

(b) Incapacity. Traditionally, the law of rape has encompassed sexual intercourse with an incapacitated female in four situations. The first is where the defendant has administered a drug or intoxicant to the woman in order to deprive her of the capacity to resist her advances. That is one variety of imposition engaged in by rapists in order to produce a situation in which they may engage in intercourse, and thus was discussed in that context earlier (see § 15.3(e)). By contrast, the concern here is with situations in which the rapist has merely taken advantage of an incapacity in the woman that he is not responsible for bringing about. This type of case arises in three separate circumstances: where the woman is unconscious; where the woman is mentally incompetent; and where neither of those circumstances obtains but the woman is under the influence of self-administered drugs or intoxicants.

Under English common law, the established rule was "that unlawful and forcible connection with a woman in a state of unconsciousness at the time, whether that state has been produced by the act of the prisoner or not, is presumed to be without her consent, and is rape."

On the infrequent occasions when the issue arose, American courts reached the same result, and in more recent times the point has often been covered by a specific provision in the applicable rape statute. There is considerable variation in the current statutes. Sometimes the statutory reference is only to a victim who is unconscious, and sometimes unconscious is listed with some alternative condition, such as asleep, physically powerless, or physically incapable of resisting. Some statutes refer more generally to where a physical condition has affected the person in some way, such as by making the person unaware that a sex act is being committed, incapable of consent, or substantially limited in the ability to resist. However, much more common is use of the broader general term of "physically helpless," usually specifically defined as including the situations where the victim is unconscious, asleep, or for any other reason is physically unable to communicate nonconsent. It must again be emphasized that unlike the situation previously mentioned, these statutes do not require that the defendant have brought about the victim's condition; the theory underlying these provisions is that "the actor may be held liable for rape even where he did nothing to cause her incapacity but merely took advantage of her helpless state."

This naturally raises the question of what mental state, if any, the defendant must have regarding the victim's condition. Some of the statutes specifically state that the defendant must have known of the condition, while some others say it suffices that the defendant was negligent in not knowing of the condition. The other rape statutes are silent on this point, which means one of two things: either some general mental state provision will come into play (as is true of Model Penal Code § 213.1(2), which consequently makes this conduct criminal only if there is recklessness with respect to the victim's disability), or else strict liability is being imposed with regarding that fact. The latter position is a troubling one, given the seriousness of the offense, but might be defended by some on the ground that the nature of the disability described in the statute provides "a veritable bright line," relatively easy "for the actor to identify."

The second situation is that in which the sexual intercourse has been with a mentally incompetent female. Under English common law this situation was considered no different from intercourse with an unconscious person, and certainly the rationale for criminal liability is essentially the same in the two situations. Here, the "critical issue is to define the degree of mental disease or deficiency that suffices to make noncoercive intercourse a crime," for the statute should not be so broad as to cover persons suffering from only a relatively slight mental deficiency, nor so narrow as to protect only those in a state of absolute imbecility. The Model Penal Code § 213.1(2)(b) solution is to describe the requisite circumstances as where the woman "suffers from a mental disease or defect which renders her incapable of appraising the nature of her conduct." A few of the state codes put the effect of the disability in essentially this way, while some others describe it in terms of the woman being unaware the act was occurring, or being substantially impaired regarding the ability to resist or give consent. About a quarter of the states put it in terms of the woman being incapable of giving consent, "a formulation that avoids rather than answers the essential question." Also unhelpful are those statutes that describe the situation only in terms of the woman being mentally defective or mentally incapacitated, thus leaving it to the courts to work out what the necessary effect of such a condition must be.

Even when the reach of such a provision is, as in the case of the Model Penal Code, limited "to instances of severe mental incapacity," the circumstances in this kind of case will be somewhat more ambiguous than in the case of the unconscious female. This is why the Model Code makes this a lower degree of offense and in addition requires that the defendant have actual knowledge of the described condition. A few states also use a knowledge mental state, but more have permitted conviction for this variety of rape because of the defendant's negligence in not appreciating the woman's disability or its extent, while others say nothing specifically on the mental state issue.

Finally, there is the situation in which the woman is affected by the consumption of drugs or intoxicants knowingly and voluntarily taken, but not to the extent as to come within either of the previous two categories just discussed. We have previously seen that about two-thirds of the states have concluded that intercourse resulting from such circumstances does *not* constitute a basis for a rape prosecution; their statutes require that the drugs or intoxicants have been administered by the defendant or some third party without the woman's knowledge and consent. And we saw in that context the argument that those states have it right because, when the woman is at fault in becoming drugged or intoxicated, it "would be unrealistic and unfair to assign to the male total responsibility for the end result."

However, a close reading of the statutes in the remaining states indicates that most of them have language—whether intended or inadvertent—which appears to extend the reach of rape law just a bit farther in this regard, so that it can be said that at least *sometimes* a man who takes advantage of a conscious but impaired woman might be amenable to conviction for rape notwithstanding the woman's self-administration of the drugs or intoxicants responsible for that condition. These statutes indicate that one or more of the following situations are included within the crime of rape (usually, only if it is also shown that the defendant perceived that such circumstances existed): (1) where the woman is incapable of appraising her conduct; (2) where the woman is incapable of resisting; (3) where the woman is incapable of communicating an unwillingness to submit; and (4) where the woman is incapable of consenting (either as a general matter, or because of such other incapacities as those listed above). Those who, contrary to the view referred to above, believe that "it matters little whether the victim is incapable of giving consent because she intoxicated herself, was knocked unconscious by a blow to the head, was drugged by the defendant, or is insensible because of disease," quite understandably believe that this minority position in contemporary rape statutes is the correct one. That position is more compelling if the requisite disability is a total lack of capacity to give consent, as compared with a diminished capacity to appraise or control one's conduct.

(c) Statutory Rape. Under early English common law, sexual relations with a child, no matter how young, was not regarded as rape if the child consented. However, an early English statute made it a felony to have carnal knowledge with a child under the age of ten, with or without the child's consent. The rationale was that a child under that age "should be regarded by the law as incapable of giving effective consent." Several states early on enacted similar statutory provisions. However, the English statute was old enough to be encompassed within the common law of the United States, which explains why in early times prosecutions based upon the above rationale were permitted in American states lacking a comparable statute. In either event, this variety of rape came to be known as "statutory rape," apparently because it was originally engrafted onto the common law by statute, and that term is so used even today notwithstanding the fact that now statutes virtually everywhere encompass the totality of the crime of rape.

As years passed, American statutes on this subject took on a form somewhat different from the original English version. One change was a raising of the age to which inability to consent was conclusively presumed; "statutes now designate 11, 12, 13, 14 or even higher ages as defining the most serious version of statutory rape." This age increase "introduced problems of relative culpability into the law of statutory rape, because–unlike the case of a sexual relationship with a girl below ten or twelve years old–it is not always clear whether sex with an adolescent female is dangerous or morally undesirable." Most states responded to that concern in one way or another. One approach was to draw upon the common law defense of promiscuity, under which the defendant could prevail by showing prior promiscuous behavior on part of the minor. This is not a particularly appealing solution; the promiscuity defense "results in an intrusive and value-laden inquiry into the victim's sexual past," and is grounded in the dubious proposition "that, by virtue of multiple sexual partners, girls become less vulnerable to coercion, and in essence, gain the capacity to consent to sex."

Another approach was to employ two (or sometimes more) age cutoffs, with higher penalties where the victim was below the lower age limit. Still another was to create exceptions to the crime of statutory rape by defining a range of age differences between the adolescent participants inside of which sexual intercourse is lawful, which wisely "excludes sexual experimentation between contemporaries from the penal law." A somewhat different type of reform of statutory rape laws has been to make then gender neutral; only five states still have gender-specific provisions. (The more traditional gender-specific statutory rape provision was upheld in *Michael M. v. Superior Court* (1981) against an equal protection challenge as being justified on grounds of pregnancy prevention, especially because of the disproportionate burden that teenage pregnancy places on women.)

Over time, there has occurred some shifting in the policy goals underlying the statutory rape statutes in this country:

> Legislatures designed early statutory rape laws to protect young females' virginity in order to ensure their eligibility for marriage. At the turn of the century, reformers and families used statutory rape laws both to protect and control the sexuality of working class girls laboring in the new urban centers. Today, two interrelated policy goals continue to motivate legislators to retain a statutory age of consent: (1) to

prevent teenage girls from consenting to sex in an uninformed manner, thereby exposing themselves to physical and emotional harm; and (2) to deter men from preying on young females and coercing them into sexual relationships.

One aspect of the mental state issue (see § 15.2(b)) has been reserved until this point: is a defendant guilty if he mistakenly believed the purported victim was above the age specified as the liability cut-off point in the applicable statute? The traditional approach initially accepted in virtually every state has been to view the crime of statutory rape as of the strict liability variety with respect to this issue, so that the defendant had no defense because of his mistaken belief as to age, no matter how reasonable the believe and no matter whether it was based upon the girl's own representations or her mature appearance. However, the "lesser legal wrong" and "moral wrong" theories, often used to justify this conclusion, hardly provided a solid basis for the imposition of such strict liability (see § 4.6(c)). And thus, starting in 1964, some courts began to recognize that a statutory rape defendant was entitled to a defense of reasonable mistake of fact regarding the victim's age. Of course, in more recent times it has been recognized that this is a policy matter that ought to be specifically addressed in the statutory definition of the crime.

Over a third of the states have adopted statutory provisions recognizing mistake-as-to-age as a defense, at least as to some ages. The great majority of these provisions require that the defendant's belief that the victim was above the age specified by statute for criminality of the conduct was a reasonable one, and one of these goes on to specify that the belief must be "based upon declarations as to age by the alleged victim." In contrast to those provisions, which make negligence the basis of liability as to the element of age, a few others utilize a recklessness standard, while yet another state says it is enough that the defendant "did not know" the victim was at the age triggering the statutory conclusive presumption of inability to consent.

Model Penal Code § 213.6(1) takes the position that reasonable mistake *is* a defense when the age at issue is a higher age setting the very upper limits of the crime, but is *not* a defense when the age at issue is a lower age which determines whether a more serious version of the crime has occurred. Although undeniably a solid argument can be made for mistake as a defense no matter what the situation, this position makes some sense. When the age level is, say, ten, then strict liability is at least tolerable, "for no credible error regarding the age of a child in fact less than 10 years old would render the actor's conduct anything less than a dramatic departure from societal norms." But when the age at issue is in the high teens, the defendant who mistakenly but reasonably believes his partner is above the critical age should have a defense, for he "evidences no abnormality, no willingness to take advantage of immaturity, no propensity to corruption of minors."

(d) The Marital Exemption. At English common law, a man could not commit the crime of rape by forcing his wife to engage in sexual intercourse with him, and this limitation on the common law crime of rape was readily accepted in the United States. This continued to be true as statutes were enacted defining the crime as rape, for these statutes either expressly stated such an exemption or else conformed to common law terminology and thus were construed to encompass it. And thus every state in the United States came to accept the marital exemption as a limitation upon how the crime of rape was defined. (But, as was frequently stressed in those cases holding that the "not his wife" exception did not have to be specifically pleaded, the marital exemption did not mean that a husband could not be guilty of rape on his wife by assisting, aiding, or procuring another to commit the act.)

None of the historical justifications for the marital rape exemption have any validity today. One traditional explanation, that "by their mutual matrimonial consent and contract the wife hath given up herself in this kind unto her husband, which she cannot retract," clearly lacks substance, for "there is no reason why agreement to enter a relation of intimacy necessarily means consent to intercourse on demand." The other traditional justifications, that a man cannot rape his wife because the husband and wife are one or because the wife is the property of the husband, are unquestionably out of keeping with modern thinking, for "nowhere in * * * modern society * * * is a woman regarded as chattel or demeaned by denial of a separate legal identity and the dignity associated with recognition as a whole human being."

A variety of "more sophisticated and less archaic" theories have been put forward in recent years and have, in turn, been seriously challenged. (1) The argument that the constitutional right to marital privacy precludes the legal system from intruding therein has been rebutted with the observation that marital privacy is not an absolute right and is outbalanced by the wife's interest in individual bodily integrity. (2) As to the claim that prosecution of marital rapes would interfere with reconciliation and jeopardize the marriage, it has been responded that "if the relationship has deteriorated to the point where the husband is raping his wife, then reconciliation is highly unlikely, and the state should intervene to protect the wife." (3) The contention that angry wives will fabricate rape claims, is met with the counter-argument that this is unlikely because of the stigma and difficulties involved in reporting and pressing charges in a rape case. (4) As for the argument that proving lack of consent is too difficult in the marital context, it is responded that the "difficulty of proof has never been a proper criterion for deciding what behavior should be officially censured by society." (5) Finally, the proposition that marital rape is not serious enough to deserve criminalization has been met with the observation that marital rape usually involves more severe physical and psychological damage than rapes where the perpetrator was a stranger.

Although the campaign to rid American law of the marital exemption has been under way for many years now, as recently as 1985 it could still be said that the exemption existed in about thirty states. More recently the changes have been more dramatic, to the point where it may now be said that "no state retains an absolute version of the common law rule that barred the prosecution of a husband or raping his wife." Sometimes this has been accomplished by state courts finding their marital exemption provisions unconstitutional, but more often it has come about as a result of legislative action.

Legislatures have responded in a variety of ways, including making spousal rape a separate crime, removing the words "not his spouse," "to whom he is not married," or "unlawful" from an existing rape statute, passing a statutory provision expressly excluding marriage as a defense to rape, or replacing the rape statute with a gender-neutral statute called sexual assault, sexual battery or sexual abuse. In a small number of jurisdictions, the changes have been modest, limited to declaring the marital exemption inapplicable in certain circumstances, such as where the couple is living apart. But about half of the states have eliminated the exemption except where there is no force or threat of force (often adding as well a prompt reporting requirement for the spouse), while a slightly smaller number have abolished the exemption entirely (as has England). A relatively small number of the states that have criminalized spousal rape make it a lesser offense than other varieties of rape. Many of the jurisdictions that have generally abolished the marital exception have wisely retained it with respect to statutory rape.

§ 15.5   Procedure and Punishment

Perceptions about rape have had an influence not only upon the development of the substantive law regarding this offense, but also upon procedural and evidentiary rules relating to the prosecution of rape charges. This being the case, it is appropriate to take a brief look at the procedural side of the law of rape, with special attention to the unique evidentiary rules that developed in that context. Also considered herein is the matter of punishment, including the need for separate levels or degrees of the crime as it takes on a broader range of conduct.

(a) Time of Complaint. Whether or not the purported rape victim made a prompt complaint is a matter often put into evidence for the jury's consideration, sometimes with instructions from the judge as to its possible significance, and in some jurisdictions it even determines whether the prosecution can be undertaken in the first place. As for the latter possibility, absence of a fresh complaint was no bar to prosecution under the common law, and this position was adhered to by every American jurisdiction at the time the Model Penal Code was drafted. But Code § 213.6(4) created "an innovation in Anglo–American law by imposing a specific requirement that the offense be brought to the attention of the public authorities within three months of the alleged occurrence," and similar legislation was thereafter adopted in six states.

In support of this provision, it was argued that it (i) guards against the fabrication of rape complaints, as where "unwanted pregnancy or bitterness at a relationship gone sour might convert a willing participant in sexual relations into a vindictive complainant," and (ii) "limits the opportunity for blackmailing another by threatening to bring a criminal charge of sexual aggression." The Code approach was severely criticized for imposing "an initial statute of limitations of unique and unheard-of brevity in the criminal law, regardless of the circumstances or justifications for delay in the particular case," thus failing to take account of "the woman who legitimately worries about the receptiveness of police, prosecutors, juries and even friends or employers to a report that she was raped" and thus delays reporting the crime. Notably, all six states have since repealed their provisions making prompt complaint a prerequisite to a rape prosecution.

Allowing the defendant in a rape prosecution to put into evidence the fact that the purported victim did not complain to anyone about the offense either at the time of the crime or shortly thereafter has been explained on the ground that such failure is "a virtual self-contradiction discrediting her present testimony"; because it is "entirely natural" that a rape victim "should have spoken out," failure to do so "was in effect an assertion that nothing violent had been done." Like reasoning underlies the rule that the defendant in a rape prosecution is entitled to a jury instruction calling the jury's attention to the fact that it may find the complainant's allegations lack credibility in light of her failure to make a prompt complaint. While the criticisms noted above might likewise be leveled at these propositions, many scholars writing from a feminist perspective have pursued a broader line of attack that includes within its compass a different proposition, usually called the fresh complaint rule, which is actually "meant to help sexual assault complainants" by ensuring that jurors are aware, when that was the case, that a fresh complaint had been made.

> The fresh complaint rule is a special evidentiary rule applicable only in sexual assault trials that permits the prosecution to introduce, in its case in chief, out-of-court statements made by the complainant shortly after the assault, alleging that the sexual assault occurred. Because the rule permits admission of fresh complaint evidence in the prosecution's case in chief, it is an exception to the general evidentiary policy that prohibits admission of prior consistent statements until after a witness has been impeached on cross-examination.

In the main, opposition to the fresh complaint rule appears to be based upon the undeniable fact that for many years the rule was inextricably tied in with a presumption that *absence* of such a complaint would be strong evidence the rape was not committed because "it is entirely natural that the victim of forcible rape would have spoken out regarding it." But in recent years, courts confronted with the question of whether the fresh complaint rule should consequently be abolished have, in the course of answering in the negative, expressly rejected the traditional rationale in favor of a contemporary explanation justifying the rule's retention: because it is still true that some jurors are likely to erroneously believe that the only normal behavior of a rape victim is to report the offense very promptly, fresh complaint evidence serves to prevent unfair damage to the complainant's credibility as a result of such beliefs. "This rationale does not assume that only those rape victims who do make a fresh complaint are credible; it simply allows rape victims who do complain promptly to eliminate any unwarranted skepticism arising from lack of evidence of a prompt complaint." And because this is so, evidence of a prompt complaint can be received for that reason without, for purposes of consistency, having to treat the absence of such a complaint as tending to show a lack of credibility.

There is another way in which the modern version of the prompt complaint rule is an improvement over its predecessor, resulting in complaint testimony being admissible in support of the prosecution's case in a much higher percentage of rape cases. While traditionally "the common law has required that the complaint of sexual abuse be 'prompt,'" this "requirement of promptness has * * * been slowly eroding," so that "it is now relatively rare for a complaint of sexual abuse to be found inadmissible as not being 'prompt.'" At an earlier time, a complaint might be deemed inadmissible as insufficiently "prompt" merely because the victim failed to complain to the first individual encountered after the event, but now a complaint much, much later is likely to be admissible as well, together with the circumstances that serve to explain why no complaint was made earlier.

(b) Corroboration. Although there did not exist at common law any requirement that the testimony of an alleged rape victim be corroborated, the requirement has a "long and varied" history in this country. A significant minority of jurisdictions came to adopt such a rule either by statute or court decision; in the 1970s, for example, seven jurisdictions subscribed to the rule "that the testimony of a female complainant must be corroborated in order to sustain a conviction for rape," while eight others required "only limited corroboration or corroboration only under certain circumstances." There was considerable variation as to what extent of corroboration was necessary, but it was generally accepted that eyewitness testimony was not necessary and that corroboration was possible by physical evidence or admissions by the defendant. Model Penal Code § 213.6(5) also adopted a corroboration requirement for rape and other felony sex offenses, but the tide moved the other direction; all of the states that theretofore had a general corroboration requirement abolished the requirement either by legislation or by court decision.

One reason given for a corroboration requirement is that "stories of rape are frequently lies or fantasies," in that a woman "may accuse an innocent man of raping her because she is mentally sick and given to delusions; or because, having consented to intercourse, she is ashamed of herself and bitter at her partner; or because she is pregnant, and prefers a false explanation to the true one; or simply because she hates the man whom she accuses." But this conclusion that false accusations of rape are "much more frequent than untrue charges of other crimes" is, at best, nothing more than "a matter of speculation," and thus hardly supplies a basis for special rules of proof in rape cases. A second reason, that the crime of rape is so heinous that jurors would otherwise be too ready to convict, is no more compelling; experience indicates otherwise, and in any event "it is difficult to believe that rape excites so much more emotional antipathy than murder that it requires a distinctive rule."

Not so readily dismissed, however, is the argument the crime of rape is unique because it is "premised on conduct that under other circumstances may be welcomed by the 'victim,'" so that the outcome will often turn upon a critical fact difficult to resolve after the fact–what the woman's state of mind was at the time of the sex act. To this conclusion, in effect that a corroboration requirement in rape cases is "only a particular implementation of the general policy that uncertainty should be resolved in favor of the accused," it has been responded that "the policy of resolving uncertainty in favor of the defendant is one which is already addressed in every criminal trial by the requirement of proof beyond a reasonable doubt," so that piling a corroboration requirement on top of the beyond a reasonable doubt standard produces an excessively low rate of conviction for rape as compared to other crimes.

(c) Prior Sexual Conduct of Complainant. At common law, there was no requirement of chastity on the part of the victim, and this has become the well-established rule in this country. Indeed, the fact that the victim is a prostitute presents no bar to a rape conviction. This latter proposition has sometimes been questioned on the ground that the prostitute's "only grievance is that she was taken without being paid," so that "the law of assault and battery would seem more appropriate than to include such an act within the scope of one of the grave felonies." But that criticism is unsound, especially under the modern rationale of the crime of rape. As one court put it: "Prostitutes, as well as virgins, and those of all shades in between, are entitled to the sanctity of their own bodies, and all of them have the right to grant or to withhold their sexual favors, as they see fit, free from the indignity of force or compulsion through fear."

The rule at common law was that the complainant's prior sexual conduct was admissible in evidence in a rape prosecution. Such evidence was very often received in rape trials in the United States for either or both of two reasons. One was that such evidence was admissible to show consent by the victim; the notion was that "it is certainly more probable that a woman who has done these things voluntarily in the past would be much more likely to consent, than one whose past reputation was without blemish." The other reason was to impeach the complainant's credibility as a witness; as one court explained, in rape prosecutions "the inducement to perjury and revenge is so great that it is of the highest importance that the motive and character of the prosecutrix should be rigidly investigated, and to that end wide latitude should be permitted in the admission of testimony throwing light upon these points."

Some variation existed depending on the type of evidence offered. Evidence that the complainant had previously engaged in consensual sexual activity with the defendant was deemed admissible on the issue of consent everywhere, and understandably so. "It simply ignores reality to suggest that past practice with the accused is not relevant to the issue of consent on a given occasion, though it is equally a distortion to regard proof of such experience as dispositive." As for evidence of specific instances of sexual intercourse with persons other than the accused, there was a split of authority;

some jurisdictions allowed such evidence as relevant on the issue of the complainant's consent while others did not, and some allowed such evidence to attack the victim's credibility while others did not. As for the third kind of evidence, the complainant's general reputation for chastity or sexual virtue, it was deemed admissible to prove consent and to discredit the veracity of the witness.

Over time, this state of affairs came under attack. For one thing, the two reasons for receiving such evidence were themselves questioned "in light of changes in attitudes toward sexual relations and the role of women in society." As one commentator put it: "Ordinarily, information that the prosecuting witness sleeps with her boyfriend or goes around with married men or has borne some illegitimate children cannot help the jury decide on any reasoned factual basis whether or not she agreed to relations with this person on this occasion or whether she perjured herself on the stand." Moreover, such inquiries of a complaining witness made it appear that she rather than the defendant was standing trial, a circumstance which contributed to the under-reporting of rape crimes in the first instance and to not guilty verdicts in the face of compelling evidence that the crime had occurred. In response to such concerns, virtually all jurisdictions have now enacted so-called "rape shield laws" limiting the use of this kind of evidence.

These laws vary considerably as to their scope and procedures. Nearly half of the states create a general prohibition of any evidence of prior sexual conduct by the complaining witness, subject only to specified exceptions, typically (i) prior sexual relations with the defendant and (ii) sexual relations with others to explain such physical evidence of sexual activity as pregnancy, semen or venereal disease. This type of provision also contains procedures to be followed when a defendant proposed to elicit evidence under one of these exceptions. Nearly a quarter of the states take the opposite approach; the law creates no evidentiary exclusions but does provide for an in camera hearing at which the judge is to decide whether the probative value of the evidence outweighs its prejudicial effects. Several other jurisdictions have adopted a third alternative; there is a general rule excluding the complainant's past sexual conduct except as to stated exceptions, typically that prior sexual relations with the defendant are admissible on the defense of consent and sexual relations with others are admissible to prove that physical evidence of sexual assault is not attributable to the defendant, but this is followed by a catchall clause stating that such evidence is also to be admitted into evidence when it is determined at a pretrial hearing that such admission is necessary to ensure the defendant's right to a fair trial. The fourth and final variety of rape shield provision, found in just a few jurisdictions, makes the admissibility turn on whether the evidence relates to consent or to credibility (though there is not agreement as to which category is admissible and which is not).

These statutory provisions have frequently been upheld when challenged on constitutional grounds. This is true of those statutes that recognize a need for a case-by-case judicial determination of admissibility based upon a balancing of the interests of the defendant and the complainant, and also of those statutes that have flat prohibitions upon certain kinds of evidence or evidence offered for a certain purpose. However, there may well be circumstances in which the constitutional right at issue, the Sixth Amendment right to present evidence, would be deemed to invalidate certain of these statutory provisions or their application in certain situations. Because the Supreme Court has in a different context found that per se exclusion of a particular kind of testimony violates the Sixth Amendment, rape shield statutes containing per se exclusions might well be vulnerable.

Even those rape shield statutes that do contemplate a balancing of interests can raise difficult Sixth Amendment issues in their particular applications, for the Supreme Court's cases appear to say that whenever certain evidence is relevant, only *compelling* countervailing state interests may prevail. In both instances, the possibility of a successful challenge by the defendant would seem most promising when he can make a strong relevancy claim, as when he wishes to put the complainant's prior sexual conduct into evidence to show a motive for false testimony, a pattern of prior conduct that was consensual and otherwise very similar in circumstances to the instant case, or (when mistake of fact is a defense, see § 15.2(b)) the reasonableness of his belief in consent because of his awareness of the complainant's prior consensual sexual activity.

(d) Cautionary Jury Instructions. Lord Hale's admonition, quoted earlier (see § 15.1(b)), gradually entered the English common law and then was exported to this country, where it became common practice in many states for a cautionary jury instruction along those lines to be given. "Though the wording varies substantially from state to state, most cautionary instructions contain three common elements. These are: (1) rape is a charge that is easily made by the victim, (2) rape is a charge that is difficult for the defendant to disprove, and (3) the testimony of the victim requires more careful scrutiny by the jury than the testimony of the other witnesses in the trial." Fortunately, the legislatures in some states have now prohibited the giving of such a charge, and in recent years every state appellate court that has confronted the issue has either barred future use of such an instruction or has so discredited the instruction that it is no longer utilized.

The central difficulty with the instruction, of course, is that it is "based upon false assumptions upon which courts can no longer properly rely." There is no supporting data that rape charges are easy to make; indeed, the fact that rape is the most under-reported crime suggests exactly the contrary. And the claim that a rape charge is difficult to defend is belied by the statistics showing that rape is the easiest accusation of violent crime to disprove. As for the claim that a purported rape victim's testimony requires closer scrutiny than the testimony of other witnesses, the available statistics on the low rate of fabricated rape charges strongly indicate that this simply is not so. Such cautionary instructions not only arbitrarily single out one of the witnesses at a rape trial and place a greater burden on her, but also usurp the jury's function by weighing the evidence for them and amount to an impermissible comment on the evidence.

Under Model Penal Code § 213.6(5), the judge in every rape jury trial would be required to give a slightly different instruction, namely, "to evaluate the testimony of a victim or complaining witness with special care in view of the emotional involvement of the witness and the difficulty of determining the truth with respect to alleged sexual activities carried out in private." This version of a cautionary instruction, adopted and later rejected in a few jurisdictions, has not surprisingly drawn equally severe criticism.

(e) Punishment; Grading. Rape was a felony punishable by death under the Saxon laws, and then for a ten year period was reduced to a trespass punishable by two years imprisonment and a fine, which gave rise to "the most terrible consequences," prompting another statute again making the crime a capital felony. In the United States, rape was likewise commonly treated as a capital offense in the early days, but at least since 1925 less than half of the states have taken that position. When in *Furman v. Ga.* (1972) the Supreme Court invalidated most death penalty statutes because of the excessive jury discretion they permitted, it was necessary for the states to enact new death penalty legislation. Of the 16 states that had allowed the death penalty for rape, only 3 allowed the death penalty for rape of an adult woman in their revised statutes, but shortly thereafter the Court held in *Coker v. Ga.* (1977) that "death is indeed a disproportionate penalty for the crime of raping an adult woman" and thus impermissible under the Eighth Amendment's cruel and unusual punishment clause.

The offense of rape has always been subject to very high penalties in this country, and at one time the authorized penalties were the same without regard to whether the particular offense was one in which force was actually used or instead was another variety of the common law crime or of a crime defined by statute in even broader terms. Beginning in the 1940's, states began dividing the offense of rape into degrees, and today this is the situation in virtually all states. For the most part, grading distinctions take into account the severity of the injury inflicted and the type of force, if any, used. Somewhat unique is the Model Penal Code § 213.1 approach, which recognizes three categories of offenses in this area: a third degree felony called "gross sexual imposition," covering in the main cases where deception or lesser threats were utilized; and also rapes of both the first degree and second degree felony variety, with the former covering instances where (i) the defendant "inflicts serious bodily injury upon anyone," or (ii) the victim "was not a voluntary social companion" of the defendant on that occasion and "had not previously permitted him sexual liberties." The second of these is most unusual and has been sharply criticized.

Chapter 16

THEFT

Table of Sections

For additional analysis of the above topics and citations to authorities supporting their discussion in this Book, consult the author's 3-volume *Substantive Criminal Law* treatise, also available as Westlaw database SUBCRL. See the Table of Cross-References in this Book.

---

§ 16.1 Historical Development

In order to understand fully the fine distinctions between various theft crimes—principally larceny, embezzlement and false pretenses—it is necessary to look backward into legal history to see how these crimes came into existence.

(a) Development and Expansion of Larceny. First came larceny, a common-law crime (invented by the English judges rather than by Parliament) committed when one person misappropriated another's property by means of taking it from his possession without his consent. The principal factor which limited the scope of larceny was the requirement that the thief must take it from the victim's possession; larceny requires a "trespass in the taking," as the matter is often stated. The judges who determined the scope of larceny (including its limitations) apparently considered larceny to be a crime designed to prevent breaches of the peace rather than aimed at protecting property from wrongful appropriation. The unauthorized taking of property, even by stealth, from the owner's possession is apt to produce an altercation if the owner discovers the property moving out of his possession in the hands of the thief. But when the wrongdoer already has the owner's property in his possession at the time he misappropriates it (today's embezzlement) or when he obtains the property from the owner by telling him lies (now the crime of false pretenses) there is not the same danger of an immediate breach of the peace. Upon learning how he has been wronged the owner may be as angry at the wrongdoer in these two situations as he is at the thief caught in the act of taking his property by stealth, but the malefactor in these two cases is generally less available for retaliatory measures than when the owner discovers him in the process of taking the property out of his possession.

As time went on, and especially during the time of the growth of manufacturing and the expansion of trade and business in England, the judges felt the need to broaden larceny in order to protect the owner's property from various sorts of misappropriation. They did not do this directly, by abolishing the requirement of a "trespass in the taking," but rather by discovering a trespass in at least three situations where in reality it is most difficult to find any trespass:

(1) A bailee in possession of another's packaged goods who "broke bulk" by breaking open the bales and misappropriating the contents was held guilty of larceny. Some of the judges thought that the bailee by wrongfully opening the bale terminated his possession, which thereupon flew back to the bailor, though he might be many miles away. Others considered that only the outside wrapper was possessed by the bailee; the bailor, though perhaps miles distant, still possessed the contents. It was all make-believe, of course, for the bailee actually had possession of the contents in the real sense of power to control and intent to control; but the judges felt it necessary to protect the mercantile trade, which was then growing apace in England.

(2) The judges also invented something called "constructive possession" where possession in the real sense of the word was not present. Whenever one comes across that favorite legal adjective— "constructive"—he may as well get himself ready to pretend that something exists which does not in fact exist—whether it be "constructive fraud" where there is no actual fraud, "constructive knowledge" or "notice" where there has been no knowledge or notice in fact, "constructive eviction" where the landlord has not in reality thrown his tenant out of occupancy of the premises, or "constructive trust" where no real trust has been created. "Constructive possession," no exception to the rule, was discovered to exist in these three principal situations: (a) A master (employer) delivers his property to his servant (employee) to use or to keep or to deliver for the master. One would think that, while the property was in the servant's hands, he has possession of it; his dominion over the property looks, feels, smells and tastes exactly like possession. But the judges, perceiving a need to protect masters against the depredations of their servants, came to decide that the servant had something called "custody" only, while the master still had "constructive possession." Thus, when the servant misappropriated the property, he took it from his master's possession, so that there was a "trespass in the taking," and hence the servant was guilty of

larceny. (b) The owner of property loses it or mislays it. While the actual possession is vacant (the owner is too far away from his property to exercise any dominion over it; moreover, in the case of lost property, he does not even know where it is), the owner is considered to have "constructive possession" of the property. Thus when a finder picks it up and, seeing earmarks of ownership thereon, nevertheless then decides to misappropriate it, he takes it from the owner's possession and is therefore guilty of larceny (see § 16.2(f)). (c) A property owner delivers the property to another person as part of a transaction to be completed in the owner's presence, as where he hands a storekeeper a large bill to pay for a small purchase, or hands a jeweler his watch to be appraised while he waits. The owner is said to have "constructive possession," while the other person has mere custody, so that, if the latter runs off with it, he takes it from the owner's possession and so is eligible for a conviction of larceny.

The development of the notion of construction possession where no actual possession existed thus had the effect of broadening the scope of larceny; for a wrongful interference with this make-believe possession constituted just as much a "trespass in the taking" as a similar interference with real possession.

(3) A wrongdoer obtains possession of (but not title to) another's property by telling him lies, intending to misappropriate the property and, at the earliest opportunity, doing so. In the leading case of *Rex v. Pear* (1779), the defendant hired a mare to go to Sutton, intending, however, to go to another place and sell the mare and abscond with the proceeds. He went to Smithfield and sold the mare. Since the owner had voluntarily delivered the mare to the defendant, it is somewhat difficult to find a "trespass in the taking" so as to make the misappropriation larceny. But the judges held it to be larceny, a majority of them indulging in the fiction that the owner of the mare retained possession until the time of its sale by the defendant. The expression "larceny by trick" is often used to identify this type of larceny, but it is the crime of larceny and not a separate crime.

(b) Creation of Embezzlement and False Pretenses. The three situations in which the judges by using fictions enlarged the notion of possession—i.e., where a bailee of property breaks bulk, where a possessor of property loses actual possession but retains "constructive" possession, and where a possessor of property is induced by lies to give up his possession—thus had the effect of enlarging the scope of larceny. But the English judges stopped short at this point. Thus in *Bazeley's Case* (1799) a bank clerk, employed by a banker, received from a depositor money for deposit in the bank; he put the money in his pocket instead of in the cash drawer, intending to misappropriate it. One might think that, as long as the judges had been pretending that, when an employer hands property to his employee, he still keeps possession, they might as easily pretend that, as soon as the depositor handed the money to the employee, possession (of the "constructive" sort) immediately lodged in the employer, the employee acquiring mere "custody," so that his misappropriation would amount to larceny. But the court held that the constructive-possession idea did not apply to property coming to a servant for his master from a third person, until the employee hands the property to the employer or puts it in a receptacle (such as a cash drawer) provided by the employer for its safe-keeping. The result was that the bank clerk was not guilty of larceny (and there was then no other crime which covered his conduct). It was of course necessary, for the protection of property in an age when shops and banks were growing into something more than a one-man or one-family operation, to make such conduct criminal; if the courts would not do it, the legislature must. Accordingly, in the very year of the court's decision in the case of the bank clerk, Parliament enacted the first of a long line of embezzlement statutes.

So too in the area of misappropriation of property by spoken lies, the judges stopped short of enlarging larceny to cover it, except, as noted above, where possession of, but not title to the property was obtained by the lies (i.e., larceny by trick). Parliament stepped in here too, creating the new crime of obtaining property by false pretenses.

It may be wondered why the English judges, who did not hesitate, in the face of need, to invent murder and manslaughter, burglary and arson, robbery and larceny and other crimes, hesitated during the late 1700's to expand larceny to include the areas of embezzlement and false pretenses. The commentary to the Model Penal Code explains the matter in a nutshell as follows:

> At this point in the chronology of the law of theft, about the end of the 18th century, a combination of circumstances caused the initiative in the further development of the criminal law to pass from the courts to the legislature. Among these circumstances were the general advance in the prestige and power of parliament and the conversion of the idea of "natural law" from an instrument for judicial defiance of monarchy to a restraining philosophy envisioning judges as interpreters of immemorial custom rather than framers of policy. Perhaps the most direct influence of all was a revulsion against capital punishment, which was the penalty for all theft offenses except petty larceny during much of the 18th century. The severity of this penalty not only made the judges reluctant to enlarge felonious larceny, but also may account for the host of artificial

limitations that they engrafted on the offense, e.g., the exclusion of growing crops, fixtures, deeds, and dogs.

It was noted above that when the English Parliament plugged the loopholes in larceny left by the judges' refusal to expand that crime, it did not do so by enlarging the definition of larceny to fill in the gaps, as it might have done. Common-law burglary, as defined by the judges, consists of a night-time breaking and entering of another's dwelling house with intent to commit a felony therein. A modern legislature may wish to stretch burglary to include similar daytime misconduct, or to include entering without a breaking, or buildings other than dwellings, or an intention to commit a misdemeanor as well as a felony. It often does so, not by creating some brand new crime, but by altering the definition of the old crime of burglary so as to cover the new areas. But Parliament elected to create the two new crimes of embezzlement and false pretenses, assigning to the new crimes a less severe punishment than that for larceny (although today in most Anglo–American jurisdictions the punishment is the same for all three types of theft). And, since the new crimes were created to fill gaps in the law of larceny, they were considered not to overlap the crime of larceny, although as to some situations their language seemed broad enough to do so. As we now look back on history, matters would have been simpler for us in the United States today if Parliament had stretched larceny rather than creating new crimes, for here in America we have generally adopted England's tripartite scheme of things, with the three separate theft crimes, larceny, embezzlement and false pretenses. We shall see, in the sections that follow, how thin and technical are the dividing lines between the three crimes and how often, as a result, difficulties stand in the way of successful prosecution of thieves. We shall conclude with a discussion of how many Anglo–American jurisdictions have, with greater or less success, dealt with the problem.

§ 16.2　Larceny—The Trespass

Larceny at common law may be defined as the (1) trespassory (2) taking and (3) carrying away of the (4) personal property (5) of another (6) with intent to steal it. American statutes dealing with larceny as a discrete offense have generally left the six elements of the crime unchanged, except that there has been considerable enlargement of the kinds of property that can be the subject of larceny.

Over the years, courts have limited the significance of the first of these elements—trespass—by declaring "constructive possession" to exist in several situations, as where an employer delivers property to his employee; the owner delivers property to another for a transaction to be completed in his presence; a bailee breaks bulk; a wrongdoer obtains possession of (but not title to) the property by lies; a wrongdoer finds lost or mislaid property; or property is delivered to a wrongdoer by mistake.

(a) Factors Negating Trespass. We have already noted in the historical survey of theft that larceny requires that there be a "trespass in the taking," i.e., that the thief take the property out of the possession of its possessor (see § 16.1(a)), who is generally, but not always, the owner of the property in question. If the wrongdoer fraudulently converts property already properly in his possession, he does not take it from anyone's possession and so cannot be guilty of larceny. Thus one who sells property to another and who then fails to deliver it cannot be guilty of larceny; nor can a repairman, who properly receives an article to be repaired, be guilty of larceny when he later carries it off with intent to steal it. Finders of lost or mislaid property, and those to whom property is delivered by mistake, who pick up the property or accept its delivery with an innocent intention (e.g., with lost or misdelivered property, an intention to return the property to the owner; or, with misdelivered property, a lack of knowledge of the mistake) do not commit a trespass and so cannot be guilty of larceny, even if later they succumb to the temptation of keeping the property for themselves.

There is, of course, no trespass in the taking, and hence no larceny, if the owner of property actually consents to the defendant's taking his property. A problem arises when the owner of property learns in advance that a thief is planning to steal his property and (often with the cooperation of the police) silently lies in wait in order to catch him in the act, perhaps even smoothing the thief's way somewhat, as by leaving the door open or the key in the lock. Does the owner's lying-in-wait state of mind amount to consent so as to preclude a conviction for larceny? It is held not to constitute consent, unless, according to some cases, the owner, himself or through directions to his employees, goes so far as actually to hand the property over to the thief.

Where two persons both have an interest in property—as in the case of partners and co-owners (for instance, tenants in common and joint tenants)—difficulties have arisen in larceny prosecutions. Suppose a partner or co-owner fraudulently misappropriates partnership or co-ownership property. The cases denying that such misappropriation constitutes larceny may be explained on the ground that there is no trespass in taking what one has a right to possess, or in the alternative on the ground that property which is partly one's own is not the property "of another." The theft statutes in the modern codes usually contain an express provision to the contrary (see § 16.4(c)).

Similar difficulties have arisen when one spouse makes off with the separate property of the other. At common law this was considered not to be larceny, the usual explanation being the rule of unity that existed between husband and wife (for, as it was sometimes said, the husband and wife were one, and the husband was that one). Later, larceny convictions were sometimes allowed in the exceptional case when the thieving married partner was leaving or had already separated from his mate. Modern statutes allowing a married woman to own her separate property free from her husband's control, thus abrogating the unity rule, have generally been held to authorize larceny convictions of either husband or wife. A few modern criminal codes expressly state that taking property from a spouse is not a theft, while a few others have adopted the Model Penal Code § 223.1(4) position that it "is no defense that the theft was from the actor's spouse, except that misappropriation of household and personal effects, or other property normally accessible to both spouses, is theft only if it occurs after the parties have ceased living together." But even absent any such statutory provision, and notwithstanding the fact that the property in question is by the law of the jurisdiction community property, it has sometimes been held that "a spouse may be criminally liable for the theft of community property" because the property of another need not be "wholly" of another.

Switching now from various situations that, because they may involve factors which negative a trespass, tend to hinder or prevent larceny prosecutions to other situations where a trespass, though perhaps difficult for the uninitiated to discover, nevertheless exists: we have already noted briefly that servants, bailees who break bulk, persons who obtain possession by lies, finders, those who receive or pick up others' property by mistake or who are erroneously overpaid are all eligible, in proper cases, for larceny convictions (see § 16.1).

(b) Master and Servant. Thus we have seen that where the master (in more modern terminology, employer) puts his servant (employee) in charge of his property, the master still has possession ("constructive possession") while the servant has mere custody. But if the property comes to the servant from a third person for the master, the servant has possession until he puts it in some receptacle (such as a cash drawer) designated by the master for its reception (see § 16.1). As to the first proposition, the cases draw a distinction between a caretaker or other minor sort of employee, who has custody only, and one to whom the employer has delegated considerably more authority, who has possession. The second proposition has led to some borderline distinctions.

(c) Transaction to be Completed in the Owner's Presence. A property owner who delivers his property to another in connection with a transaction to be completed in the owner's presence—as where he hands the other a large bill to be changed or counted or for an inexpensive purchase, or where he delivers him property to be inspected or appraised or worked upon while the owner waits—retains constructive possession, as we have seen; so that, when the other misappropriates it, he is guilty of larceny; there is a trespass in the taking, for, in taking it, he has removed it from the owner's (constructive) possession.

(d) Bailee Who Breaks Bale or Breaks Bulk. We have seen that, as a protection for England's growing trade and commerce, the English courts in the 15th century held it to be larceny for a bailee, in rightful possession of another's baled (packaged) goods to break open the bale and misappropriate a part or all of the contents, although if he misappropriated the entire bale, without breaking it open, it was not larceny. Although the rule originated in the case of a bailee for purposes of transportation, it was extended to apply to other types of bailees as well. The original rule that it is larceny under these circumstances to break open a bale ("breaking bale") was broadened to cover cases of misappropriation of a part (though not all) of unbaled goods shipped in bulk ("breaking bulk"), and even of packaged goods so shipped, where part (but not all) of the packages are taken, though none is broken open. In the United States today the situation of the misappropriating bailee who either does or does not break bale or break bulk is variously treated. In some states, it is larceny if there is such a breaking, embezzlement if not. In others there are statutes that make it larceny, or embezzlement, or a new crime (separate from larceny and embezzlement) called "larceny by bailee," or a larger new crime (encompassing both larceny and embezzlement) called "theft," without regard to whether there is such a breaking.

(e) Larceny by Trick. In our look into the history of the theft crimes we learned that one who obtains possession of, but not title to, another's property by lies, then intending fraudulently to convert the property and later doing so, is guilty of larceny. The distinction between obtaining possession and obtaining title—the principal dividing line, not always easy to draw, between larceny by trick and the separate crime of false pretenses—is discussed at some length later. The lies that will suffice for larceny by trick may be written or spoken; they are generally misrepresentations of some present or past fact, but there is authority that for larceny by trick, as distinguished from false pretenses under the majority view, a false promise (i.e., a promise which the promisor, at the time he makes it, does not intend to keep) will do. There is a question whether the defendant must intend, at the moment he obtains possession of the property by lies, to convert it, or whether a subsequently-formed intent to convert it will do. At all events, he must, in fact, later convert it.

(f) Finders. The owner of lost property or of mislaid property (with mislaid property, the owner has intentionally placed it somewhere and then forgotten it) has "constructive possession" of it as long as the actual possession is vacant; therefore, a finder who picks up the lost or mislaid property intending to misappropriate it may be viewed as taking it by a trespass from the owner's possession, so that his conduct constitutes the necessary trespass in the taking for larceny. To be guilty of larceny, however, more than a trespass is required: the finder must, at the time of the finding, (1) intend to steal it and (2) either know who the owner is or have reason to believe (from earmarkings on the property or from the circumstances of the finding) that he can find out the owner's identity. It is not larceny, therefore, for a finder to pick up property with knowledge of or means of discovering its ownership, intending to return it to the owner, or to pick up property with no knowledge of or means of discovering the owner, intending to keep it for himself, even though later, with full knowledge of the ownership, the finder converts it to his own use. And he is not guilty of larceny if he picks up another's lost property, with no knowledge or means of discovering the owner, with intent to convert it, because later he may not use proper diligence in trying to discover the owner. Modern theft statutes, it should be noted, typically deal with the theft-by-finders case in a quite different manner.

(g) Delivery of Property by Mistake. Property belonging to one person may be delivered to another under a mistake as to the nature of the property (such as delivery of gold pieces in the belief that they are nickels, or a trunk containing money or clothes although thought to be empty), or as to the amount of the property (as where one, cashing a check for $36, is paid $4,328), or as to the identity of the recipient (as where mailed property intended for one James Mucklow is delivered by the postman to another James Mucklow). It is well settled that the recipient of the mistaken delivery who appropriates the property commits a trespass in the taking, and so is guilty of larceny, if, realizing the mistake at the moment he takes delivery, he then forms an intent to steal the property. On the other hand, if, when he takes delivery, either (1) he does not realize the mistake and so cannot then have an intent to steal, or (2) he does realize the mistake but intends to return the property, he cannot be guilty of larceny even though he may later decide to steal (see § 16.5(f)), for two reasons: (1) as to the original taking of delivery, there is no trespass, for he took it with an innocent mind, and (2) as to the later intent to steal, it did not coincide with the taking.

The principal difficulty in applying the rule arises in the cases of delivery of goods or money enclosed in a package or envelope or other container, so that the defendant first receives the container without knowledge of the contents and therefore without any dishonest intent to steal anything; later (perhaps a minute, perhaps several days) he opens the container, discovers the mistake and immediately decides to steal. The cases are split between the view that he is guilty of larceny because he intends to steal when he takes the property, for he does not "take" the property until he discovers its existence, and the view that he is not guilty of larceny, for he "takes" the property enclosed in the container when he takes delivery of the container, so that his later intent to steal that property does not coincide with the taking. As with finders, doubtless the defendant is about as bad morally when the urge to steal comes over him late, so that the distinctions in the law of larceny which depend upon the time when he becomes dishonest do not make much sense. Such distinctions very often (but not always) have been abandoned in the modern criminal codes.

(h) Property Picked up by Mistake. In what seems to be a situation analogous to that of mistaken delivery, one person picks up and carries off another person's property by mistake—as where A's lamb (or bull) is placed with or wanders into B's flock of sheep (or herd of cattle) and B, not noticing the addition, takes it away with the rest, or where B, mistakenly thinking he is authorized by A to do so, carries off A's property for some lawful purpose. In a variant of this situation, B picks up A's property, not with an innocent mind, but with a bad yet not criminal purpose—as where he intends to use it and return it. Under either situation, what may happen to give rise to a larceny problem is that B later decides to steal and does so. The difficulty in holding B for larceny is not that there is no trespass in the taking, for it is clearly a trespass to pick up another person's property without legal right even if innocently done. The difficulty lies in finding a coincidence of intent to steal and trespassory taking, a requirement discussed later (see § 16.5(f)).

(i) Removal From Owner's Premises or Presence. One may be said to have taken another's property by a trespass though he has not removed it from the other's premises or from his presence.

§ 16.3 Larceny—Taking and Carrying Away

Commission of the crime of larceny requires a taking (caption) and carrying away (asportation) of another's property. A taking occurs when the offender secures dominion over the property, while a carrying away requires some slight movement away of the property.

(a) Taking (Caption). The defendant does not commit larceny of another's property unless he "takes" it in the sense of securing dominion over it. There is no "caption," as the taking element is sometimes called, if the defendant, in an attempt to steal another's property, strikes the latter's hand, causing him to drop the property on the ground where, because of the darkness, the defendant cannot find it. So too property that, unknown to the defendant when he first tries to carry it off, is chained in such a way that, although it can be moved, it cannot be taken away, cannot be "taken." On the other hand, one may "take" the property of another, although he personally does not acquire dominion over it, if he sells it as his own to an innocent third person, who then takes possession of it (see § 16.3(b)).

As we shall see, there is a question concerning the *time* of taking of another's property, which, unknown to the defendant, has been deposited within a container of some sort (see § 16.5(f)). Also, one can take another's property without removing it from the latter's premises or from his presence (see § 16.2(i)).

(b) Carrying Away (Asportation). The word "carrying" in the expression "carrying away" (the common law requirement of an asportation) is not to be taken literally, for one can be guilty of larceny of property that he cannot pick up in his hands, as by riding away a horse, leading away a cow, driving off in an automobile or pulling or pushing a heavy object along the ground or floor. The distance "away" that the property must be moved need not be substantial—a slight distance will do. But every part of the property must be moved; it is not enough, for instance, to turn a barrel, standing on its head, onto its side, in order to get a better grip on it. The movement must be a "carrying away" movement; it is not enough, for instance, merely to shoot an animal for purpose of stealing it, though it moves from a standing to a prone position when shot. As already noted (see § 16.2(i)), so long as the defendant moves every part of it, it is not necessary to move it away from the owner's premises or from his presence.

One difficult fact situation concerning the asportation element in larceny is where *A,* falsely pretending to be the owner of *B*'s property, sells it to *C,* an innocent purchaser, who after the sale takes it and carries it off. Since *A* never touched it, how can it be said that he took and carried it away? The majority and better view is that *C* is *A*'s innocent agent for the purpose of the caption and asportation requirements, so that *C*'s taking and carrying away is attributable to *A,* but there is authority to the contrary, refusing to attribute *C*'s caption and asportation to *A,* on the ground that, under ordinary agency principles, the purchaser is not the seller's agent. There has been less difficulty in finding an asportation by an innocent agent in the case where *A* switches tags on *B*'s baggage, so that the carrier *C,* following the directions on the false tag, carries the baggage to *A* instead of to *B.* Here, although *A* has not personally moved the baggage, the asportation of *C, A*'s innocent agent, is held to be attributable to *A.*

There are in some jurisdictions special larceny statutes that provide a greater punishment than for ordinary larceny where the larceny in question is "from the person" (popularly called pickpocketing) or (less frequently) "from the house" (or "dwelling house," or "building"). For larceny from the person it is not enough to move the property within the pocket; it must be moved out of the pocket. So also, the crime of larceny from the house is not committed when the only asportation occurs within the house; to be guilty the defendant must have carried the property out of the house.

We have already noted that for that special type of larceny called "larceny by trick," something more than a mere asportation is required; the defendant must actually convert the property (see § 16.2(e)).

The common law asportation requirement is generally of no significance today, as theft offenses in the modern codes are usually defined without resort to that concept. In this respect, these statutes follow Model Penal Code § 223.2. While this abandonment of the asportation requirement has sometimes been criticized, the Code position is sound. If the defendant has taken control of the property, then it is of no penological significance whether or not he has in any sense engaged in a carrying away of that property.

§ 16.4 Larceny—Personal Property of Another

Although common law larceny was limited to the taking of tangible personal property, modern statutes have generally covered other kinds of property as well. Most jurisdictions distinguish between grand and petit larceny, depending upon the value of the property. The property must be "of another," which excludes such items as abandoned property and wild animals.

(a) **Nature of the Property.** At common law, larceny was limited to misappropriations of goods and chattels—i.e., tangible personal property. It could not be larceny to carry away real property. As to those items of real property—such as trees, crops, minerals and fixtures—which become personal property after severance from the realty, the common law view was that it is not larceny to sever the property and carry it away in one continuous act, but if the severance and asportation constitute two separate acts (as where the trespasser left the premises, or a substantial period of time intervened between these two events), it is larceny.

At common law one could not steal intangible personal property, including such substantial choses in action as stocks, bonds, checks or promissory notes, all of which are in the form of documents. Written documents were considered, for purposes of larceny, to be merged into the things that they represented—so that a deed, representing real estate, or a contract, representing an intangible right to performance, could not be stolen.

Modern statutes in all jurisdictions have broadened the scope of larceny to include such intangible personal property as written instruments embodying choses in action or other intangible rights. In addition, a number of states have statutes making it larceny to steal such specific items savoring of real property as minerals, trees, crops and fixtures, with no requirement of two separate acts of severance and asportation. The trend of the modern criminal codes is to include any sort of property of value that can be moved.

Gas and electricity are commonly held, without the aid of special statutes, to be property that can be stolen, the usual method being to run a gas pipe or electrical wire around the meter. Property that is contraband may nevertheless be stolen. On the other hand, in the absence of a specific statutory provision, it has been held not to be larceny to make use of the factory, or of the labor and services, of another. Modern statutes, however, make it theft to steal labor or services or the use of property.

(b) Value of the Property: Grand Larceny vs. Petit Larceny. Following the English precedent, practically all American jurisdictions by statute divide larceny (and, usually, theft more generally) into categories, depending upon the amount stolen. There is considerable variation in the number of categories utilized. Most common are two-, three- and four-tier arrangements, but even five- and six-tier classifications are to be found. There is likewise no agreement as to what amount should escalate the crime into the felony category. The range is from $2,000 to $50, with the most common being $500.

There are some legal questions concerned with valuation of stolen property. Property value is not necessarily its cost; rather it is its market value (a matter of buying and selling) at the time and place stolen, if there is a market for it. It is the value of the property in its whole condition and in its proper place, rather than its value after removal, that controls. In the case of property of intrinsically small value that represents a contract or property right of much greater value (as where an automobile license plate made of $1 worth of metal costs the motorist $20 to obtain; or as a check, written on paper worth a cent, represents a right to receive $100), it is the latter value that is important in larceny cases, unless perhaps the owner can at a smaller cost replace the property and thereby save his right. As the statutes are generally worded, it is the value of the property taken, not the thief's estimate of its worth, that governs. As with the defendant's intention to deprive (see § 16.5), the extent of the deprivation depends on the loss to the victim and not the benefit to the thief.

A thief may steal different articles from different victims at different times and places, and such takings cannot be aggregated for the purpose of making one grand larceny out of several petit larcenies. Conversely, different articles stolen at one time and place from the same victim (e.g., theft of his wallet containing three twenty dollar bills; or theft of his money and his watch) can be aggregated (so that, in the case of the wallet with the three twenties, it is one sixty-dollar larceny rather than three twenty-dollar larcenies). Cases falling in between these two extremes give more difficulty.

In the case of the thief who takes small amounts from the same victim over a period of time before his peculations are discovered, the small thefts are aggregated into one large theft if (as is generally the case) the successive takings are pursuant to a single scheme. So too in the case of one who takes several small amounts (in the aggregate comprising a large total) from different victims at one time and place (as where, during a tea party downstairs, the thief searches the bedroom where several ladies' purses have been stowed, taking ten dollars from each of ten purses), the takings may, by the great weight of authority, be aggregated; it might be said that such takings are necessarily part of one scheme.

Of course, there are instances when the aggregation of larcenies is a benefit, not a detriment, to the defendant, as where he has taken several items of property each of sufficient value for grand larceny: it is generally better for the defendant to be guilty of one grand larceny of $1000 than of ten separate $100 grand larcenies. The question of whether several related takings constitute one big larceny or several smaller larcenies arises in criminal-law settings other than with respect to the grand-petit larceny distinction. And the question of aggregation arises in connection with theft crimes other than larceny (e.g., embezzlement, false pretenses, receiving stolen property) which commonly draw the same line between the grand and petit varieties.

It should be noted also that in practically all jurisdictions there are by statute some kinds of larceny that are felonies without regard to the value of the property taken. Such is often the case as to larceny from the person ("pickpocketing"). Then too statutes frequently make it felonious larceny to steal certain types of property regardless of value, such as automobiles and firearms. And, of course, that aggravated type of larceny called robbery is a felony which carries a severe penalty, once again without regard to the value of the property taken.

(c) Of Another. For larceny the property must be "of another." For this reason wild animals, even though on another's land, cannot be the subject of larceny; nor can property, once owned, that has been abandoned by its former owner.

The common law view of larceny is that one co-owner (e.g., a partner, tenant in common, joint tenant) cannot steal from the other co-owner. The modern trend is to provide by statute that it is no defense to larceny that the thief has an interest in the property taken, so long as the other has an interest therein to which the thief is not entitled.

Sometimes the property that A owns is in the lawful possession of B, who has a pledge or lien interest in the property to secure a debt which A owes B. From A's viewpoint such property is considered the "property of another" for purposes of larceny, so that if A takes it from B's possession with intent to deprive him of his pledge or lien interest therein, A is guilty of larceny. Similarly, if A should bail his property to B and then stealthily take it, intending to charge B with the value of the property, A would be guilty of larceny of his own property.

For larceny the thief need not take the property from its owner. A second thief is guilty of larceny even though he steals the property from the first thief. Many modern codes expressly provide, as does Model Penal Code § 223.0(7), that property may be the subject of theft even though the "victim" is a person whose interest in the property is unlawful. This is as it should be. "It is inconsistent with the objectives of the criminal law of theft to permit one who wrongfully appropriates wealth to escape from liability merely because the victim of the misappropriation has also incurred criminal liability of forfeiture of his rights with respect to the property."

§ 16.5 Larceny—Intent to Steal

For larceny there must be an intent to steal (or, as stated in the Latin form, *animus furandi*). It is, of course, not very helpful to say that to be guilty of stealing property one must have an intent to steal the property. It is more helpful to state (as it is sometimes put) that, for larceny, one must intend to deprive the owner of the possession of his property either permanently or for an unreasonable length of time, or intend to use it in such a way that the owner will probably be thus deprived of his property. Note that the matter is stated in terms of the owner's deprivation rather than of the thief's gain, in recognition of the majority view that, for larceny, there need be no intent on the part of the thief to gain a benefit for himself (or, again to use the Latin phrase, for larceny there need be no *lucri causa*—"on account of pecuniary gain").

Precisely what kind of intent is needed is usually addressed in rather specific terms in modern statutes dealing with theft. By far the most common approach is to follow Model Penal Code § 223.0(1), which defines the word "deprive" (theft requires a "purpose to deprive") as "(a) to withhold property of another permanently or for so extended a period as to appropriate a major portion of its economic value, or with intent to restore only upon payment of reward or other compensation; or (b) to dispose of the property so as to make it unlikely that the owner will recover it." Some other states use the Model Penal Code formulation without the intent-to-restore part, while a few other statutes declare either that nothing short of permanent deprivation will suffice or, on the other hand, that mere temporary deprivation is enough.

Perhaps the best way to understand the meaning of "intent to steal" is to see how the courts have handled the following types of situations that have a bearing on the problem.

(a) Claim of Right. One may take the property of another honestly but mistakenly believing (1) that it is his own property, or (2) that it is no one's property, or (3) (though he knows it is another's property) that the owner has given him permission to take it as he did. In any such event, he lacks the intent to steal required for larceny, even though his mistaken but honest belief was unreasonable. As to how the defendant can prove his claim that he actually had such an honest belief, it has been pointed out that the openness of the taking, as well as the reasonableness of the belief, though not conclusive, will buttress his claim of good faith.

(b) Intent to Return the Very Property Taken. One who takes another's property intending at the time he takes it to use it temporarily and then to return it unconditionally within a reasonable time—and having a substantial ability to do so—lacks the intent to steal required for larceny. It should be noted that it is the intent to return the property, not its actual return, which constitutes the defense to larceny: one who takes another's property intending at the time of taking to deprive the owner permanently is nevertheless guilty of larceny, though he later (becoming frightened, or his better nature prevailing) decides to return it and does so.

Conversely, an intent to return is a defense though some unexpected obstacle prevents an actual return. An intent to return, to be a defense, need not be an intent to return it to the exact spot from which it was taken if the intent is to return it to a place sufficiently near so that the owner is substantially certain to find it or get it back. The intent to return, however, must be unconditional. Thus it is no defense to larceny that the taker intended to return it only if he should receive a reward for its return, or only upon some other condition which he has no right to impose.

As noted above, it is not a defense to larceny merely to have an intent to return the property; in addition one must, at the time of taking, have a substantial ability to do so (even though, as events turn out, it may later become impossible to do so). Thus if one takes another's property intending to use it recklessly and then abandon it, the obstacles to its safe return to the owner are such that the taker possesses the required intent to steal. Even without the intent to use recklessly, an intent to abandon, accompanied by a not-too-well founded hope that the property will find its way back to its owner does not negative the intent to steal. So too, an intent to pawn the property, accompanied by an intent later to redeem the property and return it to its owner, is a defense only if the taker's financial situation is such that he has an ability to redeem it.

An intent to return the property taken, in order to qualify as a defense to larceny, must be an intent to return within a reasonable time. In determining what is a reasonable time, much depends upon the nature of the property and its expected useful life, for to deprive the owner of the property for so long a time that he has lost a "major portion of its economic value" is to deprive him for an unreasonable time. It is one thing to take another's fresh strawberries with intent to return them two weeks later, another thing to take his diamond ring with a like intention.

As we shall see in the discussion of the notion of "continuing trespass," one who takes another's property intending only to use it temporarily before restoring it unconditionally to its owner (i.e., one who normally is found not to have an intent to steal) may nevertheless be guilty of larceny if he later changes his mind and decides not to return the property after all.

A large number of states have singled out the motor vehicle for special treatment, making it a crime (generally called "joyriding," a crime somewhat less serious than larceny) to take such a vehicle with intent to use it and return it. An important federal statute makes it a felony to transport a stolen motor vehicle, with knowledge that it is stolen, across state lines.

(c) Intent to Return the Equivalent. It is not so clear that one who takes another's property intending, and having the financial ability, to pay for it or otherwise to restore the equivalent (rather than to restore the property itself) has a defense to a charge of larceny. Doubtless where the property taken is property that the owner has offered for sale, such an intent, with such an ability, does constitute a defense. If the property is not for sale, however, perhaps an intent to pay (with ability) is not a defense; although even here if the intended payment is clearly the equivalent of (or more than) the property taken, it might be considered that the defendant lacks the intent to steal. If the property is unique, for which there is no monetary equivalent, or if the owner has been made an offer which he has rejected, it is quite clear that an intent to pay for it is no defense. As noted above, the intent to pay for the property taken or otherwise to restore its equivalent is never a good defense unless there is a substantial ability to do so; a mere hope, under circumstances disclosing little foundation for optimism, that one can replace or pay for the property will not do. Of course, an intent to pay for the property with a bogus check is no defense to larceny.

(d) Intent to Collect a Debt or Satisfy a Claim. The traditional view is that it is a defense to larceny and robbery (an aggravated form of larceny), because negativing the intent to steal, that the defendant who takes another's money (by stealth or by force) intends to collect a debt which the other owes him or (even if no debt is actually owed) which he honestly believes the other owes him. The matter is somewhat more difficult if he takes the other's property, rather than his money, in satisfaction of the debt, as where he takes a cow in satisfaction of a $300 debt; or where he takes money in satisfaction of an unliquidated claim for damages. The trouble is that, although money is fungible, property is not so clearly the equivalent of money, or money the equal of an unliquidated claim. Even so, where the property or money taken is clearly less in value than the amount of the debt or claim, it ought not to be larceny. There is, of course, no difficulty in giving the defense if the property or money is taken for security, rather than in satisfaction of, the debt or claim.

The Model Penal Code § 223.1(3)(b) position, reflected in many of the modern criminal codes, is that it is an affirmative defense that the defendant "acted under an honest claim of right to the property or service involved or that he had a right to acquire or dispose of it as he did." The wisdom of this position is, at best, debatable. In support, it is contended that those "who take only property to which they believe themselves entitled constitute no significant threat to the property system and manifest no character trait worse than ignorance." On the other side, it is claimed that such a rule is "but one step short of accepting lawless reprisal as an appropriate means of redressing grievances, real or fancied," and that disputed claims "are better resolved in a court of law than by violence or stealth."

(e) Miscellaneous Defenses. As with other crimes requiring intent, the intent to steal may be negatived by intoxication (even voluntary intoxication) so great as to rob the defendant of his capacity to entertain such an intent.

The defenses of insanity, infancy and compulsion are available, in appropriate fact situations, in larceny as in other cases. Mistakes of fact or of law constitute defenses to larceny when the mistake in question negatives the intent to steal—as shown by the cases, discussed above (though not specifically in terms of mistakes) holding it a good defense to larceny that the defendant takes under a bona fide claim of right.

(f) Concurrence of Larcenous Conduct and Intent to Steal. With larceny, as with other crimes requiring both specified physical conduct and a specified state of mind (see § 5.3), the defendant's conduct and his mental state must coincide. So the taking and carrying away (the physical conduct in larceny) and the intent to steal (larceny's state of mind) must concur. Thus one who finds lost or mislaid property and picks it up intending to return it to the owner, but who later decides to steal it, cannot be guilty of larceny; for the taking and asportation, on the one hand, and the intent to steal, on the other, do not coincide. So also, for the same reason, one who, because of a mistake on the part of the deliverer, receives a misdelivery of property (including an overpayment of money) is not guilty of larceny when he receives it with an innocent mind (not then realizing the mistake), though he later, on learning of the mistake, decides to steal it. There is some minority authority, however, for the proposition that, in the case of a misdelivery of property or overpayment of money enclosed within a container (e.g., a check within an envelope, a roll of coins within a paper wrapping, clothing within a trunk), the recipient of the container takes the enclosed property from the deliverer's possession only when he learns of its existence within the container, so that, if he then decides to steal, the taking and the intent to steal do coincide for larceny purposes.

As an aid in finding that the taking-and-asportation and the intent to steal coincide, the law of larceny under some circumstances makes use of the fictional notion of *continuing trespass,* under which the original trespassory taking, although not coinciding with an intent to steal (for the taker originally has no such intent), continues until the taker does form such an intent. At that moment the taking (and, as soon as he moves the property, the asportation) and the intent to steal do coincide, so that the taker is guilty of larceny. What are the circumstances giving rise to a continuing trespass?

First, there must, of course, be a trespass in the original taking. As we have seen, the finder of another's lost or mislaid property, or the one upon whom another's property is thrust by a misdelivery, who takes the property with an innocent mind, is not guilty of a trespass at all. But it is a different matter in the case of one who innocently picks up another's property erroneously believing it to be his own, or mistakenly thinking the other has authorized him to take possession. He is guilty of a trespass. And, even more clearly, one who takes another's property knowing it is not his own and that the other has not authorized the taking (e.g., one who takes it intending to use it carefully and return it soon) commits a trespass. But he is not, in either case, guilty of larceny yet, for he has not yet formed an intent to steal.

Suppose that he does later decide to steal; does the trespass continue so as to produce the necessary coincidence of trespassory taking and intent to steal? The second requirement for continuing trespass (in America, at least) is that the original trespass be of a mentally-bad (though not necessarily criminal) type rather than an innocent-minded sort. Thus to pick up another's property mistakenly believing it to be one's own or that the taking is authorized, though a trespass, does not constitute a trespass which continues (so that, when the taker later decides to steal, he is not guilty of larceny); whereas to take it, wrongfully, intending to use it and return it, is a trespass which does continue (so as to render the taker who later decides to steal guilty of larceny).

In the modern criminal codes, however, it is generally true that a later-formed intent to steal will suffice without regard to whether this fictitious continuing trespass is present. Sometimes this is accomplished by an express statement that the intent to deprive may occur either when the property is obtained or later. But other statutes appear to accomplish the same result either by use of such words as "retains" or "withholds" in defining the requisite acts, or by attaching the intent-to-deprive element to the failure to take reasonable measures to restore the property. The change, in any event, represents sound policy, for the "objective in this area is not to prevent initial appropriation but to compel subsequent acts to restore the owner."

§ 16.6 Embezzlement

Embezzlement, a statutory crime, is defined somewhat differently in different jurisdictions, so that it is impossible to define it authoritatively in a single way. But in general it may be defined as: (1) the fraudulent (2) conversion of (3) the property (4) of another (5) by one who is already in lawful possession of it.

(a) Need for Crime of Embezzlement. As we have already noted in connection with the historical development of the theft crimes (see § 16.1), there was a large gap in larceny caused by larceny's requirement of a trespass in the taking. Thus one, already in lawful possession of another's property, who converted it to his own use with intent to deprive the owner of it, committed no trespass in the taking and so could not be guilty of larceny. (And there was then no other crime that covered this type of misappropriation.) So the English legislature created the new crime of embezzlement to fill this loophole. It did so by listing various kinds of persons who might have lawful possession of another's property—e.g., store clerks, bank employees, agents, attorneys, brokers, factors, trustees, bankers, merchants, corporate officers, partners, bailees—and by providing that any such person entrusted with another's property who fraudulently converted it was guilty of embezzlement.

In America the English pattern was for many years generally followed, although in a few states, instead of listing the various types of persons (and perhaps omitting some who should be included) who commit embezzlement when they fraudulently convert, the statutes simply provided that one in lawful possession of (or entrusted with) another's property who fraudulently converts it is guilty. This latter approach now prevails, especially in those jurisdictions with modern codes consolidating embezzlement with other forms of theft (see § 16.8). Such consolidation, resulting in a rather broadly-defined crime of "theft," has obviated many of the problems (discussed herein) that had arisen under the earlier embezzlement statutes adhering to the English model.

One further thing should be noted at the outset: embezzlement and false pretenses were new crimes created by the legislature for the specific purpose of plugging loopholes left by the narrowness of the crime of larceny. That being so, the courts have generally held or assumed that these crimes do not overlap, that they are mutually exclusive. Yet there may be some small areas where because of the wording of the embezzlement statute, embezzlement does overlap with larceny.

(b) Conversion. Although ordinary larceny requires, so far as the act is concerned, only a taking and an asportation, embezzlement requires something more: a conversion. Conversion for embezzlement purposes is not different from conversion for tort purposes. A conversion of property requires a serious act of interference with the owner's rights. Thus the mere act of moving it a short distance (the asportation for larceny), or of using it casually, or of damaging it slightly, will not do. On the other hand, using it up, selling it, pledging it, giving it away, delivering it to one not entitled to it, inflicting serious damage to it, claiming it against the owner, unreasonably withholding possession of it from the owner— each of these acts seriously interferes with the owner's rights and so constitutes a conversion. One is not a converter unless his acts are intentional (as distinguished from merely negligent); but one can be a converter though innocent-minded, as where he is a bona fide purchaser of stolen goods. (Yet an innocent-minded converter is not guilty of embezzlement, for the crime, unlike the tort, requires a fraudulent intent in addition to the conversion.)

Embezzlement statutes sometimes are worded in terms of the wrongdoer's conversion "to his own use." These words are not to be taken literally, however, for it is not a requirement for a conversion that the converter gain a personal benefit from his dealing with the property. Thus one might convert another's property though what he does is to benefit the corporation of which he is an officer or stockholder, or to benefit his wife or son.

There is a dispute as to whether it is a conversion for one in possession of another's property to secrete it with an intent to misappropriate it at a later, more convenient time. A large number of embezzlement statutes take care of the matter by specifically providing that the crime may be committed by secreting another's property with an intent to embezzle it.

(c) Property. Embezzlement statutes are sometimes worded in terms of "property which may be the subject of larceny," or words to that effect, thus incorporating by reference all the learning, discussed above, concerning the property that will qualify for larceny. As we have seen (see § 16.4(a)), larceny, originally limited to tangible personal property, has been everywhere expanded to cover such intangible personal property as specialty choses in action like negotiable instruments (checks, promissory notes, bonds, stocks) and written documents (deeds, contracts) representing intangible rights; and to include such items savoring of real estate as minerals, trees, crops and fixtures. The modern trend in larceny, in fact, is in the direction of covering all sorts of property that have value and can be moved. On the other hand, the traditional view is that use of another's property or the use of the labor or services of another, not being property, cannot be stolen. Modern theft statutes, however, very often cover both property and services (see § 16.4(a)).

In some states, however, embezzlement is defined, as to the property requirement, more broadly than is the case with larceny. The statute may punish the embezzlement of real as well as of personal property. On principle, it seems clear that, although one cannot commit larceny of a plot of real estate (for it cannot be moved, as larceny requires), yet one (e.g., a trustee, agent, guardian) who has power to sell or mortgage another's real estate, and who deprives the other of it by fraudulently transferring it to a bona fide purchaser or mortgagee, ought to be guilty of embezzlement.

The situation of the agent, with authority to draw checks upon his principal's bank account, who makes unauthorized use of the bank account for his private gain, has given rise to some problems. Thus a corporate treasurer or secretary, having authority to draw checks upon his principal's bank account to carry on his principal's business, may make out a check (a) payable to himself (or to cash) and then indorse and cash it; or (b) payable to an innocent third person and then forge the latter's indorsement and cash it; or (c) payable to a confederate third person who then indorses and cashes it and splits the proceeds with the agent; or (d) payable to his own private creditor, to whom he delivers the check in payment of his debt and who indorses it and cashes it.

In the first three situations there is not too much difficulty in holding the agent liable for embezzlement of the cash, for he took his principal's cash into his hands and then fraudulently converted it to his own use. The fourth situation is more difficult, however. It has been held that this is not embezzlement: all that the agent has control over is an intangible chose in action (the claim against the bank), which is not the sort of property which can be embezzled; and the agent never had within his possession or control the specific money actually paid to the agent's creditor. The weight of authority, however, finds an embezzlement, by stretching things to the extent of finding that the agent did have control over the money itself.

(d) Of Another. One cannot be guilty of embezzlement if he converts his own property; the property converted must be that "of another." For this reason one who borrows money and then converts the borrowed sum to his own use is not guilty of embezzlement, even though, when the time comes to repay the loan, he is unable to do so. On the same principle, an employer who, by agreement with his employee, deducts a sum of money from his employee's wages, agreeing to pay that sum to a third person, is not guilty of embezzlement when he fails to pay the third person; the money that the employer deducts, not being segregated from his other funds, is not the employee's money. So too a building contractor who receives from the landowner an advance payment on the contract and who thereafter spends the money for his own purposes and does not fulfill the contract, is not guilty of embezzlement, unless the money is earmarked to be used only for a construction purpose. Similarly, when in the context of a lessor-lessee relationship the lessee pays a sum of money as a deposit on the item (e.g., an automobile) leased, title to the security deposit funds is transferred to the lessor upon receipt, so that nonpayment to the lessee when the deposit becomes due did not constitute the taking of the property of another.

Another embezzlement problem concerns co-owners of property (joint tenants, tenants in common, partners): if one co-owner in possession of the jointly-owned property misappropriates the whole of such property for his own bad purposes, can he be guilty of embezzlement; is it not his own property rather than property "of another" that he is appropriating? In the absence of some statutory provision expressly covering such co-owners, the cases generally hold that there is no embezzlement. Another situation, which has given rise to a split of authority in the absence of a specific statutory provision, is that of the agent, authorized to collect money due his principal and to keep a certain portion of the amount collected as his commission, who misappropriates the whole amount. A chattel mortgagor and one who purchases under a conditional sales contract, who misappropriates the property in his possession with intent to defraud the chattel mortgagee or conditional seller, may not be misappropriating the property "of another"; but statutes in a number of states make this misconduct a form of embezzlement. On principle, a co-owner, or an agent working on a commission basis, who misappropriates that part of the property in his possession which belongs to his co-owner or principal ought to be guilty of embezzlement of the other's interest in the whole.

We have seen that, although at common law one spouse could not be guilty of larceny of the other spouse's separate property, modern statutes allowing a married woman to own her separate property free from her husband's control have generally been held to authorize larceny convictions of either husband or wife (see § 16.2). The crime of embezzlement has undergone the same evolution.

(e) By One in Lawful Possession. This element is the one that principally distinguishes larceny and embezzlement. For larceny there must be a trespass in the taking: the thief must take the property out of the victim's possession, which means that he cannot already have it in his possession. For embezzlement, on the other hand, the property must already be in the embezzler's lawful possession when he misappropriates it.

Yet it may be that not every case of fraudulent conversion of another's property already in one's lawful possession is covered by the particular embezzlement statute. Following the lead of the English embezzlement statutes, most American states at one time listed the various types of persons who may have another's property in their rightful possession—employees, agents, bailees, attorneys, guardians, executors and administrators, factors, bankers and the like. One trouble with undertaking to make a list is the danger of omitting someone who ought to be included. As previously noted, the modern view is to make it embezzlement (or, a form of the broader crime of theft; see § 16.8) fraudulently to convert another's property in one's possession. Some statutes limit the scope of embezzlement by requiring that the property be "entrusted" or "delivered" to the embezzler with the result that he must acquire his possession of the property by being entrusted with it or by receiving delivery of it. The following are some of the situations that have given rise to some difficulty:

(1) Employees. We have already noted that the master (employer) who hands his property to his servant (employee) retains possession of it, the servant having mere custody, so that the servant who misappropriates the property is guilty of larceny; but if the property comes to the servant for his master from a third person, the servant acquires possession, and his misappropriation, before he transfers possession to the master, is not larceny (see § 16.2(b)). The crime of embezzlement was created to plug the loophole left by this gap in larceny. A typical statute on embezzlement by servants punishes a servant, clerk or agent employed by a person, partnership or corporation who misappropriates his employer's property in his possession. Under such statutes, misappropriating employees who have possession of their employer's property are guilty of embezzlement, those with custody are not (being guilty of larceny instead).

Sometimes it is not easy to determine whether the employee has received the property from his employer (and so has custody) or from a third person (so as to have possession)—as where the employer hands his employee a large bill with instructions to get it changed, and after getting the change the employee absconds with it. Sometimes there is difficulty in deciding whether the employee, by placing the property received from a third person in a receptacle, has transferred possession to the master and thus reduced his own possession to custody. Many cases draw a distinction between minor employees (caretakers, janitors, night watchmen) who are generally considered as having mere custody of the property (and so guilty of larceny when they steal) and those employees who have been delegated greater authority, who have possession (so as to be guilty of embezzlement when they fraudulently convert).

A common type of embezzlement-by-servant statute, however, punishes an employee who fraudulently converts his employer's property "in his possession or under his care." Under such a statute, the crime is embezzlement without regard to the subtle distinction between custody and possession. Under such statutes there is thus some overlapping between larceny and embezzlement.

(2) Finders. We have already noted that a finder of lost or mislaid property having earmarks of ownership who picks it up with intent to steal it is guilty of larceny; but he is not guilty of larceny if he picks it up with intent to restore it to the owner, though he later changes his mind and decides to steal it (see §§ 16.2(f), 16.5(f)). In the latter case is he guilty of embezzlement? He is in lawful possession of another's property, to be sure; but the embezzlement statutes of the state may not specifically cover finders. Statutes that limit embezzlement to property "entrusted" to or "delivered" to the wrongdoer do not cover the finder who properly picks up property. Perhaps a finder may be considered in a sense a bailee, so that if the embezzlement statute covers bailees, then finders may be covered.

(3) Transferees of Property Delivered by Mistake. When considering larceny we noted that one to whom property is mistakenly delivered is guilty of larceny if, realizing the mistake at once, he then intends to steal; but if he originally intends to return the property—or if he does not at the time of taking delivery realize the mistake—and only later decides to steal, he is not guilty of larceny. In the latter situation, is he guilty of embezzlement? Once again, there may be difficulty in finding an embezzlement statute that covers such a misappropriation.

(f) Fraudulent. The mental state required for embezzlement generally appears in the statutes in the form of the adverb "fraudulently" modifying the verb "converts." (If the statute should instead punish one who "embezzles," it would not signify anything different, for "embezzles" means "fraudulently converts.") As with larceny, the principal mental-element questions concern the conversion of another's property done under a bona fide claim of right; or done with intent to return the very property taken; or with intent to restore equivalent property; or with intent to collect a debt.

(1) Claim of Right. One who converts the property of another that is in his lawful possession is not guilty of embezzlement (for his conversion is not fraudulent) if, when he converts, he honestly believes the property is his own or is nobody's, or he otherwise honestly believes he is authorized to convert it. It should make no difference whether this bona fide claim of right is the result of a mistake of fact or a mistake of law, nor whether the mistake is reasonable or unreasonable so long as it is real, for in any such event he lacks an intent to defraud.

(2) Intent to Return the Very Property Taken. One who, with another's property in his rightful possession, converts it, intending, however, to return the specific property (and having a substantial ability to return it) in its original condition, after a period of time, is not guilty of embezzlement, for he lacks the fraudulent intent that embezzlement requires. It is the intent at the time of conversion that is important; one who converts with a fraudulent intent is none the less guilty of embezzlement although he later decides to return the property and does so.

(3) **Intent to Restore Equivalent Property.** A person in lawful possession of another's property may convert it in such a way that he cannot return the specific property; but he may intend to return the equivalent of the converted property to the owner, and he may have a substantial ability to do so. Commonly the property involved is money: the wrongdoer spends the money for pressing purposes of his own, intending to put back other money at a later date, and sometimes having enough private resources to be able to do so and even succeeding in doing so before his misconduct is discovered. It is uniformly held that the intent to restore the equivalent property even under these conditions is no defense to embezzlement.

We earlier noted with respect to larceny that intent and ability to restore the equivalent (generally, to pay for the property taken) may be a defense to that crime, especially if the property taken is property offered for sale. Perhaps the reason why such an intent with such an ability is no defense to the companion crime of embezzlement is the fact that in most embezzlement cases there is in fact no substantial ability to restore; the converter generally uses the money to gamble, play the stock market, or to keep his mistress in appropriate style.

(4) **Intent to Collect a Debt.** Just as it is generally held a defense to larceny that the taker takes the other's money honestly believing the latter owes him that amount (see § 16.5(d)), so too it is a defense to embezzlement of money that the converter thereof believes that the money converted is the amount owed to him by the owner.

(5) **Miscellaneous Defenses.** Embezzlement requires a specific intent to defraud. As with other crimes requiring some specific intent, intoxication which is such as to negative the intent to defraud, and mistake of fact or of law which negatives such intent, are defenses to embezzlement. In addition, the substantive-law defenses of infancy, insanity and compulsion apply to embezzlement as they do to other crimes.

(g) **Embezzlement by Public Officials.** Many states have singled out state and local government officials who have public funds in their possession for special embezzlement treatment, sometimes watering down the mental element of the crime (perhaps punishing the public official who "converts" public funds, or who fails to pay them over on demand, rather than "fraudulently converts" the funds), sometimes increasing the possible punishment—all in recognition of the fact that public officials are not generally as closely watched by the public as employees or agents of private persons or corporations are watched by their employers or principals.

(h) Grand vs. Petit Embezzlement. Just as with larceny, embezzlement statutes commonly divide the crime into grand embezzlement (a felony) and petit embezzlement (a misdemeanor), depending upon the value of the property embezzled. As with larceny, a series of fraudulent conversions of small amounts of property, belonging to one owner, over a period of time, all pursuant to a single scheme, may be aggregated so as to make one larger embezzlement out of several smaller ones.

§ 16.7 False Pretenses

False pretenses, a statutory crime, although defined in slightly different ways in the various jurisdictions, consists in most jurisdictions of these five elements: (1) a false representation of a material present or past fact (2) that causes the victim (3) to pass title to (4) his property to the wrongdoer, (5) who (a) knows his representation to be false and (b) intends thereby to defraud the victim.

(a) Need for Crime of False Pretenses. We have already noted, in connection with the historical development of the theft crimes (see § 16.1), that the modern crime of obtaining property by false pretenses (often called by the shorter term "false pretenses") was created by Parliament in 1757 to plug a loophole left by larceny. Although one who, with intent to steal, obtained possession but not title to another's property by false representations, and then converted it, was guilty of larceny (this type of larceny being called "larceny by trick"), one who obtained the title to the property was not guilty of larceny; and no other crime existed to fill the gap except in limited circumstances. The 1757 English statute punished one who "knowingly and designedly, by false pretense or pretenses, shall obtain from any person or persons, money, goods, wares or merchandises, with intent to cheat or defraud any person or persons of the same."

Most American states enacted a statute similar to the original English statute. Generally speaking, there was greater uniformity among the American false pretenses statutes than among the American embezzlement statutes. Today, virtually all of the modern codes contain a comprehensive crime of theft (see § 16.8), which includes what was traditionally viewed as false pretenses (discussed herein) and often much related conduct as well. Many of the problems discussed below have been obviated by such legislation.

(b) False Representation of Material Present or Past Fact.

(1) False. For one to be guilty of false pretenses his representation must, first of all, be false. If he states a fact that he believes to be untrue but which is actually true, he is not guilty. If he represents to be gold a brick that he believes to be made of brass but which, he later learns to his surprise, is actually made of gold, he has made no false representation as the crime requires. Even when the representation is false when made, if because of changed circumstances it becomes true by the time when the victim, relying thereon passes title to the other, the crime is not committed, for the falsity of the representation and the obtaining of the property must coincide.

(2) Representation. The representation in false pretenses may be made orally or it may be made in writing. It may even be the result of unwritten and unspoken conduct, as where the wrongdoer, by wearing the cap and gown of an Oxford student, purposely produces the false impression that he is such a student and, on the basis of that false impression, obtains property from a tradesman on credit. The representation of one fact may be implied from words that literally say something quite different: thus one who, to induce purchasers to buy land, falsely states that the state is about to build a hospital on the land, or that the federal government is about to construct a canal thereon, impliedly represents that the state or federal government has already taken affirmative action according to existing plans to construct the hospital or canal. In some but not all jurisdictions the drawing and delivery of a check not postdated and without disclosure of insufficiency of funds, which states, "To the X Bank: Pay to the order of John Jones $50," is held to be an implied representation that the drawer has $50 in the X Bank to cover the check.

(3) Nondisclosure. A misrepresentation for false pretenses generally requires some affirmative conduct—ordinarily the speaking or writing of words, although sometimes affirmative conduct (like the wearing of the cap and gown of Oxford) not involving words. No doubt affirmative statements that reinforce false impressions which the defendant did not create, or affirmative conduct in suppressing the truth—e.g., the defendant actually hides information and so prevents the victim from learning the truth—will do as well. Mere silence, however, will generally not suffice, even though the silent one realizes that the other is acting under a mistaken impression. Under special circumstances there may, nevertheless, be a duty to speak to correct a misapprehension (thus making silence the basis of liability)—as where the defendant has, even though innocently, previously created the misapprehension by something he said or did, or where he stands in a fiduciary relationship to the other.

(4) Material. The false representation, to suffice for false pretenses, must be as to a material fact. A fact can be material without going to "the essence of the transaction," as required for the civil tort of fraud. One who obtains money from another by subletting his apartment to him for three months falsely representing that the lease has two years to run, is not guilty of false pretenses, though he intends to defraud, where under the applicable rent laws, though not under the lease itself, he has the right to possession beyond the three months period.

(5) Present or Past Fact. Under the traditional view, to qualify for the crime of false pretenses the false representation must relate to a present or past fact; a false representation as to a future fact will not do. It should be remembered, however, that it may be possible to find, in a statement relating to something that is to happen in the future, an implied representation that something has happened in the past.

It is quite possible to view a false statement of intention—for example, a false promise (one that the promisor, at the time he makes his promise, intends not to keep)—as a misrepresentation of existing fact, for he is falsely representing his present state of mind. And a clever criminal can defraud his victim about as well with a false promise as with other types of false statement of fact. Nevertheless, the traditional view was that false promises will not suffice for false pretenses. The argument supporting this position that one cannot ever be sure whether a borrower has made a false promise or whether he has simply later changed his mind about the use of borrowed money; and that therefore there is a grave danger that honest businessmen who do not pay their debts will go to jail—has been countered by the argument that the mental state involved in a false promise is as easily discoverable as many other states of mind recognized by the criminal and civil law, and by studies showing that in those minority jurisdictions which recognize false promises as false pretenses the jails are not flooded with unfortunate but honest businessmen. The modern prevailing view, by case law and especially by comprehensive theft legislation, is in the direction of allowing false statements of intention—including false promises—to qualify as false representation for the crime of false pretenses. (And, for some illogical reason, although in a particular jurisdiction a false promise will not do for the crime of false pretenses, it may do for the companion crime of larceny by trick.)

It is sometimes stated that an exaggerated expression of opinion, which generally concerns the value of property—e.g., "This land is worth $12,000" or "That stock is virtually worthless"—is "seller's talk" or "puffing wares" and not a misrepresentation of fact that will qualify for false pretenses. On the other hand, it has been recognized that, under appropriate circumstances, a dishonest expression of opinion may be a misrepresentation of fact suitable for false pretenses, especially where the opinion relates to a matter peculiarly within the knowledge of the one who expresses the opinion.

There is a split of authority as to whether a false statement of law (rather than of fact) will do for false pretenses—as where one induces another to buy stock by making the representation, which he knows to be false, that the stock is not subject to assessment. No doubt a clever criminal can accomplish a fraud as well by misrepresenting the law as by misrepresenting a fact; so that the better view is that intentional misrepresentations of law, done with intent to defraud, will do for the crime of false pretenses.

A statement that though literally true is nonetheless misleading because it omits necessary qualifications—the half-truth which can operate to deceive quite as effectively as the outright lie—constitutes a form of misrepresentation that, when done to deceive, ought to qualify as a false pretense.

Sometimes a clever swindler, after making oral misrepresentations to deceive his victim, gets the latter to sign a written contract which not only omits the offensive representations but contains a "merger clause" stating that the written contract is the entire agreement between the parties and that no representation has been made which is not set forth in the written contract. Such a merger clause, however, has been held ineffective to shield the swindler from a conviction for false pretenses.

(c) Cause and Result (The Element of Reliance). For false pretenses it is necessary that the swindler's misrepresentation *cause* the victim to pass title to his property or money to the swindler. Looking at the matter from the point of view of the victim, the same thought may be expressed thus: for false pretenses it is required that the victim pass title to his property *in reliance upon* the swindler's misrepresentation.

Thus if the victim, although he passes title, does not believe the misrepresentations, the crime is not committed. He may pass title, though knowing the defendant to be lying, in order to be able to prosecute him for the crime; but the prosecution for the completed crime (though not for the attempt) must fail for lack of the element of reliance. Or he may pass title, though he knows the defendant to be lying, because he nevertheless wants what the defendant offers—i.e., he would have passed title even if the defendant had told the truth. The defendant is not then guilty of false pretenses. Or he may pass title in response to a judgment obtained against him because of judicial reliance on the defendant's misrepresentations, even though he does not himself believe defendant's misrepresentations.

Often the defendant, in order to induce the victim to part with his money or other property, makes several representations, some true but one false, which, operating together upon the victim's mind, cause the victim to hand over his money or other property. It has been held that if the one false representation is "one of the material matters relied upon," or is a "controlling inducement" for the transfer of property, or "substantially contributed" thereto, even though not the sole inducement, the victim has relied upon it, for purposes of the reliance element of false pretenses. For this reason it has been held that, even if the victim has so little faith in the defendant's representation that he undertakes to investigate its truth, without however discovering its falsity, he nevertheless has relied upon the misrepresentation for purposes of false pretenses.

(d) Title Passing. The wording of the typical false pretenses statute—requiring that the defendant "obtain" property by false pretenses—is quite ambiguous on the issue of whether he must obtain title to, or possession of, the property, or whether he must obtain both title and possession. As we have already noted, however, the crime of false pretenses requires that the defendant, by his lies, obtain *title* to the victim's property. If he obtains *possession* without title by means of his lies, his crime is larceny.

Whether title to property delivered to the defendant passes to him usually depends upon whether the victim *intends* to transfer title to him—so much so that the rule for false pretenses is sometimes erroneously expressed in terms of the victim's intent. But there are cases wherein the victim, intending to transfer title, fails to do so—as, for instance, where the victim ships goods to the defendant who has ordered them by mail, fraudulently using the name of another person. In such cases, the true distinction is not the victim's intention but the actual transfer of title, so that, since title does not in fact pass, the defendant's crime is larceny rather than false pretenses.

The defendant who, in committing the crime of false pretenses, obtains title to the victim's property by lies usually obtains possession from the victim as well. Indeed, delivery of possession is generally, though not always, a requirement for title to pass. What of the rare case in which the defendant obtains title but not possession? If he fails to acquire possession from the victim only because he is already in possession, he qualifies for false pretenses. But even if, when obtaining title, he never has or gets possession— as where title passes by delivery of a deed of transfer without actual delivery of the property, which remains in the victim's possession— he would seem to be eligible for a false pretenses conviction. Although some cases have language which seems to require, for the crime, that the defendant obtain possession in addition to title, what is really meant is that, where it takes delivery of possession of property to complete the transfer of title, obtaining possession is required; but if no such delivery is necessary, obtaining possession is not necessary for the crime. On principle, it should be enough that the defendant obtains title even though, in acquiring title, he does not also acquire possession.

Normally the victim of the crime of false pretenses had the complete title to the property in question, but there may arise instances in which he has something less—such as the interest of a pledgee in possession to secure a debt, or of a purchaser in possession under a conditional sales contract with purchase payments still to be made. Under these circumstances the defendant may not be able to acquire, by his lies, the complete title, but only such title as the pledgee or conditional-sale purchaser had. Nevertheless, he may be guilty of false pretenses. On the other hand, if the victim has no interest in the property other than its possession—as is the case with the finder of lost property—the defendant by fraud can obtain only possession, and the crime must be larceny by trick.

Generally, of course, the defendant, by his misrepresentations, induces the victim to transfer title to the property to himself; but if instead he should get the victim to pass title to a member of the defendant's family, or to the corporation of which he is an officer, or substantial stockholder, the crime is nevertheless committed.

Although it is easy enough to state the rule that false pretenses involves obtaining title, while larceny by trick involves obtaining possession, it is not always so easy to determine whether that which the defendant actually obtained was possession only, or possession plus title. It may be helpful, in discussing the matter, to divide the problems into these two situations: (1) where the property obtained is other than money; and (2) where it is money:

(1) Concerning Property Other Than Money. One who induces another by lies to *sell* him his property obtains title thereto, so as to qualify for false pretenses, whereas if his lies induce the other to *lend* or *lease* him the property, his crime is larceny by trick. One who, by the use of lies, induces the victim to sell him property on conditional sale, making a small down payment and promising to pay further instalments, does not obtain the complete title, for the conditional seller keeps the "security title"—

the legal title, with the right to repossess the property if the future payments are not made as promised. And yet the purchaser has obtained something more than mere possession, since he has the right to complete ownership upon completing his payments, and since meanwhile the risk of loss falls on, and chance of gain enures to, him. It has been held that, in this situation where the aspects of "title" are thus split between seller and buyer, the buyer gets enough of the title to qualify for the crime of false pretenses. A cash-sale "buyer" who takes delivery of property upon giving a check instead of giving cash is generally held not to get title until the check is cashed; so that, if the check proves worthless, title has not passed, and (assuming a worthless check is a misrepresentation of fact, or that other such misrepresentations were made) the "buyer's" crime is larceny rather than false pretenses.

(2) Concerning Money. In most cases one who hands over money to another never expects to get that very money back; and so it might be thought that in most cases of money obtained by fraud the wrongdoer obtains title, making his crime false pretenses rather than larceny by trick. It is, of course, possible to pledge money as security, or to bail money for safekeeping, to the wrongdoer, in which case title does not pass, so that the crime, if any, falls into the larceny-by-trick category. What if the money is not pledged as security or bailed for safekeeping, but handed over to the wrongdoer to do something particular with it, something that when performed precludes any chance of the return of the identical money? It is generally held that where the victim hands money to the wrongdoer with the understanding that the latter is to spend it only for a particular purpose (thus creating an agency or trust, it would seem) title does not pass to the wrongdoer; he has only a power to pass title by spending it for the specified purpose. Thus where the victim hands money to the wrongdoer to be invested on the stock market, or to purchase specified property, or to bribe a particular official, and the wrongdoer, instead of thus dealing with the money, absconds with it, the crime is larceny by trick rather than false pretenses, the wrongdoer never having acquired title.

On the other hand, it is possible that the victim should agree or understand that the money, though desired for a particular purpose, might be used for any purpose—i.e., the defendant's lie about his need for money induces the victim to make a loan rather than to create an agency or trust—in which case title to the money does pass to the defendant, so that his crime if any is false pretenses rather than larceny by trick. One who obtains money from the victim by cheating at cards or by other forms of fraudulent betting is almost always held guilty of larceny by trick rather than of false pretenses, on the theory that possession but not title passes to the wrongdoer, although it is somewhat difficult to see why title as well as possession does not in fact pass under these circumstances.

(e) Property. The original English false pretenses statute covered only "money, goods, wares or merchandise," and thus was limited to tangible personal property and money. Modern statutes, although not uniform in language, have generally expanded this list to include "anything which can be the subject of larceny" or by adding, at the end, "or other valuable thing," "or other property" or "or anything of value." Such provisions generally are construed to include written instruments representing choses in action (stocks and bonds, checks and promissory notes, savings-bank deposit books, insurance policies) and other documents representing intangible rights (deeds, tickets, stamps). While the asportation element of larceny requires that larceny be limited to property which can be moved, false pretenses (like embezzlement) need not be so limited, there being no asportation element in false pretenses (or embezzlement). Thus one who defrauds another of title to real property should, on principle, be guilty of false pretenses; but the statutes that speak of obtaining "property" or a "valuable thing" are perhaps somewhat ambiguous, at least when read in the light of the early limitation of false pretenses to personal property; so that the cases on real property are in conflict. There are similar conflicts concerning board and lodging and labor or services. It is generally held that one who obtains the renewal of a loan, or the satisfaction of a prior debt, does not obtain property or a "valuable thing" within the false pretenses statutes. So too, a signature upon a document with business or pecuniary significance is usually held not to be "property" within such statutes.

Although it is sometimes said that, for false pretenses as for larceny, the property obtained must be the property "of another," this does not mean that the wrongdoer may not have an interest in, or even have legal title to, the property obtained, so long as the victim has an interest (for instance, a pledge or lien interest) in the property of which the wrongdoer has no right to deprive him.

(f) State of Mind. The typical modern false pretenses statute, like its original English ancestor, contains two words or phrases bearing on the mental state required: (a) "knowingly" (or, as some statutes word it, "designedly"); and (b) "with intent to defraud."

(1) "Knowingly" ("Designedly"). To be guilty of the crime of false pretenses, one must "knowingly" ("designedly") by false pretenses obtain property from another. The word "knowingly" modifies the phrase "false pretenses" so that the defendant, to be guilty, must know that his representation is false. We have already noted that one who says what is in fact true, though he believes it to be false, is not guilty of false pretenses, for the pretense must, to qualify, be actually false (see § 16.7(b)(1)). Now we are concerned with the statement that is in fact false, and the question is: When does the wrongdoer "know" it to be false within the requirements of the statute? The following may be said to be the various states of mind he may have when he states something to be a fact:

(i) He knows that the fact is untrue.

(ii) He believes but does not know the fact to be untrue.

(iii) He knows he does not know whether it is true or false.

(iv) He unreasonably believes the fact to be true.

(v) He reasonably believes the fact to be true.

Clearly, one who believes a false fact to be true does not know it to be false, and so, if his belief is honest, be it reasonable or unreasonable, he is not guilty. At the other extreme, one who knows or (since one hardly ever "knows" anything in the sense of being 100% certain) believes a false fact to be false "knowingly" makes a false representation, and so is guilty of false pretenses if the other elements of the crime are present. More difficult is the in-between case—number (iii) in the above list—of the one who states as a fact something which is actually contrary to fact, knowing that he does not know one way or the other whether it is true or false. Such a state of mind, on principle, ought to do for false pretenses, just as it will do for false pretenses' civil counterpart, the tort of deceit.

(2) "Intent to Defraud." To be guilty of false pretenses (under the typical statute) it is not enough that the wrongdoer tells what he knows or believes to be false or what he knows he does not know to be true; in addition he must have an intent to defraud. Although one does not ordinarily obtain property from another by telling an intentional lie unless he does intend to defraud, it does not necessarily follow from his use of the intentional lie that he intends to defraud. As with the analogous theft crimes, larceny and embezzlement (see §§ 16.5(a), 16.6(f)), one who tells intentional lies nevertheless is not guilty of false pretenses, because he lacks the intent to defraud, if (1) he honestly but erroneously believes the property obtained is his own property or is otherwise property to which he has a lawful right; or (2) he intends to restore the very property obtained, unconditionally and within a reasonable time, and has a substantial ability to do so; or (3) he obtains it in satisfaction of a debt which the other actually owes (or, it would seem, a debt which he honestly but erroneously believes the other to owe him).

In order for one who misrepresents a fact to have an intent to defraud, it is necessary that he intend the victim to rely upon his misrepresentation, an intention which generally can be inferred from the fact that the defendant actually obtained another's property or money by telling lies.

(g) Concurrence of Conduct and State of Mind. In the light of the basic criminal-law principle that the mental and physical elements of the crime must coincide (see § 5.3), the knowledge of the falsity of the statement and the intent to defraud must coincide with the obtaining of the title to the property. One who states what he believes to be true but which he later—before the victim, in reliance on the statement, passes title—learns to be false, has a duty to correct the misapprehension which his innocent statement has engendered, so that, if he takes title without disclosing the truth, he is guilty of false pretenses (so long as the other elements of the crime are present) (see § 16.7(b)(3)).

(h) Grand vs. Petit False Pretenses. As with larceny and embezzlement, most jurisdictions draw a distinction between grand false pretenses, generally a felony, and petit false pretenses, generally a misdemeanor.

(i) Possible Defenses to False Pretenses. Those charged with false pretenses have sometimes urged the following matters as defenses to liability, generally without success:

(1) The Victim's Gullibility. The defendant sometimes urges that, although the victim was actually deceived by the lies (exactly as the defendant intended), the victim was foolish to let himself be deceived; or the victim was negligent in not checking on the truth of the defendant's statement. Although at one time there was some authority that, for false pretenses, the lie had to be one calculated to deceive a reasonable man, the almost-universal modern rule is that the gullibility or carelessness of the defendant is no defense, since the criminal law aims to protect those who cannot protect themselves. This rule is analogous to that which holds that the victim's contributory negligence is no defense to crimes based upon some degree of negligence (such as depraved-heart murder and recklessness manslaughter or battery), and to that which states that the victim's carelessness (as in leaving his front door unlocked or the keys in his car's ignition) is no defense to burglary of the house or larceny of the car (see § 5.5(c)).

(2) Illegality of Victim's Conduct. One charged with false pretenses sometimes argues in his defense that the victim himself was involved in illegal conduct, as where the defendant obtains punchboard prize money from the punchboard operator by presenting a number which he has falsely altered to resemble the winning number; and by way of defense he points out that the victim was committing a crime by operating the punchboard or where the defendant obtains money from the victim by falsely representing himself to be a smuggler in need of funds to purchase a boat for smuggling purposes. The almost universal rule quite properly holds that the victim's illegal conduct is no defense to the crime of false pretenses. This rule is but a part of the broader principle that the victim's badness is no defense to crimes committed against him (see § 5.5(b)).

(3) No Pecuniary Loss to Victim. The defendant sometimes urges in his defense that, when the transaction which his misrepresentations brought about was over, the victim had suffered no pecuniary loss. The defendant induces the victim to buy stock in a silver-mining property by representing that a certain vein of silver ore is located near the property; though this representation is false, the stock in fact is worth what the victim pays for it, or more. (On these facts, the stock may nevertheless not be worth what it would have been worth if the representation had been true. Yet it is possible that it may be worth as much, as would be the case if the silver-mining property was weak in silver ore but contained valuable deposits of high grade gold ore.) Of course, a civil suit would not lie against the defendant when the victim suffered no damage, at least if the victim made out as well financially as he bargained for. But on the criminal side, it is generally held that the lack of financial loss is no defense to false pretenses.

§ 16.8 Theft Crimes: Consolidation

We have seen that English legal history explains the fact that in American jurisdictions the wrongful appropriation of another's property was covered by three related but separate, non-overlapping crimes—larceny, embezzlement and false pretenses. This fact, together with the fact (discussed below) that the borderlines between the three crimes are thin and often difficult to draw, gave rise to a favorite indoor sport played for high stakes in our appellate courts: A defendant, convicted of one of the three crimes, claimed on appeal that, though he is guilty of a crime, his crime is one of the other two. Sometimes this pleasant game was carried to extremes: A defendant, charged with larceny, is acquitted by the trial court (generally on the defendant's motion for a directed verdict of acquittal) on the ground that the evidence shows him guilty of embezzlement. Subsequently tried for embezzlement, he is convicted; but he appeals on the ground that the evidence proves larceny rather than embezzlement. The appellate court agrees and reverses the conviction.

(a) Technical Distinctions Between the Three Crimes. As three rival nations that face each other across common borders often experience difficulty in maintaining friendly relations, so have the technical distinctions between the three theft crimes created unfriendly difficulties in at least two common-border areas: (1) larceny (including larceny by trick) versus embezzlement; and (2) larceny by trick versus false pretenses:

(1) Larceny vs. Embezzlement. The misappropriation by an employee has created problems requiring for solution the drawing of a line between the employee's custody (the basis for larceny) and his possession (embezzlement) of his employer's property. Minor employees, such as caretakers and night watchmen, may have only custody, while employees of higher rank, like office managers, may have possession; it is not always easy to draw the dividing line between minor employees with custody and those who rank high enough to have possession. An employee who puts the money he receives from a customer directly in his pocket commits embezzlement, because the employer never has possession; but if he puts the money first in the till and later in his pocket, he commits larceny, since placing the money in the till gives the employer possession—unless he merely drops it in the till by mistake or places it there for only a minute or two before pocketing it. An employee who receives his employer's property from the employer acquires custody only, so his misappropriation is larceny; but if he receives it from a third person to give to his master, it is embezzlement.

How is it when the employer hands his employee a five-pound note to go out and get change; the employee gets the change, saying that it is for his employer; and then he absconds with the change? In a way, this is property that was handed him by the employer, and so his misappropriation constitutes larceny. But, in another way, it is property coming from a third person, so that the misappropriation is embezzlement. As a matter of good sense the prosecutor, to convict, should not have to put it in one pigeon-hole or the other. Some states have embezzlement-by-employee statutes that cover an employee who fraudulently converts the employer's property "in his possession or under his care" (or "control"); embezzlement under such a statute is generally held to overlap larceny, so as to warrant a conviction of embezzlement by an employee with custody only, though a conviction of larceny would also be upheld (see § 16.6(e)(1)).

The bailee (e.g., a carrier or warehouseman) of property that is made up into a bale (for transportation or storage), who breaks open the bale and misappropriates the contents is guilty of larceny. If, however, he misappropriates the whole bale without breaking it open, his crime in most jurisdictions is not larceny but embezzlement. What if goods are shipped or stored in bulk but without wrapper or rope—for instance, 32 tons of pig iron, consisting of 640 bars each weighing 100 pounds? This might be viewed as one big bale without a wrapper, so that the carrier who separates 100 bars and sells them as his own breaks bulk and so commits larceny. Or it might be looked upon as the shipment of 640 separate bales, so that the conversion of 100 bars by the carrier constitutes embezzlement. It is a pretty even matter.

In addition to the above difficulties the *law* experiences in pigeon-holing borderline misappropriations into the larceny or embezzlement categories, there are situations where the proper pigeon-hole depends on what is the *fact* of the defendant's intent, a matter concerning which the prosecution can often only guess. One who finds another's lost or mislaid property bearing the earmarks of ownership, or who by mistake receives an overpayment or misdelivery of property belonging to another, and who intends to steal when he first takes possession of the property is guilty of larceny, for his trespassory taking and intent to steal coincide. But, if, when he first takes possession, he intends to restore the property and only later decides to misappropriate it, or if he does not until later realize the mistake and so only later decides to misappropriate it, his crime is not larceny; whether it is embezzlement depends on whether the embezzlement statute is broad enough to cover finders and persons who receive overpayments and misdeliveries by mistake. In a state that has the broad embezzlement statute, the prosecuting attorney, not knowing whether the evidence will show an intent to steal instantly formed, or one which overcame the wrongdoer later, will generally charge both crimes; so that the trial court can leave it to the jury to find the defendant guilty of larceny if it finds that he formed the intent to steal at once, but of embezzlement if its finding is that he later decided to steal.

Similarly, it is not always easy to tell in advance whether the proof will show larceny by trick or embezzlement. Thus, the evidence may show that the defendant, who fraudulently converted another's property, obtained possession of (but not title to) the victim's property by lies, intending from the beginning to misappropriate it (larceny by trick), or it may show that he obtained the possession honestly and only later decided to misappropriate it (embezzlement). Evidence of one crime will not support a conviction of the other.

(2) Larceny by Trick vs. False Pretenses. One who obtains only possession of another's property by lies and then fraudulently converts it is a candidate for a larceny-by-trick conviction. If by lying he obtains title along with possession, his crime is false pretenses. Though this distinction is easily stated, it is not always so easy to determine whether what the defendant got from the victim was possession only, or title as well—as where the victim sells property to the defendant on conditional sale or at a cash sale where the defendant gives a bad check; or where the victim hands the defendant money to be used for one particular purpose (see § 16.7(d)).

It is thus apparent that to retain these technical distinctions between the three crimes serves mainly to present a guilty defendant with an opportunity to postpone and perhaps altogether to escape his proper punishment. Yet, as Cardozo once expressed the matter when speaking of the difference between larceny and embezzlement, "The distinction, now largely obsolete, did not ever correspond to any essential difference in the character of the acts or in their effect upon the victim. The crimes are one today in the common speech of men, as they are in moral quality." The fact that the statutory punishment is almost always the same for false pretenses and embezzlement as it is for larceny supports the notion that there is no moral difference between the activities of the thief, the embezzler and the swindler. And it can hardly make a difference to the victim whether he loses his property by another's stealth, or by his fraudulent conversion or through his falsehoods.

(b) Some Possible Remedies. In an attempt to deal with these problems, the embezzlement and false pretenses statutes of some American states provide in effect that one who embezzles, or one who obtains property by false pretenses, "shall be deemed guilty of larceny and punished accordingly." It might be thought that, under such statutes, if the charge is larceny but the proof shows embezzlement (or false pretenses) there may properly be a conviction of larceny, for embezzlement (or false pretenses) *is* larceny. Though a few courts so held, most courts held that the statute does not make embezzlement (false pretenses) larceny but merely provides that the punishment shall be the same as for larceny.

Another technique has occasionally been used to sustain a conviction where the defendant is charged with one of the three crimes but the proof shows another. As noted in *State v. Gould* (1932): "Where a defendant, by his own criminal acts, has placed himself in such a position that the evidence will support a conviction on either one of two theories, such as embezzlement by agent, or obtaining money by false pretenses, it should not be the duty of the court to draw fine hair-splitting distinctions. * * * The embezzlement statutes were enacted to remedy a defect in the common law. The courts should not, by strained constructions, add to the difficulties of the state in such prosecutions."

The fact that the prosecuting attorney may join several counts in one indictment or information is helpful, especially where the law concerning the dividing line is clear enough but it is uncertain what facts, putting the case on one side of the line or the other, the proof will disclose. Thus, if uncertain whether the proof in a borderline case will show larceny or embezzlement, the prosecution may include two counts, one for each crime. The defendant may move, when the evidence is in, to have the prosecution elect upon which count he will go to the jury. Although it is often loosely stated that the grant or denial of the motion to elect is within the trial court's discretion, the situation here (the evidence relates to but one transaction, and the difficulty is whether the disputed facts require the transaction to be pigeon-holed in one category or the other) is the one situation where the motion should be denied. Yet, because of the requirement that the jury by its verdict specify which of the two different crimes the defendant is guilty of, there is still the danger (especially where the difficulty is that the law concerning the location of the borderline is uncertain) that the jury will select the wrong one, so that the defendant, on appeal, can show that the evidence proves the other one, and thus he can secure a reversal of his conviction.

(c) Consolidation of the Three Crimes into One. We have already suggested that many of the modern American difficulties in the area of misappropriation of property would have been avoided if in the beginning the English Parliament, instead of creating the new statutory crimes of embezzlement and false pretenses to plug the loopholes discovered in the law of larceny, had by statute simply extended larceny to cover the new situations which needed to be covered. American states generally followed the English lead, recognizing the three separate crimes. But in recent years, the great majority of states (usually as a part of enacting a new criminal code) have abolished these three separate crimes in favor of a single crime, usually called "theft."

Convictions under such statutes have been upheld against the contention that the statutes are unconstitutional because the defendant, charged with the consolidated crime of "larceny" or "theft," is not sufficiently informed of the nature of the crime charged unless he is accused of a particular one of the three former crimes. That is, the prosecuting attorney who charges "larceny" or "theft" need not elect a particular one of the three former crimes; if the evidence shows any one of the three, the defendant may be found guilty and the conviction will be upheld. But it has occasionally been held that, in spite of the consolidation, an information or indictment which sounds like one of the former three will not support a conviction on evidence which shows another one of the former three. The former view is the correct one: a defendant is entitled to notice in the indictment or information of the charge against him, but this means notification of the basic facts upon which the charge is based; he is not entitled in addition to a charge that "makes a noise" like one of the three formerly separate, but now consolidated, crimes. And thus it is quite proper to provide by statute, as is commonly done in jurisdictions with a more comprehensive crime of "theft" described in its various manifestations in several statutes, that a conviction may be had upon proof that the theft was committed in any of these various ways.

(d) The Model Penal Code Consolidation. The Model Penal Code provides for an ambitious plan of consolidation of smaller separate crimes into one larger crime called "theft." Theft under Code § 223.1(1) covers not only larceny, embezzlement and false pretenses, but also receiving stolen property and blackmail or extortion. Thus "theft by unlawful taking or disposition" in § 332.2 covers what was formerly larceny and embezzlement; "theft by deception" in § 223.3, what was formerly false pretenses and larceny by trick; "theft by extortion" in § 223.4, what was formerly blackmail or extortion; and "theft by receiving" in § 223.6, what was formerly receiving stolen property. Many states follow essentially this approach.

The desirability of consolidating extortion (or blackmail) with false pretenses is illustrated by a federal case involving these facts: An English woman wrote movie star Clark Gable a letter informing him that he was the father of her child, conceived in England in September, 1922; her intent in writing him was to induce him to pay her money. Gable had not in fact been in England in 1922 or 1923, and he had never met the lady, so that the letter contained misrepresentations of fact. The lady was charged with using the United States mails to defraud, a federal crime, and she was convicted upon the above evidence. On appeal, however, her conviction was reversed, for, since she intended to frighten, not to mislead, Gable by her lies, she used the mails to extort rather than to defraud. Extortion (blackmail) may be thought of as simply another way—in addition to the ways encompassed by the three crimes of larceny, embezzlement and false pretenses—in which one person can misappropriate another's property.

It is often difficult for the police and prosecuting attorney, who find the defendant in exclusive possession of property recently stolen from the owner, to know whether he actually stole it or whether he received it from another who did the stealing. This gives a defendant, charged with larceny, a chance to urge that he received it; or, if charged with receiving, to claim that he stole it. Once again, in moral quality the two crimes, larceny and receiving, are alike, as the generally-similar statutory provisions for punishment recognize. The two crimes may be thought of as simply two ways of misappropriating another's property. Thus Model Penal Code § 223.1(1) brackets them together as merely two ways among several ways of committing the single crime of theft.

Robbery is a crime related to theft; indeed, it should be considered to be a sort of aggravated theft. Since it involves a danger to the person in addition to a danger to property, it is morally a worse crime than the other crimes the Model Penal Code collects together under "theft." Code § 221.1 therefore treats robbery not as a form of theft but as a separate crime related to theft.

Table of Cases

N

O

P

R

Table of Model Penal Code Citations

Index

747

CONTEMPT OF COURT
Proceedings, § 1.7(e).

CONTRACT DUTIES
Omission to act, § 5.2(a)(3).

CONTRIBUTORY NEGLIGENCE
Factor in criminal justice administration, § 5.5(e).
Not a defense, § 5.5(c).
Relevant to causation issue, § 5.4(f)(6).
Relevant to issue of defendant's negligence, §§ 5.5(c), 14.4(d).

CONVERSION
Embezzlement, § 16.6(b).

CONVULSION
Automatism, § 8.4(a).
Involuntary act, § 5.1(c).

COOLING TIME
Manslaughter, § 14.2(d).

CORPORATE AGENT
Liability of, § 12.5(e).

CORPORATE OFFICER
Liability of, § 12.5(e).

CORPORATIONS
See also Enterprise Liability.
As conspirators, § 11.4(c)(3).

CORPUS DELICTI
Proof of, § 1.4(b).

CORROBORATION
Rape allegation, § 15.5(b).

CORRUPT MOTIVE DOCTRINE
Conspiracy, § 11.2(c)(5).

COUNTY ORDINANCES
Proceedings for violation of, § 1.7(c).

CREATION OF PERIL
Omission to act, § 5.2(a)(5).

CREDIT CARD LEGISLATION
False pretenses and, § 16.7(j)(6).

CRIME PREVENTION
Defense classification, § 8.1(b).
Imperfect defense causing death as manslaughter, § 14.3(b).
Use of force in, § 9.7(c).

CRIME TERMINATION
Use of force in, § 9.7(c).

CRIMES
See also Administrative Crimes; Common Law Crimes.
Administrative, § 2.6.
Classification of, § 1.6.
Common law, §§ 1.6(f), 2.1.

CRIMES—Cont'd
Felony, § 1.6(a).
Infamous, § 1.6(d).
Involving moral turpitude, § 1.6(c).
Malum in se, § 1.6(b).
Malum prohibitum, § 1.6(b).
Misdemeanor, § 1.6(a).
Petty offenses, § 1.6(e)
Statutory, § 1.6(f).
Torts distinguished, § 1.3(b).

CRIMES AGAINST THE PERSON
See Assault; Battery; Manslaughter; Mayhem; Murder.

CRIMES RELATING TO PROPERTY
See Bad Checks; Blackmail; Burglary; Embezzlement; Extortion; False Pretenses; Larceny; Receiving Stolen Property; Robbery; Theft.

CRIMINAL ATTEMPT
See Attempt.

CRIMINAL INTENT
See Intent; Mental State.

CRIMINAL JURISDICTION
See Jurisdiction.

CRIMINAL NEGLIGENCE MANSLAUGHTER
Generally, § 14.4.

CRIMINAL PROCEDURE
Characteristics of, § 1.4.
Discretion in, § 1.4(c).
Evidentiary tests in, § 1.4(a).
Use of part of process, § 1.4(d).

CRIMINAL PROCEEDINGS
Contempt proceedings distinguished, § 1.7(e).
Juvenile delinquency proceedings distinguished, § 1.7(a).
Ordinance violation proceedings distinguished, § 1.7(c).
Sexual psychopathy proceedings distinguished, § 1.7(b).
Statutory penalty proceedings distinguished, § 1.7(d).

CRIMINAL STATUTES
See Statutory Interpretation.

CRUEL AND UNUSUAL PUNISHMENT
Generally, § 3.5(g).
Chronic alcoholism, § 8.5(i).
Death penalty, § 3.5(g).
Insanity defense abolition, § 6.1(d).
Narcotics addiction, § 8.5(i).

DEATH PENALTY
Constitutionality, § 3.5(g).
Cruel and unusual punishment, § 3.5(g).

MURDER—Cont'd
Felony murder—Cont'd
Conviction of felony also, § 13.5(g)(3).
Depraved-heart murder compared, § 13.5(e).
Duress defense, § 8.7(b).
First degree, § 13.7(b).
Future of the doctrine, § 13.5(h).
History of, § 13.5(a).
"In the commission of" felony,
Generally, § 13.5(f).
Causal connection, § 13.5(f)(2).
Differing views on scope, § 13.5(f)(3).
Homicide followed by felony, § 13.5(f)(4).
Time, § 13.5(f)(1).
Limited to certain felonies, § 13.5(b).
Manslaughter as felony, § 13.5(g)(1).
Vicarious responsibility of co-felons, § 13.5(c).
First degree,
In commission of listed felonies, § 13.7(b).
Lying in wait, § 13.7(c).
Other, § 13.7(d).
Poison, § 13.7(c).
Premeditation and deliberation, § 13.7(a).
Torture, § 13.7(c).
Intent-to-do-serious-bodily-injury murder, § 13.3.
Intent-to-kill murder,
Generally, § 13.2.
Causation, § 13.2(d).
Intention, § 13.2(a).
Deadly weapon doctrine, § 13.2(b).
Means of producing intentional death, § 13.2(c).
Living human being requirement,
When life begins, § 13.1(c).
When life ends, § 13.1(d).
Malice aforethought, § 13.1(a).
Partial responsibility, § 8.2(b)(2).
Premeditation and deliberation, § 13.7(a).
Intoxication negativing, § 8.5(b).
Resisting-lawful-arrest murder, § 13.6.
Second degree, § 13.7(e).
Statutory definitions of, § 13.1(b).
Year-and-a-day rule, § 13.1(e).

NARCOTICS ADDICTION
See also Intoxication.
Crime, constitutionality, §§ 3.5(g), 8.5(h).

NECESSITY
Defense classification, § 8.1(b).
Defined for particular offenses, § 9.1(a).
Examples of defense, § 9.1(c).

NECESSITY—Cont'd
Imperfect defense causing death as manslaughter, § 14.3(c).
Nature of defense, § 9.1(a).
Rationale of defense, § 9.1(a).
Relationship to other defenses, § 9.1(b).
Requirements of defense,
Harm avoided, § 9.1(d)(1).
Harm done, § 9.1(d)(2).
Intention to avoid harm, § 9.1(d)(3).
Optional courses of action, § 9.1(d)(5).
Relative value of harm avoided and harm done, § 9.1(d)(4).
Where defendant at fault in creating situation, § 9.1(d)(6).

NEGATIVE ACT
See Omission to Act.

NEGLIGENCE
See also Criminal Negligence Manslaughter; Ignorance or Mistake; Manslaughter.
"Constructive intent" including, § 4.2(e).
Criminal, § 4.4(b).
"Criminal intent" including, § 4.2(e).
Criminal law vs. tort law, § 4.4(a).
Disparity between foreseeable and actual result,
Unexpected degree of harm, § 4.4(h)(4).
Unforeseeable manner, § 4.4(h)(2).
Unforeseeable victim, § 4.4(h)(1).
Unhazarded type of harm, § 4.4(h)(3).
Gross, § 4.4(b).
High degree of, § 4.4(b).
Intoxication and, § 8.5(c).
Objective standard, § 4.4(a)(2).
Objective vs. subjective fault, § 4.4(g).
Proof of realization of risk, § 4.4(d).
Recklessness compared as basis for liability, § 4.4(g).
Recklessness distinguished, § 4.4(b).
Subjective vs. objective fault, § 4.4(g).
Tort law vs. criminal law, § 4.4(a).
Transferred, § 5.4(e).
Unreasonable risk, § 4.4(a)(1).
Violation of statute or ordinance, § 4.4(c).

NEGLIGENCE MANSLAUGHTER
Generally, § 14.4.

NO RETREAT RULE
Self defense, § 9.4(f).

NONPERFORMANCE
See Omission to Act.

†